WALTERS, C. Glenn. Marketing channels. Ronald, 1974. 524p il tab 74-80916. 11.95

Although a number of books on marketing channels have appeared, none has been as complete as this one in its coverage of the subject. Walters has organized the book logically, taking the reader from channel management through channel structure, dynamics, channel communications, decisions as to channel choice, leadership, and co-operation. This reviewer was pleased to see how much good marketing theory Walters interwove into his structural and functional explanation of channels. In addition, Walters has written quite unique chapters not treated elsewhere on such topics as Alderson's assortments model, information theory in channel communications, conflict theory, and analysis of channel decisions peculiar to the international business fields. Clearly written, modern, comprehensive, this will be a valuable addition to this area of marketing resources. It would be most suitable for intermediate-level, rather than introductory, courses in marketing, and certainly could be handled by an upper-division undergraduate student. Well indexed and illustrated.

C. GLENN WALTERS (Ph.D., University of Illinois) is Professor of Marketing at Mississippi State University. He was formerly a member of the faculty at Louisiana State University, and is a Past President of the Southwestern Marketing Association. Professor Walters has carried on extensive research in the fields of retailing and the social aspects of marketing, and is author of a book on consumer behavior.

MARKETING CHANNELS

C. GLENN WALTERS
MISSISSIPPI STATE UNIVERSITY

101444

THE RONALD PRESS COMPANY · NEW YORK

To Pat Walters

Preface

A principal objective in the writing of this textbook for the advanced undergraduate student of marketing has been to survey, organize, and integrate all of the theories and concepts relevant to today's problems of channels management. In achieving this purpose no concept has been slighted because of its complexity, although special pains have been taken to present all discussions in language calculated to promote understanding. While the student is assumed to have taken a basic marketing course, the author does not expect that every aspect of that foundation will be remembered.

A second major objective has been to encourage the student to put himself in the role of the channel leader—the person responsible for managing the coordinated efforts of the organized group of institutions that make up a particular channel of distribution.

The study of marketing institutions has traditionally been descriptive and fragmented. Discussion has generally been focused on explaining how types of businesses operate—their purpose, performance characteristics, and types of activities. At the same time, the tendency has been to treat wholesalers and retailers as separate topics. Manufacturers and agent middlemen have been given scant attention; manufacturers were included as a part of industrial marketing or treated briefly in industrial purchasing. Transportation and warehousing were discussed from the point of view of national transportation policy.

Here, the coverage of all the major institutions is integrated in a decision-making context. The text presents the relevant theory, background concepts and empirical information necessary to provide a foundation for students to understand and solve actual channel problems. The perspectives of institutional structure, functions performed, and products distributed are presented. Decision making underlies these perspectives, and the channel is treated as an organization of firms with its own structural, operational, communications, and leadership problems. A behavioral philosophy is followed, and the overall point of view is that of the dominant institution responsible for coordinating the managements of a group of businesses.

Although the book contains information about such marketing functions as purchasing, selling, advertising, pricing, transportation, and storage, no attempt has been made to explain these functions per se. Each is considered only in the sense that it involves organizational decisions of the channel group. Activities primarily related to a firm's internal operations are consistently deemphasized in favor of those involving relationships among firms.

It is hoped that the book's integrated, managerial approach will serve well the modern student of marketing, who, upon entering a large multi-level organization or embarking on a professional career, will require a broad understanding of the different types of institutions functioning as a coordinated channel of distribution.

C. GLENN WALTERS

Starkville, Mississippi
June, 1974

Acknowledgments

Help and encouragement have been received from many people in the preparation of this text, and it is all appreciated. However, special recognition is due to certain individuals. Dr. Gaines Rogers, Dean, College of Business and Industry, Mississippi State University, and Dr. Henry W. Nash, head of the Marketing Department, encouraged my efforts and cooperated in every way to facilitate work on the book. The cooperation of Dr. Guy T. Peden, Jr., Director, Division of Research, College of Business and Industry, in supplying research material and typing aid greatly contributed to the book's progress. Appreciation is also extended to Dr. Z. W. Koby, Dr. Donald P. Robin, and Dr. J. William Rush, for their advice and counseling at various points. The contribution of Mrs. Dot Hall to the book, including typing, filing, and handling correspondence, proved indispensable. Special thanks go to Professor J. F. Curry for help that greatly benefited the chapter on information systems, and to Mrs. G. Pepper Holland for her editorial assistance. The work of the members of the secretarial staff of the Division of Research is appreciated, and special mention must go to Mrs. Jo Ann Cox, Mrs. Nancy Upchurch, Mrs. Linda Crowe, Mrs. Peggy Zimmerman, and Mrs. Lynn Allen. Thanks are also extended to John Hendricks for his work on certain technical aspects of the book, and to Mrs. Sherry Coleman for her excellent work in typing the final draft of the manuscript.

C.G.W.

Contents

CHANNELS MANAGEMENT: CONCEPT, OPPORTUNITY, RESPONSIBILITY

The major purpose of this group of chapters is to present the concept of marketing channels and to trace their development; the model of channels management used in the book is also developed. In addition, Part I introduces two basic variables of channels management: the market and the environment. The market is discussed in terms of its opportunity to effect channel decision making and the environment is viewed as a restraint on this decision making. With this introduction, we can then focus more clearly on the specific management areas of marketing channels.

1

The Channel of Distribution

Consider for a moment the complexities involved in supplying all the products necessary to furnish the living room of the average American home. This one room requires, among other things: (1) paper and chemicals from the forest; (2) synthetics made from petroleum; (3) animal and plant fabrics from the farm; and (4) metal, glass, and ceramics from several mines. All these products must be extracted, fabricated, stored, transported, and sold to the home owner. These activities involve some distribution channels, and the complexity of the channel *reflects* the degree of sophistication of the social order that employs it. In the United States, the marketing channel is a highly involved and intricate mechanism and, in spite of its importance, it has been neglected by marketing educators. This book is about marketing channels. It assimilates knowledge and offers an explanation for important decisions of channels management.

DEFINITION OF MARKETING CHANNELS

In discussing the marketing channel we must first arrive at a meaningful definition. There is considerable latitude in our choice because marketing scholars do not agree on the meaning of channels. Therefore, it is necessary for us to develop a definition that is not only accurate in its description but also in its effectiveness as a basis for communications. In short, a definition that allows two people to agree on their interpretation of some real thing, idea, or situation. Intelligent conversation can proceed on the basis of this agreement.

The reality of a marketing channel, like anything else, can be perceived more than one way, depending on the intent of the conversation.

3

If the discussion is political, one person may conceive of the channel as a device for exploiting the public. Another person may maintain that a marketing channel is a vehicle of public service. Two parties possessing such different definitions may exchange words, but they are not likely to exchange any understanding. Since this book emphasizes business activity rather than social, political, or other areas of activity, a business definition of channels is sought. The time spent carefully constructing this view of the marketing channel can avoid misunderstanding later.

Historical Channel Definitions

A channel of distribution, sometimes called a trade or marketing channel, can be defined in several ways. A popular definition views it as a route or path. Revzan says a channel is "a pathway taken by goods as they flow from point of production to points of intermediate and final use." [1] This definition is restrictive in two ways. First, the term "goods" can be misleading; it is often taken to mean a physical thing. As a result, the definition tends to de-emphasize the movement of services or the combination of goods and services. Second, the definition is restrictive of those institutions making up the channel. Since it stresses physical distribution, it seems to downplay firms that move ownership. An adequate definition must include all institutions involved in the channel, and it must be sufficiently broad to include goods and services.

Nystrom says, "The channel of distribution for a product refers to the course of ownership taken in the transfer of title to it as it moves from manufacturer or producer to final consumer." [2] This definition goes to the other extreme. It includes in the channel only those institutions involved with the flow of title. The definition does point to products as the things moved rather than physical goods. "Products" is a term that typically refers to a combination of goods and services. Product is used in this broad interpretation throughout this book, and the term goods is restricted to physical goods.

The definitions committee of the American Marketing Association emphasizes institutions rather than the flow of products. The committee says that a channel is "the structure of intra-company organization units and extra-company agents and dealers, wholesale and retail, through which a commodity, product, or service is marketed." [3] This definition is

---

[1] David A. Revzan, "Marketing Organization Through the Channel," *Wholesaling in Marketing Organization* (New York: John Wiley and Sons, Inc., 1961), p. 108.

[2] Paul H. Nystrom, ed., *Marketing Handbook* (New York: The Ronald Press Co., 1958), p. 219. See also: Reavis Cox, *Distribution In A High School Economy* (Englewood Cliffs, N. J.: Prentice-Hall, Inc., 1965), p. 71.

[3] *Marketing Definitions: A Glossary of Marketing Terms.* Committee on Definitions of the American Marketing Association (Chicago: American Marketing Association, 1960).

broader than the previous two, but it is cumbersome. By playing up structure, the definition gives a static connotation to the channel. Furthermore, the reference to so many institutions is confusing. One cannot help wondering what the relationship is between the institutions. Although any of the above definitions is workable, one that overcomes some of the disadvantages is desirable.

The Channel Defined

The definition of a marketing channel used in this book is broad. It is designed to provide a foundation of communications upon which the remainder of the book can be built. Thus, a channel is defined as *a team of merchant and/or agent business institutions that functions to create and distribute assortments of products to specified markets.*

First, a channel is a team rather than a random collection of institutions; consequently there must be some cooperation among members to achieve the common goal. Second, since some members are merchants and some are agents, it follows that some pass title and some do not. The channel involves both the flow of title and the flow of physical goods, since merchants move title while physical distribution is necessary to distribute assortments. Third, the objective of the marketing channel is to reach specified markets. No single channel may attempt to reach all markets, but some market is the end result of channel activity. Fourth, the marketing channel performs two important operations in meeting its objective: it creates assortments and distributes them. The assortment refers to number of types of products necessary to satisfy the market. Both goods and services are part of the assortment, and it is understood that each product has an accompanying price.

Channels Management Defined

The concept of marketing channels developed here is decision-oriented since the channel's function cannot be achieved without some strategy. This fact makes a definition of channels management necessary. Channels management is defined as *the decision making necessary to administer the business institutions so as to achieve their purpose within the parameters of the environment.*

A decision-oriented approach means that the focus of attention throughout this book is on the development of channel strategy and decision making rather than on the description of how a channel operates. Decision making will focus on the broad *problem areas* of channels management, and how it relates to each problem. Of course, no text can tell a manager which decision is best. One can only relate alternatives and explain the factors that management must consider in the choice. Since the text is decision-oriented, it is written from the point of view of the channels manager. The decisions discussed are limited, in so far as possible, to those encompassing the integration of a group of businesses.

BASIS FOR DISTRIBUTION CHANNELS

The definitions given above only begin our inquiry into the nature of channels of distribution. Further insight can be gained by considering their economic function. That is, how do channels fit in with other economic activity? At this time the manner in which channels aid in creating economic value is considered. We can thus gain a review of important economic concepts and expand our knowledge of the nature of channels of distribution.

Factors That Create Economic Value

The operation of channels of distribution is an economic activity, and its importance rests on its ability to aid in the creation of economic value. Economic value refers to the worth of goods and services to individuals.[4] Three important factors are necessary for the creation of economic value: (1) production which makes products, (2) marketing which distributes products, and (3) consumption which uses products. Each of these factors is defined below.

It is generally agreed that production involves a transformation process in which something is created. One group, by the inclusion of service, holds that all business activity, even marketing, is production.[5] Another group sees production as the creation of physical goods.[6] The latter definition is preferred because it allows for a clear distinction from marketing which performs a distribution service. Thus, production is defined as the creation of a specific economic value associated with making physical goods.

Marketing, like production, can be defined in more than one way. It has been termed simply "the delivery of a standard of living," and as "matter in motion." The most widely accepted definition is that of the Definitions Committee of the American Marketing Association: "the performance of business activities that direct the flow of goods and services from producers to consumers or users." [7]

Any of the above definitions of marketing are satisfactory. They differ primarily in the amount of formality. Each states or implies a flow of

[4] Douglas Greenwald et al., The McGraw-Hill Dictionary of Modern Economics (New York: McGraw-Hill Book Co., Inc., 1965), p. 542.

[5] Elwood S. Buffa, Modern Production Management, 3rd ed. (New York: John Wiley and Sons, Inc., 1969), p. 29.

[6] Raymond R. Mayer, Production Management, 2nd ed. (New York: McGraw-Hill Book Co., Inc., 1962), p. 3.

[7] Marketing Definitions: op. cit., p. 15.

goods and services, but the one designated by the definitions committee is preferred because it emphasizes distribution.

Consumption can be defined as "the application of goods and services to the uses for which they were created."[8] Consumption takes place through individual people, business institutions, or non-business institutions such as governments, colleges, or charities. Although there is no complete consistency, the term consumer tends to be associated with final household consumers and the term buyer with business consumers.

Relationship Among Factors

It was pointed out that production, marketing, and consumption working together create economic value.[9] Figure 1–1 illustrates the relation-

Fig. 1–1. Relationship among economic components.

ship between these three factors. The creation of economic value is purposeful in the sense that there is always a reason for it. Production and marketing are carried out for the purpose of consumption. Marketing is uniquely placed between production and consumption. Without marketing there is no interaction between the other two economic functions because only marketing performs the essential functions of distribution in which production and distribution are brought together.

Marketing is an important factor in a cycle that begins and ends with consumer wants. Marketing must interpret consumer wants and combine them with such other market data as the location of consumers, their numbers, and their preferences for stores. This information is transmitted to production to become the basis for manufacture. The producer makes a physical good, and this good is combined with such marketing services as credit, pricing, providing information, etc. Then the finished product is moved into the hands of consumers. The cycle ends when the consumer obtains the satisfaction resulting from product ownership. Of course, many such cycles are going on continuously.

The place and importance of marketing channels can be determined from this cycle. The service performed by marketing is the movement

[8] Nystrom, *op. cit.*, p. 31.

[9] Lee Adler, "Systems Approach to Marketing," *Harvard Business Review*, Vol. 45 (May–June, 1967), pp. 105–18. Adler supports the concept of an interrelationship between production, marketing, and consumption.

of products and title through a channel by the performance of necessary activities that result in consumer satisfaction. Thus the channel of distribution is the vehicle through which products move and within which marketing functions are performed.

Marketing has a responsibility to each of the sectors with which it comes into contact. It acts as a seller for producers by promoting and physically moving goods. It functions as a purchasing agent for consumers by interpreting consumer wants and making products available when and where desired.

Channels Important in Creating Utility

Production and marketing perform their function in the society by creating utility. Utility is defined as the ability of a product to satisfy a human want. Thus, utility is the basis for all economic value. There are four types of utility that can be identified: form, time, place, and possession utility. Form utility is any change in the make-up of the product; its creation is a prerogative of production. This may involve taking out impurities; releasing the good from its natural state; changing shape or function of raw materials; determining the type of materials used; determining chemical content; changing size, shape, or other dimensions of the finished good; or changing the method of construction. It is the existence of a good that initiates channel operations. This fact is true whether the goods that exist are in a natural state, or are semifinished, or finished.

The remaining three utilities are the prerogative of marketing; they could not occur without a channel of distribution. Time utility is having the good when the consumer wishes to purchase. A product has no purpose to a consumer if it is made available either before or after it is needed. It is storage primarily that creates time utility. The channel helps create time utility by warehousing. Place utility is having the product at the location desired by consumers. A consumer cannot derive satisfaction from a product in some distant location. Thus refrigerators stockpiled at place of production serve no economic function for consumers until moved to market. The channel creates place utility by means of transportation. Possession utility refers to all the activities necessary to change ownership of goods. Neither the business buyer nor the final consumer can perform his economic function unless control over the goods can be obtained. Business seeks to own goods for the purpose of resale, and business satisfaction is obtained by acquiring profit or other objectives. Final consumers seek to possess goods in order to obtain use satisfaction. Possession utility concerns the change of title, and it must occur between two channel members or between a channel member and a final consumer.

In reality, the four types of utility discussed are inseparable. The consumer cannot obtain a finished product unless it is transported to the consumer's place of residence, stored until he is ready for it, and title passed. He also cannot possess a product that has not been produced. The consumer must obtain all utility or he obtains none. It follows that marketing and production are equally important to the channel of distribution.

Channels and Marketing Decisions

If one begins with a flow that results in the creation of time, place, and possession utility, then the major decision areas of marketing can be inferred.[10] First, a flow necessitates that something move. In marketing the thing moved is goods and services that we call products, and there can be no consumer satisfaction or marketing strategy until there is an identifiable product. Second, a flow requires a route or path over which the products move. Since the channel creates and distributes assortments, it can be called a route or path. Thus channel decisions are necessary to facilitate the movement of products.

Third, a flow does not occur automatically; activities must be performed to cause the movement to happen. Products must be picked up and shipped and institutions must be informed of their arrival and departure. These and other activities are the functions of marketing; a large number of functional decisions are necessary. Fourth, there must be a reason for the flow. Marketing flows are not random occurrences—marketing is consumer-oriented. This consumer orientation is known as the marketing philosophy.

Product Decisions

Products make up the assortment of goods available for sale. The decisions related to this area include additions and deletions, determination of product standards, product design and development, branding, and product control. Additions and deletions determine the structure of the product line and aid in maintaining product cost. The determination of product standards is a quality decision that involves what materials and ingredients make up the products and the manner of their use. Product design and development constitute the decision relating to the form of the product. Of course, determining design and setting standards are interrelated—the design affects standards and standards affect the design. Branding is the function of product identification, and can involve the brand name, identifying slogans, package design, etc., that identify the product as of one particular maker. Product control involves

[10] Neil H. Borden, "The Concept of the Marketing Mix," *Journal of Advertising Records*, Vol. 4 (June, 1964), pp. 2–7.

the decisions related to maintaining a balanced inventory. Most control decisions relate to width of the line, the number of different types of products handled; depth of line concerns the number of items of each type normally kept in stock.

Functional Decisions

The number of marketing functions cited in the literature varies according to the source. A marketing function is any activity, operation, or service necessary to distribute products. There is general agreement on six broad activities: buying, selling, transportation, storage, marketing research, and service surrounding the sale.[11] Buying is the search, evaluation, and acceptance of title to products. Buying decisions include search for sources of supply; evaluation of sources; evaluation of products; determination of amounts of purchase; consideration of prices, terms, and conditions of sale, and acceptance of title. Selling is the activity of demand creation. It includes such decisions as the methods of advertising and personal selling, the combination of promotional method, choice of media, timing of promotional methods, timing of promotional campaigns, price determination, service determination, design and layout of facilities, and presentation of title.

Transportation and storage involve movement and warehousing of goods. Decisions in these areas include choice of transportation and storage methods, combination of transportation and warehouses, inventory control, and timing of product movement. Marketing research is the collection, evaluation, and presentation of facts for decision making. In a sense, research underlies all marketing decisions. Internal decisions, within the firm, are under the functional areas. External research decisions concern the market. Market research requires such decisions as market location and customer wants, preferences, and motivations. Also important to market research are customer characteristics and the total demand for the product.

Services are less easily defined, because their numbers are large. Services surrounding the sale include such activities as credit, installation, repairs, alterations, complaints, wrapping, etc. Some functions go by two names depending on their placement in the channel (e.g., transportation and delivery and credit and financing). This fact can lead to confusion if the reader is not careful.

Channel Decisions

Since this book is about channels of distribution it is not necessary to delve deeply into this decision area at this time. Some of the broad deci-

[11] Some scholars include grading, financing, and risking with the above functions. However, since these activities are not unique to marketing (e.g., risk is inherent in all business activity), it is questionable if they are marketing functions.

sion areas covered in channels include channel selection, channel design, member cooperation, motivation, control, and channel communications. The importance of these decision areas is explained later in the chapter.

The Marketing Philosophy

The concept of the marketing philosophy has generally been recognized by marketers, but Fred Borch of General Electric was largely responsible for popularizing the concept and coining the name.[12] The fundamental idea of the marketing philosophy is consumer orientation at a profit. Everything that the business undertakes should be undertaken with the consumer's interest in mind, for this point of view is the shortest route to profitable operations. Four points are important concerning the marketing philosophy.

First, consumer orientation is not a philosophy biased toward consumers. It is not necessarily benevolent nor does it subscribe to the notion that the consumer is always right. Rather, consumer orientation recognizes that there are two sides to every transaction, and each side must be satisfied for trade to be effective. Consumers are satisfied by obtaining desired products. Businesses are satisfied by obtaining profits. If a product is desired but not profitable, it cannot be long supplied.

Second, the marketing philosophy is best described as a state of mind.[13] It is not something that the management does so much as it is the way the management thinks about everything it does. Management may develop a new product because it wants to take advantage of customers or because it wants to satisfy them, but only the latter is an example of the employment of the marketing philosophy.[14] In short, the philosophy is not an organizational or functional problem, it is a mental problem. The marketing philosophy can be employed effectively within any organization. Of course, its adoption may cause changes in the organization to better coordinate the effort toward consumers.

Third, consumer orientation is not a philosophy applied to marketing. It is a marketing philosophy applied to the business. In other words, consumer orientation should permeate the whole business, not simply marketing.[15] This does not mean that production and finance managers

---

[12] Fred J. Borch, "The Marketing Philosophy as a Way of Business Life," *Marketing Series No. 99*, American Management Association, Inc., 1957.

[13] For a more complete discussion see: Glenn Walters, "Marketing Philosophy: Buried but not Dead," *Mississippi Business Review* (December, 1970), No. 6, Bureau of Business and Economic Research, College of Business and Industry, Mississippi State University.

[14] Robert J. Keith, "The Marketing Revolution," *Journal of Marketing*, Vol. 24 (January, 1960), pp. 35–39. Keith has a good discussion of the four areas of business philosophy.

[15] Theodore Levitt, "Marketing Myopia," *Harvard Business Review*, Vol. 38 (July–August, 1960), pp. 45ff.

should hire marketers to perform their functions; they simply must be made aware of the importance of their operations to consumers.

Fourth, consumer orientation provides a consistent point of view for developing marketing strategy. This strategy can be implemented in two steps: (1) identify the consumers to be satisfied, and (2) marshal the business's activities to develop a consistent plan for consumer satisfaction. In the second step, the firm should focus on its strength in order to make a differential appeal to the market. A strategy designed on a differential appeal should give the firm the strongest competitive position. Hence the development of a consistent strategy is as important to the entire channel as it is to individual firms in the channel.

CHANNEL PARTICIPANTS

The discussion of marketing channels has proceeded in a logical manner. We defined channels, established the basis for their existence, and discussed their place in and importance to marketing. Now attention can be turned to the question of which institutions participate in the channel of distribution.

Producers Included in the Channel

The decision whether or not to include an institution within the channel of distribution should rest on some concrete criteria. First, the institution included must be a business in the sense that it performs commercial activity for the purpose of making a profit. After all, the channel concerns business operations, and such institutions as government, colleges, and fraternities do not fit the requirement. Second, the institution must create marketing utility. We have demonstrated that the channel is a part of marketing, and it follows that only marketing institutions can be included.

Based on the criteria, the producer is logically a part of the marketing channel.[16] The producer is clearly a business, but there may be some question as to whether the producer creates marketing utility. The answer to this question lies in the distinction between producer and production. Production is the function of creating products, and it is not marketing. However, producers do much more than create products. They also distribute the products produced, and create marketing utility by performing the marketing functions of buying, selling, transportation, and storage. As a matter of fact, marketing is as important to the producer as production. Marketing is interested in production because it is the

[16] Revzan, op. cit., pp. 107–42. Revzan not only justifies manufacturers but provides a good list of channel members.

existence of goods that result from production that provides the stimulus which sets the channel into motion.

Inclusion of Consumers

The inclusion of the consumer in the marketing channel depends on the point of view. The consumer is not a business in the usual sense of the word. That is to say, the consumer functions as a user of commercial output rather than as a creator of it. Also the consumer does not consume for the purpose of making a profit in the business sense. Based on these points, the consumer can quite legitimately be excluded from the channel and this position is the one normally taken by businessmen. A business executive considers that his product has moved out of the channel when it is sold by the retailer to the household consumer. He views the consumer as the object of his activity rather than a participant in it. The consumer does not cooperate with the executive to sell products, and the executive cannot figure consumer cost.

There is another point of view on consumer inclusion in the channel. This view holds that consumers create marketing utility by the performance of such marketing functions as buying, transportation, and storage. It has been said that one reason for increased marketing efficiency is that functions have been shifted to the consumer by such means as self service. It can also be argued that consumers are businesses—they are economic entities due to direct participation in the market, and they do strive for a type of profit. Of course, profit has to be defined as the satisfaction that consumers obtain from using products, rather than monetary gain.

It is felt that there is some merit to both positions. One has to strain the definitions to include the consumer in the channel, but there can be no question that marketing channels concern consumers since they are the ultimate reason for the existence of channels. Perhaps the most compelling reason for excluding consumers from the channel is that we do not know how to include them. In this book, consumers will be included or excluded as necessary.

CHANNEL MODEL USED IN THE BOOK

A model has two important purposes: one, to present the basic variables under investigation; the other, to demonstrate the overall relationships between these variables.[17] These purposes may be served by a highly complex model or by a simple one. A complex model allows the

---

[17] For a more complete discussion of models see: William Lazer, "The Role of Models in Marketing," *Journal of Marketing*, Vol. 26 (April, 1962), pp. 9–14.

reader to analyze all the relationships in detail; it represents the most accurate picture of the subject under discussion. A simple model allows a clearer picture of the more fundamental relationships, but it lacks precision. While the complex model is best suited for research and analysis leading to the extension of knowledge, the simple model is most appropriate for teaching. We shall present a simple but reasonably accurate model of the major variables that are involved in channels management.

The Channels System

The marketing channel is a part of the broader system in which we all live.[18] Any channels model developed must recognize this total system. It is generally conceded that von Bertalanffy first used the term "general systems theory" to describe a set of parts functioning as a total entity.[19] In following von Bertalanffy's lead, a system can be defined as "a set of objects with relationships between objects and their attributes."[20] Thus, systems can be found everywhere including ant colonies, radio receivers, schools, waterways, governments, and typewriters. The requirement for identifying a system is to isolate all the factors that make up that system and determine their attributes and relationships.

The channel of distribution can be considered a part of a system as shown in Figure 1–2. When defining a system it is normal to make the component emphasized the central element and to name the system after that component. In the model, the channel is presented as the central component of a total system that also includes a market and the environment. The components of the system are related in the sense that the channel operates within the opportunities and constraints of the environment to serve the needs of the market.

The idea of a system emphasizes an overall operational process rather than a collection of pieces.[21] This overall process may be subdivided; when this happens we have a sub-system. The channel system described above has three subsystems: the market, the channel, and the environment. Whether a component is a system or a sub-system often depends on the point of view taken. The channel is a sub-system of the total system presented, but taken in isolation the channel can be viewed as a

[18] Louis W. Stern and Jay W. Brown, "Distribution Channels: A Social Systems Approach," *Distribution Channels: Behavioral Dimensions* (Boston: Houghton-Mifflin Co., 1969), pp. 6–19.

[19] Eugene J. Kelley and William Lazer, eds., *Managerial Marketing: Perspectives and Viewpoints,* 3rd ed. (Homewood, Ill.: Richard D. Irwin, Inc., 1967), p. 19. See also: Ludwig von Bertalanffy, *General System Theory* (New York: George Braziller, Inc., 1968), p. 7.

[20] A. D. Hall and R. E. Fagen, "Definitions of a System," *General Systems* (Ann Arbor: University of Michigan Press, 1956), p. 18.

[21] William P. Dommermuth and R. Clifton Anderson, "Distribution Systems— Firms, Functions, and Efficiencies," *Business Topics* (Spring, 1969), pp. 51–56.

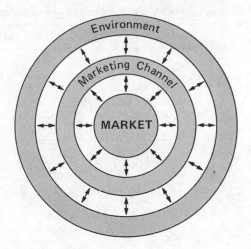

Fig. 1–2. Relationship within the channel system.

system with sub-systems of its own. Many of the sub-systems of marketing can also be viewed as complete systems in their own right.

Channel as a Team Within the System

We have seen that the channel is an important component of a total system, but what type of component it is has not been established. The channel can best be described as a team of marketing institutions operating within the system.[22] Team is used here in the sense of an organization, and the channel displays most of the characteristics of an organization.

There are six factors necessary for an organization to exist: (1) management, (2) activities, (3) communications, (4) roles and status, (5) reward, and (6) objective. Remove any factor and the organization ceases to be an entity. Table 1–1 shows how these organizational factors relate to the specific type of team called a channel.

The primary difference between the channel as a team and any other type of organization is that the channel is composed of business firms rather than individuals. We usually think of people being organized, not things. However, the difference is not so great as one might imagine. A business is most typically described in terms of its human factors rather than its physical factors. When the terms business, institution, member, or firm are used in the context of a channel team, the reference is to the collective management of the firm and not to its physical facili-

22 David O. Ellis and Fred J. Ludwig, *Systems Philosophy* (Englewood Cliffs, N. J.: Prentice-Hall, Inc., 1962), p. 3. See also: George Schwartz, ed., *Science in Marketing* (New York: John Wiley and Sons, Inc., 1965), Chapter 12.

Table 1-1   Factors of an Organization and Channel Team Compared

Organization Factors	Channel Team Factors
Management	Leadership of members
Activities	Operations necessary to achieve objective
Communications	Communications
Member roles and status	Membership structure
Reward for Achievement	Markets to satisfy (combination of reward and objective)
Objective to obtain	

ties, machinery, etc. Used this way, there is little difference in a channel team and any other type of team. Throughout this book, attention is focused on the human elements of channels, particularly management decision making.

Elements of the Channel Team

This book is organized around the channel system, with the emphasis on the management of the channel as a team. Therefore, it is important that all the elements constituting that team be understood at the outset. The five elements of the channel introduced in the previous section are arranged into the simple model presented in Figure 1–3. The market is placed in the center of the model because all channel activity is directed at satisfying some market. Also, the market is different from the other factors. It lies outside the channel membership, but it is the force that draws the members together and provides the incentive to cooperate. Both the reason for cooperation and the reward for effective performance are found in the external market. The four internal factors of channel team effort are placed around the market. This arrangement demon-

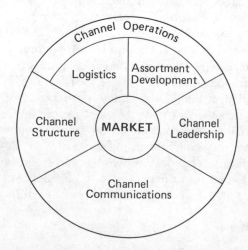

Fig. 1–3. Elements of the channel team.

strates their equal importance and emphasizes their interaction with each other and with the market. Each of the internal factors of the channel team are discussed below.

Channel Operations. Channels cannot reach desired markets without the performance of certain operations. The channel members must do something—perform some activities to achieve their objective. Channels perform the two operations of assortment development and logistics. Assortment development is the practice of combining different types of products with specific services throughout the channel. Assortment development provides customers with differential choice in the market place. Logistics is the movement of products to market. It includes both over-the-road movement, which is called transportation, and storage, which is called warehousing.

Channel Leadership. Channel leadership is necessary to focus channel members on the objective and to provide the decision making necessary to perform operations. Leadership is used in this context in much the same manner as management. The channel leader is responsible for stimulating, motivating, and coordinating members of the marketing channel.

Channel Communications. Communication is the basis for all interaction within the channel and between channel members and outsiders. Communication results from interaction through the exchange of information; without it the leader could not stimulate and control members. Internal information flow includes orders, directives, memorandum, information, etc., and passes between members. Persuasive communications take place mostly between members and the market. Both types are important to channel operations.

Channel Structure. Channel structure refers to the manner in which channel members are organized, their status, and their roles within the team. In a management sense, channel membership must be determined and individual relationships specified. The members who constitute the channel structure can be roughly divided into agents and merchants. Merchants take title to goods, and the important merchants are manufacturers, wholesalers, and retailers. Agents do not take title, and all marketing institutions except the ones specified as merchants are classed as agents.

Channel Environment

With the introduction of the environment, the model of the channels system is made complete as Figure 1-4 demonstrates. Broadly speaking, the environment consists of all external factors that influence the behavior of the channel team. The factors of the channel's environment have been grouped for ease of handling into: (1) social environment, (2) economic

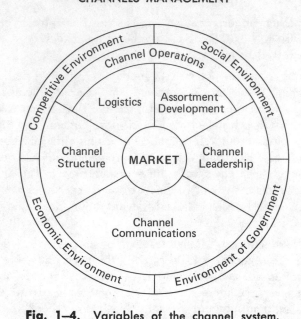

Fig. 1–4. Variables of the channel system.

environment, (3) environment of government, and (4) competitive environment. Each of these factors is discussed below.

Competitive Environment. Competition refers to the economic pressure brought to bear on a given channel, or its members, by other businesses. Competition places pressure on the channel by threatening to take away markets. The channel may have to modify operations because of this competition. It is certainly true that at no time can the channel members ignore competition. They have two basic choices in meeting competition. They can attempt to be like competitors doing the same operations but perform them more efficiently, or they can attempt to make an appeal different from that of competitors.

Environment of Government. Government is the legally constituted administrative body of any socio-economic system. It exists at the local, state, and federal levels. Government affects the channel of distribution by means of legal restraint and direct pressure. First, the legal environment is the structure of common and statutory law. The channel must operate in conformity with these laws. Second, government includes all duly appointed or elected officials. Government agencies, such as the Federal Trade Commission, the Pure Food and Drug Administration, and the Justice Department can affect channel operations by means of persuasion, economic pressure, or threat.

Social Environment. The social environment is a catch-all term used here to include both the social and cultural environments of our system.

The social environment is the factor of public opinion and it operates through the ethics, mores, folkways, and morals of the society. It is generally thought of as the majority opinion that shapes the social values of the culture; in practice, however, the social values that result may or may not be the effect of majority opinion. In any case, the marketing channel must operate within the general values established by the society. When business steps outside these values some type of persuasive or legal censure is brought to bear in order to force conformity. It is through the social factors that the market is brought into the external environmental factor. The same people who constitute consumers operate to exert external influence on the operation of the channel. In this sense the market is discussed twice: once as an opportunity and once as a constraint.

Economic Environment. The economic system refers primarily to the level of economic activity. In effect, it is the productivity or efficiency of the system. The most important concepts normally associated with the economic environment are the allocation of resources and the business cycle. Both the productivity of the system and inflation affect the channel. Inflation erodes profit while productivity contributes directly to the efficiency of channel members.

These four factors encompass the environment of channels. On the model, the environment contains the channel team within its factors. This placement emphasizes that the environment has an effect on all aspects of the team's management including structure, communications, leadership, and operations. The environment also interacts with the market, and each environmental factor influences the other environmental factors. The degree of influence among the various elements of the channel system varies from channel to channel and over time.

CHARACTERISTICS OF THE CHANNEL SYSTEM

There is more to understanding the channel system than identifying the components that make up that system. The system operates as a unit, and displays specific characteristics that largely determine the manner in which the system functions. The channel system has three important characteristics: (1) human involvement, (2) structure, and (3) closure.

Human Involvement

Systems can be classified on the basis of human involvement into physical or behavioral types.[23] A physical system is one that operates essen-

[23] Wroe Alderson, *Dynamic Marketing Behavior* (Homewood, Ill.: Richard D. Irwin, Inc., 1965), pp. 43-45. This discussion is based on Alderson.

tially as a result of non-human components. A radio receiver, a river system, or a typewriter are examples of physical systems. Humans may be involved in the operation, but the components and relationships are basically non-human. The system functions by either mechanical or natural means.

A behavioral system is one that is based on the interaction of some living organisms. While the mechanical system is mindless, the behavioral system is not. It is capable of thought. Because the system thinks, it is capable of change and development. Any system characterized by human involvement is subject to errors in judgment, emotional responses, miscalculations, and second thought. However, the human system can learn from its errors and make adjustments. Thus, while a mechanical system can never improve through its own efforts, the behavioral system can.

The system to which the channel belongs is a behavioral system. It displays many of the attributes of a living organism. The system seeks favor and avoids pain, as when the channel attempts to please consumers. The system strives for survival, but its survival depends on the separate decisions of millions of individual persons organized into necessary institutions. This fact is true of any living organism. When some part of the channel system ceases to function or when the system is otherwise threatened, it attempts to correct the situation. Pollution today is like a cancer eating at the channel system, and already the social, economic, and channel sub-systems are at work attempting to find solutions.

Structure

Systems can be defined by the amount of structure existing within them. Alderson, who has provided a successful classification of this type, describes systems as: (1) atomistic, (2) ecological, and (3) mechanistic.[24] The atomistic system has no rigid relationships among members; its components are free to associate in a completely random fashion. This type of system is similar to gas in a chamber. When turned loose, the gas fills every part of the chamber in a completely unstructured manner. In the mechanistic system, the parts are rigidly held together. A motor makes a good example—although the pistons, shaft, and other parts can move, they can move only in one prescribed way. Unlike gas that has no structure, all parts of the structured system are rigidly connected.

Ecological systems are characterized by thinking components such as those found in channels of distribution. Ecological systems lie somewhere between the atomistic and the mechanistic system. In the ecological system, the components are loosely connected. There is movement, but the

[24] Wroe Alderson, *Marketing Behavior and Executive Action* (Homewood, Ill.: Richard D. Irwin, Inc., 1957), pp. 27–30.

movement does not follow the same prescribed pattern each time. For example, in the channel sub-system, institutions can be added or dropped, they can change their function, and different strategies may be employed over time. The same is true for other sub-systems in the channel system. The attitude of consumers may differ from one time to the next, competition may increase or decrease, and government activities may vary. There is sufficient permanence to the relationships among channel components so that the system can function satisfactorily even while adjustments in the structure are taking place.

Closure

Any system can be considered as either open or closed.[25] A closed system is one in which all the components are present, relations are fully specified, and the components are efficient. In other words, a closed system is one that is complete. An open system is one that is incomplete in some manner. The channel system may be considered open if the channel needs a change in membership, if government is ineffective, if competition is inadequate, etc.

Actually, the system to which channels belong can be considered simultaneously open and closed. That is to say, the channel system is never complete, but as a behavioral system it is sufficiently complete to function. The result is that the system functions at reduced efficiency. The important point is not that the system can function, but that it always strives to achieve closure. Just as there are automatic forces in the human body that cause it to attempt to maintain equilibrium, the channel system automatically seeks closure. If management becomes too powerful, labor unions develop. When retailers are needed in the suburbs, the pressure of demand causes a movement out from the city; and when business becomes too powerful, the government begins to exercise control. The system changes so rapidly that the achievement of closure may be impossible, but striving for it is characteristic of the system. Because the channel system is open to change, expansion, and improvement it is dynamic; because it is closed, it is a practical tool of marketing.

QUESTIONS

1. Compare the historical definition of channels with the definition used in the text.
2. Discuss how the flow of title and goods progresses through the channel with and without change of ownership.
3. Discuss the industrial and final consumer markets with reference to consumption and distribution.

[25] Kelley and Lazer, *op. cit.*, pp. 25–26.

4. Discuss marketing's place with reference to channels of distribution in the creation of economic value.
5. Discuss how channels of distribution aid in the creation of utility.
6. Compare and contrast organizational factors and channel team factors.
7. Discuss the interaction of the different elements of the channel team and various environments.
8. Discuss how a system can be both open and closed?
9. Compare the function of production and marketing in the economic system.
10. Are producers a part of the marketing channel? Are consumers?

2

Development of Channels

Chapter 2 examines how channels arose, where they came from, and how they have evolved. The emphasis is not on historical description for its own sake but for its reflection of the concepts and theories of channel development.

THE SELF-CONTAINED ECONOMIC SYSTEM

Modern economic systems include production, marketing, and consumption, but it is possible to conceive of an economic system without marketing. This situation exists when the sole producing unit in the system is also the sole consuming unit. Such an economic system can be described as *self-contained*, or self-sufficient, since it operates without any exchange of goods with outsiders.[1] Production and distribution are combined in this simple system and occur simultaneously with consumption. The system requires no physical or title movement for the goods produced. Thus, there is no external route for products between producers and no marketing channel.

Early Systems

Self-contained economic systems probably existed at the dawn of history. In order for man to survive, each family provided for its members' needs and did not interact or trade in any way with other families. The children left the group early to establish their own lives independently or in association with a mate. The acquisition of food required a nomadic

[1] "Association of the Household," *The Politics of Aristotle* (New York: Oxford University Press, 1958), pp. 22–24.

existence, and once separated, the two groups drifted without regard to one another. Interaction was, at best, the result of chance. Even when it occurred, there was no assurance that the encounter would be friendly. Family loyalty had not been established.

These self-contained economic systems based on family survival are not unique to early history. Examples of such systems can be found in more recent times. The feudal system of Europe is one, and the frontier family of colonial America also qualifies. American frontier families were isolated from their neighbors and were forced by circumstances to be independent. Anything family members could not provide from the garden or forest, the family did without.

Conclusions

Several conclusions can be deduced concerning the self-contained systems. First, self-contained economic systems occur only rarely and in isolation. They do not occur where large numbers of people are concentrated, and they are of little importance to modern societies. Second, the standard of living is very low in these systems because of inherent deficiencies. The most important deficiency is the inability to take advantage of the special or unique skills of other people. There is little chance to advance knowledge because of the lack of contact with other people. Thus, improvement in efficiency occurs very slowly. Third, channels of distribution are associated with relatively advanced societies. As the economic system advances, trade based on the use of channels forms an alternative to self-contained systems.

Importance of Channels

It is true that channels of distribution are not universal to man's existence. A knowledge of the self-contained system indicates this fact. This lack of universality should not lull one into believing that channels are unimportant. Importance is determined not by frequency of occurrence but by the significance of the contribution. After all, dirt is more universal than diamonds, but the latter have greater economic value. So it is with channels of distribution. No modern economic system can exist without channels because of the separation of production and consumption as a result of specialization. The channel of distribution is necessary to bridge the gap in any specialized society.[2] It can be demonstrated that channels of distribution contribute to the overall efficiency of the system, and marketing channels are universal to all economic systems other than the very simplest.

[2] Ralph F. Breyer, "Some Observations on 'Structural' Formation and the Growth of Marketing Channels," *Theory In Marketing*, Reavis Cox, Wroe Alderson, and Stanley J. Shapiro, eds. (Homewood, Ill.: Richard D. Irwin, Inc., 1964), pp. 163–75. This article introduces several generally useful concepts of channel structure.

EXPLANATIONS FOR TRADE CHANNELS

Trade and channels both arise when the producer finds cause to look beyond internal requirements in order to dispose of all, or a part, of his output.[3] This disposal through exchange necessitates a channel. Thus, there can be no trade without channels, and no channels without trade. It follows that the explanation of how one arises is the explanation of how the other arises. There is no way that we can check with accuracy the processes that led to trade and marketing channels. Of the many attempts to explain how trade arises, some have been simple and some complex; and even today, scholars differ in their assessment of the situation. Nevertheless, there is sufficient information to draw some tentative conclusions on the origins of trade and the development of channels.

Single Explanation Syndrome

Where channels and trade are concerned, as with most other phenomena, there is a tendency to seek the single explanation. This tendency is almost an obsession with some scholars. The argument is that if one result follows from two different causes, then the researcher simply has not looked sufficiently far to find the common thread that links both causes. There has to be a single cause for mankind, poverty, theft, trade, and channels. In short, if one carries the argument sufficiently far, everything results from a single cause.

The evidence is strong that there is no single explanation that covers all the possibilities for the development of trade channels. Furthermore, it is not felt that a single explanation is necessary.

Explanations Advanced for Trade

There have been four fundamental explanations advanced for how trade arises: [4] (1) trade is instinctive, (2) trade arises out of conflict, (3) trade depends on giving, and (4) trade is explained by economic considerations.

Trade Is Instinctive. A basic argument for the development of trade holds that trade is instinctive with man. Although little concrete evidence is presented to support this contention, it is argued that trade is a type of social interaction, and man is a social animal. He instinctively seeks out his fellow man, and upon occasion his fellow woman, for peaceful social interaction. One natural way in which this socialization is mani-

---

[3] Marketing is sometimes referred to as trade, and the terms are used here to mean the same thing.

[4] George W. Robbins, "Notions About the Origins of Trading," *Journal of Marketing*, Vol. 11 (January, 1947), pp. 228–36.

fest is through trade.[5] Man supposedly has an inborn urge to swap his goods for the goods of others. This swapping may be symbolic of man's need for his fellow man. The idea of the "natural born salesman" is based on this concept. According to this explanation, trade had to emerge because man cannot exist without trading.

Conflict Theories of Trade. Another theory is that trade developed out of conflict. This explanation, which is directly opposed to the idea that trade is instinctive, holds that trade is learned as a result of hostile actions. There are two types of conflict—warfare and predation. The difference between them is one of degree. Warfare is an open conflict based on force where the object is to kill or incapacitate the enemy and take his possessions. The head hunters of New Zealand are an example of this type of society. Predation is more subtle. It is based on the stealing of possessions from an enemy through deception and cunning without the offended becoming aware of who is responsible. The Bushman of Australia and the Plains Indians of the United States are examples of societies based on predation.

In both warfare and predation, man is seen as basically hostile to his fellow man. This hostility is natural and a part of the nature of man. It also has an economic basis since it represents a means of obtaining the goods of others without giving up anything in return. The proponents of the conflict explanation see trade as an alternative to conflict. The conflict sets up social interaction, but there are inherent dangers due to the use of force. Sooner or later, man seeks ways to lessen the danger, and trade shows itself to be a superior method of gaining wanted goods.

Trade Depends on Giving. Another explanation of trade is based on gift giving and, like the conflict explanations, it has two possibilities. One is friendly gift giving and the other is hostile gift giving or "silent trade." Both of these possibilities are opposed to the conflict and instinctive explanations already presented. The gift-giving concept considers trade to be learned, but not a result of direct hostility. This concept does not recognize hostility as necessarily innate in man. Friendly giving may have grown out of natural human affection and the desire to show appreciation. Some primitive tribes in Africa and South America still display this trait. Indeed, gift giving may have developed from the self-contained economic system as the family unit became more cohesive.

Unlike friendly trade, silent trade developed between essentially cautious tribes, and in some cases there was no physical or face-to-face interaction. Overtime, a particular place became institutionalized as "holy" ground. One tribe brought gifts, placed them on the ground, and retired. The other group came at a different time, inspected the goods, and took

[5] John Wheeler, "Civil Life Lies in Fellowship; Fellowship in Government and Trade," *A Treatise of Commerce,* 1601.

them if satisfied. This second group left goods of their own in return. The first group reappeared to take the second group's goods. This form of trade is still found among some primitive tribes. Such gift giving becomes trade when the two parties begin to place values on the gifts and expect equal values in return. In this case, the discovery of the utility of exchange leads to trade.[6]

Economic Explanations for Trade. Trade may have developed for economic reasons. These include (1) the recognition of property ownership and (2) the creation of surpluses. It can be argued that for trade to take place the parties trading must have legal or physical control over the property they wish to trade. The proponents of this concept place all the emphasis on private property. Control over property can lead one to appreciate its value and to wish to increase goods he has in scarce supply. Either could precede to the idea of trade. However, it is erroneous to assume that *only* private property can lead to trade; there is evidence of trade developing with the use of community property. All that is necessary is to designate someone, such as the tribal chief or the village elder, to handle the property and act for the group in trading.

The idea of surpluses as the basis for trade is a common one. Specialization of labor leads to surpluses that are available to trade. The very existence of these surpluses causes the producer to look for methods of disposing of the goods. This explanation sees trade as the direct result of economic pressures. These pressures could lead to gift giving which in turn could lead to trade. Furthermore, a lack of goods—the opposite of surpluses—could be a reason for warfare in order to obtain the necessary goods.

PROBLEMS WITH SINGLE EXPLANATIONS OF TRADE

Each of the attempts to explain trade on the basis of a single, all-inclusive explanation runs afoul of logic. We shall discuss below the two basic causes of the difficulty. First, there is inconsistency between the several explanations. Second, the explanations explain socialization, not trade.

Inconsistency in Explanations

It is difficult to maintain that trade is instinctive when there is evidence that the Incas and early Polish peasants lived for centuries without any form of trade.[7] Warfare as a single explanation makes it hard to place

[6] Elizabeth E. Hoyt, *Primitive Trade: Its Psychology and Economics* (London: Kegan Paul, Trench and Co., Ltd., 1926), p. 104.

[7] Robbins, *op. cit.*, pp. 22–28. This discussion is based on Robbins.

the Eskimo of the Arctic and the Semang of the Malay peninsula, neither of which knew the meaning of warfare until introduced to the subject by modern man. Gift giving is also not an adequate explanation for trade, for it makes the known evidence of trade based on warfare difficult to explain. Nor does the economic theory appear logical as the single explanation of the way that trade arises. In the first place, there were few surpluses among primitive tribes. Their lives were more nearly characterized by a constant striving for subsistence rather than by abundance. Furthermore, there is some evidence that the institution of private property was developed because of trade rather than the other way around. When tribes began to trade, they developed a more formal attitude toward things. Whereas, before trade, things could be picked up and disposed of at will, trade required ownership over the things traded. One can only conclude from the evidence that there is no single explanation for the origin of trade.

Socialization Explained, Not Trade

None of the single explanation theories of how trade arises actually gets at the reason why trade develops. Each implies only that some particular type of interaction leads to trade. None of the concepts explains how the connection comes about. The fact remains that the explanations advanced for trade are, in fact, better suited as reasons for social interaction. Trade is just another type of social interaction and could have developed in the same manner as any other type of social interaction.

No doubt some types of social interaction (such as the display of affection) are instinctive. The human child is helpless at birth. If it were not for the instinctive love and care of the parents, the child would die. Thus man could not have developed into the highly intelligent being he has become without the basic family unit and the natural socialization contained therein. Other types of socialization, between families or larger groups, include warfare, gift giving, predation, and economic socialization. After all, warfare is a type of social interaction just as much as gift giving is. Both involve communications, contact, and give and take. The primary difference between the two lies in the respective purpose and means of contact. As we shall see, the emergence of trade and channels resulted from a complexity of factors. Certainly socialization was a part of the explanation, but it was only a part. Trade does not occur automatically because man socializes.

FACTORS OF CHANNEL DEVELOPMENT

The belief is that trade may have developed for slightly different reasons in different parts of the world or at different points in time. However, there does appear to be a group of factors that have a direct bearing on the emergence of trade channels. Six factors can be identified that, if present, singly or in combination, increase the chances for trade channels to develop, but it cannot be said that their presence guarantees that there will be trade. These six factors are: (1) socialization, (2) specialized production, (3) control over property, (4) surpluses, (5) appreciation of values, and (6) ordered markets.[8] All of these factors need not be present, but the more that are, the greater the likelihood of the emergence of trade.

Socialization

Socialization refers to the interactions based on communication that takes place between individuals and groups.[9] Channels cannot exist without this socialization because a channel requires an exchange between two individuals or two institutions. In a real sense, the channel is a specialized device for economic socialization based on prescribed routes or social contact.[10] Where there is socialization of any type there is greater chance that channels will result at some point in time. One type of interaction leads to other types of interaction. Man, as a curious animal, likes to experiment with different kinds of social contacts. Channels for trade are likely to emerge as a natural extension of other contacts such as gift giving or as an alternative to such contacts as predation or warfare. A people capable of inventing conflict and gift giving are capable of inventing channels.

Specialized Production

The introduction of specialized production is another factor that increases the chances that channels will develop. Specialization tends to increase interdependence among people. Interdependence tends to open channels for the exchange of economic goods. In fact, specialization goes hand in hand with surpluses which are discussed later. It allows the producer to become proficient in his work because full time can be devoted to perfecting his task to the exclusion of other duties.

Specialization does not necessarily lead to trade or channels. In the beginning, a specialized producer may simply have had fewer goods. If a man did nothing but hunt, he lived off meat to the exclusion of vegetables. He need not automatically seek a channel to dispose of some of

[8] Reavis Cox, *Distribution in a High Level Economy* (Englewood Cliffs, N. J.: Prentice-Hall, Inc., 1965), pp. 17–24. Cox offers a different explanation for the rise of distribution.

[9] Edwin H. Lewis, *Marketing Channels: Structure and Strategy* (New York: McGraw-Hill Book Co., Inc., 1968), pp. 4–5.

[10] Louis W. Stern, *Distribution Channels: Behavioral Discussion* (Boston: Houghton-Mifflin Co., 1969), pp. 13–19.

his meat for other products. Furthermore, a specialized producer does not necessarily mean the producer of a single good. There are degrees to specialization.[11] A person producing ten goods is more specialized than one producing a hundred. A specialized producer can have a sufficient variety of goods to survive without channels of trade.

A producer may restrict the number of goods produced in order to have more of the ones kept. The restriction may be due to the aversion the producer has to doing certain work. For example, one may specialize in farming either because farming is enjoyable or because of ineptitude or because of a dislike for hunting. Thus, the idea of specialization could have developed gradually as further restrictions on the number of products produced were made. At any rate, once the concept of specialization becomes entrenched in the group, the chance of channels developing is increased. The step is a logical one as each producer observes his own holdings of some goods increase and of others decrease, relative to his neighbor's. The producer can logically be expected sooner or later to want to re-establish his holding by means of trade and a channel is the result.

Surpluses

Producer surpluses complement specialization. Specialization, as a result of increased efficiency, leads to increased output of a limited number of goods. The surplus, thus created, may not be absolute in the sense that the producer has more than he can use. It can be relative in the sense that the manufacturer is able to produce more of product A in relation to product B. The concept of relative surplus has been called the law of comparative advantage. Even though the producer desires more of both goods, he is willing to swap some of A for some of B. Comparative advantage assumes some other producer can make more of B relative to A. Where surpluses exist, the chances of channels developing are increased. Actually, the relative surpluses provide the goods that are necessary to move through marketing channels. There is a tendency to try to find some outlet for the surpluses, and the use of channels to trade is a natural means for disposal of the extra goods.

Control Over Property

The opportunity for channels to develop is increased with control over property. The very idea of a movement of goods suggests that one has control over the goods that are moved. Control over property is based on either of two alternatives. First, property control can be founded on

[11] Cox, *op. cit.*, pp. 14–16.

power or force. The desire to control things by force is a possible factor that leads to socialization in the form of warfare or predation. Thus these factors interact. It is probably true that property was first based on power. A man killed an animal, and he could consume whatever portion he could forcibly keep others from taking. A weapon or tool belonged to the person who had physical possession of it. Once a thing was put down it was lost forever.

Second, control over property can be based on law. This type of control came much later in history. It was perhaps the result of a recognition that interaction based on rules removed much of the guesswork. Rule of law provided security for the fruits of one's labor and created greater incentive to work. The legal basis for property control developed slowly, probably growing out of informal rules imposed by force by a leader within the group. Later the group began making its own rules, including those for electing the leader.

The likelihood for channels is increased with control over property, but that control does not have to be private. The chances are that in the beginning community property was jointly owned. Control was in the hands of a group of tribal elders. There is evidence that any surpluses of goods were placed under communal control in this manner. In the beginning, the community goods may have been used for gift giving. Later trade developed. The elders, not the individuals, controlled trade and the channel. Private property perhaps developed out of dissatisfaction with the manner in which the elders handled the public property, or it may have resulted from a desire to have greater control over the disposal of individual goods. Communal trade is likely to result in communal use, and this method of use is at best unhandy and inflexible. At any rate, whether private or public, control over property increases the chances of developing channels.

Appreciation of Value

A proper appreciation of the value of things is certainly a factor that increases the likelihood of having channels develop. It is difficult to understand how anyone could trade without some understanding of the relative worth of the things being swapped. There must be some appreciation of value in order to initiate the idea that goods can be traded. Gift giving can be accomplished without the idea of value because nothing is expected in return. The moment something is given with the idea of obtaining something, gift giving ceases and trade begins. Even today when a mother moans, "After all the nice wedding gifts we have given to the Joneses, they have the nerve to give our daughter this little thing," it is understood that no giving has actually taken place. What we have here is simply an unequal trade.

Ordered Markets

Ordered markets may not be absolutely necessary for channels to develop, but the chances of their developing and flourishing is greatly enhanced by ordered markets. The term ordered markets means the assurance that market interactions will take place under predictable circumstances. For example, there must be some assurance that contracts will be honored, that goods will not be stolen, that quality is not misrepresented, that one actually owns the goods, etc. Without these assurances, there can be individual channels of exchange, but the use of channels as an established way of life is practically impossible. Some order is the basis for all social interaction, including trade. Man has found that even with gift giving and warfare, there have to be rules of the game and ways have always been found to enforce these rules.

EMERGENCE OF CHANNELS

We have discussed the factors that underlie the development of channels of distribution, but have said little about the process whereby these channels arise. In order to explain the process it is necessary to discuss the non-channel system: decentralized and centralized trade channels. The discussion would not be complete without reference to channel efficiency and the ratio of advantage in favor of centralized channels. The section ends with an illustration of how channel members proliferate.

Non-channel System

Suppose that a group of families decide to get together for some reason. It may be for social interaction, defense, or for any of the other types of socialization that have already been discussed. Let us say that the group gets together for defense purposes and builds a wall around their community as shown in Figure 2–1.

As the illustration demonstrates, there is no trade in the group although there is social interaction. Thus, we have a collective social system, and five self-contained economic systems, but no single economic system among the five families. The social system may or may not be quite highly advanced. There may be a community leader, and there may be status and roles of a social nature established. The defense mechanism may be highly organized with specialized functions among the members. In spite of this complexly structured social activity, there is no channel of distribution within which trade can take place. All the members of the community provide for their own needs, and each family's economic ac-

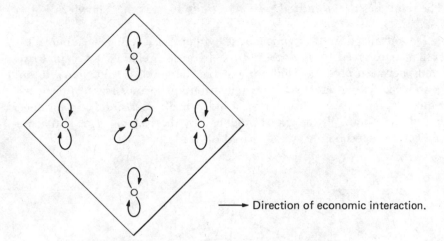

——→ Direction of economic interaction.

Fig. 2–1. The self-contained group.

tivity is turned inward. The only economic specialization that can exist must be within the family group. It is a truism of self-contained systems that there are no surpluses to trade. There is no reason to suspect that this society could not exist for an indefinite period of time, functioning in the manner described. However, it has also been demonstrated that there are possibilities for trade to develop in this group.

Decentralized Trade Channels

Once the group gets together, possibilities arise for improving the lot of all of its members.[12] The result of interaction leads to observations and assessments of individual workers. Someone is bound to notice that individual community members have different interests and aptitudes. One member may be a good fisherman but a poor gardener. The gardener may not enjoy making tools. The hunter may spend so much time on the trail that he has little time for anything else. One could not help observing that individual differences cause each person to have more of some goods and less of others. Perhaps control over property and the rule of law have already been established in order to handle problems arising out of normal social interaction. Given these or similar circumstances, the catalyst that leads to channels may be nothing more than normal discussion. One member hits on the idea of each member doing that job for which he is best suited and swapping some goods with others.

[12] Wroe Alderson, "Factors Governing the Development of Marketing Channels," *Marketing Channels,* Richard M. Clewett, ed. (Homewood, Ill.: Richard D. Irwin, Inc., 1954), pp. 5–34. This analysis is based on Alderson's article.

The result is a *decentralized system of trade* such as that shown in Figure 2–2.[13]

Decentralized trade cannot exist without marketing channels. The system is referred to as decentralized because exchange takes place directly between producer and consumer. The goods do not move to any central marketing agency before redistribution to buyers. In the decentralized system, each consumer must individually seek out every producer in order to obtain all the goods produced by the system. This is the simplest form of economic system based on trade.

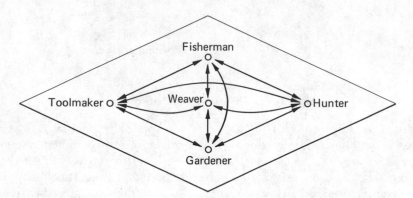

Fig. 2–2. Decentralized trade channel.

Decentralized trade offers several advantages over the self-contained economic system. First, the number of products available to each consumer is increased because more people are producing. Second, specialization and division of labor lead to more and better products. Each person in the system can spend the necessary time to become proficient in producing his own specialized product. Third, facilities can be consolidated to do a specialized task, also benefiting and further promoting efficiency. Decentralized trade obviously offers benefits. However, all the increased efficiency occurs on the production side of the market. What we have with decentralized trade is specialized production but nonspecialized marketing.

The inefficiencies on the marketing side of the decentralized system are clear. First, the number of transactions are excessive. Figure 2–2 shows that it takes ten separate trips by the consumer in order to obtain all the goods produced by the system. Second, too much time is wasted by individuals traveling. The ten separated transactions plus the fact that goods are bought in small quantity necessitates these frequent trips.

[13] Wroe Alderson, *Marketing Behavior and Executive Action* (Homewood, Ill.: Richard D. Irwin, Inc., 1957), pp. 211–12.

Small quantity purchases are the rule with direct sale and little storage since the seller must sell as he produces. Third, there is too much time wasted in negotiation. Excessive negotiation results because the consumer must dicker ten different times for the desired products. Time spent traveling and negotiating is time that the individual cannot use making goods of his own. If the number of purchases and deliveries are not simultaneous, the number of trips can expand to twenty. The end result is that marketing efficiency tends to decrease the efficiency of production as well, and the entire system suffers. Clearly, then, there is ample room for improvement in the decentralized trade system.

Centralized Trade Channels

The inefficiencies associated with the decentralized trade system are likely to create pressures leading to the development of *centralized trade*. Assume that one man located in the center of our community, as illustrated in Figure 2–3, has practically no aptitude toward production. He cannot hunt, fish, weave, farm, or make tools. He may be a thoroughly lazy man, and although he appreciates a high standard of living, he sees no chance of achieving one under present circumstances. Thus, our hero is slowly starving to death in the midst of plenty. Finally, he observes that he has two advantages over his neighbors: first, he is cen-

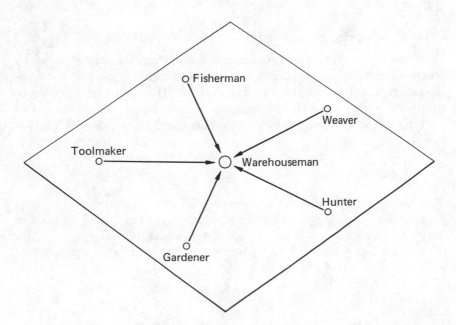

Fig. 2–3. Centralized trade channel.

trally located in the community; second, his father left him the largest hut. Armed with this knowledge, he goes to his neighbors with a proposition. Let each producer bring his output to the central location and store it with proper identification. Then each consumer in the community could make a single trip and enter into one negotiation in order to obtain all the goods produced by the community.

What we have here is an example of a centralized trade system. It is called a centralized system because goods are sold through an intermediary. The specialization and division of labor already introduced on the production side of the system are now introduced on the marketing side. Once again the entire system has increased efficiency.[14] Everyone specializes and spends less time traveling and negotiating. There is more time available for work and the standard of living goes up.

The centralized trade system contains an example of the first completely independent marketing middleman. Our warehouseman is in effect a retailer selling to final consumers, and the channel of distribution is manufacturer–retailer–consumer. The middleman is a specialist in marketing, and he performs no production activity at all. Notice that our centralized system required six members to produce the same products that were produced by five members in the decentralized system. The centralized system is a more roundabout system, but is more efficient because the roundaboutness offers opportunities to specialize in both production and marketing.

Ratio of Advantage

It was demonstrated in the above analysis that the efficiency of an economic system can be improved with the introduction of merchant specialists into the channels of distribution. This fact can be demonstrated by formula as well as by reason.[15] The formula needed to determine the number of transactions in decentralized trade can be expressed as follows:

$$\frac{N(N-1)}{2}$$

The designation N indicates the number of producers where each producer makes a single product. The minus 1 is the number of degrees of freedom. Remember in our example of a decentralized trade system there were 5 producers. If we place these 5 producers in our formula, we obtain the following results:

$$\frac{5(5-1)}{2} = \frac{20}{2} = 10$$

---

[14] Lewis, *op. cit.*, pp. 4–5.
[15] Alderson, *Marketing Behavior and Executive Action, op. cit.*, pp. 213–14.

The formula indicates that 10 transactions are necessary to obtain all the goods in a decentralized system possessing 5 producers. This is the result we discovered in the previous analysis.

In the centralized trade system, the number of transactions is simply N. Thus, in a centralized system with 5 producers, only 5 transactions are necessary. This fact coincides with our earlier findings on the centralized system.

It is possible to work out a ratio of advantage favoring the centralized system based on the above formulas. This ratio can be expressed as follows:

$$\frac{N-1}{2} = \frac{4}{2} = 2$$

Thus, in our simple example, the ratio of advantage is 2, and this figure is the same as that obtained by dividing the 10 transactions from the decentralized system by the transactions in the centralized system.

The ratio of advantage of 2 may not appear to be great, but it must be remembered that the number of producers in the example is only 5. The ratio of advantage in favor of centralized trade and the longer channel of distribution go up astronomically as more producers are added to the system. For example, with 50 producers the ratio of advantage is 24.5 and with 100 producers it becomes 49.5. Even these figures do not tell the complete story. In a modern society there are thousands of producers and each produces multiple products. It should be obvious to the reader that the channel of distribution employing specialists greatly increases the efficiency of any economic system.

Proliferation of Middlemen

The number of consumers and the distances involved in the economic system so far have been small. It is not difficult to understand how wholesalers and other types of middlemen develop when the economic system becomes more complex. Once the principle of specialization in middlemen is discovered, the types are likely to proliferate as attempts are made to gain further advantages. The development of the wholesaler and other middlemen is likely to follow (see Figure 2-4).

A manufacturer selling through a single wholesaler can reach fifteen consumers in widely scattered communities with only one transaction. Three transactions are necessary if the manufacturer sells to the consumers through retailers, and fifteen transactions to sell directly to each consumer. The introduction of the wholesaler generally brings with it the specialization of the retailer. The wholesaler does not sell to final consumers and the retailer sells only to final consumers. The channel of distribution is further lengthened and the distributions system thus be-

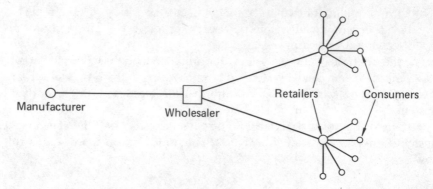

Fig. 2–4. Proliferation of middlemen.

comes more complex. Efficiency is increased by the greater specialization and even greater reduction in transactions and travel. One should not confuse complexity with inefficiency; the efficiency of specialization is sufficient to offset the problems of complexity and increased handling caused by the longer channel.

EVOLUTION OF MIDDLEMEN

In discussing the emergence of middlemen, we have not explained the sophistication of today's channel members. The evolutionary process that gave us the variety of efficient merchants constituting present channels will now be examined.

Early Producers

Lewis says, "The history of man is a progression from hunter to herder to agriculturist to craftsman." [16] This statement emphasizes man as a producer. There is no question that man was producing even before he was trading. The first producers perhaps did nothing more than scratch for berries and hunt small animals. Later man learned to control animals and became a herder. About the same level of intelligence that invents herding is necessary to invent trade, and the two probably emerged at about the same time. The producer became the first channel member in a vastly different society. The pattern of the producer was established as one who changes the physical form of goods.

It was left to the invention of agriculture to tie man to one place. Once he settled down, man's productivity and the variety of his production vastly increased. There followed an interest in the development and

[16] Lewis, *op. cit.*, p. 8.

use of tools, and man became the manufacturer of a variety of implements to aid him in his pursuits. The stone, bronze, iron, and steel ages are a tribute to man's increasingly diversified production. Gradually, man began to systematize and specialize his manufacturing. Millers, bakers, furriers, cobblers, candlemakers, and farmers resulted. Such craftsmen producers had developed by the time of the Roman empire, but they reached their zenith in colonial Europe and America. The craftsmen still tended to deal directly with the consumer. It was between 1700 to 1900 that producers grew greatly in physical size and diversity of product line. At the same time the producer become increasingly removed from consumers. Greater dependence was placed on wholesalers and retailers to distribute the manufacturers' output. Today, producers have expanded the number and variety of their skills to become among the largest institutions in America.

Combination Merchants

The first middlemen who specialized in marketing were probably retailers, but they had no allegiance to consumer sales. These merchants would sell to anyone—producers, other merchants, or consumers. Chances are that the village elders, who were basically politicians, doubled as merchants. As the tasks of merchant and politician became increasingly complex the two jobs were separated.

Later merchants specialized in shipping, and the caravans of the Mediterranean area are world famous. These shipping merchants sold at retail and wholesale. The Phoenicians were great seafarers and by 1500 B.C. had trade routes all over the known world. As civilization shifted, first to Greece and later to Rome, so did trade. In these nations where goods from all over the world concentrated, active small merchants developed around the seaports. These, like their predecessors, were combination merchants who re-shipped goods to other European and Asian ports and inland to the major cities of the time. Such channels tended to be direct although there is some evidence that specialist wholesalers may have developed by the time of the Roman empire.

Beginning of Retailing

Civilization had a drastic decline with the fall of the Roman empire. The great strides that had been made in commerce were reversed, and the known world evolved backward toward the self-contained economy. This period was known as the Middle Ages, and the re-emergence of relatively advanced industrial and marketing processes was a long and drawn-out process. The center of the resurgence of trade was England, the antecedent of modern American trade.

Merchant middlemen developed slowly in England, but by 1000 A.D. such specialists as the smith, peddler, thatcher, tailor, cooper, and miller had emerged. They were among the first of the modern retailers even though their basic function was still production. These producer–retailers sold direct to consumers, often hawking their wares in the street or from stalls located on the side of the road. About the same period can be found the English markets and fairs. These meeting places where people came together to trade were often sponsored by the church. The earliest retail centers, these fairs finally evolved into the craft guilds which were associations of merchants. Goods were produced and sold in the same store—examples can be found in the English cobbler and tailor—and sales were direct to the public.

The growth of concentrated population in the cities led to the demise of the guilds and the development of small specialist retailers.[17] These merchants had stores, and they purchased their wares from producers. The retailers kept regular store hours, and some even had warehouses where they stored their merchandise.

Early American retailers were specialty shops much like those that had developed in England. Peddlers moved West with the pioneers. These retailers grew almost unopposed until the middle of the eighteenth century when large-scale retailing began to develop in this country. The first department store in America appeared at about the time of the Civil War. R. H. Macy, John Wanamaker, and A. T. Stewart were among the early stores. The first chain stores were opened only slightly after the department stores. One of the earliest chains was the Great Atlantic and Pacific Tea Company; F. W. Woolworth was another. The late arrival on the scene was the discount house that developed after 1945.[18]

Evolution of Wholesalers

Wholesalers most likely developed after manufacturers and retailers, but there is evidence of wholesaling in dual merchant institutions as far back as the caravan merchants. Wholesalers helped to sell the ivory, linen, metal tools, oil, wines, and spices that were shipped by these caravans. There is also evidence of wholesalers in the ports of ancient Rome where they redistributed the goods brought into the seaports to merchants located inland. During the Middle Ages wholesalers suffered a decline, as did all other types of trade. But like the retailer, the wholesaler began to re-emerge in Renaissance England.

Among the first wholesalers in the United States were the full-line

---

[17] William J. Regan, "The Stages of Retail Development," *Theory In Marketing*, Reavis Cox, Wroe Alderson, and Stanley J. Shapiro, eds. (Homewood, Ill.: Richard D. Irwin, Inc., 1964), pp. 139–53.

[18] Perry Bliss, "Schumpeter, The 'Big' Disturbance and Retailing," *Social Forces*, Vol. 39 (October, 1960), pp. 72–76.

wholesalers, jobbers, and commission merchants. These middlemen operated primarily in the coastal towns and were well-established by the 1800's. Early American wholesalers sold such agricultural products as cotton, molasses, wine, wool, tea, and sugar. They were also instrumental in the storage and sale of manufactured goods, especially since the colonies were not allowed to make their own products. Agent middlemen such as manufacturers' agents and selling agents were becoming common by the middle of the nineteenth century.

The full-service wholesaler began to decline after the advent of the large-scale retailer and the wholesale institution underwent considerable change. This period saw the rise of the specialist wholesaler. By 1920, the limited line wholesaler and the cooperative wholesaler were well-established in the market. The cooperative had become especially strong in the grocery field. Since 1940 the merchant wholesaler has made a modest comeback in the market; certainly, the wholesaler's place appears secure in the modern American market.

QUESTIONS

1. Compare and contrast gift giving and warfare theories of how trade developed.
2. Explain the conditions that give rise to the development of marketing channels.
3. Compare the self-contained and decentralized channel system.
4. Give an example of the ratio of advantage equation and discuss its demonstration of efficiency in the economic system.
5. Discuss how middlemen became a necessary part of the channels system of distribution.
6. Contrast the development of retailers and wholesalers.
7. What is the single explanation syndrome? Explain.
8. Trace the evolution of retailers and wholesalers.
9. Why do you think there are so many conflicting theories for the development of trade? Explain.
10. Why is socialization so important to the development of trade?

3

Markets That
Channels Serve

Many of the differences in channels can be traced directly to the types of markets served. One type of channel can best serve a particular market, but it may take a completely different type to service another market. The emphasis of this chapter is not on explaining the reasons why buyers purchase in a given manner; [1] rather the focus is on understanding buyer attributes that more directly affect the design and operation of channels. The channel manager wants to know, among other things, where the market is located, how many buyers make up the market, and what characteristics or factors provide clues for better channel design to service consumer needs.

MARKETS AND MARKET SEGMENTS

Our subject is markets, but markets are as many and varied as people. According to the differences that exist in buyers, markets can be divided into segments and sub-segments. There may be some confusion in the mind of the reader as to what is meant by market, segment, and sub-segment.

[1] See: John H. Howard and Jagdish N. Sheth, *The Theory of Buyer Behavior* (New York: John Wiley and Sons, Inc., 1969); C. Glenn Walters and Gordon W. Paul, *Consumer Behavior* (Homewood, Ill.: Richard D. Irwin, Inc., 1970); James F. Engel, David T. Kollat, and Roger D. Blackwell, *Consumer Behavior* (New York: Holt, Rinehart, and Winston, Inc., 1968).

Definition of a Market

In a general sense a market is the group to whom a business sells or attempts to sell its products.[2] However, there are two important aspects of this definition that require clarification. The first involves the meaning of group. In marketing, there are two broad groups to whom a business may sell: final household consumers and other business buyers. Generally, these two types of buyers are quite different. Marketers are inclined to reserve the word consumer for final household consumers and to use the term buyer when referring to either final and business consumers, or when referring to business buyers alone.

Second, there is the difference between selling and attempting to sell that must be clarified. Markets can be classified on the basis of the willingness of the buyer to purchase into potential and realized markets. Either type of market may relate to household or business consumers. A potential market is defined as *buyers possessing wants and the resources necessary to satisfy these wants.* Buyers in a potential market are not actively engaged in the market; they may not even be aware of the need. They are potential because they represent an opportunity. Potential buyers can buy if they so desire. A potential market may be tapped by any enterprising business that can convince these buyers to act on their wants. This convincing may entail making the buyer aware that he has a want, persuading buyers that the firm has the best solution to their known problems, or inducing indifferent buyers to act on their wants.

A realized market exists when the buyers making up the market have committed themselves to purchase now or in the immediate future. A realized market is defined to mean *buyers who possess wants, who have the resources to satisfy these wants, and who have a desire to purchase.*

The buyer in the realized market is actively engaged in satisfying known wants. A realized market has already been tapped by some business firm; to acquire this market, another firm must induce buyers to transfer their loyalty. Unless otherwise specified, when we refer to the market in this volume it is the realized market that is meant. Of course, what represents a realized market to one firm may be a potential market to another. In a potential market, the persons or organization may or may not be aware of their wants. This condition cannot exist in a realized market, because the customer must know of his wants to be inclined to purchase.

Market Segmentation

It is practically impossible for any single firm, or for any group of firms operating as a channel of distribution, to satisfy all buyers for all

2 For a more complete discussion, see: Lee E. Preston, *Markets and Marketing: An Orientation* (Glenview, Ill.: Scott, Foresman and Co., 1970), pp. 1–5.

instances in time. Buyer wants and desires are simply too varied and individualistic and this is as true for business buyers as for final consumers. Thus, each business must take its place alongside other firms, each offering different combinations of goods, services, and prices designed to meet the needs of a particular group of buyers. Consequently, it is necessary for total markets to be segmented in line with the unique abilities of the firms making up the channel.

Market segmentation is defined as *dividing the heterogeneous market into smaller customer divisions having certain relatively homogeneous characteristics that can be satisfied by specific firms.*[3] Any identifiable characteristic of the buyer can serve as a basis for segmentation.[4] Thus, market segmentation is a process of identifying homogeneous buyer groups to which the business can direct its efforts. The identified group is known as a market segment. Inherent in any market segment is a want or a combination of wants that the business may be able to satisfy. How well the business can satisfy a particular buyer want depends on the abilities of that firm.

Segments and Sub-Segments

A market segment refers to some part of the total market, and a sub-segment is a part of a segment.[5] A market segment may be large or small, and a given total market may have several segments. As a matter of fact, one could go on subdividing a large market almost indefinitely. What constitutes a total market or a segment depends on the point of view. An example based on geographic considerations can clarify the point. If the members of a particular channel consider the United States to constitute the total market, then each state may be considered a separate segment. The counties and cities within the states are sub-segments. On the other hand, a regional seller may view a single state as his total market. If so, each county or city of that state may be seen as separate segments. Obviously, a state may be considered as a total market in one instance and a segment in another because a total market may be defined to be any size. Of course, other factors besides geography can be used to illustrate the difference in segments. A total market may exist for vacuum cleaners with separate segments that desire avocado-colored cleaners, large motor sizes, or all attachments. In the industrial market, a total market may exist for ball bearings but there may be specific segments based on size of bearing or type of material in the bearing.

[3] Adapted from *Definition of Terms* (Chicago: American Marketing Association, 1961), p. 15.
[4] John C. Bieda and Harold H. Kassarjian, "Overview of Market Segmentation," *Marketing in a Changing World,* Bernard A. Morin, ed. (Chicago: American Marketing Association, 1969), pp. 249–53.
[5] Engel, Kollatt, and Blackwell, *op. cit.,* pp. 12–13.

Consumer and Business Markets

Although both consumer and business markets constitute important buyer groups, there are important differences in the two types. The distinction between the household consumer market and the business market is based on the type of institutions involved and the purpose for which purchases are made by each group.

In the *final consumer market* the basic institution for consumption is the household, which is defined as all people living together in a housing unit. Thus, a household includes single persons living alone, people living in hotels or boarding houses, and individuals who are unrelated but happen to be sharing quarters. All products bought in the final consumer market are purchased either for individuals who live in a household or for the household in general. The purpose for final consumer purchasing is personal use satisfaction. Normally, the product is used up in the process of giving up its satisfaction in the final consumer market.

The *business market* is generally concerned with all profit-oriented organizations in the economy besides the final household. Products and services are purchased by business organizations not for personal use but for resale. Non-business institutions such as the government, universities, charities, and churches are often included with business buyers although their primary purpose is not profit. In fact, the non-business institutions constitute what may be termed special markets. There are actually many types of buying units in the business market just as there are in the final consumer market. Sometimes these businesses can all be lumped together for discussion purposes and sometimes it is necessary to make a distinction among them. The channel of distribution is concerned with both the business and household buyer. The business buyer is internal to the channel since it involves sales by one channel member to another. The household consumer market is often considered external because consumers take the product outside the realm of business. The marketing channel has a dual responsibility to meet the needs of both the business and the final consumer market segments, but the methods of reaching these two markets sometimes vary considerably.

Classification of Consumer and Business Markets

Business and the final consumer markets are not segmented in the same way. The consumer market is typically grouped according to four major characteristics: (1) location, (2) demographic factors, (3) psychographic factors, and (4) buyer behavior.[6] Table 3–1 shows these characteristics and the typical manner of their measurement in the market.

[6] Daniel Yankelovich, "New Criteria for Market Segmentation," *Harvard Business Review*, Vol. 42 (March–April, 1964), pp. 83–90.

Table 3-1 Major Segmentation Variables and their Typical Breakdowns

Variables	Typical Breakdowns
Geographic	
Region	Pacific; Mountain; West North Central; West South Central; East North Central; East South Central; South Atlantic; Middle Atlantic; New England
County size	A; B; C; D
City or S.M.S.A. size	Under 5,000; 5,000–19,999; 20,000–49,999; 50,000–99,999; 100,000–249,999; 250,000–499,999; 500,000–999,999; 1,000,000–3,999,999; 4,000,000 or over
Density	Urban; suburban; rural
Climate	Northern; southern
Demographic	
Age	Under 6; 6–11; 12–17; 18–34; 35–49; 50–64; 65+
Sex	Male; female
Family size	1–2; 3–4; 5+
Family life cycle	Young, single; young, married, no children; young, married, youngest child under six; young, married, youngest child six or over; older, married, with children; older, married, no children under 18; older, single; other
Income	Under $5,000; $5,000–$7,999; $8,000–$9,999; over $10,000
Occupation	Professional and technical; managers, officials and proprietors; clerical, sales; craftsmen, foremen; operatives; farmers; retired; students, housewives; unemployed
Education	Grade school or less; some high school; graduated high school; some college; graduated college
Religion	Catholic; Protestant; Jewish; other
Race	White; Negro; Oriental
Nationality	American; British; French; German; Eastern European; Scandinavian; Italian; Spanish; Latin American; Middle Eastern; Japanese; and so on
Social class	Lower-lower; upper-lower; lower-middle; middle-middle; upper-middle; lower-upper; upper-upper
Psychographic	
Compulsiveness	Compulsive; noncompulsive
Gregariousness	Extrovert; introvert
Autonomy	Dependent; independent
Conservatism	Conservative; liberal; radical
Authoritarianism	Authoritarian; democratic
Leadership	Leader; follower
Ambitiousness	High achiever; low achiever
Buyer Behavior	
Usage rate	Nonuser; light user; medium user; heavy user
Readiness stage	unaware; aware; interested; intending to try; trier; regular buyer
Benefits sought	Economy; status; dependability
End use	(Varies with the product)
Brand loyalty	None; light; strong
Marketing-factor sensitivity	Quality; price; serivce; advertising; sales promotion

Source: Philip Kotler, *Marketing Management*, 2nd ed. (Englewood Cliffs, N. J.: Prentice-Hall, Inc., 1972), p. 170.

Fewer characteristics are used for classification purposes in the business segment. The business buyer is typically classified according to: (1) type of industry class according to the major product, such as the automobile, appliance, steel, or furniture industries; (2) placement in the channel, such as wholesaler, agent, or retailer; (3) physical or financial size of customer; (4) size of purchase; (5) location; and (6) number of product types purchased. Actually, the business buyer has not been given the attention in recent years that the final household consumer has received.[7]

CONSUMER MARKET SEGMENTS

Final household consumers make up a very large and diverse market. Every good sold by channel members relates directly or indirectly to final consumers. Because the consumer market is so diverse, there are many segments or sub-segments within it. One important method of segmenting consumer markets is based on population. This is a logical basis since our definition of markets suggests people as the foundation of consumer markets, and wants and desires reside in people. In this section, some of the important consumer market segments based on the characteristics of the population are discussed: (1) total population—age and sex segments, (2) segments based on population characteristics, and (3) segment change by selected population characteristics.

Total Population: Age and Sex Segments

The total population of the United States has been increasing throughout our nation's history. A total population of 180.7 million people in 1960 increased to 205.2 million people in 1970. It is projected that in 1980 the United States will have 227.5 million people. The population tree in Figure 3–1 shows how the age and sex distributions of the population are expected to change between 1970 and 1980.

A male population of 100.7 million in 1970 is expected to increase to 111.2 million by 1980. The female population is expected to increase from 104.5 million in 1970 to 116.3 million in 1980. The population tree clearly shows the effect of a changing birth rate on the proportion of age groups in the population. The age group between 15–39 will increase in importance over the next ten years, and senior citizens in the group between 50 and 65 will also continue to grow. The youth group (those between 0–19 years), which has had such an impact on markets since World War II, will decrease in importance over the period. Females will

[7] Frederick E. Webster, Jr., "Industrial Buying Behavior: A State-of-the-Art Appraisal," *Marketing in a Changing World,* Bernard A. Morin, ed. (Chicago: American Marketing Association, 1969), pp. 254–60.

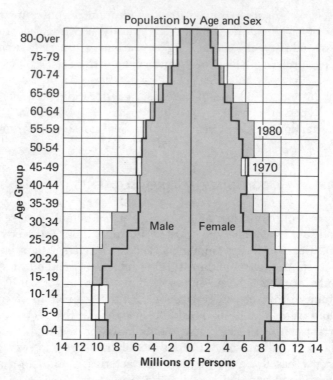

Fig. 3–1. Change in age and sex distribution between 1970 and 1980. *Source:* Helen Axel (ed.), *A Guide to Consumer Markets.* New York: National Industrial Conference Board, 1972–1973.

continue to outnumber males in the later years. The bulk of the market comprises the group between 15 to 34 years of age.

Selected Population Segments

Table 3–2 shows the composition of the population of the United States, by characteristic, as of 1971. Several interesting market segments can be discovered in these figures, some quite large, others small. Just because a segment is small does not mean that it is unimportant or un-worthy of tapping. A small segment may be ideal because no other seri-ous challenger exists in the market.

The large market segment is the non-farm population, and nearly 65 per cent of this group can be reached by sales in just 230 standard metro-politan areas. Most American consumers are married, and the majority have one child or none. Furthermore, a significant proportion—33.8 per cent—of the women in families work to contribute to family income. Nearly 70 per cent of the population has finished high school and 12.9 per

Table 3-2　White and Black Families by Selected Characteristics, 1971

	Total Families		White Families		Black Families		
Characteristic	(Thousands)	Percentage	Number (Thousands	Per Cent Distribution	Number (Thousands)	Per Cent Distribution	As Per Cent of Total Families
Total	51,948	100.0	46,535	100.0	4,928	100.0	9.5
Residence							
Nonfarm	49,600	95.5	44,328	95.3	4,804	97.5	9.7
Farm	2,347	4.5	2,207	4.7	124	2.5	5.3
Metropolitan	33,431	64.4	29,484	63.4	3,583	72.7	10.7
In Central Cities	14,531	28.0	11.538	24.8	2,807	57.0	19.3
Outside Central Cities	18,900	36.4	17,946	38.6	776	15.7	4.1
Nonmetropolitan	18,516	35.7	17,051	36.6	1,345	27.3	7.3
Age of Head							
Under 25	3,745	7.2	3,327	7.1	404	8.2	10.8
25–34	10,649	20.5	9,378	20.2	1,161	23.6	10.9
35–44	10,840	20.9	9,630	20.7	1,101	22.3	10.2
45–54	11,065	21.3	9,951	21.4	998	20.3	9.0
55–64	8,473	16.3	7,696	16.5	704	14.3	8.3
65 and over	7,175	13.8	6,554	14.1	560	11.4	7.8
Family Type							
Married, Wife Present	44,739	86.1	41,092	88.3	3,235	65.6	7.2
Wife Working	17,568	33.8	15,651	33.6	1,747	35.5	9.9
Wife not Working	27,172	52.3	25,441	54.7	1.488	30.2	5.5
Other Male Head	1,258	2.4	1,056	2.3	187	3.8	14.9
Female Head	5,950	11.5	4,386	9.4	1,506	30.6	25.3
Number of Children							
None	21,953	42.3	20,303	43.6	1,504	30.5	6.9
One	10,009	19.3	8,862	19.0	1,027	20.8	10.3
Two	9,257	17.8	8,339	17.9	819	16.6	8.8
Three and Four	8,364	16.1	7,270	15.6	998	20.3	11.9
Five or more	2,364	4.6	1.761	3.8	580	11.8	24.5
Earners							
None	4,691	9.0	4,061	8.7	588	11.9	12.5
One	19,252	37.1	17,426	37.4	1.653	33.5	8.6
Two	20,443	39.4	18,269	39.3	1,990	40.4	9.7
Three or more	7,561	14.6	6,778	14.6	697	14.1	9.2
Education of Head*							
Elementary, Total	12,624	24.3	10,602	24.5	1,892	41.8	15.0
Some High School	8,051	15.5	6,902	16.0	1,090	24.1	13.5
High School Graduate	15,423	29.7	14,196	32.9	1,091	24.1	7.1
Some College	5,405	10.4	5,091	11.8	263	5.8	4.9
College Graduate	6,699	12.9	6,417	14.9	187	4.1	2.8
Region							
Northeast	12,381	23.9	11,382	24.5	938	19.0	7.6
North Central	14,563	28.0	13,485	29.0	1,040	21.1	7.1
South	16,003	30.8	13,391	28.8	2,538	51.5	15.9
West	9,001	17.3	8,277	17.8	412	8.4	4.6

*Head 25 years and over.

Source: Helen Axel, ed., *A Guide to Consumer Markets* (New York: National Industrial Conference Board, 1972–1973), p. 69.

cent has finished college. The South has the largest proportion of families closely followed by the North Central Region.

The American population is largely white, but with a significant black segment. Black Americans make up only 9.5 per cent of all families, and there are significant differences between this market segment and the white segment. A smaller proportion of black family heads are married, but of those that are married, a larger proportion of wives work. The figures show that blacks have more children than their white counterparts. It is also notable that the female heads the household in a very significant number of black families.

The black market is more geographically concentrated than the white market. Over 50 per cent of all blacks live in the South, nearly 73 per cent live in the metropolitan areas, and 57 per cent of these live in the central city. Almost 67 per cent of the black population has not finished high school compared to approximately 39 per cent of whites. The black population has more non-earners and more multiple earners than its white counterpart. These latter two factors tend to emphasize the plight of the black market. Consumers in this market are caught in a vicious circle of low education, unemployment, and low wages. All these factors must be taken into account when appealing to the black market segment.

Change in Selected Population Characteristics

We have pointed out some important market segments in the United States based on population, but markets are seldom static. An excellent market today may be much less desirable in the future and some insignificant present market may develop into a really important segment over time. Figures 3–2 to 3–7 provide a view of some population changes that affect market composition.

We see from Figure 3–2 that although the East North Central and Middle Atlantic had the largest base of population, the rate of growth is far greater in the Pacific and Mountain regions. There is a net shift of population to the West. As demonstrated by Figure 3–3, the population wasn't only going West, it was going to the cities. The population of metropolitan areas increased from 150.5 million people in 1950 to 178.5 in 1960 and reached over 200 by 1970. A standard metropolitan statistical area consists of a central city with 50,000 population and all contiguous counties. There are slight variations in this definition, notably in New England where cities in the county rather than the entire county are included. Figure 3–3 shows that the rate of growth was greater in the suburbs of these metropolitan areas. The central cities lost a great proportion of the total population between 1950 and 1970.

Figure 3–4 emphasizes the tremendous increase in the education of the American people. Not only did the vast majority of the people finish high

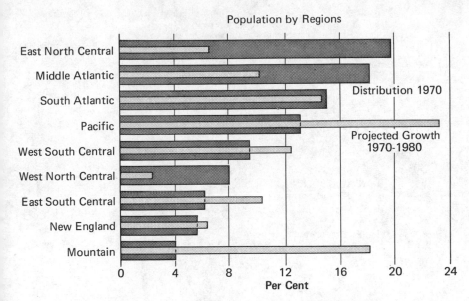

Fig. 3–2. Population by regions. *Source:* Same as Fig. 3–1.

school, but the incidence of advanced degrees granted greatly increased as well. The greatest increase in education began during the 1960's, and the predictions are for this pace to accelerate during the 1970's. Figure 3–5 demonstrates that the total labor force has increased steadily since 1947, reaching 85.9 million persons by 1970, of whom 78.6 were employed that year. Females, with 54.3 million of the total in 1970, have increased steadily since 1947. This increase in women workers as a percentage of the total was expected to level off during the 1970's. Unemployment was slightly higher among women than among men.

Figure 3–6 shows the makeup of the labor force in 1970 and its expected composition for 1980. The operatives group was the largest group of employed in 1970 followed by clerical workers and professionals, but the professional and clerical groups were expected to expand at a much faster rate during the 1970's. The difference would lead to a vastly different composition of the labor force by 1980. Sales workers and managers were expected to have the least amount of growth over the period. Figure 3–7 shows working wives highly concentrated in the clerical classification in 1960, a fact which held true also in the 1971 figure.

Total Income and Its Distribution

Income, like population, has been increasing in the United States. Personal per capita income, in 1970 dollars, was $2,340 in 1950; $2,788

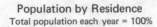

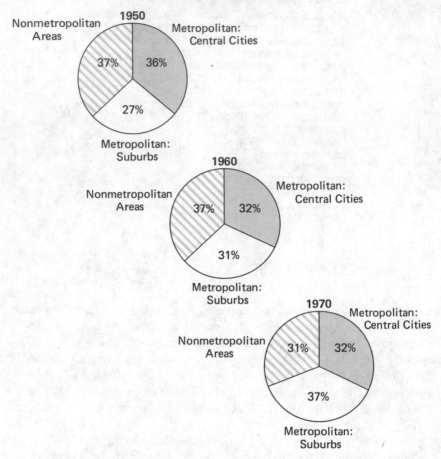

Fig. 3–3. Population by residence. *Source:* Same as Fig. 3–1.

in 1960; and $3,911 in 1970.[8] These figures represent a significant change in consumer purchasing power. Figure 3–8 shows that income was distributed regionally much the same manner as the population.[9] The bulk of American income was distributed to the East North Central and Middle Atlantic regions. There was, however, a different pattern of change in income from that observed for population. While the Pacific, Mountain, South Atlantic, and West South Central regions, in that order, were

[8] Fabian Linden, ed., *A Guide to Consumer Markets* (New York: National Industrial Conference Board, 1971–1972).

[9] Chester R. Wasson, "It Is Time to Quit Thinking of Income Classes," *Journal of Marketing*, Vol. 33 (April, 1969), pp. 54–57. Wasson points out some pitfalls of income classes when viewed as social class.

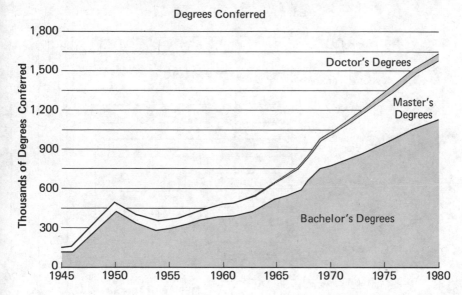

Fig. 3–4.　Degrees conferred.　*Source:* Same as Fig. 3–1.

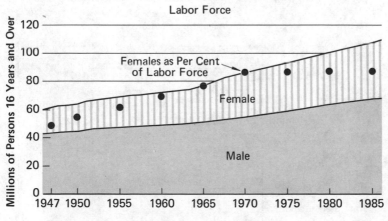

Fig. 3–5.　Labor force.　*Source:* Same as Fig. 3–1.

growing fastest for population, the South Atlantic, East South Central, Pacific, and East North Central regions were growing fastest for income.

The Income Pyramid

The income pyramid in Figure 3–9 demonstrates how income distribution by income classes in the United States changed between 1960 and 1970. Income over that period increased for most persons in the

Employment by Occupational

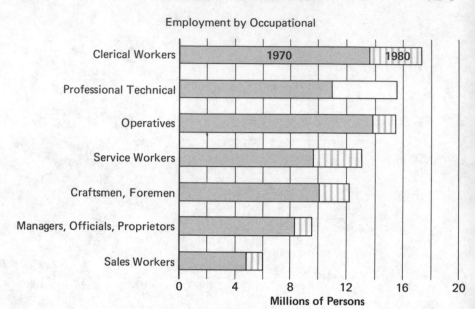

Fig. 3–6. Employment by occupation. *Source:* Same as Fig. 3–1.

Working Wives by Occupation

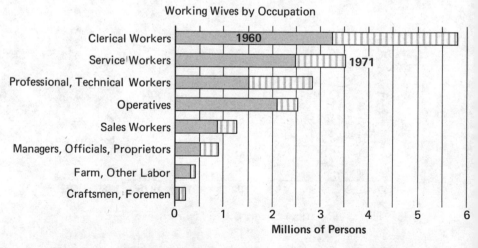

Fig. 3–7. Working wives by occupation. *Source:* Same as Fig. 3–1.

society. The largest income segment included the group between $7,000–15,000, accounting for over 48 per cent of the total population. At the same time a significant proportion of the population made below $5,000 in 1970. With all incomes going up, it simply cost more in 1970 to be poor than it did in 1960. In spite of this fact, government statistics show

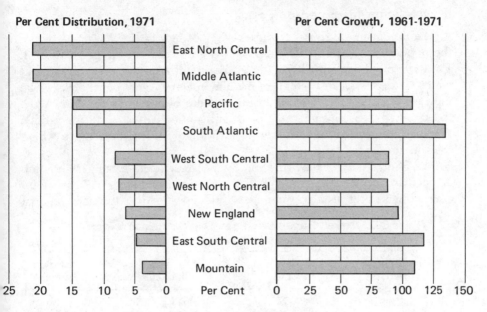

Per Cent Distribution, 1971   **Per Cent Growth, 1961-1971**

Fig. 3–8. Regional income: distribution and growth. *Source:* Same as Fig. 3–1.

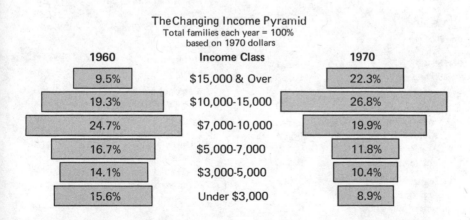

Fig. 3–9. Changing income pyramid. *Source:* Same as Fig. 3–1.

that poverty decreased over the period from 22 per cent of the population in 1959 to 12 per cent in 1970. These figures represent significant gains for the society and important markets. Basically, the quality of American markets has been on the rise.

Income Segments Based on Population

Median income displays a wide variety of figures by characteristics of the population. Some of the important figures are shown in Table 3–3. For the United States in 1970, the median family income was $9,867, and whites had significantly higher median income than did blacks. The most productive years for family heads were between 35–55, and this is the period when consumers could spend more than at any other time. Families with wives working had slightly more income than those where the wife did not work.

The figures clearly show the importance of education and occupation on median income. Median income went up steadily as education increased, with professionals, managers, and sales leading the occupational

Table 3–3   Median Family Income by Selected Characteristics, 1970
(In dollars)

Family Characteristic	Median Income	Family Characteristic	Median Income
TOTAL FAMILIES	9,867	Occupation of Head	
Race		Professional, Technical	14,482
White	10,236	Managers, Officials	14,014
Negro, Other Races	6,516	Clerical	10,471
		Sales	12,325
Age of Head		Craftsmen, Foremen	11,294
Under 25	7,037	Operatives	9,602
25–34	9,853	Farmers, Farm Mgrs.	6,138
35–44	11,410		
45–54	12,121	Residence	
55–64	10,381	Nonfarm	10,006
65 and over	5,053	Farm	6,773
Type of Family		Metropolitan Area	10,789
Husband-Wife	10,516	1,000,000 or more	11,394
Wife Working	12,276	Central Cities	9,900
Wife not Working	9,304	Outside Central Cities	12,425
Other Male Head	9,012	Under 1,000,000	10,106
Female Head	5,093	Central Cities	9,477
		Outside Central Cities	10,599
Education of Head*		Nonmetropolitan	8,348
Elementary, 8 yrs	7,649		
Some High School	9,136	Region	
H. S. Graduate	10,861	Northeast	10,696
Some College	12,346	North Central	10,327
College Graduate	14,722	South	8,552
Postgraduate	17,352	West	10,273

*Family heads 25 years and over.

Source: Helen Axel, ed., A Guide to Consumer Markets (New York: National Industrial Conference Board, 1972–1973), p. 126.

categories for median income. Incomes were much higher in the metropolitan areas, and increased with the size of the city. Within the city (for all city sizes) incomes were higher in the suburbs than in the central city.

BUSINESS BUYER SEGMENTS

The market that consists of business buyers is different in many respects from household markets—although the major function of buying is the same. These differences exist in the reason for purchasing, the size of the purchase unit, the degree of specialization involved, and the risk. It is time to establish the nature of business markets that can become the basis for a comparison with final household consumer markets.

Number and Location of Business

There are approximately twelve hundred thousand business organizations in the United States as indicated in Table 3-4. This is a large num-

Table 3-4   Incidence of Proprietorships and Partnerships in the United States by Regions, 1969 (In thousands)

Region	Number of Firms
Northeast	1,736
North Central	3,449
South	3,312
West	1,849
U. S. Total Other than Corporations	10,345
U. S. Total of all Businesses	12,010

Source: *Statistical Abstracts of the United States*, 1972, p. 470.

ber of firms, but the table demonstrates that they are not evenly divided across the nation. The North Central and the South have the largest totals of business firms other than corporations. Most of the 1,665 existing corporations are also located in these two geographic areas. Of course, the reader must remember that these organizations are legal entities and not individual plants. Many businesses have multiple plants often scattered across the nation. The figures only reflect the legal residence of the organization. Even so it is easy to observe the differences that exist, and how these differences reflect real differences in the business market. For example, fewer salesmen can call on more firms in the Northeast than in the West because of the pattern of concentration.

Table 3-5 Proprietorships, Partnerships, and Corporations—Number, Receipts, and Profit: 1939 to 1970 (Number in thousands; money figures in billions of dollars)

Item	1939	1945	1950	1955	1960	1965	1966	1967	1968	1969	1970
Number	1,793	6,737	(NA)	(NA)	11,172	11,416	11,479	11,566	11,672	12,021	12,001
Receipts	171	382	(NA)	(NA)	1,095	1,469	1,594	1,666	1,813	2,009	2,082
Net profit (less loss)	11	40	(NA)	(NA)	73	111	121	119	129	125	109
Proprietorships, number	1,052	5,689	6,865	8,239	9,090	9,078	9,087	9,126	9,212	9,430	9,400
Business receipts	24	79	(NA)	139	171	199	207	211	222	234	238
Net profit (less loss)	2	12	15	18	21	28	30	30	32	34	33
Partnerships, number	271	627	(NA)	(NA)	941	914	923	906	918	921	936
Total receipts	15	47	(NA)	(NA)	74	75	80	80	83	87	93
Net profit (less loss)	2	7	(NA)	(NA)	8	10	10	11	11	10	10
Corporations, number	470	421	629	807	1,141	1,424	1,469	1,534	1,542	1,670	1,665
Total receipts	133	255	458	642	849	1,195	1,307	1,375	1,508	1,688	1,751
Net profit (less loss)	7	21	43	47	44	74	81	78	86	81	66

NA Not available

Source: U. S. Internal Revenue Service, Statistics of Income, Business Income Tax Returns, annual.

Business Segments by Type of Organization

Not only does the market represented by businesses vary on a geographic basis but there are wide differences in the potential of different types of organizations over time. These indications can be determined from Table 3–5 below. Such data indicate a steady, but varying, rate of growth in both the number of businesses and receipts between 1939 to 1970. Profits had a rather spectacular increase over the period. However, again we observe that some types of businesses were better markets than others. Corporations, with the smallest total number of firms, completely dominated other organizational types where receipts were concerned. Clearly, the largest potential markets lay in this direction. Furthermore, corporations had more than double the profits in most years of the other two types of businesses combined.

In spite of these results, it should not be concluded that proprietorships and partnerships are relatively insignificant or unimportant business markets. What constitutes a market depends largely on what you have to sell. Just because a firm is large does not mean that it purchases in large quantity. For example, a large firm may purchase practically no castings, but it may buy large quantities of motors that use the casting of small foundries. One point is certainly clear from Table 3–5: corporations have receipts much more nearly in proportion to their numbers than do either of the other business types. It is also interesting that proprietorships represent a larger market and have larger receipts than do partnerships. This was the only group that had an increase in profits in 1969 over 1970.

Business Classed by Size of Receipts

Table 3–6 sheds more light on the importance of large business organizations. Based on the assumption that more firms and more receipts generally means larger markets (because more firms provide greater opportunity to sell and more receipts means greater purchasing power), we can draw several conclusions from the table. First, firms with receipts under $25,000 comprise nearly 69 per cent of all business firms, but they account for only 2.7 per cent of receipts. These firms constitute a relatively small market. Second, the 3 per cent of firms with receipts over $500,000 account for approximately 79 per cent of receipts. Clearly, the purchasing power is concentrated in the large firms. Any seller attempting to appeal to a business market with firms under $50,000 can expect to have to use a larger sales force, make fewer calls per day, and be satisfied with smaller orders as a general rule.

Third, proprietorships and partnerships tend to concentrate in the lower groups for receipts, where numbers are concerned, but corpora-

Table 3-6 Proprietorships, Partnerships, and Corporations—Number and Business Receipts, by Size of Receipts, 1970
(Number in thousands; receipts in millions of dollars)

Size Class of Receipts	Total		Number			Receipts		
	Number	Receipts	Proprietorships	Active partnerships	Active corporations	Proprietorships	Active partnerships	Active corporations
Total	12,001	2,035,615	9,400	936	1,665	237,727	91,774	1,706,115
Under $25,000	8,200	50,888	7,247	501	452	43,831	3,568	3,489
$25,000–$50,000	1,302	46,440	1,006	125	171	35,729	4,508	6,203
$50,000–$100,000	1,000	70,756	661	120	220	46,278	8,571	15,907
$100,000–$200,000	661	92,802	325	97	239	44,640	13,774	34,387
$200,000–$500,000	474	145,667	131	65	278	37,984	19,512	88,170
$500,000–$1,000,000	181	125,853	23	17	141	15,142	11,646	99,065
$1,000,000 or more	182	1,503,211	7	10	165	14,123	30,194	1,458,894
Per cent distribution	100.0	100.0	100.0	100.0	100.0	100.0	100.0	100.0
Under $25,000	68.3	2.5	77.1	53.5	27.1	18.4	3.9	0.2
$25,000–$50,000	10.8	2.3	10.7	13.4	10.3	15.0	4.9	0.4
$50,000–$100,000	8.3	3.5	7.0	12.8	13.2	19.5	9.3	0.9
$100,000–$200,000	5.5	4.6	3.5	10.4	14.3	18.8	15.0	2.0
$200,000–$500,000	4.0	7.2	1.4	7.0	16.7	16.0	21.3	5.2
$500,000–$1,000,000	1.5	6.2	0.2	1.8	8.5	6.4	12.7	5.8
$1,000,000 or more	1.5	73.8	0.1	1.1	9.9	5.9	32.9	85.5

*Includes businesses with no receipts.
Source: Statistical Abstracts of the United States, 1973, p. 472.

tions are much more evenly spread over all classes of receipts. However, success in obtaining receipts is a function of business size no matter which type of business is under consideration. Fourth, corporations do not appear suited for the smaller-type operations, based on the figures. Corporations had a very poor record for receipts in the smaller classifications. Ninety-one per cent of all corporate receipts were concentrated in the $500,000 or more category. Thus the figures show that not only is the business market varied by geographic area, but it is also quite varied according to the type of organization involved, Nevertheless, the corporation, and particularly the large corporation, dominates American business markets.

The 500 Largest Corporations

The 500 largest corporations are such a significant market where business is concerned that this group is worth investigating in greater detail. In this section, these organizations are broken down by size and industry to provide a greater depth of understanding of their importance to the business market.

Corporations Ranked by Sales. There is perhaps no better indicator of a business's purchasing power than that of size based on sales. Table 3–7 presents data on the sales rank of the top corporations over time. These data are divided by manufacturing corporations represented by 500 firms, and retailing corporations that are represented by 50 firms. Manufacturers make goods and retailers basically sell goods. Because of the difference in numbers, these data are not strictly comparable; however, some generalizations can be made.

First, both manufacturing and retailing sales are large, and the markets are significant. However, it is clear that the top firms in manufacturing represent a larger market than do the top firms in retailing. Second, both markets were increasing over the time period, but the manufacturing group increased the most. Third, there existed a slightly less concentration of retailing in the two largest categories than was found for manufacturing. This, of course, may be conditioned by the fact that there are only 50 retailers shown.

Corporations by Industry. Table 3–8 contains selected data on the 500 largest corporations. The first column ranks industry types according to assets per employee in 1971. We see that the top three industries were petroleum, mining, and tobacco. The bottom three industries were apparel, textiles, and electronic appliances. However, we should interpret these figures with caution. Some industries require large numbers of people and relatively small assets, while with other companies it is the opposite.

Table 3-7 Largest Industrial Corporations and Retailing Companies—Sales, by Group Rank, 1955 to 1972

Sales Group	Volume of Sales (in billion dollars)					Percent Distribution				
	1955	1960	1965	1970	1972	1955	1960	1965	1970	1972
Industrial Corporations										
First 500 largest	161.4	204.7	298.1	463.9	557.8	100.0	100.0	100.0	100.0	100.0
Lowest hundred	6.3	8.5	12.5	19.9	24.3	3.9	4.1	4.2	4.3	4.4
Second hundred	8.6	11.7	17.7	28.8	34.2	5.3	5.7	5.9	6.2	6.1
Third hundred	13.7	18.5	27.7	43.6	53.7	8.5	9.0	9.3	9.4	9.6
Fourth hundred	24.5	32.6	47.2	82.7	97.7	15.2	15.9	15.8	17.8	17.5
Highest hundred	108.3	133.4	193.0	288.9	347.8	67.1	65.2	64.7	62.3	62.4
Second 500 largest	(NA)	15.7	(NA)	48.3	58.9	(X)	(X)	(X)	(X)	(X)
Retailing Companies										
50 largest	25.6	35.7	49.0	73.6	89.9	100.0	100.0	100.0	100.0	100.0
Lowest ten	1.2	2.2	3.3	4.4	5.8	4.6	6.2	6.7	5.9	6.4
Second ten	1.7	2.8	4.4	6.8	8.2	6.7	7.9	9.2	9.3	9.1
Third ten	2.7	4.1	6.1	9.0	11.4	10.6	11.5	12.4	12.3	12.6
Fourth ten	4.5	6.4	9.0	13.9	16.8	17.6	18.0	18.3	18.9	18.6
Highest ten	15.5	20.1	26.2	39.4	47.8	60.5	56.4	53.5	53.6	53.2

NA Not available   X Not applicable.
Source: Fortune, New York, adapted from The Fortune Directory. (Copyright, by Time Inc.)

A slightly different result is found when the industries are ranked for sales. Petroleum still leads, but it is followed by beverages, tobacco, and broadcasting. The industries ranked lowest are apparel, office machinery, and textiles. A different rank is also observed when one considers return on sales, which is a most significant measure. Based on return on sales, mining ranks first, followed by pharmaceuticals. Five industries show a profit decline between 1970 and 1971, and four industries have increases in profit greater than 18 per cent. Motor vehicles led the parade of profit increase with 49.0 per cent. The importance of these figures is to point up again the variety that exists in the business market. Any of the firms shown represent large, financially strong organizations. Some are capable of supporting the output of several smaller organizations alone. Furthermore, within each firm there are literally thousands of opportunities to sell varying quantities of specific products.

Inventories and Expenditures for Business

Two other aspects of the business market may help to define its importance to various channel members. They are expenditures on new plant and equipment and change in inventories. Of course, expenditures for plant constitute a specific market, and the fluctuations in inventory

Table 3-8   500 Largest Industrial Corporations— Selected Financial Items, by Industry, 1972 (Figures are medians based on sales in 1972)

Industry	Assets per Employee	Sales per Employee	Sales per Dollar of Stockholders' Equity	Return on Stockholders' Equity	Return on Sales	Change from 1971 in—	
						Sales	Profit
	Mil. dol.	Mil. dol.	Dollars	Per cent	Per cent	Per cent	Per cent
Total	27.1	34.4	2.48	10.3	4.1	11.2	21.8
Petroleum refining	126.8	116.9	1.51	9.4	6.0	7.2	6.8
Mining	84.3	51.5	0.78	10.1	12.8	24.3	3.8
Tobacco	65.2	59.8	1.77	15.1	8.0	7.2	6.2
Beverages	57.3	63.3	2.25	13.1	5.1	10.1	6.5
Broadcasting and motion pictures	49.0	54.3	2.96	13.5	5.9	12.4	40.3
Metal manufacturing	43.5	39.2	1.83	6.9	3.3	13.2	33.4
Chemicals	38.6	38.6	1.97	9.0	4.4	10.9	27.8
Paper and wood products	36.5	37.7	1.97	8.6	4.2	12.5	47.5
Pharmaceuticals	31.4	33.0	1.72	15.3	9.1	12.6	16.0
Soaps, cosmetics	30.0	45.5	2.65	16.0	7.7	11.9	14.9
Glass, cement, gypsum, concrete	28.0	33.5	1.95	11.2	5.9	12.3	28.6
Food	27.9	57.8	4.30	9.8	2.2	7.9	9.8
Publishing and printing	27.3	35.9	2.16	11.3	4.5	13.0	17.8
Farm and industrial machinery	24.2	29.7	2.27	9.7	4.1	10.6	20.7
Rubber	23.9	29.3	2.56	10.0	3.5	10.0	13.5
Measuring, scientific, and photo equip.	23.3	29.7	1.96	13.0	6.9	14.4	21.9
Shipbuilding RR equip., mobile homes	23.2	36.4	3.20	12.3	4.6	13.5	37.2
Motor vehicles and parts	22.6	34.8	3.12	11.1	4.2	15.6	33.2
Aircraft and parts	21.6	29.5	2.97	9.5	2.7	-5.2	13.0
Appliances, electronics	19.9	25.9	2.57	11.3	4.4	12.1	29.3
Office machinery (includes computers)	19.6	21.7	2.19	7.8	3.9	10.4	18.8
Metal products	19.6	29.0	2.90	10.4	3.6	9.8	18.4
Textiles	17.1	22.4	2.70	5.9	2.5	11.2	29.3
Apparel	12.4	20.1	3.01	12.0	3.4	10.2	18.4
Leather and leather products	11.3	20.9	3.41	12.5	3.6	15.4	18.6

Source: Statistical Abstract of the United States, 1973, p. 482.

represent one of the best indicators of the willingness of businessmen to purchase.

Business expenditures increased every year between 1950 and 1972 for plant and equipment. The figure rose from 20.2 billion in 1950 to 36.8 billion in 1960. In 1965 business spent 54.2 billion on plant and equipment, but the amount had jumped again to 89.6 billion by 1972.[10]

Table 3–9 presents the changes in business inventories between 1950 and 1971. Notice that inventories fluctuated widely during these years. When inventories are high it means that businessmen are reluctant to

Table 3–9   Net Change in Business Inventories, 1950 to 1971
(In millions of dollars. Prior to 1960, excludes Alaska and Hawaii. Measures change in physical inventories, valued at average prices current during year. Difference between change in business inventories at thus measured and change in book value of inventories constitutes inventory valuation adjustment. Minus sign (−) denotes decrease)

Item	1950	1955	1960	1965	1967	1968	1969	1970	1971 (prol.)
Total	6,789	5,953	3,569	9,620	8,193	7,065	7,398	2,810	2,200
Farm	789	467	233	973	737	117	131	329	500
Nonfarm	6,000	5,486	3,336	8,647	7,456	6,948	7,267	2,481	1,700
Corporate	4,823	4,927	3,031	7,907	7,252	6,423	6,486	2,610	(NA)
Noncorporate	1,177	559	305	740	204	525	781	−129	(NA)

Source: U. S. Bureau of Economic Analysis. *The National Income and Product Accounts of the United States, 1921-1965* and *Survey of Current Business,* July 1971 and February 1972.

purchase and these are poor sales years for industrial firms. The table shows high inventories in 1965, 1967, and 1968. It is clear that 1970 and 1971 were relatively good years in the business market. The data show that farm inventories are generally smaller than non-farm inventories; industrial firms must keep a certain amount of raw materials on hand for continuous production. Notice also that corporate inventories run rather higher than non-corporate ones. When you are selling in large quantities you must keep materials on hand to produce in large quantities. This is another reason why the larger corporations are such excellent markets. They not only purchase more, but they tend to purchase many products in larger quantities than other organizations.

GENERAL COMPARISONS OF BUSINESS AND CONSUMER MARKETS

There are important differences between the consumer market and the business market and it is important for channel members to recognize

[10] *Statistical Abstract of the United States,* 1972, p. 474.

these differences since they affect channel structure, promotional methods, pricing, etc. The relationships that exist between channel members and the final household consumer are also affected.

Patterns of Size and Geographic Concentration

Interpretation of data presented earlier in this chapter indicates very clearly that the business market is much more concentrated than the final consumer market, whether the comparison is made either on the basis of size of units involved or on a geographic basis. The patterns of variation are not uniform however.

Concentration by Spending Unit. There is, of course, wide variation in the amount of money spent by individual households in the United States. Even so, the sums involved are small when compared to the expenditure of business firms. After all, the median income of families was less than $10,000 in 1969. While the median family may spend approximately $195.00 per week, a business firm may spend millions per week on raw materials alone. High income families have more to spend than low income families, but one could hardly say that household expenditures were concentrated in these high income families. The bulk of household expenditures is small and scattered throughout the population. This is not so in the business market. Although all industrial firms spend more individually than households, the bulk of expenditure is concentrated in relatively few organizations. Figures show that approximately 65 per cent of industrial value added was concentrated in firms employing 250 employees or more. It can be said that the 500 largest industrial firms in America account for the bulk of industrial expenditures, and previous figures demonstrate the economic power of these top businesses.

Geographic Concentration. Not only is the business market more concentrated by spending unit, but it is also more concentrated by geographic area. Figure 3–10 is useful in illustrating this point. First, it would be incorrect to assume that there is no concentration of households in the United States. By 1970, about 74 per cent of the American population lived in the approximately 230 metropolitan areas, but it must be noted that these large cities are scattered across the nation. To reach these consumers requires a national market effort.[11] Furthermore, there are significant numbers of small cities randomly located, not to mention the fact that over 8 per cent of the total population still live in rural areas. Thus the household consumer market was generally scattered across the entire nation.

The business market, as the map shows, has a much stronger pattern

[11] "1971 Survey of Buying Power," *Sales Management Magazine* (July 10, 1971), pp. 13–14.

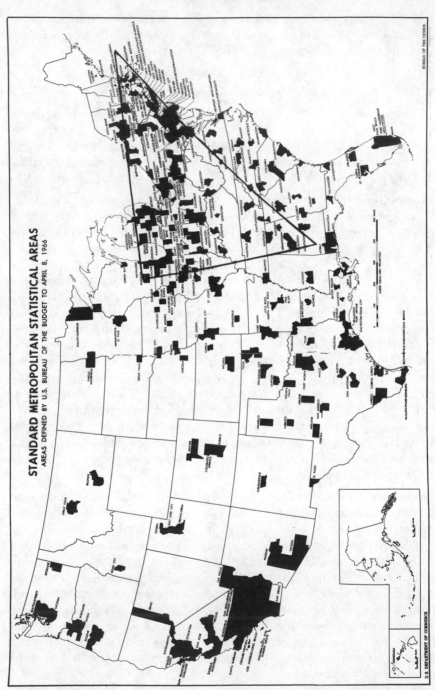

Fig. 3–10. Standard metropolitan statistical areas.

of concentration. However, one must make a distinction between manufacturing concentration and the concentration of distribution-type firms. American manufacturing is geographically concentrated in a triangle roughly from the Boston area to Milwaukee, to Birmingham, and back to Boston. This Eastern triangle accounted for 60 per cent of American industry in 1968 as shown in Table 3–10. The states in the table do not

Table 3–10   Value Added by Manufacturing for Sixteen States, 1968

State	Dollar Value Added	Percentage of U. S. Total
Illinois	$ 21,210	7.0
Indiana	11,247	4.0
Kentucky	4,031	1.0
Ohio	22,312	8.0
Michigan	19,311	7.0
Tennessee	5,543	2.0
Alabama	3,961	1.0
West Virginia	2,224	1.0
Pennsylvania	20,509	7.0
New York	26,793	9.0
New Jersey	13,509	5.0
Maryland	4,111	1.0
Massachusetts	9,056	3.0
Rhode Island	1,465	1.0
Connecticut	6,620	2.0
Delaware	1,208	1.0
Total	$151,900	60.00

Source: Department of Commerce, Bureau of the Census; *U. S. Census of Manufacturers General Summary*, 1968.

correspond exactly to the triangle because figures apply to entire states. The major exceptions to the Eastern triangle are for California and the Gulf Coast. California, with $25,472 of value added and 9.0 per cent of American manufacturing brings the total value added to 69 per cent of the U.S. total. This pattern of manufacturing concentration is changing. Fifteen years ago approximately 70 per cent of the nation's production was located within the triangle. The impetus of decentralization was initiated for defense reasons during World War II, but it has picked up steam as local governments encourage new business by giving cheap labor, tax breaks, and community help.

The incidence of distribution firms tends to be concentrated in the metropolitan areas in much the same fashion as consumers. The tendency is for intermediate distributors to locate in the central area of these cities. Final distributors to households, on the other hand, tend to follow the movement of the consumer population. Retailers are much less concentrated than industrial organizations.[12] Significant numbers of retailers are now located in the suburbs of the large cities to better service the consumer market. Thus, it would be difficult to call retailing distribution concentrated markets.

Differences in Basis for Demand

The consumer market constitutes final demand, and products in this market are used up or destroyed. The business market is characterized by derived demand. Derived demand means that the demand for goods in the business market is dependent on, or derived from, the demand for goods in the consumer market. When final consumers purchase more refrigerators and mobile homes, the demand for steel at the manufacturing level increases. It follows that, generally speaking, manufacturing demand is more elastic, although this may not be true for individual products. A small increase in consumer demand has a multiplier effect on manufacturing demand—each channel member, including distributive members, increases his inventories to be prepared for the observed sales increase. Thus, there is a cumulative effect of purchases at each stage of the channel. Of course, the opposite is true when consumers decrease their purchases. Industrial production decreases by much more than the initial consumer decrease as middlemen stop buying until their inventories run down.

Reciprocal Trade Agreements

Reciprocity means that, "I will buy from you if you will buy from me." It is very common in the business market, but rarely is a factor of purchase or sale in the consumer market. Businessmen see reciprocity as a means to increase sales, therefore, the sales departments of many organizations favor reciprocal agreements.[13] These arrangements do have their disadvantages, and often the purchasing and engineering departments do not approve of such agreements. Reciprocity tends to tie the two firms together and thus to reduce flexibility. The buyer loses the ability to shop for better prices, quality, or terms. Higher prices paid for products can result, with concomitant internal friction and moral problems. Division managers who are held strictly accountable for cost do not like to take products bought under reciprocal agreements. The seller may also lose opportunities to gain higher prices for his products because he is tied to the reciprocal firm. Finally, some of the ill feeling

---

[12] "The Giants Put In More Muscle," *Business Week* (July 23, 1966), pp. 72–75.
[13] See: H. Robert Dodge, *Industrial Marketing* (New York: McGraw-Hill Book Co., Inc., 1970), pp. 34–35.

rubs off on the seller. Of course, consumers have no such problems since they do not engage in such deals.

CONSUMER AND BUSINESS MARKETING METHODS COMPARED

Just as there are general differences in the business and the consumer markets so are there differences in the methods of marketing to these markets. Actually, the differences in the markets partly account for particular methods of marketing. In this section, some of the important marketing variations are summarized.

Differences in Channel Type

When discussing the type of channels used to reach business and final household consumer markets, a distinction must be made in the channels involved. Intelligent discussion requires dividing the business market into two types according to the product's distribution. Thus there is: (1) the manufacturing channel which involves sales only to producers, and (2) the final household industrial channel which involves sales only to households. It is common to include in the manufacturing channel such businesses as mines, manufacturers, fabricators, assemblers, and industrial distributors. In other words, the manufacturing channel involves sales from one creator of form utility to another. The final consumer channel begins with the final producing firm and includes wholesalers and retailers. These types of specific firms are discussed in more detail later.

Number of Firms by Channel Type

There are differences in the number of institutions involved in the manufacturing and the final consumer channels of the business market. Retail and service trades combined have about 1,624,082 firms.[14] Wholesalers constitute approximately 311,464 outlets. Thus the consumer channel has a total of about 1,935,546 firms. The manufacturing channel, including mining, construction, and manufacturing combined has only 602,167 businesses. The consumer market requires a great many more firms for several reasons. Lack of concentration in the consumer market is one factor. Another is the much greater variety of goods sold in the consumer market. Consumer purchases in small quantities make frequent trips to nearby stores necessary. Besides, consumers resist traveling far to buy. The nature of the business buyer makes it possible to purchase in quantity and in advance. The arrival of goods can be

[14] Department of Commerce, Bureau of the Census; U. S. Census of Business, 1963 and 1967.

scheduled in the manufacturing market. Thus, the location of the supplier is less important, and fewer outlets can service a much wider market area. A final factor is the concentration of both sales and geographic location in the manufacturing market.

Differences in Channel Length

A wholesaler in the manufacturing channel is called an industrial distributor. These industrial distributors are important in sales to small manufacturers and for fill-in buyers. For example, industrial distributors are important in the sale of air conditioning; machinery, equipment, supplies; professional equipment; transportation equipment; metals, minerals; scrap; and lumber.[15] However, the total impact made on sales volume by the industrial distributor is not great. Most of these firms have sales of less than $200,000 per year. Their manufacturing channel is characterized by direct sales from producer to producer without the use of middlemen and, consequently, it is typically short, with a high degree of control over marketing. The principal reason for this type of channel is the size and geographic concentration of the manufacturing market.

The opposite is true of the final consumer channel. Sales through wholesalers to retailers is considered the normal route to reach the final consumer market, with perhaps as much as 60 per cent of all products handled by a wholesaler at some point. The reason is basically the predominance of staple-type goods and the lack of concentration in the final consumer market. Where sales are scattered through many different types of firms, control is less in the final consumer channel.

Opportunity for Dual Marketing

A seller in the manufacturing market may be able to sell simultaneously in the final consumer market. Furthermore, within the manufacturing market the seller may concentrate sales in one producing industry or market to several essentially different types of industries. For example, manufacturers of tires and automotive parts make sales in the manufacturing market in the form of original equipment, but they also make replacement sales in the final consumer market. The manufacturer of motors has the option of selling in several different manufacturing market segments. For example, motors are used in the appliance industry, the aircraft industry, the automobile industry, the shipbuilding industry, and the toy industry. The advantage of being able to sell in different markets or in different market segments is that it (1) increases the base of sales

[15] For this and a more complete discussion of industrial distributors see: Ralph S. Alexander, James S. Cross, and Richard Hill, *Industrial Marketing*, 3rd ed. (Homewood, Ill.: Richard D. Irwin, Inc., 1967), Chapter 9.

and (2) forestalls sales decreases due to depressions in a given industry or segment.

Wholesalers and retailers in the final consumer channel have very little opportunity to sell to manufacturers; all their efforts are directed toward the final household consumer. However, retailers have one advantage— the final consumer market is much more diverse than the manufacturing market. The retailer has an opportunity to appeal to several widely different market segments at the same time. He also does not have the problems associated with attempting to sell in essentially different types of markets. Thus, we see that there are advantages to selling in each type of channel.

Use of Specialists

The manufacturing channel is characterized much more by the use of highly trained specialists than is the final consumer channel. Very often the sales representative is an engineer or has engineering training. In the consumer channel, clerk-type salesmen are much more typical. Manufacturing, buyers have great responsibilities that involve large sums of money and direct responsibility for keeping the plant operating. Their tasks are separated from other activities in order to allow them to give buying their undivided attention. In the consumer channel, buyers are often department heads with a responsibility to sales, personnel, and other functional areas. Combined responsibility is possible since the entire store need not shut down because of one or two poor purchase decisions. This combined responsibility is changing in the consumer channel. For example, buying and selling are increasingly separated in department stores. Other types of specialists are used more frequently in the manufacturing channel. These specialists include cost and quality control personnel, economists, marketing research experts, and computer personnel. This does not mean that there are not highly trained specialists in the consumer channel. Examples of high quality sales specialists can be found in the automobile retailer, specialty wholesaler, and furniture businesses. Special buyers and fashion coordinators exist in large department stores. The point is that these highly trained specialists are fewer and they are employed less frequently by firms in the consumer channel.

Difference in Appeals Used

The idea that business purchasers are more rational than consumer purchasers is illogical. After all, they are the same people, only in different purchase situations. It is true that the business purchaser has more information, better information, and more frequent information from his specialists than does the average consumer. The business consumer can obtain specific cost and engineering data to use in comparing competitive products. The average final consumer has to depend strictly on judgment when purchasing. Furthermore, the average final consumer probably has to make more significant decisions related to running a household in a given period than does the average industrial buyer. The business purchaser, may, as a result, do a better job of buying and be no more rational than the household purchaser. The difference between the two purchasers lies in the amount and type of information available rather than in the rationality of the people involved.

It is true that factual appeals to price, quality, long-term agreements, concessions, discounts, ease of handling, etc., affect the industrial purchaser more. Due to a lack of information, the final consumer may be more easily confused by the variety of products and product claims. Thus, appeals to the emotions are often more effective when dealing with the final consumer.[16] With little concrete evidence to go on, the consumer may decide on the basis of such superficial factors as the color of the carton, shelf placement, or recommendation of a neighbor. Of course, it is also true that many consumers do not want to spend the necessary time gathering facts.

CONSUMER AND BUSINESS PURCHASING METHODS

There are differences in the ways that business and final consumers purchase. Of course, there is considerable interaction between the manner of purchase, the method of sale, and the type of market. Nevertheless, the differences that exist can be important to the operation of marketing channels.

Size and Frequency of Purchase

The manufacturing firm, and the firm in the final consumer channel, are much larger organizations than the final consumer household. Thus, purchases by these business organizations are made in much larger units than those for households. Individual business purchases may run into thousands of dollars, as they do for such raw materials as coal, copper, bauxite, iron ore, parts, etc. About the only time that the final consumer commits himself for more than a thousand dollars is when purchasing an automobile, a home, or furniture. Most final consumer purchases probably involve no more than $1.00 to $50.00 at a given time. The manufacturer's purchases may run into thousands of dollars each day. Of course, business firms also make many small expenditures involving only a few dollars. Examples can be found in cleaning compounds, rags,

---

16 Walters and Paul, *op. cit.*, pp. 501–4.

lubricating oil, paper, pencils, etc. Both businesses and final consumers purchase many types of products regularly and frequently. Consumers purchase such staples as groceries, gas, cleaners, and clothing regularly. Businesses' purchasers buy a wide variety of staple items frequently, including office supplies, washroom towels, soap, food, and medical supplies. Both consumers and business users make regular payments for rent, fuel, lights, and water. The difference is in the amounts involved. The reader should not fail to note that although households purchase much less than businesses, their numbers are vastly superior, and the total market may be larger than a given business market.

Product and Store Loyalty

It is difficult to generalize concerning product and store loyalty between household consumers and business users. Final consumers depend considerably on price and brand to judge products.[17] However, this fact should not be taken to mean that they are brand loyal. Consumers have choices among many well-known brands and they do considerable switching. Consumers also display store loyalty, but some are more loyal than others. Young people tend to be very brand conscious but not very brand loyal compared to their parents.

Business firms demonstrate a definite type of product and store loyalty similar to that of final consumers. Many firms purchase known or trusted products that have given good service over time. In fact, the use of long-term contracts for the purchase of goods in the industrial market is a common practice. Certainly, there is ample evidence of strong loyalty to preferred suppliers. It is safe to say that product and store loyalty are important factors of purchase in both the final consumer and business markets and any seller is wise to cultivate this attribute on the part of buyers.

Decision Responsibility

Where large sums of money are involved, purchases of new plants and major equipment purchase decisions are often made by top management. Many decisions, such as the engineering and design of a new product, involve managers at all levels of the business. Anyone attempting to sell under such circumstances must know his way around the business and have a feel for contacting the proper person. Sales to industrial firms are, therefore, often complex and time-consuming. On the other hand, many industrial purchases are routine, even some involving large sums of money. This latter situation is particularly true if the good in question is a staple such as sand, chemicals, etc. These routine decisions are made by purchasing officers.

---

[17] *Ibid.*, pp. 507–10.

Purchases of goods for the home are quite different.[18] The housewife typically acts as the household purchasing agent about 60 per cent of the time. Joint purchases, where the wife has help from either the husband or children, usually involve such major dollar expenditures as for the automobile, furniture, home, and recreation. Even when the housewife acts as the purchasing agent, she takes into consideration the wishes of the rest of the family. Consequently, it is much easier to reach and deal with household purchases. Most of the time the housewife seeks out the store to acquire the items needed; it is much more common for salesmen to call on the industrial firm.

QUESTIONS

1. Why should markets be segmented and what factors are used in isolating a market segment?
2. Discuss consumer market segmentation with respect to channels of distribution.
3. Explain why a change in total population characteristics is important in planning channels of distribution.
4. Describe methods of segmentation in the business markets.
5. Compare today's predominant patterns of size and geographic concentration between the business and final consumer markets.
6. Explain how the size and frequency of purchase affect channels of distribution.
7. How do channels of distribution affect the policies of the different segments of the business market?
8. Summarize important consumer trends within metropolitan areas of the United States.
9. What is the significance of patterns of age, race, and sex of consumer markets to the concept of channels?
10. Explain the difference in channel length between manufacturer and final consumer.

[18] Henry Whiteside, "Interacting Roles of the Household Purchasing Agent," *Theory In Marketing,* Reavis Cox, Wroe Alderson, and Stanley Shapiro, eds. (Homewood, Ill.: Richard D. Irwin, Inc., 1964), pp. 270–80.

4

Channel Responsibility
to the Environment

The channel of distribution is a team of marketing institutions, functioning within an environment for the purpose of satisfying markets at a profit. The channel, the environment, and the markets, taken together, form an operating system. The major emphasis of the book is on the marketing team. Markets were discussed in the previous chapter; this chapter deals with another major variable of the system: the environment. The interaction of the marketing team with its environment is emphasized.

ENVIRONMENT OF THE CHANNEL

The term environment, other than markets, is very popular in modern marketing, but little effort is devoted to clarifying what it means. Yet it is difficult to discuss intelligently environmental influence on business without some clear concept of what is involved. The term environment has the general meaning of external factors or the total climate within which something functions.[1] This climate can be defined as broadly or as narrowly as one desires. Thus, we speak of the climate of the classroom, the national political climate, and the world weather climate. It is in this general sense that environment is used in connection with the marketing channel. The channel environment is defined specifically as *all the forces or factors external to the channel team which operate to influence the behavior of that team.*

[1] See: Y. Hugh Furuhashi and E. Jerome McCarthy, *Social Issues of Marketing in the American Economy* (Columbus, Ohio: Grid, Inc., 1971).

By this definition, almost everything is a part of the channel environment. The system within which the channel operates is recognized as a socio-economic system which exists for personal contact as well as for economic purposes. Although market considerations are specifically excluded from the environment, people are not. Social factors take into consideration the same people that constitute markets; we simply evaluate the consumer in a different light. In the discussion of markets, consumers were treated as opportunities—under the environment they are treated as constraints on business.[2] As a part of the social environment, people exert pressures that have a definite influence on the operation of channel.

Interaction of Channel and Environment

The channel environment is never static. The change that the environment causes in the marketing channel is not a type of one-way street. For example, consumer tastes change over time, and competitors become more or less active. The channel must be modified to furnish satisfaction to the new tastes, as it must adjust to meet changed competitive circumstances. However, the actions of the channel, in turn, affect the environments. A new retail institution, such as the discount house, alters consumer purchase patterns. Too aggressive a competitive situation may lead to new laws, etc. Neither the channel nor the environment is completely independent of the other.

It is true that at any given point in time, one or two environmental components may have more influence on the channel than others. For example, government and social considerations, as a result of the 1957 Civil Rights Act, have had tremendous impact on the conduct of business in the past years. In the early twentieth century it was employees, operating through the trade unions, that had greater influence in shaping the actions of channels. The 1930's saw competition rise in importance because of the depression. No matter what the individual influence, it is never sound for business to ignore the environment.

Types of System Influences

The channel and environment tend to influence each other in specific ways. Environmental influences on the channel can be grouped into three types. First, channel members find business opportunities in the environment in such areas as specific consumer needs, changes in social behavior, changes in tastes, etc. Generally, the business that does the best job of recognizing and handling opportunities succeeds. Second, the environment establishes the general social values under which business must

---

[2] Robert O. Harrmann, *The Consumer Movement in Historical Perspective* (University Park: The Pennsylvania State University, 1970), pp. 2–31.

operate. These social values reflect honesty, moral and ethical judgments, rewards and sanctions, and group behavior. Of course, channel members may take advantage of the rules, but if the businesses do not operate within the general standards established by society then pressures are brought to force conformity. Third, where moral persuasion fails, the environment specifies constraints on business activity.

The channel also influences the environment in three ways. First, personal opportunities for success are achieved by participating in business. In the American society, a person's achievements are largely related to work and the income that results from work. Businesses provide for the economic achievements of the individual. Second, channel members, as a group, help establish economic values. That is, total accumulated output of business in the form of factories, equipment, and products determines the economic worth of a nation. The standard of living is a reflection of these economic values. Third, business places constraints on social activity, because income determines the family's standard of living and affects social activity and social placement.

FOUNDATION FOR ENVIRONMENTAL ISSUES

The environmental issues that affect channel operations range over a variety of subjects from pollution to high consumer prices.[3] Everyone has an opinion on the nature of the questions, but there is very little consensus concerning the nature of the business response. Almost everyone agrees, however, that environmental issues must be a part of the decision process in all future business undertakings including those of channels.

Environmental Issues Reflect Society's Values

There has been much discussion recently of environmental issues.[4] This dialogue has erupted because of basic changes taking place in our socio-economic values.[5] The issues found in any society arise out of the values held by that society. Social values are defined as a society's cus-

---

[3] S. H. Gamble, "Marketing and Social Change," *Marketing and Social Issues*, John R. Wish and S. H. Gamble, eds. (New York: John Wiley & Sons, Inc., 1971), pp. 12–18.

[4] William D. Patterson, "J. Irwin Miller: The Revolutionary Role of Business," *Saturday Review* (January 13, 1968); Philip Kotler and Sidney J. Levy, "Broadening the Concept of Marketing," *Journal of Marketing*, Vol. 33 (January, 1966); Robert J. Lavidge, "The Growing Responsibilities of Marketing, *Journal of Marketing*, Vol. 34 (January, 1970); Wroe Alderson, "The Mission of Marketing," *Men, Motives and Markets*, Wroe Alderson and Michael H. Halbert, eds. (Englewood Cliffs, N. J.: Prentice-Hall, Inc., 1968).

[5] Thaddeus H. Spratlen, "The Challenge of the Humanistic Value Orientation in Marketing," Paper presented to the Boston Conference, American Marketing Association, August 31, 1970.

toms, mores, institutions, and ideals. These values provide guidance for human actions and play a large part in shaping our moral, ethical, social, competitive, religious, and political activities. Actions that are in line with social values are deemed right and correct, while those that deviate are said to be wrong or incorrect. However, it must be remembered that social values are not necessarily ultimate truths. They simply represent the will of the majority. They are subjective judgments of what is significant and worthwhile in society. Because values are subjective they vary from one society to another. For example, Eskimos found nose rubbing socially acceptable, while Americans prefer kissing. The early American Indians' predatory action against his enemies was simply business as usual. Modern societies frown on any type of theft.

Overall, the United States has made a rather abrupt shift in the direction of its social values in recent years—from those stressed under individualism to the social values emphasized under collectivism.[6] Neither of these terms is intended to be associated with specific socio-economic systems, and the author does not apply the labels good or bad to either. Each is simply descriptive of a type of social trend. What has happened is that society is losing some of its old *individualistic* emphasis on self-reliance, personal reward, technological advancement, and personal honor. These values are being replaced by a *collectivist* emphasis on group interdependence, controlled technology, public protection, and equal rights to minorities. The major environmental issues before our nation demonstrate the shift in values. Historically, America was concerned with expansion, personal productivity, private technology, corruption, and unionization. These were issues that grew out of individualism. Today's more socially oriented issues include pollution, the population explosion, the urban crisis, social injustice, and the quality of life.[7] Even as our society moves increasingly toward collectivism there are opposing currents of individualism within the movement. For example, the desire of the court system to provide maximum freedom for individuals has made it very difficult to enforce laws designed for the good of all.

Determination of Social Values

Social values can be determined by: (1) individuals, (2) pressure groups, or (3) a combination of the two. When individuals set broad social values it means that each person acts in his own self-interest.[8] The

---

[6] Sen. Warren G. Magnuson, *Consumerism,* Ralph M. Gaedeke and Warren W. Etcheson, eds. (San Francisco: Canfield Press, 1972), p. 3.

[7] National Goals Research Staff, "A Report Toward Balanced Growth: Quantity with Quality" (July 4, 1970), pp. 25–35.

[8] Keith Davis, "Understanding the Social Responsibility Puzzle: What Does the Businessman Owe to Society?," *Business Horizons,* Vol. 10 (Winter, 1967), pp. 45–50.

values that result are a summation of all the individual values. Presumably, the prevailing social values are those held by the majority of individuals. Of course, in such a society as ours, there are likely to be important currents of dissenting values held at any time. For example, most consumers may feel that they would rather have gasoline at cheaper prices than oil conservation, but many individuals may prefer conservation. An even worse situation exists when large numbers of people want both objectives. This situation creates internal conflicts within individuals that may show in very inconsistent and erratic behavior patterns. For example, a person may insist on a fuel-consuming automatic transmission for his car to drive to a conservation rally.

When broad social values are established by pressure groups, it means that one person, or a small minority of people, interprets social values for the entire group. In a sense, this is rule by minority, and it happens frequently in a modern society. When a board of censure can decide what is immoral or obscene in movies, it is acting as the conscience for all moviegoers. In our society, almost anyone can be a pressure group. Ralph Nader has recently been acting as the social conscience of the automobile industry and has now moved into politics. Censors of all types serve this same purpose. Legislators, to the extent that they act for their constituents, also fit this category. It typically happens that the values of the pressure groups become formalized in legislation. In effect, the government becomes the ultimate pressure group. Partly as a result of Nader's efforts the government has set standards of emissions for the automobile industry. Of course, neither of the above extremes is typical. Most of our society's values are set jointly as a result of the interaction of individuals and groups.

Consequence of Value Determination

Neither individually determined values nor those set by small groups are ideal for a society, simply because there are serious drawbacks to either extreme. When social values are established by the individual he tends to: (1) set short-run goals, (2) be personally motivated, and (3) lack social perspective. The individual is not interested in long-run social gains. He wants gas for his car today even if the resource is depleted in another twenty or thirty years. His attitude is, "they will find a way." The individual wants the advantages of city life even if the city breeds pollution and ghettos. Personal motivation means that the individual does not want to become involved in the problems of others. Such group action as aid to the poor is not in line with this thinking. Lack of social perspective means that the individual does not see the larger picture. He cannot understand that throwing one beer can really causes litter, or that his cheating on his income tax hurts anyone. If society religiously followed the dictates of the individual, there would be little public activity designed to aid groups as a whole.

Values established completely by small pressure groups have as many pitfalls as those established by the individual. Pressure groups tend: (1) to substitute their own values for those of others, (2) to have little consideration for the individual's needs, (3) to lead to a loss of personal freedom, and (4) to be too idealistic. The substitution of the values of the pressure group for those of the individual can be called the "Priscilla Goodbody Syndrome." This syndrome is exemplified by the movie censor who delights in reviewing dirty movies but bans such movies for the general public. Another example is the critic who informs the public how to feel toward a play, a fashion, or a political candidate. The danger in letting an individual or small group set values is that they often abuse the privilege. They get carried away with their own power and really believe that their judgments are superior to those of "other" people.

When social values are set by small pressure groups, the needs of the individual tend to be forgotten. However, individuals do need many things that may not be compatible with the needs of the pressure group. Low income consumers want inexpensive goods, and these people have difficulty accepting extra charges, such as elaborate emission abatement auto systems, that create social values. Of course, when a group decides for the individual, that individual has given up his freedom of choice. Some people see this as the most serious fault of group determination of social values. Idealism tends to be inherent in group-set values. The group wants things perfect now, and there is often an unwillingness to compromise. For example, the automobile industry has informed the government that it can achieve 85 per cent pollution control at a reasonable cost. In time, this figure can be raised to 90 or 95 per cent. The government, reacting to group pressure, is insisting on 95 per cent control in 1975. One has to wonder if the added cost of 10 per cent more control immediately is worth the price. If social values were set exclusively by small groups, there would by tyranny by the few. The more desirable social values are those determined jointly. In this way each interested party can act as a brake on the other. The resulting standards are more likely to reflect careful judgment.

How Social Values Affect Channels

The manner of channel member response to environmental issues depends on the social values established by society. Remember, channel members reside between the market and environments. These businesses must interpret broad social values from the environment and translate them into concrete products and services to be delivered to consumers in acceptable form. There may be some question whether business has, or should have, a social conscience,[9] but it really doesn't matter. Generally, the channel member is quite willing to perform in a manner consistent with the goals established, and actually a business does not care whether the goals are established under individualism or collectivism. The only requirement for effective business performance is that society's values be clear and that there be agreement among the interested group on the values established. The channel can just as easily make and distribute pollution abatement devices or automobiles, stay open on Sunday or close, or employ advertising to promote good health or cigarettes.

There is no problem about channel responsibility to the environment when the individual, business, and other social groups are in harmony about social values. Trouble arises when some parts of society and consumers do not agree on social goals and three types of problems may result.

Management Misinterpretation of Goals. First, business may misinterpret the conflicting goals (see Table 4–1). Thus, the action taken by

Table 4–1   Critic and Businessmen Perspectives

Key Words	Critics View	Businessman's View
Competition	Price competition	Product differentiation
Product	Primary function	Differentiation
Consumer needs	Directly related to primary functions	Any customer desired
Rationality	Efficient matching of product to needs	Any customer decision
Information	Any data that facilitates product fit to needs	Information that truthfully makes product attractive

Source: Raymond A. Bauer and Stephen A. Greyser, "The Dialogue that Never Happens," *Harvard Business Review*, Vol. 45 (November–December, 1967), pp. 2ff.

channel members may not conform to the majority will. This situation can result in the misdirection of channel activity and in inefficiency. Many times the problem is a difference in consumer and management perceptions. One study shows that consumers and management do not perceive key market phrases in the same manner. Misdirection of channel activity occurred when an automobile manufacturer distributed a "safe" car only to discover that consumers valued looks and power above safety. Consumers did not purchase the car in sufficient quantity to

[9] Peter Drucker, "Consumerism: The Opportunity of Marketing," Address, Marketing Committee of the National Association of Manufacturers, (April 10, 1969). The author takes the position that the existence of consumerism is evidence of the failure of the marketing concept, and ends by showing how the movement can offer opportunities to marketing.

warrant continued production. The result of this channel action was high-cost production, socially unacceptable cars, and dissatisfied customers. The whole question of consumer sovereignity is involved. One author argues that the concept of consumer sovereignity is, "incomplete, highly ambiguous, and lacks independence." [10]

Forced Channel Inefficiency.   Second, channel members can be forced, by law or social pressure, into the inefficient position of satisfying the desires of a minority. Some feel our society has shifted from one essentially controlled by business to one controlled by consumers. [11] Small pressure groups in America have considered seat belts for automobiles desirable, based on clear evidence that they save lives. However, most consumers steadfastly refuse to use the belts, and they complain about the extra cost and discomfort. It is not a question of right or wrong, but rather of whom business pleases. The channel leader is caught in the middle when there is disagreement between factions in the environment. No matter which way the business turn it is open to criticism. For example, if channel members oppose seat belts they are accused of fostering unsafe cars. Much criticism of business is of this type. For example, people want the output of industry, but they do not want the pollution it brings.

Disagreement in Channel and Social Goals.   Third, the goals of society may not agree with those of channel members. When this situation happens, the tendency is to accuse businesses of dishonesty for acting in their own self-interest. The criticism is often justified, as when channels push unimproved or no longer desired products. It is justified when managers lie, cheat, or steal. Examples can be found in false, unjust, or misleading advertising. Too much advertising fails to meet its overall responsibility of persuasion based on sound facts. However, much criticism of channel members is not justified. Businesses are often criticized for such actions as profit seeking, failing to compete, fostering obsolescence, and advertising when such actions are a necessary part of business. [12] Each channel member must make a profit to survive. If businesses do not survive, everyone is hurt. Recently, housewives have been upset with food chains over high prices; they accuse the chains of making excess profits and wasting money on advertising when government reports show that these food chains have not shared in the recent rise in profits. There is considerable evidence that large numbers of people favor obsolescence

[10] G. William Trivoli, "Has the Consumer Really Lost His Sovereignty," *American Business and Economic Review*, Vol. 1 (Winter, 1970), pp. 33–39.

[11] E. T. Grether, "From Caveat Emptor to an Emerging Caveat Venditor: Whither?" *Changing Marketing System*, Proceedings of the American Marketing Association, Series No. 26, 1967, pp. 174–77.

[12] Lee E. Preston, "Fair Competition," *Social Issues in Marketing*, Lee E. Preston, ed. (Glenview, Ill.: Scott, Foresman and Co., 1968), pp. 112–14.

and change in the products they buy. For example, change and obsolescence are typically undertaken at the insistence of consumers. Regular business advertising is necessary to inform the public, and it is a basic competitive weapon of our economic system. The system cannot perform as effectively without honest advertising.

ENVIRONMENTAL ISSUES THAT AFFECT CHANNELS

The United States presently finds most of its environmental issues in the value of collectivism. These issues can be grouped under five headings: (1) discrimination, (2) quality of life, (3) business behavior, (4) social conflict, and (5) the level of life.

1. National attention was first focused on the problem of discrimination by the Civil Rights Act of 1957. This act was first applied to blacks, but in recent years women, Mexicans, Cubans, Asians, Indians, and youth have been involved in an expanding interpretation of discrimination. Women, youth, and minority groups are seeking expanded job opportunities, equal pay, non-discrimination in buying, equal use of facilities, and greater participation in the good things of life.

2. There has been an increased awareness in the American economy of the importance of the quality of life, which refers to the condition of the environment in which one lives. The principal issues in the fight for a better quality of life include the population explosion; poverty; water, air and noise pollution; and the urban crisis. Much of the blame for the environment falls on channel members although the evidence is that municipal governments, with their archaic waste disposal methods, poor zoning, and fire laws, are as guilty. Even the consumer, when he litters, is polluting the environment. It is probably accurate to say that the blame for pollution lies with all of us. The environment cannot be improved until the ordinary citizen is convinced of the need to do so. Nevertheless, the business community is faced with increased social and political pressure and needs to become involved.

3. As the emphasis of the society shifts from an attitude of independence to one of public concern, the behavior of channel members comes under increased scrutiny. The American public has become very critical of business in general, and the credibility gap appears to be widening. The principal problems are product quality, price discrimination, product safety, economic power, monopoly, collusion, and truth in communications.[13] In the future, the business community will have to conform to the standard of conduct desired by society.

4. Social conflict has been increasing in recent years as those who are

[13] Lester G. Telser, "Abusive Trade Practices: An Economic Analysis," *Law and Contemporary Problems*, Vol. 30 (Summer, 1965), pp. 488–505.

underprivileged and discriminated against become impatient with waiting to share in the good life. Social conflict takes the form of violence and crime. Both are a threat, not only to channels, but to the very society in which we live. Channels have a place in making the good life available to everyone. It is to the advantage of businesses to act in this area. Violence and crime destroy property, disrupt business activity, and increase insurance and other costs. Business communications in this area, backed by honest endeavors to help, should be undertaken.

5. The level of living concerns the manner in which family income is spent. The socio-economic problems our nation faces today that relate to the level of living are high prices, unemployment, productivity, and foreign imports. Use of government controls is also an issue related to the level of living. The country has gone through a period of rather constant inflation since the late 1930's which erodes the family's life style. Personal dissatisfaction is a natural result.

MANAGEMENT RESPONSIBILITY TO ENVIRONMENT

The new emphasis on collective issues in the society has greatly changed the understanding of management's responsibility. In this section we shall investigate this new responsibility. Three principal topics are discussed: (1) how management views its responsibility, (2) how society views management's responsibility, and (3) conflict in the views of management's responsibility.

Management Attitude Toward Environmental Responsibility

Under the concept of individualism, management looked out for itself. The attitude was that if every member of the society performs its own function efficiently, the system will operate smoothly. This concept recognized no broad environmental responsibility for channel members. In a society increasingly governed by collectivism, this attitude can only lead to antagonism toward the business community.[14] Table 4-2 indicates that the viewpoint of channel managers is changing, but it is still self-oriented. That of the chief executive is changing faster than comptrollers, possibly because the chief executive has a broader view of business responsibility. Neither group of executives gave a high rank to social responsibility. It is obvious from this data that executives are not keeping up with the changing times. Furthermore, there is little evidence to support adoption of the marketing concept by these businesses. However,

14 "How Business Responds to Consumerism," *Business Week* (September 6, 1969), pp. 94–108.

Table 4-2   How Business Executives View Their Responsibility

Group Ranked	Percentage Chief Executive Giving Rank of 1	Percentage Comptroller and Financial Executive Giving Rank 1	Percentage Total Giving Rank of 1	Composite Rank
Stockholders	81.9	86.2	84.2	1
Employees	12.1	10.5	11.3	3
Customers	26.1	0.0	17.6	2
Creditors	11.8	11.0	11.3	3
Society	5.5	0.0	2.4	4

Source: Arthur Lorig, *Business Horizons* (Bloomington: The University of Indiana Press, 1967), p. 51–54.

it is encouraging to see the chief executives becoming more interested in customers.

Environmental Expectations From Management

Society has come to view the responsibility of channel managers in a much different way from these managers. The new attitude is that businessmen cannot escape responsibility for the environment. The participants in the environment have come to expect certain things from business.

Market Expectations from Management. Consumers constitute an important environmental element. They have become much more active toward business in recent years, and these activities are showing results. The growth of consumerism is one evidence of this activity.[15] Consumers are banding together across the nation in order to acquire economic power. These groups are putting pressure on marketing channels both directly by verbal and written confrontation and indirectly through the government. Not everyone agrees on the perceived purpose of these consumer organizations as indicated in Table 4–3.

In spite of different perceptions, consumerism has had its effect. Consumer pressure has led to the establishment of the Consumer Advisory Council under the office of the President. Charged with studying and making recommendations in areas of consumer interest, this council has defined four rights of consumers in their dealing with channel managers.[16]

[15] Richard H. Buskirk and James T. Rothe, "Consumerism—An Interpretation," *Journal of Marketing*, Vol. 34 (October, 1970), pp. 61–65.
[16] Based on: *Consumer Advisory Council, First Report*, Executive Office of the President (Washington, D.C.: United States Government Printing Office, October, 1963), pp. 5–8, 18–31; Magnuson, *op. cit.*, pp. 3–7.

Table 4-3 Perception About Consumerism

Perceived Purpose	Business Oriented Responses	Consumer Oriented Responses	Federal Government Responses
Political in nature	67%	29%	47%
Economic in nature	5	29	39
Social in nature	14	21	0
Psychological in nature	9	0	0
Combination of above	5	21	14

Source: Ralph M. Gaedeke, "What Business, Government, and Consumer Spokesmen Think About Consumerism," *Journal of Consumer Affairs*, Vol. 4 (Summer, 1970), pp. 7–18.

1. *The Right To Safety.* This right refers to protection against the production and sale of goods that are harmful to life and health. Examples can be found in flammable clothing, unlimited sale of drugs, and defective equipment.
2. *The Right To Be Informed.* This right has two aspects. It refers to protection against the dishonest, deceitful, and grossly misleading information sometimes distributed by business. It also refers to the consumer's right to have business furnish sufficient facts for the consumer to use in selecting products. Examples of the former are found in the gross claims of advertisers and salesmen. The latter occurs when business fails to disclose vital information about a product's performance.
3. *The Right To Be Heard.* This is the assurance that the consumer has available a sympathetic outlet where his opinions and complaints can be voiced.
4. *The Right To Choose.* This is the right to have access to a variety of products. Considerations include effective competition among businesses, the availability of market entry, and restraint of monopoly.

The evidence is clear that the consumer can no longer be ignored when management develops its marketing strategy. The increased emphasis on the marketing concept by many educators and practitioners is a recognition of this fact.

Socio-Economic Expectations. Because of their close relationship, socio-economic environmental factors are discussed together. Both aspects of the system have rights relative to the operation of channels. The social side of the system can expect businesses to function morally and ethically in all their interactions with consumers, competitors, government, or employees. Ethical conduct does not deny the profit motive, but it does require that the profit motive operate under a positive system of social values.[17] These social values determine the right and wrong way to make profit. The channel member is rewarded when it conforms to the social value system, and is punished when it does not conform. The following code of ethics has been prescribed for managers:

1. The professional manager affirms that he will place the interest of his company before his own private interests.
2. He will place his duty to society above his duty to his company and above his private interest.
3. He has a duty to reveal the facts in any situation where his private interests are involved with those of his company, or where the interests of his company are involved with those of society.
4. He must subscribe wholeheartedly to the belief that when business managers follow this code of conduct, the profit motive is the best incentive of all for the development of a dynamic economy.[18]

The channel owes to the economic system a proper allocation of resources and efficiency in operations. This allocation means that business must distribute what the society desires in accordance with the various incomes of the people. Channels exist to distribute goods and services. Channel efficiency means that the task of enterprise must be accomplished by employment of the best tools, management, and techniques available. Where it is deficient, management must strive to improve efficiency. Only by accomplishing these ends can the channel discharge its responsibility to the system. Of course, when economic responsibility and social responsibility are in conflict, some compromise must be found. How to compromise is a decision for the total environment, and business wishes constitute only one voice in the decision.

Government Expectations. The government has the right to expect channel operations to conform, not only to the letter of the law, but also to its spirit.[19] The laws passed by ordinary men are not always good for business, and sometimes these laws are not even good for society. Nevertheless, ours is a nation founded on law and not on men. The law is, and should be, greater than any individual, enterprise, religion, race, or particular social persuasion. Channel managers must live up to the law. A good example of channel cooperation was observed in the recent price controls established by the government. While there were some individual attempts to circumvent the law, most businesses attempted to abide by the letter and spirit of the legislation.

---

[17] Kenneth Boulding, "Ethics and Business: An Economist's View," *Beyond Economics* (Ann Arbor: The University of Michigan Press, 1969); Henry O. Pruden, "Which Ethics For Marketers?" *Marketing and Social Issues*, John R. Wish and Stephen H. Gamble, eds. (New York: John Wiley and Sons, Inc., 1971), pp. 98–104.

[18] *Business Week* (June 17, 1961).

[19] Marshall C. Howard, *Legal Aspects of Marketing* (New York: McGraw-Hill Book Co., Inc., 1964), pp. 1–4.

If a law is bad for channel members, or if management feels it is bad for society, there is the right of any pressure group to attempt to change the law through persuasion. No one can doubt that business is a significant pressure group able to make its point with government. If the law cannot be changed in this manner, one can only assume that it represents the will of the people. In such a case, business has the moral obligation to abide. Any other conclusion can only lead to anarchy and chaos. There has been, in recent years, increasing encroachment by gangsters on the arena of legitimate channel activity. While such encroachment is not the responsibility of business, it is the responsibility of managers to discourage such activity and not to deal with known gangsters.

Competitive Expectations. The society has the right to expect the competitive environment to be reasonably free and sufficiently responsive to carry out its economic function. The system has the right to expect channel members to compete honestly and directly based on legitimate differences in product, operations, or promotion. It must be recognized by all agencies of the system that every business has two basic competitive rights: the right to try to succeed and the right to fail. The right to try to succeed means there must be reasonable freedom of entry for new firms into the various trades. There is no place in competition for trade boycotts, collusion, or other attempts to restrain trade. Each business must have the right to independent action so that it has some degree of control over its own success or failure.

The right to fail goes hand in hand with the right to succeed. This right means that the slow to adapt, underfinanced, or inefficient channel members must get out of industry in order to make room for the efficient. Obviously, if any group tampers with the right of a company to fail, it is denying some other company the right to try. The sheer intimidation of large businesses can sometimes keep smaller ones from entering a field, and the financial requirement of entry can also be prohibitive. Government aid to small business, and the recent disclosure that the government loaned Lockheed enough money to continue operations is not in the best interest of competition.

Management Response to Environment

The response that channel managers make to the environment varies. Actually, three different types of response are possible. Members may ignore the environment, adjust to it, or change it. Different managements may use different approaches. Even within the same business, all three of the approaches may be in use simultaneously, and a business may utilize different approaches at various times. The particular method used depends on the disposition of management and the circumstances.

Ignore the Environment.   The possibility does exist that channel managers can ignore the environment by refusing to take any action. This is a do-nothing policy, but it may be sound to avoid environmental action for several reasons. First, not everything that happens in the environment applies to every channel. Emission standards applied to auto channels do not apply to others. The ban on cigarette commercials on television does not apply to cigars.

Second, channel managers can often ignore the environment in the short run, even if they must conform in the long run. Some environmental elements, such as the political, social, and cultural areas, tend to change slowly. The environments of the government, consumers, and competition change rapidly. Business managers may assume that slow-moving environments do not affect short-run channel operations. Management may ignore these areas and devote attention to the more volatile environments. Some businesses have disregarded such social change as women's liberation and the emancipation of blacks. It is seldom a good policy to ignore change in the more dynamic environments.

Third, managers may avoid environmental action because they do not wish to conform. This is a poor reason, and it often leads to antagonism from people and loss of competitive position to more flexible channels or firms. Some businesses attempted to ignore the Civil Rights Act, but social and legal pressures have brought most of them around. It is sometimes possible for managers to ignore issues of small consequence. Many small firms ignored the price freeze because they thought themselves too small for the government to bother.

Adjust to the Environment.   One alternative available to channels is to adjust to present conditions of the environment. Under this policy, managers affect active policies, but take little initiative. A policy of adjustment is a cautious approach to environmental problems. The channel managers read conditions existing in the environment and modify operations to conform. Inherent in this policy is the channel members' acceptance of the environment as it exists. If consumers become price conscious, the business begins to emphasize sales and bargains. If government decrees that labels must show product content, then business adjusts its packages. Adjustment is often a sound channel policy, and sometimes it is the only acceptable course. It is impossible for business managers to anticipate every type of environmental change. Many changes are accomplished facts before business is aware of their existence. Thus, when business becomes aware, channel members may have to adjust.

Change the Environment.   Channel managers can take the lead in effecting environmental change. This policy is aggressive and designed to give the channel control over its interaction with the environment. Under this policy of innovation, management recognizes that change is inevitable. Every time a firm introduces a new product it fosters this type of change. Most new products are resisted by consumers who must be convinced that it is a good idea and often management must change social patterns in order to have the product accepted. For example, it took years of creative promotion before the automobile became widely adopted. People's concepts of travel had to be changed in the process. Many felt the body could not take the pressure of moving at 40 m.p.h.; others took the attitude that the buggy was good enough; and still others objected to the way the automobile frightened the horses. Many adults had to be convinced that long hair was not related to a person's sex or work habits.

There is a question of how active channel members should be in causing environmental change. Some feel that business conditions customer responses. Others feel that business has no effect. The truth probably lies somewhere in between. Most people feel that industry is a good thing, but does a factory have to contribute to environmental problems? Would it not be better if automobiles were sturdy rather than beautiful? Most people feel that aspirin is a worthwhile medicine, but is the psychic satisfaction derived from using a particular brand necessary? Only society can decide. Clearly, business must be persuasive in order to function, but it is doubtful if business can cause consumers to act against their basic instincts.

CHANNEL SELF-REGULATION

Channel conformity to environmental standards is not left to chance in the American system. There are important forces at work to insure that industry complies. These forces include self-restraint, government restraint, and competition.

Perhaps the most important type of restraint on the activity of channel managers is self-regulation.[20] Self-regulation means that channel members conform to environmental standards because of self-interest. Self-regulation does not necessarily imply that member firms be benevolent or socially oriented. As a matter of fact, many businesses are benevolent and/or socially oriented. Many contribute regularly to worthy causes, and the managements of some firms take an active part in community life.

---

[20] Louis L. Stern, "Consumer Protection Via Self-Regulation," *Journal of Marketing*, Vol. 35 (July, 1971), pp. 47–53; Harper W. Boyd and Henry J. Claycamp, "Industrial Self-Regulation and Public Interest," *Michigan Law Review*, Vol. 64 (May, 1966), pp. 1239–54.

Other firms consciously gear operations to achieve social ends. Examples can be found in firms that deliberately keep prices low, or that develop and promote products highly beneficial to mankind. The majority of businessmen do attempt to conduct themselves in an honest, moral, and ethical manner, because business does recognize the inherent advantage of serving the public.

The point is that social orientation, while desirable, is not necessary for a channel to conform to socially acceptable standards. The channel may conform because of external pressure or the threat of pressure. Firms recognize that compliance is the best route to achieve overall goals such as survival and profit. The average firm attempts to make or sell products that keep customers happy, putting as much quality material into the product as possible, consistent with what customers can pay. The threat of competitive action or government intervention often is sufficient to induce self-regulation.

Many channel members have made specific responses to the consumer movement.[21] First, they have established divisions of consumer affairs that are alert to all areas having consumer implications. Second, many firms have changed practices considered unfair or deceptive. Third, channel leaders have undertaken the education of channel members to consumer interests. Fourth, the total cost of consumer protection has been incorporated into the operating budget of many firms. It makes good sense for management to keep its options open. Very little is gained from pushing the environmental sectors to take positive action because the result is nearly always increased restriction of business. A good rule for management is, "Use your power in such a way as to maintain the ability to use your power." [22] A firm should not take action that will cause a curtailment of its power to act in the future. For example, by abusing workers in the 1800's, management caused the growth of labor unions, which, in turn, restrained management prerogatives in many areas. It would have been better if management had led in worker reforms.

GOVERNMENT RESTRAINT OF CHANNELS

The government effects considerable restraint on channel operations. Local, state and federal governments all play a part in restraining member activities, but the most critical effects are those administered by the federal government.

[21] Buskirk and Rothe, *op. cit.*, pp. 61–65.
[22] See: Wroe Alderson, *Marketing Behavior and Executive Action* (Homewood, Ill.: Richard D. Irwin, 1957), pp. 51–52.

General Government Restraint

General government restraint refers to a broad spectrum of specific local, state, and federal acts that directly affect business.[23] The number and types of general restraint vary between geographic areas; enforcement also differs. The more important ones include tax collection, zoning laws, licenses, and building codes. Taxes and licenses can be collected at all levels of government. Taxes are levied directly on individual business such as the corporate tax, on customers such as the sales tax that business must collect, or on products such as the excise tax. There are also taxes on imports and exports. Usually, zoning laws and building codes are locally administered. Many laws are also designed to apply to specific businesses. Two important examples include federal and local meat inspection, inspection of food handlers and restaurant operations, and the auditing of banks. Such restraint can be critical for a particular business.

Consumer Protection by Government

Government protection of consumers covers a wide range of activity, mostly overseen by the federal government.[24] It is designed to assure that consumers get a fair shake in the market place. Our discussion is organized around the four rights of consumers previously discussed.[25]

First, the federal government acts in the area of consumer safety by controlling unsafe products and by establishing product standards. The government limits the sale of unsafe products such as narcotics and diseased meat, controls the sale of ethical drugs, and administers highway safety.[26] Important legislation in the area of unsafe products includes the Pure Food and Drug Act of 1906, the Meat Inspection Act of 1907, and the 1962 Drug Amendments, Flammable Fabrics Act, 1953, and the Cigarette Labeling Act, 1966. State governments have been very active in the area of false advertising, and most states have laws against false, misleading advertisements. Responsibility for administering to consumer protection is centered in the Department of Health, Education, and Welfare and the Department of Agriculture. The Treasury Department

[23] Howard, *op. cit.* This is a general summary of the legal structure of marketing.

[24] Richard J. Barber, "Government and the Consumer," *Michigan Law Review*, Vol. 64 (May, 1966), pp. 1203–17; Virginia H. Knauer, Federal Role In Consumer Affairs, Hearings before the Subcommittee on Executive Reorganization and Government Research of the Committee on Government Operations, United States Senate, 91 Cong., 2nd Session, January 20, 1970, pp. 245–51.

[25] The following discussion is based on: *Consumer Advisory Council, op. cit.*, pp. 5–8, 18–31.

[26] National Committee on Product Safety, "Perspectives on Product Safety," *Final Report of the National Committee on Product Safety* (Washington, D.C.: June 30, 1970), pp. 1–8.

has responsibility for narcotics and alcohol control. The federal government also sets standards for products, and responsibility is primarily centered in the National Bureau of Standards. Legislation affecting standards includes the Standard Container Acts of 1916 and 1928, and the Alcoholic Beverages Administration Act of 1936. We have already noted that the government is setting pollution standards for automobiles, steel and other factories, and airplanes. Timetables are presently set to begin eliminating these health hazards.

Second, in the area of consumer information the federal government has been very active.[27] The Wheeler-Lea Act of 1938 prohibited false or misleading advertising. Authority over this and similar legislation was centered in the Federal Trade Commission established in 1914. The concept of full disclosure introduced in the Wheeler-Lea Act has been gradually extended to include a variety of products. The Securities Act of 1933 and the Security Exchange Act of 1934 are designed to protect the purchaser of securities. The Fair Packaging and Labeling Act of 1965 sets standards for packaging and labeling.[28] The government provides information through the Department of Agriculture, the Food and Drug Administration, and the Cooperative Extension Service.

Third, the right to choose is affected by competition, and the government has important legislation in this area.[29] The Sherman Act of 1890 was landmark legislation that prohibited all combinations in restraint of trade. This act led to several others that clarify conditions of monopoly, fraud, and restraint of trade. These include the Clayton Act of 1914, the Robinson-Patman Act of 1936, the Wheeler-Lea Act of 1938, the Trade Mark Act of 1946, the McCarran Insurance Act of 1948, and the Celler-Kefauver Anti-Merger Act of 1950. These acts are administered by the Justice Department and the Federal Trade Commission.

Fourth, little has been done in the area of the right to be heard. Of course, all the agencies previously mentioned keep an ear to consumer interests. The Consumer Advisory Council is one of the better agencies that are interested in consumer opinions.
the use of inducements and punishments to obtain business conformity.

Special Treatment by Government

The federal government and, to some extent, state and local governments, restrain channels by special treatment. Special treatment refers to

[27] *Report of the ABA Commission to Study the Federal Trade Commission* (Washington: The Bureau of National Affairs, 1969), pp. 36–54.

[28] H. E. Dunkelberger, Jr., "The Fair Packaging and Labeling Act—Some Unanswered Questions," *Food, Drug, and Cosmetic Law Journal*, Vol. 24 (January, 1969), pp. 17–36.

[29] James R. Withrow, Jr., "The Inadequacies of Consumer Protection," *1967 New York State Bar Association—Antitrust Law Symposium* (New York: Commerce Clearing House, 1967), pp. 58–73.

For example, state and local governments may give industry tax breaks, lower land cost, and similar inducements in order to get the industry to locate in the state. Location in turn affects channel structure and cost.

The most important types of special treatment occur at the federal level. The federal government uses purchase contracts, subsidy, threat, and direct control to obtain business conformance. Purchase contracts are manipulated either as a reward or threat. The federal government gives contracts to firms it wishes to favor. Often the contracts of primary supplies of defense products contain clauses that specify small business subcontractors must be used where possible. The government can threaten to take away a contract to gain compliance.

A subsidy is a grant of some type. For example, the federal government subsidizes air lines with grants on air mail. Government subsidizes the building of ship and air line terminals. Everyone is familiar with the farm subsidy. Agencies such as TVA even subsidize consumers by providing lower cost electricity. In recent years we have seen the first examples of direct government control over the economy since World War II. Direct control occurs when the government sets prices. The threat of control is often as effective as the control in restraining some businesses. It should be clear to the reader that the government at some level is very much involved in all phases of business activity.

COMPETITIVE RESTRAINT OF CHANNELS

A third type of restraint on channel activity comes from competition. This section deals with the manner of competitive restraint and discusses three important subjects.

How Much Competition Is Necessary

Most channel members in the American economy feel that they do not lack for competition. As we shall see, these managers are probably right. It is true, however, that competition in the United States does not always conform to a textbook description. It is also true that non-competitive behavior occurs more often than one would like. Traditional economics makes competition a function of numbers of competitors. Thus, there is a tendency to conclude that duopoly is twice as competitive as monopoly, four-firm competition is twice as competitive as duopoly, eight-firm competition is twice as competitive as four-firm, etc. Competitiveness increases directly with the number of competitors in a completely predictable fashion in the traditional view. This view is deficient because it leaves out of consideration emotions and the nature of the competition.[30]

[30] Eugene V. Rostow, "The Ethics of Competition Revisited," *California Management Review*, Vol. 5 (Spring, 1963), pp. 13–24.

Competition has more dimensions than simple numbers.[31] It is a highly emotional activity, and what a manager feels about competition may be as important as what he knows. If management perceives it has effective competition, that firm is going to perform in the same way whether competitors are effective or not. Management's feelings about the likelihood of new firms entering the industry are equally important. A business may price, and otherwise act highly competitive, in order to forestall competition. It is easier to act competitively than to be competitive, but the results can be the same from the environment's point of view. Uncertainty is an important factor in the competitive process. How can a given business determine exactly how effective a competitor's strategy is, or whether the competitor is likely to become more or less competitive in the future? Where there is competitive uncertainty, it is better to operate as if you have effective competition.

The fallacy of numbers is particularly interesting since there is no evidence to suggest that competition increases proportionally with more competitors. If a business has just one competitor, and that one is beating his brains out, figuratively speaking, the firm doesn't need more competitors. Thus, it may be that the aluminum, automobile, computer, aircraft, and similar industries with low numbers of producers, are highly competitive. It could even be argued that some of the erratic social behavior of these firms is due to the intensity of competition. When competition is cutthroat, the idea of collusion is much more appealing than when competition conforms to more acceptable standards.[32] In spite of these facts, the government continues to evaluate competition based on numbers.

Along this same line, it is often argued that a lack of competition is a function of large size. Competition is a function of real and imagined competitors, no matter how many or what their size. Competition, or the lack of it, can only be determined by observing the total behavior pattern of the firms involved. Perhaps no better example of monopoly can be found than the old country general store: small, isolated, inefficient, but having a limited market competely within its control. Where competition is lacking, the government has the means, already described, to discourage the practice.

Types of Competition

The average channel member is faced with more than one type of competition. Two concepts of competition are necessary to understand this point. First, the channel members compete horizontally and verti-

[31] William Lazer, "Competition, Innovation, and Marketing Management," *Competition In Marketing*, T. W. Melon and C. M. Whitlo, eds. (Los Angeles: University of Southern California, 1964), pp. 9–22.

[32] Robert C. Brooks, "Businessmen's Concepts of Injury to Competition," *California Management Review*, Vol. 3 (Summer, 1964), pp. 89–101.

cally. *Horizontal competition* occurs between firms at the same level in the channel, such as retailers competing with retailers. *Vertical competition* refers to competition between firms at different levels in the channel, such as wholesalers competing with manufacturers. Second, there is individual and system competition. *Individual competition* means that each firm in the channel acts individually. *System competition* occurs when two entire channels compete, each as a unit. Given these two concepts, we can divide the discussion of types of competition into: individual firm competition and team competition.

Individual Firm Competition. Individual horizontal competition means that each firm competes individually with firms at its own stage in the channel.[33] There are three possibilities for this type of competition. First, the firm may compete with another firm exactly like itself. This is the case of a shoe store competing with another shoe store, a hardware wholesaler competing with another hardware wholesaler, or an auto manufacturer competing with another auto manufacturer. Second, the firm may compete with dissimilar firms that have a few overlapping lines. Thus, the shoe store competes with the shoe department in the department store even though the stores have nothing else in common. Third, all individual businesses compete for the consumer's dollar. The firms may be completely different with no overlapping products, but if the consumer purchases from one, he cannot purchase from another.

Team Competition. Team competition is a different type of competition. The average person does not think of an entire marketing structure competing with another marketing structure. Team competition may involve several firms at a given level in the channel, but it may also involve more than one level. This type of competition stems directly from recognition of the channel of distribution as a complete organization. Team competition, as Figure 4–1 shows, occurs when one entire channel of distribution competes with another entire channel of distribution. Each is attempting to satisfy the same market. The diagram demonstrates two types of team competition. In example 1, the channels are alike in the sense that they have the same type of middlemen and perform about the same services at the same prices on similar products. This channel is similar to the automobile industry. In example 2, the channels are different. Here a short channel and a long channel compete. This channel may exist for small appliances. One channel sells through franchised dealers to the consumer while another sells through wholesalers to retailers. The point is that the entire team competes. There is cooperation among members on advertising, personal selling,

---

[33] Chester R. Wasson, Frederick D. Sturdivant, and David H. McConaughy, *Competition and Human Behavior* (New York: Appleton-Century-Crofts, Inc., 1968), pp. 107–8.

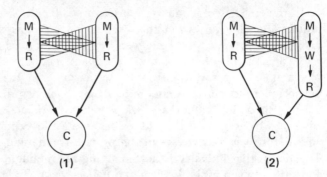

M = Manufacturer
W = Wholesaler
R = Retailer
C = Consumer

Fig. 4–1. Channel team competition.

display, margins, etc. Of course, the cooperation may be greater in the short channel of example 2 than for the long channel in the same example. Notice also that individual competition may still occur even when the entire systems are competing.

HOW WELL HAVE CHANNELS PERFORMED

The question of how well channel members have performed is a difficult one to answer, and much depends on the criteria used.[34] Since ours is a socio-economic system, the answer has social as well as economic aspects.

The performance of channels in the economic sphere has been quite good. The American people have the highest standard of living the world has ever known. Even the ghetto family is vastly better off than most people in most countries of the world. This statement is a fact, not a suggestion that we cannot improve the condition of the poor. American industry is virile, flexible, and progressive. In fact, American industry is the envy of the world. Productivity is high and has been increasing. Nevertheless, there are difficulties. Unemployment, while not excessive, has been a high four to six per cent of the labor force in recent years. Part of the explanation can be traced to the dislocations caused by the Vietnam war—the return of servicemen has placed an overload condition on the system.

Since inflation has been high recently and there is no easy solution for controlling it, government has resorted to artificial restraint. It is doubtful that such control can continue indefinitely. Finally, American productivity has slipped compared to that of other nations. This fact has resulted in an unfavorable balance of trade and a poor competitive position for some American products.

[34] Lee E. Preston and Norman R. Collins, "The Analysis of Marketing Efficiency," *Journal of Marketing Research* (May, 1966), pp. 154–62.

In the social sector, answers are more difficult. Values are currently undergoing change. Even the consumer himself is not always sure of his objectives. One study suggests consumer motives in the market vary by money involved, time, and energy expended.[35] Variations in consumer objectives lead to instability in the market. It is difficult for channel members to perform adequately until society provides a clear mandate as to which values are important. American industry apparently continues to adhere to the old values while the system is adopting new ones. However, business is in the process of changing. Currently, there is criticism that industry is not changing fast enough. Many individuals are torn between individualism and collectivism. Even so, channel members are responding to the broad social needs of the society. Clear evidence of this is seen in programs to hire the handicapped; to clean up air, noise, and water pollution; to provide employment for underprivileged and minority groups; and to respond to consumer desires for better products and information. Crime is one area where it appears a great problem still exists. Criminals are moving into legitimate industry, and crime against industry in the form of robbery, shoplifting, employee theft, etc., are increasing. The curbing of criminal activities may require the average businessman to improve the moral and ethical conduct of his association with known criminals.

In short, there is much good and some bad in the present conduct of American business. As a people we need to recognize the advantages and to continue to work on the problems.

QUESTIONS

1. Explain the meaning of environment to channels of distribution.
2. Discuss the ways in which the channel and the environment interact.
3. Discuss the recent shift in American social values. How are social values determined?
4. Discuss the problems associated with individual determination of social values, with group determination of social values.
5. A business may be at odds with the society because of (1) misinterpretation of goals, (2) forced inefficiency, and (3) disagreement in goals. How does each affect channel performance?
6. Discuss the major environmental issues of our day.
7. How do businessmen view their responsibility to the environment? Explain. Do you think this attitude is likely to change?
8. Discuss the manner in which business responds to the environment.
9. Distinguish between self-regulation, government restraint, and competition in affecting business behavior.
10. Compare governmental effect on business by legal means and special treatment.

[35] Anthony Downs, "A Theory of Consumer Efficiency," *Journal of Retailing*, Vol. 37 (Spring, 1961), pp. 6–12, 50–51.

PART II

CHANNEL STRUCTURE

Part II deals with channel structures; its purpose is to introduce the variety of structural problems faced by the channel's manager and to discuss the manner in which these problems are handled. The clear understanding of channel structure is the foundation upon which channels management rests.

5

Institutions of the Marketing Channel

In a sense, the wide variety of channels emerges to meet the requirements of the market and environment. Chapter 5 deals with the different
types of middlemen that comprise these marketing channels.

TYPES OF CHANNEL MEMBERS

The channel of distribution is too complex to explain in a short space.
Although this chapter focuses on member types, it is necessary to understand the relationship between these types in order to clarify member
differences. Presently, we want to identify the major types of middlemen and demonstrate their general placement and function to the channel.

Merchant and Agent Middlemen

There are two broad types of marketing institutions that make up any
channel of distribution. They are merchants and agent middlemen. The
term *merchant* is used to designate businesses that are in the direct line
of product ownership. That is, merchants always take title to products,
although they may or may not have physical possession of them. There
are three major types of merchants—manufacturers that make products,
wholesalers who sell to other businesses, and retailers who sell to house-

holds. It is the merchant channel members that most of us visualize when we consider the marketing channel.

Agent middlemen or *agents* are defined for our purposes as institutions that perform for merchants some specialized service or function related to the sale or distribution of goods, but who do not take title to the products in performing this service. The Definitions Committee of the American Marketing Association has a different definition. To the committee, an agent is an institution that purchases or sells goods for others. These institutions are seen as operating primarily at the wholesale stage in a channel. This definition is not suited for our purpose for it leaves out transportation agencies, as well as such agents as banks, doctors, public warehouses, etc. Furthermore, agents can operate at all levels in a marketing channel. The definition of agent must include all the possibilities, and it is for this reason that the broad definition is preferred.

An agent acts for his principal and is bound by his wishes. Agents may act for their principal in any matters surrounding the movement or sale of products, but they never own the goods. Agents, like merchants, may or may not have physical possession of the products. Thus it is clear that one cannot distinguish a merchant from an agent on the basis of possession of goods. It can only be done on the basis of ownership.

Distinction Between Agents

All merchants transfer ownership, but agents exist for a variety of purposes. Agents may be divided into two major groups by purpose: facilitating agents and supplemental agents. To facilitate is to assist, help, or lighten the work of someone, and that is exactly what a facilitating agent does. *Facilitating agents* specialize in some aspect of the movement of goods and services, and these middlemen can be subdivided into: (1) bulk transportation agents, (2) storage agents, (3) specialty shippers, and (4) purchase and sales agents. Facilitating agents help to move products so they can enter into direct contact with both buyers and sellers. These facilitating agents serve the needs of each group simultaneously. Facilitating agents may, in fact, be employed by either the sender or receiver of the goods. For example, freight shipments may be paid by either the shipper or the buyer of merchandise. An agent may be hired either by the manufacturer to sell or by the buyer to purchase.

Supplemental agents also derive their name from the nature of their responsibility. To supplement is to add something, especially to make up a deficiency. Supplemental agents perform a service for a single type of institution or business in the channel and their responsibility is to that type of institution. Unlike facilitating agents, supplemental agents are not go-betweens. They typically perform services that the institutions either cannot perform for themselves or services that the merchant finds too expensive to perform for himself. Thus, most supplemental agents render a wide variety of financial, advisory, information, or special services to their principals. It should be clear to the reader that it is impossible to designate the importance of a middleman by whether he is an agent or a merchant. The fact is that practically no marketing channel can exist without both types.

It must be understood that agents can, upon occasion, hire other agents. For example, an advertising agency may employ radio and television just as easily as the advertising department of a company, and a transportation company is as likely as a merchant to hire an agency. Agents acquire their designation from their relationship with merchants and not from their relationship with each other. There may be a principal–agency relationship between two agents.

Line and Staff Relationships Among Members

We have noted how the marketing channel functions as a team; it is an organization and displays many of the attributes of other organizations. The interaction that takes place between merchants and agents adds a great deal of the complexity to channels. One important organizational attribute displayed by the channel team is the existence of clear line and staff relationships (see Figure 5–1).

Merchants in the channel function as the line members because the right to decide all aspects of the product's disposition, including buying, selling, promotion, pricing, delivery, and service lies within the domain of the merchant. In short, the right to command follows the movement of title except where responsibility is delegated. The facilitating and supplemental agents act in the capacity of staff members. These agents do not have direct decision responsibility over products. Rather they advise and/or carry out specific instruction assigned by the line members. For example, a management consultant may be brought in by the wholesaler to study and to advise the company concerning inventory and related functions. However, his recommendations do not have to be followed by the wholesaler. Consider also that the various transportation companies perform their function of moving goods at the discretion of the merchant members of the channel. The merchant could exercise his right to move the goods in his own equipment. Transporters are delegated the act of movement, and the owner of the goods is in no way relieved of this responsibility.

The inclusion of agent middlemen makes our channel much more realistic. Figure 5–1 demonstrates how each type of channel member makes a specific contribution to the total operation of the channel. The difference in the function of facilitating and supplemental agents to the line

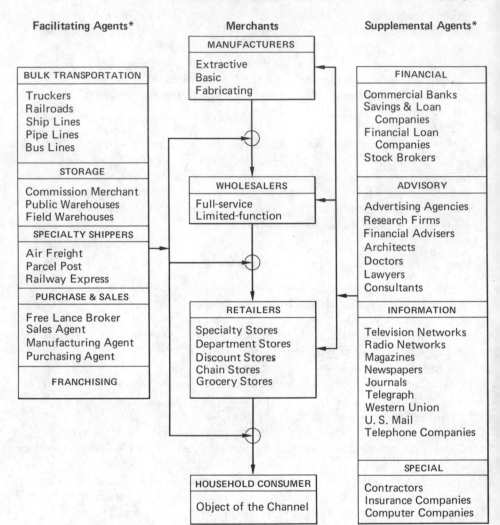

*The types of middlemen are intended to be illustrative rather than inclusive.

Fig. 5–1. Relationships between merchants and agents.

members is clearly shown. It is particularly important to realize that other types of agents besides those of physical movement operate between merchant channel members. Some of these are agents of purchase and sale, and some are franchise agents. In both these cases, it is possible to mistake the agent institution for a regular line member if one is not aware of the organization of the businesses involved. We should also be aware of the large number of supplemental agents—marketers are prone to forget that these institutions are members of the channel, and the contribution they make to its operation.

RETAILERS

The field of retailing is complex, thus, in order to provide system to the discussion, the treatment of retailing has been grouped into six broad categories: (1) total retail stores and sales, (2) width of product line, (3) number of stores, (4) use of facilities, (5) retailer ownership, and (6) retailing operating characteristics.

Total Retail Stores and Sales

Retailers are defined on the basis of whom they sell to. Thus, retailing involves all the marketing activities related to selling to final household consumers. A *retailer* is "a merchant, or occasionally an agent, whose main business is selling directly to the ultimate consumer." [1] Retailers sell only to final household consumers. Although the reader is infinitely familiar with retail stores, it is doubtful that one can begin to name all the different types that operate.

Actually, the total number of retail establishments has changed little in recent years. The figures (in thousands) show 1,722 establishments in 1954, 1,795 in 1958, 1,708 in 1963, and 1,763 in 1967 according to the Bureau of the Census.[2] In 1972, there were still just over 1,700 retail establishments in the United States. In spite of the small change, retailers represent the largest single type of channel member.

Table 5-1 shows the major types of retail establishments by sales volume. These data indicate that retail sales have shown rapid increase since 1965, with non-durable goods representing the largest sales potential compared to durable goods. The most important types of retail stores for sales in 1971 were food stores, automotive stores, and general merchandise stores.

Retailers engage in a very wide variety of activities including: combining specific types of goods, relating retail services to the products, locating sources of goods for customer convenience, affecting a proper balance between price and quality of merchandise, providing goods when consumers want them, informing consumers of their choices, and engaging in competition.[3] Each consumer is unique, and the tremendous variety of retail operation is needed in order to cater to the specific

---

[1] *Marketing Definitions* (Chicago: *American Marketing Association*, 1960).

[2] U. S. Department of Commerce, Bureau of the Census, *Census of Manufacturers*, 1970.

[3] Leonard Rubin, "Today's Retailer Must be a Man of All Seasons," *Stores* The NRMA Magazine (October, 1969), p. 27.

Table 5-1   Retail Trade—Sales, by Kind of Business, 1965 to 1972
(In billions of dollars. Quarterly data are not adjusted for seasonal variation
or trading day differences)

Kind of Business	1965	1968	1969	1970	1971	1972 1st qtr.
All retail stores	284.1	341.9	357.9	375.5	408.9	97.8
Durable goods stores*	94.2	111.2	115.5	114.3	131.8	32.1
Automotive group	56.9	65.7	68.2	65.0	78.9	19.5
Passenger car, other automotive dealers	53.5	61.0	63.1	59.4	72.5	18.1
Tire, battery, accessory dealers	3.4	4.7	5.1	5.6	6.4	1.4
Furniture, appliance group*	13.4	16.7	17.3	17.8	18.6	4.8
Furniture, homefurnishings stores	(NA)	(NA)	10.5	10.5	11.0	2.8
Household-appliance, TV, radio stores	(NA)	(NA)	5.7	6.1	6.2	1.6
Lumber, building, hardware, farm equipment group*	17.1	14.3	19.7	20.5	23.0	5.2
Lumber yards, building-materials dealers†	9.7	11.1	11.6	12.0	13.7	3.2
Hardware stores	2.6	3.2	3.4	3.4	3.6	.8
Nondurable goods stores*	189.9	230.7	242.4	261.2	277.0	65.7
Apparel group*	15.8	19.2	19.9	19.8	20.8	4.5
Men's and boys' wear	(NA)	(NA)	4.8	4.6	4.7	1.0
Women's apparel, accessory stores	(NA)	(NA)	7.5	7.6	8.2	1.7
Shoe stores	(NA)	(NA)	3.6	3.5	3.5	.8
Drug and proprietary stores	9.2	11.6	12.2	13.4	13.7	3.4
Eating and drinking places	20.2	25.7	27.0	29.7	31.1	7.5
Food group*	64.0	67.9	78.3	86.1	89.2	22.1
Grocery stores	(NA)	(NA)	72.9	79.8	83.0	20.6
Gasoline service stations	20.6	24.8	25.9	28.0	29.2	7.1
General merchandise group, including nonstores*	42.3	54.1	57.6	61.3	68.1	14.6
Department stores**	25.0	33.1	35.7	37.3	42.0	8.7
Mail-order (department store merchandise)	(NA)	(NA)	3.5	3.9	4.3	1.0
Variety stores	(NA)	(NA)	6.4	7.0	7.0	1.5
Liquor stores	5.7	7.0	7.4	8.0	8.8	2.1

NA   Not available.

*Includes data not shown separately.

†In addition, includes paint, plumbing, and electrical stores.

**Includes sales made by mail-order catalog desks located within department stores of mail-order firms.

Source: U. S. Bureau of the Census, Monthly Retail Trade Report. Monthly data in U. S. Bureau of Economic Analysis, Survey of Current Business, April, 1972.

requirements of customers. Retailers normally perform their activities in a local market but a few may draw customers from great distances.

Width of Product Line

Of the many methods of classifying retailers, perhaps one of the more important is by width of product line.[4] Based on width of product line,

[4] Paul H. Nystrom, Marketing Handbook (New York: The Ronald Press Co., 1958), pp. 230–32.

we can divide retail stores into specialty stores and departmentalized stores. The *specialty store,* one of the oldest forms of retailers, sells a single or narrow line of merchandise such as shoes, dresses, records, candy, furniture, groceries, or novelties. It is generally small, independently owned, and operated as a proprietorship or partnership. Specialty stores in the grocery field are often referred to as "mom and pop" stores. Among these small grocery stores, one of the fastest growing groups, is the convenience grocery store.[5]

Specialty stores provide their customers with personalized attention, good depth of merchandise within the narrow line, and delivery. They typically do not grant credit, although exceptions exist. Measured by the number of stores, specialty stores constitute the largest category of retail outlet. Of course, this grouping is very heterogeneous when compared to other types of retailers. There are almost as many specifics of operation as there are types of these stores.

Departmentalized retail stores are far fewer in number than specialty stores, but they make a much greater impact on retailing when measured by volume of sales. In this class are included the traditional department store, discount department house, supermarkets, and variety stores. Department stores alone accounted for approximately 6 per cent of total retail sales according to the Census of Business.[6] Although individual characteristics of these stores' operations differ, they all have certain traits in common. Departmentalized stores are typically large, financially strong, and usually operated as a corporation. They carry a wide line of merchandise, separated into departments, and they are frequently chains. Each type of departmentalized store differs primarily in the services and prices offered.

Traditional *department stores* offer a good example of service-minded institutions, for they provide the most service and the widest variety of services including credit, delivery, wrapping, parking, liberal returns, extensive advertising, alterations, etc. On the other hand, prices in these stores tend to be somewhat higher. *Discount houses* and supermarkets greatly restrict service and make a price appeal. For example, grocery stores typically do not offer credit, delivery, or aid in selecting merchandise. Often, the customers must package their own groceries and perform their own carry out. *Variety stores* provide a mixed service appeal. They offer some services but not others, and there is great variety among their offerings. In the discount house and the traditional department store the line between service and price is beginning to blur. It will be interesting to see whether this trend continues or whether it will lead to new types of institutions.

---

[5] See: "A Convenience Store Chain is Born," *The Voluntary and Cooperative Group,* A Mulville Publication (June, 1970), pp. 13–16, and 50–52.

[6] U. S. Department of Commerce, *Census of Business,* 1958.

Number of Stores

Based on the number of stores, retailers can be divided into independents, branches, and chain stores. Independent is a term reserved for the ownership and operation of a single store. *Independents* are usually specialty shops, although there are notable exceptions. Goudchaux's of Baton Rouge is an outstanding example of an independent department store. Most independents are small, and most retail stores fall into this category.

Chain stores were originally defined by the Census as four or more stores under one management offering a similar line of merchandise. Today, twelve or more stores is often taken as the breaking point for a business to be classed as a chain. Traditionally, *branches* referred to small suburban editions of a downtown store. The main store and the branch were confined to a single city, and the chain of command and all operations were controlled by the downtown store. The growth of large suburban stores and the movement toward suburban store independence has made this distinction meaningless. One can say that retail store operations that have between four and eleven stores may be considered branch operations. In this sense, the branch falls somewhere between the independent and the chain store. Now, most branches operate like chains, and there is little to distinguish between them. Both chain stores and branch operations tend to perform some wholesaler functions. Furthermore, retail chains tend to be characterized by centralized management. Most important decisions are made from the home office and the retail stores tend to be primary selling units whose managers have very limited authority. The exception is the chain department store which continues to employ autonomous management.

Use of Facilities

Retailers can be classified according to whether or not they employ facilities in their final contact with consumers. The two-way classification is: (1) store retailers and (2) non-store retailers. Retailers employing stores are usual, and most of the types of retailers that we have already mentioned sell out of stores. Specialty stores, grocery stores, department stores, and discount houses are examples of retailers who sell out of stores.

The important types of non-store retailers are door-to-door salesmen and mail order houses. *Door-to-door salesmen* are outside sales representatives who call on final household consumers. They canvass up one side of the street and down the other or they use lists, telephone books, and similar means to discover prospects. The door-to-door salesman depends on the law of averages to make sales. His sales presentation does not vary greatly from that found in retail stores except that it is in the home and restricted to high margin, portable merchandise. Sometimes there is more planning, as with the canned sales talk. Door-to-door sales-men are usually employed by manufacturers. The Avon lady and the Fuller Brush man are outstanding examples.

Mail order selling involves the use of a catalog. Customers send in orders by mail, using the catalog to obtain merchandise information. The mail order house operates a warehouse from which goods are dis-tributed. The orders are processed and the merchandise is shipped direct to the customer from the warehouse. Typical mail order operations place their warehouses strategically around the country so that orders can be processed and products shipped on the same day. Customers can typi-cally receive the merchandise within four to ten days. Although Sears, Roebuck and Company and Montgomery Ward operate retail stores, they are outstanding examples of mail order retailing.

Retailer Ownership

Retailers can also be classified according to the owner of the operation. The possibilities include manufacturer-owned retail operations, self-owned retailer and consumer-owned retailers. Of course, most retailers are self-owned. Manufacturers often own retail outlets. For example, refineries often own and operate some gasoline service stations and tire manufacturers have their own retail outlets. It is also true that retailers sometimes own manufacturing operations as do Sears and Proctor and Gamble.

Some retail operations are owned by consumers—that is, the customers own the outlets from which they purchase. This type of operation is known as a *consumer cooperative*. Many rural power companies are consumer-owned, and approximately one per cent of the grocery sales of the United States are generated from consumer cooperatives. The phi-losophy of the cooperative is essentially non-profit, and its purpose is to get products to the consumer at the lowest price. The consumer buys stock in the retailer but accepts limited dividends. Since every business must make profits in order to expand and provide for contingencies, the cooperative charges prevailing retail prices. However, all profits not needed for the business are returned in the form of a patronage dividend paid according to the amount of business the customer-owner does with the cooperative. Each member of the cooperative has one vote in its operation to insure that no person is able to take over its operation. Man-agement is either hired on a permanent basis or contributed by the membership on a rotating basis.

Retailing Operating Characteristics

As a channel member, the various types of retail operations offer an almost endless combination of opportunities to distribute products. It is impossible to characterize all the combinations. Table 5–2 illustrates

Table 5-2 Important Activities of Some Major Retailer Types

	Advertising	Personal Attention	Delivery	Width of Line	Product Quality	Price	Special Service	Integrated	Customer Attention	Warranty	Parking	Fancy Fixtures	Multi-unit	Salesmen	Credit	Location
Department Store	heavy	yes	yes	wide	good	moderate	yes	yes	yes	yes	yes	yes	yes	yes	yes	central
Discount House	heavy	no	varies	wide	low	mixed & low	no	yes	no	yes	yes	no	yes	some	no	central
Supermarket	heavy	no	no	wide	good	low	no	vary	no	yes	yes	no	yes	no	no	area
Variety Store	light	yes	no	wide	low	medium & low	no	yes	some	yes	no	no	yes	yes	no	central
Specialty Stores																
Furniture	moderate	yes	yes	narrow	mixed	mixed	yes	varies	yes	yes	yes	mixed	sometimes	yes	yes	central
Drug	light	no	yes	wide	good	mixed	some	yes	some	yes	yes	yes	often	some	yes	area
Convenience Grocery	heavy	yes	some	narrow	good	high	no	no	no	yes	yes	no	yes	no	no	neighbor-hood
Clothing Shop	light	yes	yes	narrow	vary	vary	vary	no	yes	yes	no	yes	some	yes	varies	area
Shoe Store	light	yes	no	narrow	vary	vary	vary	no	vary	yes	vary	vary	some	vary	no	area
Auto Dealer	heavy	yes	yes	narrow	good	high	yes	no	yes	yes	yes	yes	no	yes	yes	central
Gas Station	light	yes	no	narrow	good	vary	yes	no	yes	yes	yes	yes	vary	yes	yes	neighbor-hood
Jewelry Store	moderate	yes	no	narrow	good	vary	yes	no	yes	yes	no	yes	vary	yes	yes	central
Hardware Store	light	yes	no	wide	vary	vary	vary	no	no	yes	vary	no	vary	no	no	area

some of the important possible combinations of activities performed by retailers. These examples are intended as generalizations, and many exceptions can be found. Such possible combinations offer variety to both the manufacturer and the consumer.[7] For example, a producer of furniture has a choice of the department store, discount house, drug store, furniture store, and variety store as possible outlets. Each one offers a different type of companion merchandise, as well as different prices and services.

The consumer looking for specific merchandise can select from the several specialty shops that offer a variety of services and prices. If he wants to make multiple purchases, he may choose between the department store and the discount house, depending on the type of activities desired. In the illustration, compare the choice that a consumer has between the supermarket and the convenience grocery store. The many possibilities mean that each consumer can find some preferred outlet where he can satisfy his price, quality and convenience desires.

WHOLESALERS

Wholesalers, like retailers, are defined according to markets served. However, the terms wholesaler and wholesaling do not necessarily mean the same thing. Broadly speaking, *wholesaling* can refer to all sales by merchant institutions in a channel of distribution except those to final household consumers. Sales to final household consumers are always reserved for retailing. Thus, institutions which sell to manufacturers, wholesalers, retailers, and such non-business institutions as fraternities, universities, and the government are involved in wholesaling. By this definition manufacturers, some agents, and even some retailers are often involved in wholesaling.[8] When this broad definition of wholesaling is used, there are only two types of activities in a channel of distribution— wholesaling and retailing.

Use of the term wholesaler involves a narrower interpretation of wholesaling. The *wholesaler* is a particular type of institution that performs wholesaling. A wholesaler is a "business unit which buys and resells merchandise to retailers and other merchants and/or to industrial institutions and commercial users but which does not sell in significant amounts to ultimate consumers." [9] Thus, the term wholesaler specifically excludes manufacturers and other industrial sellers in the channel. Wholesalers in the business market are known as industrial distributors

[7] Stanley Marcus, "Retailing: Past, Present, and Prospects," *Business Horizons* (Spring, 1967), pp. 45–50.

[8] Thomas Jule, "What Is a Wholesaler?" *Air Conditioning, Heating, and Refrigeration News* (June 13, 1966), p. 35.

[9] *Marketing Definitions, op. cit.*

or supply houses. The wholesaler is placed between manufacturers and retailers in the channel. Like the retailer, he is uniquely a marketing specialist. The Census lists approximately 301,114 wholesalers in the United States in 1970, employing about 4,243,583 persons. Of this total only 54,471 were non-merchant, or what we call specialty wholesalers. This figure represents approximately 18 per cent of the total in any given year with some variation. Table 5–3 shows the number of merchant

Table 5–3   Merchant Wholesalers—Estimated Sales, by Kind of Business, 1960 to 1972
(In millions of dollars)

Kind of Business	1960	1965	1969	1970	1971	1972 1st qtr.
Merchant Wholesalers	139,866	187,141	236,708	246,643	267,357	68,706
Durable Goods*	58,581	82,691	109,578	111,778	122,420	31,244
Motor vehicles, automotive equipment	8,222	12,243	18,493	20,203	24,506	6,410
Electrical goods	8,941	12,518	15,748	15,809	16,800	4,284
Furniture, homefurnishings	3,065	3,803	5,422	5,343	6,096	1,424
Hardware, plumbing, heating equip., etc.	6,525	8,366	10,748	10,634	11,813	2,967
Lumber, construction materials	7,295	9,758	11,750	10,836	13,003	3,288
Machinery, equipment, supplies	14,436	20,711	18,093	28,515	31,044	8,016
Metals, metalwork (except scrap)	5,748	8,990	11,794	12,625	12,353	3,186
Scrap, waste materials	3,335	4,777	5,542	5,986	4,882	1,216
Nondurable Goods*	81,285	104,450	127,130	134,865	144,937	37,462
Groceries and related products	27,902	37,541	47,771	50,430	53,610	13,821
Beer, wine, distilled alcoholic beverages	7,396	9,380	11,913	12,862	14,071	3,270
Drugs, chemicals, allied products	5,470	7,267	9,369	9,619	10,397	2,787
Tobacco, tobacco products	4,200	4,992	5,752	6,118	6,498	1,598
Dry goods, apparel	6,713	8,766	10,157	10,391	11,799	3,129
Paper, paper products (excl. wallpaper)	4,250	5,546	7,296	7,317	7,600	1,952
Farm products (raw materials)	11,969	13,794	13,449	18,336	15,741	4,222

*Includes data not shown separately.
Source: U. S. Bureau of the Census, Monthly Wholesale Trade Report.

wholesalers in the United States between 1960 and 1973 along with their sales volume. These figures indicate that the number of wholesalers was far smaller than the number of retailers previously shown, but that merchant wholesalers did increase over the period. Sales for wholesalers followed the same pattern as that found for retailers, with non-durable goods having higher values than durable goods. However, the difference between the two for sales was much more nearly alike than was found for retailing. Groceries, machinery, and automotive equipment led in sales for merchant wholesalers in 1971. There can be no question from the figures that wholesaling represents a large group of channel members with tremendous purchasing power.

Full-Service and Limited-Function Wholesalers

There is not the variety of institutions found among wholesalers that one observes at either the manufacturing or retailing stages in the channel. The most important method of classification is by function performed and the two broad classes are: (1) the full-service wholesaler and the (2) limited-function wholesaler.[10] The *full-service wholesaler* is the oldest form. This enterprise performs most of the functions of marketing such as buying, selling, transporting, storing, dividing, and pricing. Here, the middleman also renders most of the expected services such as the granting of credit, delivery, accounting and inventory advice, and sometimes financial aid.[11] The full-service wholesaler carries a relatively complete stock and typically employs outside salesmen who call regularly on the retailer. There are over 90,000 full-service wholesalers in the United States.

Just as the name implies, the *limited-function wholesaler* restricts his functions, his service, or both. His development arose from attempts by full-service wholesalers to increase their efficiency and cut the cost of operation because manufacturers and retailers had bypassed their operation. Some important types of limited-function wholesalers with their limitations are listed below: [12]

Mail order wholesaler—No salesmen, central handling of products
Cash and carry wholesaler—No credit and delivery; restricted number of goods
Drop shipper—No storage, telephone operation, low overhead
Rack jobber—Service specialist, services his own racks in retail store
Wagon jobber—Specializes in speedy handling of perishable goods

The important point is that a wide variety of combinations can be obtained in the channel, depending on the type of wholesaler the goods move through.

Area Served by Wholesalers

Wholesalers can be classified according to the area they serve into national, regional, and local wholesalers. A national wholesaler covers, at least, the continental United States; a regional wholesaler covers one

---

[10] Nystrom, *op. cit.*, pp. 246–48.

[11] Margaret Hall, "The Theory of Wholesale Distribution," *Marketing Channels: A Systems Viewpoint*, William G. Maller, Jr., and David L. Wilemon, eds. (Homewood, Ill.: Richard D. Irwin, Inc., 1971), pp. 165–74.

[12] Edwin H. Lewis, *Marketing Channels: Structure and Strategy* (New York: McGraw-Hill Book Co., Inc., 1968), pp. 24–25.

to five states; and a local wholesaler typically services customers within a fifty-mile radius of his business. This close proximity offers the opportunity for speedy delivery and personal working relationships between the wholesalers and the retailer. Almost eighty-five per cent of all wholesalers are local and only about one-half of one per cent are national. Even regional wholesalers are not of any great importance in the market. The explanation for the concentration of wholesalers lies in the nature of their function. These middlemen concentrate on staple or convenience goods and such goods are not tolerant of long order periods, special transportation, etc. They must be locally available when needed.

Integrated Wholesaling

It was pointed out previously that not all wholesaling is accomplished by the institutions called wholesalers. Sometimes wholesaling is combined with either manufacturing or retailing. This type of arrangement is called *integrated wholesaling* because it involves the ownership of more than one type of channel middleman.

Wholesaling Combined with Manufacturers. One type of integration occurs when the wholesaling function is combined through ownership with the manufacturer. An example of the integration of wholesaling with manufacturing can be found in the manufacturer's branch.[13] A *manufacturer's branch* is "an establishment maintained by a manufacturer, detached from the headquarters establishment and used primarily for the purpose of stocking, selling, delivering, and servicing his product."[14] These warehouses usually coincide with regional sales territories. The Census reports approximately 15,000 manufacturer's branches with over 40 billion dollars in sales. These branches carry stock and very nearly duplicate the activities of the full-service wholesaler. The principal difference is that the branch does not stock competing lines; it may handle complementary lines of other manufacturers. The branches sell mostly to wholesalers and retailers. Manufacturer outlets that do not carry stocks are called *sales offices*. Sales offices provide facilities from which company salesmen operate.

Wholesaling Combined with Retailers. An example of wholesaling integrated with retailing is the retail chain operation (see Figure 5-2). Many large retailers such as department stores, chain grocery stores, and discount houses purchase directly from the manufacturer and sell to final

[13] Theodore N. Beckman, "Changes In Wholesaling Structure and Performance," *Marketing and Economic Development,* Peter D. Bennet, ed. (Chicago: American Marketing Association, 1965), pp. 603–18.
[14] *Marketing Definitions, op. cit.,* 1960.

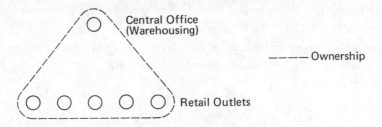

Central Office (Warehousing)

————— Ownership

Retail Outlets

Fig. 5–2.   Chain store organization.

consumers. These retailers perform their own wholesaling through a central office. They have their own warehouses, often on a regional basis like the manufacturer. Each warehouse may service a large number of retail stores. There are about 4,000 wholesalers integrated with retailers in the United States. Often the retailer will process his direct purchases from manufacturers through his regional warehouse right along with other purchases made from independent wholesalers. Thus the retailer's warehouse operation is very similar to the regular wholesaler's.

There are several important advantages to chain operations. These include: (1) common name; (2) joint advertising; (3) use of specialists in wholesaling, retailing, research personnel, etc.; (4) discounts from quantity purchases; (5) mass merchandising; (6) wide market coverage, and (7) centralized decision making.[15] Of course, one also has to consider the problems of coordinating unlike operations, providing quality managers, and accounting for geographic sale techniques. It is certainly true that many chains have been extremely successful.

Semi-Integrated Wholesaling

Integrated wholesaling involves the ownership of wholesaling operations by either the manufacturer or the retailer. Another way to gain control over wholesaling is through some type of contractual arrangement, a method that has been increasing in importance.[16] When control is gained through contract, the result can be called *semi-integrated wholesaling* because the two stages in the channel do not become completely one; they simply operate as if they were. The importance in semi-integrated wholesaling is that it provides most of the advantages of chain operations without having the middleman give up his independence.

[15] John McDonald, "Sears Makes it Look Easy," *Fortune* (May, 1964), pp. 120ff.
[16] Bert C. McCammon, Jr., "The Emergence and Growth of Contractually Integrated Channels in the American Economy," *Marketing and Economic Development,* John Varino, ed. (Chicago: American Marketing Association Fall Conference Proceedings, 1965), pp. 496–515.

The voluntary wholesaler and the cooperative wholesaler are examples of semi-integrated wholesalers.[17]

The Voluntary Wholesaler. The voluntary, such as I.G.A. and Associated Grocers, is initiated by the wholesaler who binds a group of retailers to cooperate with him through a contract as shown in Figure 5-3.

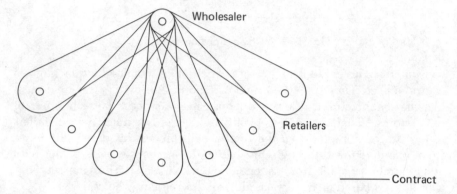

Fig. 5–3. Organization of the voluntary wholesaler.

The retailer agrees to buy primarily from the wholesaler and to purchase by order form. This not only provides a sure market and quantity orders but eliminates the salesmen. Deliveries are by schedule. The wholesaler may or may not eliminate some functions, but he usually offers advice to the retailers and helps with advertising. The retailers typically use a common name although it may be incorporated with the owner's own identification. There is specialization of function, quantity purchases, wide market appeal, mass merchandising, and most of the other advantages of the chain. Voluntaries have been particularly important in such lines as groceries and hardware. In the general grocery line they increased their business from 27.5 per cent in 1948 to about 45 to 47 per cent today.[18]

The Cooperative Wholesaler. The cooperative wholesaler is initiated by the retailers. Piggly Wiggly is an example of such an operation. The arrangement is demonstrated in Figure 5-4; a group of retailers get together on a contractual basis and buy, as a group, the wholesaler. They then hire their own management and operate the wholesaler. The co-

---

[17] Seymore Freedgood, "Uncle to 1,700 Grocers," *Fortune* (March, 1965), pp. 130–33; Edwin H. Lewis, "Channels Management By Wholesalers," *Marketing and the New Science of Planning*, Robert L. King, ed. (Chicago: American Marketing Association, 1968), pp. 137–41.

[18] Lewis, *Marketing Channels: Structure and Strategy, op. cit.,* p. 18.

Fig. 5–4. Organization of the cooperative wholesaler.

operative has most of the same advantages of the chain as those previously mentioned. However, not only does the organization of the cooperative differ from the voluntary, but the philosophy of the two also differs. Since the voluntary is initiated by the wholesaler, its philosophy is service-oriented. This service tends to insure the retailer's cooperation. The cooperative has a price philosophy because the retailers want to get the goods at the lowest price and make their profit off the retail operation. Of the two types, the voluntary has been the more successful. The need for joint ownership by retailers restricts the use of the cooperative.

Nature of Wholesaling Operations

The wholesaler has always been considered in a rather poor light, and twenty-five years ago the picture looked gloomy.[19] The view has been one of slowness, inefficiency, and indifference, but this is changing. The following is a generally accepted characterization of the modern wholesaler.

Advantages	Disadvantages
1. Serves a wide market	1. Slow to move goods
2. Reaches a variety of institutions	2. Slow to introduce new products
3. Convenient for manufacturing a ready-made sales force	3. Little manufacturer cooperation
4. Inexpensive for manufacturing	4. Lacks aggressive selling
5. Shifts transportation and storage responsibiilty away from the producer	5. Poor market penetration

On balance, the modern wholesaler, as a marketing specialist, is one of the more productive and stable of channel members.[20] Over fifty per cent of all goods move through wholesalers, and all goods must flow through some type of wholesaling operation whether the wholesaler institution is involved or not. The criticism of the wholesaler as an institution is oversimplified, for there is a great variety in his performance. As a group,

---

[19] Richard S. Lopota, "Faster Pace In Wholesaling," *Harvard Business Review* (July–August, 1969), pp. 130–43.
[20] Hall, *op. cit.*, pp. 75–78. Hall emphasizes the economic worth of wholesalers.

wholesalers are probably no more inefficient than other type of middlemen.

Wholesalers, because of their proximity, can often service retailers faster than direct sales from manufacturers. Some specialty wholesalers (such as the drop shipper) lower cost and speed delivery by consolidating orders from several buyers. Cooperation among middlemen can be extremely high for rack jobbers or other specialty wholesalers and for the full-service wholesaler. However, it is admitted that cooperation tends to be an individual matter. The aggressiveness of the sales effort also varies among wholesalers. Some have done an outstanding job. The wide range of wholesalers offers the manufacturer considerable variation in the type of service and performance he wishes to obtain. The inclusion of integrated wholesaling increases the variety even more. Without integrated wholesaling the speed and efficiency of direct sales could not be accomplished.

MANUFACTURERS

There is a tendency among marketers to ignore manufacturers, but there can be no marketing channel without manufacturing. Manufacturers take the natural resources, such as ore, timber, vegetables, fish, game, or petroleum, and change their form to more nearly fit the needs of specific consumers. These changes may take place in type of materials, quality of components, chemical content, shape, function, style, package, etc. Marketing is vitally concerned with manufacturers. Marketing's involvement occurs in two ways. First, it acts as a consultant to the manufacturer. Marketing is concerned with having the goods engineered to consumer specifications, although the responsibility for design and development of the product remains an engineering activity.[21] Second, marketing is directly involved in the manufacturer's activities relating to the purchase of raw materials and the sale of products output.

Manufacturers Classified by Industry

One of the most important methods of classifying manufacturers is by industry type. An industry classification refers to the major type of manufacturers with which the producer is engaged. Although an industry may be quite diversified, it is usually classified by the most important product group manufactured and sold. Table 5–4 shows the four major manufacturing classes established by the Bureau of the Census.

A more casual listing of manufacturers would include such well-known

[21] Robert D. Smith and Karl Shilliff, "Balancing Production and Marketing Effort," *Manufacturing, Engineering, and Management* (March, 1970), pp. 55–58.

Table 5–4   Number of Manufacturing Firms by Industry Class

Manufacturing	Total Reporting Units 1970
Total	3,520,930
Agricultural services, forestry, fisheries	31,078
Agriculture services and hunting	27,811
Forestry	537
Fisheries	2,730
Mining	23,802
Metal mining	896
Anthracite mining	263
Bituminous coal and lignite mining	2,640
Oil and gas extraction	14,275
Nonmetallic minerals, except fuels	4,826
Administrative and auxiliary	902
Contract construction	298,595
General building contractors	80,507
Heavy construction contractors	29,069
Special trade contractors	188,382
Administrative and auxiliary	637
Manufacturing	297,770
Ordnance and accessories	467
Food and kindred products	28,579
Tobacco manufactures	362
Textile mill products	7,009
Apparel and other textile products	24,319
Lumber and wood products	28,942
Furniture and fixtures	9,414
Paper and allied products	6,032
Printing and publishing	36,310
Chemicals and allied products	11,389
Petroleum and coal products	1,858
Rubber and plastics products, N.E.C.	6,840
Leather and leather products	3,430
Stone, clay, and glass products	14,162
Primary metal, industries	6,833
Fabricated metal products	26,224
Machinery, except electrical	37,839
Electrical equipment and supplies	11,342
Transportation equipment	7,813
Instruments and related products	4,471
Miscellaneous manufacturing industries	13,132
Administrative and auxiliary	11,003

Source: U. S. Department of Commerce, Bureau of the Census, Census of Manufacturers, 1970.

industries as aircraft, automobile, canning, shipbuilding, frozen foods, television, clothing, drug, shoe, cosmetics, computer, and office machine.

Manufacturers and the Stage of Production

Goods, particularly in the business channel, may be in one of several stages of production. Thus we can identify manufacturers as (1) extractive, (2) basic, or (3) fabricating. *Extractive producers* are engaged in separating natural resources from the environment. Here we have primarily mining, agricultural, and fishing businesses. *Basic manufacturing* involves separating the resource from waste products and putting it into a basic shape to be shipped and used by other industries. The steel and copper industries are examples. *Fabricating industries* make products by combining finished or semi-finished raw materials. Their function is mostly a putting together of materials or parts. Examples are producers of sewing machines, automobiles, and washing machines.

Brand Ownership by Producers

Manufacturers produce a great variety of goods. Some produce under their own brand name, some produce goods that are branded by distributors, and some combine producer and private brands. It is extremely important who owns the product brand, because the brand carries with it channel control. The business owning the identification has control over such marketing factors as establishing product specifications, type and amount of advertising, price levels, number and type of services, and method of shipment. Some manufacturers produce no products under their own name, and others produce only under their own name. It is fair to say that at some time most producers make some private brand products. Although private branding requires the manufacturer to give up sales control, it does have the advantages of (1) expanding markets, (2) cutting price without hurting brand prestige, (3) utilizing excess plant capacity, and (4) placing much of the cost of selling on the brand owner.

Geographic Area Served by Manufacturers

Some manufacturers distribute over wide geographic areas and some do not. The geographic area served can be divided into national, regional, and local segments. A *national producer* makes and distributes his goods throughout the United States with the possible exception of Alaska and Hawaii. A *regional producer* generally refers to one who sells in one geographic area of the country such as the Southeast or the West. As a general rule, two to six states are involved. A *local producer* is one who produces and sells in his immediate area, usually not greater than one state, and most manufacturers, based on volume of sales, serve a national market; regional producers are second in importance; and local manufacturers are rather specialized such as contractors, foundries, canners, producers of bricks, etc.

Manufacturer Operating Characteristics

Manufacturers initiate the first combination of goods, services, and prices that flow through the channel. They accomplish this combination by the character and variety of their operations. Manufacturers in the channel traditionally take the primary responsibility for: product research, brand research, product development, mass media advertising, and distribution planning.[22] There are large, financially strong manufacturers such as DuPont, General Electric, and United States Steel. There are also small producers with limited financing such as Howard Furniture Company of Starkville, Mississippi, and the Economy Casket Company of Opelousas, Louisiana. There are wide line producers such as Lever Brothers and Allied Chemical, and there are producers of a narrow line of products such as Coca-Cola and Campbell's Soups. Some manufacturers concentrate on high quality products, some have low quality, and some have mixed quality products. There is just as much variety in manufacturer services and prices. Some manufacturers render complete service and some restrict service and concentrate on low price. Some manufacturing is efficiently run and some is not. There are heavy advertisers like General Motors, and others who spend very little on advertising like Hershey's. It should be obvious that the possible combination of manufacturers in any given industry is large and the variety of operations is almost infinite. It is the responsibility of the channel to provide outlets to market for all these possible combinations.

FACILITATING AGENTS

Agent middlemen are extremely important to the channel of distribution; they are specialists in helping merchants to do their job better and more efficiently. We saw earlier that facilitating agents aid the merchant in the movement of goods and that supplemental agents make up some deficiency in the merchant's operations. It is now time to take a closer look at the agents and their operations in the channel.

Facilitating agents can be divided into three types based on the function they perform: (1) agents that facilitate purchases or sales, (2) agents that facilitate physical movement, and (3) agents that facilitate storage.

[22] Bert C. McCammon, Jr., Alton F. Doody, and William R. Davidson, "Emerging Patterns of Distribution," *Marketing Channels and Institutions*, Bruce J. Walker and Joel B. Haynes, eds. (Columbus, Ohio: Grid, Inc., 1973), pp. 211–18.

Agents of Purchases and Sales

It often happens that because of limited finances or the need for specialized market talent a merchant desires to hire an agent to negotiate his purchasing or his selling.[23] The merchant has his choice of four types of brokers that perform these tasks: (1) the freelance broker, (2) the manufacturer's agent, (3) the sales agent, and (4) the purchasing agent.

Each type of agent is an independent business that operates on the basis of a contract and receives a commission for services rendered to the principal. These four agents do not normally take physical possession of the goods that they sell for the principal and they cannot act for competing principals. The purchasing agent negotiates sources, the other types normally negotiate for sales. Usually these agents have earned their commission when they bring the buyer and seller together.

1. *The freelance broker* has no permanent ties with any principal, and he may negotiate sales for a large number of principals over time. There is no limitation on the territory in which sales occur, but the agent is strictly bound by his principal for prices, terms, and conditions of sale. A man who owns a truck and contracts with a strawberry grower in Hammond, Louisiana, to sell his berries in the St. Louis area is an example of the freelance broker. The agent is bound by the grower's terms but may get the price changed by request. Once the berries are sold, the agent is free to obtain another principal in St. Louis for whatever purpose.

2. *The manufacturer's agent*, like freelance brokers, negotiates for the sale of products for his principal. The manufacturer's agent has a rather loose arrangement with his principal that is seldom permanent beyond a year.[24] This arrangement is usually renewed but can also be terminated on notice. The agent is strictly bound by his principal for the territory, prices, terms, and conditions of sale.[25] Manufacturers' agents normally negotiate sales for several principals, but they have jurisdiction over only a part of the manufacturers' total output. A merchant using a manufacturer's agent does not need a sales force, but must have a sales department with a head to coordinate the activities of the agents and to establish policy.

3. *The sales agent* has long-term arrangements with from one to a very restricted number of principals. This agent sells the entire output for his principal and has no limitation on the territory in which he operates or on prices, terms, or conditions of sale. The sales agent also frequently finances his principals. When a merchant uses a sales agent there is no

---

[23] Lewis, *Marketing Channels: Structure and Strategy, op. cit.,* p. 14–15. Lewis provides an excellent summary of the operating characteristics of agents.

[24] Richard McLaughlin, "The Case of Using the Manufacturers Agent," *Industrial Marketing* (November, 1966), pp. 82–85.

[25] *Marketing Definitions, op. cit.*

need for any sales department because the agent handles all sales functions.

4. *Purchasing agents,* sometimes known as resident buyers, specialize in seeking out sources of supply for some merchant principal. They operate on a contractual basis for a limited number of customers and receive a commission just as sales agents do. Purchasing agents usually operate in the central market headquarters for a particular type of product. They are specialists on sources, prices, quality, shipping, fashion, and other considerations surrounding the purchase of merchandise. Chain stores make considerable use of resident buyers; so occasionally do department stores.

Agents of Physical Movement

There are two types of agents that facilitate movement: bulk transportation agencies and specialty shippers. In the former category are truckers, railroads, ship lines, pipe lines, bus lines and air lines. Each offers its own combination of services to the merchant. For example, the air lines offer speed, but the truckers offer accessibility. The rails offer bulk shipment and economy over the long haul.

Specialty shippers include air freight, parcel post, and railway express. They specialize in speed but generally handle only relatively small packages. None of this group can handle bulk shipments of such things as raw materials. Specialty shippers are used where the need is urgent or where the item is small or expensive.

Agents of Storage

Two types of agents facilitate storage: the commission merchant and public warehouses. The *commission merchant* operates in a manner similar to the broker, but differs in that he physically handles the merchandise. Commission merchants are frequently found in the agricultural market. Grain elevators are an example. Generally, the commission merchant takes the grower's goods on assignment and negotiates their sale. This means that the agent stores the goods until sold.

Public warehouses are agents that specialize in the storage of goods for pay. The warehouse receipt issued must be presented to obtain the goods, and it makes good security for a loan. Public warehouses do not attempt to sell the goods that they store, but they do often provide desk space for the manufacturer's salesman or representative. Sometimes it is not convenient to take goods to a public warehouse. In such cases, the public warehouse may come to the goods—that is, the warehouseman may lock up goods in the merchant's own storage facilities, but he issues a warehouse receive that the merchant can use as collateral on a loan. The warehouseman keeps the goods under lock until the warehouse receipt is presented. This operation is called field warehousing because the warehouseman goes into the field to secure the goods rather than bringing the goods to his own terminal.

Franchising

Franchising is a special type of agency arrangement between a buyer and a seller. It could be listed under agencies of purchase and sale, but we chose to make it a separate category because of the special considerations involved in franchising.[26] In its simplest form, franchising means that a seller gives a buyer exclusive rights to market the seller's product; in return, the buyer agrees to follow policies desired by the seller and not to sell competing products. Franchising usually involves close cooperation on price, advertising, and other policies.

As franchising has evolved, there are now two distinct types: the franchising of individual product lines and the franchising of entire businesses. *Product franchising* involves exclusive agency arrangements to sell individual goods.[27] The retailer may sell hundreds of non-competing goods, but he agrees not to sell any competing products. Jantzen bathing suits and Florsheim shoes have been franchised in this manner.

Today, many exclusive agency arrangements have been identified with the entire organization; they are called *business franchises*. The automobile dealer is the best known illustration, but this type of franchise also includes hamburger stands, restaurants, motels, and service stations. Examples of franchised businesses are Kentucky Fried Chicken, McDonald's, and Shoney's. Franchising leads to increased cooperation and communications within the channel, and it is a way for a small retailer to obtain professional management help and financial assistance without giving up his business.

The franchised business functions in the following fashion.[28] The franchiser perfects the product and the method of production. He then enters into contractual agreements with independent retailers to sell the product under guidance, utilizing policies established by the franchiser. The franchiser provides management consulting on advertising, store location, accounting, inventory control, services, and operating methods. He may also help with financing. The retailers all use a common name. In return, the retailer returns a percentage of the profits on operations

---

[26] See: B. J. Lender and Wayne Lucas, "The Nature of Franchising: Part 1: Its History," *Atlanta Economic Review* (October, 1969), pp. 12–14; Wayne Lucas and B. J. Lender, "The Nature of Franchising: Part 2: Legal Difficulties," *Atlanta Economic Review* (November, 1969), pp. 18–21.

[27] Leonard J. Konopa, "Exclusive Dealing Arrangements in Marketing," *Business Topics* (Summer, 1964), pp. 63–72.

[28] See: "A Business of Your Own—The Growth of Franchising," *U. S. News and World Report* (December, 1969); William P. Hall, "Franchising—New Scope on an Old Technique," *Harvard Business Review*, Vol. 42 (January–February, 1964), pp. 60–72.

to the franchiser. Some agreements have provided for the franchiser to buy back the retail business within a specified length of time. This has caused some friction between the parties, and there are presently court actions based on this practice.

SUPPLEMENTAL AGENTS

Supplemental agents make up a deficiency in other channel members. There are four broad types of supplemental agents: agents that supplement finances, agents that supplement decisions, agents that dispense information, and special agents.

Agents That Supplement Finances

From time to time, every business gets into financial trouble. Actually, financial stress is more likely to occur with the growing, prosperous firm than with any other kind. When financial problems arise there are agents that can help this situation. They include commercial banks, savings and loan asociations, loan companies, and stock brokers. These agents provide financial advice and other services, such as secured and unsecured loans to deserving businessmen. The stock broker provides advice on investments that can be a real source of income to the business. Of equal importance is the fact that when the business needs money, the stock broker, operating through the stock exchange, can often obtain capital by the sales of company stocks or bonds.

Agents That Supplement Decisions

Companies have access to many types of agents that can take a part or the full burden of making decisions. Some of these include advertising agencies, research firms, financial advisors, architects, doctors, lawyers, and consultants. The advertising agency can plan and execute the entire advertising program or simply give the company advice about particular advertising problems. Research firms and consultants can analyze everything from customer relations to how to come up with new products. The field of management consulting has grown rapidly in the past few years. One may wonder about the inclusion of doctors, architects, and lawyers in the group but these men really represent private businesses that offer important and specialized advice to business. Of course, the business may also employ such people on a permanent basis.

Agents That Dispense Information

A whole group of agents that tend to become lost in the discussion of marketing channels are the media. They are separate from advertising although they may perform advertising functions. Their primary function is as an agency of transmittal of information. Included in this category are television networks, radio networks, magazines, newspapers, journals, telegraphy, Western Union, telephone and the United States Postal Service. Most businesses could not function adequately without these agencies. The U. S mail alone performs a tremendous service to business although technically it is not a member of the channel because the government is not a business. The efficiency that use of the telephone has brought to business is immeasurable.

Special Supplemental Agents

Special agents include contractors, insurance companies, and computer companies. Contractors do all the building that is so vital to American industry. Most are small independently owned businesses, with the exception of those that build in the industrial field. Insurance companies are generally very large organizations which perform a special service in providing the business with a hedge against risk. In the process they are a prime source of funds for business enterprises through their investment of funds entrusted to their care. Computer companies give advice and provide information to management. In some cases, computer companies combine these activities with management consulting They may either rent or sell their equipment to business firms. The computer has been extremely important in recent years to scheduling production, computing payrolls, inventory control, personnel records, quality control, etc.

QUESTIONS

1. Explain the line and staff relationship between merchants and agents.
2. Discuss the importance of manufacturers to the marketing channel.
3. Contrast the chain store with the voluntary and cooperative wholesaler.
4. Distinguish between specialty and departmentalized retailers.
5. Distinguish between facilitating agents and supplemental agents.
6. Explain the difference in a manufacturer's agent and a sales agent.
7. To what do you attribute the importance of franchising in recent years?
8. What is the importance of understanding middlemen to channels management?
9. Discuss the important ways of classifying manufacturers.
10. Distinguish wholesaling from wholesaler.

6

Design of
Marketing Channels

In the previous chapter the members of a channel of distribution were introduced and discussed in order to show the types of institutions that may be combined into a channel. This chapter presents an analysis of channel design using the institutions previously introduced. Certainly, channels management begins with an understanding of the anatomy of the channel. A doctor would not dare to operate on a patient to remove the appendix without understanding basic body structure; in the same manner, the manager of a marketing channel can encounter great difficulty tampering with its parts without a clear realization of the effect on the entire structure. The channels manager must understand the placement, function, and relationships that exist between members within a channel before he can make effective decisions on the selection, implementation, and control over the operation of the channel.

STRUCTURE OF MARKETING CHANNELS

Webster's *New World Dictionary* defines structure as "the arrangement or interrelation of all the parts of a whole." It is exactly in this sense that we mean structure when referring to a marketing channel. The marketing channel is an immensely complex structure. Figure 6–1 provides some insight into its complexity, even though it shows only the institutions that move ownership in the channel. There are two aspects to the structure of any marketing channel: (1) the placement of institutional types in relationship to each other, and (2) the number of different institutional levels or stages included in the channel.[1] Placement of institutions concerns the order in which institutions occur; Figure 6–1 demonstrates a basic order of manufacturer, wholesaler, retailer, and household consumer.

The levels, or stages, in a channel refer to how many different separate types of institutions are involved. In a general sense, each institutional type, such as wholesalers as a group or retailers as a group, constitutes a level. Thus the illustration has four levels when the consumer is included. Some idea of the relative importance of the various levels of marketing channels can be provided. The figures below show what percentage of the $336,911 million sales in wholesale markets were considered representative of one, two, or three or more intermediaries as of 1963. The evidence is that most wholesale sales move through one or two intermediaries, but there are wide differences in the use of intermediaries.

No Intermediaries	15.4%
One Intermediary	37.5
Two Intermediaries	33.9
Three or More Intermediaries	13.2
Total	100.0%

A marketing channel is much like a house. The number and variety of different rooms and floors pretty much determine the type of house. So the types of institutions and the number of stages determine the structure of a marketing channel.

PERFORMANCE OF FUNCTIONS IN CHANNELS

Any discussion of the design of marketing channels has to take into account the patterns of functional performance that exist. After all, the incidence of how functions are performed and who performs them has much to do with the strategy that the channels manager must employ.

Variations in Member Performance of Functions

The marketing functions of buying, selling, transportation, storage, etc., must be performed no matter which type of channel is utilized. Therefore, the difference between the structure of channels of distribution lies not in functions performed, but in the type of institution used, the distribution of functions, and the manner in which the functions are performed by specific institutions. For example, drop shipper wholesalers do not store, and discount retailers often curtail specific services.

[1] F. E. Balderston, "Design of Marketing Channels," *Theory In Marketing*, Reavis Cox, Wroe Alderson, Stanley Shapiro, eds. (Homewood, Ill.: Richard D. Irwin, Inc., 1964), pp. 163–75.

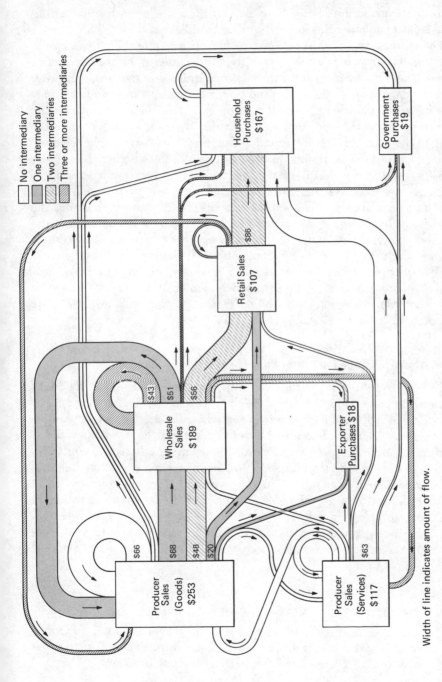

Width of line indicates amount of flow.

Fig. 6–1. Title flow of goods and services among major types of middlemen. Source: Adopted from Joseph C. Seibert, *Concepts of Marketing Management* (New York: Harper & Row, Inc., 1973), p. 368.

Thus, the distribution of functions differs in channels using such institutions from channels using other types of middlemen.

The manner in which functions are performed depends on the operational philosophy of the firm and its independence in the marketing channel. A retailer may perform functions quite different from the way a wholesaler performs them, and the performance by a manufacturer may vary from that of either of the other two. As a rule, independent channel members, unless they are tied to the leader by some contract, have the right to perform marketing functions in their own way. The channel leader is interested in results, and he does not care whether the retailer sells his product by means of personal selling or promotion so long as total revenue is satisfactory. If the retailer does not perform effectively and sales decrease, the channel leader will consider either changing the middleman or changing the structure of his channel. A channel's structure may be changed by utilizing more cooperative members of the same type presently employed, or by employing different types of members. If a full-service wholesaler is not selling effectively, the manufacturer may utilize a more cooperative full-service wholesaler or he may go to a cash and carry wholesaler who usually has a faster turnover of a limited line of merchandise.

How Agents Affect Functional Performance

The seller achieves control over the performance of many functions without the ownership of a separate channel stage when he uses agents. Agents are used by the channel leader when financial or other considerations make it impossible for him to integrate, but he needs specialized abilities.[2] Since all types of agency arrangements are based on contracts, it is impossible for the manufacturer to specify certain conditions relating to the middleman's operations in the contract. For example, an agent may be allowed to warrant the goods or even to set prices, terms, and conditions of sale, but all are subject to the approval of the principal. In a franchise arrangement, the manufacturer may set sales quotas, factory train the middleman's sales force, establish prices and service policy, and coordinate promotion.

Functional Performance and Length of Channel

There is a direct relationship between the performance of functions and channel length. Specifically, channel structure affects functions as they relate to: (1) control over the performance of functions, (2) speed

[2] See: Bert C. McCammon, Jr., and Malcolm L. Morris, "The Changing Structure of Automotive Retailing," *Business Horizons* (Winter, 1965), pp. 5–24.

of delivery, and (3) cost of operations.[3] These are important aspects of channel operations that concern the manager. When a decision is made on the structure of the channel, it affects many other facets of channel operations.

Generally, the shorter the channel the greater the channel leader's control over functions.[4] With increased control comes greater speed of delivery, and the opportunity for lower operating cost. The increase in cost is directly related to the efficiency of the seller in performing more of the marketing function. If a seller wishes either control or speed within the channel, that seller would tend toward the use of a more direct channel. The fact that Avon and Fuller Brush choose to sell door-to-door is no doubt partially explained by the desire to control activities associated with the sale of their products. Thus, the increased channel cost may be offset by increased sales volume causing total cost to decrease. The competitors of Avon and Fuller Brush feel their interests are best served by giving up channel control and employing wholesalers and retailers. This distribution structure is preferred if lower sales volume is offset by greatly reduced operational cost. The point is that both Avon and its competitors may be quite successful using different channel structures. Perishable goods such as fresh fruit or seasonal items like fashion clothing use a short channel because short life makes speed a necessity. In the same channel canned goods or work clothes may be sold through food brokers or wholesalers respectively.

As a general principle, the greater the need for control over functions in the channel, the greater the total cost to the manufacturer. Less need for control is associated with less cost for the manufacturer. Thus, in a long channel with both wholesalers and retailers, these middlemen assume much of the cost burden otherwise borne by the manufacturer.

Sears offers an excellent example of effective channel management.[5] We do not mean to say that the longer channel is always preferred because it has lower cost. The preferred channel is the one having the greatest profit and offering consumer satisfaction.

BASIC OWNERSHIP STRUCTURE OF CHANNELS

The channels manager should base structural design on a knowledge of the alternatives available. This cannot be presented or understood

[3] Louis W. Stern, "Channel Control and Interorganizational Management," *Marketing and Economic Development*, Peter Al Bennett, ed. (Chicago: American Marketing Association, 1965), pp. 655–65.

[4] William R. Davidson, "Innovation In Distribution," *Marketing Channels and Institutions*, Bruce J. Walker and Joel B. Haynes, ed. (Columbus, Ohio: Grid, Inc., 1973), pp. 71–78; "Evans Products Cuts Out The Middleman," *Business Week* (July 31, 1971), pp. 70–71.

[5] John McDonald, "Sears Makes It Look Easy," *Fortune* (May, 1964), pp. 120–27ff.

in one simple composite picture; it is necessary to develop the idea of channel structure carefully and in steps. In this section, we discuss: (1) basic structure of ownership members, (2) concentration and dispersion, and (3) the normal channel.

Types of Ownership Structure

The phrase *basic channel structure* is used to mean the relationship among channel members who affect the movement of ownership. Structure that involves the physical flow of goods is discussed later. Figure 6–2 demonstrates eight types of possible channel structures involving

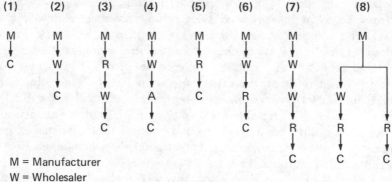

M = Manufacturer
W = Wholesaler
R = Retailer
C = Consumer

Fig. 6–2. Types of channel schematics.

product ownership. When discussing channels, the usual demonstration is with schematics such as those shown.[6] These schematics are very useful for explaining simple channel relationships, but they must be understood by the reader to be effective. There are three assumptions upon which these schematics are based:

1. The channel consists of complete institutions or organizations
2. Manufacturer's agents and selling agents are included with merchants [7]
3. Physical movement follows exactly the movement of ownership

[6] For a more detailed discussion, see: Louis P. Bucklin, "The Classification of Channel Structures," *Vertical Marketing Systems*, Louis P. Bucklin, ed. (Glenview, Ill.: Scott, Foresman and Co., 1970), pp. 16–31.

[7] There is no logical reason to include these two types of agents and exclude others; we are simply following tradition.

Since the channel is made up of complete institutions rather than parts of institutions, manufacturer's sale organizations, manufacturer's branch houses, retailer warehouses and similar facilities are not included as separate parts of the channel. The inclusion of only institutions of ownership means that all transportation agencies and other types of agents can only be implied by the dashes contained in the schematics. By making physical movement and ownership movement simultaneous, the channel becomes one flow process. Thus the channel schematic is not a picture of an actual channel; it is the definition of a channel in terms of its merchant members. A great deal about channels is left unsaid when this type of schematic is used. However, these schematics do provide a basis for expanding our knowledge of channel structure.

Legitimate Ownership Channels

The first problem with the basic channels presented in Figure 6-2 concerns whether or not all illustrate actual marketing channels. The fact is that the channels illustrated as one through four are not possible. The reason for their exclusion is definitional, because we know they exist in a practical sense. (After all, Fuller Brush and Avon both sell directly from manufacturer to consumer.) Since only retailers can sell to final household consumers, there can be no marketing channel that does not have a retailer as its final member.

We might assume that an easy way out of the dilemma would be to change the definitions. However, there is no known way of effectively distinguishing retailers from wholesalers except on the basis of whom each sells to. Both wholesalers and retailers create time, place, and possession utility, and it even is true that they perform generally the same marketing functions. One might argue that although the functions are the same, the degree to which they are performed differs between wholesalers and retailers. Wholesalers buy in larger quantity, transport in larger quantity, sell more, etc. Actually this reasoning does not stand up to logic or fact. Large retailers, such as Sears, Korvette's, Woolworth's, etc., buy, sell, transport, store, etc., in larger quantities than many wholesalers. If we are to distinguish wholesalers from retailers we must base the distinction on the markets that they serve.

Why distinguish between wholesalers and retailers at all? Since they are so similar, it hardly appears worthwhile but there are actually very practical reasons for doing so. First, the placement of each in the channel is different. This affects determination of price discounts, shipment preferences, and coordination of members. Second, each does sell to different markets—and this is a real distinction. The channel would be chaotic if every member could sell to anyone, and control would be impossible. Third, retailers and wholesalers are required to collect and pay different types of taxes by the several governments. Wholesalers do not collect sales tax but retailers do. The two types of institutions have different inventory taxes. Fourth, the government requires different types of information from the wholesalers and retailers. It keeps a much closer check on income tax, profits, revenue, and cost for manufacturers and wholesalers than for retailers. Therefore, one can only conclude that it is important to be able to distinguish the two types of marketing institutions.

Dual Institutions Solution

It is possible to explain the existence of all the channels presented in schematic form, and to preserve the definitions at the same time. The solution lies in relaxing the assumption that the channel consists of complete institutions. If we allow it to include institutions which are partly one type and partly another, the definitions work. That is, in any given institution we need to identify those aspects that are wholesale and those that are retail. This identification can be based on the market in exactly the same manner used as when the institution is considered as a whole. The dual nature of institutions is illustrated in Figure 6–3.

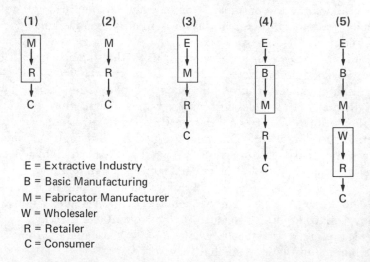

E = Extractive Industry
B = Basic Manufacturing
M = Fabricator Manufacturer
W = Wholesaler
R = Retailer
C = Consumer

Fig. 6–3. Concept of dual institutions.

A manufacturer who sells directly to consumers is a manufacturer–retailer. A wholesaler who sells to consumers is a wholesaler–retailer. Any institution that employs an agent simply combines that agent with its own operations. In practice, each channel is redefined in such a way as to include a retailer. In many cases these dual institutions can be clearly distinguished. For example, a manufacturer who sells directly to consumers probably has branch sales offices located regionally from which his salesmen operate. These sales offices become identifiable retail facilities within the manufacturer's operation. A manufacturer may produce clothes on the second floor of a building and sell these clothes on the first floor. In this case, the floors separate the different operations. Where agents are concerned, any agent is simply an extension of his principal, but the two function as separate units.

The dual institution concept is employed by both the government and the manufacturer when dealing with channel members. The government, for tax purposes, divides an institution according to the majority of its sales. Thus, an institution that has sixty per cent of its sales at retail and forty per cent at wholesale is classified sixty per cent retail and forty per cent wholesale. The firm's taxes are established according to these proportions. A retailer who makes some purchases direct from the manufacturer may be classified a wholesaler for these purchases and given what amounts to a trade discount by the manufacturer.

Structural Width of Channels

So far the discussion of channels has tended to concentrate on how a single manufacturer moves his products to market. However, it would be a mistake to assume that each symbol in our channel schematic represents a single business. A channel has the characteristic of width as well as length. Figure 6–4 shows the relationships between the numbers of institutions, by channel levels, in the United States. There are more retailers than any other type of institution, a fact true both for the total number of firms or by separate industries. The next largest group of institutions is in the extractive industry followed by fabricators. Wholesalers have the smallest number of institutions in the United States. Thus, a channel involves two broad processes of concentration and dispersion that are caused by the nature of the structure. *Concentration* is the process of bringing goods from the mines, farms, sea, and air together in one place. It involves a movement through fabricators to the central wholesale markets. *Dispersion* is the process of disseminating goods from central wholesale markets through a large number of retailers to the final household consumer.

Normal Channel of Distribution

The channel M—W—R—C is generally considered the normal channel in marketing literature. Actually, the concept of a normal channel is largely a myth. This channel is normal only in the sense that most goods flow through wholesalers most of the time. However, nearly every retailer on some occasion or another purchases some of his products direct from the manufacturer. Furthermore, manufacturers often sell through wholesalers to small retailers, but deal directly with large re-

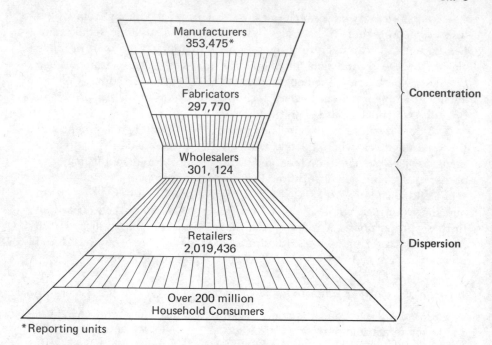

*Reporting units

Fig. 6–4. Concentration and dispersion of channels. *Source:* U. S. Department of Commerce, Bureau of the Census, 1970.

tailers and chain store retailers. Actually, the normal channel of distribution is a multiple channel, shown as number 8 in Figure 6–2. It has a route through the wholesaler to the retailer, but it also has a direct route that bypasses the wholesaler. Both concepts of a normal channel are useful to the marketing manager.

STRUCTURAL LINKAGE OF CHANNELS

Discussion of the design of marketing channels has, to this point, assumed the existence of a particular structure. Very little has been said about the mechanism that links one part of the channel to another part. Nor has there been any treatment of the various types of linkage that may exist between parts of the marketing channel. Coordination, motivation, and control require that the channels manager be aware of various types of linkage.

Flow Concept in Channels

The channel of distribution involves some flow and it is this flow mechanism that ties the channel memberships together for the purpose of satisfying the wants of some market segment. We are in the habit of thinking about the movement of ownership and physical movement when we think of channel flow, for without these two flows the channel would have no reason for being. However, several other important types of flows have been demonstrated in the channel. There flows include: promotion, negotiation, financing, risking, ordering, and payments. In a sense, the channel of distribution is caught up in a whole *web of relationships* involving these various types of functional flows that take place. All these flows occur between institutions in the channel, but, as between any two channel members, the functional flow of goods depends on whether title passes at the seller's plant or the buyer's Payment normally follows physical flow, but risking occurs concurrently with all functional flows.

Direction of Channel Flows

In a channel of distribution, the different types of flows have direction as demonstrated in Figure 6–5.[8] There may be either vertical or horizontal flows. *Vertical flows* take place between members participating in the same channel. The flow is between separate channel stages or levels. It is this type of flow that is primarily depicted in Figure 6–5. It is a flow that directly involves the channel team's fulfillment of its purpose. Vertical channel flows may be directed from the consumer back to the producer, or forward from the producer to the final con-

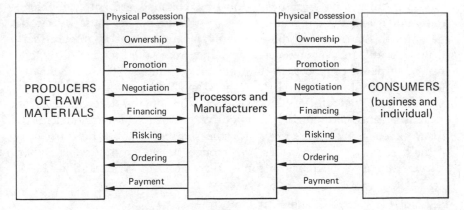

Fig. 6–5. Market flows by direction of the flow. *Source:* R. S. Vaile, E. T. Grether, and Reavis Cox, *Marketing in the American Economy* (New York: The Ronald Press Co., 1952), p. 113.

[8] Reavis Cox and Thomas F. Schutte, "A Look At Channels Management," *Marketing Involvement In Society and the Economy* (Chicago: American Marketing Association, 1969), pp. 99–105. These authors provide a different flow concept.

sumer. Orders and payments flow vertically to the producer, while physical movement, ownership, and promotion flow vertically toward the final consumer. A dual vertical flow is illustrated by negotiation, financing, and risking.

Horizontal channel flows occur between institutions that are not a part of the same channel. The horizontal flow takes place between institutions at the same stage in the channel. It typically involves competitive information on such things as new products, promotion, employee training, plant openings, layoffs, and sales volume where possible. Horizontal information is vital to channel operations, but most channel members feel that they do not have sufficient information of this type.

Rate of Flow Over Time

Not only do flows take place in different directions in the marketing channel, but there are different rates to the flows. Leo Aspinwall has offered a tentative explanation for these different rates called the *depot theory of distribution*.[9] The basic idea of this concept is that goods move through the channel at a controlled rather than at an uncontrolled rate. The rate at which these goods move is established by the final consumer; the more he purchases the faster the goods move.

In a perfect channel with no friction, the goods would never need to be stopped for storage and handling. This situation would eliminate storage and handling cost, and there could be no profit from holding goods for speculative purposes. However, channels are not frictionless, and storage and handling are necessary. Thus, depots must be established for this purpose and these depots typically become an integral part of the operation of channel members. They serve the function of matching the output of producers to the wants of consumers. There is a steady flow of goods into and out of the depots, and the reserves normally kept in the depots fluctuate up or down depending on the different rates of consumer wants. Supposedly, competitive pressures cause channel members to keep goods in the depot for the shortest possible time because of the cost involved. Of course, in practice, a seller can offset a higher cost of storage by efficiency in some other aspect of his operation.

Physical Flow and Ownership Flow

The assumption was made in dealing with the basic channel structure that the movement of goods followed exactly the flow of ownership over the goods. In fact, this is not always true. Many times in a channel

---

[9] Leo V. Aspinwall, "The Depot Theory of Distribution," *Managerial Marketing: Perspectives and Viewpoints*, William Lazer and E. J. Kelley, eds. (Homewood, Ill.: Richard D. Irwin, Inc., 1962), pp. 652–59.

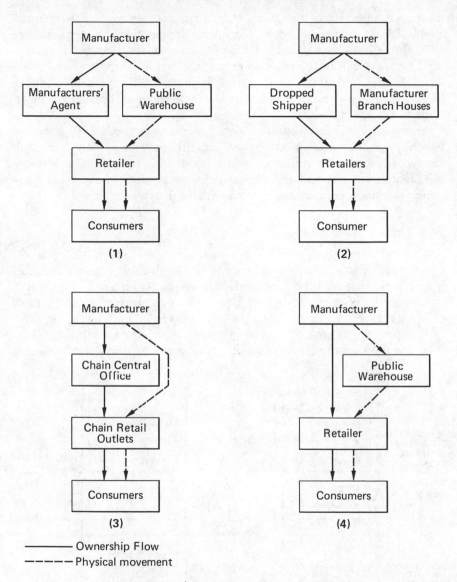

Ownership Flow
----- Physical movement

Fig. 6–6. Ownership and physical flow.

the goods flow in one direction and the ownership flows in another.[10]
Figure 6–6 demonstrates four possibilities for dual flow in a channel of
distribution. In example 1, sale is through an agent directly to the re-

[10] Donald J. Bowersox, "Changing Channels in the Physical Distribution of Finished Goods," *Marketing and Economic Development* (Chicago: American Marketing
Association, 1965), pp. 711–21.

tailer, and shipment of the goods is through another agent. In example 2, the sale is through a wholesaler, and shipment is direct to the retailer through the manufacturer's branch. In example 3, central buying is used by the chain in the wholesaler market, but all shipments are made direct to the individual retail stores. In example 4, the sale is direct from the manufacturer to the retailer, but the physical goods move through an agent middleman.

There are other possibilities. For example, the goods may pass between the retailer and the consumer, but title may be held by the bank until the goods are paid for. It is easy to see that there are many combinations of physical and contractual flow possible in channels. Certainly channel structure must account for both types of flow.

Two-Channel Structure

The "M" used to designate manufacturer in our schematics, has referred to all manufacturers who operate in the channel. Thus, discussion has been built around the final household consumer channel. Figure 6–7 illustrates the concept that many times manufacturers may sell to each other, and this leads to the manufacturing channel.

It is possible to view a channel of distribution as one continuous flow from the mine to the final household consumer. In many instances this

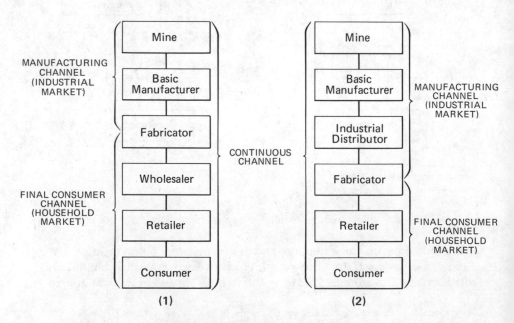

Fig. 6–7. Two channel structure.

point of view is very useful, such as when studying the total cost of marketing and production, when making sequence studies of the production–distribution process, or when comparing production operations to distribution operations for a given product.

For most management decisions the channel is divided into two. The manufacturer channel concerns the sale of goods and services to production firms. It is often referred to as the industrial channel. The manufacturing channel tends to be engineering-oriented while the final household consumer channel tends to be marketing-oriented. When the channel is considered as two rather than one, the fabricator of the final product is the last consumer in the manufacturing channel and the initial member of the final household consumer channel. Notice also that the manufacturing channel can have as many types of middlemen as the final household channel. It may even have wholesalers in the form of the industrial distributor. However, the manufacturing channel cannot have retailers because retailers sell only to final household consumers. Each firm in the entire channel is an industrial consumer of some type.

LEVELS OF CHANNEL STRUCTURE

The subject of channel levels basically involves horizontal and vertical integration in channels. The manager must be aware of what integration does to structural design of channels and how this affects his decision making.

Vertical Integration

It often happens in a channel of distribution that a member at one stage wants to take over the operations or functions of another stage. The reasons may be to reduce cost of operations, to stabilize activities and performance, to assure sources of supply, and to provide better control over operations.[11] This combining of different stages through ownership is called vertical integration. It occurs when the management of one stage purchases a business operating at another stage, but it also takes place when the management of one stage simply begins performing the duties or functions of another stage through expansion.[12] An example of the latter situation occurs when a retailer begins to perform the wholesale function by building and operating warehouses. One study of in-

---

[11] Frederick D. Sturdivant, "Determinants of Vertical Integration In Channel Systems," *Science, Technology, and Marketing,* Raymond M. Haas, ed. (Chicago: American Marketing Associaiton, 1966), pp. 472–79.

[12] H. O. Ruhuke, "Vertical Integration: Trend for the Future," *Advanced Management Journal* (January, 1966), pp. 69–73; Bert C. McCammon, Jr., Paper Presented to *National Association of Wholesalers,* 1969, Las Vegas, Nevada, January 15, 1969.

dustrial firms shows a direct relationship between size of firm and vertical integration with large firms displaying more integration.[13]

A definitional problem of vertical integration arises concerning what is meant by a step or stage in the channel. Earlier in this chapter, a stage was defined as any institutional level such as the manufacturer stage, the wholesaler stage, and the retailer stage. This definition must now be modified because it lumps too many dissimilar operations together. This is particularly true at the manufacturing stage in the channel—would the manufacturers of parts, motors, refrigerators, ball bearings, stoves, and electrical wire all be viewed as a whole? Obviously, the definition requires broadening in order to take in such situations. We shall now define a step or stage in the marketing channel as: *any group of business firms, or separate operations within a business, that perform similar functions or operations within the flow of process of production or distribution.*

By this definition, retailing and wholesaling are stages because each contains a relatively homogeneous group of institutions. It would not be difficult to identify mining, basic manufacturer, and fabrication as individual stages, though all occur in production. Even in our illustration above, it is possible to determine stages in the flow. We observe that the manufacturer of motors precedes the fabrication of refrigerators and stoves as part of a continuous flow of process. Parts, electrical wire, and ball bearings precede the manufacture of motors. Refrigerators and stoves are essentially the same type of operation since they both require fabrication. Thus these latter two operations would be classified at the same stage in the channel. The definition, therefore, provides a finer-edged tool for making valid determinations about vertical integration. Any firm that performs any of the above activities in sequence is vertically integrated.

The existence of vertical integration in a channel of distribution is relative, as shown in Figure 6–8. The reader should not think of vertical integration as something that happens only between the wholesale and the retail channel members; it can occur between any of the members. If channel 5 in Figure 6–8 is assumed to be the longest channel available, then each of the other channels is relatively vertically integrated in comparison. In channel 4 the wholesaler and the retailer of channel 5 have been combined as the retailer in channel 4. This description of the combination does not imply anything about the performance of functions when a channel member is eliminated. It only illustrates that where there were previously two identifiable channel members, there is now only one.

---

[13] Robert E. Weigand, "The Marketing Organization, Channels, and Firm Size," *Journal of Business,* Vol. 36 (April, 1963), pp. 228–36.

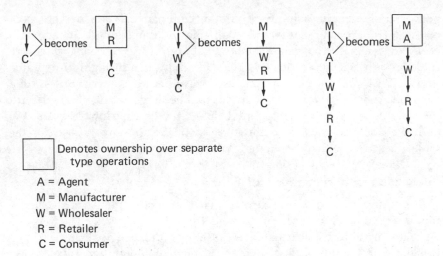

Denotes ownership over separate
type operations

A = Agent
M = Manufacturer
W = Wholesaler
R = Retailer
C = Consumer

Fig. 6–8. Vertical integration.

Horizontal Integration

Horizontal integration is normally used to designate the combination of two or more separate enterprises through ownership at the same stage in the channel of distribution. A wholesaler buying out a wholesaler or a manufacturer buying out another manufacturer are examples of horizontal integration. There is a great similarity between horizontal integration and product diversification and we shall use the terms synonymously. *Product diversification* consists of a firm handling multiple lines of products, especially if the products appeal to essentially different markets.

If a large sawmill seeks to extend its product line to include the manufacture and sale of paperboard boxes, it has two choices. It can attempt to locate and purchase a manufacturer of paperboard boxes—this would be considered horizontal integration. The sawmill may also consider building a paperboard plant and making its own cartons—in this case, product diversification. In either instance we have a wider product line. The problems of product management, sales, channel selection, and control are very similar in both situations, and these problems can be serious.[14] The primary difference between the two is that with horizontal integration one competitor is replaced by another, whereas with product diversification there is a net gain of one competitor in the market.

Simultaneous Vertical and Horizontal Integration

Normally, when a channel displays vertical integration it also displays horizontal integration. The two types of integration tend to occur to-

[14] "The Dent in American Can," *Dun's Review* (April, 1970), pp. 38–41.

gether. For example, the Ford Motor Company is one of the more completely vertically integrated companies in the United States. This company owns its own mines, steel mills, and fabricated cars which are sold through franchised dealers. The company is also highly integrated horizontally. Ford is in the appliance business, the parts business, and is involved with government contracts. The large retail chain department stores are vertically integrated since they do their own wholesaling and some do manufacturing, but these department stores also carry the wide lines of merchandise found at retail.

Integration and Elimination of Functions

It has already been demonstrated that the greater the vertical integration in a channel, the fewer levels there are in that channel. The question naturally arises as to what happens to the performance of such marketing functions as buying, selling, and service when integration takes place. We can answer in two ways. Marketing functions can be eliminated within any given stage of a channel at will. We have already observed examples of this when discussing the types of middlemen. For example, a drop shipper does not perform the storage function. All types of limited-function wholesalers eliminate some function or service to increase efficiency and to reduce the cost of operations. At the retail level, we find that some retailers grant credit and deliver while some do not. Thus, it is apparent that activities can be eliminated by any given member of the channel.

Whether marketing functions can be eliminated from the channel as a whole depends on the understanding of functions. If one middleman does not perform the function some other middleman must pick it up. However, the number of times a function is performed in the channel can be changed. In a M–W–R–C channel, selling is performed three times and buying is performed twice. In the integrated channel M–R–C, selling is performed only twice and buying once. The number of performances has been reduced in the integrated channel.

Functional Shifts Caused by Integration

Figure 6–9 illustrates what can happen to the performance of functions when a wholesaler is eliminated from the channel. The functions are pushed forward to the retailer, back to the manufacturer, or simultaneously forward and back. Suppose a manufacturer sells through 100 wholesalers to 1,500 retailers who, in turn, reach one million consumers. Suppose also that each salesman can service 50 institutions—either wholesaler or retailers. Now let us assume that the manufacturer decides to eliminate the wholesaler. What happens to the buying, selling, transportation, and storage functions? In the non-integrated channel the manufacturer needed 4 salesmen, but he requires 60 in the integrated channel.

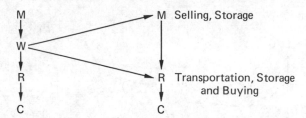

Fig. 6–9. Shift of marketing function with integration.

His performance of selling has increased 15 times. The retailers may have to spend more time on transportation because of the longer distances involved between manufacturer and retailer with the integrated channel. Thus, transportation is pushed forward to the retailers. In the integrated channel, the retailers and the manufacturer both have to store in larger quantities because shipments take longer. The manufacturer needs more products on hand for the larger quantities in which the retailers must buy, and the retailers must store more because they cannot obtain quick-fill orders from the wholesaler.

STRUCTURAL CHANGE IN CHANNELS

Professor Malcolm McNair advanced the concept some years ago that the structure of retailing continually changes until it arrives back at the same place. He called his concept the *wheel of retailing*.[15] The concept might have been better named the *wheel of marketing* since it applies to all levels in the channel, and that is the context in which it is treated below.

The Wheel of Marketing

Figure 6–10 can aid in an understanding of the concept of the wheel of marketing. The basic idea is that new marketing firms enter the market because of a rejection of the policies of firms already in the market. For example, at points A and C services are great, costs are high, margins are squeezed, and prices are up. This situation creates a need for a low price type of firm which enters the market at point B. The new entry may be illustrated by limited-function wholesaler, chain grocery store of the 1930's, or discount house of the 1950's. The new firms begin with low status, low prices, but wide margins because of limited service, streamlined operations, and low capital cost due to use of out of the way locations.

[15] Malcolm P. McNair, "Significant Trends and Developments in the Postwar Period," A. B. Smith, ed., *Competitive Distribution in a Free High-Level Economy and Its Implications for the University* (Pittsburgh: University of Pittsburgh Press, 1957), p. 17. The concept has broader applications besides those to retailing; this discussion is based on Professor McNair's ideas.

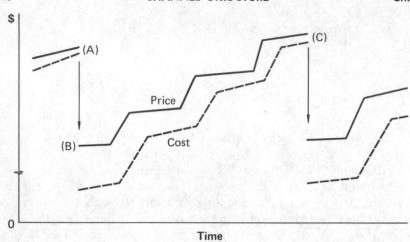

Fig. 6–10. The wheel of marketing. *Source:* Based on Malcolm McNair's concept of the wheel of retailing.

As time goes on, marketers observe opportunities to increase the market by appealing to different consumer groups. In order to attract the new market some service must be added. The service, for example, increased promotion or higher quality products, causes cost to increase just a little. Thus, prices have to rise with increased cost and margins are squeezed. Then the sellers observe another possible market if they just offered credit, and cost and prices go up a little more. Each increase in service, cost, and price is hardly noticeable in the short run, but it adds up over time. As the business gradually moves out of the low status market, a vacuum is left and many customers go unsatisfied. In time, a new business observes the market opportunity and enters the low status market. The structure has come full circle.

The cycle described was followed in the case of all the marketing institutions just mentioned. Chain grocery stores and discount houses began selling goods in abandoned warehouses. They did not advertise, sold out of original cartons, used few clerks, and did not offer such services as warranty, credit, delivery, returns, etc. In time these institutions have moved downtown, made their stores attractive, begun to advertise, and included most services.

Evaluation of Wheel Concept

The basic idea of the wheel is excellent, but it simply does not extend far enough.[16] It does provide a basic explanation for a major portion of

[16] Bert C. McCammon, Jr., "Alternative Explanations of Institutional Change and Channel Evolution," *Toward Scientific Marketing*, Stephen A. Greyer, ed. (Chicago: American Marketing Association, December, 1963), pp. 477–90.

the structural change that takes place in the marketing channel. However, three important points concerning the wheel must be made.

First, it has application to both wholesaling and manufacturing as well as retailing. For example, in wholesaling the full-service wholesaler had very modest beginnings. Later, as the service wholesalers upgraded their operations, limited-function wholesalers of all types entered the channel. At the manufacturing level of the channel, a great many of America's major corporations began very modestly—Ford, duPont, and Georgia Pacific.

Second, it is restrictive to assume that all businesses begin as low status organizations and work toward higher class markets. It is possible for a firm to begin as a low status firm, a middle status firm, or a high status firm and to move either up or down in its market appeal. Firms tend to enter wherever there is a vacuum in the marketing structure, and customers are going unsatisfied. For example, department stores began as status businesses, but with the competition from discounters they have either streamlined their operations or opened low status operations of their own. Likewise, many full-service wholesalers have streamlined their operation downward. J. C. Penney began in the middle and has been steadily moving into the vacuum created by the upgrading of merchandise by Sears and Wards. While there is merit in the wheel concept, it is a mistake to assume that the movement is always in one direction.

Third, it must be pointed out that the wheel concept does not explain all structural changes in the marketing channel. Some businesses begin at a particular level and remain there. This situation is, perhaps, more usual at the manufacturing level than at the wholesale or retail level, but it happens everywhere. For example, chain grocery stores have resisted adding credit and delivery. Even when an institution does not change over time it has an impact on channel structure. If the institution remains the same this may indicate the need for it in the marketing structure. Furthermore, many firms enter the market only to fail.

QUESTIONS

1. What is meant by channel structure? Why is it important to channel decision making?
2. Discuss the advantages of long and short channels of distribution and illustrate the use of each.
3. What is a "dual institution?" In which forms do they exist? Give examples.
4. Define and compare vertical and horizontal channel flows.
5. Can the flow of the physical good and ownership of that good ever be separated? If so—how?
6. How is vertical integration used by business and what are its advantages?
7. Give an example of horizontal integration and how it affected the company.

8. Trace the channels of distribution your most recent personal purchase went through.
9. Select a product for each of the four legitimate channels of distribution and trace its movement through the channel.
10. What does the wheel of retailing have to say about the status of a business remaining constant?

7

Channel Selection

Channel selection involves the determination of the most effective route to market, given the environment in which the business finds itself. In one sense, channel selection is the natural outgrowth of understanding channel design; in another sense, channel design is the result of selecting a particular type of channel. In any case, the importance of channel selection cannot be underestimated. It is the fundamental decision of channels management, and the particular channel selected affects each of the other decision areas of that management: leadership, information flow, logistics, and assortment development.

BASIC CONSIDERATIONS OF CHANNEL SELECTION

The determination of an effective channel is never complete. The channel leader must, at least, face the problem periodically. In this chapter the term channel selection is used to refer to three broad decision activities. First, *channel adoption* occurs when the firm initially decides on a preferred route to market from among available channel alternatives. Channel adoption typically occurs only once in a product's life, but may occur often in an innovative firm that frequently adds products. Second, *channel modification* is defined to mean the process of continual re-evaluation, adjustment, and change that occurs with a channel over the life of the product. Channel modification occurs continually for both products and companies. Third, *channel creation* is development from the ground up of a channel where no alternative previously existed. Channel creation typically involves designing new institutions or using existing institutions in a new manner. The development of discount houses and shopping centers illustrates channel creation.

149

Ideal Channel of Distribution

At this point, we must understand what kind of channel is being selected. The tendency is to assume that the channel's manager seeks the one ideal channel.[1] In fact, this is never true. The concept of an ideal channel is attractive, but it does not stand the test of sound theory or practical application.

Such a concept is also logically deficient, even for two similar businesses selling one homogeneous product to the same market. Perhaps the executives of the two firms are not equally competent. It may also be that buyer perceptions of the two organizations differ even though no real differences exist in the firms. It follows that two firms can attempt the same channel and one will fail while the other succeeds. In short, the ideal channel concept can be based on a logical construct, but the firm and/or the market are often emotional in their behavior.

The most important reason refuting the concept of the ideal channel is the fact that markets differ. Frequently, it is feasible to sell a given product direct in concentrated markets while it may be necessary to use wholesalers in the sparse or thinly settled markets. In addition, we must remember that every customer is in some ways unique. That each consumer's wants and desires differ in many respects may cause the firm to modify its basic product offered, and such differences will affect the channel of distribution used. For example, built-in appliances may be sold through wholesalers to the final consumer, or they may be sold direct to consumers by building contractors.

The concept of an ideal channel is even less logical when we consider that the same product is sold by competing firms that differ in some important respects. Often both firms are successful, or one or the other may fail. Differences in markets sought, operating costs, profit requirements, management ability, etc., affect a firm's channel. One firm may seek a direct channel to control sales promotion and physical distribution, while another firm uses a longer channel in order to keep the cost of distribution low. Another example can be found in manufacturers that sell direct to department stores but use wholesalers to reach the independents who purchase in small quantity.

There are other reasons to refute the concept of the single ideal channel. The particular basis for a channel may change over time. Given an adequate period of time, the market may develop sufficiently in size to warrant using a different channel or the company may change its channel objectives.[2] For example, a company that starts out using a manufactur-

---

[1] "What Determines The Correct Channel of Distribution," *Industrial Marketing* (March, 1966), pp. 27–30.

[2] Thomas L. Berg, "Designing the Distribution System," *The Social Responsibility of Marketing*, Peter D. Bennett, ed. (Chicago: American Marketing Association, 1961), pp. 481–90.

er's agent either because of limited finances or because the market is small may change to its own sales force if either of these conditions changes. The concept of a single ideal channel is deficient because often the firm is not in a position to seek an ideal. It may not have the ability to conduct the necessary research to determine the ideal channel, even if it existed. Furthermore, if such an ideal channel were actually discovered, the company might not possess the finances or the management talent to exploit the find. In the final analysis, the marketing manager settles for the selection of an effective channel of distribution.

Channel Selection Is Important

Too many businesses do not realize the importance of channel selection. First, the existence of an effective channel is important because it can greatly improve operating efficiency.[3] A well-chosen channel may lead to lower shipping costs through reduced delivery time and better matching of products to middlemen needs. A sound channel may also improve efficiency by providing for shorter routes to market, better control leading to a reduction of inventories, and more cooperation among channel members.[4] Second, the channel is important because of the consequences of ineffective channels. The channel is one of the basic elements in the competition that takes place between firms. Everything competitive that happens between firms relates—directly or indirectly—to the channel used. Thus, the selection of an ineffective channel may cause such consequences as: (1) increased promotional cost, (2) poor market coverage, (3) ineffective sales effort, (4) a misbalance of production and sales, and (5) slow or misdirected physical distribution of the company's products. It is for these reasons that channel selection is never simple or easy.

Factors of Channel Selection

Any attempt to discuss all of the important points associated with channel adoption, modification, or creation on an individual basis would probably prove to be cumbersome and disjointed.[5] Fortunately, it is possible to group the major decision areas into six meaningful categories: (1) final consumer considerations, (2) product considerations, (3)

---

[3] Bruce Mallen, "Interaction of Channel Selection Policies in the Marketing System," *The Marketer: Journal of the Marketing Association of Canada* (Spring, 1965), pp. 14–16.

[4] Wroe Alderson and Paul E. Green, "Bayesian Decision Theory in Channel Selection," *Planning and Problem Solving In Channels* (Homewood, Ill.: Richard D. Irwin, Inc., 1964), pp. 311–17.

[5] See: Helmy H. Baligh, "A Theoretical Framework for Channel Choice," *Economic Growth, Competitive and World Markets*, P. D. Bennett, ed. (Chicago: American Marketing Association, 1965), pp. 631–54; Delbert J. Duncan, "Selecting a Channel of Distribution," *Marketing Channels*, Richard M. Clewett, ed. (Homewood, Ill.: Richard D. Irwin, Inc., 1954), pp. 367–403.

membership considerations, (4) management considerations, (5) competitive considerations, and (6) cost and profit considerations.

FINAL CONSUMER CONSIDERATIONS OF CHANNEL SELECTION

One of the major factors affecting channel selection is the final consumer market to be served. A channel suitable to reach one household market may not necessarily be suitable for another. Demographic factors, customer preference, market size, and customer location will affect the channel selection.

Demographic Factors

It is difficult to generalize about the effect of customer characteristics on the selection of channels. You cannot say that all young people, or all women, or all low income people require a specific type of channel that is different from a channel required by older people, men, or high income customers. You can say that for a given product, customer characteristics affect the channel selected. A retailer may specialize in the sale of odd size shoes, clothing, etc., appealing to size characteristics in people who cannot find satisfaction in regular outlets. A manufacturer may produce and distribute both men's and women's clothing, but it is not uncommon for the producer to specialize by sex. The channel used to distribute jewelry to high income consumers may be quite different from one designed to reach low income consumers. The former may sell direct to specialty stores while the latter may sell costume jewelry through wholesalers to specialty and department stores. Blacks, Chinese, and other races represent, for some products, distinct markets that can be reached with special channels. Furthermore, patterns of living caused by discrimination and income differences necessitate difference in the channels designed to serve these groups. There are no simple answers, but the manager must be aware of the effect of customer characteristics on the design of the marketing channel, or he can miss large and significant market segments.

Customer Preferences

Customer preferences concern specific and individualistic desires of customers. Similar customer preferences may be possessed by tall people, middle income people, people in the same occupation, etc. On the other hand, people with the same characteristics may have different preferences. In any case, customer preferences do affect channel selection, but, as with customer characteristics, their effect is difficult to generalize. The problem is that there are numerous consumer preferences, and their influence is widely diverse. The important consideration is for the business manager to isolate those preferences that affect his particular channel and give sufficient attention to each one.

Some consumer preferences are rather obvious in their effect on channel selection. Customers expect outlets with such names as hardware stores, record shops, grocery stores, shoe stores, dress shops, etc., to carry appropriate merchandise, and the channel must be selected to reach the appropriate retailer. Customers do not expect to find quality products and brands in retail stores with low price images. The seller of quality furniture would not use the same channel as the seller of junk furniture, because each is aware of the preference of his chosen market. Customers often expect specific services to accompany their purchases of products. For example, some customers, whether tall or short, blue collar or white collar, male or female, expect such services as credit, delivery, and installation when purchasing appliances. Others may prefer low prices to appliance service. A channel that includes the Appliance Specialty Shop is appropriate for the preferences of the first group of customers but a channel using the discount outlet is better suited to the desires of the latter group.

Some customers' preferences are not so obvious in their effect on channel selection. The desire by consumers for multiple purchases and one-stop shopping has led to a blurring of lines of merchandise carried by retailers. *Scrambled merchandising* is a term that has been defined as retailers carrying merchandise not normally thought of as being carried by that particular type of store. This scrambling of line has been a direct result of customer preferences for one-stop and multiple-purchase shopping. In turn, these wide-line retailers have generated greater pressure for wide-line wholesalers. The desire of consumers to trade in suburban shopping centers has influenced the structure of trade channels. Sellers must now move products through a variety of wholesalers to reach the inner city, suburbs, and rural areas. The multiple channel has become normal because of the variety of retailers that can be reached by a single manufacturer or wholesaler.

Market Size

Both market demand and sales volume have an impact on the selection of a channel of distribution.[6] Other things being equal, the greater the number of potential customers the greater is the tendency to use a shorter channel of distribution. Markets with smaller potential tend to increase the chance of using longer channels. More potential sales mean that the

[6] Fabian Lenden, "Consumer Markets: Families by Age, 1: Characteristics," *A Graphic Guide to Consumer Markets Monthly Supplement,* National Industrial Conference Board, (April, 1964).

opportunity exists to spread sales over more units of output.[7] Business often tends to use the channel that reflects the ultimate size of the market rather than its actual size. Thus, it is sometimes feasible to use a short channel when the potential in a market is great even though sales volume may presently be low. For example, the sale of encyclopedias has historically been direct because the potential market is large but the product is difficult to sell.

The greater the sales volume, generally, the greater the temptation to use a short channel of distribution, and the smaller sales volume the greater the opportunity to use a long channel. A maker of pneumatic air tools sold its products direct to industrial users. Research demonstrated that in the southeastern part of the United States the market potential was not sufficient to support direct sales. The company then converted to use of industrial distributors in that part of the country and greatly increased profits. Very often large retail operations such as Sears, Ward's, Wanamaker's, Macy's and other similar stores can purchase convenience goods direct from the manufacturer because of the high sales volume these stores have. Seasonal sales also affect channel selection. If a product has high seasonal demand, it may be purchased direct during the peak of the season and purchased from wholesalers during the other months. Toys, lawn furniture, and some clothing are examples of merchandise that retailers purchase in this manner.

Customer Location

As a rule, the farther away from the seller customers are located, the greater the tendency to use a longer channel. Close proximity is conducive to direct sales, other things being equal. Besides these generalizations, the location of customers has some specific and individualistic influence on channel selection. We are all aware of how retail channel members had to adapt to the movement of consumers from the central city to the suburbs. The changes brought about by this movement are still going on. In the beginning the suburban centers had the advantage because they were new, coordinated, and only competed with a downtown area. However, as more centers develop, they begin to compete with each other. Meanwhile, the downtown areas are starting to modernize. The eventual outcome of these changes is still in doubt.

The concentration of minority groups and low income groups in the central core of the cities of our nation has created special channel problems there. The better quality department stores and specialty shops are beginning to vacate the central city for the more affluent suburbs. Thus, retail members of the channel are adjusting to the location of the market.

[7] Ernest Dale, "The Changing Channels of Distribution: Lower Costs, New Freedom on Consumers," *Printers' Ink* (July 11, 1958), pp. 21–27.

Rural markets have always created special channel problems because of their sparse customer population. The dual channel where the seller sells direct to large retailers or chains in the city and sells through manufacturers or selling agents or uses wholesalers to reach the smaller rural markets is an example of how the channel accommodates the market. The location of the market also affects the channel for individual products. Grits have never been sold in quantity in the North, but this item is a big seller in the South. Obviously, the channel for winter clothing also differs because of the climatic differences between the areas.

Market Concentration

The concentration of customers is also important to channel selection. Generally, the more scattered the market, other things being equal, the greater the tendency to use a longer channel. Scattered markets increase the cost of travel and reduce the number of calls a salesman can make in a given period of time. Thus, the cost of each call is increased. The tendency is to leave such scattered markets to the wholesaler who can spread cost over many different products rather than just a limited line. One reason a manufacturer uses agents is that they are well suited to reach scattered markets since they sell more than one line of products.

PRODUCT CONSIDERATIONS OF CHANNEL SELECTION

There is a direct correlation between the type of product and the type of market. After all, specific products are differentiated in such a way as to appeal to specific markets. Therefore, we must consider the effects of products on channel adoption, modification, and creation.

Type of Products

The product can have a varied effect on channel selection, but it is always important. Generally speaking, products that are bulky or perishable, have high unit value, involve fashion, or require service tend to move through shorter channels. That is, convenience goods tend toward long channels while shopping and specialty goods tend toward short channels. Staple groceries tend to flow to market through a long channel using brokers or wholesalers. However, if the product is perishable, such as fresh fruits and vegetables, the channel tends to be shorter. Diamonds, with a high unit value, tend to move directly to the retailer. Specially made or bulky industrial goods such as machine tools and special stamping or cutting equipment, tend to follow direct channels. Shopping goods or products with an element of high fashion tend to use short channels. Examples can be found in fashion clothing, watches, and shoes. These products are perishable in much the same way as products that physically deteriorate. Of course, a management may improve its competitive position by being a non-conformist in distribution. Maytag has for years depended heavily on private brand appliances sold directly to large department stores. Several makers of cookware sell door-to-door instead of through the traditional wholesalers.

Order Size

Where the size of the order is large, there are some significant savings possible between the manufacturer or seller and buyer. First, variable costs are affected and can be reduced by order size. Large orders make it possible for the owner of goods to take advantage of carload rates from the railroad, rates which are generally lower. Second, large order size from buyers makes it possible for the seller to employ larger cartons which are cheaper to produce since carton suppliers also provide quantity discounts. The use of large cartons by the seller makes goods easier to handle and store, thereby increasing the seller's efficiency. Third, larger orders also provide the manufacturer savings in order processing. A single order of 100 gross transistors requires less processing than 4 orders of 25 gross each. Thus there are savings in secretarial time as well as in wear and tear on the equipment. Besides, the larger order necessitates fewer supplies and uitlizes less management time.

Not only are variable shipper costs reduced by large order size, but fixed costs are spread over more units which makes unit cost lower. The manufacturer may be willing to pass on some of these savings to the retailer, thus encouraging the short channel. Furthermore, some of the advantages of large orders that reduce cost for the shipper also reduce cost for the buyer. This is particularly true of handling and processing costs. For these reasons, the tendency is to employ more direct channels when orders are large and longer channels when orders are small.

Because some savings from order size are internal to the firm and some are external, various types of channels affect the savings that result from order size. Figure 7–1 illustrates this concept. In example 1 we have the standard situation described above. The retailer is bypassing the wholesaler because of savings in transportation and processing cost. Example 2 shows a chain processing orders through a central office but shipping direct. There are savings in order processing but little in shipping. In example 3 the chain is processing both orders and transportations through the central office, effecting savings on both. In some ways example 3 is just like example 1 because the business is purchasing direct. The difference is that the chain has multi-unit retail outlets and must do some reprocessing internally.

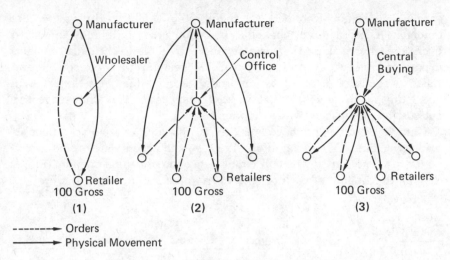

Fig. 7–1. Channel type and order size.

Examples 2 and 3 may be obtained in ways other than those described. A drop shipper or freight forwarder could be substituted for the central chain office in example 2. These middlemen would consolidate orders for independent retailers. Use of voluntary and cooperative wholesalers offers most of the advantages shown in example 3. The difference is again contractual rather than ownership-based.

Width of Product Line

The width of product line has a direct effect on the channel of distribution selected because it affects the quantity purchased.[8] Generally, the greater the variety of products handled, the greater the opportunity to use direct channels. This point assumes that many of the items of stock can be bought from a single supplier or manufacturer. Thus, even though individual items may be purchased in small quantity, the total order that results from combining many different items together may be sufficient to take advantage of the cost savings from buying quantity. Where this advantage of combination does not exist, the channel is likely to use the wholesaler.

Order Frequency

The frequency of orders is another important factor affecting the selection of marketing channels. Generally speaking, where no order size is

[8] Lee E. Preston and Arthur E. Schramm, Jr., "Dual Distribution and Its Impact on Marketing Organization," *California Management Review*, Vol. 8 (Winter, 1965), pp. 59–69.

specified, the more frequent and regular the purchase, the greater the tendency to use a direct channel. The total order is thereby increased over time, thus making the customer more valuable to the seller. It also makes possible good continuous working relations between buyer and seller. Regularity of orders is important because this helps the seller in predicting needed facilities, labor, equipment, etc. This knowledge can cut cost by eliminating wasted motion.

Cumulative discounts have been given by manufacturers on purchases made over time. The seller allows the buyer to accumulate orders over a period of time and gives a discount based on the total amount rather than on the amount of each order. In example 2 Figure 7–2, the Federal

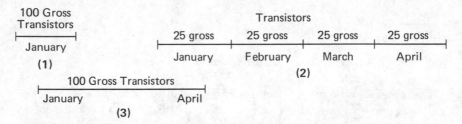

Fig. 7–2. Order frequency and channel size.

Trade Commission would frown on giving a discount on a quantity of 100 gross transistors when separate orders of 25 gross each were placed each month and shipped individually. In example 1 there is no problem with giving a quantity discount on 100 gross transistors. There would also be no problem if the business ordered 100 gross each month. Example 3 is also satisfactory because one order and delivery of 100 gross transistors covers the entire four month period. Even if the company cannot receive the cumulative quantity discount, a shorter channel may be indicated when orders are made frequently. Frequency often relates to urgency, and direct relations may be called for to maintain control over needed goods. It may also be that the total quantity is sufficient even without cumulative discounts to indicate a shorter channel.

The above generalizations must be considered with care. If purchase is frequent but in small quantities, a longer channel may be called for. If purchase is regular, say one time a year, but not frequent, a wholesaler channel may be more advantageous. If the purchase is non-regular but the quantity is sufficient when purchase is made, a direct channel may be indicated. As pointed out above, the effect of frequency and regularity of purchase is often dependent on other things, particularly width of lines and sales volume.

MEMBERSHIP CONSIDERATIONS OF CHANNEL SELECTION

There are important considerations revolving around the types of channel membership that affect adoption, modification, or creation. Every channel of distribution is a joint operation, and each of the members that make it up has some influence on that channel. Five membership considerations are important to channel selection: (1) member performance of functions, (2) assistance rendered to members, (3) cooperation expected from members, (4) speed of operations, and (5) need for multiple channels.

Performance of Functions

The selection of a channel of distribution is very much dependent on what each middleman is capable of accomplishing for the unit.[9] One cannot generalize on this factor except to say that the channels manager seeks members who perform necessary functions at reasonable cost. The capabilities of middlemen do vary considerably.[10] Direct sales provide control but place a great burden on the business' management.

The use of agent middlemen, such as the manufacturer's agent, selling agent, and purchasing agent, allows the channel manager to maintain reasonable control over operations, gain the use of a specialist, and keep cost of operations to a minimum. Frequently, of course, the seller must compete for the agent's time, employ effective incentives to get the agent to perform properly, and trust the judgment of an outsider on important business decisions. The seller must also recognize that agent middlemen specialize in one task such as buying or selling. They do not perform many of the normal functions expected of merchant middlemen.

If the channel's manager seeks the greatest functional performance by channel members, then the wholesaler may be the best choice. The full-service wholesaler performs nearly all expected functions, such as buying, selling, storing, breaking bulk, granting credit and delivery, taking telephone orders, etc. Limited-function wholesalers may not perform some specific function such as storage or the granting of credit, but they do typically provide most of the functions. However, when the channel coordinator employs any type of wholesaler in the channel, he gives up

9 William R. Davidson, "Changes In Distributive Institutions," *Journal of Marketing* (January, 1970), pp. 7–10.

10 Bert C. McCammon, Jr., Alton F. Doody, and William R. Davidson, "Emerging Patterns of Distribution," Paper presented to the National Association of Wholesalers, Annnal Meeting, Las Vegas, Nevada, January 15, 1969; Edwin H. Lewis, *Marketing Channels: Structure and Strategy* (New York: McGraw-Hill Book Co., Inc., 1968), pp. 126–29.

control over the performance of marketing functions. It is also difficult to get wholesalers to take on new products.

Assistance to Members

The amount and type of assistance that the channel coordinator expects to give to the channel members is an important consideration in channel selection. Assistance is more generally associated with a longer channel of distribution. Thus, the more assistance the seller is willing to give and the greater his ability to work with middlemen, the greater the opportunity to use a longer channel of distribution. For example, wholesalers can be induced to perform better for the manufacturer if the manufacturer provides such assistance as joint advertising, factory training of salesmen and servicemen, aid with accounting and inventory problems, and with pricing. Where good working relations cannot be maintained the seller is probably advised to use a shorter channel.

Cooperation From Members

The cooperation expected from channel members is as important to channel selection as the assistance given to these members by the manufacturer.[11] The seller of many types of convenience goods such as tooth brushes, nails, plastic dishes, and pocket books does not expect a lot of sales cooperation from middlemen. The products either must sell themselves, or the manufacturer assumes the total burden of direct consumer advertising. On the other hand, the distributor of power tools, desks, typewriters, and furniture expects close coordination of the sales effort with that of the middlemen. Many manufacturers expect their middlemen to extend credit to customers, install equipment, perform repairs, warrant merchandise, and make deliveries. Also important to channel selection is how well or efficiently the middlemen perform these tasks. If a clear understanding on the services is not forthcoming, the manufacturer is ill advised to use a channel where he is dependent on middlemen for their performance.

Speed of Operations

Speed is an essential factor in channel selection. The problem is that there are two types of speed in a channel, a fact seldom clarified in the literature which can lead to confusion. One type of speed has to do with the total time goods are in process in the channel—that is, the time it takes the goods to move through the channel from producer to consumer. This type of channel speed was discussed under types of products. The other

---

[11] Roger M. Peysom, "Selecting and Evaluating Distribution," *Business Policy Study*, No. 116 (New York: National Industrial Conference Board, 1965), p. 93.

concept of channel speed concerns the reaction time between two channel members or two successive stages in the channel. For example, it is true that a short channel direct from producer to retailer may keep the product in process for the shortest total length of time because of more rapid adjustment to market changes. Thus, this type of channel is preferred for fashion or other perishable goods. Generally, it takes a long total time to move goods through wholesalers, but if a retailer wishes to obtain a convenience product, a product in regular use, or a fill-in order, he can often call his local wholesaler on Thursday and have the goods delivered on Friday. This speed of delivery for staple items cannot be accomplished if the retailer has to buy direct from the manufacturer who may be located two thousand miles away. An agent, because he is an expert in markets, may be able to interpret a market trend long before a full-service wholesaler. The wholesaler, on the other hand, may be very sensitive to competitive conditions. It is obvious that both concepts of channel speed are important for channel selection.

Need for Multiple Channels

Channel selection must take into consideration the diverse nature of the seller's manufacturing or distributing operations. It was pointed out earlier that the normal channel is a multiple channel. Thus, the choice for most manufacturers is not which channel to select, but which combination of channels is best suited for the business. It is often true that the manufacturer makes and sells types of products that require different channels. In the appliance industry, for example, major appliances and small appliances are both sold by franchised agencies, department stores, and discount houses. However, small appliances are also sold by hardware stores, drug stores, and variety stores that do not generally handle large appliances. A manufacturer of motors in the industrial market may need different channels to reach such industries as shipbuilding, the aircraft industry, appliance fabricators, builders of road building equipment, etc.

Multiple channels may also be necessary because of the type of customer the manufacturer sells to. Sellers of such items as cooking utensils, hardware, television and associated products, and office paper typically sell direct to large buyers, but sell through wholesalers to the small buyers.

MANAGEMENT CONSIDERATIONS

There are factors related to management of the enterprise that have an important bearing on the selection of marketing channels. The management considerations taken into account at this time are those that have a rather direct bearing either on the business organization or on the operation of the business.

Channel Objectives

There is nothing in the operation of a business enterprise that is more important than establishing clear, precise objectives to act as business guidelines for daily operations. It follows that no channel of distribution can be adequately selected unless it meets the test of the objectives set down by the channel coordinator.[12] The objectives that are important to channel selection relate to the degree of market exposure sought by the firm. Three types of market coverage objectives apply to channel selection. (1) *Intensive distribution* occurs when the firm attempts to get its product into the largest number of different types of firms and the largest number of firms of each type. Intensive distribution provides the firm with the largest possible market. (2) In *selective distribution*, the firm wants a large market but not necessarily the largest. The manufacturer wants to select his outlets to provide better quality performance. This selection may be made on the basis of cooperativeness, financial strength, progressiveness, future development possibilities, or sales ability. (3) In *exclusive distribution* the seller selects only one outlet in each market to sell his output. Exclusive distribution goes with the exclusive agency and provides the highest quality outlet but restricts the market coverage to some degree.

Generally, intensive and selective distribution tend to call for longer channels using wholesalers or agent middlemen. Exclusive distribution is more compatible with direct sales. It should be noted that if the entire market is local, the seller may be able to accomplish intensive distribution and do it with a direct channel. If the market is regional or national, this is more difficult to accomplish.

Available Channels

In selecting the trade channel, the manufacturer wants to make sure that he considers all the possible alternatives. Thus, once there has been a decision on the market and the coverage desired, the manufacturer should give careful attention to the types of channels available to serve this market. Available channels are typically the ones in use by competitors, but may include any known method of distribution. In the process of studying these channels the channel's manager must pay careful attention to the advantages and disadvantages of each type available. Information on competitive channels can often be gained by talking directly to the middlemen involved. It is entirely possible that one of the

[12] Baligh, *op. cit.*

existing channels is exactly what the manufacturer is seeking. It may also happen that the producer will want to do something different. In either case, the decision must be based on knowledge, not on guesswork. A careful analysis may show weaknesses in the present approach to the market that the seller may take advantage of with an entirely different type of channel.

Financial Requirements

The financial condition of the company plays an extremely important part in the selection of a channel, but this part is very often of a limiting nature.[13] Given unlimited finances, the business can have almost any type of channel that it desires, even an inefficient one. Finances place restrictions on the company's ability to select any channel. Generally, the greater the financial strength, the greater the opportunity to use a direct channel of distribution. The reason for this generalization is quite simple. It takes money to perform marketing functions. Every marketing activity has an associated cost, and the more direct the channel the greater the performance of marketing functions by the channel leader and the greater the cost of operations. The leader must have the financial strength to cover the cost of performing these functions. One of the primary reasons for using such agents as the manufacturer's agent is to reduce the cost of performing the buying or selling function. A business may prefer to sell direct but finds that it has to compromise on the use of agents because of financial considerations.

Financial limitations can show up in many ways because they affect the entire base of the business. A lack of finances may cause the firm to restrict its market, and the smaller market may cause the company to shift from wholesalers to its own sales force. Limited finances may cause a firm to restrict its product offering, thus having an effect on sales volume and the channel; they may also affect the ability to attract high quality management, and channel selection may suffer as a result.

Company Organization

Channel selection is affected by the organization of the business. An integrated firm has chosen to perform some functions itself, and has reduced the number of middlemen. A non-integrated firm delegates the performance of more activities to middlemen.[14] Businesses that are orga-

---

[13] Eugene W. Lambert, Jr., "Financial Considerations In Choosing a Marketing Channel," *Business Topics* (Winter, 1966), pp. 17–26. Lambert considers channel selection more of a financial decision than a marketing decision; Lewis, *op. cit.*, p. 126.

[14] Bert C. McCammon, Jr., and Albert D. Bates, "The Emergence and Growth of Contractually Integrated Channels In the American Economy," *Economic Growth and Competition In World Markets* (Chicago: American Marketing Association, 1965), pp. 496–515; Norman J. Gallop, "Manufacturer's Representatives or Company Salesmen," *Journal of Marketing*, Vol. 28 (April, 1964), pp. 62–63.

nized around separate product divisions where each is autonomous may come up with different types of channels. This fact may result either because of a lack of communications between divisions or because of special divisional problems that call for different channels. Research-oriented businesses may find that they have a rather continual pressure to develop channels because of the new or improved products coming from that research. DuPont is a case in point. This company has had to develop channels in the textile industry, munitions industry, sports fields, and automotive industry just to name a few. A business organized around the production process will have a different attitude toward channel selection than one organized around the marketing function.

Management Preference

There is no use denying that the preferences of the executive affect channel selection. Management preference pertains to the attitude and competence of management in taking the facts of the situation and making the proper decision.[15] Management preference is the result of training, experience, intelligence, and judgment. There is really no substitute for it. A management can have the best facts available and gain nothing unless it is capable of taking these facts and arriving at the correct decision. Nevertheless, it is impossible to generalize about the effect of management on channel selection. Two managers, equally competent, may take the same facts and arrive at different channels of distribution. We have already pointed out that there is no ideal channel, and likewise, there is no correct interpretation of some of the factors of channel selection already discussed. The simple truth is that these factors are capable of being interpreted in more than one way.

Sometimes management simply wants to use a particular channel of distribution, and there may be no sound basis for the decision. This type of unfounded decision is called management bias. One management may select a direct channel even though it is aware that financial considerations dictate the use of wholesalers. Another manager may have friends in the wholesale business and insist on selling through close friends even though they have a record of poor performance. It is very likely that the desires of management will triumph over any arguments for economy. How management perceives the risk of various alternatives enters into the decision.[16] In the final analysis, any company is going to do what its management wants to do. One simply hopes that what management wants to do has been carefully considered and is based on the facts in the situation and not on simple preference or bias. Thus, while management

[15] Thomas J. Murray, "Dual Distribution Is the Small Retailer," *Dun's Review and Modern Industry* (August, 1964).

[16] Louis P. Bucklin, "Postponement, Speculation, and the Structure of Distribution Channels," *Journal of Marketing Research* (February, 1965), pp. 26–31.

bias is not the most scientific way of selecting a channel, it certainly is an important consideration.

COMPETITIVE FACTORS AFFECTING CHANNEL SELECTION

Competition, another important consideration in the adoption, modification, and creation of marketing channels, is difficult to categorize. The effect of competition on channel selection is diverse. Some businesses attempt to cause competitive change, other businesses attempt to maintain the status quo, and still others are completely defensive in their competitive strategy.

When a business selects a channel of distribution it is establishing a policy, and every time a business sets a policy or takes a position it introduces some degree of rigidity into the organization. A policy prescribes the course of action to be used by the firm each time the situation covered by the policy is encountered. It is a fact of business life that a policy may be both a foundation for business success and an open invitation to competition. The establishment of policies invites competition in two ways. First, a business may duplicate a competitor's operation, but with the intention of performing more efficiently. The increased efficiency can provide a competitive advantage. Second, a business can grant the competitor his course of action and try instead to follow a different course of action. In this case competition is based on a differential advantage. Either procedure can be a successful competitive strategy.

In the automobile industry every competitor has decided to compete on the basis of the same type of channel. Competition becomes a question of who can develop the strongest system of dealers. On the other hand, Electrolux has chosen to sell door-to-door when most vacuum cleaner manufacturers sell through wholesalers or direct to retailers. While we cannot generalize on the effect of competition, we can say that competition must be carefully taken into account when selecting a channel. The following questions should be asked. How will competition react to the channel selected? What advantages do my competitors have in using the same channel or in using some different channel? What will be the reaction of middlemen? Who will my competitors be, given each possible channel I might select? Can I effectively meet competition?

COST AND PROFIT CONSIDERATIONS OF
CHANNEL SELECTION

Every business exists to serve customers at a profit. This fact is equally true in the industrial and the final household consumer markets. The act of service has an associated cost which the firm willingly incurs because of the anticipation of making a profit. A channel of distribution provides the service of assortment, development, and delivery, but there is an associate cost.

The costs associated with using different channels of distribution are not the same. Direct sales are typically more costly to the channel leader, whether the sales are to industrial users or final household consumers. Direct channels also typically increase cost to consumers. The channel coordinator must build his sales staff, provide for the storage of large amounts of products, develop delivery schedules, assume large credit and financial burdens, find means for understanding the market, and supply the several services required by customers. Of course, the offsetting advantage is speed. Sales to retailers shift part of these costs from the manufacturer to the retailer, but the channel is still costly. The exact cost depends on the type of retailers selected and their efficiency. Sales through wholesalers or industrial distributors generally provide the least costly channel to the manufacturer. The reason is that the wholesaler and retailer together assume an even greater burden of the storage, sales, financial, credit, and service operations of the manufacturer. Actual cost of the total channel is again a function of the type of middlemen and their efficiency. This entire discussion of cost is from the point of view of the manufacturer.

If cost were the only consideration for the manufacturer, the selection of a channel would be a simple matter. The manufacturer would simply choose to sell through the most efficient wholesalers and that would be the end of the matter. However, cost is not the only consideration. The profitability of the channel must also be considered. The appropriate channel is not necessarily the least costly one; it is the one that comes closest to achieving the firm's objectives including the revenue or profit objective. A channel that keeps cost low but does so by relinquishing a disproportionate revenue is not a good channel for the manufacturer. A more profitable channel may be one in which the manufacturer has more control over sales and distribution, or it may be a channel where the manufacturer has greater speed of delivery. Obviously, much depends on the efficiency with which the firms making up the channel perform marketing functions. One firm may have a more efficient sales force than another, and this firm may be able to bring in sufficient sales volume to offset the higher cost of selling.

FACTOR INTERACTION AND TIME

Limitations of language have made it necessary for us to discuss several considerations that affect channel selection separately. This method was used purely as a convenience and to aid the clarity of the presentation. The reader must be aware that in an actual business there is never a situation where only one factor affects channel selection.[17] There may be managers who consider only one factor, but there is always more than one factor at work. When this is true, there is an interaction among factors. No single factor discussed can stand alone, and there is often a conflict between individual factors that pulls the manager in different directions. In the final analysis, the channel selected will be a compromise between factors that influence the selection.

Let us take a look at the implications of the above statement. We generalized that the larger the order size the greater the opportunity to use a direct channel. The answer to channel selection is quite clear so long as we consider only this one factor. However, besides order size being large, suppose the market is scattered and the firm has limited finances. In the first instance the channel leader would be likely to use a short channel, but in the second the decision is not so clear. We also generalized that a seller with a wide product line would tend to use a short channel. This decision is not so clearly indicated if a wide-line seller sells mostly convenience goods, sells in small quantity, and is faced with competition that sells through wholesalers. Obviously, the channel decision is extremely difficult when dealing with several factors at one time. The manager must bring his best judgment to bear on the problem. He must rate the importance of each factor. In a sense, he must assign weight to the factors and figure the probabilities of one course of action as opposed to another; it often happens that one factor clearly dominates the others. For example, a firm with a weak financial position may use manufacturer's agents to distribute its product even though every other indicator pointed toward the use of the company's own sales force. The financial position may be such that the use of a sales force is just not a possible choice. The complexity of the decision increases with the number of factors involved, and channel selection becomes hazardous. It is safe to say that all the relevant factors should be considered as carefully as possible to reduce the chance of error.

Channel development is endless. Every time the channel manager induces a new retailer to handle his product, changes wholesalers, uses a broker for a special job, or negotiates a new arrangement with a channel member, the whole channel is changed. What happens in practice is that the manufacturer adopts the basic marketing channel, then throughout the life of the business that channel undergoes subtle change and modification. It is sometimes amazing even to company executives to look back at the changes that can occur over as short a period as ten years. Therefore, the factors that have been introduced in this section cannot

[17] Mallen, *op. cit.*

be considered and then forgotten. These factors, one at a time and in pairs, occur weekly and monthly over the entire life of the business.

QUESTIONS

1. What is an ideal marketing channel? Explain.
2. How do the services required by customers affect the channels that would be used?
3. Explain why markets with small potential would increase the length of marketing channels.
4. How do different types of products affect channel selection?
5. Illustrate how the size of an order affects channel decisions using the material in the text.
6. Compare the effect that one large order has on the channel as opposed to several small orders.
7. When may a manufacturer be forced to use multiple channels for distribution of his products?
8. Describe the three market coverage objectives and tell how they relate to channels of distribution.
9. How does competition affect the selection of channels of distribution?
10. Describe a channels system you would use to market a consumer good, shopping good, staple good, and convenience good.

PART III

MANAGEMENT OF CHANNEL OPERATIONS

The purpose of Part III is to discuss the major decisions associated with the performance of channel operations. Two principle operations—assortment development and logistics—are presented. The discussion begins with an explanation of assortments, the purchasing of goods necessary for assortments, and the pricing of the assortment. Next, the operation of logistics systems are explained along with an examination of the logistical decisions of the shipper. The overall purpose of Part III is to develop understanding of managing groups of products and then physical movement within the channel.

8

The Nature of Assortments

The team of institutions that comprises the marketing channel must have some activity or operation to perform. As the model of channel management shows, it is through the performance of specific operations that the channel accomplishes its goal of providing satisfaction to the market. These operations include the development of assortments of products and physical distribution. The channel must create combinations of products designed to satisfy some group of consumers, then physically place these products in the consumer's hands. All other activities performed within a channel, from designing its structure to providing leadership, relate directly or indirectly to the performance of these overall operations.

MEANING OF A PRODUCT

Products are the building blocks from which assortments are made. Therefore, it is essential that we begin our discussion with some clear understanding of products. The term *product* is defined as: *the benefits perceived by industrial or final consumers in the combination of physical goods with specific services.*

The first consideration in identifying a product is to distinguish it from goods. The term *goods* is typically restricted to mean some physical thing such as slab steel, copper, wire, machinery, furniture, appliances, shoes, etc. The term product has a broader meaning that not only includes the physical good but all the services that surround it. Thus, the furniture mentioned above is surrounded by such services as credit, delivery, advertising, personal selling, provision for parking, store lighting, display, etc. The product includes everything for which the industrial or final consumer pays. Buyers are not willing to pay for goods or services in which they observe no benefit.

Every single undertaking by a channel member has some cost connected with it. The industrial or final customer pays to be informed by advertising or personal selling; he pays for the convenience of parking and delivery; he pays for pleasant store surroundings; and he pays for the need for deferred payment. The final consumer may purchase a television—plus credit, delivery, and a pleasant store atmosphere. The price paid for the product could be less if some of these services were excluded, because price reflects the seller's total cost of production and/or distribution.

The second consideration in identifying a product is to distinguish the product sold from the customer benefit received. Products, in the form of goods and services, have no interest for either industrial or final customers per se. That is, it is not the collection of chassis, wire, tube, transistors, credit, or delivery that causes the customer to purchase the television. He purchases what the product can do, and we call this benefit or satisfaction. In the case of the television, the final customer may purchase the specific entertainment of the "Super Bowl" or "As the World Turns." The television may represent companionship after the spouse has retired or status among the owner's neighbors. The industrial buyer may purchase a particular type of television because of the opportunity to turn a profit through resale, to provide better customer service from a full line, or to provide some competitive differential advantage. In terms of customer sales it is always better for channel members to focus on the benefit their products have to offer than to push the physical goods themselves.

Product and Brand

It is not quite enough to define a product as perceived benefits. Every product can be perceived in both real and symbolic terms. The products' *real existence* is the observable benefits that result from the combination of goods and services. Services, such as credit and delivery, are intangible, but their real existence is a provable fact. The products' *symbolic existence* refers to anything that is used to stand for the perceived real product.

Brand is the most important symbol used to identify real products. A brand is any name, term, symbol, or design that identifies the product as being of one owner. Brand is a broad term used to refer to any means of product identification through symbolism. The *brand name* is a particular word or two that means the same thing as the product in the buyer's mind. Thus the brand name can be spoken, but it is not the same as a slogan—a group of words that identifies the product by some feature or characteristic. Take, for example, the Budweiser label. Everything on the label is a part of the brand. The name Budweiser or Bud are the brand names, and the phrase, "That Bud—that's beer," is a slogan.

The diagram below shows that there are two types of brands:

A. Manufacturer's brand ⎫ 1. Local recognition
B. Dealer (private) brand ⎬ 2. Regional recognition
                          ⎭ 3. National recognition

manufacturer's brands, which are identified with the maker, and dealer or private brand, which are identified with a middleman other than the maker. Any brand, like other marketing devices, can be classified by coverage into local, regional, or national brands. A *local brand* usually means one confined to a single state. *Regional brands* are those recognized in two to six states, and *national brands* are recognized throughout the continental United States. Either manufacturer's brands or dealer brands can be recognized locally, regionally, or nationally. For example, Sears Kenmore brand is a national dealer brand, and United States Steel is a national manufacturer's brand.

CONCEPT OF ASSORTMENTS

The term *assortment* has traditionally been associated in the marketing literature with physical goods. Alderson, one of the first to develop the concept, says:

An assortment is a collection of two or more types of goods which either complement each other directly or in total possess some degree of potency for future contingencies.[1]

This view of assortments is restrictive because the use of the term "goods" tends to de-emphasize service as a part of the product. Thus for our purposes, the term assortment is defined as: *the combination of similar and/or complementary products that, taken together, have some definite purpose for providing benefits to specific markets.*

Assortment refers to the product combination found within any identifiable organization of marketing. In this sense, the assortment is akin to the *product line.* It is the total line of products carried by a business unit.[2] Thus assortment can be meaningfully discussed for an individual firm, or as the result of several firms operating together within the channel. Assortments, like individual products, are benefit-related, and they exist to satisfy buyer wants. The assortment is a meaningful concept to

---

[1] Wroe Alderson, *Marketing Behavior and Executive Action* (Homewood, Ill.: Richard D. Irwin, Inc., 1957), p. 199.

[2] Harry L. Hansen, *Marketing,* 3rd ed., (Homewood, Ill.: Richard D. Irwin, Inc., 1967), pp. 460–62.

explain either business purchase patterns or final household purchase patterns. In other words, our definition does not restrict assortments to businesses. Households develop assortments when they combine the products necessary for meeting household needs. However, the attention of this book is restricted for the most part to business assortments.

Purpose of Assortments

It was noted in the definition that the overall purpose of assortments is to benefit specific markets. In order to accomplish this objective the assortment must be constructed to: (1) implement market exchange and (2) forestall competition. Exchange is a type of market interaction whereby buyers and sellers achieve satisfactions. Competition tends to be interaction that either takes place between firms at the same stage or between complete channels. The assortment must be so constructed that competitors cannot encroach on the market but exchange is facilitated.

Assortments Implement Exchange. *Exchange* is defined as the act whereby buyers trade money for the goods and services offered by businesses. Because it involves an interaction of supply and demand, exchange occurs across the market. The consumer has unique wants and desires. Likewise, the firm has unique abilities to provide products. The assortment is the common denominator that matches this heterogeneous demand to heterogeneous supply.[3]

In spite of the old wives' tales that there are always a winner and a loser in trade, the fact is that the assortment provides a basis upon which both the seller and the buyer can benefit from trade. Furthermore, such dual benefit is normal in trade. The reason both parties can win—in fact, must win, if there is to be any exchange—is that each approaches the exchange from a different market perspective.

The seller's perspective is that he has products in large supply but a relative shortage of money. Thus he wants to get rid of the products in his assortment so that a profit can be turned and new inventory purchased. The buyer's perspective is that he has money but a relative shortage of needed products. Thus the buyer wants the product in order to obtain the benefit contained therein. Since both the buyer and seller can benefit from the exchange, trade is likely to occur. The consumer is satisfied by the physical and/or emotional benefits received, and the business is satisfied by profit, survival, market share, or some other designated goal. It follows that at the time of purchase both the buyer and the seller must feel that they are getting more than they are giving

---

[3] Philip Kotler, *Marketing Management*, 2nd ed. (Englewood Cliffs, N. J.: Prentice-Hall, Inc., 1972), p. 154. Kotler discusses different types of assortments as a basis for strategy.

up. It is not rational for a person to enter into exchange if he thinks he is getting less than he is giving up. Of course, the reader is reminded that we are talking about mental attitudes, not actuality. Either the consumer or the business may decide at some time after the trade that they made a bad bargain. New information may be found, or the product may be discovered at a lower price. This fact is beside the point. At the moment of exchange each side must *feel* that it is benefiting.

Assortments Forestall Competition.   Whereas exchange occurs across the market, much competition occurs between firms at the same level in the channel. Since each business has unique abilities in the form of management talent, physical plant, location, suppliers, equipment, employees, and finances, it develops heterogeneous assortments. Those individualistic assortments have been given the name *product differentiation*. Product differentiation may be based on variation in the physical goods like packaging, branding, product quality, flavor, etc., or it may be some variation in the services of promotion, personal selling, delivery, credit, etc.[4] It is true that the assortment of every business is differentiated to some degree, and the variations that exist form the basis for most competitive advantages or disadvantages. If the physical goods are similar, firms compete on the basis of some difference in price or service. If services are similar, firms compete on the basis of differences in price or physical goods. Even as they compete, all competitors are attempting to provide the best differentiated assortment designed to satisfy a particular market segment.

Assortment Utility

The understanding of assortments is central to any discussion of marketing channels, because in meeting its market and competitive purpose, the assortment creates marketing utility.[5] *Assortment utility* is defined as the satisfaction derived from differential choice in the market place. Before the concept of assortments, any change in the goods was considered completely the prerogative of manufacturing. Marketing could only distribute *goods* (time and place utility) and change the ownership of *goods* (possession utility). The existence of goods was always a precondition to the creation of marketing utility. Only manufacturers could affect the satisfaction contained in the goods, and this effect always involved a specific change in the form of the good itself.

In fact, marketing does affect the form of the goods. Although marketing cannot change the physical form of the goods, it can change physical

---

[4] Irving S. White, "New Product Differentiation: Physical and Symbolic Dimensions," *Marketing In A Changing World,* Bernard A. Morin, ed. (Chicago: American Marketing Association, 1969), pp. 99–103.

[5] Alderson, *op. cit.,* pp. 198–99.

goods into products by combining individual physical goods with other goods or with specific services.[6] Marketing creates products as surely as manufacturing creates physical goods. A dress is a physical good, but a dress in combination with a handbag, scarf, and hat is an entirely different product known as an ensemble. No manufacturing is involved in the creation of the latter assortment. Note also that while assortment utility makes use of transportation and storage, it is not simply in the sense of movement and storage. Assortment utility involves how goods are moved and stored in combination. Thus, assortment utility includes the way in which goods and services are structured. A single good transported creates time utility. A single good stored creates place utility. Several individual goods moved, stored, and structured into a rational combination create the utility of differential choice. This is not the same thing at all as simple movement or storage. Thus, assortment utility involves all the activities and decisions related to structuring combinations of goods. It provides infinite choice among products available for consumption and it recognizes the satisfaction derived from: (1) more suitable products, (2) multiple purchases at a single location, (3) variety in purchase and use, and (4) shopping and comparing.

ASSORTMENT CREATION AS A CHANNEL ACTIVITY

It is difficult to proceed very far into the discussion of assortments without coming to grips with the effect of the channel on their creation. There are three specific dimensions to assortment creation in channels. First, there is the dimension of the *individual firm assortment*. This assortment dimension is limited to the specific products handled by an individual business, and it reflects that member's interpretation of its market. Second, there is the dimension of *channel interaction*. The final assortment achieves results from the contact that each channel member has with other institutions. The individual firm's assortment becomes modified as a result of this contact. Third, there is the dimension of *consumer reaction*. Assortments are developed for consumers, and the final test of the assortment is how well it meets customer needs. These three dimensions of assortment creation are the subject of this section.

Individual Firm Assortments

Ultimate control over assortment creation rests with the individual channel member because of the necessity to specialize. There is no manufacturer, wholesaler, retailer, or agent sufficiently large, financially

---

[6] Louis W. Stern and J. W. Brown, "Distribution Channels: A Social Systems Approach," *Distribution Channels: Behavioral Dimensions,* Louis W. Stern, ed. (Boston: Houghton Mifflin Co., 1969), p. 7.

powerful enough, or possessing sufficient plant and equipment to produce and distribute everything that final household consumers want for every instance of time. As a result, it becomes necessary for each channel member to take its place alongside other similar and dissimilar institutions, each specializing according to the number and combinations of goods and services handled. The difference between individual firm assortments lies in the degree of specialization of products.

Assortments for Mass and Segmented Markets. The individual firm assembles its assortment in response to the market.[7] Sometimes major markets are sufficiently homogeneous so that a single homogeneous product satisfies everyone. Such products have mass market appeal. Trim fingernail clippers and Chapstick are examples of products that appeal to mass markets. Where market segments exist, the problem of assortment development is complicated. An example can illustrate the problem of dealing with segmented markets.

Let us say that a business recognizes the basic desire of a large number of consumers for clean floors and decides to produce a vacuum cleaner to satisfy this want. The firm designs a standard vacuum cleaner: it is average size, has an adequate motor, comes in black, and includes only the essential attachments. The vacuum cleaner is good quality and completitively priced. Thus it meets the basic needs of many consumers in the market, and sales are good. However, substantial numbers of customers do not like the standard model cleaner. They will purchase only if there is no adequate substitute. Some of these customers want a more powerful motor, some want colors, and still others want more attachments. Therefore, the seller begins to add these extras in different combinations to attract the different segments. He may make three motor sizes, four colors, and eight different combinations of attachments. The seller may end up with an assortment consisting of a standard model cleaner, an economy model, and a deluxe model. Furthermore, the different types of cleaners carry varying services. For example, the economy model may not have a warranty. The deluxe model may include lifetime free servicing. All three models may provide for credit. Of course, the more complex assortment is reflected in different prices for each cleaner.

Types of Sorts by Channel Levels. There are specific types of sorts conducted by individual channel members at each level of the channel of distribution. Each group of manufacturers, wholesalers, or retailers makes a specific contribution to the overall assortment structure. The

[7] Alan A. Roberts, "Applying the Strategy of Market Segmentation," *Business Horizons,* Vol. 4 (Fall, 1961), pp. 65–72; Theodore Levitt, "Management Myopia," *Innovations In Marketing: New Perspectives for Profit and Growth* (New York: McGraw-Hill Book Co., Inc., 1962), pp. 43–50, 54–71.

three types of sorts are: (1) the initial sort, (2) the intermediate sort, and (3) the final sort.

Manufacturers, or producers, execute the *initial sort*. The initial sort means that goods found heteogeneously scattered throughout the mines, farms, forests, air, and oceans must be organized into relatively homogeneous groups and processed. The initial sort is necessary because no single firm can produce everything needed by consumers. Thus the manufacturer makes a narrow range of products and adds the initial service package such as promotion, warranty, branding, and repair service.

Wholesalers and agent middlemen perform an *intermediate sort* in the channel. The output of specific goods from producers is combined in the intermediate sort with other products and differential groups of services. The general activities of the intermediate sort have often been referred to as breaking bulk. *Breaking bulk* is taking the large variety of products (usually in bulk containers) distributed by producers, sorting them out by market destination, breaking the quantity down into units normally used by retailers, and moving the goods closer to consumers. For example, the wholesaler may purchase work socks by the gross, combine them with work pants purchased by the gross, and redistribute both to retailers by the dozen.

The *final sort* occurs at the retail stage in the channel, and it creates the last combination of services to goods. It is the final sort that determines the specific number and types of choices of products available to households. Retailers, because there are so many different types, add even greater combinations of similar and complementary goods and services to the original product started through the channel by the manufacturer. It follows that the final sort is the most heterogeneous of all.

Channel Interaction Affects Assortments

The implication of the previous section is that no single firm can do more than initiate or add to the channel assortment. The final assortment that results at the retail level is a cooperative action on the part of the entire channel. This channel interaction is the second dimension of assortment creation previously mentioned.

Sorting Process in Channels. Although natural resources may be found in nature according to some divine plan, they are certainly not located according to the design of man. Natural resources are scattered indiscriminately in their natural state. They are not structured in any purposeful manner for the direct benefit of man. This completely unstructured state of the raw materials of business may be referred to as conglomerates.[8] A *conglomerate* is the exact opposite of an assortment. The concept of assortment creation concerns the manner in which conglomerates of raw materials are structured for the benefit of mankind. This creation of assortment through the channel involves a total process that consists of four aspects: (1) sorting out, (2) accumulation, (3) allocation, and (4) assorting. See Figure 8-1 for an illustration.

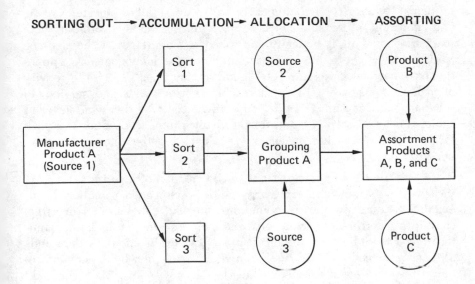

Fig. 8–1. The sorting process. *Source:* Donald Bowersox, Edward W. Smykay, and Bernard J. LaLonde, *Physical Distribution Management* (London: The Macmillan Co., 1969), p. 41.

Sorting out is the first step in the process. Sorting out occurs at the manufacturing stage in the channel and involves classifying the individual raw materials in natural conglomerates into relatively homogeneous groups necessary for the production of specific products. This operation adds structure to the resources from the mines, fields, forests, oceans, and atmosphere. It is necessary for each firm to concentrate production on a few relatively similar products. *Accumulation* is the building up of substantial quantities of the homogeneous supply of products sorted. There must be sufficient quantities of the goods for the market and to provide an inventory cushion. Accumulation provides these quantities. Accumulation, like sorting out, is accomplished at the

[8] Alderson, *op. cit.*, p. 200.

manufacturing stage in the channel, but it is itself a different type of activity.

Allocation involves breaking the accumulated products down into the smaller homogeneous amounts normally used by retailers. In the allocation stage goods are divided out of bulk cartons into smaller quantities and shipped. Accumulation and allocation should not be confused with storage. Each aspect of the process involves storage, but storage of a particular type. Accumulation is building up supplies during storage, and allocation is breaking down supplies during storage. Storage, as a marketing function, is typically performed at most stages of the channel.

Assorting is the operation that combines the homogeneous supplies that have been allocated into heterogeneous assortments. It is the activity of making a logically structured combination of goods and services to suit particular consumer wants. Assorting occurs at the retail level in the channel and involves putting the many products produced and allocated in relatively homogeneous types back together into heterogeneous groups.

Irreversible Channel Assortment. The creation of assortments within the channel is inevitable and irreversible.[9] Assortment creation is inevitable because product combinations, no matter how small or large, constitute assortments. An assortment includes one single item manufactured and sold direct to the consumer, and it also includes thousands of items produced and sold through a wide variety of wholesalers and retailers. To create and sell any product is to create an assortment. To add other products or services to the original does nothing more than complicate the existing assortment. Assortment creation is irreversible because, once an assortment comes into existence within the channel, you may change its nature by changing the combination of products, but you cannot make a non-assortment out of it. If products previously included are eliminated, the assortment is only restructured. The only way to eliminate the assortment is to completely eliminate the channel of distribution.

Consumer Reaction to Assortments

It has been said that assortments are created for customer satisfaction; this is the third dimension of assortment creation within channels. Customer satisfaction is difficult to achieve because assortments come into existence in anticipation of demand. This is, customers are not waiting at the end of the assembly line to immediately take the goods and services produced. In fact, goods and services are produced for storage in warehouses. Sales take place from these warehouses as the anticipated demand materializes.

[9] *Ibid.*, p. 198.

Three problems can arise because of anticipated demand. First, the institutions comprising the channel may sometimes produce the wrong products. Since firms are forecasting only what consumers want, the channel may supply Edsels when the market wants Fords or Chevrolets. Second, the channel members working together may supply the correct products but in the incorrect quantity. There may be too many shoes on the market forcing the prices down and not enough natural gas which forces rationing.

Third, the products supplied may not be exactly what the consumers want. This is perhaps one of the most common problems of mass production markets. Most people have had the feeling when purchasing that, "this product is not exactly what I had in mind, but it is the closest I'm going to find." All mass-produced goods have to be made for the average customer, and there is no such person. The result is that goods made for the average may not exactly suit any particular person. For example, most cars, private homes, and living room suites are designed for a family of five. The size of your toothbrush fits the average size mouth, and telephone booths are made for right-handed people. It follows that not everyone can find the exact fit, color, texture, size, price, etc., to suit his needs as he could if each product were tailor-made. The result is that most people must be satisfied with a little less than their ideal. However, the important point concerning assortments is that the variety of products in channel assortments is sufficient so that most consumers can find a preferred solution to their problems.

ASSORTMENT CREATION AS PRODUCT CLASSIFICATION

In the previous section, assortment creation was treated as an activity that occurs as a result of individual channel members functioning throughout the marketing channel. In another sense, the entire concept of assortment rests on the classification of products. We have already discussed the fact that products make up the assortment, and, in one sense, the assortment is a classification system through which these products are combined into a rational structure. There is no real conflict with these two positions. We could say that assortments are created as a result of individual channel members interacting with other channel members to classify their products. Closely related to the effect of the channel on assortment creation is the subject of product classification.

There is no general agreement among marketers on the best method of classifying products and this explains why product classification has received so much attention in the marketing literature in recent years. It also accounts for the wide variety of classification schemes presently used.

Fallacy of Two Markets—Two Classifications

Traditionally, consumer and industrial goods have been classified in distinctly different ways. The separate methods for identifying the two major types of products probably evolved from the separation of buyers into consumer and industrial markets. It was noted earlier that there are differences in these markets. The implication of this view is that there can be no comprehensive strategy designed to operate simultaneously in both industrial and consumer markets. The simple philosophy is: two markets, two products, two channels, and two strategies. This attitude by scholars denies reality. It is common practice in business to sell in both the consumer and industrial markets. It follows that the separate classification of products leaves much to be desired.

There is no question that differences exist between the consumer and industrial markets; however, there are equally important differences between segments within the consumer market and within the industrial market. Yet similar methods of sale and distribution are applied to these segments. The same reasoning can be applied between the consumer and industrial markets. As a matter of fact, when one begins to look upon the marketing channel as a team effort, one has to start thinking in terms of similarity in all things rather than differences. This fact may be one of the great contributions of the team approach to marketing channels.

Consumer Goods Classified by Method of Purchase

The method of classifying consumer goods most often used by marketers is based on method of purchase. It is so important that it has become traditional in marketing literature. The original classification was made by Melvin T. Copeland.[10] The classification by method of purchase divides products into dichotomous convenience and shopping types with an overlapping group called specialty goods. This method of classification is illustrated below.

1. Convenience goods
2. Shopping goods ———————⟶ 3. Specialty goods

Convenience goods are defined as products for which the probable gain from shopping and making comparisons is small compared to the time, effort, and mental discomfort involved in the search.[11] Consumers

---

[10] Melvin T. Copeland, "Relation of Consumer Buying Habits of Marketing Methods," *Harvard Business Review*, Vol. 1 (April, 1923), pp. 282–89.

[11] The definitions of convenience, shopping, and specialty goods are based on: Richard H. Holton, "The Distinction Between Convenience Goods, Shopping Goods, and Specialty Goods," *Journal of Marketing*, Vol. 23 (July, 1958), pp. 53–56.

buy convenience goods close to home, and they would rather go without temporarily than go to much trouble. Convenience goods are characterized as: (1) low in price, (2) standardized, (3) non-service oriented, (4) branded, (5) bought frequently, and (6) bought regularly. The consumer is typically aware of the attributes of the product before purchase as well as the attributes of most substitutes. Goods such as candy, staple groceries, work clothes, lawn rakes, cigarettes, and work shoes fall in the convenience category.

Shopping goods can be defined as products for which the probable gain from shopping and making comparisons is large compared to the time, effort, and mental discomfort involved in the search. Shopping goods are characterized as: (1) high in price, (2) non-standardized, (3) service oriented, and (4) bought infrequently. Brand may or may not be important for shopping goods, and they may or may not be purchased regularly. The consumer is quite willing to shop around comparing prices, services, and other features of shopping goods. As a matter of fact, one of the pleasures of purchasing this type of good for many people is the fun of shopping. Such goods as fashion clothing, automobiles, vacuum cleaners, furniture, watches, and appliances are typical shopping goods.

Specialty goods are distinguished by brand preferences. In all other respects this group may be exactly like either convenience or shopping goods. The only distinguishing factor is that the consumer will not willingly accept a substitute. For example, bread, a convenience good, becomes a specialty good when a customer prefers one brand over all others. An automobile, normally a shopping good, becomes a specialty good when the consumer insists on one brand.

Disadvantages With Method of Purchase Classes

There are four problems with the classification of consumer goods by method of purchase. First, the group of specialty goods is unhandy. It tends to negate both convenience and shopping goods because it fits into both groups. Second, the same product may be classified differently by two consumers. For example, an Arrow shirt may be a shopping good to one consumer and a specialty good to another. Third, the same consumer may classify a given product differently at different times. For example, an ash tray, bought for the purpose of putting out a cigarette, may be a convenience good. When the same consumer is seeking an ash tray to complement the general decor of her living room, it may become a shopping good. This consumer may spend hours looking for just the right color and shape ash tray. Fourth, the categories are often too broad for effective decision making. A product may have some attributes of a convenience good and some attributes of a shopping good. There is no room in the classification for such a product.

Other Consumer Classification Methods

There are four methods of classifying consumer goods besides method of purchase that are frequently used by marketers: (1) generic product type, (2) type of store, (3) elasticity of demand, and (4) nature of expenditure.

Generic type of product is a method of classifying consumer goods based on the individual nature of the item. Any product such as nails, eyeglasses, watches, toothpaste, or radios represents generic product types. This method is useful for identifying specific products, but it tends to be too unstructured to be very effective for channel decision making. Consumer product classification by type of store groups similar generic product types according to particular businesses. Examples of this method are hardware stores, dress shops, music stores, and shoe stores. The idea is that we expect to find certain types of products in a hardware store or a shoe store. We can identify these products by the name of the store. The assumption is that only a narrow line of relatively homogeneous products are sold by each store. This class is useful in identifying stores, and it is frequently used by businesses. However, it is not sufficiently distinctive for most channel decisions. The continued practice of scrambling merchandise lines makes the classification particularly difficult to use.

Elasticity of demand is the traditional economic way of classifying consumer goods. It divides products into three classes of demand: elastic goods, inelastic goods, and unitary elastic goods. A product has *elastic demand* when the change in quantity of product sold is greater than the change in price. A product has *inelastic demand* when the change in quantity sold is less than the change in price. *Unitary elasticity* occurs when the change is proportional. This method of classification has limited application in business price strategy, but it is also helpful in explaining how price operates in our economy. The problem is that the elasticity of a group of products is not always the same as the elasticity of a single product within the group. For example, the demand for food is inelastic, but the demand for individual food types such as steak or canned peas may be highly elastic.

Consumer goods classified by nature of expenditure refers to the broad groups of necessities and luxuries. Consumers use this classification all the time. When a husband says to his wife, "We cannot afford that mink coat," he implies that the coat is a luxury. The method of classification is frequently used in this informal manner. The difficulty with the classification is that one cannot easily decide what is a necessity and what is a luxury. One person's necessity is another person's luxury. One consumer may consider a dishwasher essential but to a ghetto family it is a gross luxury. The determination of necessity and luxury also varies from country to country. Most countries consider owning such items as refrigerators, lawn mowers, can openers, door bells, and electric toothbrushes, that Americans take for granted, as living in the lap of luxury.

Classification of Industrial Goods

Industrial goods are typically classified by one of four different methods: (1) type of operation, (2) industry, (3) stage of process, and (4) product features.[12] Each method is important in the industrial market. The choice of classification usually depends on the purpose to which the classification is applied.

First, there is the classification based on the type of operation. Under this class, products are grouped according to extractive industries, basic manufacturer, and fabricators. *Extractive industries* generally involve mining, *basic manufacturers* involve the production of semi-finished goods such as iron and steel, and *fabricators* simply put finished products together from finished or semi-finished goods. Second, there is the classification by industry. This group is self-explanatory and includes the steel, automobile, and aircraft industries. Third, industrial goods can be classified by stage in process into raw materials, semi-finished goods, and finished goods.

Fourth, and perhaps one of the more popular methods of classifying industrial goods, is by product features. This classification divides the goods into: (1) installations, (2) accessory goods, (3) raw materials, (4) parts, (5) supplies, and (6) services. The characteristics of these types are summarized below.[13]

1. *Installations*—These are capital goods. Bolted to the floor, installations become a part of the building. The goods are already finished goods. They are used in the production of other goods but do not enter into the final product. Installations are highly specialized and very expensive. They are often made to order. Machines that stamp out automobile body tops or bore engine blocks are examples of installations.
2. *Accessory equipment*—These goods are similar to installations except that they are more standardized, cost less, and are not typically bolted to the floor of the plant. They are generally finished goods used in the manufacture of other goods. Examples of accessory equipment are lathes, drill presses, and power saws. Each machine is capable of a variety of uses.
3. *Raw materials*—These are goods used in the production of finished goods or that are used up in the production process. They are

---

[12] Richard M. Hill, *Industrial Marketing*, 3rd ed. (Homewood, Ill.: Richard D. Irwin, Inc., 1967), Chapter 2. This author has an excellent discussion of industrial goods.

[13] *Ibid.*

typically staple goods, and they are low priced and bought in bulk. They are usually unfinished or semi-finished. Coal, iron ore, limestone, timber, raw vegetables and water are examples of raw materials.

4. *Parts*—This category includes semi-finished or finished goods that become part of the finished product or are necessary to the equipment used in manufacturing of the finished product. Parts may be used as original equipment or as replacement. Examples of parts are batteries, spark plugs, tires, motors, and ball bearings.

5. *Supplies*—These industrial goods are not directly associated with the production process, but are necessary to facilitate production. Such items as machine oil, paper, carbons, sweeping compounds, wiping rags, etc. are examples of supplies.

6. *Services*—This group includes all specialized talent purchased by the industrial firm. It includes laundry service, doctors, management consultants, advertising agencies, lawyers, contractors, etc.

There is much less criticism of the industrial classification than there is of the consumer classification. The reason may be because there is less inference about purchase behavior in the industrial classification. Nevertheless, the categories are broad, making analysis for decision making difficult. There is also the difficulty of deciding whether a particular good is an industrial good or a consumer good. For example, parts, supplies, and services are sold in both the consumer and industrial markets. The same product is at one time an industrial good and at another a consumer good. Furthermore, none of the classifications are compatible with the classification of consumer goods.

UNIVERSAL CLASSIFICATION OF PRODUCT TYPES

There is another method of classifying products referred to as the characteristics of goods method. This classification scheme is based on a common set of attributes possessed by all products whether industrial or final consumer. As we shall see, the method overcomes some of the problems of the traditional classification methods.

Classification by Characteristics of Goods

The characteristics of goods method of classifying goods was advanced by Leo Aspinwall.[14] Although Aspinwall uses the term goods in his concept, the meaning is the same as product. The characteristic of goods is simple in concept, but more difficult to administer. The basic thesis

---

[14] Leo V. Aspinwall, *Four Marketing Theories* (Boulder, Colorado: Bureau of Business Research, 1961). The presentation is the author's, based on Aspinwall's concept.

behind Aspinwall's classification is that there is a common group of characteristics possessed by every product. If these characteristics can be
identified, measured, and combined they provide a sound basis for typing
specific products. Although every product is different from every other
product in some ways, these differences are based on how the common
characteristics are combined in the product. In other words, every
product has the same characteristics but not in the same *amount*. The
differences in amount become the basis for classification.

Aspinwall selected five characteristics as the basis for his classification
method. To be selected the characteristic has to be common to every
good; measurable, at least relatively; and related to the other characteristics. The characteristics selected are: (1) replacement rates, (2) gross
margin, (3) adjustment, (4) time of consumption, and (5) searching
time. *Replacement rate* is defined as the frequency of purchase of a good.
An automobile may be bought each year, whereas groceries may be
bought weekly. *Gross margin* is the difference between the selling price
of a product and its cost price. This definition is in line with common
business usage. *Adjustment* is a term used to identify all the services and
extras added to a product to fit it to the needs of particular customers.
Adjustments may take the form of product variations or specific services
such as credit and delivery. *Time of consumption* is defined to mean the
exact time it takes to consume a given good. A restaurant meal may be
consumed in a matter of minutes while an automobile may last for years.
Searching time is the actual time physically spent in seeking the product.
It includes all travel, parking, and shopping, but not time spent at home
thinking about purchasing. Searching time and replacement rate may be
identical but not necessarily. In the case of the automobile, if a new one
is purchased as soon as the old one wears out, they would be identical.
On the other hand, one does not replace a bottle of aspirin immediately
after using the last one. One usually waits until the next headache to buy.

Use of the Color Continuum

The number of possible ways in which the five measured characteristics of goods can be combined is infinite, but it is very difficult to discuss
an infinite classifications scheme. It is also true that seldom in business
practice does management require an infinite classification of products.
It is more common for the firm to require an individualistic classification.
Therefore, a color continuum, such as the one illustrated in Figure 8–2,
is ideal for both purposes.

It is common knowledge that colors can be combined in infinite ways,
but they can also be grouped by major types such as red, orange, and
yellow. If more types are needed, each color such as red can be sub-
divided into light, medium, and dark or some other combination. Thus,

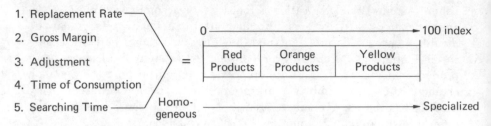

Fig. 8–2. Color continuum. *Source:* Adapted from Leo V. Aspinwall, *Four Marketing Theories* (Boulder, Colo.: Bureau of Business Research, 1961).

the use of a color continuum, in conjunction with the summation of the characteristics of goods, provides the business with as many classes of products as needed. Each firm can develop its own classification to meet particular needs.

The amount of space on the continuum devoted to each product varies. Red products take less space and yellow products take more. There is a reason for this arrangement. Red products tend to be more homogeneous; that is, the total scores from combining the measured characteristics of red products tend to be low and fall within a more narrow range of difference. Red goods are characterized as having high replacement rates with low margins and little service or extras. Buyers do not spend long periods consuming or searching for red products. Purchases can be put off.

Yellow products require more space on the scale because there is greater variety among these products. These are the specialized, non-standardized products of our society. Replacement rate is low, but margin is high. There is great variety both in the physical goods and services offered. The products generally last longer and customers spend considerable time shopping and comparing before purchase.

Orange products can occur in either of two ways. First, you have an orange product when the summation of all the characteristics gives a medium score on the continuum. Second, orange products may occur when a medium score results from a combination of low scores for some characteristics with high scores from other characteristics. In other words, the product has some of the characteristics of red products and some of yellow products and averages out as orange.

Measurement of Product Characteristics

The difficult task related to the classification of products by characteristics concerns measurement. Measurement can be a problem for any decision area within the channel, so it is not unusual to find the problem cropping up with the classification of products. The two problems with measurement are: (1) deciding on the type of measure to use, and (2) obtaining information.

Types of Measures.   Judgment of the executive is an important aspect of selecting measures for the individual product characteristics. Some typical types of measures are suggested by the characteristics themselves. Aspinwall does not describe specific types of measures; he does demonstrate that characteristics can be measured. Replacement rate may be measured by the number of times purchased or by product turnover figures. Gross margin is the difference in cost and selling price. It can be obtained either as a dollar figure or a percentage. Since selling price can be viewed as the accumulated margin from all previous stages, the selling price may even be used within a channel. Adjustment may be measured by a count of variations in either product, or services, or both. Time of consumption can be measured in terms of hours, days, weeks, months, or years.

Whatever measure is selected, it should be given careful consideration. For example, candy may take a higher percentage markup than an automobile, but the dollar markup of the automobile is much greater. In this case dollar margin is probably the better measure. Percentage may be appropriate for more similar products. Adjustment is another characteristic that is difficult to measure. Do you count only the store services such as credit and delivery or do you include all the extras such as models, styles, colors, sizes, advertising, credit, etc.? There is no simple answer to these questions.

Information Acquisition.   The problem of obtaining the information is equally difficult. Replacement rate, gross margin, and adjustment can often be obtained from internal records of the firm. However, it may be necessary to conduct surveys to determine time of consumption and searching time. Where possible, replacement rate and time of consumption can be combined in the same measure. Once obtained, the weighting of the characteristics should be considered. The author knows of no method for determining the relative importance of each characteristic. This means that in practice the factors are weighted equally.

Product Placement by Type

Replacement rate is the key characteristic of products. All other characteristics are related to replacement rate in an inverse manner. This must be considered when measuring the five characteristics. The problem is handled by reversing the scale for replacement rate as demonstrated in Figure 8–3. With the information available, a sample classification of automobiles is possible.

It remains only to average the five characteristics in order to classify an automobile as a red, orange, or yellow good. At this point, we encounter the final obstacle. Since we are adding unlike quantities, each characteristic must be reduced to a percentage. This step is accomplished by dividing the largest number on each scale by the figure for the char-

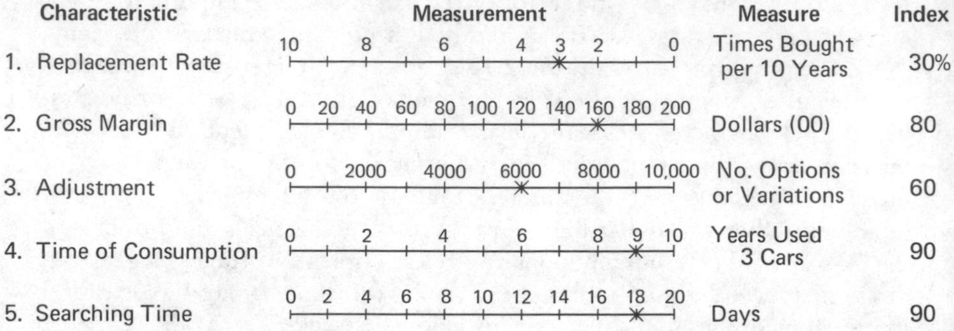

Characteristic	Measurement	Measure	Index
1. Replacement Rate	10 8 6 4 3 2 0 (mark at 3)	Times Bought per 10 Years	30%
2. Gross Margin	0 20 40 60 80 100 120 140 160 180 200 (mark near 170)	Dollars (00)	80
3. Adjustment	0 2000 4000 6000 8000 10,000 (mark near 6000)	No. Options or Variations	60
4. Time of Consumption	0 2 4 6 8 9 10 (mark near 9)	Years Used 3 Cars	90
5. Searching Time	0 2 4 6 8 10 12 14 16 18 20 (mark near 19)	Days	90

Fig. 8–3. Color continuum characteristics measured for automobiles. *Source:* Same as Fig. 8–2.

acteristics placement on the scale. Thus 3 divided by 10 gives a 30 per cent replacement rate for automobiles. The total of the 5 indices must be added and divided by 5 in order to obtain the single index for auto- biles. Figure 8–4 shows the classification of automobiles on the color continuum. Automobiles score 70 per cent. If we had also measured canned food, using a different set of values, this product might have scored only 20 per cent on the continuum. A comparison of the two products shows that canned food is a red good, and automobiles are yellow goods. Some other product might fall at a different place on the continuum.

Advantages and Disadvantages of the Method

The characteristics of goods classification is not a cure-all for all product typing. As with most concepts, there are certain advantages and disadvantages associated with the use of the characteristics of goods method of classifying products. However, it is the author's opinion that the advantages far outweigh the disadvantages.

Advantages of Characteristics of Goods. First, the characteristics of goods classification is based on a logically sound group of five characteristics. These characteristics do relate directly to the manner in which all types of goods are purchased. Second, the characteristics of goods provides a universal method of product classification. Only this method works for all types of products and services, and it can be applied both in the consumer and industrial market. This one advantage is sufficient to make the method extremely desirable to any channel manager. Third, the characteristics of goods method provides an infinite number of classes upon which the manager can base his judgment. No longer is

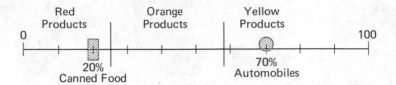

Fig. 8–4. Product placement on color continuum. *Source:* Same as Fig. 8–2.

the manager handicapped by the simple dichotomous convenience-shopping classification. The characteristics of goods method is a workable one that has sufficient variety to account for all the variations found in actual products. This advantage is nearly as important as the universality of the method. Fourth, the method can be applied in a very practical manner in the real world.

Disadvantages of Characteristics of Goods. While there are advantages to the characteristic of goods method, there are also disadvantages. First, there is the problem of measurement. Measures can be found, but it is not always easy. For example, how would one determine the adjustment applied to cigarettes? There is little service, but there are a large number of brands in several lengths, some with and some without filters and menthol. Another problem is the difficulty in measuring searching time and time of consumption without taking a sample. Samples are both tricky and costly. Second, there is some overlap of replacement rate, time of consumption, and searching time. These characteristics are different, but there is some similarity in each. As a result, there may be a degree of double counting among the characteristics. The general factor of search has more weight in the scheme than do adjustment and margin. Third, the classification does not work for all goods. For example, bread, a red good is sold direct because of the overriding influence of perishability. Furthermore, under the characteristics of goods classification, there is no equivalent to specialty goods. Of course, there is no reason why specialty goods cannot be related to the characteristics of goods as they now relate to method of purchase. Specialty goods are really a separate category that can be used with any classification scheme.

Parallel Systems Concept

Leo Aspinwall developed a companion theory to his classification of goods known as the parallel systems theory.[15] The basic idea is that the placement of the good along the color continuum makes possible the de-

[15] Leo W. Aspinwall, "Parallel Systems of Promotion and Distribution," *Cost and Profit Outlook* (October, 1956).

termination of the best method of distribution, and the method of promotion parallels the method of distribution. This concept provides the best basis for channel strategy available. Figure 8–5 is used as the basis for discussing the parallel systems theory.

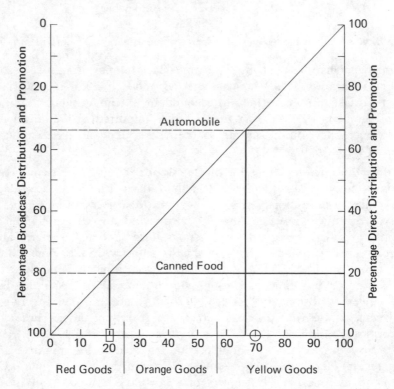

Fig. 8–5. Diagram of parallel systems theory. *Source:* Same as Fig. 8–2.

The diagram is based on the assumption that more direct distribution and promotion are associated with yellow goods. The horizontal line at the bottom of the scale is the color continuum on which the graph has been superimposed. Canned food and automobiles are used for illustration purposes because we have already been working with these products.

Let's say that the channel's manager wants to know how to distribute and promote automobiles. He draws a line from the product placement on the classification continuum vertically until it intersects the 45° line. A horizontal line is drawn from this point of intersection. The manager reads to the left and finds he should use broadcast (employing as many firms as possible) distribution thirty-five per cent of the time. By reading to the right the manager discovers that direct distribution is best sixty-five per cent of the time. Since our hypothetical automobile promotion parallels distribution, we observe that direct mail, handouts, and point-of-sale aids along with heavy doses of personal selling are appropriate for automobile sales. These methods of promotion should be used sixty-five per cent of the time with such mass promotion as radio, television, magazines, and newspapers used about thirty-five per cent. In practice, there is a little more emphasis placed on mass promotion than our hypothetical data would indicate.

Significance of Parallel Systems Theory

When channel strategy is based on the characteristics of goods a more sound basis for decision making is provided for several reasons. First, this method dispels the notion that a particular type of good uses a particular channel and requires one type of promotion. Only in the case of extreme yellow or extreme red goods is a single channel of distribution or a single type of promotion indicated. This finding is in line with actual practice. Seldom is any good distributed or promoted one hundred per cent by a single method. This finding is in line with our earlier discussion of the use of multiple channels. Second, strategy based on the classification of goods allows decision making with products that display mixed characteristics. With the convenience-shopping classification there is no room for products that do not conform to one of the other classes. Third, the universal method provides variety to the combinations that are possible. Of course, the percentages should not be taken literally. They are intended to reflect strong tendencies; their use must be tempered with judgment.

STRUCTURE OF ASSORTMENTS

The natural culmination of the classification of products is the creation of assortments within the firm and within the entire channel. The channel manager usually finds both his problems and his opportunities in the structure of his assortment. Therefore, the channel manager cannot know too much about assortment structure.

Attributes of Assortments

An assortment has three universal attributes: (1) purpose, (2) status of items, and (3) completeness. First, the total assortment and each element or individual item included, has a purpose. *Purpose* is the assortment's reason for being. For example, the assortment may have the purpose of satisfying consumers and providing profit for channel members. Therefore, each product must make a contribution to this purpose, or it has no place in the assortment. The management decisions that necessitate adding and dropping products from the line are found in this characteristic. An individual product may be fine for customers but not included in the line because it is not profitable. It has been said that a light bulb can be produced to last a lifetime, but what company would invest in plant, equipment, or personnel to produce such a product at a reasonable price. Of course, managers make mistakes, and a given item may be temporarily included in the assortment that makes no real contribution to the overall purpose.

Second, the individual items that comprise the asortment have *status* in the sense of relative importance to the whole. In the assortment of women's clothing in a department store, dresses may rank above shoes in status, and shoes may rank above handbags. The status of a product in the firm's assortment is typically based on contribution. Firms do not devote much time to products that cannot deliver. High sales volume can compensate for a low margin as in grocery sales, or a high margin can compensate for low volume as in the sale of diamonds. Many grocery stores can operate on one half per cent net margin, whereas jewelry stores typically have a markup of over one hundred per cent on many items. The manager's decisions relating to upgrading turnover, deciding amounts to stock, and allocating promotion, etc., are based on consideration of the status of items in the assortment.

Third, any assortment may be open or closed in the sense of *completeness*.[16] An assortment is said to be *closed* when each needed item is present in the required amount, that is, the assortment is complete. An *open* assortment means item or items are missing. When an assortment is open, there is a need for the business to take some action. A missing product or service can be the stimulus causing the channel member to enter the market. It is characteristic of assortments that they strive for closure. The absence of closure typically shows up as a problem for some manager who must seek a solution. An open assortment is not a desired state, because it means that the firm is operating at reduced efficiency and may not be obtaining its objectives.

Assortment Structure

Assortment structure refers to the particular manner in which products and services are combined for a specific purpose. There may be great differences in the particular assortments handled by individual members of the marketing channel, but all assortments display three structural elements: width, variety, and depth.[17] The *width* of an assortment refers to the number of major types or categories of products carried. A manu-

[16] Alderson, *op. cit.*, p. 197.
[17] See: William R. Davidson and Alton F. Doody, *Retailing Management*, 4th ed., (New York: The Ronald Press Co., 1973); John W. Wingate and Joseph S. Friedlander,, *The Management of Retail Buying* (Englewood Cliffs, N.J.: Prentice-Hall, Inc., 1963), Chapter 6.

facturer may make only one major category of product such as motors, but a retail department store may have such major categories as housewares, women's clothing, men's clothing, children's clothing, furniture, hardware, appliances, and toys. *Variety* refers to the number of different types of products carried under each major product category. In the department store's appliance department there may be washers, dryers, vacuum cleaners, stoves, sinks, etc., and there may be several models of each type mentioned. The manufacturer of motors may also make a wide variety of motors from large to small, each having a different power rating. *Depth* refers to the number of each individual item carried. The depth of items constitutes the amount on hand for sale or use. Thus, the manufacturer may have an inventory of fifty of each type of motor. The department store may keep only three or four of each appliance in stock because of the ability to acquire replacements quickly from the warehouse.

Differences in Assortments

The differences in assortment structure can be demonstrated by use of the two assortment grids illustrated in Figure 8-6. It is difficult to demonstrate the combination of goods and services on the same table so the emphasis is on types of products. However, the reader is reminded that the types of products included already contain a great many services. Two manufacturers are used in the examples, but wholesalers or retailers can be just as easily substituted.[18]

The difference among assortments hinges on how the product characteristics are handled. No business can carry complete width, variety, and depth of products. If a firm wants greater width, it must typically sacrifice some variety, depth, or both. If a firm wants greater depth, it must typically sacrifice some variety, width, or both. In Figure 8-6, producer A and producer B have the same width of assortment, but producer B has restricted variety and increased depth. Still another appliance manufacturer could restrict his width by producing only major appliances. This manufacturer may then be able to have greater variety and depth than either producer A or B shown above. It follows that the management of assortment structure is a problem of balance between the three elements.

Some blank spaces were left in each illustrated assortment in Figure 8-6 because at any given time the seller may wish either to expand or contract his assortment. The blank space can also represent an "out condition" which signals the firm to enter the market. We must re-

---

[18] C. Glenn Walters and Gordon W. Paul, *Consumer Behavior* (Homewood, Ill.: Richard D. Irwin, Inc., 1970), Chapter 9. The authors discuss assortment structure for final consumers.

Assortment Grid 1 — Appliance Manufacturer A

Major Appliances		Minor Appliances	
Number of Items	Product Types	Number of Items	Product Types
1000	Stove	800	Mixer
1000	Refrigerator	1500	Iron
800	Washer	600	Fry Pan
800	Dryer	500	Can Opener
300	Vacuum cleaner	200	Hair Dryer
200	Freezer	100	Manicure Set
100	Dish Washer	1000	Clock
600	Oven	700	Blender

Assortment Grid 2 — Appliance Manufacturer B

Major Appliances		Minor Appliances	
Number of Items	Product Types	Number of Items	Product Types
2500	Stove	2000	Iron
3500	Refrigerator	1500	Mixer
2000	Washer	1200	Blender
1500	Dryer		

Fig. 8–6. Differences in product assortments.

member that an assortment is never static. Both the firm and the channel as a whole are continually adjusting and modifying their assortments as customers, competitors, employees, suppliers, and others place pressures on the organization. Each of the assortments illustrated is simple, but the reader must bear in mind that assortment complexity is relative. For example, each item listed under product type could be considered a major category (width) and the number of types and colors could then be representative of product variety, giving each specific style a depth of its own. Such a further division would greatly add to the complexity of the example, but even further divisions are possible in practice.

Importance of Service to Assortments

Grid 3 in Figure 8–7 can help to overcome the problem of demonstrating the combination of goods and services. Notice that the concept of width, variety, and depth can be applied to services in much the same way as demonstrated for products. The producer's assortment decision includes combinations of major and minor services. Major services are those that customers consider important or that have a significant cost

Assortment Grid 3 Services—Appliance Manufacturer A

	Product Width		Service Width	
Product Variety	Major Assortment Depth	Minor Assortment Depth	Major Service Types	Minor Service Types
Stove	1000	—	5 Warranty, repair, delivery, installation, credit	5 Returns, insurance, shopper information, complaints
Refrigerator	1000	—	5 Warranty, repair, delivery, installation, credit	5 Returns, insurance, shopper information, complaints
Mixer	—	800	3 Warranty, repair, credit	5 Returns, insurance, shopper information, complaints, wrapping
Iron	—	1500	2 Warranty, repair	5 Returns, shopper information, complaints, wrapping

Fig. 8–7. Combinations of services offered.

associated with their performance. Major services include: (1) warranty, (2) repairs, (3) delivery, (4) installation, (5) alterations, and (6) credit. Minor services are useful to customers but most customers can do without them and their cost is not great for the business. There are too many types of minor services to list, but some of the more important ones include: (1) return, (2) repair insurance, (3) shopper information, (4) complaints, and (5) wrapping.

As Figure 8–7 demonstrates, our appliance manufacturer offers most of the services mentioned. However, these services are offered in different combinations depending on the product involved. Some other producer or seller may not offer all the services shown. Thus, the inclusion of services to the assortment further complicates the structure. The particular combination is based on the judgment of the executive based on the particular types of products offered for sale.

QUESTIONS

1. What is an assortment? Discuss the purpose of assortments.
2. How does marketing create a product? How does assortment utility aid this process?
3. How does the sorting process work in channels? Trace a raw material through the process and discuss each step.
4. What is the two market, two classification fallacy? Explain.
5. Explain the classification of consumer goods by methods of purchase. What are the advantages and disadvantages?
6. List five examples of convenience goods and five examples of shopping goods. Illustrate how the knowledge of each class will help in the marketing of these goods.
7. Discuss what you consider to be the reasons for the different ways of classifying consumer and industrial goods.
8. Give a brief discussion of the classification of goods. How are goods measured under this concept and what is the significance of the color continuum?
9. Select a red good and a yellow good and classify it according to the characteristics of goods theory.
10. Explain the parallel systems theory. Relate this theory to the characteristics of goods. Take the two products you used in Question 9 and illustrate the manner of distribution and promotion.

9

Channel Purchasing
Decisions

Although all marketing planning begins with the wants of consumers, the development of specific tactics to satisfy these consumers is always founded in the product assortment. It is the product, individually or in combination, that is branded, priced, moved to market, serviced, promoted, and researched. Without a product to sell the business has nothing. Even in the area of operating results most activities center on the product. Such important channel efficiency concepts as cost, revenue, and profit are directly identified with specific products or product lines. Of course, the first decision is to provide for products to sell. This chapter deals with purchasing problems and decisions that are important to developing a channel product assortment.

DEFINITION OF PURCHASING

Purchasing is a basic component of assortment management because it brings order to individual and group product decision making. Purchasing can be defined as: *the process of acquiring, for a consideration, the products necessary to maintain a balanced product assortment and implement business objectives*. Purchasing is broader than ordering. Ordering implies the very restricted activity of requesting products, while purchasing includes all the pre-planning that precedes ordering combination of products and the follow-up that comes after. Purchasing and buying are used to mean the same thing. However, buying is an activity of final household consumers as well as business institutions. The general area of purchasing discussed in this chapter is limited to business buying. Thus, purchasing is understood to involve products bought either to become a part of some finished assortment or to be used up in the process of manufacturing or selling the finished product. Institutional purchasing such as that by governments, colleges, and non-profit agencies does fit within the meaning of purchasing as used in this chapter.

Procurement and purchasing are not defined to be the same thing. Procurement is a broader term than purchasing since it includes not only the buying of products but such activities as receiving goods, inspection, storage, salvage, scrap recovery, and inventory control. These activities are not included in purchasing as it is used here. This chapter focuses on the specific decisions that are made in acquiring products.

TYPES OF PURCHASE MANAGEMENT

That there is a close relationship between assortment development and purchasing management can be clearly demonstrated.[1] How product purchase decisions are made largely determines the type of assortment developed. There are two separate types of purchasing decisions that directly affect the assortment. They are: (1) assortment balance decisions and (2) product acquisition decisions. The two types of decisions are illustrated in Figure 9–1.

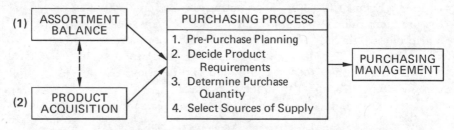

Fig. 9–1. Types of purchase management.

Assortment balance, as discussed earlier, involves manipulating the proportions of assortment width, variety, and depth.[2] *Product acquisition* is deciding on the amounts of specific types of products to buy. There is an obvious interaction between assortment balance and product acquisition shown in the illustration by the dotted line. Both assortment balance and product acquisition operate through the purchase process,

---

[1] Mark E. Stern, *Marketing Planning* (New York: McGraw-Hill Book Co., Inc., 1966), pp. 47–58. A good general discussion of product strategy.

[2] Ronald R. Gist, *Basic Retailing* (New York: John Wiley and Sons, Inc., 1971), Chapter 9.

a new concept that requires explanation. The *purchase process* is a rational decision sequence. While most marketers do not agree on the exact number of steps involved in this process, there is agreement on the broad decision areas that apply. Four steps to the purchase process are outlined for our purpose: (1) pre-purchase plans where purchase guidelines are established; (2) decide on product requirements, where needs and specifications are determined; (3) determine purchase quantity, where product amounts by type or brand are decided; and (4) select sources of supply, where suppliers are picked, negotiations conducted, and title passed.

Assortment balance decisions can be made that affect one or more of the structural factors without directly involving the purchase process. For example, the decision to add or drop a product, which concerns width or variety, may be made independently of any specific act of purchase. The action may be initiated by sales volume or profit consideration, and it may not even involve the purchasing officer. However, the purchase process is brought into play as soon as the balance decision is acted on. It may also happen that the assortment balance decision is made simultaneously with the act of purchasing. This is true of the purchasing officer, in the act of buying, who has decided to add a product just observed. The product acquisition decision always involved the purchase process. This chapter is designed to explain how the purchase process facilitates both the balance of assortments and product acquisition.

THE PURCHASE PROCESS IN CHANNELS

The purchase process underlies all assortment development decisions. It is particularly important to recognize that while the process is fundamentally the same in all buying situations, there are differences in how purchasing is accomplished by the individual channel members. It is the function of this section to explain to the reader the four steps in the purchase process and to contrast the differences in purchasing that exist between manufacturers, wholesalers, and retailers.

Purchase Process Summarized by Type of Middlemen

The steps in the purchase process are illustrated on Table 9–1 along with the activities involved, and the tools used by middlemen to accomplish the particular step in purchasing.[3] Several important points about

---

[3] See: John W. Wingate and Joseph S. Friedlander, *The Management of Retail Buying* (Englewood Cliffs, N.J.: Prentice-Hall, Inc., 1963); David A. Revzan, *Wholesaling in Marketing Organization* (New York: John Wiley and Sons, Inc., 1961), Chapter 12; Ralph S. Alexander, James S. Cross, and Richard M. Hill, *Industrial Marketing*, 3rd ed. (Homewood, Ill.: Richard D. Irwin, Inc., 1967), Chapter 4.

Table 9–1　The Purchase Process

Steps in the Purchase Process	Retailers	
	Activity Involved	Tools Used
1. Pre-purchase planning	Decide purchase routine Decide purchase responsibility Provide for purchase policy review	Executive judgment
2. Decide product requirements	Determine suitability to product line Estimate sales potential Select product type or brand	Executive judgment
	A. *Staple Products*	
3. Determine purchase quantity	Establish minimum and maximum inventory quantities Estimate rate of product usage Decide amount of cushion Figure reorder point Calculate amount to buy	Basic stock list (Mini-max System)
	B. *Fashion Products*	
	Estimate brand fashion trends Keep records of product staple aspects (size, color, type, price, vendor, etc.) Determine average inventory by staple aspects Select current styles in proportion to average inventory	Model stock plan
4. Select source of supply	Locate alternative sources Decide product suitability Agree on prices, terms conditions of sale Evaluate supplier operating practices Select source Transfer of title	Executive judgment

Among Channel Members

Manufacturers		Wholesaler
Activity Involved	Tools Used	Similar to
Decide purchase routine	Executive	Retailer
Decide purchase responsi-	judgment	and
bility		manu-
Provide for purchase		facturer
policy review		
Establish finished product	Value	Retailer
performance	Analysis	
Evaluate components to		.
provide performance		
Estimate cost and revenue		
Assign specifications for		
materials and product		
design		
Select products that meet		
specifications and cost		
requirements		
A. *Staple Products*		
Establish minimum and	Mini-max	Manufacturer
maximum inventory	system	
quantities		
Estimate rate of product		
usage		
Decide amount of cushion		
Figure reorder point		
Calculate amount to buy		
B. *Fashion Products*		
Not applicable		
Locate alternative sources	Vendor	Retailer
Decide product suitability	analysis	
Agree on prices, terms,		
conditions of sale		
Evaluate, supplier oper-		
ating practices		
Select source		
Transfer of title		

purchasing can be made using this table. First, it is not necessary for each middleman to perform each step with every purchase. For example, the first two steps need not be performed with routine purchases after the initial purchase decision. Second, it is generally true that retailers take a more informal approach to purchasing. They depend on executive judgment except where the determination of purchase quantity is concerned. Third, the activities performed in a given step may vary among institutions. Notice the difference in how retailers and manufacturers select product requirements. The retailer has a dual problem in deciding purchase quantity that the manufacturers do not have. Fourth, there may be differences in the intensity with which an institution performs an activity. Retailers approach pre-purchase planning much more casually than do manufacturers, either omitting some steps or performing them very informally. It is not often necessary for manufacturers to put into determining purchase quantity the effort retailers must exert.

Fifth, the methods used to accomplish the purpose of a particular step often vary by institution. Notice the differences in steps 2, 3, and 4. Sometimes the activities are the same and the methods the same. Sometimes the activities are the same but the methods are different. Sometimes the activities are different and the methods are different. Manufacturers actually have no activity completely comparable to that of the retailer's need to determine purchase quantity for fashion goods. Sixth, wholesalers are sometimes similar to the retailer and sometimes similar to the manufacturer in purchasing, but overall purchasing among wholesalers tends to be similar to retailers.

Pre-Purchase Plans

The previous summary of the purchase process is useful, but we need a more detailed understanding of each step. Thus, we begin with pre-purchase plans. Pre-purchase planning is the step where overall policies are established to guide the purchasing process.[4] As the illustration shows, guidelines must be established on purchase routines and responsibilities. The types and manner of review of purchasing decisions must also be established. Purchase routines include such policies as: which supplier to contact, how to treat suppliers, company attitude toward negotiation, how to handle problems and differences, what constitutes normal supplies of products, etc. The decision on purchase responsibility becomes important only if the product is not to be bought through the purchasing officer, or if some joint consideration is involved in the purchase. In these cases guidelines of responsibility must be established.

---

[4] Wingate and Friedlander, *op. cit.*, Chapter 1; Raymond R. Colton, *Industrial Purchasing* (Columbus, Ohio: Charles E. Merrill Books, Inc., 1962), Chapter 1.

One particularly important task of this stage is that of review. Because of the necessity for review, pre-purchase planning is typically a continual process. Feedback from the entire process is funneled into this stage in order to make any necessary adjustments in purchase policy. Most of pre-purchase planning is accomplished on the basis of executive judgment, and the activities and the methods are the same for all members of the marketing channel.

Decide Product Requirements

The selection of goods and services varies considerably among retailers, wholesalers, and manufacturers. For this reason the activities involved in deciding product requirements also vary. Manufacturers are seeking products to be further procesesd. They have to evaluate the nature and function of each material or product in relation to its contribution to the finished product as well as the potential of the finished product to sell. This evaluation necessitates consideration of finished product and component performance, estimates of cost, revenue, assignment of specifications, and selection of satisfactory products.

Wholesalers and retailers seek finished goods for the purpose of resale. These middlemen face only three major decisions: whether the product fits the assortment, whether it has the potential to sell, and which particular type or brand to choose. Since the decision for wholesalers and retailers is a specific product or brand choice, there is no need for these middlemen to establish specific product specifications. The brand name identifies the quality of the product.

The product line is seldom static for retailers and wholesalers who must constantly assess the composition of their assortments. As the tool for adjusting the product line, retailers and wholesalers use *executive judgment*. The activities involved are listed in Table 9–1. The retailer may hedge his decision by making his initial order small, and if the product does not measure up, by dropping it. If it does measure up, a large reorder is made immediately.

Manufacturers require a more formal means of deciding product requirements. The method used, *value analysis*, is the analysis of the total performance of the product and its market potential.[5] It may involve the testing of materials, components, services, cost, and sales potential of the product where possible performance ratings may be established. This method is used by manufacturers to establish, or to improve, product standards and more nearly fit the product to customer needs. Applicable either to the company's own products or to the products of prospective suppliers, value analysis is founded on the idea that the product should fit as nearly as possible the need for which it was designed. Materials

[5] Colton, *op. cit.*, Chapter 18.

that go into the product should not be of too high quality because this runs up the cost and restricts sales. On the other hand, materials should not be of too low quality as this can cause poor performance and customer dissatisfaction. In fact, value analysis is used to establish acceptable standards, and actual products are measured for closeness of fit to these standards.

Through value analysis a balance between cost and performance is sought that provides the greatest overall profit. Materials, design, and production methods are analyzed in order to find whether materials or processes can be eliminated or changed to reduce cost without hurting performance materially. Perhaps production shortcuts can be found that reduce cost without significantly reducing performance. The entire technique seeks to modify, simplify, substitute, or standardize to maintain or improve quality at lower cost. The market may also be analyzed to determine sales potential of the completed product.

Determine Purchase Quantity

The third step in the purchase process is the determination of the amount of the product to buy. This may be the first step for recurring purchases where pre-purchase plans and the decision on product requirements have already been settled. Certainly, it is the one step where the decision is more complex for retailers than for wholesalers or manufacturers. The reason for this fact is the importance of fashion merchandise to the retailers.

Purchase Quantity for Staples. Manufacturers, wholesalers, and retailers all use some variation of the same mini-max system to determine purchase quantity for staple items of inventory.[6] For retailers, this system is referred to as the *basic stock list*.[7] In all cases, it is used to purchase relatively standardized merchandise. Just as the name suggests, a *mini-max system* involves establishing minimum and maximum inventory quantities; estimating rate of product usage; deciding amount of cushion; figuring reorder point; and calculating amount to buy.

Figure 9–2 demonstrates the operation of a mini-max system. The *rate of usage* is the average amount of the product consumed in a specified period. *Delivery time* is the measured period from placement of the order to receipt of the product from the supplier. The *cushion* is the amount of goods above zero that is kept on hand to avoid running out. It allows for errors in judgment and timing. In a perfect system new

[6] G. Hodley and T. M. Whitin, *Analysis of Inventory Systems* (Englewood Cliffs, N.J.: Prentice-Hall, Inc., 1963), Chapter 4. This book contains a good mathematical explanation of order size; Arthur J. Schomer, "An Approach to Inventory Management," *New Jersey CPA* (Winter, 1965), pp. 17–21.

[7] Pearce C. Kelly and Norris B. Brisco, *Retailing*, 3rd ed. (Englewood Cliffs, N. J.: Prentice-Hall, Inc., 1957).

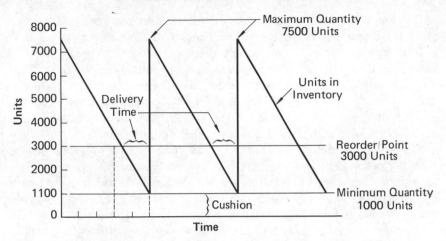

Fig. 9–2. Operation of the mini-max system. *Source:* Adapted from Arthur J. Schomer, "An Approach to Inventory Management," *New Jersey CPA* (Winter, 1965), pp. 17–21.

goods would arrive just as you run out so no cushion would be necessary. Since it costs money to maintain an inventory cushion, the firm would like to keep it as low as possible without running too great a risk of an "out condition" occurring frequently.

Let's say our company makes motors. The company uses approximately 1,000 armature brushes per week, and it takes two weeks for delivery. It has been decided that 7,500 brushes, or about four weeks' supply, constitute the maximum inventory. The company wants a cushion of 1,000 units because it may use more than the estimated amount some weeks or deliveries may be unusually slow. With these figures, it is determined that the purchasing officer automatically reorder armature brushes when the amount in inventory reaches 3,000 units. In the two weeks it takes to receive shipment, inventory drops to the minimum desired level of 1,000 units. Therefore, the order quantity is 6,500 units which, when added to the cushion of 1,000, provides the maximum inventory amount desired of 7,500 units.

Purchase Quantity for Fashion Products. The *model stock* is used by retailers for the purchase of fashion or perishable merchandise.[8] Since manufacturers and wholesalers do not typically sell fashion merchandise, the decision does not apply to them. A model stock can be defined as a representation, by selected staple classifications, of the average amount of stock carried. The model stock may be carried as physical units of stock or by dollar value. Although it is recognized that fashion is un-

[8] Wingate and Friedlander, *op. cit.*, pp. 168–70.

stable, there are aspects of even the most fashionable goods which vary little from one period to the next. These include size, supplier, basic colors, type of material, type of cut, price ranges, etc. The model stock is kept in terms of the proportions of these predictable elements. Thus, the purchasing officer is freed to devote his attention to the style changes that are not so easily forecast. In short, the purchaser knows the proportion of various sizes and colors he is going to buy, no matter which style he decides will be in fashion for the coming year.

To build a model stock is nothing more than to determine the proportion of stock normally carried by size, colors, type of material, etc. The steps in determining model stock are: (1) estimate broad fashion trends, (2) keep records of proportions of products by staple elements, (3) determine average inventory by staple aspects, and (4) select current styles in proportion to coverage inventory. For example, although a retailer does not know which dress styles will be in fashion next year, he does know enough about dresses in general to model his stock. The retailers knows that women buy about the same proportion of their wardrobe in: (1) dresses, suits, and skirts; (2) basic colors such as brown, black, blue, and white; and (3) specific sizes such as 10, 12, 14, and 16. A check of his past records can show what these proportions are, and the buyer can plan to purchase any style selected in these proportions. The selection of the particular type is done on the basis of executive judgment after carefully analyzing all available information on fashion trends.

Select Sources of Supply

The final step in the purchase process is the selection of the source of supply from among the alternatives available. Activities involved in this step are the same for all the members of the marketing channel: (1) locate alternative; (2) decide product suitability; (3) negotiate prices, terms, and conditions of sale; (4) evaluate supplier operations; (5) select source; and (6) transfer title. Sources are located on the basis of manufacturer catalogs, trade directories, resource files, salesmen calls, and advertisements. Agreement on prices, terms, and conditions of sale is a problem of negotiation. Terms and conditions of sale refer to all the factors surrounding the sale. Some important terms are discounts, delivery schedules, allowances for damaged merchandise, payment periods, and credit. Negotiation can involve nothing more than accepting the conditions set by the seller, but it often involves considerable haggling and the use of economic power. Manufacturers frequently select sources based on predetermined specifications and sealed bids. Some large retailers duplicate this method of selecting suppliers. The low bidder is typically chosen although there is no obligation to select the low bidder or any bid.

Retailer and Wholesaler Source Selection. Retailer investigation of sources is typically casual and informal, and the same statement can be made for wholesalers. Each depends primarily on past experience and executive judgment. A *resource file*, which lists previous suppliers and sometimes comments on the performance of various sellers, may be kept by large retailers and wholesalers. The buyer may get some information from competing salesmen. Retailers use supplier catalogs, telephone directories, and advertisements in trade journals to find sources of supply. Very often retailers and wholesalers make no investigation of sources. This is particularly tru of small middlemen. If the supplier's products are not satisfactory, the retailer drops the source.

Manufacturer Use of Vendor Analysis. Manufacturers employ *vendor analysis* to evaluate sources. Vendor analysis should not be confused with value analysis previously discussed. Vendor analysis is the formal investigation into all pertinent aspects of the source company's operations that are important to the purchasing company.[9] This analysis usually involves consideration of technical skill, financial ability, management competence, and service ability. The purchaser may use a combination of: (1) financial analysis and (2) physical investigation, including on-site inspection. Pertinent financial data can be obtained from such secondary sources as *Standards and Poor's*, or *Moody's Manual*. In some cases, the seller may furnish a financial statement. Some types of physical investigation can be made at the buyer's place of business. For example, product reliability, delivery, service, product performance and quality, and the handling of complaints can be obtained from inspecting physical goods or from the buyer's past experiences. On-site inspection is typically used to check on the supplier's management, facilities, and production techniques but it is time-consuming and costly, and some suppliers consider it an invasion of privacy. Not every supplier will cooperate with such inspection.

The purchaser frequently devises some type of rating system as a basis for comparing various vendors. These rating systems typically involve two factors. First, judgment is used to evaluate the intangibles such as management ability and service. The judgment can be assigned a numerical value perhaps from one to ten. Next, quantitative measures are found for price, product quality, and service. For example, price can be measured by performance standards, the number of defective items, or customer complaints. Delivery can be rated according to the number of times goods arrive on or ahead of schedule or by the number of late deliveries. Third, all the measures are combined into one composite evaluation for comparison purposes. This step involves addition of the values involved and dividing by the number of values. Direct compar-

[9] Alexander, Cross, and Hill, *op. cit.*, Chapter 5.

isons can then be made item by item or for the total. Item evaluation may be preferred because some factors may be more important to the decision than others.

PURCHASING IN NON-INTEGRATED CHANNELS

The manner in which the purchasing process applies within the channel varies with the type of channel under consideration. The location of purchase decision making, the amount of control, and the degree of cooperation all vary by type of channel. Variations occur between: (1) non-integrated channels and (2) integrated channels.

Purchase Control in Non-Integrated Channels

In non-integrated channels each member is responsible for buying the goods necessary to its own operation; that is, each business pursues its individual buying interest. There may be varying degrees of cooperation between independent members necessitated by the nature of buying, but there is no coordination of the purchasing process for the channel as a whole. The purchase process still applies, but is employed independently. Whatever control the channel leader has over purchasing by members is informal and depends heavily on persuasion. The purchase process in such a channel, however, may be quite efficient. Independence of action in changing sources of supply and negotiating for products may cause vendors to keep on their toes. The channel members are bound together by their common interest in a group of goods. Thus, the assortment of goods offered by the channel is a composite of individual decisions.

Responsibility by Type of Channel Member

The type of channel member determines the basic organization for purchasing in non-integrated channels. Small independent retailers concentrate all buying effort in the hands of one person, usually the owner or manager of the business. In larger, non-integrated retail stores, such as independent department stores and discount houses, prime purchasing responsibility is placed in the hands of the managers of the individual sales departments. For example, in the department store, each merchandise manager is responsible for purchasing the products sold in his department. Retailers feel this organization provides better coordination of buying and selling and establishes clear responsibility.

Independent manufacturers of all sizes typically concentrate purchasing in the hands of a purchasing agent. If specialization of the function is required, the purchasing agent is made the head of a purchasing department which may have several buyers. These *buyers* may be assigned purchase responsibility by operating divisions, specific customers, or categories of products. Manufacturers, unlike retailers, seldom combine sales and purchasing because of the vast difference between providing raw materials for production and the sales function. Manufacturers feel that each area requires special attention. In retail organizations both buying and selling involve the same product or brand, and there is less need for specialization.

The wholesaler in non-integrated channels has an organization for purchasing similar to both the manufacturer and the retailer. Wholesale buyers are similar to purchasing agents for manufacturers in that they are responsible for specific classes of merchandise and they do not have dual responsibility over sales. The wholesale buyer is similar to a retail buyer in that each is responsible for a particular category of goods and not for the entire purchasing function. Like retailers, wholesale buyers purchase both staple and perishable merchandise.

Responsibility With Purchase Importance

In non-integrated channels purchasing responsibility often varies according to the importance of the purchase decision. If this decision is sufficiently important it is taken away from the merchandise manager or purchasing agent and given special attention. For example, in some independent retail stores the purchase of fashion merchandise is often placed in the hands of a *fashion coordinator*. This person is responsible for purchasing fashion goods for the entire store regardless of departmental lines. The fashion coordinator may have buyers who are responsible for specific types of fashion products. The tendency in retail stores to separate buying and selling in the merchandise departments is another example. There is an increased use of buyers at retail who are responsible for purchasing specific categories of merchandise.

Responsibility by Nature of Purchase

The responsibility for purchasing in non-integrated channels varies with the nature of the purchase. For example, routine purchases are left in the hands of the purchasing agents, buyers, or department heads. However, purchases of a specialized nature may be handled by a committee. At the retail or wholesale level, decisions to purchase real estate or to locate new stores may be given to a committee. At the manufacturing level, decisions to build a new plant or to take on some new line of products requiring different materials are often placed in the hands of a committee. If the amount of purchase is large, say, building a new plant, the committee may consist of top management personnel. Once the decision is routinized, it may be turned back to the purchasing agent. The need for technical assistance affects purchasing. The purchasing agent may have basic responsibility for the buying decision, but he may draw on the knowledge of the engineering, finance, and design departments for recommendations where technical products are concerned.

PURCHASING IN INTEGRATED CHANNELS

In integrated channels, the organization of purchasing varies according to whether decision making is centralized or decentralized. Thus, both aspects of purchasing in integrated channels deserve attention.

Decentralized Buying

Even though all, or part, of the channel of distribution may be under one ownership, the management of various functions or entire operations may be decentralized. When all the business functions are decentralized the divisions are said to be autonomous. *Autonomy* means that each division is operated essentially as a separate business. The autonomy of divisions varies from almost complete to practically none. The management of the completely autonomous division is fully accountable for all cost and revenue aspects of the operation. The individual divisions within the same company may actively compete. Any ties with the parent organization are loose and frequently limited to financial matters or overall policy. There is little meddling into divisional operations. If the division does not meet expectations, the head is replaced and the new head is allowed to make his own decisions in line with overall corporate objectives. In completely automous divisions, the organization of purchasing is similar to that in the non-integrated channel. There is independence of action in purchasing and its placement depends on the type of division, purchase importance, and the nature of the purchase just as in the non-integrated channel.

In some integrated organizations autonomy is not complete. There is central office control that varies from reasonably strict to lenient. Purchasing, like any other function, is affected in direct proportion to the control applied to the division from above. Three examples can illustrate the manner of control and coordination. First, top management may decide that the purchasing division can purchase from any source with no obligation to buy from other company divisions. Second, management may decide that the purchasing division must give first priority to the company's own producing divisions, but can take a better deal outside the company if the internal division cannot meet the competition. Third, in some instances the purchasing division may be required to purchase the company's own products regardless of better deals offered by competition. In this case, the purchasing division can go outside the organization only when other company divisions cannot furnish needed goods.

The coordination and control of purchasing are always greater in integrated channels than in non-integrated ones because no matter how autonomous a division is, there is always recognition of possible influence from above.

Nature of Central Buying

The opposite of autonomy in integrated channels is centralization where decisions in the functional areas of the business are concentrated with top management. Divisional, or individual store managers, have little authority other than making routine operational decisions. *Central buying* is a concept that has been identified with the chain grocery store in retail trade.[10] In practice, the concept is just as important for manufacturers where the purchase decision is centralized in the main office of a multi-divisional business or branch operations. Central buying involves the concentration of purchasing responsibility at the home office with top management employees responsible for all the buying.[11] Typically, the central office is located in a city with a concentration of suppliers or raw materials.

Central buying is used primarily for staple merchandise; the method is simply too slow to have great importance for purchasing fashion goods. The need for extensive records alone complicates this method. There is a significant flow of information between individual units and the main office. The buyer located in the central office must be informed concerning all conditions affecting the divisional sales of individual units such as rates of sale, inventory on hand, product arrivals, products on order, and transfers among divisions. From this basic information, the headquarters buyer determines needs, selects sources, and places the order. The merchandise may be shipped from the manufacturer to the headquarters or direct to individual stores. Chain grocery stores and variety stores such as Kroger, A & P, Winn-Dixie, F. W. Woolworth Company, and W. T. Grant have long used central buying. Even department stores are using the method for staple goods. Now such firms as J. C. Penney and Sears utilize some central buying.

Central Buying by Store-Owned Offices

Central buying can be accomplished by means of store-owned offices in the central market, or by the use of resident buyers. Store-owned offices are discussed in this section.

There are three types of central buying offices owned by the retailers: (1) private offices, (2) associated offices, and (3) chain or syndicated

[10] Kelley and Brisco, *op. cit.*, pp. 244–47.
[11] Wingate and Friedlander, *op. cit.*, pp. 41–44.

offices. The *private office* is owned by a single retail store. The *associated office* is owned jointly by a group of independent retailers and its cost is based on a flat monthly fee, a per package fee, or a combination of both. The association among the retailers is based on a contract. The *chain office* is owned by a single organization, but the office does the purchasing for a large number of retail outlets. The cost of private offices and chain offices is the regular operating expense of the division to the company.

When store-owned central buying offices are employed there is co-ordination of the overall buying process for all segments of the channel. The central office offers the advantage of purchasing specialists. These specialists bring efficiency to the purchasing process by: (1) keeping abreast of product and market trends, (2) quickly adjusting for drops and adds, (3) allowing local buyers and merchandise managers to concentrate their efforts in sales, (4) facilitating bargain hunting, and (5) providing a thorough knowledge of available suppliers.

Some problems with the use of central buying include the following. The morale of local buyers can be lowered by taking away their purchase responsibility. It is not always easy for a buyer located hundreds of miles away to know the type of merchandise that is best for a given locale, a fact which can lead to poor assortments in some local stores. It is difficult to coordinate buying and selling, and there is also the problem of cost involved in keeping the central office. Of course, if all decisions are centralized, then buying is responsible for only a small part of the overall cost.

Central Buying by Resident Buyers

An alternative to the use of store-owned central offices is the use of agents. Agents used for buying in central markets are known as *resident buyers*, and they are classified according to the principals that they represent.[12] The two types of resident buyers are: (1) salaried, paid, or independent office and (2) the merchandise broker.[13]

The *salaried office* operates on a contractual basis and is paid by the retailer. It provides continual central market representation for the retailer, and the agent is paid a commission or fee or approximately .25 to .5 per cent of the retailer's sales. The contract typically runs for one year with renewal usually automatic. The salaried office is the most common type of resident buyer, but it is retained primarily by larger retailers such as department stores and discount houses.

The *merchandise broker* or manufacturer's representative is paid a

---

[12] *Ibid.*, p. 249.
[13] See: Edwin H. Lewis, *Marketing Channels: Structure and Strategy* (New York: McGraw-Hill Book Co., Inc., 1968), p. 15.

commission by the vendor of about .5 per cent of sales. The merchandise broker services smaller retailers who do not need continual central market representation. In most other respects this operation is similar to that of the salaried office. Merchandise brokers have no contractual basis for their relationship. Resident buyers provide most of the advantages of central buying but without the cost of maintaining an office with employees in the central market. Resident buyers also cut down on the cost of executives having to travel to central markets.

CHANNEL DECISION AFFECTING ASSORTMENT WIDTH

The second major type of purchasing decision lies in the areas of structural balance. There are several structural decisions that have been grouped under width, variety, and depth. In this section channel decisions affecting assortment width are discussed.

Types of Lines To Carry

The decision by each channel member concerning the number of different major product lines to handle is basic to the overall channel assortment. The factors that enter into the decision are the same whether made by the manufacturer or by other middlemen. These factors are customer requirements; financial strength; facilities needed to produce and/or warehouse; management attitude toward width; and profitability.[14] The larger number of different categories of products carried by each channel member increases purchase importance to the firm, because the buying of more individual types of products from more different types of sellers is involved.

In an integrated channel, the channel leader decides on the product line for all the members of the channel. The leader in such a channel tends to favor vested interest products. If the leader is a manufacturer, he may restrict the channel to the sale of his products. Purchases from other firms are restricted. This situation tends to result in a more narrow assortment for the channel. In a non-integrated channel each member makes his own decision as to the width of product line. Purchases in such channels are likely to show a wider range of individual member attitudes between narrow and wide lines, and the complexity of the assortment is likely to increase. Even so, it is normal to find in most channels that some members handle a wide line of products and some a narrow line. Basic to the inclusion of any product in the line is the opportunity to make a profit.

[14] Joel Dean, "Product-Line Policy," *Journal of Business,* Vol. 23 (October, 1950), pp. 248–58; Charles H. Kline, "The Strategy of Product Policy," *Harvard Business Review,* Vol. 33 (July–August, 1955), pp. 91–110.

Purchases Direct or From Wholesalers

The decision on whom to buy from has a direct bearing on the width of the channel assortment because intermediaries offer different combinations of types of goods. Any channel member has two choices relative to the source of his products. The middleman can purchase direct from the producer or he can purchase through the wholesaler or industrial distributor in the case of the industrial market.[15]

Conditions that tend to lead to purchase from wholesalers include: (1) when order size is small, (2) when goods have low unit value, (3) when goods are purchased frequently, (4) when goods are staple, (5) when filling in between major orders, (6) when in an "out" condition, (7) when making regular purchases, and (8) when transportation costs from the manufacturer are significant. Conditions that tend to lead to direct manufacturer purchases include: (1) when purchasing special or made to order goods; (2) when goods require significant service, installation, employee training; (3) when goods have a high margin; (4) when the manufacturer is local; (5) when order size is large; (6) when exclusive agency arrangements exist; and (7) when speed in getting goods to market is essential.

The decision on whom to purchase from is not difficult so long as the purchaser is dealing with one condition at a time. However, in practice this seldom happens. For example, the rule is that one buys staple, low-cost goods through the wholesaler. Nevertheless, if these staple goods happen to be bought in large quantity, such as coal or iron ore, one makes the purchase direct. How does one purchase specially made goods bought in small quantity and having a low margin? How does one purchase staple goods in large quantity when the margin is low and the purchase is not to be repeated?

The wholesaler offers more different types of goods in a single location because this institution brings together the output of several manufacturers. In order to obtain the same width of assortment as that supplied by the wholesaler, the channel members must make purchases from several different producers. Frequently, this action greatly increases the cost of obtaining a wide assortment. As the above discussion shows, the types of goods normally purchased through wholesalers are quite different from those purchased from the manufacturer, and the resulting assortments also differ. In practice, many products are bought both direct and through wholesalers.

CHANNEL DECISIONS AFFECTING ASSORTMENT VARIETY

The variety of products offered by members of the marketing channel flavor the final consumer assortment available as much as if not more

[15] Revzan, *op. cit.*, pp. 595–604.

than the width of assortment. Just as with width, each channel member has his own idea concerning the types of products or brands to carry under each major category. Product variety generates as many major purchasing decisions as any other aspect of the product assortment. These decisions can be grouped under three major headings: (1) additions and deletions, (2) concentration of purchases, and (3) make or buy decisions.

Product Additions and Deletions

Assortment variety is never a constant. A business may decide its product width and more or less stick with that decision for years. This is not so with variety—the individual products or brands that make up the categories change constantly.[16] In this section we investigate the circumstances that surround this change.

Need To Adjust Assortment Variety. Products go through a four-stage life cycle somewhat similar to living things. As Figure 9–3 demonstrates, products are born, they grow, they stabilize in maturity, and they

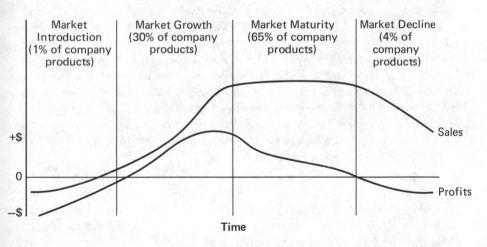

Fig. 9–3. Product life cycle.

decline and die. *Product introduction* is the period when the product is planned and placed on the market. Introduction normally includes preplanning and pilot plant stage. *Product growth* is the period of rapid sales and profit increase. Competition normally enters and becomes a problem toward the end of this stage. *Product maturity* is the period of

---

[16] Donald K. Clifford, Jr., "Leverage in the Product Life Cycle," *Dun's Review* (May, 1964).

market saturation with sales coming primarily from replacements, and everyone who wants one has one. Competition has stabilized typically at this stage. In this period sales may drift up or down. An upward drift may be accounted for by inducing customers to purchase more than one of the items. For example, we observe an upward drift in automobiles, refrigerators, and even homes. This may also result from normal population increases which expand the market. *Product decline* is the period of sales decrease. The decline may be due to more competitive products or to displacement by newer products. Products in the growth stage make the greatest contribution to profits. In fact, growth products frequently carry the remainder of the line. It is possible for a product in the decline stage to be rejuvenated by changing strategy, developing new markets, or modifying the product.

The single product life cycle is of little importance, because each product is a member of some assortment. In a firm's assortment, some products will be at each stage in the life cycle at a given point in time.[17] This is demonstrated in Figure 9–3 by showing the percentage of products at each stage for a hypothetical firm. We can identify a structure to the firm's assortment based on the product cycle percentages. Furthermore, the overall channel assortment has many products at each stage in the life cycle, just as the firm has. Therefore, the channel assortment shows a similar type of overall structure.

The fact that individual products and assortments have some products at each stage in the life cycle makes the addition to and deletion of products from the line a necessity. Adding growth products is necessary to insure profits and to replace declining products. Deletions are necessary to rid the assortment of unprofitable items and to keep the total investment in the line balanced as new products are added. The result is that assortments are constantly changing.

Product Adoptions. The addition of new products to the line should not be left to chance because this policy leads to an uncoordinated assortment.[18] Besides, a firm cannot continue to add new products indefinitely since the cost of physical goods is prohibitive. Estimates for new product failures range from as high as four out of five down to about seventeen per cent.[19] Therefore, the cost of poor product selection comes

[17] See: Charles H. Sevin, *Marketing Productivity Analysis* (New York: McGraw-Hill Book Co., Inc., 1965), pp. 55–57.

[18] Taylor W. Meloan, "New Products—Keys to Corporate Growth" (Chicago: Winter Conference of the American Marketing Association, 1960); David Novick, "What Do We Mean by Research and Development," *California Management Review* (Spring, 1960), pp. 9–14.

[19] Taylor W. Meloan, "New Products and Corporate Strategy," *Managerial Marketing, Perspectives and Viewpoints;* Eugene J. Kelley and William Lazer, eds. (Homewood, Ill.: Richard D. Irwin, Inc., 1967), p. 418; James W. Russell, "Developing New Products for Profit," *Management Review*, Vol. 47 (August, 1958), pp. 9–13ff.

high.[20] The adoption process illustrated in Figure 9–4 is recommended to assure that adequate attention is given to the selection of products. This process is essentially a narrowing of alternatives since only a few of the possible products discussed ever make it to market. The process works satisfactorily for manufacturers as well as wholesalers and retailers, but there are differences in methodology between institutions.

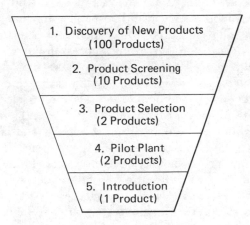

1. Discovery of New Products
(100 Products)

2. Product Screening
(10 Products)

3. Product Selection
(2 Products)

4. Pilot Plant
(2 Products)

5. Introduction
(1 Product)

Fig. 9–4. Product adoption process. *Source:* Adapted from H. Robert Dodge, *Industrial Marketing* (New York: McGraw-Hill Book Co., Inc., 1970), p. 168.

1. *The discovery of new products* for wholesalers and retailers involves finished products. These middlemen seldom need to take overt action at this stage because new products are thrust on them by salesmen, catalogs, advertisements, and competitor offerings. It is different for the manufacturer. His problem is to innovate better ways to satisfy customers and translate these ideas into products. The manufacturer makes use of all types of research facilities and a variety of people to generate new product ideas. It is common to employ regular brainstorming sessions using customers, workers, or managers for this purpose.

2. *Product screening* is a narrowing of alternatives generated by means of product evaluation. Retailers and wholesalers use informal methods of screening. A retailer or wholesaler may do no more than review the literature about the product, talk to a salesman, or observe the product's physical characteristics. Some analysis may be made of product turnover for products already in the line. This data can be used to discover weak products to replace, or as a measure against the estimated

[20] Richard C. Christian, "Increasing the Success Odds in Marketing New Products," *Journal of Marketing*, Vol. 25 (January, 1961), pp. 74–75.

sales volume of products that may be added.[21] Large retailers follow a policy of continually attempting to upgrade their turnover. They will add a product with a higher turnover sometimes, even if doing so means dropping a profitable product. Of course, the product added must be more profitable than the one dropped.

Product screening is more complex for the manufacturer. It may involve a complete system of value analysis where a study is made of raw materials, material sources, cost and revenue estimates, production feasibility, and potential markets. Many hours of research may be involved.[22] In any case, the narrowing process follows for all types of middlemen until a few relatively equal opportunity products are left.

3. *Product selection* is approximately the same for all institutions. Selection is based on the judgment of the selector, or selection committee, using all the data already made available. If several products of equal potential are involved, they may all be selected. If all are not selected, the judgment may be based on some minor preference. One fact is certain—the company goals should be considered. Products, even good ones, that do not fit in with the firm's profit, market, service, distribution and other objectives are not likely to succeed. Often the final choice narrows down to the product or products that fit these company goals.

4. *The pilot plant stage* is the point where the most likely products selected are given a thorough testing.[23] Some testing is done in screening, but this testing centers on the product itself. At the pilot plant stage it is the production and sale that are tested. For the retailer or wholesaler the step may simply involve placing the product on the shelf in a small trial quantity. It can also involve extensive test marketing. The manufacturer may have to build a complete miniature factory to work out the bugs of assembly-line operations and of distributing the product. The product could be rejected even at this late date if production is not possible at a reasonable cost, or if it cannot be made in sufficient quantity to justify its inclusion in the line.

5. *Product introduction* is the final stage of the adoption process. At this stage the product is introduced to the entire market. Thus, the final step of adoption is the first step of the product life cycle.

Deletion of Products. Where there is a conscious policy of adding products to the assortment, there must be a conscious policy of dropping products.[24] Any other conclusion would lead to a continually expanding

---

[21] The Adoption Process," *The Adoption of New Products: Process and Influence* (Ann Arbor, Michigan: Foundation for Research on Human Behavior, 1959), pp. 1–8.

[22] Lee Adler, "Time Log In New Product Development," *Journal of Marketing*, Vol. 30 (January, 1966), pp. 17–21.

[23] See: Edgar A. Pessemier, *New Product Decisions* (New York: McGraw-Hill Book Co., Inc., 1966), Chapters 4 and 5.

[24] R. S. Alexander, "The Death and Burial of 'Sick' Products," *Journal of Marketing*, Vol. 28 (April, 1964), pp. 1–7.

assortment with accompanying imbalance and prohibitive cost. The decision to drop products is easier than the decision to add products, because there is more historical data available on which to base the decision.[25] The decision to drop a product can occur: (1) when the product is losing money for the firm or (2) when a product can be added that either has a higher turnover with the same margin or a higher margin with the same turnover as some product presently in the line. In either case more profit results. Chain grocery stores, discount houses, and specialty wholesalers follow a policy of continually attempting to upgrade the turnover of the assortment.

In practice, the decision to drop a product is never automatic, even if the product is losing money. Before dropping a product that is losing money, four possible alternatives should be considered. First, an investigation should be made to determine how costs are allocated to the product. Cost allocation is an inexact business, and it may be that the product has too large a cost burden. Removal of some cost may cause the product to show a profit. Second, the product may not have been handled properly. The firm may keep it but change some policies relating to its production or sale. For example, product quality may be changed, price or margin could be altered, the product may be advertised more or differently, etc. Third, the firm may consider keeping the product and doing nothing. That is, it may continue to lose money. This is not necessarily a bad policy. Possibly it would be a good decision if the product is a part of a complete line, and if possessing a complete line is an important factor in the sale of all the products in the line.[26] In such a case the losses on the product may be written off as a type of promotion cost. Fourth, of course, is the decision to drop the product.

Concentration of Purchases

The decision to concentrate purchases with one or a few suppliers is as valid for wholesalers and retailers as it is for manufacturers. The voluntary and cooperative wholesaler requires members to concentrate purchases with the wholesaler. Retailers who are involved in exclusive agencies often concentrate purchases with one supplier. In private branding, the manufacturer often requires a concentration of purchases before agreeing to supply the private branded goods. Frequently, he purchases all raw materials from a single supplier. The advantages of concentrating purchases are: (1) assurance of supply, (2) good working relations, (3) favorable treatment, and (4) quantity discounts. The advantages of utilizing several suppliers include: (1) ability to shop for bargain prices, better quality merchandise, and favorable terms; (2)

[25] Sevin, *op. cit.*, pp. 59–62.
[26] Alexander, *op. cit.*

greater recognition from the supplier; (3) independence of action in all matters; and (4) no threat of having supply cut off. Either policy, for a given situation, can be quite correct.

Make or Buy Decisions

The decision on whether to make needed products or to purchase them from outside sources is a serious one, not confined just to manufacturers. In integrated channels of distribution this decision can affect the cost structure of the entire channel including the wholesaling and retailing operations. A company will probably make its own goods when: (1) it has excess plant capacity, (2) doing so is cheaper than buying, (3) sources of the material are not available, (4) it is necessary to control product quality, (5) management talent and labor are available, and (6) management prefers to produce.

The company will probably buy its materials when: (1) doing so is cheaper than producing, (2) the plant has no capacity to produce, (3) the seller's brand is important to the company's finished product, (4) the company must obtain fill-in orders or emergency goods, and (5) the company lacks the financial ability to produce. Considerable care should be taken in making the final decision. It is particularly difficult to reverse the decision to make your own products.

CHANNEL DECISIONS AFFECTING ASSORTMENT DEPTH

The depth of product lines carried by members affects the product assortment of the channel. How channel members individually and collectively view the amount of goods to carry partly determines the nature of the final assortment put together by that channel.

Amount To Purchase

The amount of each item to be purchased depends on a number of factors. First, there is the purchase philosophy which underlies all purchase decisions. It concerns whether management wants to keep complete stocks or limited stocks. Second, there is management's attitude toward the possibility of an out condition. Customers become angry when the firm runs out of merchandise, but to carry sufficient supplies to meet all contingencies is very costly. Most firms try to balance the chance of running out against the cost. Third, there is sales volume. Purchases cannot be separated from sales. Products that sell faster must be purchased in larger quantity. Slow sellers do not require large stocks. For many items middlemen attempt to determine the approximate rate of sale and use this figure to determine the quantity to purchase.

Fourth, there are seasonal considerations. Retailers and wholesalers, for example, purchase larger quantities at the beginning of a season and gradually decrease reorders as the season progresses and sales volume drops. Fifth, there is the reorder to consider. On new merchandise, it is sometimes better to order small quantities of several types, determine which is selling best, and reorder quickly and in quantity on this best seller. Sixth, there is the sale to consider. Some retailers and wholesalers order in large quantity specifically for the purpose of putting the merchandise on sale. Other middlemen reserve sales for season-end merchandise or to clear stocks.

Forward vs. Hand-to-Mouth Buying

The attitude taken by the purchasing agent toward forward buying is important to the depth of assortment. *Forward buying* means buying in larger quantity for longer periods into the future than normal; it is buying for long-range needs. *Hand-to-mouth buying* refers to purchases made for immediate short-run needs when the purchase involves smaller quantities than normal. The factors that influence forward buying are: (1) economic conditions, (2) attitude toward speculation, (3) stock piling, and (4) anticipated price changes.

The economic conditions revolve around the business cycle. As a general rule, middlemen use forward buying during inflationary periods because it provides a windfall advantage over competitors who purchase later at higher prices. Middlemen buy hand-to-mouth during depressed economic conditions because with prices falling they are at a disadvantage to competitors who purchase later.

Speculation is a policy that is used more by manufacturers than by wholesalers or retailers because manufacturers are more involved in the purchase of basic raw materials where prices may be very volatile. The purchase agent can speculate by using either forward buying or hand-to-mouth buying. Speculation is not determined by which method is employed or the amount of the purchase; rather it is a mental attitude, and its exists because of the reason for the purchase. If the buyer is acting to make money off the broad movements in the basic commodity price, there is speculation. In normal operations the seller attempts to make money from the sale of the finished product and not by anticipating price changes in the commodities that are used to produce that product. The purchasing agent can use hand-to-mouth buying to speculate if he feels that prices are going to drop. He will plan to stock up with large quantities of the lower-priced good. Forward buying is used to speculate when the purchasing agent feels that the price of commodities will rise.

Stock piling is closely related to speculation because one stock piles when forward buying. Stock piling need not involve speculation, however. The purchasing agent may decide to stock pile because of an impending labor strike, an expected shortage of materials, anticipated increases in production at a later date, or because the plant plans to begin producing a new product. Postponement of purchases may also constitute speculation if the postponement is based on an expected drop in market price. On the other hand, postponement for regular operating reasons, such as a slack sales period, is not speculation.

Long-Range Contracts

The type of contract entered into by the purchasing agent directly affects the amount of goods purchased. Most products are purchased on the basis of short-range contracts. Each order is a separate contract, and the company is not bound beyond execution of the one order. All types of middlemen enter into long-range contracts, but they are most commonly associated with manufacturers. Such contracts commit the buyer to a specific quantity of goods, typically a year's supply, in advance. The contract usually provides for regular shipment over the life of the contract with the price and the life of the contract established in advance. Normally, the price on long-range contracts is a very favorable one for two reasons: first, the seller may have been decided upon on the basis of sealed bids with the contract going to the lowest bidder. Second, the seller may consider the total amount of goods involved in the order when establishing the price rather than the amount involved in each individual shipment. Of course, there can be some problems with the Federal Trade Commission if the contract calls for cumulative discounts.

QUESTIONS

1. Define purchasing. Distinguish purchasing from ordering and procurement.
2. Explain each step in the purchase process. How does the decision on product requirements differ for retailers and manufacturers?
3. Compare a mini-max system and the model stock plan.
4. Discuss the concept of vendor analysis. Contrast vendor analysis and value analysis.
5. Explain the concept of central buying. Differentiate store-owned offices from resident buyers.
6. What type of factors should the purchase officer consider in deciding on product lines to carry?
7. Discuss the importance of the product life cycle to product conditions and deletions.
8. If a product is losing money should it be dropped from the line? Explain.
9. Discuss the product adoption process.
10. What is speculation? How does it relate to forward buying and to hand-to-mouth buying?

10

Assortment Pricing
in Channels

Once the assortments structure has been decided and the products purchased, it must be priced. Price is one of the more volatile variables associated with channels management, and the channels manager must watch member pricing very carefully. In one sense, price is the common denominator that ties together all aspects of assortment management and relates this strategy to the buyer. For this reason price deserves our careful attention.

CHANNEL PRICE: ITS NATURE AND FUNCTION

When the word price is mentioned among businessmen or consumers, most people have a picture of what is meant. In their minds, price is the amount paid by the buyer for goods and services offered by the seller. In fact, this point of view is an oversimplification. The problem occurs because there is more than one concept of price, and not all concepts even require actual payment. For example, we can identify a list price, selling price, offered price, fair price, and sale price. All these terms are in common business usage. In order to accommodate the different types, price is defined for our purposes as: *the perceived value of goods and services measured in some legal exchange.* Price is value, and it is the difference in perceived value or worth that leads to the several concepts of price mentioned above. The seller may perceive more in the product than the buyer, but the selling price is always the result of an agreement between the buyer and seller on the worth of the product.

A *list price, asking price,* or *suggested price* is the amount that the seller seeks to obtain for goods and services. It is the original price placed on the merchandise. A list price is not necessarily an average sale price, a fair price, or a just price. For example, a seller can set a high list price, discount it 40 per cent and still sell above competition. List prices are often printed in the manufacturer's product catalog or on the price tags of wholesalers or retailers. The *selling price* is the amount actually received for the goods. The difference between list price and selling price is the *reduction* or *discount,* and, of course, the list price and selling price are the same if there are no reductions. The term *sale price* is used primarily for promotional purposes to designate that products have been marked down temporarily. It is supposed to suggest a bargain. An *offered* price is the amount a buyer is willing to pay for goods and services. The list and offered price can be the basis for price negotiations. The selling price can be considered a fair or just price when both parties agree to the price on the basis of free negotiations. On the other hand, society, as a whole, may consider a just price only one that achieves broad social goals.

Price serves four specific channel functions: (1) a payment to channel members for services rendered, (2) a competitive weapon, (3) a communicator of information, and (4) a device of channel control. Each of these channel functions carries with it specific responsibilities for the channel leader, and there is some feeling that the leader does not devote sufficient attention to pricing. Payment to channel members necessitates an adequate profit strategy. The use of price as a competitive weapon requires that effective policies be developed as a basis for competition, and that members be guided in the effective application of these policies. Communications is an overriding function of price in that it affects both of the other strategy areas.

Besides developing profit and competitive price strategy, the channel leader must also control the internal administration of these price policies among channel members. Thus, control of price is an essential ingredient of any discussion of channel pricing practice. In the process of performing his function, the channel manager develops his price strategy. That is, a combination of prices results from administering profit strategy, competitive strategy, price control, and price communications.[1] This chapter is organized around these four considerations of pricing.

PRICE AS A CHANNEL COMMUNICATOR

We begin our discussion with price communications because this function pervades all the others. Price communicates many things to

[1] "The Perplexing Problem of Pricing," *Grey Matter,* Vol. 37 (December, 1966).

several different groups of people. Some of these communications are intentional and some are unintentional. For example, the seller intends to convey to the buyer how much the product costs, but he may not intend to convey to buyers that the price is too high. Much of what price communicates depends on the perception of the parties involved. To better understand these points we have divided the discussion of price communications according to the major groups addressed.

Price Communicates to Household Consumers

The price of products communicates quality and value to the household consumer. The consumer depends explicitly on price and brand as the two most important indicators of product quality. This dependence is necessary (by consumers) because they have so little factual information. At least price and brand are observerable. However, the consumer can interpret price incorrectly. There are two types of price generalizations made by consumers that can lead to incorrect interpretations. First, the consumer generalizes that the higher the price the better the product quality and vice versa. There is no consistent evidence to suggest a direct correlation between product price and quality. Price may be a good indicator of quality, and it may not be because product quality is dependent on many things including the consumer's intended use. Some low-priced products perform just as well for a specific purpose as higher priced products. There are also many products whose quality is reflected in the price. The point is that the consumer should consider other factors than price consistent with his or her capability and attitude toward the expenditure of time and effort.

Second, the consumer reads "sale price" or "discount price" to mean value in purchase. He generalizes that a reduction from list price means the same quality for less money. In a great many cases the generalization is correct, but there is no necessary correlation between a sale price and a bargain. Merchants sometimes set the initial price artificially high before placing the product on sale. Merchants also use factory seconds and damaged merchandise as the basis for sale prices. This tactic is frequently employed without informing the consumer. Nevertheless, the price does convey definite meaning to consumers, and they act on the basis of perceived price.

Price Communicates to Middlemen

Product price communicates sales opportunity, margin, and competitive worth to the middleman. The price of the product is one of the factors a middleman takes into account when evaluating the chances of the product's meeting a market need sufficiently to sell in volume. The margin that accompanies price tells the middleman if it is worthwhile to merchandise the product. Competitive worth is the price of a product compared to similar products of competing firms. This factor indicates to the middleman how difficult the sale of the product will be. Most middlemen are fairly shrewd business judges, and price communicates information about the character of suppliers. For example, an exorbitantly high price on a supplier's product may communicate the notion that if the supplier will cheat the customer, he will cheat me. Of course, the middleman and the supplier may perceive price communications differently. A product deliberately set with a low margin by the supplier to encourage sales volume may be viewed by the middleman as an attempt to cut into his profit.

No matter what the communication, price perceptions directly affect dealer–supplier relationships in the marketing channel. Middlemen make judgments concerning the supplier's honesty, business objectives, reliability, and cooperation from the price of his product. They are much less likely to cooperate if they do not feel they have been treated fairly. Of course, middlemen are perfectly capable of deliberately misunderstanding the supplier's price policy as a means of gaining some bargaining advantage.

Price Communicates to Competitors

Price communicates to competitors relative market strength. Much of competitive strategy is a reaction to someone's price policy as perceived by the competitor.[2] Price is one of the best indicators a business has of its product's competitive position. Retailers, wholesalers, and manufacturers all need competitive information. Thus, considerable effort is made at all channel levels to evaluate competition. At retail, *comparison shoppers* are used to actually trade with competing stores. They compare merchandise features, prices, and promotional methods. Many manufacturers also purchase and analyze competing products, and it is common to seek sales and promotional information. Wholesalers, retailers, and manufacturers talk to salesmen about competitor's products and prices, compare catalogs for similar information, and survey competitive promotional efforts in the media. Many middlemen have a policy of not being undersold. If a customer can find a lower price the business will meet this price. Price can be misunderstood by competitors as easily as by consumers or middlemen. For example, a competitor may take a sale price for the regular price. And competitors are much less likely to misjudge quality based on price, though this happens. False or misleading perceptions about competitor's prices can lead to poor price strategy.

    [2] Jon G. Udell, "How Important Is Pricing In Competitive Strategy," *Journal of Marketing*, Vol. 28 (January, 1964), pp. 44–48.

Other Groups to Whom Price Communicates

Other groups are interested in the price businessmen place on their products. First, the company's own salesmen may view price as a sales advantage or as a hindrance. Salesmen frequently attempt to get product price lowered. Indeed, many salesmen devote their efforts to low margin products that require little sales effort rather than pushing the more difficult, higher margin goods. Second, various agencies of the government receive communications from price. Our present laws against unfair prices reflect the manner in which the government perceives business' pricing. The government interprets the meaning of fair prices, monopoly prices, and competitive prices and the laws reflect these interpretations. Third, consumer social organizations are concerned about prices. These groups feel that consumers are not receiving full value from the prices paid for products, and there are attempts to apply pressure to have these prices changed. How these groups view price directly affects the price policies of each channel member and the channel as a whole. A failure to respond can lead to even more restrictions on channel pricing practices.

CHANNEL PRICE AS A TEAM PAYMENT

One important function of price is to generate profit for the members of the marketing channel. Of course, price alone is not responsible for profit as we shall see, but it plays an important part in the determination.

Margin as a Payment for Member Service

When the marketing channel is viewed as an operating team, margin can then be considered a payment to the members for services rendered to the leader.[3] In this sense, margin is the reward, or price, for performance. This view is extremely important to channel pricing. It takes pricing out of the realm of an automatic occurrence based on pure competition and admits to a degree of control by some institution(s) in the channel. When viewed as a payment for services, margin becomes an important element of channel strategy that can be manipulated by the leader to obtain objectives. Margin, viewed as a price, works on channel members much as any other payment. Raise the price and channel members are more interested in pushing the leader's products. Lower the price and thus decrease interest. Margin can be used in combination with other strategy, such as changes in product quality, to achieve an even greater effect.

[3] See: Martin R. Warshaw, "Pricing to Gain Wholesalers' Support," *Journal of Marketing*, Vol. 26 (July, 1962), pp. 50–54. The concept of price as a payment is presented.

Rationale for Margin as a Payment

The concept of margin as a payment to channel members has a logical foundation in the concept of value added.[4] Figure 10–1 demonstrates this point. Assume that production begins at the mining stage, and the entire selling price is paid out to land, labor, and capital, because there is no input cost from a previous stage. Thus, we disregard input cost and margin becomes the only payment at this stage. Each of the other stages has an input cost plus margin.

We can observe several items from Figure 10–1.

1. Selling price for one stage becomes cost price for the next stage
2. Margin and value added are the same for any stage in the channel
3. The separate margins for the members when added equals the selling price to the consumer
4. The selling price of any stage is the equivalent of total accumulated value added to that point
5. The consumer receives full value for his money since he pays the accumulated value added

Under assumed conditions of maximization and perfect allocation, each factor of production, land, labor, or capital is paid at the point where marginal cost equals marginal revenue. Said another way, the amount paid a marketer (marginal cost—MC) is equal to the contribution, or value added, by that marketer (marginal revenue—MR). This accounts for margin and value added being the same. If the middleman does not perform he doesn't get paid, and if the middleman performs less efficiently than some other channel member of some competitor, then he gets paid less. In actual practice, there may be some difference between the payment and the service because of the firm's unwillingness or inability to operate exactly at the point where MC equals MR. After all, the concept is a theory and not a proven fact, even though it is the best explanation presently available.

The payment to any group of middlemen can be determined by adding the margins of the stages involved. In the example, firms specializing in producing receive $1.00 for their services to the system, and marketing firms also receive $1.00. Of course, this statement assumes that manufacturers perform no marketing, and we know this does not conform to fact. These contributions can be used as the basis for comparing various parts of the channel. Figure 10–1 demonstrates that production and marketing each take about 50 per cent of the consumer's

---

[4] Theodore N. Beckman, "The Value Added Concept As a Measurement of Output," *Advanced Management* (April, 1957), pp. 6–8; "The Value Added by Distribution," *Marketing In Progress,* Hiram C. Barksdale, ed. (New York: Holt, Rinehart and Winston, Inc., 1964), pp. 34–46.

Calculations on Margin* and Value Added	Mining Firm		Fabricators		Wholesaler		Retailer		Consumer
	Cost Price	Selling Price	Cost Price	Selling Price	Cost Price	Selling Price	Cost Price	Selling Price	Cost Price
	$.0	$.50	$.50	$1.00	$1.00	$1.50	$1.50	$2.00	$2.00
Margin of a Stage	$.50		$.50		$.50		$.50		$2.00
Cumulative Margin	$.50		$1.00		$1.50		$2.00		$2.00
Value Added by a Stage	$.50		$.50		$.50		$.50		$2.00
Cumulative Value Added	$.50		$1.00		$1.50		$2.00		$2.00
Totals	Value Added by Manufacturers = $1.00				Value Added by Wholesalers and Retailers = $1.00				Value Received by Consumers = $2.00

*Some definitions are in order as a basis for understanding the table. Margin is defined as the difference between cost and selling price. Value added refers to the contribution or worth added to the product by the factors of production. Cost is defined as the payments made to factors of production. This cost is based on the economic concept and includes the cost of capital or profit.

Fig. 10–1. Value added concept in the marketing channel.

dollar expenditure and this condition approximates the facts.[5] It also suggests, but doesn't prove, that production and marketing are about equally productive in the society.

Payment as a Salary or a Profit

The reader should not be confused about margin as a payment because it is difficult to observe one channel member actually turning over money to another. In one sense, all the channel members are working for the team, and it is the team that pays. In another sense, any payment can be called a salary or a profit, and, depending on who makes the payment, both types can be identified in the channel. First, when a channel leader sets the margin for another member it is the equivalent of a salary.

[5] Reavis Cox, *Distribution in a High Level Economy* (Englewood Cliffs, N.J.: Prentice-Hall, Inc., 1965).

When a channel member generates his own payment it is the equivalent of a profit.

Actually, responsibility for the payment of margin may reside with the individual channel member, or with a channel leader. The best example of a channel where the leader makes the payment is a completely integrated channel or one with franchised members. Channels that practice resale price maintenance allow the manufacturer to establish all margins for all members. In a non-integrated channel, where each member functions autonomously, each channel member partially determines his own payment, although the member may be influenced by another member.

Determination of Member Payment

In the American economy, prices are referred to as administered prices or judgment prices.[6] These terms are defined to mean that price is set on the basis of executive judgment (supply) and then tested in the market place (demand). There are a great many factors that have a direct bearing on the determination of price, and no doubt in a particular pricing situation several factors are considered.[7] In a practical sense, channel members from the manufacturer on down to the retailer do not have sufficient information or time to consider all the variables. Experience or judgment has to substitute. The three most important factors taken into account for practical pricing decisions are cost, demand, and competition. Basically, in the process of price determination: (1) cost determines the lower limit of price, (2) demand determines the upper limit, and (3) competition influences the difference between the two extremes.[8] What is referred to as price determination actually involves the manner in which these three factors are combined.

Cost Plus Pricing. The pricing process is highly inexact, but it typically involves some variation of the cost plus method. Cost plus is the basis for pricing, in a practical sense, at all stages in the marketing channel, and this fact holds true whether the price set is stated in advance or whether the price involves haggling.[9] The formula for cost plus pricing is demonstrated on the top of the next page.

---

[6] Robert F. Lanzillotti, "Why Corporations Find It Necessary to 'Administer' Prices," *Challenge, The Magazine of Economic Affairs,* Vol. 8 (January, 1960), pp. 45–49.

[7] H. W. Huegy, "Price Decisions and Marketing Policy," *Challenging Perspectives In Marketing,* Hugh W. Wales, ed. (Urbana: The University of Illinois Press, 1951), pp. 228–42. This is an excellent discussion of the factors affecting price.

[8] Kristian S. Palda, *Pricing Decisions and Marketing Policy* (Englewood Cliffs, N.J.: Prentice-Hall, Inc., 1971), pp. 1–7.

[9] Jules E. Anderson, "How To Price for Maximum Profit," *Management Methods* (November, 1958), pp. 37–40. A good discussion of the general question of cost plus pricing methods; William Longworth, "The Formation of Product Pricing Policy," *Scientific Business,* Vol. 2 (February, 1964), pp. 343–47. This article contains a discussion of the pitfalls of cost plus pricing.

$ Invoice Cost of Goods + $ Markup = $ Asking Price

Most marketers begin pricing with cost because it is the only figure they know, and frequently even it has to be estimated. Consequently, the margin is the only factor requiring judgment. We know that any margin established should be sufficiently high to cover operating cost and provide the firm with its profit objective.[10] In practice, the margin may be determined in one of two ways, depending on whether there is haggling or not. Cost plus pricing is compatible with economic theory, but judgment must substitute for the marginal revenue and cost curves.

First, if there is no haggling, the margin may be decided on the basis of some historical percentage, competitor's margins, industry average, or suggested manufacturer's markup. Once the margin has been estimated, added to cost, and list price estimated, the product is placed on sale. At this point, demanders enter the price picture. If the demand is high and the product moves faster than expected, the seller may consider raising the price. If the product is a slow mover, the seller finds himself with increasing inventories, so he may consider reducing the price. Experience over time with a variety of price situations gives the seller a "feel" for about what margin he can add to the invoice cost of most goods he carries in stock.[11] The number of times that the executive has to adjust price becomes less with experience.

Second, if haggling is involved, the price process can begin with either an offer to buy or an offer to sell. The two cases only affect the manner in which cost plus is applied. If the seller makes the initial offer he has already made a cost plus estimate of price. As previously described, an offer to buy simply causes the seller to quickly figure how much the offer is above his cost. It amounts to the same thing. The only difference is that with haggling, offers and counter offers may be made. The two sides begin with extreme figures, and the amount of margin is adjusted until the two parties agree on a mutually satisfactory price.

The Effect of Competition on Pricing. The one important factor in addition to cost and demand that directly influences the margin in cost plus pricing is competition. The seller may either price above or below competitors depending on such other factors as quality of the product, business location, or advertising to account for the price differences. It is only in rare cases that a merchant, at any level in the channel, completely ignores his competition. One variation of cost plus pricing is inverted pricing, and industrial sellers frequently use this method (for example, in the automobile industry). Inverted pricing occurs when the

[10] F. E. Brown and A. R. Oxenfeldt, "Should Prices Depend on Costs?" *Business Topics,* Vol. 16 (Autumn, 1968), pp. 73–77; "Airline Takes The Marginal Route," *Business Week* (April 20, 1963).

[11] Bill Darden, "An Operational Approach to Product Pricing," *Journal of Marketing,* Vol. 32 (April, 1968), pp. 29–33. Darden presents an alternative to the experience concept of pricing; also discusses the obstacles of any pricing method.

middleman knows the price of a competitor's product and must meet it. The engineering department of General Motors may be told to build a car to compete with the Mustang. This car must sell to the dealer for $2,000 and profits must be $400. Thus, the engineer is told that there is $1,600 of cost to work with and is instructed to build the best car possible for $1,600. In other words, with inverted pricing the seller works back from selling price to cost price.

Channel Price Objectives

Any attitude that the marketing firm takes toward pricing must be based on some objective. Price objectives may be quite formal and stated, or they may exist only in the mind of the owner or some executive of the business, but they always exist. These price objectives, when properly understood, provide direction and consistency to price policies. The important price objectives are summarized below. Notice that any one of these objectives may apply in the short run or the long run. Most businesses employ some combination of objectives, and they are selected on the basis of top management judgment.

I. *Profit Objectives*
   1. *Profit maximization*—attempts to charge what the traffic will bear in the short or long runs.
   2. *Satisfactory profit*—attempts at an amount that will reasonably satisfy either management or stockholders.
   3. *Minimum profit*—basically a humanitarian objective. Considers profit a necessary evil. Firm takes minimum necessary to survive and seeks other objectives.
   4. *Target return*—usually stated as a percentage of sales or investment. It is whatever management considers desirable and can be a high, reasonable, or low return. It often substitutes for maximization where there is inadequate information.

II. *Competitive Price Objectives*
   1. *Market share*—firm can pursue large share, small share, or stable share. Prices set to obtain some specified percentage of the market.
   2. *Sales maximization*—prices set to obtain greater sales volume. Typically means low price and low margin. Often attempted in mistaken belief that greater sales mean more profit.
   3. *Competitive stability*—price set to maintain the competitive status quo. Prices typically set defensively.
   4. *Survival*—all price policy designed to maintain the ability to function as a business.
   5. *Fair prices*—this is social pricing done in an effort to meet broad social need in the system.

III. *Price Objectives of Internal Control*
   1. *Management security*—prices are set to keep the manager's

job secure. Usually very conservative pricing and margins. Mostly use defensive pricing with little price innovation.

2. *Member satisfaction*—prices set to maximize the profit of channel members. The price leader may sacrifice profits in deference to member satisfaction.

3. *Leader growth*—aggressive pricing by channel leader with little consideration for the needs of members. More typical of non-integrated channels with loose affiliations.

Under each one of these price objectives the firm's attitude toward price as a payment is important. The leader may wish to pay itself or its channel members a lot or a little. As a general rule, the channel leader, as well as members, perform better when they are well-paid, so higher margins generally lead to more enthusiastic performance. The exceptions are found in objectives of satisfactory profits, minimum profits, and competitive stability. Even with these exceptions, a channel leader would make a mistake in attempting to induce a member to perform with a higher margin when the member was pursuing a minimum profit objective.

COMPETITIVE PRICE POLICY IN THE CHANNEL

The third function of price, that of a competitive weapon, is as important to channel operations as its function as a communicator and a payment. The effectiveness of competitive price policy is one of the major factors determining the success of the channel of distribution. Every member of the channel, whether coordinated or uncoordinated as a group, has a stake in competitive price strategy. Even in an uncoordinated channel if one member prices too high this restricts sales throughout the remainder of the channel and has a multiplied effect on the total.

Decision on the Type of Price Policy

The first price decision that any channel member has to make is whether to use a one-price or a negotiated price policy. A *one-price policy* means that the seller sets the price in advance of sale, and the buyer's choice is to purchase or not at the set price. There is no haggling and the seller does not reduce price except on special occasions such as the end of the season or if the merchandise is old or damaged. A *negotiated price* occurs when the two parties haggle by means of offers and counter offers until a mutually agreed upon price is set.[12] Both types

---

[12] Franz Edelman, "Art and Science of Competitive Bidding," *Harvard Business Review*, Vol. 43 (July–August, 1965), pp. 53–66.

of policies are found at all levels in the marketing channel. While whole-sale and retail prices are characterized as one-price policies, you find automobiles, appliances, furniture, homes, etc., that are negotiated. Ne-gotiated prices are associated with industrial buyers, but in the industrial market there are many items such as nuts, bolts, accessories, small equip-ment, office machinery, etc., that employ a one-price policy. It is not uncommon in the same channel to discover some members relying more on the one-price policy and other members relying more on negotiated prices. Even within a given business, use of the two methods may vary by type of product or time. For example, appliance dealers may nego-tiate over refrigerators, washers, freezers, etc., but stick to a one-price policy on small appliances. A firm that uses the one-price policy may be willing to negotiate during a sale or under other particular situations.

A negotiated price is likely to be used when the following conditions prevail:

1. Merchandise is nonstandardized
2. Sale involves a trade-in
3. Sale involves a long-term contract
4. Price fluctuates greatly
5. Single order purchases are made in quantity
6. Sealed bids are used
7. Price is high or margin is greater than average

In the industrial market, such items as installations, raw materials, and parts have negotiated prices. Consumers negotiate their automobiles, homes, appliances, and furniture.

A one-price policy is typical where the following conditions exist.

1. Products are standardized
2. Purchase quantity is small
3. Product price is low or has small margin
4. Sales volume is regular
5. Product quality is known
6. Items are branded

Such consumer products as food, cosmetics, clothing, and shoes have one price. Industrial goods such as accessory equipment and supplies have one price. Which type of overall price policy is used is not a serious channel problem because the policy is dictated more by circumstance than by channel considerations.

Channel Price Level Policies

Competitive price levels refer to the relationship of prices for a single firm, or for a marketing team, to the prices of competing firms or channels.

Price levels can also compare to general market prices for the nation. The price may be set above competitor's levels, at competitor's levels, or below competitor's levels. In a given channel, the members may be allowed to establish their own price levels or the channel captain may attempt to coordinate price levels for the team.

Coordinated price levels may be of several types.[13] First, the leader may coordinate all prices at the same competitive level. For example, the basic price of automobiles is the same for all retail outlets, and it is set near the market price. Second, the leader may allow for price level differences among types of channel members at different stages in the system. In appliance channels, wholesalers may be required to price at the level of competitors, while retailer's price levels may be below those of competitors. Third, the price level may be set, but different channel members at the same stage may have different prices. For example, retailers may be required to price above the market generally, but the specific prices of individual retailers may vary from just above to far above competitor's prices. Fourth, the leader may attempt to coordinate prices for some members and not for others at the same stage in the channel. For example, appliance manufacturers have found themselves in the ambiguous position of holding the line on appliances to franchised dealers while allowing discounters to cut price.

There are valid reasons why individual channel members may need different price levels. First, competition at different stages in the channel may vary. Second, price objectives often differ among members. Third, buyer attitudes toward product and service requirements differ. Fourth, there are often differences in the cost structure of channel members. Fifth, variations exist in buyer willingness to pay a given price. An example can tie these five points together. Competition may be intense at the retail stage in the channel but only mild at the manufacturing stage. As a result the manufacturer wants to pursue a don't-rock-the-boat price policy, but the retailer wants an aggressive below-the-market price. Too, service may not be important in the sale of refrigerators between the wholesaler and retailer, but it may be vital in sales to final consumers. The retailer may need a margin sufficiently high to cover these services even if it means pricing above competition.

Multi-Product Pricing

It is one thing to establish the price of a single product that is sold through a single channel. The problem becomes more complex when multiple products are sold sometimes through more than one type channel. There are several channel policies that relate to multi-product pric-

---

[13] Warshaw, *op. cit.*, pp. 52–54.

ing decisions. Before getting into these policies let us review the important specific price policies that are associated with multiple products. There are no specific rules to guide the selection of multiple product prices.

1. *Psychological pricing*—involves setting the price below natural breaks in 100 such as $.49, $1.98, and $399.95.
2. *Leader pricing*—involves reducing the price of expensive nationally recognized products as a promotional device to induce customers to come into the store.
3. *Price lining*—involves grouping products with varying cost around 3 to 5 price points such as $3.95, $5.95, and $10.95. These points are the only sale prices so that a less normal markup is taken on some items and more than normal on others.
4. *Full line pricing*—involves utilizing three different quality lines of merchandise with the highest quality line priced above the market, the average quality line priced at competitive levels, and the lowest quality line priced below the market.

Although leader pricing and psychological pricing are generally associated with retailing, the fact is that all four of these pricing policies are used in varying degrees by all channel members. Full line manufacturers often keep products in the line that they lose money on in order to help sell the remainder of the line, and manufacturers and wholesalers alike use varying forms of psychological pricing. Multi-product lines create special channel problems. First, a full line of products may be developed and priced to suit a single channel. The oil industry manufactures and sells a full line of products through service stations. Second, the channel leader may develop a full line of products and price them to sell to two or more completely different channels. For example, a furniture manufacturer may sell a low quality, low priced line of furniture direct to discount houses, while selling a full line of high quality, high priced furniture direct to exclusive furniture specialty stores. Third, the leader may sell part of a full line of products to two or more different channels of distribution. An appliance producer may private brand and sell washers to large department stores while distributing them full line through franchised dealers.

In some channels, the leader has full control over pricing and in others there is only partial or little control. Some channels require higher prices than others, and some are more competitive. It is even possible for a manufacturer to compete with itself at the final retail level because of the channels selected. For example, anti-freeze is sold at service stations for list price, and at discount service stations at reduced prices. The same groceries can be found in chain stores, convenience stores, and drugstores and there may be different prices at each of these outlets.

New Product Pricing in Channels

The two principle policies for pricing new products in any channel are skimming and penetration. The method used depends a great deal on demand elasticity.[14] One or the other policy is considered when determining the original markup on new products. Figure 10–2 illus-

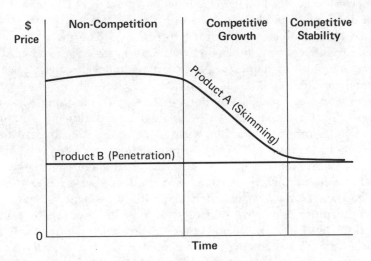

Fig. 10–2. New product pricing.

trates these two policies. A *skimming policy* is essentially charging what the traffic will bear. The price is set high and the executive expects to bring the price down as competition develops until the long-run competitive price level is reached. A skimming policy effects a quick recovery of cost connected with introducing the product and may allow high profits initially. The policy is used: (1) when products have a short economic life, (2) when large expenditures are necessary for research and start-up to production, (3) when patent protection is available, (4) when capital is in short supply, (5) when competition is expected to develop quickly, and (6) when there is no initial competition.

A *penetration policy* occurs when the executive sets the original price as near the long-run competitive figure as possible.[15] The idea is to take a slower recovery of start-up cost. A penetration policy is typically used: (1) when attempting to forestall competition, (2) when the product is

[14] Stephen F. Welch, "A Planned Approach to New Product Pricing," *Pricing: The Critical Decision* (Chicago: American Management Association, Report No. 66, 1961), pp. 44–57.

[15] Joel Dean, "Pricing a New Product," *The Controller*, Vol. 23 (April, 1955), pp. 163–65.

easily copied, (3) when seeking a favorable customer image, (4) when humanitarian goals are sought, and (5) when competition already exists in the market, or is quick to develop.

The essential channel problem with the introduction of new products is how to get middlemen to handle the product. Most wholesalers and retailers know that only about one-third of the products introduced can be expected to succeed. These middlemen prefer that the manufacturer assume the cost of product introduction. If the product proves successful, then the middleman will add it to his line. The manufacturer can use price to induce the middleman to stock and promote the new product. In general, middlemen prefer a penetration policy because it leads to more and quicker sales, creates market goodwill, and simplifies pricing. However, there are many exceptions to this generalization. The manufacturer can also manipulate price to favor the middleman during introduction. A price set low but with an above-average margin for the middleman can be effective at the introduction stage. The problems with this policy are two. First, it reduces the manufacturer's margin even more than with normal penetration. Second, it is always easier to reduce price than to increase it. Customers object to price increases. Therefore, the manufacturer may have difficulty getting the price up to a normal competitive level. The problem is much easier to handle in an integrated channel. In fact, a skimming policy is more typical in channels that are short or controlled by the leader. It is simply too difficult to keep a price up when there are several independent middlemen.

Decisions on Price Differentials

Price differentials are defined as the variations around the seller's list price that may increase or decrease buyer cost. The two types of price differentials are discounts and transportation cost.[16] Price differentials operate through a change in the invoice price to the buyer. *Discounts* lower invoice price to the buyer, and the lower cost can either be passed on to customers in lower prices or retained by the middleman in a higher margin or both. *Transportation costs* involving product movement must be covered in the long run.

Types of Price Differentials. The channel leader has a choice among several types of discounts and several methods of handling transportation cost. The important choices are summarized below.

    A. *Discounts*
        1. *Trade or functional discounts*—reduction from list price for performing a specific function in the channel or because of the

[16] Robert A. Lynn, *Price Policies and Marketing Management* (Homewood, Ill.: Richard D. Irwin, Inc., 1967), Chapter 10. An excellent discussion of discounting and transportation cost in channels.

location in the channel. It is the wholesaler discount or the the retailer discount.

2. *Cash discount*—reduction from list price for making payment before the grace period ends. The statement 2/10/net 30 means a 2 per cent discount for paying in 10 days or the net amount of the bill due in 30 days. The dating period is usually from receipt of goods (R.O.G.); first and fifteenth of the month (M.O.M.); or end of the month (E.O.M.).

3. *Quantity discount*—a reduction in list price for purchasing in quantity. Usually involves a schedule of successively larger quantities and correspondingly larger discounts. Quantity discounts can be cumulative or non-cumulative, but the government frowns on cumulative discounts where separate orders can be placed over time and the discount based on the total amount.

4. *Promotional allowance*—reduction from list price because the middleman assumes a portion of the manufacturer's cost of promotion. For example, the manufacturer may pay 50 per cent of the retailer's advertising of his product up to a total of $5,000.

5. *Seasonal discount*—reduction from list price for purchasing early or out of season. Allows the manufacturer to even out his production.

6. *Product allowances*—reduction from list price for taking less than normal in the product. The purchase of factory seconds, odd sizes, or damaged merchandise usually takes an allowance.

B. *Transportation Costs*

1. *F.O.B. plant*—buyer pays the freight and title passes at the manufacturer's loading dock. This method is preferred by the Federal Trade Commission.

2. *F.O.B. destination*—seller pays the freight and title passes at the buyer's receiving dock.

3. *Zone pricing*—manufacturer sets up geographic price zones across the country and charges the average cost of shipping into a zone. Some middlemen overpay and some middlemen underpay depending on their location in the zone. May increase competition because everyone has same transportation cost.

4. *Basing point pricing*—F.O.B. plant pricing but using one or more bases from which to measure cost. It can lead to phantom freight (goods shipped from a near base but freight charged from a more distant point) or freight absorption (goods shipped from a distant point but freight charged from a near point).

Policies of Price Differentials.   The selection of price differentials can be a problem no matter what policy is followed. It may appear that the simplest policy is to give everyone exactly the same discounts. However, this would not work because there are legitimate bases for the differences in discounts and transportation charges. Some of the price differentials are given automatically, such as the trade discount. On the other hand, seasonal discounts, promotional allowances, and zone pricing are given at the discretion of the channel leader. In most cases, the decision reflects the needs of specific types of customers and management's discount policy.

Channel members who purchase in larger quantity or pay their bills on time are unhappy when they receive the same discount as members who did not do these things. If goods are purchased in quantity in the industry, such a discount is profitable to both parties because of savings involved. On the other hand, the owner of a small local garage has a difficult time understanding why a large discount house can sell automobile parts for less than he can purchase them from the same company. The garage dealer does not care about differences in quantity purchased. He knows only that he has to compete with that discount house, and he is at a disadvantage. The dealer in a price zone located close to the seller does not care that averaging the cost of shipping into the zone makes the price less to all channel members and the consumer. He is interested in the fact that he is paying more than dealers who are located further from the seller.

Effect of Price Wars on Channels

Sometimes competition does not follow prescribed patterns in a marketing channel, and a price war can be one important result. The most important reason for price wars is the accumulation of surplus stock by some manufacturer.[17] Other important reasons include the entry of a new competitor, a seller attempting to increase market share, some cost cutting innovation, and a sudden decrease in demand. The classic example of the price war is found in the gasoline industry. Some refinery finds it has excess gasoline, and it is cheaper to dump the excess on independents at very low prices than to incur the cost of shutting down the refinery. The independent may use the low priced gasoline as an excuse to cut price in order to increase market share. The war is on when the brand stations cut price in an attempt to maintain the differential between brand stations and independents.

Price wars can have a disastrous effect on the channel unless there is cooperation among members of the same channel. As the price dips lower, the margins of retailers are squeezed, and losses result. Left to

[17] Ralph Cassidy, Jr., "The Price Skirmish—A Distinctive Pattern of Competitive Behavior," *Californian Management Review*, Vol. 7 (Winter, 1964), pp. 11–16. A good discussion of price wars.

their own devices, many retailers are forced out of business. The war is soon over with the channel in shambles unless the manufacturer makes offsetting price reductions to retailers. Typically, the manufacturer sets his price to allow the retailer a nearly normal margin, and the losses are absorbed by the manufacturer. Trouble can also develop between retailers. Generally, the price gradually rises as one moves out from the center of the price war. This fact places peripheral retailers at a price disadvantage because their customers find it worthwhile to travel to the lower priced stores. On the other hand, the retailers participating in the war do not feel the competitive situation is their fault. In any event, the war continues until the surplus is worked off or the manufacturer takes direct action. The action usually comes in the form of a refusal to maintain the retailers' margins. Faced with losses, the retailers must raise prices back to normal.

POLICIES FOR CHANNEL PRICE CONTROL

No matter which combination of price policies the channel leader selects, there are problems in controlling these prices among the channel membership. Control is never easy, and few channel leaders, even in highly integrated channels, are able to maintain complete control over prices. However, there are policies that can greatly aid in controlling channel prices.[18]

Need To Maintain Prices

There are two types of price differences that can develop between the channel leader and the members. First, there are *price level variations* that occur when individual channel members do not hold the line on prices desired by the leader. The member may set the price either above or below that promoted by the leader. Price level variations do not refer to "sale" or other temporary prices, but regular list prices. Any variation either above or below the desired level can be harmful to the leader's overall channel strategy, and the leader may feel the need to discourage such practices. Of course, not all variations are harmful to the leader. In fact, it is often necessary to recognize differences in the member's customers and operating considerations.[19]

Second, there are *variations in price reduction* that involve markdown from list price. Reductions are normal in any marketing channel, but

[18] Louis W. Stern, "Approach to Achieving Retail Price Stability," *Business Horizons*, Vol. 7 (Fall, 1964), pp. 75–86. This study presents a different approach to control.

[19] E. Raymond Corey, "A Concept of Price Strategy," *Industrial Marketing* (Englewood Cliffs, N. J.: Prentice-Hall, Inc., 1962), pp. 215–34.

the leader wants them to conform to his strategy. Markdowns are taken to promote the store's sales interests and to correct operating mistakes. Reductions designed to promote the store's interests include: (1) promotional sales undertaken to increase volume, (2) season-end markdowns taken to clear stock and make way for new merchandise, (3) reductions to eliminate discontinued merchandise, and (4) sales for the purpose of introducing new merchandise. Reductions made necessary to correct mistakes include: (1) markdowns to eliminate damaged or dead stock, (2) reductions to correct buying mistakes, (3) going out of business sales, and (4) markdowns to correct pricing mistakes.

The channel manager is primarily interested in reduction control. Because the channel operates efficiently when individual members can adjust their prices to meet special circumstances, the channel manager may not seek to control all types of price variations. He wants the level kept within reasonable limits, and he wants reductions to be sensible and planned. Thus the problem in the channel is not the elimination of price variations but the management of these variations toward the overall goals of the channel. This fact may be equally true in an integrated or non-integrated channel.

Informal Methods of Price Control

The informal methods of price control include the use of suggested list prices, persuasion, pre-pricing, and brand withdrawals.[20] For many small wholesalers and retailers, it is simpler to follow list prices than to get involved in the pricing function. The manufacturer usually provides for an adequate margin in the suggested price. In fact, some retailers appear to believe that suggested list prices must be followed. Persuasion is the use of salesmanship and needs no further comment here. It is often used in conjunction with the other methods, and can be most effective when employed this way.

Pre-pricing, or pre-marking, occurs when the manufacturer puts the price on the good before shipment. Pre-pricing can be done at the buyer's suggestion, as with private brand goods sold by large department stores, or at the seller's discretion as with potato chips. In any case the convenience for the retailer gives the manufacturer a lever to use in keeping price in line. If the manufacturer has a valuable brand with wide and strong customer acceptance, the threat of its withdrawal can be the most effective weapon of price control. Brand withdrawal hits the middleman where it hurts, and that is in his sales. The company's salesmen can spot check dealer performance as a basis for the withdrawal decision.

[20] A. J. Alton, "Pricing Practices and Channel Control," *Marketing Channels: A Systems Viewpoint,* William G. Moller, Jr., and David L. Wilemon (Homewood, Ill.: Richard D. Irwin, Inc., 1971), pp. 233–39.

Legal Methods of Price Control

There are several important laws that have a direct bearing on the seller's ability to control price in the channel. Some of these laws provide a legal argument for the leader's actions, and some restrict the leader's flexibility when dealing with middlemen. Table 10–1 summarizes the more important laws that have a direct bearing on channel price policies. The law most applicable to price discrimination today is the Robinson-Patman Act. It sets the pattern for what constitutes price discrimination. There is nothing in the law against discrimination against buyers of a different class, which implies that a trade discount is legal. An interesting feature of the law is the fact that the suspect firm is guilty until it proves innocence by supplying accounting records that show the discrimination was based on a cost savings.

The Resale Price Maintenance laws apply to price control by the seller.[21] In 1963, forty states had Fair Trade Laws and thirty-one had Unfair Practices Acts.[22] States having Unfair Practices Acts require markups from four to twelve per cent. The conditions under which sales below cost can be made include sale of damaged merchandise, shop worn or distress merchandise, and when the seller has been given an opportunity to repurchase his goods. It should be obvious that in setting the resale price the seller is setting the margin, or payment, to all middlemen and is removing price from competition. Actually, neither of the Resale Price Maintenance Laws are effective because there is no provision for any enforcement agency. This fact may be their greatest advantage since it makes the laws practically unenforceable which benefits competition.

Organizational Methods of Price Control

The organizational methods of price control include: (1) use of a short channel, (2) use of contractual control, and (3) sale on consignment. The short channel reduces the number of middlemen the manufacturer has to deal with. Use of persuasion and the means of checking on prices are both made easier in a short channel. The franchise provides more complete control since it involves the total retail operation, but exclusive arrangements usually call for limited competition and price control. Consignment sales are conditional sales where the manufacturer does not give up ownership of the goods. The retailer is acting as an agent in consignment selling, and although he has physical control of the goods, he has no control over prices, terms, or conditions of sale.

[21] Palda, *op. cit.*, Chapter 7.
[22] Marshall C. Howard, *Legal Aspects of Marketing* (New York: McGraw-Hill Book Co., Inc., 1964), pp. 39, 44.

Table 10-1 Summary of Price Legislation

Name of Law	Agency	Major Provisions Summarized
I. Sherman Act of 1890	Federal	Made illegal all contracts, combinations, conspiracies in restraint of trade.
II. Clayton Act of 1914	Federal	Unlawful to discriminate in price between buyers of the same class where the effect of such discrimination is to materially lessen competition or tend to create a monopoly. Exceptions are made for differences in grade, quality, or quantity of product sold.
III. Robinson-Patman Act, 1936	Federal	Unlawful to discriminate in price between buyers of the same class where the effect of such discrimination is to materially lessen competition or tend to create a monopoly unless the difference is based on an actual cost savings. 1. Placed burden of proof on the offender. 2. Commissions or brokerage allowance can be given only for actual services rendered. 3. Made it illegal to receive a discriminatory price knowingly. 4. Made it illegal to differentiate in price in different sections of the country for the purpose of destroying competition. 5. Any appropriation of value created by a competitor is illegal. 6. Allows a seller to meet a discriminatory price initiated by a competitor.
IV. Resale Price Maintenance Law	State	Allows the seller a degree of control over the resale price of his merchandise.
A. Unfair Practices Acts	State	Prevent sales below cost except under specified circumstances. Cost is typically defined as invoice price plus a stated percentage markup.
B. Fair Trade Laws	State	Make it legal on a contractual basis for a seller to "fix" the resale (retail) price of his product. Typically includes a non-signers rider which allows blanket coverage in a state once a contract is signed with a single retailer.
C. Miller-Tydings Act, 1937	Federal	Both these laws attempt to make the non-signers clause legal in interstate commerce.
D. McGuire Act, 1953	Federal	

Consignment selling is unhandy because of the contract, but it can be effective.

Differentials Used for Price Control

Price differentials are a problem to the channel leader. However, these same price differences offer an opportunity to the channel leader to help control overall channel prices. This is particularly true for discounts. Discounts can be given to members who cooperate on price practices in the channel, but they cannot be given indiscriminately. For example, the manufacturer may make promotional allowances available to all retailers who cooperate on prices, and refuse to sell to other retailers. Factory seconds and odd lot merchandise may be made available to cooperative customers along with their price reductions. This merchandise can be legally withheld from uncooperative members. The channel leader may be willing to increase his cash discount if the channel members cooperate on price. No tool of price control in the channel has to be used alone, and this is true of discounts. Most often the channel captain uses a variety of tools simultaneously on the channel membership. The likelihood of effective price control is increased when the tools are combined.

PRICE PRACTICES USED TO PROTECT CHANNEL MEMBERS

So far we have discussed price practices used to constrain channel members and obtain their compliance. We do not mean to imply that channel members are naturally antagonistic toward the leader. The fact is that all the control devices discussed may be needed even in highly cooperative channels, and there are many occasions when price is used to protect the middleman's status or position in the channel.

Figure 10–3 indicates that the channel leader can do much to protect

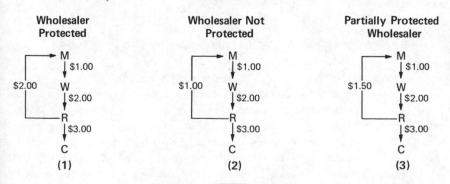

Fig. 10–3. Middleman protection by channel leader.

the integrity of the entire price structure by how he applies the margin to different channel members. Given the price structure, and a channel with normal sales through wholesalers, at what price should the manufacturer sell to a retailer who makes occasional direct purchases? The answer, of course, depends on whether the manufacturer wants to protect the wholesaler's position in the channel. In example 1 the wholesaler has high status in the channel and is fully protected. The manufacturer will only sell to the retailer at the same price the wholesaler would sell to the retailer. In this situation, the manufacturer may remit to the wholesaler his normal margin. The wholesaler has greater status and importance than the retailer, and the retailer is discouraged from making direct purchases.

In example 2, the wholesaler is not protected, and the retailer receives the same price for which the manufacturer would sell to the wholesaler. The retailer has greater status in this channel. In such a channel the wholesaler cannot continue to sell the manufacturer's products unless the incidence of direct sales is small, or the product is relatively unimportant to the wholesaler's profit.

Notice that example 1 is unfair to the retailer who receives no price break from the direct purchase that may be less costly to the manufacturer. Example 2 is unfair to the wholesaler who may perform valuable services to the manufacturer. Example 3 recognizes these problems. It provides some cost break to the retailer for purchasing direct, but not enough to force the wholesaler out of the channel. Actually, depending on the degree of wholesaler protection, the retailer's price could fall anywhere between $1.00 and $2.00.

Other means of member protection can be cited. Resale price maintenance can be devised to protect retailers from each other because it takes price out of consideration as a competitive weapon in the channel. The leader can provide considerable protection by not giving under-the-counter discounts. Such discounts may be illegal, but some sellers continue the practice, thereby hurting everyone in the channel.

RE-NEGOTIATION OF PRICE AMONG CHANNEL MEMBERS

Once the price of a product has been established, the job is not necessarily finished. No price is permanent. There comes a time when the price must be re-negotiated. In basic metals the price may remain constant for months and move up in definite stages. Retail prices are more volatile and change frequently. When a re-negotiation becomes necessary, the manufacturer has three choices. They are notification and persuasion, threat of product discontinuance, and creation of price competition.

Notification and Persuasion

Most of the time price re-negotiation is a routine matter. It may require no more than the manufacturer deciding on the new price and notifying the membership. Notification may be handled through a change in the catalog or by letter. In either case, the effective date of the change should be made very clear. At worst, a little gentle persuasion, perhaps by a salesman's routine call, may be required. Members of the system are usually receptive to a sound argument. This is particularly true if the manufacturer is economically stronger than the collective membership.

Product Discontinuance

Sometimes, the membership resists the proposed price change. When this happens the problem becomes more serious for the channel captain. The leader may turn to the threat of product discontinuance to obtain his way. The middleman is informed, usually by letter, that he is abusing the privilege of handling the manufacturer's product and is asked to bring his price in line. Very often the manufacturer will attempt to drive a wedge between individual middlemen by inducing a few key channel members to accept the new price. If, for example, a large chain department store can be induced to make the price change, the competition from this member may cause the other retailers to fall in line. Of course, the manufacturer may have to give the department store something in return for the change. This is one place where the use of discounts and other methods suggested previously can become helpful.

Creation of Price Competition

The most serious step in re-negotiating price in the channel is to create new competition for channel members who do not go along with price change. This is drastic action and is not undertaken until other methods of re-negotiation have failed. The method involves favoring channels of distribution that have members who are receptive to the leader's price policies. If the leader is lucky, an alternative channel may be available, or there may be key members in his present channel who will reduce price. By favoring the price cutters or the low price channel, the leader may bring the other channel members into line with his price policy. Sometimes there are no alternative methods of creating competition within the existing (traditional) channel. In such a case, the leader must develop new competitors. The manufacturer may continue to sell to the "traditional" channel at the established price while seeking new types of outlets never used before. When the new channel is strong, the manufacturer discontinues sale to the traditional channel.

The creation of price competition within a channel is both time consuming and costly. New types of marketing institutions are not created overnight. There must be a place for them in the competitive scheme, and they must be encouraged in their growth. In the meantime, the channel leader is incurring two types of cost. He is losing money on the products sold at lower prices in the traditional channel, and the development of the new channel is costing money. The new channel probably requires help from the manufacturer in the form of price concessions, financial aid, and help with organizational, accounting, and managerial problems. Obviously, the creation of new price competition should be carefully considered.

The emergence of the discount house is mostly explained by the need of appliance manufacturers to re-negotiate prices among traditional department stores and appliance dealers. Discount houses developed in the appliance channel because prices and margins were high due to long established fair trade practices. Manufacturers wanted prices reduced because they realized sales were being lost. Retailers did not want to give up the high margins that they were able to acquire because fair trade kept prices artificially high. The manufacturer created competition by encouraging some merchants to: (1) establish businesses in low rent districts, (2) streamline operations thus reduce operating costs, and (3) reduce product margins. In turn, the manufacturers gave these merchants substantial discount in violation of their own fair trade laws. The result was an efficient low priced retail outlet for appliances. Once the discount channel was established the leaders had sufficient leverage to negotiate prices down among traditional retailers. However, it took over ten years to develop the competitive situation.

QUESTIONS

1. What is meant by price? Explain the several types of price one may find in business.
2. Compare price communications to middlemen with price communications to competitors.
3. Explain and illustrate the concept of value added. How does this concept of value added relate to margin as a payment?
4. How are prices determined in the American economy?
5. How would you relate profit objectives to competitive price objectives in the business firm?
6. Discuss some of the problems associated with coordinating product price among different levels in the channel.
7. Explain the meaning of multi-product pricing.
8. Discuss the methods of price control over channel members.
9. Explain price practices used to protect channel members.
10. Discuss the methods of price re-negotiation among channel members.

11

Operations of
Logistics Systems

It has been pointed out that assortments are created as the result of the cooperative efforts of the several members of a marketing channel, each performing activities that further the combination of goods at particular prices. Assortment creation necessitates a progression of activities; the transfer of goods between institutions is necessary to keep the progression moving to its logical completion. This movement between channel members is the general area of logistics, the second of the major channel operations.

BUSINESS LOGISTICS

The terms logistics and physical distribution, used to describe a common group of activities, have had a varied history. In its original use, logistics was a military term referring to a complete system of moving, supplying, and quartering troops. Businessmen broadened logistics to include any type of transportation and storage. Marketers specialized the use of the term to mean the physical handling of products; they also began employing the term physical distribution in place of logistics.[1]

The Definitions Committee of the American Marketing Association defines logistics as: *the movement and handling of goods from the point*

[1] Norman E. Daniel and J. Richard Jones, "The Nature and Scope of Business Logistics," Norman E. Daniel and J. Richard Jones, eds., *Business Logisticis* (Boston: Allyn and Bacon, Inc., 1969), pp. 1–8. The authors provide a good overview of the relationship of logistics to marketing.

of production to the point of consumption or use.[2] Historically, logistics has been divided into transportation and storage, and both these aspects of the activity can be identified in the definition. *Transportation* is defined as over the road movement of goods that takes place between marketing firms or between marketing firms and the consumer.[3] *Storage,* used here synonymously with warehousing, means all activities associated with the safekeeping of goods until needed. Each of these activities was usually viewed as a separate business function, and there was little integration of decision making.

The modern view is that logistics is a complete operating system comprising one of the major sub-systems of the channel team.[4] Figure 11–1 has two common methods of handling logistics; one in the final consumer channel and one in the industrial channel. The three basic elements of a logistics system can be identified in each of these distribution methods: (1) institutions engaged in physical movement, (2) functions necessary to perform physical movement, and (3) a specialized communications network.[5] Notice that both transportation and storage are involved with each of the system elements. There is some feeling that logistics has been a neglected member of the channel's team which has tended to increase marketing inefficiency.[6] This neglect is beginning to change. The importance of logistics is accounted for by the fact that it takes approximately six per cent of gross national product. A breakdown of logistics cost can provide further insight into this importance. One breakdown shows: carrier charges, 44 per cent; warehousing and handling, 20 per cent; inventory, 18 per cent; shipping room, 11 per cent; and administration, 7 per cent.[7] Thus the management of logistics is the least expensive item cited.

INSTITUTIONS THAT PERFORM LOGISTICS

The first requirement for the design of logistics systems is knowledge of the institutions that comprise that system. Some of these institutions are merchants and some are agents.[8]

[2] Definitions Committee of the American Marketing Association, "1948 Report," *The Journal of Marketing* (October, 1948), p. 202.

[3] Mark E. Stern, *Marketing Planning: A Systems Approach* (New York: McGraw-Hill Book Co., Inc., 1966), p. 84.

[4] E. Grosvenor Plowman, "For Good or Ill, Users Influence Transportation," *The Annuals of the American Academy of Political and Social Sciences* (January, 1963).

[5] Wendell M. Stewart, "Physical Distribution: Key to Improved Volume and Profit," *Journal of Marketing,* Vol. 29 (January, 1965), pp. 65–70. The author takes a more restrictive view of the logistics system as a group of steps or cogs in the movement of goods—a view that tends to be more mechanical than behavioral.

[6] Bud Reese, "Physical Distribution the Neglected Marketing Function," *Industrial Marketing* (October, 1961).

[7] Robert P. Neuschel, "Physical Distribution—Forgotten Frontier," *Harvard Business Review* (March–April, 1967), pp. 125–34.

[8] J. L. Heskett, Robert M. Ivie, and Nicholas A. Glaskowsky, Jr., *Business Logistics* (New York: The Ronald Press Co., 1973), Part II.

Merchant Institutions of Logistics

Every channel member who owns goods is responsible for their transportation and storage. The marketer has two basic choices for transporting and storing. He can obtain the necessary equipment and personnel and privately perform logistics, or he can delegate the task to some agent specialist. Merchants who ship and store are the manufacturers, wholesalers, and retailers explained earlier.[9] It typically happens that when one considers the firms that perform logistics, the merchants are ignored in favor of discussion of railroads, airlines, truckers, etc. Yet merchant middlemen are the most important of all logistics firms. In fact, nearly all merchant channel members perform some logistics and most perform substantial amounts. The only explanation for the lack of attention to the performance of logistics by merchants is that logistics is only a part of their total activity and tends to become lost in the overall operation of the business.

Warehouse Agents

The agent used for storage in the channel is the public warehouse.[10] There are approximately 9,433 public warehouses in the United States with revenues of $1,624,632,000 and payrolls of $634,429,000 per year.[11] Public warehouses can be broadly classified as: (1) terminal and (2) field. A *terminal public warehouse* is one that operates out of its own facilities and merchants who seek to store goods there transport their goods to it. Terminal public warehouses can be further subdivided, according to the type of facility used, into (1) general merchandise, (2) specialty, (3) refrigerated, (4) bonded, and (5) bulk storage. Of this group, bulk storage with approximately 519,601,000 gallons of storage, and refrigerated warehouses with 533,960,000 square feet are most important.[12] *General merchandise warehouses* handle a wide variety of goods. *Specialty warehouses* handle a limited line of goods such as hardware, household furnishings, or soft goods; or they specialize in commodities difficult to store. *Refrigerated warehouses* handle farm products and other goods that must be kept cool or frozen. *Bonded warehouses* are those insured against loss. *Bulk storage facilities* specialize in the storage of liquid goods such as gasoline, petroleum, natural gas, and oils from food products.

---

[9] Donald J. Bowersox, Edward W. Smykay, and Bernard J. La Londe, *Physical Distribution Management* (London: The Macmillan Co., 1968), pp. 41–43.

[10] Heskett, Ivie, and Glaskowsky, *op. cit.*, p. 47.

[11] U. S. Department of Commerce, Bureau of the Census, *Census of Business, Wholesale Trades,* Subject Reports, 1967, Section 8, p. 1.

[12] *Ibid.*

A. LOGISTICS FOR A CONSUMER APPLIANCE MANUFACTURER

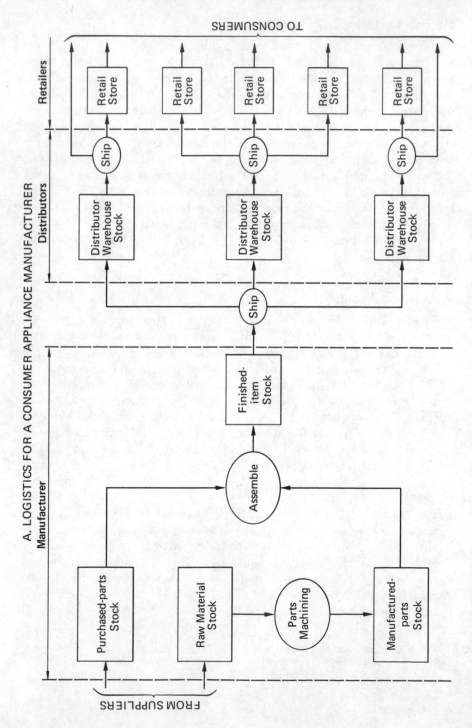

B. LOGISTICS FOR A MANUFACTURER OF BASIC METALS

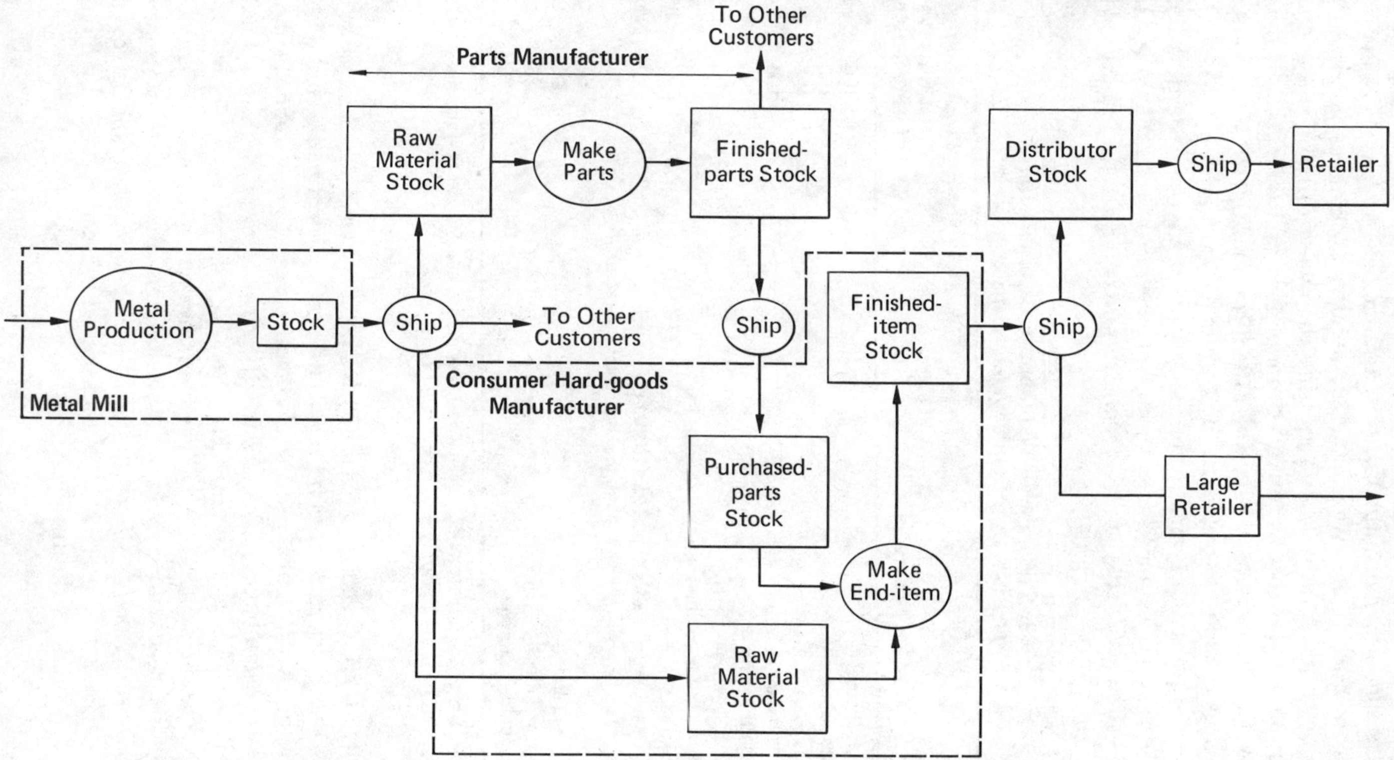

Fig. 11–1. Two logistics methods. *Source:* John F. Magee, *Physical Distribution Systems* (New York: McGraw-Hill Book Co., Inc., 1967), pp. 12–13.

Field warehouses are typically operated by the same company that operates the terminal, although this arrangement is not necessary.[13] A *field warehouse* is one where the warehouseman isolates goods in the owner's own plant rather than requiring the owner to bring the goods to the terminal. The goods are placed under lock and the owner is denied entry without a warehouse receipt. In all other respects the goods are handled as though they were in the terminal.

Public warehouses typically receive goods, reship, provide desk space for salesmen, divide merchandise, and fill customer orders, among other services shown in Table 11–1. A *warehouse receipt* is issued to the owner

Table 11–1   Public Warehousing Services Offered
by 120 Larger Public Warehousing Companies

Service	Proportion of Firms Surveyed Offering Service
Inventory records	100%
Warehouse receipts	100
Storage	100
Break bulk handling	100
Marking and tagging	100
Over, short, damage reports	93
Prepaying freight (on behalf of warehouse users)	88
Local pickup and delivery	72
Accredited customer lists (for credit and other purposes)	72
Recoopering and repairing (for broken and damaged packages)	68
Packaging	52
Field warehousing	32
Make bulk handling	28
Loans on goods in storage	23

Source: James L. Heskett, Nicholas A. Glaskowsky, Jr., and Robert M. Ivie, *Business Logistics*, 2nd ed. (New York: The Ronald Press Co., 1973), p. 64.

of the goods as a receipt for the goods and a contract for their storage. The warehouse receipt may be negotiable or non-negotiable, but either type can be used as collateral for credit purposes. The warehouseman is liable as a legal bailee. This means the firm is responsible for taking reasonably good care of the merchandise. Negligence must be proved in court before an owner can collect from the warehouseman. Typically, merchandise stored in the public warehouse is obtained by presenting the warehouse receipt which describes the merchandise and gives the quantity. Thus, it is possible to obtain partial release of goods by having them marked off on the receipt.

Transportation Agents

The major transportation agents, often called carriers, can be classified by method of movement into railroads, air lines, bus lines, truckers, ship lines, and pipe lines. All types of carriers operate similarly and haul goods for pay. The relative importance of transportation types is demonstrated in Table 11–2. Tons originated refers simply to the total amount loaded, while ton miles is one ton moved one mile.

Table 11–2 Transportation Agents by Tons and Ton Miles, 1963

Type Transport	Tons Originated	Ton Miles
Rail	32.8%	36.4%
Trucks	42.1	18.8
Air	—	0.1
Water	24.5	44.0
Other	0.6	0.7

Source: Census of Transportation, Commodity Transportation Survey, Part 1, 1963, pp. 5–25.

Differences among carriers are found primarily in the type of personnel and equipment used, and differences caused by the environment within which each carrier operates. The result is that each carrier has advantages and limitations based on its equipment and personnel.[14] Airlines are fast; ships and railroads can carry great weight; trucks have great flexibility of movement; and pipe lines are highly dependable. Each carrier has strengths and weaknesses. These carriers will undoubtedly reach their peak of efficiency to shippers when they can fully cooperate, and for the first time management is becoming concerned with utilizing a combination of the best means available.[15]

Common and Contract Carriers. The major types of carriers can be subdivided according to their legal form into common carriers and contract carriers.[16] Technically, any one of the carrier types can be a common or contract carrier, but in practice railroads do not operate as contract carriers. *Common carriers* haul for the general public over specified routes on a regular schedule at rates set by the government.

[13] Heskett, Ivie, and Glaskowsky, *op. cit.*, p. 48.

[14] Frank H. Mossman and Newton Martin, *Logistics of Distribution Systems* (Boston: Allyn and Bacon, Inc., 1965), pp. 51–55.

[15] "New Strategies to Move Goods," *Business Week* (September 24, 1966), pp. 112–36.

Common carriers are quasi-public utilities, and they are closely controlled by the federal government in all aspects of their operations. *Contract carriers* operate for a limited number of specific shippers based on individual contracts established between the two parties. Contract carriers haul a limited number of goods, do not have regular routes or schedules, and are more flexible in rates to particular situations than are common carriers. These contract carriers are less rigidly controlled, but they must be licensed by the Interstate Commerce Commission.

A *bill of lading* is given to a shipper using a common carrier. This bill, a receipt for the goods and a contract for their shipment, is not necessary with contract carriers because the agreement serves the same purpose. The goods are carefully listed on a bill of lading, and it may be either negotiable or non-negotiable. The owner obtains his goods by presenting his copy of the bill to the carrier at the carrier's terminal or at the owner's own loading dock. Common carriers have unlimited liability for the goods that they carry, while contract carriers are liable only for taking reasonably good care of the goods. In this respect the contract carrier has similar liability to the public warehouse. No transportation agent is liable for acts of God, acts of the owner, or acts of an enemy power.

Services of Common Carriers. Like their manner of operation, the services offered by common carriers are similar. The most important of these services are listed below.

1. *Protection.* Common carriers provide whatever protection is necessary for the goods including refrigeration, heat, and ventilation. In the case of some goods, such as cattle, the agency will feed or exercise the animals during shipment.
2. *Diversion.* This service allows a change in the routing of a shipment while in progress. In order to save time a shipper may start perishables moving to market with a tentative destination. When the best market is located, the destination is changed. The carrier considers the distance between the origin and final destination as one haul.
3. *Reconsignment.* This service allows a change in the consignee for a shipment while in progress. In most instances, diversion and reconsignment are treated the same.
4. *Transit privilege.* This service allows the shipper to unload a shipment for further manufacturing or processing at an intermediate point between origin and destination. The carrier treats the haul as continuous.
5. *Piggy back and containerization.* These services are similar. Piggy back occurs when one transporter allows the equipment of

[16] Bowerson, Smykay, and La Londe, *op. cit.*, pp. 126–27.

another to be hauled with the load inside. For example, the railroads allow trucks to be shipped on special rail flat cars. Containerization is a total system where the container of goods is designed to be loaded and hauled equally well aboard two or more types of carriers. For example, truck trailers are made to be loaded, as a unit, aboard either ships or railroad cars.

Special Shippers

There are several types of special institutions that transport goods. These include: (1) parcel post, (2) air express, (3) united parcel post, and (4) REA express. These institutions tend to be used on a limited scale mostly when small amounts of goods are to be shipped or when speed is important. Their use can be extremely important for some high unit value goods of small weight such as rare books or diamonds.

FUNCTIONS OF PHYSICAL MOVEMENT

The second element in the logistical sub-system is the physical movement of goods. Design of the logistics system requires knowledge of the activities involved. The four primary activities of logistics are: (1) traffic, (2) scheduling, (3) inventory control, and (4) material handling.[17] These functions must be performed whether the channel member uses private or agent institutions to execute logistics.

Traffic

Traffic is defined to mean the transporting of a firm's raw materials and/or finished goods. Traffic is the overall guiding function of logistics [18] and, consequently it overlaps all other functions. Traffic is the responsibility of the traffic manager, who has many duties that can be summarized under five areas. First, there is the selection of the carrier type. Second, the control of shipments status. This responsibility involves documentation of shipping dates, arrival dates, and en route status of merchandise. Records must be checked against planned status and communication established with suppliers or customers to maintain the schedule.

Third, there is the responsibility for payments. The amount of payment is established at the time of shipment, but the actual transfer of

---

[17] *Ibid.*, pp. 47–51; Heskett, Ivie, and Glaskowsky, *op. cit.*, Part IV.

[18] Heskett, Ivie, and Glaskowsky, *op. cit.*, Chapter 15; Roy J. Sampson, "Evolution of the Traffic Management Function," *Northwest Business Management* (Spring, 1966), pp. 13–17.

money is made after the arrival of the goods. Although the check may be dispatched from accounting, the traffic manager has overall responsibility. Usually, a schedule for payment is established and checked each day to determine which payments are necessary. These checks insure that prompt payments are made and that the company takes advantage of all discounts and allowances both from the transportation agencies and the suppliers.

Fourth, there is the coordination of the other logistics functions.[19] The status of goods in transit affects inventory control. Scheduling cannot be effective between production and inventory unless the status of goods in transit is known. Traffic also needs to know when materials will be ready for shipment in order to plan for carriers. Material handling requires knowledge of incoming and outgoing goods to schedule internal movement of goods effectively so that shipping and receiving are coordinated with inventory and traffic.

Fifth, there is activity analysis. This responsibility involves the measurement of carrier performance, evaluation of rates and services offered by carriers, and the measurement of internal efficiency of the traffic function.

Inventory Control

Inventory control is defined as the management of stock. Inventory control directly affects wide areas of the business enterprise including sales, production, and finance.[20] Inventory exists as a necessary device to coordinate the production of goods with the consumption of goods.[21] Some goods, such as wheat, are produced seasonally but consumed all year around. Others, such as toys, are produced all year around but consumed seasonally. Some goods, such as clothing, are produced and consumed all year around, but the rates of production and consumption vary widely. It is inventory that adjusts for all these differences. Figure 11–2 demonstrates the relationship between orders, inventory, and production output. It is easy to see how critical timing is to the entire distribution system. The lag in orders from each channel member results in a late start on production by the manufacturer. Initially, the manufacturer must meet increased orders by selling from existing supplies and backordering against future production. As inventories begin to build up, production is cut and unfilled orders decrease. The discrepancy between orders, production, and inventories evens out over time unless there is a new spurt of buying at retail. It is the nature of this response

---

[19] Raymond LeKashman and John F. Stoller, "The Total Cost Approach to Distribution," *Business Horizons* (Winter, 1965), pp. 33–46.

[20] Harlan C. Meal, "Policy Conflicts and Inventory Control," *Financial Executive* (December, 1963), pp. 13–17.

[21] Heskett, Ivie, and Glaskowsky, *op. cit.*, Chapter 11.

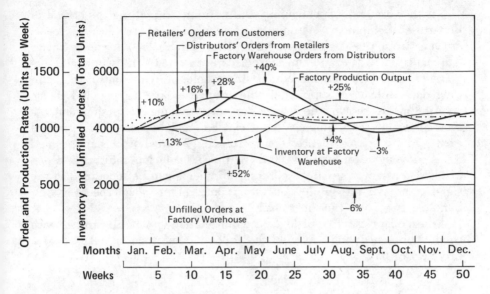

Fig. 11–2. Simulated production distribution system response to a sudden 10 per cent increase in sales at the retail level. *Source:* Jay W. Forrester, "Industrial Dynamics," *Harvard Business Review* (July–August, 1958), p. 43.

that makes monitoring of all the functions of distribution so important to management.

Scheduling

Scheduling is an essential factor in any logistics system. It is defined as the task of specifying times for the arrival and departure of goods and coordinating these times with the other logistics functions. Scheduling is a basic management device useful in many types of decision or choice situations. The function of scheduling where logistics is concerned is to coordinate receipt of raw materials, production, inventory, and ship-ments.[22] A variety of information may be needed to perform this func-tion and the actual data requirements would depend on the situation. Some of the more common information used in scheduling logistics in-cludes: (1) production, use, or sales rate, (2) order quantity, (3) set up time, (4) shipping time, (5) normal inventory, and (6) priority. Pro-duction, use, or sales rates may be forecast or determined from past ex-perience. Set-up time (the time necessary for the supplier to set up machinery and begin production) and shipping time can be estimated from averages. Normal inventory is estimated from usage rates, and priorities are set according to importance of the product or material.

[22] *Ibid.,* Chapter 14.

Another example of scheduling can be found in plotting the arrival or departure of shipment. Assume that a wholesaler of steel has shipments arriving from twelve different mills. The wholesaler can process two shipments each day, and three orders are crucial to the wholesaler because of urgent customer needs. If the wholesaler can control the shipping date from each supplier, if the properties are known, and if the transit time is known, the wholesaler can schedule these shipments to increase efficiency. Shipment dates can be staggered so that: (1) steel arrives in a proper sequence by importance, (2) steel arrives at specified times convenient for handling, and (3) there is sufficient interval between arrivals so as not to tax the facilities. Shipments can be scheduled in the same manner if the production rate is known for each type of goods, handling time, and time in transit.

An excellent example of logistics coordination can be illustrated with production scheduling. Assume the following information relative to a producer of large generators:

1. Advance order time $O = X$
2. Order quantity $Q = 500$ items
3. Set-up time $S = 5$ days
4. Shipping time $T = 10$ days
5. Production rate $P = 100$ items per day

The formula for figuring advance order time is:

$$O = S + T + \frac{Q}{P} = 5 + 10 + 5 = 20 \text{ days}$$

Other mathematical techniques that have been applied to logistics problems include MILSTRIP and PERT.[23] MILSTRIP involves determining priorities in terms of the speed of a shipment's movement. Twenty priority designations are used, based on the rated strategic importance of the shipping organization and the estimate of importance of the shipment to the receiving organization toward fulfilling its mission. An example, using PERT (Program Evaluation Review Technique), is shown in Figure 11–3. The example involves warehouse construction, but PERT has a variety of uses in logistics. As shown in the illustration, the values for a, m, and b are estimated by management, and the formula is applied to determine the mean elapsed time, t_e, for each activity to be performed. This knowledge provides a basis for planning the arrival of material and performing the necessary tasks. The *most critical path* is the one requiring the longest elapsed time. It is shown in Figure

[23] For a complete discussion see: Powell Niland, *Production Planning, Scheduling, and Inventory Control* (London: The Macmillan Co., 1970), Chapter 4; G. Hadley and T. M. Whitin, *Analysis of Inventory Systems* (Englewood Cliffs, N.J.: Prentice-Hall, Inc., 1963).

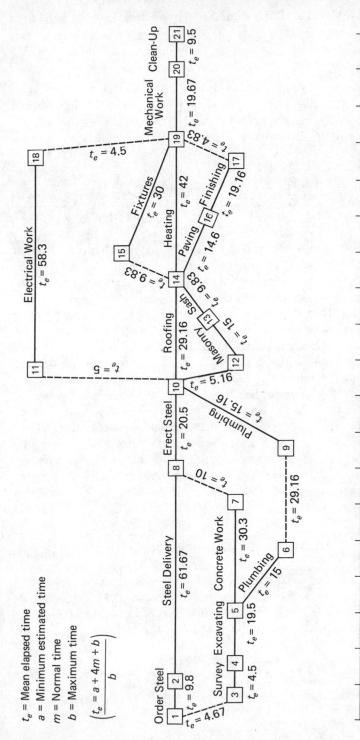

Fig. 11–3. Warehouse construction PERT network with mean elapsed time. Source: Donald J. Bowersox, Edward W. Smykay, and Bernard J. LaLonde, *Physical Distribution Management*, rev. ed. (London: The Macmillan Co., 1968), p. 392.

11–3 as 1–2–8–10–14–19–20–21, and the elapsed time can be added to 192.3 hours.

Material Handling

Material handling occurs within the plant, whereas transportation takes place outside the plant or between plants. Material handling is defined as the processing of goods internally through the organization.[24] Five specific activities are involved in material handling:

| Receiving Goods | Mixing Goods | Storing Goods | Internal Movement | Shipping Goods |
| (1) | (2) | (3) | (4) | (5) |

The reader is familiar with all activities of material handling except possibly the product mix. The mix is simply the arrangement of goods for some purpose. Both a receiving mix and a shipping mix can be identified, but only in the sense of the purpose for the mix. In a receiving mix, goods are put together that are to be stored together and are checked while being mixed to make sure the proper goods are received. In a shipping mix, goods are placed together for storage that are to be transported to buyers. These are complex activities, and more businesses are turning to automation for the performance of material handling. There is no sequence to activities of material handling. Some activities, such as movement, may be done several times. In small warehouses, the task of material handling may be accomplished in the same general area. Shipping and receiving may occur from the same platform and the storage facilities may be located nearby. In larger warehouses, these activities become specialized, with separate areas designated within the warehouse for each activity. Of course, storage requires the most space, but even this activity can be separated.

LOGISTICS COMMUNICATIONS

An integral element of all logistics sub-systems is communications.[25] Effective management of the logistics system requires a thorough knowledge of the communications processes involved. Logistics communications exactly parallels the institutions used and the functions performed

[24] Heskett, Ivie, and Glaskowsky, *op. cit.*, Chapter 14.

[25] See: John Dearden, "How to Organize Information Systems," *Harvard Business Review* (March–April, 1965). A good general discussion of how information systems function in the three stages of development: (1) system specifications, (2) data-processing implimentation, and (3) programming.

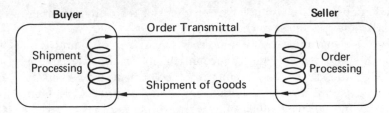

Fig. 11–4.   Order cycle.

in the logistics system. Therefore, some logistics communications are internal to the firm and some are external between the buyer and the seller.[26] Figure 11–4 is a simplified representation of logistics communications based on the order cycle.

The *order cycle* is defined as the elapsed time from determination of a need to the receipt and placement of goods in inventory. The order cycle has four steps: (1) order transmittal, (2) order processing, (3) shipment of goods, and (4) shipment processing.[27] The order cycle has two phases. *Phase one* involves purchase information. It extends from the time a buyer submits an order until the seller's warehouse is made aware of the need. *Phase two* begins with the accumulation of goods for shipment by the seller and ends when the buyer has placed the goods in inventory. This phase involves the physical movement of goods. The functions of traffic, inventory control, scheduling, and material handling are involved in both phase one and phase two of the order cycle, and each phase has its own specialized communications.

Order Transmittal

Order transmittal is the time from the discovery of a product need by the buyer to the receipt of an order by the supplier.[28] Several activities are performed at this stage, such as: (1) determining need, (2) initiating purchase, (3) informing departments of action, and (4) following up on order status. The knowledge of a need may come from several sources within the firm. Inventory records available to the purchasing department are typically the source of routine needs. While production may be the first to become aware of emergency needs or new product needs, top management is usually the first to recognize the need for capital goods. Supplier salesmen may play a part in all of these sources of needs.

---

[26] Robert M. Ivie, "Information Systems for Logistics Management," in Norton Marks and Robert Taylor, eds., *Marketing Logistics: Perspectives and Viewpoints* (New York: John Wiley & Sons, Inc., 1967).

[27] *Ibid.*, pp. 128–30. The author gives his interpretation of order processing systems; Bowersox, Smykay, and La Londe, *op. cit.*, pp. 200–1.

[28] Hesket, Ivie, and Glaskowsky, *op. cit.*, pp. 165–66.

Initiation of the purchase involves making out the purchase order, a routine task, and placing it in the mail.

Several departments may require information on purchases. Thus, copies of the order may go to accounting, manufacturing, shipping and receiving, and sales. The accounting department may need to begin processing payments and to initiate inventory control. Manufacturing is interested in the availability of raw materials and sales has the same interest in finished goods. Shipping and receiving must be made aware of goods expected to arrive. Follow-up involves correspondence between the purchasing department and the supplier to determine how the order is progressing. This information is necessary for production and sales planning and for scheduling.

Order Processing

Order processing is carried out by the supplier, not by the buyer. The shipping and receiving department is frequently responsible for this activity. Order processing is the time necessary to receive and route incoming orders to the appropriate action departments.[29] It involves receiving the order, informing action departments, and acknowledging the order. Order receipt is mechanical, but copies of the order may be forwarded to interested internal departments. The accounting department needs a copy in order to facilitate billing, the inventory control department must have a copy to make goods available for manufacturers, the production department must be informed for scheduling problems, and the sales department requires acknowledgment of sales activity. Acknowledgment of receipt of the order is automatically transmitted to the buyer. Order processing ends phase one of the order cycle.

Shipment of Goods

Shipment of the goods occurs after the manufacturing process and begins the second phase of the order cycle that pertains to the movement of goods. This second phase entails its own communications. The shipment period is the time necessary to collect goods at the shipper's plant and move them to the buyer's plant. This operation is typically carried out jointly between the store's department and the shipping and receiving department. Two important types of communications occur at the time of shipment. First, the invoice is transmitted to the buyer, placing him on notice that goods are en route. Sometimes the invoice accompanies the goods and also serves the buyer as a check on the goods. The invoice is checked against the order to determine if the desired goods were shipped, and it is checked against the actual goods to see if the correct

29 *Ibid.,* pp. 166–67.

goods arrived and what their condition is. The invoice becomes a part of the buyer's permanent record. Second, copies of the invoice are distributed internally to communicate the status of shipments to interested departments. The invoice may go to any of the same departments that received notice of the order transmittal.

Shipment Processing

The time from receipt of the goods by the buyer until their storage is called shipment processing. At this step in the order cycle the goods are unloaded, checked, and moved to inventory. The most important communication at this point comes in the form of payment transmitted to the supplier. This payment results from the internal movement of the invoice. A copy goes to the accounting department where payment is made on a regular schedule. Copies of the invoice may be sent to other interested departments including the production, sales, purchasing, and stores departments. This is also the point at which any communications concerning problems between shipper and buyer are handled. For example, communications involving bargaining, discounts, damaged goods, incomplete orders, and quality standards may be transmitted to the seller as needed. When the goods are received into storage the order cycle is complete. Of course, in practice, some goods are at one stage in the order cycle, and some are at another.

COST OF PRIVATE LOGISTICS

Every logistics system, whether privately operated or utilizing agents, has an associated cost, and management must understand this cost if the system is to be effectively designed and operated. There is evidence that logistics costs more than it should largely because business has not devoted adequate attention to logistics management. One study measured the performance of logistics and discovered that in twenty-six large and profitable companies only five rated good in logistics management.[30] The companies were tested on the basis of: (1) generation and use of information, (2) competence of personnel, (3) concern for distribution economics, and (4) capacity to deal with distribution problems.

The cost of a business performing its own logistics is the combined expense of warehousing and transportation including the cost of communications. Logistics is a major activity of the channel and the associated cost can be great. For this reason, only the larger business organizations typically attempt to maintain complete private logistics systems.

[30] Robert P. Neuschel, "Physical Distribution—Forgotten Frontier," *Harvard Business Review* (March–April, 1967), pp. 125–34.

Types of Private Logistic Cost

The major cost of warehousing includes: (1) cost of the facility, (2) cost of equipment, (3) labor cost, (4) cost of keeping and handling goods, (5) depreciation, (6) maintenance and repairs, (7) cost of record keeping, and (8) shortages. Capital and labor costs are two of the most important warehousing costs. Equipment includes items necessary to receive and ship goods and items for internal movement. Shortages are caused by theft, errors in handling, and errors in reporting. The dollar figure for warehousing varies from business to business, depending on the efficiency of operations. It is an important cost in almost any business.

The major costs of private transportation include: (1) cost of rolling stock, (2) labor cost, (3) depreciation, (4) supplies, (5) repairs, (6) handling cost, and (7) cost of facilities. Rolling stock—mostly trucks, although some firms have their own ships—and labor are the most important transportation costs. Repairs include the cost of servicing the rolling stock and other equipment while supplies consist mostly of fuel and parts. The facilities involved are repair shops and garages.

Leased Facilities and Equipment

The facilities and equipment necessary for private logistics may be either owned or leased. Leasing is the rental of buildings, land, or equipment from the owner for a fee, either in the form of rent, as in leasing warehouses, or in the form of a "use fee." [31] A use fee involves not only the basic rent of the item such as a truck, but it includes an extra charge, similar to a commission, related to the distance over which the vehicle is used. Leasing of facilities or equipment has the general advantage that the charge is known in advance and the cost does not vary in the short run. Leasing rolling stock has the specific advantage of shifting the cost of such stock to the leasor. It has the further advantage of shifting many headaches of operation such as maintenance, scheduling, and leads problems to the leasing company. Of course, leasing rolling stock necessitates relinquishing some control over the equipment and restricts the firm's flexibility in using this equipment. Many firms who do their own transporting, such as A & P, follow a policy of leasing wherever possible.

Leased warehouses are more common than leased rolling stock. The decision to lease warehousing facilities involves basically a financial problem. Leasing can greatly reduce the cost of capital for a firm, but it is not always easy to find facilities when and where the firm wants them. In fact, leasing warehouses may place a greater burden on transportation if effective placement cannot be obtained, and much of the advantage of

---

[31] Vincent M. Jolivet, "Equipment Lease Financing," *University of Washington Business Review* (February, 1961).

leasing the warehouse may be offset by increased transportation and handling cost. A great many firms use a combination system of private ownership and leasing where both transportation and warehousing are concerned.

PUBLIC WAREHOUSE AND CONTRACT CARRIER RATES

The rate structure of public warehouses and contract carriers are discussed together because of the similarity in how the two charge for their services. The basic rate charged by a public warehouse is a *per unit per month rate*. It amounts to a rental for volume of space utilized. Volume, usually measured in tons, is substituted for units in the case of bulk items such as corn, wheat, steel, or other commodities or raw materials. Public warehouse rates are controlled by the Interstate Commerce Commission, and the commission does allow deviations from the rate for special circumstances. The merchant who uses the public warehouse may receive discounts based on a regular schedule of amounts for storing in large quantities. There are sometimes special charges levied by the public warehouse for such services as providing desk space for salesmen, special handling of bulky equipment, or breaking cartons for reshipment. Rates for field warehousing are handled the same as for terminal warehousing except that the warehouseman charges out-of-pocket cost for setting up the field warehouse.

It is very difficult to generalize about contract carrier rates because the rate is contained in an individually determined contract. Any legal action can be included in a contract, so rates are an individualistic matter. In practice, a contract carrier can charge any amount that is agreeable to the shipper. Contract carriers normally establish the rate either as a per package charge or a cost plus charge, or the rate is fixed on the volume of goods hauled. In some instances the shipper is quoted a lump sum figure.

COMMON CARRIER RATES

The structure of common carrier rates is much more complex than that of the contract carriers, and they are strictly regulated by the federal government.[32] This is partly due to the several different types of common carriers, the particular conditions under which common carriers operate, and the special services offered by common carriers. However, the common carriers do employ similar rate structures although the terms placed on some rates may reflect industry practices. Common carrier rates can

[32] Charles Luna, *The Handbook of Transportation in the United States* (New York: The Popular Library, 1971), Chapter 3. A good summary of regulation history.

be divided into three types: (1) basic rates, (2) discount rates, and (3) service charges.[33]

Basic Rates

Basic rates are the standard rates around which all variations are figured. These rates are determined on the basis of ton miles or tons originated. There are two types of basic rates: class rates and commodity rates.[34] *Class rates* are standard rates that are designated by particular groups of merchandise. Any goods moved by common carrier can be shipped under class rates where each type of goods shipped is given a classification with similar goods, and a rate is assigned to each class. *Commodity rates* are lower than class rates. They also fit the general idea of a standard rate because they are regular rates assigned to basic commodities. The term commodity rate does not necessarily refer to farm commodities, although that may have been the original idea. Commodity rates are established on all types of goods that move regularly between two points in sufficient volume. The low rate is justified because of the economy of scale involved in the handling of such shipments. Commodity rates have precedence over class rates. Thus, a good may be assigned a class rate that applies unless it moves in sufficient tonnage to make a commodity rate feasible. Approximately ninety per cent of all goods shipped on rails take a commodity rate.

Discount Rates

Discount rates are applied to either the class rate or the commodity rate. Discount rates are reductions from the basic rate because of some particular factor or circumstance.[35] There are three types of discount rates: exception rates, distance rates, and quantity rates. *Exception rates* are granted for particular circumstances and are lower rates than either class or commodity rates. Exception rates may be established because of the problems of back haul, large volume shipment, competition, or any other special circumstances. *Distance rates* are discounts granted because of the distance goods are shipped. The high fixed cost of most common carriers makes it economical to ship for long distances. As a result, all basic rates increase with distance, but the increase is not in proportion to the increase in distance. Thus, the total cost increases for shipping longer distances, but the unit cost decreases. These distance rates are often associated with "key" points. When key points are grouped together into

[33] Heskett, Ivie, and Glaskowsky, *op. cit.*, pp. 93–110.

[34] Bowersox, Smykay and La Londe, *op. cit.*, 136–39.

[35] William H. Dodge, "Purchasing Transportation Service," *Journal of Purchasing*, Vol. 1 (May, 1965), pp. 24–37. Discount rates are identified and explained in this article.

the same rate group either at the destination or the origin the result is a "blanket rate" system.

Quantity rates are exactly the same as any quantity discount. These rates are reductions from the class or commodity rates granted for shipping in large amounts. The standard unit for measure is a carload in the rail industry, a truckload in the trucking industry, and a planeload in the aircraft industry. Thus, in the rail industry these rates are listed as LCL or CL. LCL rates mean less than carload while CL rates refer to carload rates. The carload rate is a lower rate than the less than carload rate.

Service Charges

Common carriers do levy special charges for extra services rendered. Diversion, consignment, transit, and split delivery all carry special charges. For example, diversion and reconsignment typically involve a flat fee of $10 or less. The charges for split delivery and the transit privilege vary, but in no case is the charge sufficiently large to offset the advantage of using the service. Protection generally carries no extra charge, but one may be levied if the shipper asks for special protection. This charge is typically a flat fee. Besides the service charges noted above there are two other important charges levied by the transportation agencies. One is called demurrage. This is a flat charge made for not unloading the car or truck on time. The consignee typically has forty-eight hours of free unloading time, after which the charge is made. The other charge is a switching charge. This charge is made when the agency switches the consignee's car to the point of unloading.

Responsibility for Freight Charges

Responsibility for freight charges basically involves who pays the freight and is determined as a part of the terms of sale of merchandise. The two types of terms are f.o.b. (free on board), shipping point and f.o.b., destination. *F.o.b., shipping point* means that title to the goods passes at the shipper's plant. Along with title passes the responsibility for the payment of freight, the determination of shipment routing, and responsibility for the goods while in transit. *F.o.b., destination* means that title passes at the buyer's plant, responsibility for shipment and routing are in the hands of the seller, and the seller is responsible for the safety of the goods. The term, f.o.b. plant, may include the statement "freight allowed." Freight allowed means that transportation charges are paid by the seller even though title passes at the seller's plant.

It is difficult to judge the fairness of the two methods as Figure 11–5 illustrates. Under f.o.b. plant, buyer A and B pay in proportion to the actual distance shipped. This arrangement would appear fair, except that buyer B can charge that he is being discriminated against because of his

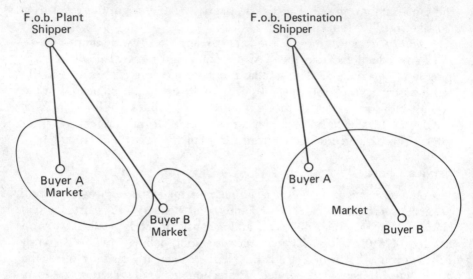

Fig. 11–5. Comparison of f.o.b. plant and f.o.b. destination.

farther location. In fact, f.o.b. plant pricing does give buyer A a competitive advantage if the two are sufficiently close to compete. An argument could be made that the result is to divide the market and reduce competition. Under the terms of f.o.b. destination, both buyer A and buyer B receive the goods at the same price because there is no freight charge. The shipper pays the freight to each buyer out of a portion of his margin, a practice known as freight absorption. Under freight absorption, buyer A can claim discrimination because buyer B is not paying his share for the extra distance the goods are hauled. It is assumed that the shipper must raise the price of his goods to both A and B sufficiently to cover the cost of transportation. In any case f.o.b. destination terms tend to cause buyer A and B to compete and to expand the total market of both. Nevertheless, the government tends to prefer f.o.b. plant when freight charges are assigned.

Basing Points

The previous discussion assumed that the freight charge was made from the same point as the shipment of goods. Historically, this agreement did not always occur, especially for businesses where freight was a large part of the total cost of goods. Some shippers, particularly in the steel and concrete industries, employed basing points. A basing point is a city used as a reference for figuring the standard shipping cost to any

---► Distance freight charged

——► Distance goods shipped

Fig. 11–6. Basing point system.

other city. The reference city is utilized to calculate freight, no matter where the goods are shipped from. Basing points can be either single or multiple.

A single basing point means that the freight is charged from a single city, say Chicago, no matter where the goods originate. Examples 1 and 2 in Figure 11–6 illustrate the operation of a single basing point where farm equipment is shipped from two different points but freight is charged from Chicago. The single base may apply to all sellers in an industry, as shown in example 3. Although the suppliers are located far apart, the freight charged is the same. A multiple basing point system operates the same as the single basing point, except more bases are used.

There is discrimination involved in the use of basing points because of freight absorption and phantom freight. *Phantom freight* is the practice of charging freight in excess of the actual distance shipped. There is phantom freight in example 1. *Freight absorption* occurs when the shipper assumes all, or a part, of the freight cost out of operating margin. This happens in example 2. Example 3 has both freight absorption and phantom freight. In example 1, the customer is discriminated against because of the overcharge. In example 3 the Memphis shipper is discriminated against because he pays the same freight as the Los Angeles shipper in spite of his closer location to the market. Notice, that in spite of the discrimination, the basing point system may increase competition by equalizing freight cost to competitors in the same market. In effect, no competitor has a cost advantage based on freight alone. The problems of phantom freight and freight absorption caused the government to become interested in basing points after World War II. Because a series of court decisions were handed down against the practice, the use of basing points has been so restricted as to make them impractical. The Interstate Commerce Commission tends to encourage f.o.b. pricing.

Freight Zones

The cost of figuring the freight between the warehouse and each buyer can become serious even when f.o.b. terms are quoted. The cost of time, labor, supplies, and depreciation add up. Often it is simpler for the seller to establish zones across the United States and compute the average cost of shipping into each zone (see Figure 11–7). The average cost of shipping into each zone can be automatically applied to all shipments into the zone. The resulting savings can be passed on to customers, sometimes lowering the cost of transportation to all.

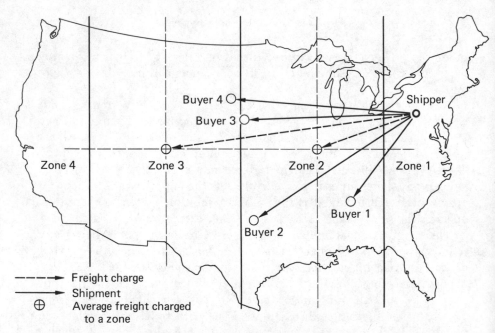

Fig. 11–7. Zone pricing of shipments.

There are two problems with zone rates. First, buyers located nearer the shipper within a zone claim they are discriminated against because they pay a part of the freight of buyers located farther from the shipper. In the example, buyer 1 is discriminated against compared to buyer 2 in zone 2. Second, there is the problem of competitors who are located close together (buyers 3 and 4) on the line between two zones. Buyer 4 in zone 3 pays considerably more freight than buyer 3 in zone

2, thereby placing him at a competitive disadvantage. Actually, the two buyers may be located only a few miles apart. As a result, the government has been interested in zone pricing for years and some prices have been declared illegal. The result is that shippers tend to use zone pricing only when there are vastly greater costs of shipping into one zone compared to another. For example, we often see in advertisements the statement: slightly higher on the west coast. This is a two-zone system, with the west coast one zone and the remainder of the country another.

QUESTIONS

1. Define logistics. How does logistics differ from transportation? Storage?
2. Discuss the operation of agent warehouses.
3. Compare and contrast common and contract carriers for manner of operation and services rendered.
4. Discuss the traffic inventory, scheduling, and material handling functions of physical movement.
5. Discuss how communications affects shipment processing and shipment receipt.
6. Explain basic common carrier rates.
7. Explain common carrier discount rates and relate them to basic rates.
8. Contrast f.o.b. plant and f.o.b. destination terms. Is f.o.b. plant or f.o.b. destination more competitive?
9. What is meant by basing points?
10. Discuss the operation of freight zones.

12

Logistics Decisions
of the Shipper

Chapter 12 emphasizes the types of logistics systems that the shipper may utilize as well as his logistics decisions. Logistics is viewed from the point of view of the channel's manager who is faced with the problem of the physical movement of goods.

MANAGEMENT OF THE LOGISTICS SYSTEM

Logistics is an integral part of the whole channel operation, and management in this area is as important as in any channel function. The management of a logistics system has the same general task as management of any other activity of the business: to balance cost and revenue in order to contribute profit to the business and satisfy customers.[1]

Physical distribution management can be defined as: "that responsibility to design and administer systems to control raw materials and finished goods flow."[2] The responsibilities of the logistics manager in meeting his general obligation to the firms may be grouped under seven general headings. These seven responsibilities are: (1) to decide the type of logistics system to use, (2) to choose between private or agent logistics, (3) to select the type of common carrier, (4) to design the logistics organization, (5) to determine the logistics mix, (6) to de-

[1] John F. Gustafson and Raymond Richard, "Customer Service In Physical Distribution," *Transportation and Distribution Management* (April, 1964), pp. 19–23. A good discussion of the importance of customer service to physical distribution.

[2] Donald J. Bowersox, Edward W. Smykay, and Bernard J. LaLonde, *Physical Distribution Management* (London: The Macmillan Co., 1969), p. 5.

termine warehouse locations, and (7) to decide warehouse operations. These decision areas are the subject of the remainder of the chapter.

TYPES OF LOGISTICS SYSTEMS

The logistics elements of institutions, functions, communications, and reward can be combined in the marketing channel in a number of different ways. It is the purpose of this section to demonstrate these different types of logistical systems. We also seek to show how the use of various logistical systems affects integration in the channel.

Combination of Logistics Elements

The logistics manager has several choices for combining transportation and storage within the marketing channel. Figure 12–1 demonstrates these choices. The three basic types are: (1) to move goods wholly by private means, (2) to use agent specialists for the entire logistics job,

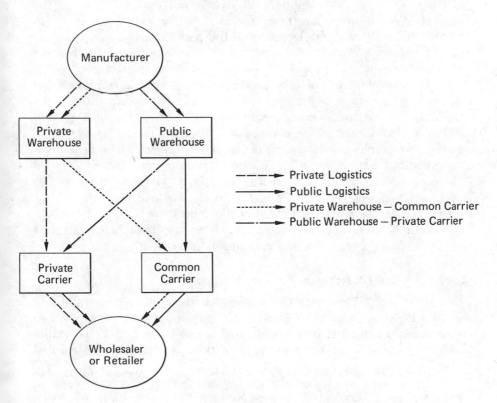

Fig. 12–1. Methods of combining logistics.

and (3) to use some combination of public and private logistics. The most common logistics channel is a combination of public and private with its movement: manufacturer–private warehouses–common carrier–wholesaler or retailer. Another choice exists where a combination of private and public warehouse is used in conjunction with a combination of private and public carriers. This multiple distribution system is more common than one might think.

There is considerable variation in the functions performed, communications employed, and cost incurred when the various logistical combinations are used.[3] The choice made by management depends on how these variations are evaluated. When logistics is privately carried out, it means that the firm is responsible for all the functions of logistics. Thus, the firm performs traffic, inventory control, scheduling, and material handling. Private logistics also implies that the entire burden of communications falls on the firm. When the firm uses public warehousing and common carriers, the shipper's responsibility is reduced. These agents assume all the logistics functions, although their liability is limited to those functions. The shipper still has overall responsibility for the products. When agents are used, communications may be reduced to routine follow-up and checks made on the performance of agents. The cost of logistics is flexible to control under private performance, but the use of agents routinizes cost and makes it relatively predictable.[4]

When a combination of private and agent logistics is employed, the system may become quite complex. In effect, the performance of the logistics functions and communications is duplicated between private and agent institutions. This complicates the tasks in two ways. First, there is the problem of each type of institution keeping track of its own performance. Second, there is the new element of coordinating internal and external logistics. Furthermore, the cost of logistics also becomes more involved when private performance is combined with the use of agents. Some costs are routinized while others are not, and the coordination of costs becomes necessary. However, total logistical costs may be reduced because of the specialization provided.

Logistics Used To Achieve Vertical Integration

Any attempt to integrate the channel of distribution must take into account logistics. Figure 12–2 shows how logistics can be important to integration. In the first case the channel is non-integrated. The wholesaler is responsible for the movement of title and for the physical dis-

---

[3] Raymond Lekashman and John F. Stolle, "The Total Cost Approach to Distribution," *Business Horizons* (Winter, 1965), pp. 33–46; Marvin Flaks, "Total Cost Approach to Physical Distribution," *Business Management* (August, 1963), pp. 55–61.

[4] Ronald J. Lewis, "Strengthening Control of Physical Distribution Cost," *Management Services* (January–February, 1968), pp. 36–46.

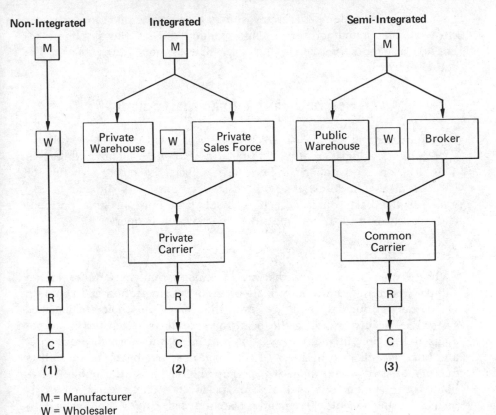

M = Manufacturer
W = Wholesaler
R = Retailer
C = Consumer

Fig. 12–2. Logistics and vertical integration.

tribution of the product. In the second case, the channel is fully integrated. The manufacturer has taken over the physical movement, as well as the transfer of title to the product. The manufacturer has duplicated, through private logistics, the wholesaler's function, and the wholesaler has been bypassed. In this second case, a common carrier can be substituted for a private one, and the logistics becomes partly public and partly private. The end result is the same.

The third case demonstrates how the public warehouse can be combined with the use of brokers to duplicate the wholesaler's function. This is an example of a semi-integrated channel. Although the wholesaler is eliminated, he is eliminated by the use of independent agent middlemen who can only be partially controlled by the manufacturer. The brokers referred to can be either manufacturer's agents or sales agents. The public warehouse receives goods from a carrier, warehouses, breaks goods down for reshipment, receives orders from salesmen, and manages carriers. The manufacturer's agent, working out of the public warehouse, can handle sales in the territory. The common carrier makes the actual deliveries.

CHOICE OF AGENT OR PRIVATE LOGISTICS

A fundamental choice of every shipper is whether to take full responsibility for logistics or to transfer a part of it to agent middlemen. This decision is so important because it affects the entire structure of logistics in the business. As with most decisions, it is difficult to say which is the best course of action. Each firm must make a personal choice according to the unique situation in which it operates.

General Factors Affecting Logistics Choice

There are certain factors that are of almost equal importance to the shipper in choosing between private or agent transportation and storage.[5] Called general factors, there are seven that affect the choice of logistics systems. The first factor is the need for specialists. Logistics is a specialized function in many ways different from the normal production and sales aspects of a business. If the firm does not have the specialists or cannot easily obtain them, it is perhaps better to use the public warehouse or common carrier that are specialists. The second factor is financial requirements. Tremendous amounts of capital are needed to construct warehouses, purchase rolling stock, provide for repair shops, acquire labor, etc. Unless the business has this capital it may have no choice but to use agents. The limitation of finances is one of the most important deterrents to the use of private logistics.

The third factor is control. Control refers to the assurance that logistics is performed in the manner that the firm desires. A business may require quick delivery or special handling of merchandise. If control is important, and if the firm has the finances, then private logistics is called for. The fourth factor is management preference. Management's preference for performing logistics may be based on sound facts or not, but it is a factor that must be considered in any case.

The fifth factor is operating cost. Cost is predetermined when agent logistics is used, but it varies according to performance with private logistics. If the company can perform logistics at about the same cost as the agents, other things being equal, then private performance is

---

[5] For a case history of how one firm dealt with the physical distribution system's efficiency see: Kenneth W. Hessler, "Assignment—Design and Phase-In a New Distribution System," *Transportation and Distribution Management* (January, 1965), pp. 35–43.

indicated. The sixth factor is the product. Some products are so specialized or bulky that private logistics is the only feasible manner of handling them. Heavy machinery or equipment and automobiles are examples. Standardized items that are shipped regularly and in bulk call for agent logistics. The seventh factor is the customer.[6] The shipper must consider the customer's desire for speed and service. There is also the customer's tolerance for delays, incorrect shipments, damaged goods, overcharging, etc. The shipper cannot long abuse the customer and survive.

Factors Affecting Warehousing Choice

Besides the general factors affecting the choice of agent or private logistics, there are several specific factors that relate to the choice of warehousing. These specific factors must be considered with the general factors.

Most merchant businesses cannot avoid the use of some private warehousing. The most important reason is the difficulty of moving goods directly from the assembly line to buyers or to public warehouses; it is very hard to coordinate production and shipping perfectly. At least some temporary storage is necessary to hold goods for the carrier. Once the decision is made to do some private warehousing, the cost to take on the entire burden may not be significantly greater. The difference in cost is the difference between operating a small warehouse or a large one. While capital cost and labor cost may increase some, the cost of equipment and of running the office may not increase significantly. Thus, private warehousing tends to be normal in most American industries. There are other advantages to private warehousing including: (1) better control, (2) fewer errors in handling, (3) low cost if volume is high, (4) inadequate public warehouses, and (5) special design requirements.[7]

Five factors influence the merchant to use public warehouses: (1) lack of storage space, (2) seasonal product variations, (3) need for a warehouse receipt, (4) customer service requirements, and (5) greater efficiency of public warehouses. A company may supplement its own warehouse with public warehouses when the company is producing more than its own warehouses can accommodate. This situation may occur in periods of peak economic activity. Seasonal product variations is slightly different. It occurs regularly and predictably. A company may build its warehouses for normal production output and use public ware-

---

[6] E. Grosvenor Plowman, "For Good or Ill Users Influence Transportation," *The Annuals of the Academy of Political and Socal Science* (January, 1963); Bud Reese, "Boosting Sales Through Customer Service," *Industrial Marketing* (November, 1961).

[7] E. M. Maney, "How to Cut Warehousing Costs: Some Practical Guides for the Distribution Manager," *Management and Physical Distribution Function* (Chicago: American Marketing Association, Management Report No. 49, 1960), pp. 40–47.

houses for the seasonal peaks. This utilization keeps capital costs down and makes maximum use of the facilities. A company may also use public warehouses to obtain the warehouse receipt which can be used as collateral on loans. Merchandise makes good collateral because it is tangible and easily disposed of.

Customers may require quick delivery and constant attention; public warehouses may be the only feasible way to handle some of these customers without building excessive warehouses. Public warehouses, because of their numbers, type, and locations, are very flexible to customer needs. Public warehouses are strategically located to service most customers and they are flexible to the space needs of their principles. In "their" markets there may be no alternative to the public warehouse because of excessive cost of private warehousing. The efficiency of public warehouses is extremely important since they are frequently less costly due to the fact that costs are spread over several principals, they employ experts, equipment is the most modern, and warehousing gets their complete attention.[8]

Factors Affecting Transportation Choice

There are factors that specifically relate to the choice of transportation that deserve the shipper's careful attention. Most merchant middlemen are biased toward the use of common or contract carriers for transportation. The bias is logically based on added responsibility and cost. Actually, most of the seven factors that apply directly to the choice of the type of carrier favor the use of agent carriers.

First, there are services to be considered. The agent carriers offer a variety of services, such as the transit privilege, reconsignment, and containerization, that are difficult to duplicate at the same cost privately. Where these services are not important, the opportunity to use private carriers is increased. Second, the availability of different methods of transport must be considered. Relatively low cost rail and relatively fast air carriers are generally not available privately and, in order to use these carriers, the shipper must go to the agent carriers. The most popular private carrier is the truck. Third, the shipper must consider the amount of flexibility needed in shipment. Because there are so many common carriers, there is great flexibility in cost, routing, speed, and handling among the common carriers. Private carriers are more likely to be used where transportation takes place regularly between well-defined points that are easily accessible.

Fourth, it is necessary to consider the amount of product to be shipped. Certain basic raw materials such as coal, iron ore, or timber are shipped

[8] Gerald A. Fitzgerald, "Why Not Public Computerized Distribution Centers," *Distribution Age* (May, 1967), pp. 51–57.

in such large quantities that it is almost impossible for private carriers to handle the load. Fifth, the availability of facilities is an important factor. Most private carriers cannot match the terminals, yard, loading and unloading equipment available with common carriers. Furthermore, the cost of public transportation is usually less than that of private means. However, if these items are not important in the shipment, there is the possibility of using private transport. Sixth, there is the risk of shipment. Risk is of two types. There is the normal risk of owning goods. If the shipper uses his own means, he must bear the risk burden of damage, loss, or delay himself. The other risk is theft. In recent years, hijacking has become relatively commonplace in the United States. When common carriers are used, these risks are shifted to the agent. Seventh, there is control. When the shipper uses public carriers he loses control over shipping. Some firms prefer to incur the cost of owning, operating, and maintaining equipment plus the added labor cost to gain this control. Control may sometimes be essential to service customers properly.

Interaction of Factors

All the factors discussed above interact. The decision concerning which type of logistics to use may be quite clear when considering only one factor at a time, but it becomes less clear when dealing with more than one factor. For example, if the cost of private transportation is considerably greater than the common carrier, we would say to use the latter. However, suppose the cost of private transportation is great and the company does not have the necessary specialists for private transport, but the product requires special handling, and loading equipment. Now, what course of action would the manager recommend? In most cases, a trade-off of factors is necessary, and the choice is seldom ideal. Each management must make its own evaluation.

SELECTION OF COMMON CARRIER TYPE

The decision by management to use common carriers leads to evaluation of the operating characteristics of the several common carriers. There are five operating characteristics: speed in delivery, frequency of service, dependability of service, movement capability, and availability of service.[9] Each carrier has its own distinct behavior patterns, based on these characteristics, which make it more or less suitable for a particular transportation task.[10]

[9] Based on: J. L. Heskett, Robert M. Ivie, and Nicholas A. Glaskowsky, Jr., *Business Logistics* (New York: The Ronald Press Co., 1973).
[10] Thomas F. Dillon, "What's the Best Way to Ship," *Purchasing* (August 10, 1964). A good discussion of the specific advantages and disadvantages of each method of transport.

Carrier Rank by Operating Characteristics

Table 12–1 gives the rank of the major common carriers by operating characteristics.[11] Each rank represents an overall tendency and does not mean that the carrier ranks first in every single operating instance. For

Table 12–1   Rank by Operating Characteristics

Type Carrier	Speed of Operation	Frequency of Service	Dependa- bility of Service	Movement Capability	Avail- bility of Service	Composite Rank
Air lines	1	3	5	4	3	3.2 (3)
Railroads	3	4	3	2	2	2.8 (2)
Truck lines	2	2	2	3	1	2.0 (1)
Ship lines	4	5	4	1	4	3.6 (5)
Pipe lines	5	1	1	5	5	3.4 (4)

example, air lines rank first in speed of delivery, but a truck can make the haul from Chicago, Illinois, to Milwaukee, Wisconsin, faster because of the short distance involved and because of the slowness of terminal operations for the air line. The railroads rank high in capacity and availability.[12] Where speed is concerned, the air lines can make one-day deliveries across country. By comparison, trucks average approximately 35 mph; railroads 19.5 mph; ship lines between 20–25 knots; and pipe lines 1–5 mph.

Pipe lines are far ahead of the other carriers in both frequency and dependability of service. They can be operated constantly day and night, and there is very little equipment to break down. Ships have the greatest haul capacity, followed by the railroads. Trucks are the most available. Even when ships or rail are used for the long haul, the goods are generally delivered to and from the ship or rail by truck. Trucks can go anywhere that roads exist. Each of the other carriers is restricted either by dependence on scarce terminals, as in the case of ships and planes, or by fixed roadbeds as in the case of railroads and pipe lines. Notice that trucks rank first in overall performance, even though they rank first in only one characteristic. This is due to their relatively high rank in all categories. Ship lines have the poorest overall rank, although a ship may be just the right carrier for a given shipper.

[11] See: Frank H. Mossman and Newton Morton, *Logistics of Distribution Systems* (Boston: Allyin and Bacon, Inc., 1965), p. 55.

[12] Henry G. Hohorst, "The Role of Railroads in Future Distribution Systems," *Transportation Research Forum* (1964).

Choice of Common Carrier

Table 12–1 illustrated clearly that each carrier has its own distinct operating characteristics which make it more or less suitable for a particular logistics task. However, this is insufficient information for arriving at a choice between carriers. Any particular selection by a business must result from a comparison of desirable operating features and the cost involved. The actual cost of shipping is an individual matter with each firm, reflecting tonnage, distance, handling, inventory, etc., but it is possible to generalize on the relative cost of different methods of transport. Table 12–2 shows the proportional use of carrier types related to distance.

Water carriers rank first for having the lowest cost. Ships cost about .006 cent per ton mile, trucks .04 cent per ton mile, railroads .01 cent per ton mile, and air lines .10 cents per ton mile.[13] Thus, there is an almost inverse relationship between speed and cost. Table 12–3 demonstrates how shippers tend to evaluate the use of common carriers for selected products.

In practice, a carrier may be selected because of one of the overriding operating characteristics in spite of the specific cost. Perishable goods, fashion goods, or goods of high unit value and low bulk tend to use the faster means of transportation. The choice may be based almost entirely on the cost of shipment with bulk purchases such as basic raw materials. Most decisions involve some combination of cost and operating characteristics. For example, trucks fall in the middle range on all operating characteristics, and the cost of trucks is also relatively low. This fact, no doubt, accounts for the popularity of truck shipment.

DESIGN OF THE LOGISTICS ORGANIZATION

No matter whether the firm's management selects private logistics or decides to use public warehouses and common carriers, it organizes to accomplish its goal and to complement the other activities of the business. Management can utilize a centralized organization, a decentralized organization, or a combination of the two. The choice is serious, and the consequences important to the business. A mistake can cost the firm millions of dollars in facilities, equipment, and personnel without providing for efficient performance. The particular organization utilized for logistics reflects management evaluation of: (1) size of the firm, (2) importance and/or cost of logistics, (3) available management talent, (4) customer service standards, and (5) nature of the product.[14] Each factor should be considered carefully and its contribution to company objectives estimated.

---

[13] Bowersox, Smykay and LaLonde, *op. cit.*, p. 131.
[14] Heskett, Ivie, and Glaskowsky, *op. cit.*, Chapter 17.

Table 12-2 Relationships Between Distance Shipped and Modal Choice, for Selected Shipper Classes, 1967

Shipper Class and Method of Transportation	Proportion of Total Tons, By Distance Shipped					Percentage of Total Tons
	Under 200 Miles	200–399 Miles	400–599 Miles	600–999 Miles	1,000 Miles and Over	
Shipper Class 021—Canned Fruits and Vegetables:						
Rail	11.6%	39.8%	55.9%	60.2%	85.2%	51.8%
Motor carrier	36.3	32.0	25.5	29.4	6.4	23.7
Private truck	49.4	28.2	18.5	7.8	3.7	21.8
Water	2.5	–	–	2.6	4.4	2.5
Other	.2	–	.1	–	.3	.2
Total	100.0%	100.0%	100.0%	100.0%	100.0%	100.0%
Percentage of total tons	25.3%	19.6%	8.0%	13.8%	33.3%	
Shipper Class 052—Women's, Misses', Girls', and Infants' Clothing:						
Rail	–	.1%	24.3%	19.1%	6.0%	10.0%
Motor carrier	53.5%	70.3	60.0	49.6	69.3	59.0
Private truck	36.4	9.0	.3	12.2	–	14.1
Other	10.1	20.6	15.4	19.1	24.7	16.9*
Total	100.0%	100.0%	100.0%	100.0%	100.0%	100.0%
Percentage of total tons	29.1%	10.3%	20.0%	21.0%	19.6%	

of Petroleum Refining:

Rail	8.4%	8.1%	19.6%	3.3%	1.4%	5.7%
Motor carrier	27.9	8.2	5.8	.5	.2	9.9
Private truck	12.4	2.3	.4	.1	–	4.0
Water	51.1	81.1	74.2	96.1	98.4	80.3
Other	.2	.3	–	–	–	.1
Total	100.0%	100.0%	100.0%	100.0%	100.0%	100.0%
Percentage of total tons	29.7%	14.0%	4.8%	22.4%	29.1%	100.0%

Shipper Class 242—Measuring, Controlling, and Indicating Instruments:

Rail	.2%	2.1%	.6%	5.9%	11.6%	3.9%
Motor carrier	90.1	85.9	71.1	78.5	71.8	81.3
Private truck	4.2	3.8	7.5	6.7	2.1	4.6
Other	5.5	8.2	20.8	8.9	14.5	10.2†
Total	100.0%	100.0%	100.0%	100.0%	100.0%	100.0%
Percentage of total tons	28.2%	22.6%	11.6%	18.9%	18.7%	100.0%

*Includes 1.4 percentage points for air and the remainder for parcel post and privately owned small-package transportation services.

†Includes 2.2 percentage points for air, 1.1 for water, and much of the remainder for parcel post and privately owned small-package transportation services.

Source: James L. Heskett, Nicholas A. Glaskowski, Jr., and Robert M. Ivie, *Business Logistics*, 2nd ed. (New York: The Ronald Press, Co., 1973), p. 64.

Table 12-3   Percentage of Shipment of Selected Product
by Specific Carrier, 1963

Rail-oriented Products	Percent by Rail
Cereal preparations	97.3
Canned meat	88.5
Animal byproducts (inedible)	87.7
Iron, steel scrap, and tailings	86.7
Metal, scrap wastes, and tailings	83.5
Lumber and dimension stock	81.6
Cigarettes	72.6
Canned specialties	72.3
Food and kindred products	66.1
Motor-Carrier-oriented Products	Percent by Motor
Gloves and mittens	98.1
Envelopes, except stationery	96.2
Show and trophy cases	92.4
Architectural and ornamental metal work	85.9
Bedspreads and bed sets	85.1
Nonferrous metal castings	84.3
Special dies and tools, die sets, jigs, and fixtures	83.0
Rubber belts and belting	80.8
Specialty cleaning and sanitation preparations	78.6
Water-oriented Products	Percent by Water
Distillate fuel oil	98.4
Residual fuel oil	95.3
Products of petroleum refining	94.2
Petroleum and coal products	93.0
Air-oriented Products	Percent by air
Computing and accounting machines	25.0
Calculating and accounting machines	8.3
Special dies and tools, die sets, jigs, and fixtures	6.6
Millinery—caps and hats	5.8
Parts and attachments for pumps	3.9
Miscellaneous apparel	3.8
Hardware and saw blades	2.7
Nonferrous metal	2.3
Rubber belts and belting	2.1
Women's handbags and purses	2.1
Heat exchangers and steam condensers	1.8

Source: Donald J. Bowersox, Edward W. Smykay, Bernard J. LeLonde, *Physical Distribution Management* (London: The Macmillan Co., 1968), p. 130.

Centralized Organization for Logistics

When logistics is centralized it means that authority and responsibiilty
are centered in the business's top management. There is little diffusion
of decision making throughout the lower management levels of the firm
concerning transportation and storage. Figure 12-3 demonstrates the

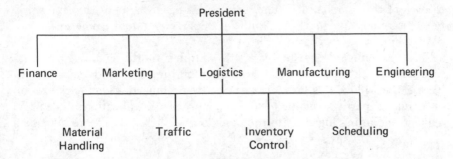

Fig. 12–3. Centralized logistics for a manufacturing plant.

organization of a manufacturing firm with centralized logistics.[15] The logistics manager is equal to the other business managers organizationally, and he reports directly to the president. This type of organization is typical for single plant operations. There is a single warehouse from which traffic material handling, inventory, and scheduling emanate. Each of these activities may have a manager in a large organization, or, in smaller firms, some activities may be placed under one manager. For example, material handling and inventory may be under the same manager. It is not uncommon to have a warehouse manager in charge of all the logistics functions. The warehouse receives shipments from suppliers and handles all shipments to customers.

Department stores at the retail level are organized in a manner similar to the manufacturing plant (see Figure 12–4). The primary difference

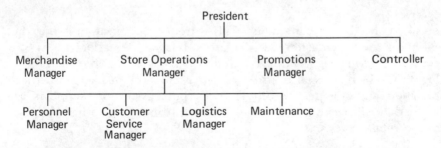

Fig. 12–4. Centralized logistics for a department store.

is that the store operations manager in a department store has responsibility for more activities than logistics. Logistics is generally referred to simply as shipping and receiving in retail stores, but it is an important function. Physical inventory may be scattered throughout a department store. There is a central storage area, but forward stock is generally kept

[15] See: H. G. Becker, Jr., "Physical Distribution Management: A View From the Top," *Handling and Shipping* (1967), pp. 41–46.

in each of the merchandise departments. It often happens that the warehouse is physically removed from the department store, sometimes even placed in a different part of the city.

The handling of logistics is more complex in the chain store organization, because of the greater number of functions and departments. Figure 12–5 illustrates how chains may be organized. This organization of chains is partly explained by the historical centralization of decision making, including logistics, in the home office. The retail store managers

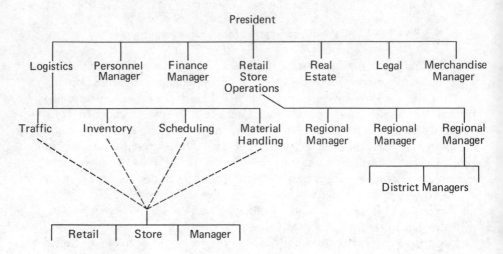

Fig. 12–5. Centralized logistics for a chain store.

operated strictly as selling units. This extreme centralization is breaking down for some chain store decision areas, but not where logistics is concerned. Logistics is centralized in the warehouse. The managers of logistics have functional control over the retail store managers for transportation and storage. Typically, goods purchased from suppliers are shipped to the central warehouse and redistributed in private carriers to the retail stores.

Decentralized Organization for Logistics

The decentralization of logistics occurs more often at the manufacturing and wholesale stage in the channel than at retail. Decentralization takes place when the logistics decisions are pushed down in the organization. Figure 12–6 applies to a multi-plant operation. In this example, logistics is placed at the plant level; only engineering and finance are centralized. What we have illustrated are essentially autonomous manufacturing plants. Each plant may have its own warehouse and is responsible for its own storage and transportation. This results in a duplication of the

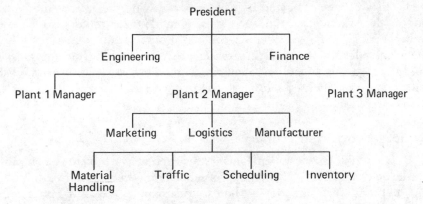

Fig. 12–6. Decentralized logistics for a manufacturing plant.

logistics function between plants, but the activity may be coordinated so that plants can supply each other. Although the illustration shows one warehouse, the organization could be further decentralized by the use of multiple warehouses by each plant. Either private or agent logistics can pertain to Figure 12–6.

Figure 12–7 shows a manufacturing firm that is centralized for production and sales but decentralized for logistics.[16] This business uses

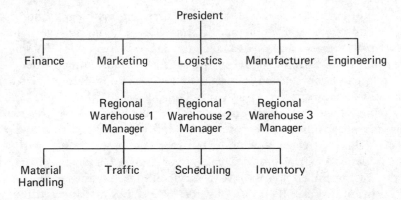

Fig. 12–7. Decentralized logistics for branch warehouses.

branch warehouses, but it could just as easily utilize public warehouses and brokers. The goods are produced and stored at the main manufacturing plant for shipment to the regional warehouses. All local shipments to customers are handled out of the regional warehouses. The salesmen working the regions send their orders directly to the main plant. How-

[16] Bowersox, Smykay, and LaLonde, *op. cit.,* pp. 274–79; Heskett, Ivie, and Glaskowsky, *op. cit.,* pp. 377–81.

ever, this arrangement could be changed by having the salesmen operate out of the warehouses. In such a case marketing would also be decentralized. The above example could also apply to a wholesaler. For the wholesaler, finance and marketing are centralized while logistics is decentralized in regional warehouses. The wholesaler can also establish autonomous warehouses across the country with salesmen working out of each warehouse.

Partially Centralized Logistics

It is possible to organize logistics in such a way as to accomplish partial centralization. This type of organization occurs less often in practice, but it is worth mentioning here. For example, a manufacturer may centralize all scheduling and traffic control in the home office but place inventory and material handling in the hands of regional warehouse managers. Another possibility is for the manufacturer to handle all the logistics functions from the central plant where certain classes of customers are concerned, say very large customers, while using regional warehouses for smaller customers. If the reader studies the illustrations, a number of other possible variations will present themselves.

THE LOGISTICS MIX

So far in the discussion of logistics no mention has been made of the proportions of transportation and storage that are necessary. The assumption was made that any amount needed was available. In spite of the need for cooperation between transportation and storage, there is a definite area of competition between the two which, in turn, affects communications. Transportation and warehousing can, within limits, substitute for one another.[17] Thus, a trade-off is possible between the two in which more transportation can substitute for more warehousing and vice versa.[18] The relative proportion of transportation and storage used by a seller is defined as the *logistics mix*. Every seller has some specific logistics mix, but the composition may vary considerably among businesses. The logistics mix and, therefore, the cost of logistics are affected by four factors: (1) shipment speed, (2) the amount and type of customer service, (3) size and frequency of shipment, and (4) forward production.[19] Figure 12–8 can aid in understanding the logistics trade-off.

First, shipment speed is very important to the logistics mix. Generally,

[17] Bowersox, Smykay, and LaLonde, *op. cit.*, Chapter 11.

[18] A good example of how one company evaluated the trade off is found in: W. Clayton Hill, "Reorganizing Distribution for Higher Profit," *Industrial Marketing*, Vol. 48 (February, 1963), pp. 77–84.

[19] John F. Magee, "The Logistics of Distribution," *Harvard Business Review* (July–August, 1960).

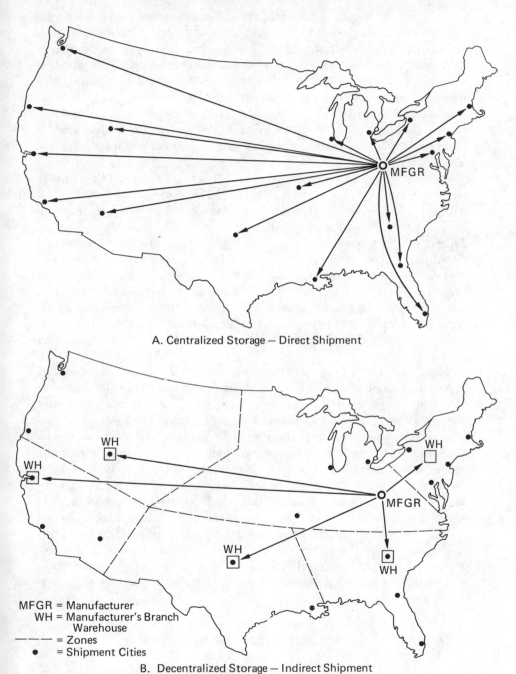

A. Centralized Storage — Direct Shipment

B. Decentralized Storage — Indirect Shipment

MFGR = Manufacturer
  WH = Manufacturer's Branch
          Warehouse
——— = Zones
  ● = Shipment Cities

Fig. 12–8.   Logistics trade-off.

more speed in transportation reduces dependence on warehouses. Assume a company's customers require speedy delivery. The manufacturer can use air freight that offers two to three day delivery from the manufacturer's home plant to any place in the United States. This situation is shown in Figure 12–8a. Air freight is expensive, but the total cost of speedy service may be reduced because the firm does not have to build warehouses.[20] Only a limited number of cities are shown, but the shipments can be direct to retailers in each city or to a local independent wholesaler. Communications problems are increased because of the distance.

Second, the amount and type of customer service can affect the logistics mix. Assume a seller's customers require frequent product service, installation, and personal attention. The manufacturer may construct regional warehouses to provide these services. The warehouses reduce dependence on transportation by reducing the large number of individual shipments to individual customers and by reducing long distance servicing. This type of logistics mix is shown in Figure 12–8b. If the number of customers is large, then the warehouses may be cheaper than using greater proportions of transportation. As in the first instance, the regional warehouses may sell to independent wholesalers or to retailers. The close proximity of buyer and seller provides a basis for improved communications.

Third, size and frequency of shipment go together in the logistics mix. Larger and less frequent shipments decrease transportation but increase the need for storage. Smaller and more frequent shipments decrease storage but increase transportation. Generally, large shipments make possible quantity discounts and the use of less costly, but slower, carriers. Bulk shipments can reduce the cost of logistics if the savings from the manner of shipment are not offset by the increased warehousing cost.

Fourth, forward production is the final factor to affect the logistics mix. This factor refers to whether the goods are produced for immediate or for future consumption. Made-to-order goods require little or no storage because they are shipped directly to the user. Transportation cost is the bulk of the logistics cost. When goods are produced in quantity for future consumption they must be kept until needed. The further in advance the goods are produced the greater the proportion of storage that is necessary.

WAREHOUSE LOCATION DECISIONS

In this section the management decisions relating to warehouse locations are presented. Several points are necessary to lay the foundation

[20] Donald D. Parker, "Improved Efficiency and Reduced Cost of Marketing," *Journal of Marketing* (April, 1962).

for the discussion. First, the same basic factors influence warehouse location, whether the warehouse is a part of a producing unit, a wholesaler, or a retailer. These factors briefly are: (1) product type, (2) transportation cost, (3) markets, (4) rent, (5) labor supply, (6) taxes, (7) geography, and (8) competition.[21] The relative importance of each of these items for manufacturing, wholesaling and retailing may vary according to the situation, but the factors are the same. The emphasis of the discussion is on privately owned facilities, but the selection of a public warehouse is based on the same general factors.

Product-Oriented Locations

A product-oriented location is one where production and/or warehousing is located near the source of raw materials.[22] The business may favor this location for several reasons. First, a business gravitates toward the factor of production used in greatest quantity because of the cost of shipping and maintaining inventories.[23] The basic extractive industries such as mining, farming, and lumbering, locate near the raw materials. Second, products that are weight losing cause the firm to locate near raw materials because of the transportation cost involved. Examples are sugar cane and timber. Third, there is the perishability factor; perishable products cause a shift toward that product. Examples are found in canning and processing fresh vegetables.

When more than one raw material is involved the producer may favor one or the other because of relative shipping cost. The shift in basic steel production in the United States can be explained by what has happened to the relative use of coal and iron ore. Historically, the steel industry was located in Pennsylvania because it took approximately two tons of coal to make one ton of steel. Cheap water transportation across the Great Falls was also a factor. The industry located near the coal because it was more costly to ship. Since the quality of iron ore found on the western side of the Great Lakes has decreased in purity, the steel industry has shifted west and to eastern tidewater. The westward movement is accounted for by increasing cost of shipping iron ore. The eastward movement is attributed to the increased availability of low-cost, high-grade iron ore from foreign countries.

Market-Oriented Locations

Market-oriented locations are those where the manufacturer and/or warehousing are located near the customer rather than near the raw

21 Maney, *op. cit.*, pp. 40–47; Donald Bowersox, "The Distribution Center Location Problem," *Houston Business Review* (Winter, 1964–65), pp. 39–54.

22 Heskett, Ivie, and Glaskowsky, *op. cit.*, Chapter 6.

23 Edward W. Smykay, "Distribution Selection and Site Selection," *Industrial Development* (September, 1961), pp. 6–8.

materials.[24] Products that gain weight in the production process, such as soft drinks, locate near the market.[25] For example, soft drinks gain significant weight when local bottlers add water to the syrup. Bulky or hard-to-ship products such as machinery and automobiles tend to locate near the market. (The automobile industry has been decentralizing in recent years.) If the finished product is perishable, there is a tendency to locate near the market. We observe this tendency in bakery products and meats. Highly concentrated markets tend to attract plants and warehouses because of the ease of servicing. Differential freight rates when they favor shipments to market are a factor in market-oriented locations. It is generally true that rates get higher the nearer the goods are to a finished product. Packaging can enter into the location decision for many finished goods. Good packaging may make it possible to ship difficult goods that could not otherwise be moved long distances.[26] Bananas are a good example. Until recently the highest grade bananas were consumed by the producing nation because their sensitive skin made shipment difficult. New types of protective containers changed this situation.

Footloose Locations

Footloose industries received the name because there is nothing inherent in their operations to cause them to favor either raw materials or markets in so far as locations are concerned. Given only these factors to consider, such firms can locate wherever they desire. In practice, the decision is not so simple. There are universal factors affecting the decision of all types of firms, including the ones previously discussed. These universal factors become important to footloose firms.

Rent on facilities and real estate are universal factors of location.[27] The question of owning or renting as well as the amount of the cost in different locales is important. Another factor is taxes. There is a great difference in taxes between states and cities; these taxes require careful investigations. Some states or cities give tax breaks as well as low rent for a specified period in order to attract industry. The labor market is another factor. The three important considerations concerning labor are whether trained people are available, the status of unionization, and the comparative cost of labor. Competition is a factor that cannot be ignored. A business may have to locate in a certain place simply because com-

[24] Edward W. Smykay and Ward A. Fredericks, "An Index Based for Evaluating Warehouse Locations," *Transportation Journal* (Fall, 1963), pp. 30–34.

[25] Heskett, Ivie, and Glaskowsky, *op. cit.*, Chapter 6.

[26] D. B. Carmody, "The Impact of Packing on Physical Distribution," *Packaging's Role In Physical Distribution* (Chicago: American Marketing Association: Management Bulletin No. 77, 1966), pp. 1–6; Walter F. Friedman, "The Role of Packaging in Physical Distribution," *Transportation and Distribution Management* (February, 1968), pp. 34–39.

[27] Irvin R. Whitman, "New Reasoning In Choosing A Warehouse Location," *Journal of Marketing* (January, 1964).

petition will have an advantage otherwise. Finally, there is geography. The proximity of the Great Lakes to the states of Ohio, Illinois, and Michigan provides cheap transportation. The Rocky Mountains are a serious barrier for Eastern companies to transport West.

Retail and Wholesale Locations

Wholesale and retail stores follow the location trends indicated by market-oriented locations. There are some special considerations, however. The majority of wholesalers serve a local market, with their sales generated within a fifty mile radius of the business. The main office and warehouse are located together, usually in the largest city serving the area. Wholesale warehouses tend to locate either in the wholesale district of the city or in outlying low rent districts. Thus, it is primarily a problem of selecting a site. The factors that enter into the decision include rent, availability of large space, loading and unloading facilities for trucks or rail, and sufficient power for operations. A few wholesalers operate on a national scale, but location of the several warehouses follows the same general principles as that for single locations.

Most retail stores are small and the storeroom accompanies the store. Such stores are located on the basis of knowledge of the neighborhood, rent, and availability. Large retailers, such as chains, department stores, and discount houses do a complete analysis before locating warehouses. This analysis typically includes evaluation of site cost, traffic flow past the site, loading and un-loading facilities, adjacent rail spurs, and accessibility to retail outlets. Department stores and discount houses and other large retailers have a tendency to locate the warehouse away from the main store but in the same city. However, mail order retailers may use regional warehouses similar to those described for manufacturers.

Multiple Warehouse Locations

There are three situations that involve multiple warehousing. First, there are multiple plants where each plant makes the same product. The basic factors of plant location apply here with exceptions. In locating the new plants, particular attention must be paid to the division of markets, and the location of raw materials. Market considerations may require plant separation, but the placement of raw materials may restrict choices. Fortunately, new plants are typically added one at a time, and each can be treated as a separate location problem consistent with how each plant fits into the logistical system. Second, there is the problem of multiple plants where each plant produces a different product. In this case the factors of single plant location already discussed apply. Third, there is the problem of branch warehouses for either manufacturers, wholesalers, or retailers. The factors of location discussed for wholesalers and retailers apply. In the case of manufacturer's branches, the business must pay particular attention to the location of customers.

WAREHOUSE OPERATIONS

There are four important decision areas of warehouse operations that require our attention: type of warehouse facilities, layout, stock placement, and equipment. All aspects of warehouse operations are dictated by the objectives of the company. The overriding factors that dictate the operation of warehouses are: (1) type of plant to be operated and (2) carriers utilized.

Warehouse Facilities

A variety of warehouse facilities is operated by American industry, but most fall into two basic types: single story or multiple story. The multiple story warehouse has been traditional, but is not as popular in recent years. Warehousemen are finding that it is less costly to move goods horizontally than to move goods vertically. Although a single story warehouse may involve more in cost of land, it allows for offsetting lower building cost utilizing metal construction and prefab buildings. The single story warehouse also makes use of conveyor belts, automated trucks, and other modern techniques available for moving goods. It is also more capable of integrating the use of trucks and rails with the internal movement of goods into a complete distribution center.[28] Thus, single story warehouses are desired because of their low cost. There are two exceptions to the above generalization. In some areas, such as the larger cities, land cost may be sufficiently high to discourage the single story warehouse that sprawls over one or more city blocks. Second, where the warehouse facilities are already available in multi-story form, they may be utilized. The type of product involved influences the decision. For example, it may be impossible to use a multi-story warehouse because of the bulkiness of the product or because the product requires heavy machinery and equipment on the second floor.

Warehouse Layout for Producers

The number of possible types of layout that can be utilized in a warehouse is almost infinite. A few illustrations can demonstrate how the activities are arranged. Figure 12–9 and 12–10 show two possible layouts for a production plant using a single carrier.[29]

In both cases storage is needed for raw materials and for finished

[28] Arthur H. Klawans, "The Distribution Center Concept of Tomorrow," *Handling and Shipping* (November, 1967), pp. 53–56.

[29] Bowersox, Smykay and LaLonde, *op. cit.*, pp. 274–79; Heskett, Ivie, and Glaskowsky, *op. cit.*, pp. 377–81.

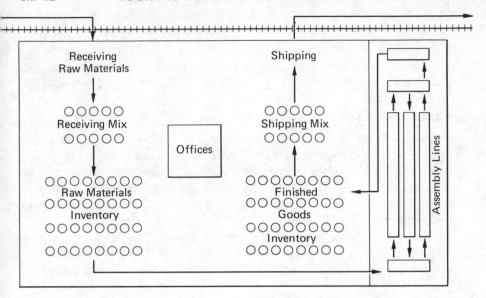

Fig. 12–9. Logistics in a production plant: single carrier.

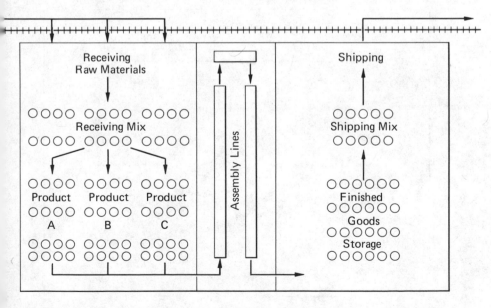

Fig. 12–10. Logistics in a production plant: single carrier—two warehouses.

goods. In the first example a single warehouse is used and the goods are segregated according to type or production status. In Figure 12–10, two different warehouses are employed. The second example also illustrates how the warehouse may be arranged when production requires three distinct types of products. This operation involves a more complex arrangement for raw materials than for finished goods. Figure 12–10 shows goods moving directly into inventory, but in fact, if there is a rush, they may be moved directly to the production line. Either example can be modified to utilize two carriers but allow for dual receiving, mixing, and shipping.

Warehouse Layout for Wholesalers and Retailers

Figure 12–11 shows a warehouse layout for a retail or wholesale operation which does not involve the storage of raw materials.[30] The goods are finished when received and may be processed in and out of the same storage facilities. They may be reshipped to retailers if the facility is a wholesale warehouse; if a retailer warehouse, the reshipment may be to individual retail stores.

Figure 12–11 also demonstrates how a typical two-carrier warehouse may be operated. The reader should bear in mind that two carriers can be used by producers as well as other middlemen. The biggest job in

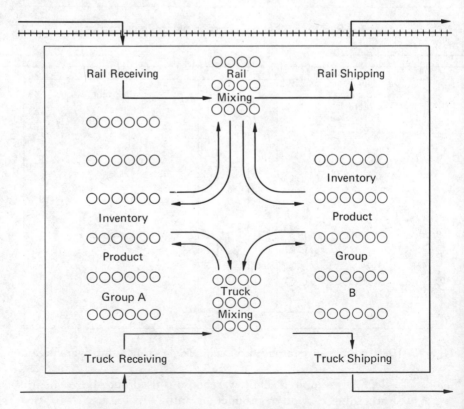

Fig. 12–11. Retail or wholesale logistics: two carriers.

[30] Heskett, Ivie, and Glaskowsky, *op. cit.,* p. 378.

this type of warehouse is mixing the goods between the two carriers. Notice that the selling side of the retail or wholesale business may be located some distance from the warehouse. Sales of retailers and wholesalers are less dependent on the location of the goods because no production is involved in the operation.

Stock Placement and Equipment

The combination of stock placement and the equipment used has a direct bearing on warehouse efficiency. Figures 12–12 and 12–13 illustrate

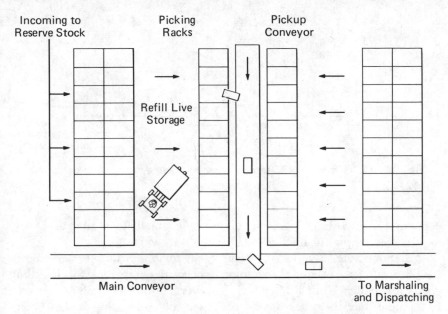

Fig. 12–12. Rack and conveyor system. *Source:* John F. Magee, *Physical Distribution Systems* (New York: McGraw-Hill Book Co., Inc., 1967), p. 76.

some typical arrangement and equipment. On-the-square stock placement requires less room for the bin or pallet, but it necessitates more aisle space for the movement of equipment. Angular placement requires less aisle space, but the pallets or bins take up more room. Generally, on-the-square placement is preferred for goods that do not require fork lift trucks or other equipment. Thus, the size, standardization, and protection of goods from packaging can greatly facilitate stock placement and handling.[31] The general rule of stock placement is to put popular goods closer to the shipping dock or conveyor. Very often zones of popularity are established in the warehouse and goods are placed accordingly. Ex-

[31] Friedman, *op. cit.*, pp. 34–39; Russ Cornell, "Packaging Function Moves UP," *Materials Handling Engineering* (April, 1967), pp. 79–84.

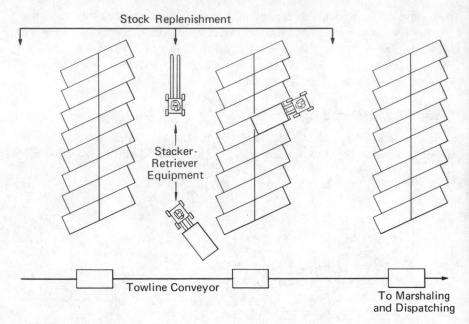

Fig. 12–13. Pallet, rack, and stacker-receiver system. *Source:* Same as Fig. 12–12, p. 77.

ceptions to this rule do occur. For example, small items that are easily moved may be placed further back in the warehouse.

Warehouses use a variety of equipment, some of which is depicted in the illustrations. The most common pieces of equipment for handling goods are pallets, fork lift trucks, conveyors, automatic rails, and carts. Equipment may be either owned or leased, but ownership is more common. In some warehouses, the heavy or bulky goods require the use of cranes, or overhead conveyors; such equipment is sometimes leased. Increasingly, warehouses are being fully automated all the way from computer interpretation of the order to carton selection and loading.[32] The type of equipment used in a particular warehouse depends on the size of the facility, the type of merchandise, and the care necessary in handling plus the relative cost of alternatives.

QUESTIONS

1. Compare and contrast the several methods of combining logistics elements.
2. Discuss the use of logistics to achieve vertical integration.

[32] James C. Tanner, "Warehouses Shakeup: Mechanized Buildings Speed Order Handling, Cut Many Firm's Costs," *Wall Street Journal* (January 24, 1963), pp. 1, 14.

3. Discuss the factors involved in choosing between public and private warehouses; the choice of private or public transportation.
4. Assume you are the manager of a company selling a variety of motors in a national market. Which type of common carrier would you use for shipment? Why?
5. Discuss the factors affecting the choice of a common carrier.
6. Contrast centralized and de-centralized organization of the logistics function.
7. What is meant by a trade-off of logistics elements? Explain.
8. Explain the difference in product-oriented warehouse locations and market-oriented warehouse locations.
9. Explain and illustrate how you would lay out the warehouse facilities for a manufacturer of furniture.
10. Discuss the importance of stock placement on warehouse operating efficiency.

MANAGEMENT OF CHANNEL COMMUNICATIONS

Part IV has a single encompassing purpose: to explain the decisions that affect the interaction of channel members through communications. Two types of communications essential to the functioning of marketing channels are discussed. They are: information systems that relate primarily to the internal operation of the channel and persuasive communications that involve selling either channel members or others on the goals and wishes of the channel leader.

13

Channel Communications

One of the elements of the channel team is communications, whose importance to the team can be easily stated. The information provided by communications unites channel members and provides the basis for cooperation. Communications is also the foundation for interaction between the channel team and the environment. Part IV deals with management of communications.

INFORMATION IN THE CHANNEL

Since information is so important to the operation of the channel team, it is necessary to develop an understanding of this subject as a foundation for the discussion of communications. The discussion is divided into: (1) types of information, (2) purpose of information flow, (3) information flows based on communications, (4) channel problems of communications, and (5) types of communications in channels.

Information Flow and Function Flow

The concept of functional market flows was previously introduced; at that time it was not pointed out that a great deal of rather specific information exactly parallels the functional flow.[1] Some information is necessary to perform the functions and to keep the channel team operating effectively, but too much information can be bad because it is costly,

---

[1] Gerald Albaum, "Information Flow and Decentralized Decision Making in Marketing," *California Management Review,* Vol. 9 (Summer, 1967), pp. 59–70.

unused, and misunderstood.[2] It is necessary to determine information needs and provide enough data to meet these needs. All the types of information flowing in the marketing channel are impossible to list, but several types are particularly important. First, ownership, promotion, and physical movement entail a parallel downward flow of information in the channel.[3] The function of ownership involves information concerning price levels, types of services offered, contract terms, discounts, and margins. Physical movement necessitates information on amounts in inventory, lead time for delivery, delivery dates, time in transit, method of movement, and destination. The promotional function requires information on types of merchandise, salesmen, campaigns, advertising, market appeals, media effectiveness, salesmen routing, and product performance.

Second, the functions of risking, financing, and negotiation have parallel information flows both up and down the channed. The risking function necessitates a wide variety of data on the market, suppliers, and competitive conditions. Negotiation involves the dual flow of offers and counter offers. The financing function entails information on money sources, loan rates, types of financing, and finance needs.

Third, the functions of ordering and payments have corresponding upward flows of information. It can be argued that these two functions are in themselves information. Nevertheless, orders necessitate further data on needs, sources of supply, quality and performance requirements, and rates of usage. Payments involve information on financial ability, deliveries, and terms of payment. Obviously, a great deal of information must flow to keep the channel functioning.

Purpose of Information Flows

The flow of information between members of a marketing channel has two overall purposes.[4] First, information flows to satisfy operational requirements. This type of information is frequently referred to as information system data or simply information systems. That is to say, the coordination of internal operational systems in a marketing channel requires certain types of informative data. In the above examples, information on such factors as orders, payments, delivery, price levels, and money sources are samples of operational information. Notice that operational information may flow toward the leader or from the leader.

---

[2] Howell M. Estes, "Will Managers Be Overwhelmed by the Information Explosion," *Armed Forces Management*, Vol. 13 (December, 1966), pp. 75–84; Oliver W. Tuthill, "The Thrust of Information Technology on Management," *Financial Executive* (January, 1966), pp. 18–27.

[3] Belden Menkus, "Information Systems In Marketing," *Systems and Procedures Journal* (July–August, 1963), pp. 10–14.

[4] William T. Kelley, "Marketing Intelligence for Top Management," *Journal of Marketing*, Vol. 29 (October, 1965), pp. 19–25.

Second, there is persuasive information. This is designed to affect the behavior of either some channel member or some group of buyers. Thus, persuasive information may be directed internally within the channel or externally toward the market. Sales campaigns and advertising are persuasive information. Persuasive information may be directed by the channel leader at members of his own channel in order to obtain performance, motivate to action, or promote an idea or product. Persuasive information may be directed at firms in competing channels to induce some change in purchase patterns. Third, persuasive information may be directed at household customers in order to hold or increase the market for the entire channel.

Information Flow Based on Communications

In a channel of distribution, as in any other group or team effort, both organizations and persuasive information flow as a result of communications.[5] Thus, to understand information flow it is necessary to delve into the subject of communications. Communication means to make common or to share information. Channel communication, a particular type of communications, is defined as [6] *the sharing of market-related information, ideas, or attitudes between institutions comprising the channel of distribution.*

Effective channel communication occurs when the meaning of the information is the same for the institution sending it and the institutions receiving it.[7] *Ineffective communication* occurs when the meaning differs between the parties. For example, a channel leader, feeling a desire to keep in touch, may inform a channel member that the district manager will call soon. If the middleman perceives this communication as a desire to keep in touch, the communication is effective. If the middleman believes the manufacturer is checking up because of suspected poor performance, the communication is ineffective.[8]

Operational efficiency and communications efficiency are not necessarily the same. For example, if the ineffective communication cited above causes the middleman to do things that improve his operations, we have better performance as a result of ineffective communications. The

[5] Erwin P. Bettinghaus, *Persuasive Communications* (New York: Holt, Rinehart and Winston, Inc., 1968), pp. 11–13.

[6] Based on: Wilbur Schramm, "How Communications Works," *The Process and Effects of Mass Communications,* Wilbur Schramm, ed. (Urbana: University of Illinois Press, 1955), p. 3.

[7] John R. Grabner, Jr., and L. J. Rosenberg, "Communications In Distribution Channel Systems," *Distribution Channels: Behavioral Dimensions,* Louis W. Stern, ed. (Boston: Houghton Mifflin Co., 1969), p. 228.

[8] Frank R. Hartman, "A Behavioristic Approach to Communications: A Selective Review of Learning Theory and a Derivation of Postulates," *Audio-Visual Communications Review* (September–October, 1963), pp. 182–86. This article contains a list of 28 generalizations about communications.

effective communication cited above may actually reduce performance because it can lead to complacency by both institutions. Generally, one prefers effective communications because the chances of good performance are greater when channel members understand each other.

Channel Problems of Communications

Communication can be a unifying factor to the team, or it can be a source of constant dissatisfaction or conflict. There are channels that spend as much time attempting to improve communications between members as dealing with the problems of competition and customers. The reason is that the marketing channel is a particular type of team with built-in problems that can place a heavy burden on communications. Four of these communications problems are particularly important: (1) spatial separation, (2) different type of organizations, (3) complexity of institutions, and (4) human differences.

Spatial Separation.   Spatial separation refers to the physical distance between channel members. To be effective, communication must reach the intended receiver, but separation reduces face-to-face communication that is so important to group cohesion. It places great dependence on human and mechanical intermediaries such as salesmen, home office representatives, memorandum, and telephone conversations to make the message meaningful. Furthermore, physical separation causes operational differences that are difficult to account for in communication. For example, operational units in different parts of the country may have to modify inventory, prices, or opening days and hours because of real differences in consumers or workers (e.g. a manufacturer in the South who has to close down on the first day of hunting season). Customer fashion does not hit all sections of the country simultaneously. Where one store unit needs to keep on top of fashion another may find that customer desires change slowly. As a result, home office policies may not apply to individual units of the channel, and attempts at strict enforcement can cause difficulties. The difficulty is in perceiving the differences. It is the burden of communications to bridge this gap of spatial separation.

Different Type of Organizations.   Communications in the channel are complicated by the fact that types of organizations differ. A wholesaler is not like a manufacturer or retailer, and there is no automatic basis for them to communicate.[9] The manufacturer may be a multi-plant corporation while the wholesaler may be a large partnership and the retailer a small scale proprietorship. The manufacturer or

[9] Walter Gross, "Profitable Listening for Manufacturers and Dealers: How to Use a Communications System," *Business Horizons*, Vol. 11 (December, 1968), pp. 35–44.

wholesaler may be able to employ specialists in purchasing, sales, accounting, etc., that are too costly for retailers. Each type of organization faces a different market, and each has its own goals, operating methods, and problems. As a result, the philosophies and attitudes of the several managers may be quite different. Table 13–1 illustrates the results

Table 13–1   Firms Indicating They Have Communication Problems

Type of Firm	Size of Firm		
	Large No. of Firms	Medium No. of Firms	Small No. of Firms
Manufacturers	15	32	28
Wholesalers	3	19	5
Retailers	16	10	21
Service Firms	0	3	6
Government	1	0	0
	35	64	60

Source: Walter Gross, "Profitable Listening For Manufacturers and Dealers; How To Use A Communications System," *Business Horizons*, Vol. 11 (December, 1968), pp. 35–44.

when channel members were asked if they had had any problems with getting information concerning inventory, product features, market conditions, prices and terms, sales promotion, and changes in company policy.

Everyone has some communication problem, but manufacturers have more than other firms. Small retailers also have difficulty obtaining information. What seems a reasonable course of action or a tenable position to the manufacturer may be completely unsatisfactory to the other middlemen. For example, the manufacturer announces that no shipments below a minimum amount will be made. He may seek to cut shipping costs, but the middlemen may not be able to purchase the quantities designated. A retailer may want high margins or retail price protection that is not necessary for the wholesaler because of his greater operational efficiency. Where different perspectives exist, communications become strained.

Complexity of Institutions. The differences in complexity of middlemen place a burden on communications. There are large multi-level corporations as well as small corporations. Sometimes the channel leader fails to account for the differences that exist, and when this happens communications break down.[10] In complex organizations, communica-

[10] Warren J. Wottreich, "Misunderstanding the Retailer," *Harvard Business Review* (May–June, 1962), pp. 147–52ff. This is a good study of manufacturer communications problems with several types of retailers.

tions may be required between a manufacturer and other channel members on several levels.[11] There may be communications between: (1) purchase and sales departments, (2) logistics departments, (3) top executives dealing with each other, and (4) sales discussing problems with engineering or service groups. In some cases, the manufacturer may be training the retailers, sales, or service people. In a large organization there are likely to be times when one area of interaction is not aware of what is going on in others. This can lead to crossed purposes and confused language. Crossed purposes refers to a failure to communicate because of differences in goals. Confused language implies a basic lack of understanding resulting from misinformation, misinterpretations, contradictions, etc. In the former case there is often an unwillingness to communicate, and in the latter there is an inability to communicate. These factors naturally place strain on the relationship.

Human Differences.   There are human differences that tax the ability of communications to keep the channel running smoothly. Intellect, emotional stability, security, economics, and prestige are the principle sources of these differences. Consider for a moment that marketing communications reaches consumers, dealers, financial institutions, government, and suppliers.[12] Most of the problems encountered can be summed up as differences in status. For example, a salesman may be more important in a large organization than the owner of a small retail store with whom he deals. The retailer may feel insecure, and the result may be belligerence toward the salesman. The nature of the sales task may also bring the company's representative regularly into contact with top executives who have great status in their own organizations. When unequals deal with each other communications are difficult; one party deals from strength and the other from weakness. Some firms give all their salesmen the rank of vice-president in order to compensate for their lack of status, but the lack of status of small retailers is difficult to compensate.

Types of Communications in Channels

Communications in the channel take place in many different forms, but can be grouped by four major methods. First, classed by type, there is personal or mass communication. *Personal communication* takes place throughout the channel any time two representatives meet face to face. Perhaps the best known example is the personal salesman. Advertising

---

[11] Grabner and Rosenberg, *op. cit.*, p. 230.
[12] James H. Myers and William H. Reynolds, "Communications In Marketing," *Consumer Behavior and Marketing Management* (Boston: Houghton Mifflin Co., 1967), pp. 263–76.

exemplifies *mass communications*. Second, classed by method, there are *written, verbal,* or *physical* communications. Literally everything that one channel member does communicates something. Personal selling is mostly verbal, but the salesman's movements also communicate. Furthermore, the salesman may employ written reminders, handouts, etc. Advertising typically employs a combination of written, verbal, and physical means of communications.

Third, classed by purpose, there are *casual, informative, persuasive,* or *reminder* communications. Casual communication is the type that just happens, such as when two executives run into each other at a football game. A considerable amount of personal selling falls into this category. Informative communication distributes basic facts, while persuasive communication distributes biased facts. Reminder communication is any repetitive message. Fourth, classed by significance, are the *formal* or *informal* methods of communications. Formal communication is that which flows up and down the chain of command. Informal communication occurs outside the regular chain of command. When the purchasing agent contacts the sales representative of a manufacturer, there is formal communication. When a salesman contacts the purchasing agent's secretary there is informal communications.

THE COMMUNICATIONS PROCESS IN CHANNELS

Communication can be described as a process that takes place between a sender of messages and a receiver of messages. As a part of this process the message must be encoded, decoded, and conducted through a media.[13] This process is common to all communications, and it needs only to be adapted to the channel of distribution. Figure 13–1 illustrates one interpretation of the communication process in the marketing channel.

The *sender,* in this example a manufacturer, has some information to be transmitted. It may be information about a new product that is scheduled for introduction. The information is *encoded* in the sense that it is interpreted as a set of symbols (words, pictures, feelings, gestures, voice inflections, etc.) to be passed on. In the encoder step an idea is given some concrete form that can be conveyed and understood. In Figure 13–1, the advertising agency is the encoder; thus, the encoder is different from the sender. However, the sender and encoder may be the same, as when the manufacturer has his advertising department handle the encoding.

[13] Mark E. Stern, *Marketing Planning: A Systems Approach* (New York: McGraw-Hill Book Co., Inc., 1966), pp. 59–63.

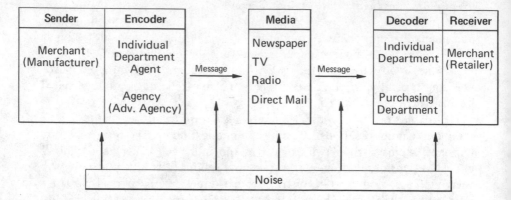

Fig. 13–1. The communications process. *Source:* Adapted from Claude Shannon and Warren Weaver, *The Mathematical Theory of Communications* (Urbana: University of Illinois Press, 1949), p. 5.

The information, now in the form of a *message,* is transmitted through some *media* (air, cables, paper, etc.) which may or may not be a commercial establishment. For example, when a salesman talks directly with a prospect the message moves directly through the air. In the example, the media are shown as establishments that specialize in transmitting information. This latter type of media is more appropriate for the marketing channel. The message proceeds through the media to a decoder who represents the receiver. The *decoder* observes the sender's symbols, interprets them as ideas, and decides on a response to the ideas. Like the encoder, the decoder may, or may not, be the same as the receiver. In Figure 13–1, the decoder is the receiver's own purchasing department, but the decoder could be a purchasing agent. The *receiver* is the institution, or its representative, for which the message is intended. In the example, the receiver is the wholesaler or retailer management. The receiver can use the message in whatever manner desired.

Noise is any type of interference with the communications; it corresponds to static on the radio. Noise most often occurs as misunderstanding or misinterpretation of the message and is not considered here as a part of the communications process. However, noise is a factor that must be contended with in communications. It can literally occur anywhere in the process, but the most likely places are indicated in Figure 13–1. There is less likelihood of noise when the sender and encoder are the same and when the receiver and decoder are the same. This combination reduces the chances for noise in the communication from five to three. Obviously, the more times a message is transferred, the greater the chance for misunderstanding.

Feedback typically follows communications. Feedback is the response made by the receiver. In Figure 13–1, feedback is just the reverse of what is shown. The receiver becomes the sender and the sender becomes the receiver. The communications process involves the same elements as shown for any communications. Feedback may occur in any form, but it is typically some acknowledgment of receipt or adherence to some prescribed channel behavior desired by the leader. For example, a letter of acknowledgment of an order is feedback and so is behavior that leads to the purchase of the product. Notice that the complete communication process is necessary between the sender and encoder and between the decoder and receiver when these are not the same institutions.

SENDER–RECEIVER RELATIONSHIP

The sender and the receiver of communications can be anyone in a marketing channel. As many messages flow from the retailer to the manufacturer as in the other direction. Wholesalers and agents must communicate with both the other parties. The relationships that result are varied and complex.

Basis for Channel Communications

Communications between marketing institutions of any type depend on four considerations. First, there is *membership* in a common channel. Channel membership is typically established by the purchase and sale patterns of the firm, but the business may not have complete control over deciding to which channel it belongs. For example, a wholesaler may wish to belong to a particular manufacturer's channel, but the manufacturer prefers to bypass the wholesaler and sell directly to retailers. Second, there is the factor of *physical proximity*. Middlemen located near to each other, or in channel sequence, tend to work closer together and communicate more. That is, a retailer tends to communicate much more with a local wholesaler than with a more distant wholesaler or manufacturer. Physical proximity is one reason why retailers prefer wholesalers over direct dealings with manufacturers. If there is no wholesaler in the channel, the retailer communicates more with the manufacturer because they are in direct sequence.

Third, *organizational proximity* is as important to communications as physical proximity. Institutions with closer organizational ties in the channel tend to communicate more. There is greater communication between integrated operations than within non-integrated channels. Even in non-integrated channels closer organizational ties lead to more communications. Agents tend to communicate more with principals than with other channel members, even those whom they buy from or sell to. Fourth, there is the matter of *identification*. Channel members communicate more when they feel they have something in common. In the marketing channel the common element can be found in such goals as profit, survival, sales volume, expense control, etc. Communications relate to achieving these goals.

Fifth, there is the consideration of *stimulus*. Communications must be prompted by cause; there must be a specific reason to communicate between institutions. The stimulus is usually found in some problem, policy, or plan that requires attention. Many communications are routine and exist simply to keep parties informed. Some plans may even be routinized. The most urgent communications typically relate to unanticipated problems or difficult ones. Long-standing or recurring problems also evoke more communications. One can generalize that the greater the problem level in a channel, the greater the flow of communications between institutions.

Channel Communications Hierarchies

The team of institutions comprising a marketing channel exists at different levels, and the market widens at each level as one proceeds down the organizational hierarchy. This fact creates a pyramid-type of structure for communications similar to that found in other organizations.[14] Figure 13–2 shows two types of communications hierarchies. When the structure has several institutional levels, it is described as a *vertical hierarchy*. A *horizontal hierarchy* exists when there are fewer institutional levels. In Figure 13–2, the two hierarchies reach the same size market. In practice, the flatter organization tends to appeal to a smaller market, because of the associated problems of span of control and communications.

The communications task increases in complexity for the channel as a whole when: (1) the number of institutional levels increases and (2) the number of institutions at each level advances. A larger number of different institutional levels increases spatial distance and the times that a single communication must be handled. This augments the need for encoding and decoding, and it places greater strain on the media. The number of levels increases the handling of a given message as well as the chances of mishandling, slowing the flow, or forgetting to include a member. Furthermore, each institutional level must interpret the message. The more interpretations, the greater the chance of changing the original

14 Grabner and Rosenberg, *op. cit.*, p. 230.

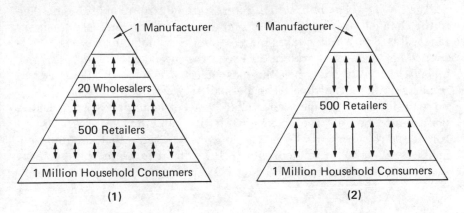

Fig. 13–2. Communication hierarchies.

meaning. The result can be miscommunication. A larger number of firms at each channel level increases the chance of not getting the message to some members or of having some members misinterpreting the message.

Aspects of Sender–Receiver Relationships

Three important aspects of the sender–receiver relationship in communications can be defined. Guetzkow explained these aspects as: (1) components of the communications system, (2) timing of communications, and (3) permanence of communications.[15] *Communications components* are the manufacturers, wholesalers, retailers, and agents of the market channel. Communications can occur between these institutional components in the following manner.

1. A single sender and a single receiver—when a manufacturer sells to a retailer
2. A single sender and multiple receivers—when a manufacturer distributes new product information throughout the channel
3. Several senders and a single receiver—when a group of retailers purchase from a single manufacturer
4. Several senders and several receivers—when a buyer association distributes orders among several manufacturers.[16]

[15] Harold Guetskow, "Communications in Organizations," *Handbook of Organizations,* James G. March, ed. (Chicago: Rand McNally & Co., 1965), pp. 537–39.
[16] Grabner and Rosenberg, *op. cit.,* pp. 232–33.

The *timing of communications* refers to the distribution of the message to the channel membership. This timing can occur in sequence or simultaneously. *Serial timing* takes place when the manufacturer sends a message to his wholesalers who in turn send the message to retailers. *Simultaneous timing* occurs when the message is sent to all wholesalers and retailers at the same time. The permanence of communications has to do with how long the message is effective. Personal messages have little permanence because the spoken word dissipates quickly. Written, recorded, or pictorial messages last longer. Messages that use multiple media, such as those written with pictures, tend to be more permanent than single media messages.

ENCODER–DECODER INTERPRETATIONS

In any communications system the encoder and decoder have a serious responsibility. The success of communications lies directly on their interpretations. No communications can be more effective than the understanding evolved by these two parties. The three factors that most directly affect these interpretations are: (1) experience of channel interpreters, (2) signals used in the channels, and (3) channel perceptions.

Experience of Channel Interpreters

Encoders and decoders act as interpreters for all messages in the channel. They are found in situations of: (1) purchase–sales, (2) shipping–receiving, (3) credit–shipping, (4) receiving–payment, (5) sales–credit, and (6) service–promotion. One factor affecting the interpretation of messages is the field of experience of the encoder and the decoder, that is, whatever common ground exists in knowledge, language, work experience, personal experience, and outlook that can lead to a common understanding of ideas.[17] Generally, effective communication increases in direct proportion to the similarity of the fields of experience between interpreters toward a common problem or situation. Figure 13–3 shows the fields of experience of encoder A and decoder B. The shaded area indicates common fields of experience. As depicted, interpreters or firms in competing channels may not share exact products, plans, policies, aspirations, abilities, or rewards, and communication is more difficult. Interpreters in an integrated channel have most of the above items in common

---

[17] James H. Campbell and Hal W. Hepler, "Persuasion and Interpersonal Relations," *Dimensions In Communication*, James H. Campbell and Hal W. Hepler, eds. (Belmont, Calif.: Wadsworth Publishing Co., Inc., 1965), pp. 87–95. Some of the ideas in this section were based on thoughts advanced in this article.

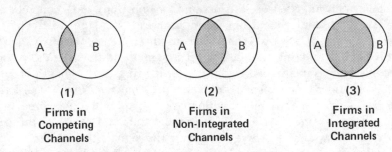

(1)

Firms in
Competing
Channels

(2)

Firms in
Non-Integrated
Channels

(3)

Firms in
Integrated
Channels

Fig. 13–3. Communication fields of experience.

and communicate much more effectively. However, a common field of experience does not guarantee successful communications. Too many other factors are involved to make such a statement valid.

Effective communication does not require exact experiences, and such a condition does not exist in practice. Thus, even in the integrated channel the fields of experience do not overlap exactly. In most cases, it is only necessary that the two parties can relate to the particular problem at hand. For example, the channel leader may be highly educated, while the wholesaler may have pulled himself up by his bootstraps. However, experience may have taught them both to use a cautious price strategy on a price cutting discount house. Their experience overlaps on the important issue of competition. The encoder and decoder may be totally different in other respects. The experience of a product manager for a large manufacturer may be completely different from that of the buyer for a small retailer, nevertheless, the two may share common knowledge of the product and communicate about its virtues quite easily. Furthermore, communication can be used to make the fields of experience more compatible before proceeding to the problem. A salesman, for example, can summarize important points of his company's history before proceeding to sell his product.

Signals Used in Channels

Channel encoders and decoders operate by means of signals. A signal is any sign or symbol representing a thought or feeling. There is no practical direct transfer of ideas from one person to another. The thought must be interpreted into signals by the encoder, the signals transmitted, and the signals interpreted back into ideas by the decoder. All thoughts transfer in the form of signals. In order to convey satisfaction with a retailer's performance, the channel manager slaps him on the back, uses words such as "great job," and smiles. All three actions are signals that the retailer can interpret as satisfaction.[18] Almost anything concrete can serve as a signal and typical signals are found in language, behavior, and physical objects. The word "channel" is used frequently in this book; this word is not a marketing channel, but it is something that stands for one. When the word is mentioned to a marketer it brings forth images of institutions, functions, movements, policies, etc., associated with marketing channels. To one not familiar with marketing, the word channel may mean a clear passage in a body of water, a band on a radio, or the path of a river. Thus, one must remember that the signals themselves are not the focal point; what is important is that the signal, because of prior agreement, conveys to the mind the total complexity that marketers call a channel.

Every field of experience develops a specialized language to signal meaning to the initiated. Think how difficult it is to communicate with doctors, lawyers, and space technicians. Channel members have their own language. Some of this language is common to all channels, and some of it applies only to a particular channel. For example, any marketer knows that institution means a business, but the term dealer may refer to an agent in one channel and a merchant in another. The term 2/10/30 may carry an understanding in one channel that dating begins with arrival of the goods, while in another channel it may mean dating begins at the end of the month. However, all channel members know that dating is a term refering to the grace period before payment is due on a shipment of goods. Signals simplify communications for the initiated. To the uninitiated, they are a real barrier to the transfer of messages.

Channel Perceptions

Perception is the particular awareness or interpretation one has of an idea, event, or thing. A firm has as many different perceptions of occurrences as it has encoders or decoders. Consider three different perceptions members of a refinery may hold toward a supplier of needed chemicals. The sales department may consider the supplier a valued customer because of reciprocal trade agreements. The purchasing department may consider the supplier a costly luxury because of low product quality. The warehouse may consider the supplier a bottleneck in the production process because of late arrival of goods. The perception one firm in the channel has of another can be thought of as the combined interpretations of the encoders and decoders who represent that firm. In the example above with two departments unfavorable and only one favorable to the

---

[18] Randall Harrison, "Nonverbal Communications: Explorations into Time, Space, Action, and Object," *Dimensions In Communications*, James H. Campbell and Hal W. Hepler, eds. (Belmont, Calif.: Wadsworth Publishing Co., Inc., 1965), pp. 158–74.

chemical supplier, top management is not likely to perceive that supplier as satisfactory.

Four characteristics determine the nature of individual channel members' perceptions of each other. First, perception is *subjective* in the sense that each representative of the firm interprets information according to his experience.[19] A buyer who has been snubbed by a particular manufacturer tends to hold this manufacturer in low esteem. The buyer may pay more for products of another manufacturer rather than purchase from the offender. Second, perception is *selective* in the sense that the firm's representative selects from a total body of information certain facts upon which to base his judgment. In this sense, perception is always based on insufficient information. A manager, in seeking to stimulate a branch to greater sales effort, may not be capable of interpreting effectively that branch's efforts to keep cost down or to service customers. The manager interprets the branch's entire performance in terms of the one item—sales.

Third, perception is *temporal* in the sense that it is of short duration. An attitude held can be quickly forgotten by the manager. In the above example, the manager may ignore the branch's sales deficiency when reviewing its overall performance. Because perception is temporal, it is necessary to continually reinforce favorable perceptions. Advertising to branches or independent middlemen can help to maintain the attitude of these middlemen toward the business. Fourth, perception is *summative* in the sense that the selected facts become representative of the total business. A buyer who has obtained good performance from a manufacturer's product tends to perceive all that manufacturer's products as being of high quality.

MESSAGES IN THE CHANNEL

All communication is based on the exchange of messages. We shall now examine: (1) message networks, (2) types of message networks, (3) interaction of message networks, (4) two-way communications, and (5) message effectiveness.

Message Networks Between Channel Members

The *content* of a message refers to what that message says. Messages in the channel tend to be specialized by content. That is, each message carries a narrow range of ideas associated with a single specific channel operation, problem, policy, solution, etc. Between any two channel members, various types of messages (e.g., order status, sales, complaints, pur-

---

[19] C. Glenn Walters and Gordon W. Paul, *Consumer Behavior* (Homewood, Ill.: Richard D. Irwin, Inc., 1970), pp. 278–81.

chases, prices, payments, etc.,) are necessary. Thus, identifiable message networks begin to emerge over time to handle the specialized routine information. The *message network* is the route, including stopover points, that the message takes between an encoder and decoder. A simple message network is shown in Figure 13–4 based on the major functional areas of marketing. This is an overall message network, but it is not the only type in existence. The network includes the internal routing as well as the routing between the firms.

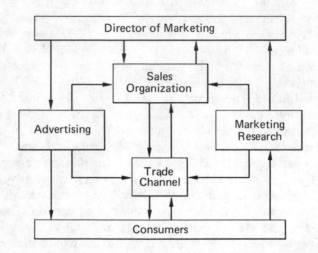

Fig. 13–4. Flow of messages in a channel system. *Source:* "Communications in a Marketing System," *Cost and Profit Outlook* (August, 1951).

Individual message networks can be classified as temporary or permanent. *Permanent message networks* develop where messages of a similar nature must be transmitted periodically on a regular basis. The message networks become routinized as in purchases and complaints. *Temporary message networks* must be established for non-recurring messages. The decision to build a new plant requires establishing a temporary message network between top management, architects, banks, and building suppliers. Once the plant is complete, the network is dismantled.

Between any two channel members message networks become superimposed on one another. In our example, one serial communications network can be identified as that from the director to advertising to the consumer and back through research to the director. Another serial network loop goes from director to sales to the channel to consumers and back through the channel to sales to the director. Other networks also are in simultaneous operation, for example, sales and advertising. In the final analysis, these networks are not separable except for the purpose of discussion. There is one master message network in the channel made up of a large number of identifiable permanent sub-nets. Each sub-net is highly specialized to perform a particular task, but it must also make a direct contribution to the master network. Temporary sub-nets must find their place within the master network.

Types of Networks

Based upon the content of the message, five types of message networks can be identified in the channel of distribution: (1) authority networks, (2) information networks, (3) task-expertise networks, (4) friendship networks, and (5) status networks.

Authority Networks. In the marketing channel, authority networks refer to the transfer of orders or commands from the leader down through the institutional levels.[20] Messages typically include directions or instructions for performing some task. When General Motors tells a balky dealer to repair a customer's car the authority network is in operation. Messages that instruct dealers on service standards or how to handle complaints fall into this same network. The authority network is typically considered to be a one-way flow because commands are basically dictatorial; there is little room for argument in this network. Nevertheless, authority messages do allow for response at least in the form of acknowledgment or clarification.

Authority networks tend to exist in tightly organized channels such as contractual channels or fully integrated channels. For the most part, the right to lead rests on the willingness of subordinates to follow, but the subordinates' will is much more apparent in non-integrated channels. Independent middlemen are much more capable of restricting the leader's authority. The middleman gives up much of his authority to the leader in a contractual channel. Where strong authority networks exist, the channel leader tends to be authoritarian; when authority networks are weak the channel becomes more democratic.

Information Networks. Information networks exist for the purpose of exchanging facts which are transferred from member to leader as well as from leader to member. Thus, there is a two-way transfer.[21] Information may be either persuasive or operational and the type of messages relates to specific problems, policies, goals, abilities, etc., that the channel members need for normal operations. Examples of the information network can be found in product advertising, personal selling, expense ac-

[20] Grabner and Rosenberg, *op. cit.*, pp. 234–38.
[21] *Ibid.*, pp. 235–36.

counting, purchase records, personnel performance records, etc. The information net is much less dictatorial than the authority net, but it may handle some of the same types of information. The difference lies in the purpose of the message and the manner of its transmittal. Information networks tend to operate on a voluntary basis, and feedback is normal and desirable. The idea is to obtain the greatest knowledge about the subject at hand. Of course, at different levels in the channel, authority and information networks may exist simultaneously.

Task-Expertise Networks. An important communications network is the task-expertise net which operates to handle specific problems that require highly technical experts where the information is generally non-routine. If the problem is routine or ordinary, the information network can normally handle it. The general idea is to bring the best methods, procedures, and facts to bear on the task. The network may be in regular operation, or it may operate only in emergencies. A regular task-expertise message network operates when an advertising agency or research firm is employed by the channel member on a regular basis. Examples of emergency use include hiring a management consultant to check operations, engaging an architect to design a building, or hiring a lawyer only when the organization is being sued. The experts may be given great authority to act on a limited time basis when engaged. Messages tend to move directly between the problem area and the expert. Thus, specific levels in the channel or specific managers may be completely bypassed.

Friendship Networks. The friendship information network is in some ways the most pervasive message network of all. This net involves messages of affection, trust, and sociability between members of organizations in the marketing channel. Therefore, the friendship network can exist simultaneously with any or all of the other channel communications nets. The messages in this network may be personal, humorous, or social, but they bear on the work of the channel because they condition the mood of the parties. When two channel members like and trust each other the work proceeds more smoothly. Simple joking, the exchange of gifts, playing golf, etc., are examples of communications in the friendship network. The feelings of friendship grow up over time as the members of the channel interact. The friendship network is basically informal, and it may exist in either integrated or non-integrated channels.

Status Networks. The status network conveys messages about the position or importance of members of the channel. In effect, the status network deals with channel prestige, and it frequently parallels the friendship network. Status can be derived from the size of firm, financial strength, position in the channel leadership, and expertise. Status of channel members can lead to problems when the members do not perceive their status in the same light as the channel as a whole. Status is equally important in integrated and non-integrated channels. Messages can be antagonistic, and they can offer a challenge. A salesman calling on a purchasing agent may resent the plush office of the purchasing agent and this may lead to antagonism. Another salesman may see the quarters as a challenge to do better to obtain a similar office.

Message Feedback in the Channel

Communicated messages may be either one-way or two-way depending on whether or not there is feedback.[22] Feedback is any information the sender obtains from the receiver about the reception of the message.[23] Feedback is, in a way, reverse communication. *One-way communication* does not involve message feedback. An institution's ad, designed to foster goodwill for the channel leader among members, may not involve any determinable feedback to the leader. Most advertising and sales promotion are considered one-way communications. Needless to say, this is an important type of transmittal. Communication is considered to be *two-way* when there is a give and take of messages between parties.[24] The feedback may be immediate as in the case of a personal salesman calling on a retailer or it may be delayed as in the case of policy decisions by the channel leader. Two-way communication is also important in the channel. It often occurs in face-to-face situations but this is not absolutely necessary. Two-way communication can take place by phone or mail.

Message Effectiveness

There are two methods for measuring the effectiveness of channel communications. One is the accuracy of the message transmitted, and the other is the result obtained from the message. In the final analysis, the effectiveness of any communicated message depends on whether it accomplishes its purpose or not. The message may be poorly stated, employ incorrect media, and be sent to the wrong person, but if it gets the job done, it is an effective message. One factor that cannot be overlooked in messages is tact; it may be considered as the proper tone of voice, and

---

[22] Bruce H. Westley and Malcolm S. MacLean, Jr., "A Conceptual Model for Communications Research," *Journalism Quarterly* (Winter, 1957), pp. 31–38.

[23] Bettinghaus, *op. cit.*, p. 207.

[24] Schramm, *op. cit.*, pp. 3–26.

the sender must know when to be hard and when to be considerate. Other factors affecting the effectiveness of messages include:

1. Saying what is intended
2. Using clear wording
3. Employing the least number of words consistent with the objective
4. Selecting methods of emphasis carefully
5. Using a channel that is appropriate to the timing required
6. Getting the message to the proper person
7. Being alert for feedback and clarifying where necessary

COMMUNICATIONS MEDIA IN CHANNELS

Theoretically, the communications media is the physical device that carries a message. Thus, the media includes air, paper, visual light, electric current, or physical movement. This definition of media is more suited for person-to-person communications, particularly those of a casual nature. A more practical explanation of media is needed to explain the operation of marketing channels.

In the marketing channel, the media is the person or institution responsible for physically transmitting the message. Frequently, it is a business organization that specializes in message transmission and engages in all the normal activities of a business. Communications media in the channel include the television and radio broadcasters, telegraph, telephone, movie companies, Western Union, newspapers, magazines, sign companies, painters, salesmen, agent buyers and sellers, etc. Some of these media, such as the telephone, telegraph, and Western Union, are used more for internal operational communications. Others, such as salesmen, magazines, newspapers, and radio, are used more for persuasive communications.

It frequently happens in a marketing channel that the encoder and the media may be the same just as the encoder and sender may be the same. Other possible combinations in the communications process are shown in Figure 13–5. In example 1 the manufacturer uses a television network that encodes and transmits to final consumers. These final consumers both decode and act as receivers of the information. Example 2 is similar, except that the decoder and receiver are different. In this case, the sales manager decodes for the retail firm. Example 3 has a combined sender–encoder media in the form of a selling agent. This is an illustration of a small manufacturer who turns the entire sales task over to the agent. The agent sells direct to industrial buyers. The one agent accomplishes the entire communications task. In example 4, the

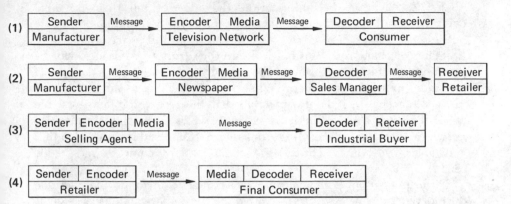

Fig. 13–5.   Use of communications media.

retailer encodes his own message by the goods placed on the shelves. It is a self-service store and, without benefit of personal selling or advertising, the consumer browses through the store making selections from the products offered. Thus the consumer acts as a combined media, decoder, and receiver.

NOISE IN CHANNEL COMMUNICATIONS

We have stated that noise is not an element of the communications process; actually, the perfect communications system contains no noise. Unfortunately, there are few such systems. Therefore, it is necessary to deal with the subject of noise, even though it does not really belong in the communications network.

Nature of Noise

Noise can be defined as any interference with the communication of ideas. In any organization, such as the marketing channel, where the coordination of widely separated operations is performed, noise is a very serious matter. The two broad causes of noise in a marketing channel are omission and distortion.[25] *Noise omission* refers to a failure to perform and has three causes. First, noise occurs when a complete message is sent but not received. There may be a failure to send the message. Channel secrecy is important here. Channel members frequently have information useful to other members but fail to send it. Although agents

[25] Grabner and Rosenberg, *op. cit.*, p. 239.

possess excellent market information, they do not tell their principal everything for fear their sales quotas may be changed. Manufacturers do not inform wholesalers or retailers about expected price changes or promotional changes because of a desire for surprise. Messages may be lost in transit, missent, or sent at the wrong time. The capacity of media to handle messages is limited. When this capacity is reached, mistakes in handling occur. It is also possible that the receiver is not available to take the message. Second, noise occurs when an incomplete message is sent or received. This type of omission is usually the result of either encoding or decoding. Third, there is noise when a complete message is sent but ignored.

Distortion is noise that results from some change in the message during the transmission. It is caused by misunderstanding of signals sent, signals that become confused in transit, and senders or receivers who change the emphasis of the facts. Signals may be misunderstood because of differences in the meaning of words. This fact is also a principal reason why messages get distorted in transit. The effect of emphasis is a major cause of message distortion in the marketing channel. The wholesaler informs the manufacturer that he simply cannot compete at these prices when he means it's tough competing. The manufacturer informs the manufacturer's agent that the agent's performance amounts to stealing when the manufacturer means that the agent should try to sell harder. Exaggeration causes two communication problems. It changes the meaning of the original message, and it may lead the receiver to discount all future messages as distorted.

Methods of Reducing Noise

Noise can occur anywhere in the marketing channel. Even the sender can contribute to noise by not obtaining all the facts or by using the wrong facts. However, noise is most likely to occur anyplace that messages are transmitted between specialized institutions. Reference to the communications models presented in Figure 13–5 shows where these points are located. Since the communications process is different in different channels, it follows that the handling of noise must conform to fit the situation. The greatest possible chance of noise occurrence is in a channel where all the institutions are separate.

There is no way for all the noise in marketing channels to be eliminated. As long as there are humans involved in the transmission of messages there will be omission and distortion of the messages sent. However, five important methods can be employed to reduce the incidence of channel noise. First, the marketing channel should use competent encoders and decoders. Nothing can quite substitute for intelligence brought to bear on the interpretations. Errors in interpretation will be made, but they can be reduced when the people know their job. Second, the channel should employ a common language in all messages. All parties in the channel should know the definitions of terms utilized. One of the more important language devices that can be used to reduce noise is language specialization. Specialized language allows shortcuts in working and places unique interpretation on common words and symbols. In the marketing channel, the use of standardized procedures, abbreviations, code words, etc., can greatly improve communications.

Third, the channel should use multiple media for message transmission. The chance of overloading a single media is decreased, and distortions are reduced. Multiple media allow for greater opportunities to time messages. It is characteristic of most channel information that its value decreases with time. Shipment delayed on an order, a price change not made, or a complaint not handled immediately do damage to the firm. The use of multiple media also provides an opportunity to send the same message more than one way.

Fourth, the channel should use machines wherever possible. Machines substitute for human subjectivity and, when working properly, they make few mistakes. Such machines as the teletype and computers can handle more data at a much faster pace than humans. Fifth, the channel should encourage feedback. Feedback serves two purposes. It verifies that the message has been received and there should be no problem with missent or forgotten messages. When the feedback does not come it signals that something has gone wrong. The sender then can use follow-up to determine what the problem is. Feedback also serves to determine whether the correct message was received. This determination is made by the nature of the feedback. Questions indicate some problem, and the type of response may show a deficiency or failure to comprehend the message. These problems can also be handled by follow-up.

QUESTIONS

1. How does channel communications differ from channel information?
2. What are communications problems created by spatial separation in channels?
3. Explain the communications process. How does noise enter into this process?
4. How do sender–receiver relationships affect channel communications?
5. What is meant by communication hierarchy? What affect does this hierarchy have on the communications problems in channels?
6. How does encoder-decoder interpretation of channel information affect channel communications?

7. What is a signal? How does it relate to fields of experience, communication, and channels?
8. What is a message network? Illustrate a message network between a clothing manufacturer and a department store.
9. How does the media relate to the communications process?
10. Discuss the methods of reducing noise in channels of distribution.

14

Information Systems
in Channels

We now turn to the subject of information systems and how they provide operational data. Chapter 15 discusses persuasive communications; in a practical sense, these two types of communications operate together and both are essential to channels management.

DESIGN OF INFORMATION SYSTEMS

Every channel of distribution possesses a system for providing operations facts. The first necessary ingredient in any design is to understand the nature of the thing being designed. The term information system has been used in several ways. Some scholars employ it almost synonymously with marketing research. Others consider information systems to be the flow of paper within the organization. Still others see the information system as the total processing of all types of information in the business.[1] Thus, information is needed on the environment, product, channel, promotion, and price. Since these subjects permeate this entire book a different definition is needed. For our purpose, an information system is defined more narrowly as: *the orderly flow of pertinent financial operational data, both internally and between firms, for use as the basis*

[1] See: Philip Kotler, "A Design of the Firm's Marketing Nerve Center," *Business Horizons*, Vol. 9 (Fall, 1966), pp. 63–74; Lee Adler, "Systems Approach to Marketing," *Harvard Business Review*, Vol. 45 (May–June, 1967), pp. 105–18; Preston P. Le Breton, *Administrative Intelligence—Information Systems* (Boston: Houghton Mifflin Co., 1969), pp. 10–35.

for decision making in specified responsibility areas of channels manage-ment.[2] In other words, we seek to delve into the cost and revenue aspects of performing functions in the channel.

Usually, information systems are used to refer to the employment of men, machines, and procedures within a single organization for the purpose of management decisions.[3] Obviously, this usage has to be broadened where the channel is concerned. When the channel itself is considered as an organized team, a dual loop in the information flow is required to understand its nature. First, there is the collection, flow, and use of data internally within a single firm, and, second, there is the same process between the channel membership and the leader. Although the source of information may be external to a given firm, or to the channel, its use is always internal.

Components of Information System

In a general sense, the information system consists of management that utilizes methods and equipment to collect, process, and utilize pertinent information for decision making. These three components of the information system are illustrated below.

Human Component		Tools		Process	
Management }	Uses {	Methods Equipment }	for the	Need determination Collection Processing Storage Use	of Information

After someone in management recognizes a need for information, the other steps occur in a relative time sequence. *Collection* encompasses acquiring and placing the raw data in the mind. *Processing* is taking the data from the mind and arranging, modifying, interpreting, and getting it into the hands of the user. *Storage* is the simple act of keeping information until needed. It may be done in the mind of someone or in a computer or other machine. *Use* concerns the application of information to the solution of some management problem for which a need was originally recognized.

---

[2] Adapted from: Samuel V. Smith, Richard H. Brien, and James E. Stafford, "Marketing Information Systems: An Introductory Overview," *Readings In Marketing Information Systems,* Samuel V. Smith, Richard H. Brien, and James E. Stafford, eds. (Boston: Houghton Mifflin Co., 1968), p. 7.

[3] Le Breton, *op. cit.,* pp. 10–14. The author presents a good organization of men, tools, and methods into an information system.

Sources of Channel Information

Types of information needed include assumptions, facts, figures, and anticipated occurrences that are important to the various operational decision areas of the channel. Much of this information can be located internally in the form of personal conversations, reports, letters, records, computer printouts, and memorandum.[4] However, it is sometimes necessary to go outside the business to obtain data. External sources include market or competitive studies, suppliers, comparison shoppers, trade journals, newspapers, magazines, radio, television, and government publications.[5]

The responsibility for providing operational data is a complex matter.[6] The two most common mistakes made in supplying information are: (1) providing too much data which is costly, and (2) providing too little data for which no sound decision basis results. These incorrect decisions have a cost of their own in terms of inefficiency.

There is a tendency to think that providing channel data is the sole responsibility of marketing research, a point of view that does not hold up in practice. The evidence is that data acquisition occurs throughout the firms that comprise a channel; it also takes place in every department or functional area of each firm.[7] No single unit appears to be more important in this activity. Most information needed to operate a specific organizational unit such as a territory, department, or office is generated from within that unit. For instance, a sales department knows units of output, salaries, and merchandise returned. Information that has general application throughout the business is usually generated by special departments designed for that purpose. It takes the marketing research department to survey consumer attitudes or evaluate competitors' promotions. In practice, the special departments generate information for their own internal use at the same time they are providing others with data. Organizational units that collect information primarily for their own use include individual sales departments of territories, warehousing, purchasing, and store operations. Those units that are specialized to provide other units of the firm with data include accounting, legal, credit, real estate, and marketing research.

Data acquisition is complex within the channel. In non-integrated channels and uncoordinated but integrated channels each unit is more

---

[4] Smith, Brien, and Stafford, *op. cit.*, p. 3.

[5] Allan D. Dale and Richard J. Lewis, "A Corporate Information System for Distribution Management," *Business Review* (Winter, 1964–65), pp. 11–22.

[6] Le Breton, *op. cit.*, pp. 14–28.

[7] William T. Kelley, "Marketing Intelligence for Top Management," *Journal of Marketing*, Vol. 20 (October, 1965), pp. 19–24.

concerned with acquiring information beneficial to internal operations than with furnishing information to other members.[8] When the channel is not coordinated, only a small part of the information generated is passed between members. Indeed, uncoordinated channels make little provision for providing information that is useful collectively. This fact no doubt hinders the effectiveness of these non-integrated channels. In coordinated channels, the specialized departments are established in a manner previously described, but they may be located at the home office or in individual plants or units. In either case, it is difficult to get all the necessary information passed between separate divisions in proper form and in time to be useful. Even when data arrives there is no assurance that it will be utilized.

Allocation of Channel Information

The design of the information system must provide for the use of information that has been collected.[9] The three most common mistakes made in the use of data are: (1) improper allocation to users, (2) failure to employ available information, and (3) misuse of data. Failure to employ data is often caused by the fact that the information does not fit the problem. One study suggests that daily pressures, insistence on a rigorous methodology, the tendency to specialize, and fascination with new techniques are the principle causes of the data not fitting the problem.[10] That is, the data is incomplete, inconclusive, or confusing. It is also often true that the manager simply cannot conceive of the proper method of using information. For example, one study shows that retailers have a considerable amount of credit information which includes customer name, location, credit rating, payment record, type of merchandise bought, amount paid, etc.[11] The only use made of this information is to figure the ratio of credit to cash sales when it could be utilized for such things as profiling customers, determining sales area, planning purchases, etc.

It often happens that the users of information in the channel are the same managers as the ones who collect the information. The manager who collects information about specific activities in his department does so because the information is useful for departmental planning. It often happens that departmental data collected primarily for use internally within the department is useful throughout the business. Sales information, for example, is employed for planning by accounting, shipping and

[8] Gerald Albaum, "Information Flow and Decentralized Decision Making in Marketing," *California Management Review*, Vol. 9 (September, 1967), pp. 59–70.

[9] Le Breton, *op. cit.*, pp. 29–33.

[10] Lee Adler, "Phasing Research into the Marketing Plan," *Harvard Business Review*, Vol. 38 (May–June, 1960), pp. 113–22.

[11] Thomas Greer and Glenn Walters, "The Effective Use of Credit Information," *Northwest Business Management*, Vol. 4 (Fall, 1966), pp. 2–7.

receiving, and warehousing. As a general rule, a greater variety of information is used in coordinated channels than in uncoordinated channels. It takes more information to relate operating units separated by stage in the channel or geography, and the coordinated channel typically has the specialized talent necessary to use data effectively. The more complex the channel, the greater the dependence on data by individual managers.

Purpose of Information Systems

The purpose of any communications is found in the use made of the information. Thus, the overall purpose of the information system is to provide facts for decision making. However, operational facts can be used in several different ways, each of which provides a purpose for gathering facts. These purposes can be summarized under: (1) type of use, (2) level of use, and (3) impact of use.

The *type of use* refers to what is done with the facts or information collected by the information system. Operational information gathered in the channel is used for planning and for evaluation.[12] *Operations planning* is forward looking and involves some type of forecasting. These forecasts either provide goals to aim toward or they provide insights into future conditions that affect daily decision making. *Evaluation* is backward looking and concerns past results. It is used to compare results to plans and to provide a basis for control of future plans. Thus, evaluation and planning are interrelated, and to some extent each depends on the other. The *level of use* refers to where the operations data is applied in the organization. Within a business, or a channel, there are two broad levels for planning and control. They are the channel leader and the channel members. The channel leader is interested in summarized results because of an emphasis on broad team goals. The channel members are interested in the specifics necessary for daily decisions.

The *impact of use* refers to whether the facts are used for long-range planning and evaluation or for short-range planning and evaluation. Both the channel leader and channel members are concerned with each type of use for internal firm objectives. Where the channel as a whole is affected, the channel leader is usually more conscious of the long run. All planning should be limited to the reasonably foreseeable future. Retailers and wholesalers consider weekly, monthly, and quarterly plans to be short run, and most planning by these firms fits this designation. Long-run plans to retailers and wholesalers typically mean between three to ten years. Manufacturers plan on a monthly and quarterly basis in the short run, and may make long-run plans between three, five, or ten years.

---

[12] David Bendel Hertz, "Information Flows and the Coordination of Business Functions," *Marketing and the Consumer,* Wroe Alderson and Stanley J. Shapiro, eds. (Englewood Cliffs, N.J.: Prentice-Hall, Inc., 1963), pp. 80–95.

MASTER PLAN OF THE INFORMATION SYSTEM

All financial data in the channel can be integrated into a master plan based on a type of income statement. The income statement can contain planned or actual figures. An example of a forecasted income statement is shown in Figure 14-1. Five important items are included on the

Forecast Income Statement: XYZ Company
(Data extrapolated from actual company records)

Item	19—5 Forecast	
	Dollars	Per Cent
Gross Sales*	$1,792,200	103.00%
Less: Reductions*	52,200	3.00
Net Sales	1,740,000	100.00
Cost of Goods Sold		
Beginning Inventory	198,000	11.38
Purchases	1,250,000	71.84
Goods Available	1,448,000	83.22
Ending Inventory*	206,000	11.84
Cost of Goods Sold	1,242,000	71.38
Gross Margin*	498,000	28.62
Operating Expenses*	353,000	20.28
Net Income before Taxes	145,000	8.33

*Indicates items typically forecast by business.
Source: Professor J. F. Curry, Mississippi State University.

Fig. 14-1. Forecasted income statement.

master plan: (1) sales, (2) stock, (3) expenses, (4) reductions, and (5) profit.[13] These items have an asterisk as identification. All the other information on the income statement can be determined from these figures. This income statement can serve as the basis for planning future dollar expenditures. When the forecast figures are compared to actual operating results, the statement becomes a device for evaluation. Most of the discussion in this chapter is based on this income statement, and wherever possible the figures quoted are taken from it.[14]

[13] Delbert J. Duncan, Charles F. Phillips, and Stanley Hollander, *Modern Retailing Management*, 8th ed. (Homewood, Ill.: Richard D. Irwin, Inc., 1972), Chapter 14.
[14] Robert E. Weigand, "The Accountant and Marketing Channels," *The Accounting Review*, Vol. 38 (July, 1963), pp. 584–90. Weigand argues for greater use of accounting in the marketing channel, though he only indirectly discusses sales and expense data.

Use of Dollar or Unit Control

The income statement is illustrated in dollar amounts and is referred to as *dollar control*. In fact, information systems can provide much data in either dollars or units. In *unit control* the physical items are the basis for the data rather than their monetary value. Both types of control are needed in nearly every business.

Dollar control is the tool of top management because this group is primarily interested in the inflow and outflow of money for the business or channel. Middle management in charge of departments or divisions seeks unit information, where it applies, because it is more suited for such daily decisions as how many units to purchase, which items to mark down, and where goods can be stored. Typically, the business keeps both types of data. Once the units of a product are known along with the price, it is a simple matter to determine the dollar value. This chapter focuses on dollar data, because of the emphasis on the channel leader's coordination of the entire team effort. However, in most instances where the data applies equally to unit management, this fact is considered in the discussion.

Frequency of Data Collection and Use

Data can be obtained and used in the channel as frequently as management desires. This fact is particularly true for dollar information. A *perpetual system,* sometimes called a book inventory, is a running account of all pertinent data needed for planning or evaluation. The data may be kept daily, weekly, or monthly, and it is derived from reports. This method requires that elaborate records are kept in the form of sales tickets, tapes, invoice receipts, returns to vendors, returns by customers, internal stock transfers, markdown, and markup. Shortages must also be estimated. A *periodic system* simply means that the physical goods are counted on a regular time sequence. Most businesses take a physical inventory at least once a year and some firms take such an inventory more frequently. Most medium and large firms utilize both methods. Periodic physical inventories are necessary to meet government requirements and to update the accuracy of the book inventory. Once the physical amount and price are known, it is a simple multiplication to determine the dollar value of the inventory. Thus, keeping a periodic and dollar inventory simultaneously is not a great problem for larger firms.

SALES FORECAST: THE PLANNING GOAL

The sales forecast is the overall planning figure for any business, and it appears first on the income statement. It is an estimate, for some future period, of the volume of output that the organization can reasonably expect to dispose of. Not only do expected sales determine the overall objective of the firm, but they are involved, to some degree, in planning stock, purchases, promotion, expenses, and profit.[15] Most of these latter figures could not be determined without planned sales. There are two basic steps to sales forecasting: (1) estimation of total company sales and (2) allocation of total sales. The discussion of sales forecasting is organized around these two steps.

The first step in sales forecasting is to estimate total company sales. Unfortunately there is no single method for accomplishing this task, and each management must select a method suited to its needs. The more important methods available to channel members are discussed at this time.

Executive Opinion

Executive opinion is perhaps the least sophisticated of the methods for forecasting total company sales, but it is frequently used. It entails nothing more than the manager's estimate of sales based on his personal judgment.[16] The manager may give specific facts such as economic conditions or changes in promotion some casual consideration on a limited basis. However, there is no systematic review of all the factors that influence sales. A variation of the use of executive opinion is to average the opinion of several managers. The actual forecast may be picked out of the air, based on a standard increase of last year's sales, or based on plant output or plant capacity. Executive opinion is a popular method for forecasting total sales with small retailers, wholesalers, and manufacturers. Its primary virtue lies in its simplicity. For many firms, without adequate personnel or equipment, it is the only feasible method of sales forecasting. There have been some outstanding successes using the method; results largely depend on the "feel" that the executive has for the market.

Sales Force Composite

Total company sales can be estimated by salesmen. The sales force composite is determined in the same general manner as executive opinion. Basically, the method depends on the personal judgment of salesmen, but there are two differences between this method and executive judgment. First, joint judgment of salesmen is built into the composite. Second, when using the salesmen composite, total company sales can be estimated

---

[15] William Lazer, "Sales Forecasting: Key to Integrated Marketing," *Business Horizons,* Vol. 3 (Fall, 1959), pp. 61–67.

[16] Ralph S. Alexander, James S. Cross, and Richard M. Hill, *Industrial Marketing* (Homewood, Ill.: Richard D. Irwin, Inc., 1967), pp. 123–24.

in either of two ways. First, each salesman can make direct estimate of total company sales, and the manager can average these estimates to arrive at a single forecast. Second, each salesman can estimate sales in his own territory or department, and the sales manager sums up these individual estimates to arrive at the company total.

Used more by medium-sized wholesalers and manufacturers, the sales composite is particularly important for middlemen who have salesmen in the field. The method is simple, and it uses the excellent experience of individuals closest to the problem. Its difficulty lies in having salesmen estimate their own objectives. Overoptimism may lead to high sales estimates, or a desire to look good on the salesman's part may lead to low estimates. Salesmen may also make mistakes, since this type of activity is not a part of their regular duty. Of particular importance is the fact that salesmen have a poor perspective for determining general economic conditions. Any accurate forecast must give some consideration to this factor.

Expert Opinion

Instead of asking the manager or sales force to forecast the total company sales, the company may have the task performed by an outside expert. The only difference in this method and executive opinion lies in who does the estimating. Economists, bankers, large business executives, and educators are frequently used as experts. Many outside experts have an excellent grasp of general economic conditions but they may lack knowledge of the industry and company. Some businesses combine the use of expert opinion and executive opinion in an attempt to take advantage of the abilities of each. Small companies sometimes base predictions on expert opinion reported in journals and magazines. Large financially strong channel members are more likely to employ experts.

Time Series

Estimate of total company sales based on time series takes a primarily historical approach to the problem. Time series is used by manufacturers and wholesalers to estimate sales, but it is the overwhelming choice of retailers. Figure 14–2 demonstrates time series analysis. Two steps are involved in the method. First, a record of the level of dollar company sales is kept over time and a trend line is fitted, either by sight or by the use of statistical techniques. The statistical method is preferred because of greater accuracy. In Figure 14–2, the trend is established to 1973.

Second, the trend must be extrapolated for the forecast period.[17] Fig-

17 William F. Hoffman, "Improved Forecasting Based on Sales History," *Systems and Procedures Journal,* Vol. 17 (January–February, 1966), pp. 28–30.

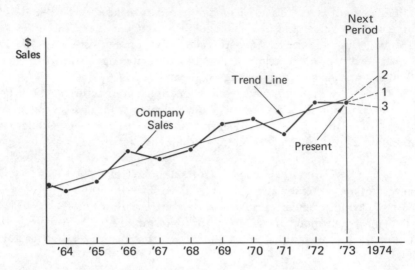

Fig. 14–2. Time series used for forecasting.

ure 14–2 illustrates a forecast for one year. If future conditions were expected to be exactly like the trend of the past, then the trend line could simply be extended, as shown by position 1. However, this situation seldom exists in reality. In fact, both internal conditions of the firm and external conditions of the environment change. The forecast must be adjusted higher or lower depending on the best estimate of how conditions are expected to affect sales volume. Some of the important internal and external factors the manager may consider in his estimate include the following:

   I. Internal Factors
       1. Change in product line
       2. Store additions or modifications
       3. Changes in store services
       4. Changes in advertising
       5. Price policies
       6. Changes in the firm's organization
       7. Changes in sales training
       8. Employment

  II. External Factors
       1. Competition strategy
       2. General economic conditions
       3. Government action
       4. Industry change
       5. Actions of suppliers
       6. Market changes

The evaluation of these facts is based on available information and executive judgment. Usually, more internal facts are available than external facts. For example, management should know if it plans future additions or an increase in advertising. Even when these internal facts are known, there is no way to determine their exact effect on future sales. Thus, executive judgment is an important part of all forecasting and what is most important is for the manager to consider the influence on sales for each factor separately. No manager can keep all of the internal and external factors in mind simultaneously; only individual attention can assure adequate consideration of each factor.

Many managers make three separate forecasts simultaneously. Position 1 in Figure 14–2 becomes the average forecast, with position 2 optimistic and position 3 pessimistic. Alternative sale strategies are designed for each forecast. This method provides flexibility. As the firm moves into the forecast period, the manager can shift strategies according to which trend is more appropriate to market conditions. A great many medium and large retailers use this method of forecasting. Because it is relatively simple, it can provide adequate information for planning. Trend analysis does relate sales to reality. One problem is that past sales include past errors. Past sales show what the company accomplished, at the time, rather than what it should have accomplished. The use of past figures for planning compounds these errors. There is also no consideration of sales potential with the method—that is, what sales are actually available in the market that the company should be attempting to attract.

Market Survey

Market surveys are used by a variety of manufacturers and some wholesalers to estimate total company sales. These surveys are typically undertaken by companies with single products or when a total forecast is needed for a specific product in the line. The method has limited use because it is time consuming and costly to conduct original research in the market. Technique involves sampling the market and extrapolating total sales from the sample. Usually based on a questionnaire, the survey follows the normal procedure of marketing research. Customers may be asked if they have the product on their shelves, if they have purchased it recently, or if they intend to purchase the product. Another type of market survey, particularly useful for new products, is the test market. The company actually puts on a complete sales campaign in a limited area. Sales results from the test are then interpolated for the market as a whole.

Factor Association

A relatively simple and easily used method for forecasting total company sales is factor association. It is frequently used by manufacturers. The method, highly reliable when used, involves associating company sales with some known factor(s) in the economy. The factor may be another product, population, magazine circulation, income, etc. A direct relationship between the existence of the factor in the market and possible company sales is assumed. Thus, where number of units (or percentage) of the factor is known, company sales can be estimated directly. For example, if the number of tape recorders in the United States is known and the number of tapes sold per recorder, a seller of tapes has a basis for forecasting tape sales. Total tape sales can be determined by multiplying average tape sale by the number of recorders. If the manufacturer of tapes knows his share of industry sales, a simple multiplication provides his total company sales. In the same way, automobile registrations provide a good measure of the opportunity to sell tires.

Allocation of Total Sales Forecast

The second step in sales forecasting is the allocation of total company sales by some method meaningful to the company. Most businesses in the marketing channel need to know more than total company sales. Total figures hide a lot that takes place within the organization. For this reason, total company sales are typically allocated by: (1) organizational unit, (2) product line, (3) customers, (4) salesmen, and (5) time. The fundamental breakdown is by organizational unit. For example, in retail stores sales are divided by merchandise departments. In wholesale and manufacturing firms the division is typically by territories. Multi-level or multi-unit organizations may allocate data by plant or operating division. The reason for these allocations is that the organizational unit is the typical unit of control in most businesses. Even divisional or plant figures may be further sub-divided, either by departments or territory.

Once the organizational breakdown is made, the other types of allocation are used. Product figures indicate which items sell well and which sell poorly. Total sales can be divided by product classes, price lines, or individual products. The deciding factor is the depth of information desired. Total sales allocated by customers augment an analysis of where profits are generated. Data may be kept on large, medium, and small customers. A breakdown of total sales by time is typical, no matter which of the other types of allocation is used. The sales data can be sub-divided by weeks, months, or quarters. It is particularly important for planning to know what proportion of sales occur each month. Of course, these methods of allocation can be combined. Product, customer, and period sales are usually allocated under the organizational unit. Product lines sales can be kept by month for specific customers. Other combinations are also possible.

FUNCTIONAL PLANNING TO ACHIEVE SALES FORECAST

The remaining functional items are illustrated on the income statement; advertising, expenses, reductions, profit, and stock can be planned once the sales forecast is available. Each of these functional areas involves a cost, but that cost is incurred in order to achieve the sales volume forecast. As the income statement demonstrates, it is this relationship between sales and functions that leads to profits.

Planned Advertising

The advertising forecast, which is an estimate of the amount to be spent on promotion, is based on the same two types of steps discussed for sales. First, the total advertising appropriation for the business must be determined. Second, the total appropriation must be meaningfully allocated. Advertising is an expense, and it could be grouped with the other expenses for the discussion of forecasting. It is discussed separately because of its importance, and because the forecast of advertising differs in some respects from the forecast methods used for other expenses.

Total Advertising Forecast. The total advertising appropriation can be established by the percentage-to-sales method or by the research-task method.[18] The *percentage-to-sales method* for figuring the advertising appropriation is simple to use and easy to calculate. The manager simply decides what percentage of the store's total dollar sales can be applied to advertising. Frequently, the advertising percentage is based on an industry average, the company's historical percentage, the opinion of some expert, the national average, or simply management judgment. If sales are $1 million, and the manager feels he can allocate three per cent to advertising, then $30,000 is the total advertising appropriation. The percentage can be applied equally well to past or forecast sales. Forecast sales are preferred because this method ties the appropriation to the sales goal. *Advertising Age* estimates that between 1954 and 1964 businesses spent approximately between 1.07 per cent and 1.18 per cent of sales on advertising.[19] In 1970, advertising expenditures were 1.1 per cent of business receipts. The high figure was for 1964 and there was a gradual increase over the period. The percentage-to-sales method is the one

[18] Harry D. Wolfe and Dik W. Twedt, *Essentials of the Promotional Mix* (New York: Appleton-Century-Crofts, 1970), Chapter 6.

[19] Internal Revenue Service Sources, Tax Returns, *Advertising Age* (September 18, 1967).

most used for figuring total advertising expenditure, but it is illogical. It makes advertising dependent on sales when, supposedly, it is advertising that helps to generate sales. Nevertheless, the method has proved successful for many marketers.

The *research-task method* requires an estimate of dollar advertising expenditure that is necessary to achieve the previously forecast sales volume. Of course, if sales have not been forecast, this must be done prior to making the estimation. The estimate of the advertising appropriation requires some judgment of advertising's effectiveness. In other words, the amount of advertising must build by considering each factor of promotion that can help to generate sales. The use of mass advertising, publicity, and sales promotion must be given individual attention. The manager may have to consider the relative effectiveness of each media used to promote the product. For example, is a dollar spent on television more effective than a dollar spent on radio? Perhaps the greatest advantage of the method is that it forces the manager to consider, individually, the various factors of advertising that affect sales volume.

The research-task method is the most logical for determining the total advertising appropriation because it places advertising and sales in proper perspective. The sales goal is set and whatever amount of advertising necessary to achieve this goal is developed. The method is not often used because it is difficult to apply in practice; the major problem is the inability to estimate advertising effectiveness. Furthermore, the influence of external factors on the effectiveness of advertising is difficult to determine. For example, who can predict the effect of a competitor's promotion on the ability of one's own advertising to attract customers? What is the effect of weather, past promotion, or the sales force on advertising?

Allocation of Advertising. The second step in deciding on the advertising appropriation is to allocate the total figure. The appropriation can be allocated by: (1) operational units, (2) product lines, (3) time, and (4) media, and is usually based on past data. The firm keeps records over time on how much is spent for advertising by whatever means of allocation is used. For example, a breakdown by media may show that the business averaged over the past five years 40 per cent of the advertising budget on newspapers, 20 per cent on television, 10 per cent on direct mail and 30 per cent on magazines. Similar, records can be kept for average advertising expenditures by month, territory or department, and product or price lines. The appropriation for the coming period is allocated according to these past averages. In the above example, if the total advertising appropriation is $30,000 then $12,000 is allocated to newspapers and $6,000 to television. The manager may make minor changes because of known circumstances. A special promotion in January may dictate slightly higher advertising in that month, or the company may be shifting its advertising from newspapers to television and might need to make this change.

Expense Planning

The planning for total expenses is as important as any other aspect of the channel's operations. Total expenses along with total sales form the building blocks from which profits are derived. Most expense planning is considerably more routine than sales, stock, or promotional planning since many expenses are relatively stable in the short run. For example, salaries, rent, and utility payments are known and they are made on a regular basis. Some typical business expenses include the following:

1. Salaries	10. Interest
2. Supplies	11. Travel
3. Advertising	12. Taxes
4. Depreciation	13. Bad debt losses
5. Rent	14. Insurance
6. Delivery	15. Donations
7. Communications	16. Membership dues
8. Utilities	17. Miscellaneous
9. Repairs	

Expenses are nearly all planned on the basis of historical data. This fact is true for every type of channel member. For each expense, records are kept over time and averaged; this percentage is then multiplied by forecast sales to obtain the dollar expense. Notice that expenses are normally expressed as a percentage of sales; they are allocated in exactly the same manner as sales, because of the frequent necessity to compare the two categories. Although the allocation varies from business to business, it may include operational units, products, time, customers, and salesmen.

Planned Reductions

The term reductions is used to refer to markdowns, employee discounts, and shortages collectively. Reductions may be intentional or unintentional. For example, some markdowns, such as promotional markdowns and distress merchandise sales, are intentional as are employee discounts. Reductions due to shortage, poor buying, or fashion trend are unintentional.

Markdowns occur any time there is a lowering of list prices on merchandise. They are necessary in any business because of promotions, poor buying, changes in economic condition, customer mistakes, and damaged and distressed merchandise. Employee discounts are the reductions in price granted to employees. Shortages occur because of clerical errors, employee theft, shoplifting, and misplacing of merchandise. Whatever their source, reductions need planning in the business. The alternative is to allow these reductions to drift. In such a case, the manager does not have full knowledge for his planning of other areas such as sales and expenses. Furthermore, the manager gives up any opportunity to control reductions if he does not plan.

Reductions are planned on the basis of historical data as already described. The figures can be kept as percentages or dollar amounts. Past data is an excellent predictor in this case because, in a going business, the amount of reductions tends to stabilize over time. Employees purchase about the same amount each month. Customers manage to steal about the same amount no matter what control techniques are employed, and the same is true for employees. Although the use of store detectives, electronic devices, etc., have a short-run effect, they seem to only offer a challenge to the thief who improves his methods. Markdowns also follow a pattern based on seasons, holidays, etc. Like the other factors planned by past data, reductions are typically expressed as a percentage of planned sales. Reductions and employee discounts are not normally broken down; shortages may be classified by product line or reason for the shortage.

Stock Forecast

Stock planning is not complicated, but it is extremely important. There are two types of stock figures used: (1) forecast end-of-the-period stock and (2) beginning-of-the-period stock. Only ending stock is planned. The beginning stock figure is historical and can be obtained directly from the previous accounting statement.

Forecast of Stock. The primary methods for forecasting stock are the week's supply method and the stock–sales ratio. Variations on these two methods are employed by manufacturers, wholesalers, or retailers. The *week's supply method* means the number of week's stock that must be kept in advance of sales in order to assure that orders can be filled. The formula below can be used to determine week's supply.

Week's supply = Weeks in the Period ÷ Average Stock Turnover

Stock turnover is defined as the number of times stock is depleted in a given period of time. Suppose, plans in a retail store are based on four weeks, and the average stock turnover is two. This means that all the stock in the store is sold on the average two times every four weeks. We see in the above situation that the business must plan for two weeks of stock. A manufacturer who operates on a fifty-two week basis and has a yearly turnover of eight needs approximately six and one-half weeks of inventory. The turnover figure may be based on the average composition of total store stock, or it may be based on the proportions of each product or price line. Very seldom is the week's supply method used on each item of stock unless the company has a very limited product line. In either case, planned turnover is favored over historical turnover.

The *stock–sales ratio* refers to the dollar amount of stock that must be kept in relation to planned dollar sales. The formula is shown below:

*Stock to Sales Ratio**

$$\text{Planned Stock} = \text{Planned \$ Sales Volume} \times \text{Stock Ratio}$$
$$\$292,700 = \$1,792,200 \times .16$$

$$\text{Stock Ratio} = \frac{\text{Average \$ Stock †}}{\text{Average \$ Sales}}$$

$$.16 = \frac{\$ 292,700}{\$1,792,200}$$

In the retail store where forward stock is kept in the selling area, stock planning can be accomplished by departments and by product line. In wholesaling and manufacturing operations, where stock is kept in central warehouses, planning can be calculated for each warehouse. Manufacturers may have stock located in a central warehouse or in branches throughout the country. In the case of a branch operation, stock may be planned for each branch and integrated into a total stock plan. Planned stock can be determined on a unit basis by simply substituting quantities in the formula for dollar figures.

Purchase Planning. Stock to meet operational requirements is provided by means of purchases. Many types of purchases are made informally, based on observations. This situation is particularly important in small retail and wholesale firms. Manufacturers frequently decide purchases based on the rate of projected output or upon plant capacity. They may establish contracts for the regular delivery of specific amounts of goods periodically for some specified period such as a year. In most cases purchases tend to be routine.

Purchase planning can be based on a formula when all the forecasts previously discussed are available. This method is used by large retailers and producers where purchases and stock must be closely controlled. The formula can be stated: **

---

* Data taken from Figure 14–1.

† Because stock is kept in cost terms on the income statement in Figure 14–1, it is necessary to convert it to retail for planning purposes. This is accomplished by subtracting the gross margin of 28.6 per cent from 100 and multiplying the result by the cost of goods sold.

** Data taken from Figure 14–1. Cost data converted to retail.

$$\begin{aligned}
\text{\$ Planned Purchases} &= \text{\$ Planned End-of-the-Period Stock} + \text{\$ Planned Sales} + \text{\$ Planned Reductions} - \text{\$ Beginning-of-the-Period Stock} \\
&= \$298{,}550 + \$1{,}740{,}000 + \$52{,}200 - \$286{,}957 \\
&= \$1{,}803{,}793
\end{aligned}$$

In the formula, planned sales, stock, and reductions are taken from the forecasts. The figure for beginning-of-the-period stock is derived from the accounting records. The period may be a week, a month, a quarter, or a year, but purchase planning on a monthly basis is common. Purchases are normally planned in dollars rather than units, and they are typically figured at selling price rather than cost price. The operating manager wants to know how many units of each item he must purchase, but the figures are computed in dollars. The purchasing officer can determine the number of items to purchase when he knows the unit price of the item. Unit purchases are obtained by dividing the unit price into dollar-planned purchases. In order to obtain order quantity, planned purchases and unit price must be known for each item of merchandise. Planned purchases can be kept by operating unit, such as department or territory, as well as by products, and time is always implied in planned purchases.

Open-To-Buy.   A retail term that applies to purchase planning in any type business is open-to-buy (OTB). This term refers to the amount of uncommitted money left to the purchasing officer. OTB can be computed as follows:

OTB = Planned Purchases − Goods Received during the Period −
Goods Bought To Arrive during the Period
$653,793 = $1,803,793 − $950,000 − $200,000

As with purchases, OTB can be translated into units by dividing the figure by unit price. OTB is derived by the same operational units and products previously discussed for purchases. As the manager purchases more, his OTB decreases.[20] Ideally, the manager should just run out of money at the end of the period. Early buying, changes in wholesale prices, increased competition, and unexpected sales increases usually make this ideal difficult to achieve in practice. Furthermore, even if the purchasing officer has overbought, he may still have to purchase. Purchases may be necessary because of out-of-stock conditions, or because a good buy on new merchandise becomes available. OTB is merely a guide to decision making; it cannot always be followed religiously. It is more important that the manager have the merchandise needed to support sales than to follow OTB exactly. However, when a manager is overbought, that does signal a need to use care in purchasing by being aware of better purchase control.

[20] Pearce C. Kelley and Norris B. Brisco, *Retailing* (Englewood Cliffs, N. J.: Prentice-Hall, Inc., 1957), pp. 336–39.

Profit and Margin Planning

Profit planning is an important area in which the channel members use forecasting. Total profit is the most important single figure for planning because profit determines whether the business survives or not. However, there is no completely objective method for profit planning. The decision on how much profit the business desires is based on executive judgment. It may be as simple a determination as the manager picking a figure out of the air. Most often, though, the profit goal is based on some type of benchmark data such as average industry profit, average company profit, or profit of similar firms. In most cases, the profit goal reflects what the management feels is an adequate or reasonable return for the firm's efforts.[21]

Profit planning evolves directly into margin planning because the margin must be sufficient to pay expenses, cover reductions, and provide the planned profit. The formula for planned markup, shown below, requires all the previously planned figures including the manager's estimate of profit.

$$\text{Planned Markup} = \frac{\$\,\text{Planned Expenses} + \$\,\text{Planned Profit} + \text{Planned Reductions}}{\$\,\text{Planned Net Sales} + \text{Planned Reductions}}$$

$$\text{Planned Markup} = \frac{\$353,000 + \$145,000 + \$52,200}{\$1,740,000 + \$52,200}$$

$$\text{Planned Markup} = 31\%$$

There is a difference between planned markup and the markup actually achieved. Expenses, sales, and reductions do not normally coincide exactly with plans.[22] This point is further discussed under evaluation. Profit planning is normally conducted by departments or territories. However, profit may be planned by customers and product lines. The markup can be figured either as a dollar value or as a percentage. When percentages are substituted in the formula, it is necessary to replace planned net sales with one hundred per cent.

EVALUATION OF OPERATING RESULTS

The second major use for the channel information system is to provide the facts necessary to evaluate operations. Stated simply, evaluation is the analysis of business results. It is undertaken to assure that the results of the channel or its members conform to plans.

[21] Duncan, Phillips, and Hollander, *op. cit.*, pp. 400–1.
[22] Douglas J. Dalrymple and Donald L. Thompson, *Retailing An Economic View* (London: The Macmillan Co., 1969), p. 263. A good diagram of the effect of the total marketing program on net profit.

Data Summarized for Analysis

Evaluation is important to every phase of the firm's operations to which forecasting applies. Thus, businesses evaluate sales, stock, advertising, expenses, purchases, and profit. In most cases the information must be summarized in some meaningful manner in order to be properly utilized. Examples of how information may be classified in the functional areas are found in Figure 14–3, 14–4, and 14–5. Figure 14–3 has total com-

Income Statement
Forecast and Actual for XYZ Company: 19X2–19X4

| | Forecast 19X4 | | Actual Operating Results | | | |
| | | | 19X4 | | 19X3 | 19X2 |
Item	Dollars	Per Cent	Dollars	Per Cent	Per Cent	Per Cent
Gross Sales	1,792,200	103.00	1,600,000	103.00	102.98	102.94
Less: Reductions	52,200	3.00	48,000	3.00	2.98	2.94
Net Sales	1,740,000	100.00	1,552,000	100.00	100.00	100.00
Cost of Goods Sold						
Beginning Inventory	198,000	11.38	170,000	10.95	10.70	10.02
Purchases	1,250,000	71.84	1,114,000	71.78	70.94	70.06
Goods Available	1,448,000	83.22	1,284,000	82.73	81.64	80.08
Ending Inventory	206,000	11.84	198,000	12.76	11.82	11.41
Cost of Goods Sold	1,242,000	71.38	1,086,000	69.97	69.82	68.67
Gross Margin	498,000	28.62	466,000	30.03	30.18	31.33
Operating Expenses	353,000	20.28	344,000	22.17	22.52	23.93
Net Income before Tax	145,000	8.33	122,000	7.86	7.66	7.40

Source: Professor J. F. Curry, Mississippi State University.

Fig. 14–3. Forecasted income statement with total company figures.

pany figures, Figure 14–4 contains company totals broken down by territories, and Figure 14–5 has company totals broken down by products. These statements are only illustrative of the methods of summarizing results.

Other types of classification can be used. The company data can just as easily apply to separate plants or departments, or it can apply to separate retail and wholesale operations in an integrated business. Data can be organized to show separate figures for customers. Individual items such as expenses or purchases can be extrapolated from the above and shown in more detail. For example, each type of expense can be

Income Statement XYZ Company
Forecast and Actual by Territory: 19X2–19X4

Territory 1 Items	Forecast 19X4 Dollars	Forecast 19X4 Per Cent	Actual Operating Results 19X4 Dollars	Actual Operating Results 19X4 Per Cent	Actual Operating Results 19X3 Per Cent	Actual Operating Results 19X2 Per Cent
Gross Sales	640,200	103.25	531,600	103.10	102.80	102.90
Less: Reductions	20,200	3.25	15,600	3.10	2.80	2.90
Net Sales	620,000	100.00	516.000	100.00	100.00	2.90
Cost of Goods Sold						
Beginning Inventory	109,000	17.68	106,400	20.54	24.00	22.00
Purchases	400,200	64.55	336,400	65.12	66.40	64.00
Goods Available	509,800	82.23	442,800	85.66	90.40	86.00
Ending Inventory	110,000	17.74	109,600	21.24	23.20	21.00
Cost of Good Sold	399,800	64.49	333,200	64.42	67.20	65.00
Gross Margin	220,200	35.51	182,800	35.58	32.80	35.00
Operating Expenses	175,200	28.26	148,100	28.70	28.30	29.05
Net Income before Tax	45,000	7.25	34,700	6.88	4.50	5.95
Territory 2 Items						
Gross Sales	338,600	104.50	326,100	104.52	104.60	104.20
Less: Reductions	14,600	4.50	14,100	4.52	4.60	4.20
Net Sales	324,000	100.00	312,000	100.00	100.00	100.00
Cost of Goods Sold						
Beginning Inventory	81,600	25.19	78,400	25.13	24.10	21.00
Purchases	220,300	67.99	220,900	70.80	70.35	68.05
Goods Available	301,900	93.18	299,300	95.93	94.45	89.05
Ending Inventory	75,000	23.15	81,600	26.15	26.25	22.50
Cost of Goods Sold	226,900	70.03	217,700	69.78	69.20	66.55
Gross Margin	97,100	29.97	94,300	30.22	30.80	33.45
Operating Expenses	102,000	31.48	106,100	34.00	32.53	31.67
Net Income before Tax	(4,900)	(1.51)	(11,800)	(3.78)	(2.65)	1.78
Total Net Income before Tax	145,000	8.33	122,000	7.86	7.66	7.40

Parentheses indicate loss.
Source: Professor J. F. Curry, Mississippi State University.

Fig. 14–4. Forecasted income statement with totals by territories.

Income Statement XYZ Company
Forecast and Actual by Products: 19X2–19X4

| | Forecast 19X4 | | Actual Operating Results | | | |
| | | | 19X4 | | 19X3 | 19X2 |
Product 1 Items	Dollars	Per Cent	Dollars	Per Cent	Per Cent	Per Cent
Gross Sales	464,400	102.75	430,300	102.80	102.60	102.70
Less: Reductions	12,400	2.75	11,700	2.80	2.60	2.70
Net Sales	452,000	100.00	418,600	100.00	100.00	100.00
Cost of Goods Sold						
Beginning Inventory	52,600	12.30	52,300	12.49	11.50	11.91
Purchases	330,000	73.01	303,800	72.58	71.42	71.85
Goods Available	385,600	85.31	356,100	85.07	82.92	83.76
Ending Inventory	60,100	13.30	55,600	13.28	12.10	11.86
Cost of Goods Sold	325,500	72.01	300,500	71.79	71.82	71.90
Gross Margin	126,500	27.99	118,100	28.21	28.18	28.10
Operating Expenses	81,600	18.05	77,600	18.53	18.70	18.62
Net Income before Tax	44,900	9.94	40,500	9.68	8.48	9.48
Product 2 Items						
Gross Sales	711,600	103.10	669,800	103.15	103.12	103.10
Less: Reductions	21,400	3.10	20,400	3.15	3.12	3.10
Net Sales	690,200	100.00	649,400	100.00	100.00	100.00
Cost of Goods Sold						
Beginning Inventory	110,400	16.00	112,500	17.32	19.30	15.25
Purchases	474,100	68.69	454,600	70.00	75.35	71.01
Goods Available	584,500	84.69	567,100	87.32	94.65	86.26
Ending Inventory	108,700	15.75	110,400	17.00	18.61	16.00
Cost of Goods Sold	475,800	68.94	456,700	70.32	76.04	70.26
Gross Margin	214,400	31.06	197,700	29.68	23.96	29.74
Operating Expenses	171,200	24.81	163,700	25.21	25.70	26.09
Net Income before Tax	43,200	6.25	29,000	4.47	(11.74)	3.65
Total Net Income before Tax	145,000	8.33	122,000	7.86	7.66	7.40

Source: Professor J. F. Curry, Mississippi State University.

Fig. 14–5. Forecasted income statement with totals by products.

shown over time, or purchases can be itemized by product line. Retailers often use expense center accounting. The particular method of classification depends on the type of organization, desire of management, type of analysis desired, and the use to which the data is applied.

Functional Comparisons

Once the data has been classified, several types of comparisons can be made. Internal comparisons include only data made available from the business's own records. External comparisons relate internal figures to those made available from outside the firm. Valuable conclusions about the operation of the business can be drawn from using both types of comparisons, with reference to the statement in the figures.

Internal Comparisons. Internal comparisons are basic, and evaluation should begin with this type of analysis.[23] The following list shows types of internal comparisons that can be made. In every case the items referred to are sales, stock, promotion, purchases, expenses, and profit.

1. Compare the forecast to actual results, by items, for the most recent period. This shows whether results coincide with the forecast.
2. Compare the forecast, by items, to actual figures for each past period. This shows how the forecast has changed over time.
3. Compare actual figures, by item, in the most recent period to each past period. This indicates the trend in actual figures.
4. Compare forecast to actual figures in the most recent period, by items, between each territory, between each division, or between each department. This illustrates how the organizational units measure up to each other.
5. Compare, by items, forecast to actual figures in each previous period between each territory, between each division, or between each department. This gives the time comparisons between organizational units.
6. Compare the items to each other in each period, by actual figures, as a percentage of net sales. This provides a study of the importance of each item.

External Comparisons. External comparisons are important to evaluation because an impartial standard is used. Internal comparisons reflect company mistakes and omissions. External comparisons show how the business, with all its successes and failures, relates to other businesses. The following types of external comparisons can be made.

[23] John J. Clark and Pieter T. Elgers, "Evaluating the Sales Forecast," *Michigan Business Review*, Vol. 20 (May, 1968), pp. 14–19; Elisha Gray II, "A Decision-Maker Looks At Forecasting," *Business Topics* (Summer, 1966).

1. Compare company's latest results, by items, to industry or national results for the latest period. This gives an indication of relative position.
2. Compare company's latest results, by items, to industry or national results for several previous periods. This provides a picture of the trend in company position.
3. Compare company results, by items, to other industries. This provides an indication of the company's relative position in the economy.

Of course, no single business is likely to use all the described methods of comparison. Each channel member must select the combination of comparisons most suitable to its operation. The actual type of comparisons utilized depends on the size of the firm, financial strength, degree of integration, use of formal control, and intended use of the data. The effectiveness of the comparisons depends on the accuracy of the original forecasts.[24]

Ratios and Other Data

So far the discussion has centered on overall evaluation. There are a great many individual ratios, percentages, and values in the specific functional areas that are useful to management. It is impossible to discuss all of these devices for evaluation at this time, but some of the important types are demonstrated in Table 14–1.

PROFIT EVALUATION

The effectiveness of overall planning and control in the channel of distribution culminates in the profit position. As long as profit evaluation is made for the business as a whole there is no problem. Total business expense is compared to total revenue. If revenues exceed expenses, the company made a profit. If expenses exceed revenues, the company lost money. The problem with using company-wide profit is that many individual successes and failures are covered up. It is known how the total channel fared, but it is not known how various parts of the channel contributed to dollar progress. Since profit is a comparison of revenue and expense, it follows that profit can only be determined for company units that have both values. Expenses occur throughout the business, but revenues are generated only in selling departments. Thus, profit allocation can only be made by sales departments, individual plants, or other sales units such as retail stores or wholesale stores or territories. Because

---

[24] "Sales Forecasting: Is 5% Error Good Enough," *Sales Management,* Vol. 99 (December 15, 1967), pp. 41–49.

Table 14–1   Typical Information for Evaluation by Functional Area

Function	Evaluation Data
Sales	Frequency of customer order, average sale, number of calls, sales per call, average sale expense, type of purchase, percentage of returns, customer complaints
Warehousing	Frequency of shipment, amount of shipment, frequency of payments, order destination, order status, average shipping time, conditions of shipments
Credit	Percentage of credit sales, delinquent accounts, average collection time, bad debt losses, new accounts, cost of credit, size of credit sale, types of credit sale
Accounting	Acid test ratio, liquidity, return on investment, profit, fixed assets to net worth, fixed assets to sales, times carrying charges earned, cash flow
Marketing Research	Market share, market size, new product opportunities, test marketing, market profiles
Advertising	Advertising effectiveness, advertising cost, ad pre-test, ad post-test, media cost, ad cost by product
Purchasing	Order frequency, out condition, price changes, average department needs, market trends, vendor reliability, product characteristics
Inventory	Stock turn over, fast movers, slow movers, stock condition, out condition

expenses are generated in other parts of the business than sales, some method of handling expenses must be devised when profits are determined by sales area. Two methods are used based on the handling of expense: the net profit plan and the contribution to overhead plan.

Net Profit Plan

The net profit plan is simple in concept, but difficult to apply.[25] It requires assigning all *direct expenses* (those that are generated completely within each selling unit) and all *indirect expenses* (those that occur outside the selling units or that apply to more than one unit) to the sales units. Once expenses are assigned to each sales unit, they are compared to revenue in the same manner as described for the business as a whole. This method is used by manufacturers, wholesalers, retailers, and integrated divisions. When dealing with individual plants, retail stores, or wholesale units, there is no problem since each sales unit is treated as a complete business. The problem arises in assigning indirect expenses to either departments or territories. There is no com-

[25] Richard H. Holton, "A Simplified Capital Budgeting Approach to Merchandise Budgeting," *California Management Review* (Spring, 1961), pp. 82–99.

Table 14-2   Methods for Assignment of Expenses to Selling Units

Type of Expense	Assignment
General management	Net sales
Real estate costs	Weighted floor space
Furniture, fixture, and equipment costs	Weighted floor space
Control and Office management	Net sales
Accounting and payroll	Net sales
Accounts payable	Number of invoices
Cash office	Net sales
Sales audit	Gross sales transactions
Credit	Gross credit sales transactions
Accounts receivable	Gross credit sales transactions
Publicity and display management	Column inches of advertising
Advertising	Direct
Display	Direct
General telephone service	Net sales
Protection	Weighted floor space
Miscellaneous customer services	Net sales
Cleaning	Weighted floor space
Maintenance of properties and utilities	Weighted floor space
Personnel	No. of employees (full-time equivalent)
Employee welfare	No. of employees (full-time equivalent)
Receiving and returns to vendors	Dollars of mer. received
Checking and marking	No. of pieces marked
Transfer hauling	Net sales
Delivery	Pieces delivered
Maintenance of stock	Direct
Selling supervision	Direct
Selling service	Net sales
Merchandise management	Direct
Buying	Direct

Source: Adapted from William R. Davidson and Alton F. Doody, *Retailing Management* 3rd Ed. (New York: The Ronald Press Co., 1966), p. 814.

pletely adequate basis for assigning indirect costs, but Table 14-2 indicates how some of the more important retail expenses are assigned. The advantages of the net profit plan are that it makes managers cost conscious, and profit provides the most reasonable basis for control. The problems are that the manager is held responsible for costs which he cannot control, and the assignment of cost leaves much to be desired.

Contribution Plan

The contribution plan does not require an allocation of indirect expenses. This method requires implementing three steps. First, direct expenses are allocated to the selling units. All indirect expenses are grouped together for the business as a whole and are called overhead.

Second, direct expenses are compared to revenues for each selling unit. The difference is called contribution to overhead. Third, the contribution to overhead is summed for the individual selling units and compared to overhead. If the contribution is greater than overhead the business made a profit. If the contribution is less than overhead the business lost money. The contribution plan is used more by retailers or manufacturers that have clearly defined sales departments, branches, or territories. Wholesalers also encounter the problem of expense allocation.

The problem with the contribution plan is that there is no way to determine profit for the individual sales units. Only contribution can be determined because indirect expenses are not allocated. However, the method is more fair to managers since it holds them responsible only for direct expenses over which they have control. Most firms use both the contribution and net profit plans, making it possible to take advantage of the good points of each method. It should be apparent that once the net profit plan is decided upon, all the necessary information is available to determine contribution. At this point, the only requirement is to rearrange the information.

STEPS IN CHANNEL INFORMATION FLOW

There are several steps in the information flow process whether it occurs in a single firm or between several units of an integrated business. First, the accounting department furnishes summary data to department, plant, or divisional managers. Where plants operate as autonomous units, each may have its own summary of data. The summary includes previous forecasts and actual figures over time as discussed in this chapter. It may also show holidays, number of working days, special events, etc., where appropriate. Second, the manager uses the summary data for evaluating past results and as a basis for forecasting. Of course, the same data may be sent at different times either for forecasting or evaluation. These functions do not necessarily have to be performed together.

Third, after the manager completes his planning, he sends the data back to accounting for checking and verification. Fourth, the group of operating managers gets together with accounting and top management in a group meeting. Here each manager explains his plans. Changes and modifications are made where necessary and the managers' results are combined into a master plan for the coming period. Obviously, these steps take time. Thus, planning must begin sufficiently far in advance so that all work is done a week or two before the planned period. This assures time to make last minute corrections and to have everyone in the organization informed in advance.

QUESTIONS

1. What is an information system? How do information systems relate to the communication process? What is their purpose?
2. What is the nature and purpose of an income statement? Explain briefly the purpose of each element of the income statement.
3. Contrast the sales force composite, the executive opinion, and expert opinion as methods of forecasting sales.
4. Advertising appropriation is decided in two steps: (1) determination of the total advertising budget and (2) the allocation of this total. Discuss each step.
5. What is meant by expense planning?
6. What is a stock forecast? Contrast the two methods of forecasting stock.
7. Explain and differentiate planned purchasing and open-to-buy.
8. Discuss the types of functional comparisons used in information systems.
9. Compare and contrast the net profit plan and the contribution plan.
10. Discuss in any way you can the relationship between information forecasting and information evaluation.

15

Promotion as Persuasive Communications

This chapter, with its presentation of persuasive communications, follows logically the discussion of communications for internal operational decisions. The subject of persuasive communications is what the businessman refers to as promotion or advertising. Unlike the information system that is basically informative, promotion exists to change someone's mind. Such change may be accomplished by facts or by the manner of presenting facts. Even when presenting basically factual information, promotion has as its object to persuade by the simple logic of these facts. Thus, promotion is always aggressive; the difference between promotions lies only in the degree of aggressiveness applied. In this chapter promotion is considered as an important ingredient in channel management.

INTRODUCTION TO CHANNEL PROMOTION

Promotion is an inclusive term that pervades all types of persuasive communications in business.[1] For our purposes, promotion can be defined as *any attempt by business to inform, persuade, or remind consumers about the company, its products, or its ideas in order to achieve company objectives.* The major activities related to promotion are per-

[1] James Engel, Hugh G. Wales, and Martin R. Warshaw, *Promotional Strategy*, rev. ed. (Homewood, Ill.: Richard D. Irwin, Inc., 1971), pp. 3–4. These authors present a different perspective concerning promotion and related activities.

sonal selling, advertising, sales promotion, and publicity.[2] Each of these activities is defined below:

1. *Personal selling*—any paid personal presentation of the company, its products, or ideas for the purpose of persuading buyers to adopt favorable attitudes or market behavior. May be presented within or outside the business.
2. *Advertising*—any paid non-personal presentation of the company, its products, or ideas by the use of independent media for the purpose of persuading buyers to adopt favorable attitudes or market behavior. Advertising employs such media as newspapers, magazines, posters, road signs, television, radio, direct mail, and handouts.
3. *Sales Promotion*—any paid non-personal presentation of the company, its products, or ideas used within the store for the purpose of persuading buyers to adopt favorable attitudes or market behavior. Decorations, posters, stamps, and merchandise premiums are types of sales promotion.
4. *Publicity*—any non-paid commercially significant news in a public media concerning the company, its products, or ideas that can persuade consumers to favorable attitudes or market behavior.[3]

Personal selling, advertising, and sales promotion are directly controllable by the business. Publicity is slightly different. It can be planned for in the sense that the company can be sure to take advantage of all opportunities that come along, but those opportunities are difficult to control. The firm tends to employ publicity on a hit or miss basis. For this reason, it is not included regularly in our discussion of promotion.

Promotion Compared by Components

The striking similarity of all the activities of promotion should be immediately clear. Each has the common purpose of persuading the buyer to believe or behave in some manner favorable to the business. To this end, similar appeals to fact or emotions can be utilized by each type of promotion. Factual appeals to price, performance, efficiency, or cost can be employed with advertising, personal selling, or sales promotion as can emotional appeals to fear, prestige, affection, security, pride, etc. As Table 15–1 shows, even the methods of appealing correspond exactly.

Product ads and *product salesmen* promote the firm's products in the short run. They are concerned with today's sales. *Creative ads* and *creative salesmen* aggressively try to change the buyer's mind. *Reminder*

[2] Harry D. Wolfe and Dik W. Twedt, *Essentials of The Promotional Mix* (New York: Appleton-Century-Crofts, 1970), pp. 8–12.
[3] Definition adapted from: *Marketing Definition: A Glossary of Marketing Terms,* Ralph S. Alexander (Chicago: American Marketing Association, 1960).

Table 15-1   Comparison of Promotional Methods

Advertising and Sales Promotion	Personal Salesmen
Product advertisements	Product salesmen
Creative advertisements	Creative salesmen
Reminder advertisements	Clerk salesmen
Institutional advertisements	Institutional salesmen

ads build repeat sales by reassuring customers. Such ads focus on brand name and location of source. *Clerk salesmen,* like reminder ads, reassure customers about known products. The salesman answers final questions and completes the sale.

Institutional ads and *institutional salesmen* are specialists in selling the company and its image. Institutional promotion is designed for long-run advantage. Institutional ads tend to emphasize the company as a good place to work as well as to play up its community contribution, progressiveness, and interest in the environment. Institutional salesmen, often called missionary salesmen or detail men, specialize in image formation. They call on prospects, introduce the company and its products, and leave samples, but they do not ordinarily take orders. As a matter of fact, there is only one basic difference among the methods of promotion, and that concerns whether it is a personal or impersonal presentation. This difference is significant only for the manner of presentation of information. Advertising and sales promotion utilize public or mass media, and personal selling utilizes face-to-face conversation. Each type of media is designed to move the buyer through the four steps of the purchase process: (1) gaining attention, (2) turning attention to interest, (3) building desire, and (4) effecting action. They differ only in how each does the job.

Methods of Classifying Promotion

The similarity between promotional methods pointed out in the previous section continues when the activities are classified. The four major methods of classifying promotional types are by (1) geographic coverage, (2) user, (3) type of market, and (4) degree of market exposure. Personal selling, advertising, and sales promotion can all be classified each way.

First, promotion can be classified by *geographic coverage* into local, regional, and national promotion. Second, promotion can be classified by user into *manufacturer* or *dealer* promotion based on who controls the promotional effort. Dealers may be wholesalers, agents, or retailers. Typically, manufacturer promotion is associated with national coverage, and dealer promotion is connected with local coverage. This thinking does not hold up in practice. Many retailers such as department stores or chains advertise nationally, and there are many local manufacturers. Thus local, regional, or national coverage can be associated with either manufacturer or dealers.

Third, promotion can be classified by type of market into *industrial* or *final consumer* promotion. This classification is based on the type of customer the promotion is designed to reach. As with geographic area, either manufacturers or dealers may appeal to either market. Fourth, promotion can be classified by degree of market exposure into broadcast or selective. *Broadcast promotion* is aimed at the mass market. It makes general appeals, and attempts to reach the largest number of people possible. *Selective promotion* is designed to reach a particular market segment such as youth, farmers, women, children, men, senior citizens, lonely people, etc. Again, either the manufacturer or the dealer may use either type of exposure.

Channel Leaders' Promotional Planning

Promotion is not employed randomly within a business nor does it lack cooperation between levels of the marketing channel. Rather, the channel leader's promotion is organized around a definite process that involves practically all the stages of the channel. Promotional planning, as it applies to channels, can be defined as *the combination of personal selling, advertising, and sales promotion among various institutional stages in the channel into a coordinated marketing effort.*[4]

One of the great disadvantages of analyzing manufacturers, wholesalers, and retailers separately is that the view does not allow for the coordination of their functions. By taking a team view of the channel, it is possible to give recognition to the fact that more than one combination of personal selling, advertising, and sales promotion may be in progress in the channel.[5] Different expenditures on advertising or personal selling may be characteristic of each level in the channel.

Table 15–2 demonstrates that different types of channel members do not employ advertising in the same amounts. Manufacturing leads all channel members in advertising expenditures, followed by retail trade. Wholesalers do not spend large total amounts on advertising. A different pattern is noted for the use of salesmen. Mining, manufacturing, construction, and transportation account for 11.8 per cent of the total United States sales force, with 10.8 per cent distributed to wholesale trade, and

---

[4] Adapted from: Robert V. Zacher, *Advertising Techniques and Management,* rev. ed. (Homewood, Ill.: Richard D. Irwin, Inc., 1967), p. 581.

[5] Sidney J. Levy, *Promotional Behavior* (Glenview, Ill.: Scott, Foresman and Company, 1971), pp. 13–15.

Table 15-2   Advertising Expenditures by Industry, 1970

Industry	Dollars Spent (Millions)	Percentage
Agriculture, forestry, fisheries	51	.3
Mining, construction, manufacturing, transportation	10,344	57.2
Wholesale trade	1,060	5.9
Retail trade	4,155	22.3
Other	2,462	13.7

Source: Statistical Abstracts of the United States, 1973, p. 761.

58.0 per cent to retail trade.[6] The remaining 19.4 per cent of the sales force is in "other trades." Thus, while manufacturing does the most advertising, retail trade employs the most salesmen. Wholesale trade that is very low in advertising expenditures ranks high in the use of salesmen.

One study of industrial salesmen bears out the inverse correlation between the amount of advertising expenditure and sales salaries when the two are used in combination.[7] The study indicated an average annual salary of $12,100 for salesmen. However, there was great variation among industries. Industries utilizing little advertising, such as manufacturers of footwear, averaged $22,500 for salesmen while the cigarette industry, which depends primarily on advertising, paid salesmen an average of only $6,500 per year.

Promotional planning is necessary to achieve a proper combination of personal selling, advertising, and sales promotion. Four steps may be identified in the development of a channel leader's promotional planning and to some degree these steps apply to any promotional planning. The steps are: (1) pre-promotional planning, (2) designing specific consumer, dealer, and local campaigns, (3) implementing a coordinated plan, and (4) evaluating the campaign's effectiveness.[8] The remainder of the chapter is developed around the four steps of promotional planning. It is assumed that the total promotional effort is under the direction of the channel leader. For ease in discussion, the second step is divided according to the consumer, dealer, and local campaign.

LEADER'S PRE-CAMPAIGN PLANNING

Pre-campaign planning is a stage that occurs before any specific promotional technique is undertaken. At this point, all the necessary ele-

[6] Department of Commerce, *Census of Population,* 1970, Characteristics of the Population, Part 1, U.S. Summary.

[7] Richard C. Smyth, "Financial Incentives For Salesmen," *Harvard Business Review,* vol. 46, No. 1 (January–February, 1968), pp. 109–17.

[8] Engel, Wales, and Warshaw, *op. cit.,* p. 34. These authors use a similar procedure but with fewer steps; there is also no recognition of division elements by channel members.

ments of the campaign are brought together, and the basic elements of the campaign along with the method of proceeding are decided.

Decide Promotional Mix

The combination of personal selling, advertising, and sales promotion is known as the promotional mix. Many factors affect the promotional mix, and some of these cannot be controlled. These include weather, long-term consumption patterns, and national income. One study has demonstrated a direct correlation between sales and weather, but an inverse correlation between sales and broad price changes.[9] Other factors are controllable, and they should be considered by the channel leader. The decision on the promotional mix is typically based on judgment tempered by experience.[10] While it is impossible to make the promotional mix decision here, it is possible to demonstrate the more important factors that enter into that decision.

Effectiveness of Promotional Types. The idea has grown slowly among marketers that advertising, sales promotion, and personal selling complement rather than compete in their market applications. Because of the difference in media used, sales promotion and advertising almost exactly complement personal selling in their market impact.[11] Thus, the decision for the channel's manager is not whether to use one promotional method, but rather which combination of methods can be most effective. Table 15-3 draws the comparison. Advertising is therefore best suited to reach mass markets, and personal selling is most appropriate for small groups or individuals. Sales promotion tends to fit in between but is more like advertising. Results vary by type of salesmen and type of advertising media, but we can generalize that because of its appeal to the masses, advertising is often effective in paving the way for the salesman, creating initial attention, and generating product interest. The salesman can concentrate on closing the sale and coping with difficult sales situations. The personal salesman tends to be used in concentrated markets or where great persuasion, perhaps over long periods of time, is necessary. Both advertising and personal selling are about equally effective in maintaining repeat sales. Advertising works through repeat ads and personal selling works through the clerk in the store.

[9] "Making Sales Factors Work for You," *Printers' Ink*, Vol. 283 (June 28, 1963), pp. 23–32.

[10] Aspinwall's Parallel Systems as previously discussed. His theory has application at this point and is an excellent method for estimating promotional requirements.

[11] Harold C. Cash and W. J. E. Crissy, "Comparison of Advertising and Selling," *The Psychology of Selling* (Flushing, N.Y.: Personal Development Association, 1965); Robert C. Brooks, Jr., "Relating the Selling Effort to Patterns of Purchase Behavior," *Business Topics* (Winter, 1963), pp. 73–79.

Table 15-3 Promotion Compared by Market Characteristic

Market Characteristic	Advertising Rating	Sales Promotion Rating	Personnel Selling Rating
Market coverage	Wide	Narrow	Narrow
Sales per call (contact)	Low	Low	High
Cost per prospect reached	Low	Low	High
Customer contact frequency	High	Medium	Low
Flexibility in presentation	Poor	Medium	Good
Ability to get attention	High	Low	High
Quality of appeal made	High	Medium	High
Customer image	Low	Low	High

Cost of Promotion. All promotion costs something, but there are economies of scale. Network radio and television, national magazines and newspapers can reach more people economically than local media. Advertising is less costly per prospect reached than personal selling, but reaching the larger market may run up the total cost. An hour on national television can cost over $100,000. A salesman can be hired for less than $15,000 per year. Thus, a limited amount of money may force the company to use more salesmen in the mix. On the other hand, advertising can be considered an investment. It builds goodwill and future sales.[12] Advertising may also be a factor in the mix if cheaper local advertising can be employed, or if the advertising can be addressed to specific prospects. The ability to acquire publicity as the automobile industry does with its trade shows and new model coverage can reduce the cost of promotion.

Market Considerations. The promotional mix is directly affected by market size. Advertising is more effective for reaching mass markets, so personal selling is de-emphasized in these markets. Advertising can reach more people for the same dollar cost than can personal selling. Personal selling is better able to adjust to the customer's wishes. It is effective in specialized household markets, and in appealing to middlemen. For example, the salesman can question customers concerning needs, meet objectives directly, and sense the proper moment to close the sale. Advertising can only utilize appeals that can be anticipated, and any objection not anticipated must go unanswered.

Type of Product. Some products can be more effectively promoted by means of advertising and others by personal selling. Products that are technical, sold in quantity, involve fashion, require installation or

[12] Joel Dean, "Does Advertising Belong In the Capital Budget," *Journal of Marketing*, Vol. 30 (October, 1966), pp. 15–21.

sewing, or have high unit value typically require more personal selling. Usually convenience and staple goods use more advertising in the mix; there is no need for personal attention with these types of products.

Type of Campaign. A manufacturer's campaign directed at final consumers tends to use more advertising because of the need to inform masses of people; when directed at middlemen it will usually employ more personal selling. There are fewer middlemen and they want more factual information as well as more personal attention. Local dealer campaigns directed at consumers tend to use more specialized advertising.

Product Life Cycle. It was pointed out earlier that products, like people, have a life cycle. The stage in this product life cycle has a direct bearing on the composition of the promotional mix. Different mixes are commonly associated with specific stages, although the actual amounts can vary from product to product.

At the introduction stage, both advertising and personal selling may be used more than at any other stage, but advertising is more important. The reason for the emphasis is that the product is unknown, and large numbers of people must be informed about the general type of product. Thus, the emphasis is on creating primary demands. The product incurs losses because of the extra cost of promotion, cost of development, and low sales volume. Market growth causes a shift in the mix to more personal selling because masses have been informed about the generic product, and the problem becomes one of promoting the particular company's brand. Promotion is directed at generating selective demands. Furthermore, at this stage middlemen must be persuaded to stock and promote the product. Personal selling is suited to these tasks. This is the stage of greatest product profit because sales volume increases faster than cost.

At the maturity stage, the shift is back to relatively more advertising in the mix, and the task is primarily on keeping the market informed of a product on which it is already sold. Thus, reminder advertising tends to predominate. Profits begin to stabilize or decline slightly at the maturity stage. With the occurrence of the decline stage the total spent on all types of promotion declines, but either advertising or personal selling may dominate the mix. Other factors such as the size of the market, concentration, and type of product become more important at this stage. The firm is mostly interested in retarding sales decline until capital can be transferred to more profitable opportunities.

Competition. It is difficult to state the exact effect of competition on the promotional mix since it varies.[13] An absence of competition may

---

[13] Jules Backman, *Advertising and Competition* (New York: New York University Press, 1967).

cause an expansion of the market, necessitating more advertising. A firm in a highly competitive market may be forced to follow the lead of larger, more powerful businesses. On the other hand, the firm may be effective by promoting its product in ways different from competition. Each firm must base the combination of personal selling and advertising resulting from competition on management judgment.

Plan Promotional Coverage

The promotional coverage desired should be decided at the pre-campaign planning stage. Of course, each campaign type implies something about the intensity of market coverage. In a national campaign the leader takes responsibility for all promotional cost. National media are used for advertising, and salesmen are important only if the product can be sold door to door. The entire country is looked upon as a single market, and a highly coordinated campaign is conducted. The same ads appear typically throughout the country with perhaps minor difference to account for local conditions. Middlemen are passive agents responding primarily to sales. A national campaign reaches a lot of people in an impersonal way, but is costly to the manufacturer and inexpensive to middlemen.

If a local campaign is planned, the middlemen control promotion. Each middleman conducts a separate campaign in his specific market, using local media and his own sales force. There is no participation by the manufacturer. Appeals, slogans, ads, information, etc., are specifically designed for the local market. The overall campaign is uncoordinated, but the promotion is tailored to specific market needs. Local campaigns can gain very intensive coverage of a concentrated market. The total cost of a local campaign is less than for a national campaign because of the use of less expensive local media. Because of sharing, the cost is low for each participant. A series of local campaigns can cover the national market sometimes as well as a national campaign. These campaigns can also be used to concentrate on special or highly sensitive markets.

A combination of national and local promotion places overall control in the leader's hands, but allows the middleman discretion over local activities. Such a campaign provides both width or depth of market coverage. The leader handles the national campaign, motivates the middlemen, and coordinates the total effort. This type of campaign spreads the cost of the campaign between manufacturer and middlemen, and the overall market coverage is complete while maintaining flexibility. In practice, the type of emphasis employed in the channel depends on such factors as: (1) dealer willingness to assume some promotion, (2) local adaptability of products, (3) leader control in the channel, (4) suitability of the product to mass promotion, (5) leader preference, and (6) cost.

Rough Out Promotional Campaign

If it is assumed that the channel leader is in control, then the broad campaign features must be roughed out in pre-campaign planning. Nothing specific is done at this stage (such as designing ads, laying out canned sales talks, selecting media, etc.); the emphasis is on providing broad guidance for these activities that come later. One of the first things done at this stage is to select the product or products to be promoted. The selection is no problem for the single product company, but it can be serious for multiple-product firms as Table 15–4 demonstrates. Only in a

Table 15–4   Number of Brand and Amount of Advertising

Number of Brands	Pages Per Brand Per Year in Magazine	Percentage of Increase or Decrease
5	13	6.8
17	8	5.5
12	5	1.2
29	1	−3.7
40	0	−6.0

Source: Daniel Starch, "Retailing AD Dollars to Dollar Sales," *Printers' Ink,* 1964.

very narrow line business can all products receive equal promotional attention at the same time. Most firms tend to alternate emphasis between products, or decrease promotion as brands increase.

The decision on products to promote presupposes that the channel leader has available some consumer knowledge. For example, a customer profile is desirable. This profile is a description of the average customer in terms of such specific characteristics as location, age, sex, occupation, education, etc. The product decision is based on special features that can appeal to consumers and on sales potential, time since last promoted, enthusiasm of the sales force for the product, proven saleability from records, and potential margin. On the other hand, many decisions of this nature are based on executive judgment. Once the products are selected they are studied carefully to determine specific features, advantages, and disadvantages. Out of these considerations, management decides broad appeals, slogans, information to emphasize. Several alternative means of presenting the product may be offered. Management may rough out tentative ideas for presenting the product. These ideas may include media suggestions and suggestions for salesmen. Comments may be made on amount of coverage, campaign timing, and overall channel coordination at this stage.

Integrate Promotion

What happens in one area of a business affects other areas. It is also true in a channel that what occurs in one business affects other channel members. This is certainly true with promotion, and interaction must be considered in pre-planning. Promotion is designed to influence sales, and sales have an impact on every facet of each channel member's operations. It is necessary to plan for this impact of the promotion in advance to assure that the channel's goals are achieved.

Some of the important business activities affected by promotion include: personnel, shipping and receiving, inventory, service areas, purchasing, and accounting.[14] The personnel department must provide the sales personnel and other personnel needed to handle the increased activity in all departments of the business. In order to meet personnel needs it may be necessary to employ new people, transfer personnel, or take on part-time workers. The shipping and receiving department must be alerted to increased activity. Docks and ramps must be made ready and equipment placed in good repair. Transportation must be scheduled so that goods will arrive and depart on time. A breakdown in this department can lead to serious "out conditions" and unhappy customers. Promotion cannot be effective if there are no goods to sell. Inventory must check current stock levels and inform purchasing of amounts on hand. Stock must be planned well in advance so that it is available prior to the beginning of the promotion period. The purchasing department needs to initiate any orders necessary to build and keep stock at proper levels. Service departments, such as credit, complaints, delivery, alterations, and maintenance, receive increased activity from promotion. These areas must be made ready. The accounting department will have increased activity in financing inventories, transportation, and other activities. This department must also keep increased records, make payments, and record financial transactions.

CHANNEL LEADER'S CONSUMER CAMPAIGN

It was established earlier that the channel leader can utilize national consumer promotion, dealer promotion, or local promotion in a national consumer campaign. The leader's consumer campaign is directed at households and emphasizes the manufacturer's specific products.

---

[14] "How Systems Selling Is Revolutionizing Marketing," *Business Management*, Vol. 32 (June, 1967), pp. 60–86.

Establish Campaign Responsibility

The first decision in developing any promotional campaign is to determine responsibility. The determination of responsibility entails more than just designating someone to do the job; the decision actually involves the organization of the business.

Internal Responsibility. There are two important internal organizational considerations in assigning campaign responsibility: the relationship between sales and advertising and the amount of decentralization in the business. If the company is organized around the marketing philosophy, personal selling and advertising are often coordinated under some marketing executive. Even top executives in the company may devote considerable time to selling.[15] There should be little friction in this arrangement because relationships are established in advance. Besides, the marketing manager can arbitrate differences. When the marketing manager concept is used, advertising and personal selling are centralized in one department. Many industrial firms use the product manager where promotion is decentralized; he is responsible for coordinating all aspects of a specific product sale.

In companies where advertising and personal selling have developed as organizational co-equals, the task is more difficult. This situation often exists in large retail stores such as department or discount stores. Sales responsibility is in the hands of department heads, but advertising is often a separate department. Either a way must be found to get the two managers to cooperate effectively, or one department head must be given authority over the other. The first solution creates problems because it is difficult for each manager not to promote his department's vested interest. The latter procedure is difficult to administer because it gives one co-equal authority over another.

No matter what the specific relationship between personal selling and advertising, decentralization affects the assignment of promotional responsibility. Three possibilities exist. First, both advertising and personal selling may be *centralized* in the same office. Second, both functions may be *decentralized* in retail units, branch offices, or autonomous plants. Third, one function may be centralized and the other decentralized. Where this latter situation exists, it is usually advertising that is centralized. Decentralized responsibility means that each organizational unit can promote its own products without interference from above. Under this arrangement, it is possible for the business to run several different promotional campaigns simultaneously. Even different products can be promoted. Where promotion is centralized, a single, coordinated

---

[15] "The Unclear Role of Top Management in Selling," *Business Management,* Vol. 30 (July, 1966), pp. 32–40.

campaign results. The most difficult arrangement exists when there is mixed centralization. This arrangement gives more authority to the centralized function, and coordination of the two is made difficult by physical separation and differences in philosophy. Chain grocers have mixed centralization, with advertising centralized and personal selling in the retail stores. However, this arrangement works because personal selling is relatively unimportant. Chain grocers operate a self-service business.

Use of Specialists.   The entire responsibility for promotion, or some part of it, can be shifted out of the business by the use of specialists. Specialists in selling include such agents as the freelance broker, manufacturer's agent, and selling agent. Agents that specialize in advertising include advertising agencies and the various media such as radio, television, newspapers. magazines, billboard companies, and poster manufacturers.[16] These advertising specialists are more frequently used by modern businesses than are the agent salesmen. Very few firms transfer personal selling to independent businesses. Actually, it is possible to have either an advertising agency or one of the media take over the entire advertising aspect of the promotion campaign. Large businesses tend to administer their own promotions or use agencies. Small firms tend toward the use of media. Of course, if responsibility is placed outside the firm, then there is no further planning or decision making necessary by the organization. The remaining decision areas are necessary only if the firm does its own promotion.

Select Media for Advertising

The decisions relating to advertising normally begin ahead of personal selling decisions because of the lead time necessary to develop ads and test them. One or two meetings are usually sufficient to plan the personal selling aspects of the promotional campaign. One of the first decision areas in advertising is to decide on the type of media to use.[17] This step precedes design of the advertisement because the type of media has a direct bearing on the design to be utilized. For example, if ads are to be placed in newspapers or magazines, or on television, visual considerations become important. Ads designed for radio depend entirely on the use of sound. In a personal letter campaign, the information is much more important than in other ads. Table 15–5 shows how advertising expenditures were divided among media to 1972. The importance of

[16] Wolfe and Twedt, *op. cit.,* pp. 153–57. These pages contain a complete listing of the elements that make up an ad.
[17] Dennis H. Gensch, "Media Factors: A Review Article," *Journal of Marketing Research,* Vol. 8 (May, 1970), pp. 216–25.

Table 15-5 Advertising—Estimated Expenditures, by Medium, 1950 to 1972
(In millions of dollars, except percentages)

Medium	1950		1955		1960		1965		1970		1972 (prel.)	
	Expenditures	Per cent of total	Expenditures	Per cent of total	Expenditures	Per cent of total	Expenditures	Per cent of total	Expenditures	Per cent of total	Expenditures	Per cent of total
Total	5,710	100.0	9,194	100.0	11,932	100.0	15,255	100.0	19,600	100.0	23,060	100.0
National	3,257	57.0	5,407	58.8	7,296	61.1	9,365	61.4	11,460	58.5	13,100	56.8
Local	2,453	43.0	3,788	41.2	4,636	38.9	5,890	38.6	8,140	41.5	9,960	43.2
Newspapers	2,076	36.3	3,088	33.6	3,703	31.0	4,457	29.2	5,745	29.3	6,960	30.2
Radio	605	10.6	545	5.9	692	5.8	917	6.0	1,308	6.7	1,530	6.6
Television	171	3.0	1,025	11.1	1,590	13.3	2,515	16.5	3,596	18.3	4,110	17.9
Magazines	515	9.0	729	7.9	941	7.9	1,199	7.9	1,323	6.7	1,480	6.4
Farm papers	21	0.4	34	0.4	35	0.3	34	0.2	31	0.2	29	0.1
Direct mail	803	14.1	1,299	14.1	1,830	15.3	2,324	15.2	2,766	14.1	3,350	14.5
Business papers	251	4.4	446	4.9	609	5.1	671	4.4	740	3.8	770	3.3
Outdoor	143	2.5	192	2.1	203	1.7	180	1.2	234	1.2	290	1.3
Miscellaneous	1,125	19.7	1,836	20.0	2,328	19.6	2,959	19.4	3,857	19.7	4,541	19.7

Source: McCann-Erickson Advertising Agency, Inc., 1950–1965, compiled for Decker Communications, Inc., New York, in *Printers' Ink* (copyright). Beginning 1970, compiled for Crain Communications, Inc., in *Advertising Age* (copyright).

direct mail may surprise some readers. Actually, it ranks just behind newspapers and ahead of television for advertising expenditures.

Five important considerations should be evaluated when selecting the media. First, the market must be considered. Some media are better suited for a given market than others. Magazines require different levels of reading competence. *Time* magazine reaches a different type of prospect than does *Playboy*. Some media, such as television, can contact different audiences in the same day. For example, the soap operas appeal to the housewife while the news is directly aimed at men. Second, the cost of the media must be considered. National television may be ideal for a product, but the seller may have to settle for a series of newspaper campaigns because of cost. In cutting cost, some combination of media may be useful. The amount of usage also influences cost, for example, a full page ad or an hour television show as compared to a smaller ad and less time.

Third, past experience must be considered. One of the best guides to the effectiveness of various media is experience. It is a good idea for business to keep a record of the effect on sales of using various media. These records can then be used to guide future decisions. It is even possible to obtain clues to advertising effectiveness when amounts spent by various media, time, periods, etc., are compared to changes in sales. While the measure is rough, it is usable. Fourth, media characteristics must be considered; that is, one must determine the media's strong points. Television excels in visual effects, and that is why it is so popular with food companies, beer manufacturers, and beauty aid firms. Newspapers and magazines can provide in-depth information; a product that needs explaining can use these media. Radio offers the opportunity to appeal to the audience frequently. Finally, the sales potential of the media must be considered. A low cost media that does not offer much sales potential may not be a bargain. Of course, sales potential is related to the market because the media that more nearly fits the needs of the market is likely to have greater sales potential.

Design the Advertisement

It is impossible at this time to discuss all the important decisions that go into the makeup of an advertisement and our interest actually lies in the channel leader's design management. It is not necessary that the advertising manager design the ad, but it is necessary that the manager appreciate and judge good design. With this thought in mind, the major ingredients to ad design can be summarized under technical factors of design and content factors of design. These factors are shown below:

A. *Technical Factors*
   1. Balance—objects, words, white space, ideas must be balanced; creates interest and appeals to the emotions

  2. Color—attracts attention, provides realism
  3. Gaze Motion—brings mind to desired features in the ad
  4. Sound—attracts attention, provides emphasis
  5. Movement—attracts attention, provides emphasis

B. *Content Factors*
  1. Headlines—creates interest, makes first point, causes to read further
  2. Body—provides persuasive information, facts; creates desire for the product
  3. Close—final points, tells what action is expected [18]

The particular manner of combining advertising factors is an art that defies technical description. It is not a matter of following principles but of following emotions. In the firm, ad development is typically placed in the hands of an expert. The ad manager's job is essentially to judge the results of the creative effort. The principal point is whether the ad achieves the desired result, for results are more important than any combination of technical and content factors.[19] The firm may design an esthetically perfect ad, but if it does not sell the product, it is a failure. To many people, the beer commercials, as a group, are among the best ads on television, but the evidence is that they have not had that much effect on total beer sales in the United States. Ad design requires a combination of experience, skill, and judgment. No two ad men will come up with the same advertisement when asked to present a given idea. Yet, either or both achievements may or may not sell the product.

Pre-Test Advertisements

Management may obtain some idea of the soundness of an advertisement by pre-testing. The two most popular methods of pre-testing are consumer jury or panel and checklist rating. The consumer jury requires the selection of a representative group of consumers. These consumers are shown several prospective ads, and they are then asked to rate them for effectiveness. Sometimes the jury is asked to rate specific features. When this is done, the best features may be combined into a single ad that is used in the campaign. Checklist rating involves rating the ad to a pre-determined standard. Specific points are checked and rated from one to ten. The checklist may include such items as, "Is the ad balanced?; Does the headline gain attention?; Is there effective gaze motion?" Both types of testing are subjective, but checklist rating is more subjective. Either method can be useful for designing effective ads when care and judgment are applied to their use.

  [18] Wolfe and Twedt, *op. cit.*, pp. 145–74.
  [19] Julian L. Simon, *The Management of Advertising* (Englewood Cliffs, N. J.: Prentice-Hall, Inc., 1971), Chapter 1.

Indoctrinate the Sales Force

Before the advertising is ready to be presented to the public, salesmen must be brought into the picture. Without question, they are as important to the promotional campaign as advertising, but the manner of planning sales participation is different. There are three decision areas in sales force indoctrination: (1) organize the sales meeting, (2) decide content of the sales meeting, and (3) build enthusiasm among salesmen.

Organize the Sales Meeting. How the sales meeting is organized depends on the particular business. A large retail chain may simply have store managers discuss the campaign some morning before the store opens and the talk may take only a few minutes. Businesses with field sales forces typically conduct formal sales meetings, often at the home office.[20] Some firms bring only managers in for indoctrination. These managers are expected to return and hold sales meetings in their territories. Many firms bring the sales force into the meeting. In some cases, home office personnel travel to the sales districts to carry out indoctrination. The advantages of bringing personnel to the home office are to create high morale and enthusiasm and provide a relaxed, carefully planned, and detached atmosphere for the exchange of ideas. Sales people are impressed when the home office shows interest in them. When indoctrination takes place in the field, it reduces the carnival atmosphere, involves less loss of work, and is less costly.

Decide Content of the Sales Meeting. Any sales meeting, no matter how important, should be: (1) planned in advance, (2) cover all important aspects of the promotional campaign, and (3) define the salesman's function. It is particularly important that the salesman knows the entire campaign. If he does not know the type of ads, appeals, slogans, etc., that are to be used, it is difficult for him to integrate his own presentation. The salesman must be shown how the advertising is designed to help him perform his job, and it is certainly true that the salesman's role is expanding. A part of the meeting should be devoted to the product and customer, for knowledge of both is the cornerstone of all sales activity. Every aspect of the product—its features, advantages, and disadvantages—should be reviewed. Customer profiles should also be reviewed.

The product and customer considerations should then be integrated into the sales presentation. Some companies use a canned sales talk. This canned talk should be presented and explained. In other companies, the salesman may be given facts, figures, points of emphasis, and visual aids, but allowed to develop his own sales presentation. Both

[20] R. A. Johnson, "Motivating a Far Flung Sales Force," *Personnel*, Vol. 45 (January–February, 1968), pp. 29–32.

methods can be effective, and there are no general rules for their use. However, most sales managers feel individual initiative is preferred to a canned presentation.

Build Enthusiasm Among Salesmen. Enthusiasm is essential to an effective personal selling campaign, and it is an intangible, not easily achieved or maintained.[21] Of course, a certain amount of enthusiasm is inherent in salesmen, especially since the man's income and well-being depend on his performance. However, a salesman's enthusiasm has peaks and valleys, and the company can do things to affect it.[22] One of the most effective methods for gaining enthusiasm is a strong emotional sales talk backed by a clearly sound product. Competition among salesmen can also be an effective means of stimulation. Many companies give points for calls made, keeping cost down, sales volume, etc. Bonuses are based on these point accumulations. Contests are also popular for stimulating salesmen and these contests take a variety of forms. Basic enthusiasm is developed at the sales meeting, but the territorial manager is charged with the responsibility for keeping enthusiasm high. Of course, the sales manager does not want enthusiasm too high so that the salesman overloads customers, uses coercion, etc., that can be harmful to the company in the long run. It is a part of the manager's job to obtain the correct amount of enthusiasm.

Test Marketing

Once the personal selling and advertising necessary for a national consumer campaign are ready, the business may consider test marketing. This is not a necessary decision, but it does tend to insure success because mistakes can be corrected before national promotion is undertaken. Test marketing is more frequently undertaken for new products than for existing ones, however, it may be used at any time for any type of product. Test marketing necessitates three steps. First, a market must be selected that is reasonably typical of the total market. The market is chosen on the basis of population characteristics such as age, sex, politics, occupations, conservativeness, and income. Next, retail stores are stocked with the product, advertising is begun, and salesmen begin making calls. Some businesses advertise heavily before stocks arrive to build up demand. Other businesses have the merchandise available when the advertising begins. The salesmen are particularly important for getting dealer cooperation. Finally, the effect of the test market campaign on sales is evaluated. This evaluation is usually a comparison of sales in

---

[21] Daniel D. Howard, "What to Do When Salesmen Run Out of Steam," *Management Review,* Vol. 56 (September, 1967), pp. 4–11.

[22] "Six Deadly Diseases that Can Affect Your Sales Force," *Business Management* (November, 1967).

the test market with sales in other company markets where the new campaign was not used. The ads and sales force may be reindoctrinated on findings before full-scale promotion is begun. Sometimes competitors deliberately increase their promotional efforts in the test market in order to confuse the firm's evaluation. Such tactics are often successful. When this is done, competitive promotion becomes another factor in the market that must be evaluated. When testing is complete, the national consumer campaign of promotion can begin.

CHANNEL LEADER'S DEALER CAMPAIGN

The manufacturer's national dealer campaign is directed at middlemen. The primary purpose of the campaign is to obtain maximum dealer effort toward selling the leader's products. Although it was necessary to discuss the consumer campaign first, this sequence is not indicative of practice. The leader's promotional campaign directed at the dealer may be planned and executed concurrently with the national consumer campaign. While the consumer promotion employs advertising as the primary ingredient in the mix, the dealer campaign is heavily dependent on personal selling. Some producers direct nearly all their efforts at the final consumer, and other producers do no consumer promotion. The two important leader decisions when promoting to dealers are how to build continuous cooperation and what specific type of promotion to select.

Build Continuous Cooperation

There is no question that repetitive advertising is more effective than one-shot advertising. Nevertheless, it is not necessary to advertise continuously. Within limits, promotion can be intermittent. However, the regularity of promotion may be more important for dealers than for consumers. The dealer must be regularly influenced to promote the leader's product actively, because the dealer feels more like a partner and requires the attention of a close association. If promotion doesn't reach a consumer, only a sale is lost, but if the dealer becomes uncooperative, the entire business can be lost. Therefore, the manufacturer must build continuous cooperation among his dealers.

There are no specific rules for keeping dealers happy. What works with one dealer may not work with another. In fact, some dealers cannot be pleased no matter what the leader does, but usually these dealers are in a minority. There are general rules that, when employed with good judgment, can aid in building dealer cooperation. The first rule is to provide an effective sales force.[23] The task of building continuous

[23] Theodore Levitt, "Communications and Industrial Selling," *Journal of Marketing*, Vol. 31 (April, 1967), pp. 15–21.

cooperation basically falls on the firm's sales force. These salesmen call on dealers regularly, and they hear the dealers' successes, problems, compliants, and aspirations. How the salesman, on a one-to-one basis, handles these communications largely determines the success of long-run dealer relations. Where communications with dealers are concerned, the salesman is the company, and a sales force carefully selected, properly trained, and effectively motivated to serving middlemen is the best promotional weapon.

The second rule is to follow good human relations when dealing with dealers. Keep channel members informed about activities and decisions that affect their operations; it is particularly important to have them up-to-date on the consumer promotional campaign. The dealer's part should be carefully explained. Middlemen should also be informed, often in advance, of price changes, changes in margin, the introduction of new products, package changes, changes in salesmen or territorial organizations, etc. Dealers should be treated fairly and impartially. A concession given to one should be given to all; if it cannot be granted, the reasons must be explained. It is better to have a dealer mad temporarily because you won't grant an advantage than to have him upset because you are playing favorites. The manufacturer should not take advantage of a dealer, even if he possesses the economic power to do so. The dealer will frequently find a way to get back.

The third rule is that the manufacturer must listen to dealer complaints, deal with them promptly, and inform the dealer of the action. If the complaint is not justified the dealer should be told. The fourth rule is that the leader should adjust to dealer needs where possible. For example, carton sizes can be suited to the dealer's order quantities, payment periods can be suited to dealer requirements, discounts can reflect typical order quantities, etc.

Select Type of Dealer Promotion

Selection of the type of dealer promotion is important because of the great heterogeneity among dealers. The promotion selected should be constructive to goodwill and cooperation among as many dealers as possible. The dealer campaign may entail nothing more than indoctrinating these salesmen on how to present the campaign to the middlemen as described in the previous section. However, the leader may wish to augment the regular sales force for a particular dealer promotional campaign. The decision is then to coordinate the various types of promotion. The leader has several choices:

A. *Personal selling*
1. Missionary salesmen
2. Manager visits

B. *Advertising*
  1. Joint advertising
  2. Point-of-sale aids

C. *Other promotional devices*
  1. Product deals and specials
  2. Dealer deals
  3. Advice with local campaigns
  4. Publicity concerning dealer operations

Most of these promotional methods require no explanation, but a word or two is necessary about items in B and C. Joint advertising occurs any time the manufacturer shares the cost of the dealer's local advertising. For example, the manufacturer may agree to pay fifty per cent of the dealer's advertising up to $2,000. Of course, the manufacturer pays only for dealer's advertising of the manufacturer's product. Point-of-sale aids are handouts, placecards, banners, etc., that are placed in the dealer's store to advertise the manufacturer's product.

Product deals and specials refer to concessions given to the consumer by the manufacturer. They are usually incorporated on the product package in the form of stamps, premiums, price reductions, or gifts. These deals make the sale of the product easier for the dealer and influence his attitude toward pushing the product. Product deals include such things as inclusion of a gift in the package, coupons that can be redeemed for money or gifts, stamps, and contests where the consumer can win prizes or money. Specials refer to any reduction in price such as 1¢ sales, two for the price of one offers, and reductions in list price of the product. Dealer deals refer to concessions given to the dealer directly and they include thirteen items in a dozen, higher margins on sale items, and discounts on sale items. Sometimes dealers are invited to participate in sales contests for prizes, trips, etc. Some combination of promotional factors is usually employed in the dealer campaign and it is generally based on management judgment backed by knowledge of previous successful combinations. A word of caution where deals are concerned: if used too frequently they lose their impact. The customer or dealer begins to expect the deal as his right. Thus, care should be taken with this type of promotion.

DEALER'S LOCAL CAMPAIGN

The dealer's local campaign is instituted and directed by the middleman. It may, or may not, be coordinated with the manufacturer. The campaign promotes dealer selected brands and store image to a limited market. The local dealer's campaign may be the only one conducted, or it may be a cooperative effort with the national consumer and dealer campaigns. It is more likely to be fully integrated with the manufacturer as integrated channels or channels employing franchised dealers. Most dealers are independent businesses, however, and their promotional campaign is independently run; the most the manufacturer can expect is cooperation, and very often he gets a lot less. The dealer has products of many producers to sell—how he promotes any particular one is a matter of his own judgment.

When the dealer's campaign is coordinated with the manufacturer's national promotion, the local campaign is supplementary. Its function is to bridge the gap between generalized national appeals and specific local problems.

Emphasis on Local Store and Products

The local promotional campaign tends to revolve around the middleman. Both sales people and advertising emphasize the store over the manufacturer or his product. Many wide-line retailers and wholesalers feel only small allegiance to the manufacturer. From a variety of manufacturer's products, these dealers promote the ones that offer the greatest advantage to the local firm. This is not as true for narrow-line dealers or integrated units. When promoting these products, the retailer or wholesaler stresses local price, store location, and dealer prestige. The emphasis is always on the middleman's overall value to the customer. Even product features, such as warranty, quality, and service, are related to the firm and only incidental to the manufacturer. Of course, the amount of cooperation between manufacturer and dealer does affect the emphasis. It should also be clear that it is usually in the manufacturer's interest for the consumer to identify with the retailer so long as the manufacturer's product is adequately promoted. The national consumer campaign can build prestige for the manufacturer.

Greater Dependence on Media

The local markets, wholesalers, and retailers tend to depend on the media for advertising to a greater extent than is true of manufacturers. Many wholesalers and retailers do not have advertising departments, and those that do employ only a manager and a very small staff. Dealers cannot afford the large national advertising agencies, and local agencies are few and unpopular. Therefore, it is not uncommon for dealers to turn the planning of the entire advertising campaign over to the local television or newspaper. The basic function of the firm's advertising man is to determine the advertising budget and pass judgment on the campaign outlined by the media. The media selects appeals, designs ads, selects ad size, decides timing, etc.; it also furnishes the dealer with market information and some evaluation of advertising results.

Different Sales Force Emphasis

There is a different emphasis in the sales force at the dealer level, just as was found for advertising. Though less for wholesalers than for retailers, the difference exists in both places. Wholesalers employ outside salesmen as do manufacturers, but they do not sell alike. The manufacturer's salesman, handling a narrow line of goods and often selling to industrial users, is highly creative. The wholesale salesman may have a catalog with 5,000 to 10,000 items listed and it is impossible to do a creative job on all these items. Thus, he acts more like a clerk on the road, offering suggestions, answering questions, and taking orders. He promotes the wholesaler's interest over that of the manufacturer. Since consumers have less information upon which to base judgments there is more use of deceptive practices at the retail level. Some of these include: bait and switch, phony contests, and outright fraud.[24] Such practices are not condoned by the majority of retailers.

Although there are notable exceptions, most retail salesmen are clerks. Overall, retail clerks answer questions and handle the sales transaction. Generally, the salesman is much less important to the sales mix at the retail level since the burden of promotion is on advertising.

IMPLEMENT A COORDINATED CAMPAIGN

When the separate promotional campaigns are approaching completion, it is time to plan their implementation. All the ingredients are put together and presented to the market and, at this point, the channel leader must make sure that all the necessary promotional components are available, and there must be effective timing of market entry. Problems are less likely to occur in the leader's promotional campaign compared to other areas because the business has more control over its own promotional planning. Slips may occur in building up inventories from suppliers, making deliveries to dealers, or obtaining personnel. These problems must be handled on an individual basis. The most serious consequence is that the campaign may be delayed, yet most channel leaders provide for a little slippage in promotional planning.

The timing of market entry may or may not be critical. It depends on such considerations as whether seasonal merchandise is being promoted, how many campaigns are being operated, and the importance of the campaign. The leader's national campaigns must be timed to the local campaign. For example, the leader may wish to begin his dealer campaign slightly before the national consumer or local campaigns be-

[24] "The 10 Most Deceptive Sales Practices of 1968," *Sales Management* (September 15, 1968).

cause of the critical part played by dealers in selling the product. Entry timing involves letting everyone know the action expected in advance. For example, salesmen are told when to begin pushing the product. Media are informed when the ads and other promotion data are to begin their run and the length of the run. Dealers are told when to display the products in special packages, and when to begin sale prices. A little foresight can save a lot of trouble at this stage and greatly enhance the total impact of the campaign. The timing of the campaign may be critical if the leader is attempting to meet a specific date such as Easter, Christmas, etc. The best hedge against a timing mix-up is to begin the planning well in advance.

EVALUATE PROMOTION'S EFFECTIVENESS

The final step in promotional planning is the evaluation of promotional results. Any method of evaluation must recognize that there is no known method for computing the contribution of personal selling or advertising that is numerically accurate. There are too many factors affecting sales besides promotion, and both personal selling and advertising interact. The interaction makes it impossible to isolate the effect of either factor.

General Evaluation

The general evaluation of the promotion effort concerns the overall effect. The two most important measures used for this purpose are profits and sales.[25] Profit is a desirable measure but it is difficult to isolate the importance of promotion on profit. However, it is possible for management to estimate sales by product type during the promotional campaign. Analysis of these product sales can not only show whether the promotion had a greater effect on high or low margin items, but also provide general conclusions about profits. Computers are being used more and more for promotional analysis.[26] Sales volume is the most used general indicator of the worth of promotion. The evaluation may involve nothing more than determining the change in total sales during the promotional campaign compared to some previous period. Some firms calculate the ratio of sales to advertising, or sales to personal selling, or sales to total promotional expenditure. If such a figure is computed for each campaign, the management can make comparisons over time. The sales analysis can be conducted from territories, departments, divisions, product lines, or individual salesmen.

[25] Jon R. Katzenbach and R. R. Champion, "Linking Top-Level Planning to Salesman Performance," *Business Horizons* (Fall, 1966).

[26] Thayer C. Taylor, "Sales Analysis," *Sales Management* (March 4, 1968).

De-Brief Salesmen

The general figures do not tell management what actually took place in the operational units during the promotion. Problems vary, competition fluctuates, and the condition of the sales force changes. Therefore, salesmen should be encouraged to provide a critical analysis of the promotional campaign. The criticism can result from an informal discussion with the manager, or it can take the form of a written report. Most managers routinely evaluate a salesman's customer calls, orders, travel, and expenses by means of periodic reports. The critical analysis can be attached to one of these reports that deals specifically with the promotional period. The salesman should be encouraged to explain the good and the bad points of the campaign. Besides the information gained, this report gives the salesman a chance to express his opinions, which can have a good effect on his morale. Of course, reports do take up the salesman's time and he often resents having to submit them.

The salesman's efforts are frequently compared to a sales quota [27] which has been established in advance of the promotional period. The growth is management's best judgment, based on some type of sales forecast as discussed in the previous chapter, of what the salesman should produce. The salesman's results are compared to the expected value, and he is evaluated according to the percentage of quota achieved.

Check Dealer Reaction

The dealer's reaction provides another aspect of the promotional campaign and in some respects it may be less biased than the report of the salesman. The salesman's job depends on his performance; he is likely to overemphasize the difficulties, but the dealer does not have this vested interest. The same general procedure is followd with the dealer as with the salesman. The difference is that the manager has little actual control over an independent dealer, which usually necessitates collecting the information informally. The manager may have the dealer fill out a form and mail it in, or the information may be obtained in informal conversations with the sales representative. It is possible to have the salesman submit the dealer's report along with his own report.

Post Test Advertisements

The reports submitted by the salesman on his activities during the promotional campaign constitute a post test of his activities. It is common also to post test the advertisement used in the campaign. These evaluations are based on samples of the population included in the

[27] Leslie Rich, "The Controversy in Sales Quotas," *Dun's Review* (May, 1966).

campaign. The post test may be conducted by the media and forwarded to the company or it may be conducted by the company's own advertising department. Most testing is done by agencies and media.

There are two broad types of post tests made of advertising: recognition tests and recall tests. As the name implies, the recognition test is based on the respondent's ability to recognize an ad when it is shown. The Starch Readership Service was instrumental in developing this test. A sample of approximately 200 persons, who have admittedly read the magazine, are shown ads of a particular page in the magazine. The respondent is asked to say whether he:

> *Noted*—remembers only seeing the ad
> *Seen—Associated*—can associate the product with the ad
> *Read—Most*—read 50% or more of the ad

Per dollar advertising cost is related to the number of individuals in each of the above categories.

The recall method does not provide the respondent with the actual ad. Rather the respondent is asked to recall ads from memory. There are three types of recall tests based on how many clues are given to help the respondent recall.

> *Unaided Recall*—individual is simply asked to remember any ads seen recently.
> *Aided Recall*—individual is given a clue, such as a slogan, "When it rains it pours," and asked to identify the ad to which the slogan applies.
> *Triple Association*—two clues are given and the individual must associate them with the ad. For example, the individual may be asked what gasoline uses a tiger in its ads. The clues are gasoline and tiger which must be associated with Exxon.

There is general feeling that recognition tests overstate the readership of ads, and recall tests understate readership. Therefore, some advertisers use a combination of the two types of tests.

Combine Evaluation Methods

Very few business managers use all the evaluation techniques illustrated here. Some managers do nothing more than check sales volume. However, we must remember that all the evaluation techniques explained involve considerable judgment. For this reason, it is better if the manager uses some combination of techniques; for example, he may combine general evaluation with sales force and post test of ads. The sales force is continually evaluated in most companies anyway, and sales evaluation is complicated only to the extent that the data are related to a particular campaign. The difficult information is the post test of ads, provided the agency or media does not furnish the information. Thus, it makes good management sense to evaluate.

QUESTIONS

1. Define and distinguish promotion, personal selling, advertising, sales promotion, and publicity.
2. Discuss and compare the methods of classifying advertising and personal selling.
3. Explain the steps in the channel leader's pre-campaign planning.
4. What factors should one consider in deciding the composition of the promotional mix? Show clearly the effect of the product life cycle in the mix.
5. Discuss important factors of integrating promotion with the other business activities.
6. Explain the relationship between the manufacturer's consumer promotion and the leader's dealer promotion.
7. How does the dealer's local promotion differ from the channel leader's consumer promotion? Explain.
8. In what ways are advertising and personal selling related in the dealer's campaign?
9. What are the problems of evaluating a promotion's effectiveness?
10. Discuss why salesman and dealer reaction to the coordinated campaign is important.

PART V

DECISIONS OF CHANNEL LEADERSHIP

The subject of Part V is channel leadership, the last of the major components of channels management. We have emphasized the channel as a behavioral team, with leaders and followers, conflict and cooperation, all requiring motivation and control; thus, we turn now to the decision areas related to leadership and how they concern the human aspects of channels management.

16

Channel Leadership

One of the purposes of this book is to provide a balanced approach to the explanation of marketing channels. What we recognize as a channel of distribution can be viewed from several perspectives. We may consider its (1) structural, (2) operational, (3) decision, (4) behavioral, or (5) environmental aspects as they relate to decision making. The team concept, and the discussion of communications, have emphasized the behavioral considerations of channels management, but we have not really come to grips with the behavioral interactions specific to coordinating the overall channel operations. We can now view the entire channel concept and focus attention on the management of the people that causes channels to function effectively.

NATURE OF LEADERSHIP IN CHANNELS

A natural first step in the discussion of channel behavior is to develop some common ground concerning the nature and meaning of leadership. Leadership is the heart of channel behavior, and channel leadership is a particular type of leadership. The concept of leadership is not clearly defined, even among management scholars who have serious differences of opinion. Some writers view leadership as the ability to get subordinates to work willingly; others regard it as a facility for matching the individual's personal goals to the goals of the organization. Almost everyone does agree that leadership is a *quality* rather than an *activity*. That is, leadership is not something one does so much as it is an innate ability to affect the activities of others. A definition consistent with the aims of this book is provided by R. C. Davis: *leadership is the principal dynamic force in organization that stimulates, motivates, and coordinates the organization in the accomplishment of its objectives.*[1]

Leadership obviously has a relationship to management, and we view this relationship as being very close. Davis says, "Management is the function of executive leadership anywhere. Business management is the function of executive leadership in business institutions."[2] Leadership and management are not the same thing, but there can be no management without leadership. Management *consists* of planning, organizing, directing, and controlling the activities of people in the enterprise to achieve company goals. Leadership directly concerns the *manner* in which these activities are performed. To plan is management, but to plan in such a manner as to stimulate or coordinate the people is leadership. The leader causes managers to want to perform their tasks efficiently.

There are degrees of executive leadership, but it is a characteristic of all social organizations. Some considerations of planning, organizing, directing, and controlling operations are routine; others are unique and highly complex. We generally think only of acts of loyalty arising from inspiration as leadership. This view is much too restrictive. It is not possible to find a management situation in which there is not some degree of leadership. Leadership, no matter how little, always provides the basis for willing performance. For example, regular delivery or cycle billing may be performed routinely in the business and without *inspired* leadership. The presence of the manager, or the knowledge that results must be reported to him, may be sufficient to gain desired performance. On the other hand, it may take creative leadership to motivate channel members to willingly reduce price or to sell the manufacturer's product aggressively. Thus, leadership may run the gambit from being practically non-existent in the routine situation to highly inspired in the less routine examples. Very often the lack of a sufficient degree of inspiration accounts for poor performance by business employees.

Leadership Applied to Marketing Channels

The definition of leadership provided by Davis can be applied to marketing channels viewed as a team. The leader institution is responsible for providing that dynamic force that stimulates a coordinated effort among businesses to achieve the overall team goal. Thus, most of the discussion in the next three chapters deals with the achievement of coordination through leadership. Underlying this presentation is the knowledge that any behavioral system, such as a channel of distribution, must

---

[1] Ralph Currier Davis, *The Fundamentals of Top Management* (New York: Harper & Row, Inc., 1951), p. 13.
[2] *Ibid.,* p. 6.

deal with member roles, conflict, cooperation and motivation, power, and communications.[3]

One has to question whether leadership is a term that applies to an organization of institutions such as the marketing channel. In its normal usage, leadership is applied to people rather than to physical things such as an institution. People can be led or managed, things cannot. Things can only be arranged, placed in sequence, ordered, etc. People, on the other hand, can be influenced through thought processes to make decisions or arrange things on their own to accomplish an end desired by the leader. The justification for the use of leadership in association with institutions rests on the fact that, in one real sense, marketing firms are not things. The marketing institution consists of people, not the physical building or equipment. Individuals run the organization and make the decisions, and the physical components are only means to an end. Thus, when we speak of retailer or wholesaler leadership, we are talking about the people, collectively, who run these organizations. When we mean an individual leader, we refer to him by name such as sales manager or credit manager.

Leader Role in the Channel

There can be no meaningful discussion of leadership in the channel without mention of the leader–led relationship. In every group activity some persons decide and others perform on these decisions. Both the leader and the led have specific roles to play in the channel.[4] A role is defined as a set of prescriptions or characteristics of behavior that identify a member's position within the group. In a marketing channel it is the functions or activities of the participants that determine position.

The channel leader is in a position of authority over the institutions that follow. To be a leader, the firm must be out in front of the situation. The leader thinks and plans for the group. Thus, the leader's primary role is to make policy, evaluate results, motivate performance. The leader must be intimately aware of the needs of the entire channel, including the need for effective roles, often before the channel members are aware of their own needs. Furthermore, the leader must anticipate the roadblocks that stand in the way of need fulfillment and he must plan in advance the most effective course of action for the channel to take in surmounting these obstacles. The channel leader must assume a role of assurance, knowledge, and preparedness and convey to the chan-

[3] Louis W. Stern and Jay W. Brown, "Distribution Channels: A Social Systems Approach," *Distribution Channels: Behavioral Dimensions,* Louis W. Stern, ed. (Boston: Houghton Mifflin Co., 1969), p. 12.

[4] Lynn E. Gill and Louis W. Stern, "Roles and Role Theory In Distribution Channel Systems," *Distribution Channels: Behavioral Dimensions,* Louis W. Stern, ed. (Boston: Houghton Mifflin Co., 1969), pp. 22–44.

nel members a feeling of confidence in their own ability to achieve mutual success. The leader must be strong when needed but fair in all dealings with those institutions he leads. It is probably safe to say that few channel leaders live up to the requirements of their office.

Follower Roles in the Channel

Where there is a leader, there must be a follower because the two are mutually dependent. Ideally, the follower's role in a channel is to willingly accept the policies of the captain and to perform his function with diligence, enthusiasm, and efficiency. Thus, the follower institution assumes the primary role of carrying out channel policy. As with leaders, few channel followers live up to the ideal. In fact, to follow does not require blind allegiance by the channel member in any case. The follower must also provide meaningful feedback to the captain that can be used for correction and future planning. The follower must be loyal, but not necessarily subservient to his leader. As we shall see, even some level of conflict is expected from channel followers.

Problems arise in the leader–led relationship for several reasons. First, there are difficulties when either the leader or the members do not understand the roles they are to play.[5] Leaders sometimes get too far in front of their channel members, and the led do not follow willingly because they do not understand the leader's motives or actions.[6] It may also happen that some follower feels he is a leader and seeks to play this role. This situation results in a conflict of interest. Second, the leader or the members may not understand their channel roles. A leader may not convey confidence or knowledge of the channel problem, or members may not perform up to the leader's expectations. The leader may not see himself as a leader, and members have expectations which he is not willing to fulfil. Third, there may be a failure of communications, with the result that the leader and his followers pursue different goals by separate means. Fourth, there may be a lack of ability to perform by either the leader or the led. When any of these circumstances prevail, there is a breakdown in the leader–led relationship and the channel fails to function properly. If the problems are not corrected, the channel can be destroyed as an effective unit of commerce.

Leadership and Channel Variables

In Chapter 1 we defined a channel of distribution as a team of institutions; the remainder of the book was structured around this idea of

---

[5] *Ibid.*, pp. 36–37.
[6] Henry L. Tosi, "The Effects of Expectation Levels and Role Consensus on the Buyer-Seller Dyad," *Journal of Business,* Vol. 39 (October, 1966), p. 518.

a marketing team functioning within a system. Our discussion of channel leadership pertains to the team rather than the environment, since only in a limited way can the channel leader affect the environment, but there is a direct effect on the institutions of the team. Specifically, channel leadership involves channel operations, channel structure, and channel information flow. Leadership provides the necessary decisions that cause things to happen where each of these variables is concerned. In channel behavior, leadership is vital. It is the unifying ingredient in the channel. Leadership coordinates and stimulates relationships among people by means of communications to achieve the system's purpose through the performance of specific operations. Without leadership, marketing institutions are a random collection rather than a coordinated system of action.

CHANNEL LEADERSHIP CHARACTERISTICS

In a channel of distribution, like any other organization, the leader and the members participate because of some particular group purpose that agrees with their own aims. Communication is the basis for channel relationships as in any organization, and specific operations must be performed to achieve the channel's purpose. The channel, like any organization, displays division of labor, specialization, and reward for good work. However, there are particulars of a marketing channel that differ in some respects from the properties of other organizations.

Team of Organizations

The channel is a team made up of institutions. Each institution that comprises the team is a complete operating organization in its own right. We normally think of an organization as a rather close-knit group where individuals deal with each other on a direct, or *one-to-one basis*. The leader tells the subordinate, or group of subordinates, what he wants done and expects the result to be forthcoming. It requires a little adjustment to think of one entire organization dealing with another complete organization. *Collective leadership* (firm-to-firm) is more complex than personal (one-to-one) leadership, but it is more common in the business world. Figure 16–1 demonstrates the different types of leadership found in the business community. In example 1, individual A exerts direct and personal leadership over other individuals. Within a given organization, we may find any number of leaders exercising authority over others. The president is a leader over the marketing, production, and finance managers, but these managers, in turn, lead large numbers of subordinates. Thus, a hierarchy of leadership is possible within the organization. Leadership within the organization is generally face-to-face and

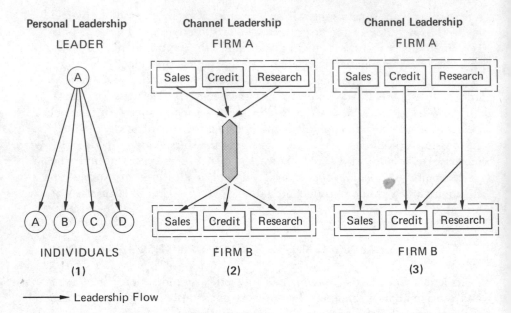

Fig. 16–1. Channel leadership situations.

the entire concept of span of control is based such a relationship between the leader and the led. This concept of leadership falls a little short of reality when dealing with a team of institutions.

In example 2, we have a different situation. Here, one complete firm exerts leadership over another complete firm. This collective leadership is a matter of the separate parts, or departments, of the leader firm creating a single consistent impression or image to the collective management of the member firm. The leader influences general policy and a majority of individual decisions made by the member firm's management. Examples can be found in the price leadership in the steel industry or the leadership that General Motors exerts over the remainder of the automobile industry. Example 2 implies that the organization is greater than the sum of its parts.

There is also the possibility demonstrated by example 3. In this case, one department of a leader firm exerts direct leadership over one or more departments of a member firm. For example, the sales or credit department of the leader may exercise leadership over corresponding departments in a member firm. It may also be true that the leader's credit department has leadership over such other member departments as research. Example 3 differs from example 2 in that leadership is not based on a single consistent image. There may actually be little interaction between the two businesses as a whole. Leadership influence is based on functional interaction between firms rather than overall interaction. For example, the knowledge that some small retail grocers have of Proctor and Gamble may be based entirely on contact with its sales department. The two managements never get together. In most channels, collective and functional leadership exists simultaneously, and either may exert the more dominant influence.

The leadership that one business exerts over another business is not necessarily consistent or uniform throughout the organization or over time. The overall image that the member firm has of the leader may vary periodically so that more leadership is exerted at one time than at another. Remember, the firm being influenced has a complete hierarchy of leaders of its own. Each is an individual who may reach in varying degrees to the channel leader. Overall leadership may be strong, but the leadership exerted between departments may be either strong or weak. For example, the sales manager may be a more effective leader than the credit manager. Even the credit manager, with dual leadership, may be more effective in regard to the credit department than to research.

Member Independence

In a person-to-person leadership situation, the goal is usually fairly clearly defined. The goal, perhaps to elect a political candidate or to win football games, is often the force that brings the group together. For some period of time, each individual is committed to achieving the goal through the organization. It is somewhat different with a channel of distribution. Each business is an independent agency. An independent firm may leave the channel if it desires; however, the channel is capable of continued performance through replacement. Many times a firm may simultaneously function within and outside the channel. For example, a single business may be a member of several channels. The business has channel goals and personal goals. Although the relationships with the leader and other channel members are important, they are often casual. Frequently, the firm is motivated more by self-interest than by group interest and is often a member of the channel not so much by choice as by necessity. Consequently, it is difficult to keep channel members focused on the overall objective of the channel. Furthermore, the activities of the individual firms often differ. The channel goal may be to distribute a certain product, but a member firm—operating simultaneously in other channels—may see its self-interest to lie in pushing some different product. As a result, the member does not perform the activity of selling the leader's product as aggressively as it could.

Member Separation

Another factor that makes goal and functional identification difficult in a channel is member separation. In most working organizations the membership has a fairly frequent and close person-to-person relationship. This is not true in marketing channels. Two types of separation exist. First, there is *physical separation.* The leader, who may be located thousands of miles from the member firm, finds it difficult to lead under these circumstances. The whole problem of business communications is compounded, and suspicion and distrust often result. Second, there is *organizational separation.* It often happens that the leader firm is much larger, more financially secure, and much more complex organizationally than the member firms. Policies, rules, procedures, and functions that work for the larger organization often do not apply as well to the member firms. The differences can lead to further communications problems. It is also true that firms that are organizationally so different just do not have the same goals. It may be that the large firm can afford to be satisfied with smaller profits or is more interested in community service and the environment. These goals may be totally unacceptable to the smaller organization that is struggling just to stay alive in the market. Indeed, the very small firm probably cannot be influenced toward any goal other than profit.

Member Status

Member status in the marketing channel refers to the position and/or importance of a firm to the channel of distribution.[7] There are two aspects of status in the channel. Each channel member has his own status within his particular channel, and each type of channel member, as a group, (wholesalers or retailers) has status in the channel. The status of a channel member varies from channel to channel and from time to time. The status of particular middlemen may be based on many considerations, but among the more important are: (1) economic factors such as finances, physical size, volume of purchase or sales; (2) effective cooperation; (3) prestige; (4) admiration; (5) seniority in the channel, and (6) personal friendship.[8] When a leader refuses to sell to retailers who purchase less than ten gross, concentrates on city outlets, or decides to sell through financially strong retailers, this leader is making a status decision on individual retailers.

The status of a particular group of channel members, such as wholesalers, can be summed up by the consideration of whether the leader can do without this group. This statement implies that a group's status depends on whether the leader can perform the group's function effectively or not. For example, a channel that eliminates the wholesaler through vertical integration is, in effect, saying that the wholesaler has no status. In another case the wholesaler may be important most of

[7] Gill and Stern, *op. cit.,* p. 34.

[8] Emile Benoit, "Status, Status Types and Status Interrelationships," *Role Theory, Concepts and Research,* Bruce J. Biddle and Edwin J. Thomas, eds. (New York: John Wiley and Sons, Inc., 1966), p. 77.

the time for regular sales, but might be bypassed during some peak period in favor of direct sales to the retailers.

Particular problems arise in the channel because of these differences in status. A member that has low status does not receive the same treatment as one with high status. The low status member may receive only token calls from the leader's salesmen. Order handling and shipping may be delayed because of low priority. Requests and complaints from low status members may be ignored, delayed in handling, or dealt with in a very highhanded manner. There may be very little effective cooperation on any matter between the leader and the low status member. As a result, the low status member may fail to provide effective service or sales effort. This action by the low status member may simply reinforce the leader's opinion, and the result is a self-fulfilling prophesy. There are always leader problems of explaining why certain actions unfavorable to a low status channel member were taken.

High status members are typically treated just the opposite of low status members. Their problems are often handled by phone. Thus, orders are expedited, their complaints given prompt attention, and their executive may be wined and dined when the occasion permits. Such action tends to insure better performance by these high status members, but not always. A member that has high status may begin to feel his own importance because of favored treatment and demand higher margins, better shipping terms, or more service. This position can cause difficulties for the channel leader in attempting to keep the member in his proper place without affecting the institution's motivation or efficiency.

WHO LEADS THE MARKETING CHANNEL

The manufacturer has been assumed to be the team leader simply because this institution is the first member in the channel sequence. Actually, any channel member can be the leader of the distributive system and we will now examine other possibilities.

Manufacturers as Channel Leaders

We do not wish to slight manufacturers, for they do make excellent channel leaders.[9] Examples of manufacturer-led channels are found throughout industry. Who would be the effective leader of a channel that contained any one of the following producers: Proctor and Gamble, Singer, Kodak, or Schwinn? Of course, the answer is that these producers

---

[9] Robert W. Little, "The Marketing Channel: Who Should Lead This Extracorporate Organization," *Journal of Marketing*, Vol. 34 (January, 1970), pp. 31–38; Louis P. Bucklin, "The Locus of Channel Control," *Marketing and the New Science of Planning* (Chicago: American Marketing Association, 1968), pp. 142–47.

lead their respective channels. We say effective leader because seldom does a channel leader control every aspect of the channel. Furthermore, a leader can only lead participating members. Most of these examples are found primarily in the final consumer channel. In the industrial market, one might naturally expect DuPont, United States Steel, Boeing, Alcoa, and Minnesota Mining and Manufacturing Company to lead their respective channels. Manufacturers that lead in channels that overlap both markets include General Electric, Ford Motor Company, and Standard Oil of New Jersey. Manufacturers make excellent leaders in integrated channels, although the simple fact of integration does not mean that the channel is automatically led by the manufacturer.

Retailers as Channel Leaders

Contrary to what most people think, the retailer is often the channel leader.[10] Can you imagine a channel containing Sears, Roebuck and Company in which this business would not be the leader? Sears is larger, more economically powerful, and has greater sales volume than the average American manufacturing firm. Retailers, like manufacturers, operate integrated channels. Such a retail organization has great influence in any channel to which it is a party. Department stores, discount houses, chain stores, and variety stores are retailers that make good channel leaders. Examples include Globe among discount stores; Kroger, A & P, and Winn Dixie among food chains; Rexall among drug stores; Penneys and Montgomery Wards among department stores; Fred's among discount variety stores; and Western Auto among hardware stores. It is true that the small independent retailers are very seldom channel leaders, but sales volume is concentrated in the larger retail types that do make good leaders. Thus, retailers are probably as important as the manufacturers in channel leadership.

Wholesaler and Agent Leaders

The number of wholesalers in the American marketing system is small compared to the number of manufacturers and the number of retailers. It follows that wholesalers lead the channel much less often than the other two types of members. Nevertheless, there are outstanding examples of wholesaler leadership and the best illustrations can be found in the cooperative movement.[11] Associated Grocers and Independent Grocers of America are cases in point. Here, aggressive wholesalers have provided leadership over large numbers of independent retailers. These

[10] Bucklin, *op. cit.*

[11] Edwin H. Lewis, "Channel Management by Wholesalers," *Marketing and the New Science of Planning*, Robert L. King, ed. (Chicago: American Marketing Association, 1968), pp. 137–41.

wholesalers are also powerful enough to exert influence over manufacturers in their channel.

Good examples of agent-led channels are found in the selling agent and food broker. The reader should not be confused because brokers do not take title to goods. Their position of leadership is based on the ability to influence members of the channel, not on ownership. Very often these agents are larger and more financially sound than the manufacturers they represent. In limited instances, agents make excellent channel leaders.

BASIS FOR CHANNEL LEADERSHIP

The concept of channel leadership used in this book implies that the leader has influence over the members led. However, the authority to lead a channel of distribution does not come automatically. It is either (1) taken by the leader because of some power over the led, or (2) bestowed on the leader by the led because of some influence by, or confidence in, the leader. Of course, what happens in practice is that leadership is based on a combination of these two factors. When a channel member assumes leadership, it typically rests on product ownership, economic power, or position in the channel. The basis for bestowed leadership comes from either technical skill or the ability to persuade.

Product Ownership

The ultimate basis for leadership in the marketing channel rests on the right of private property. This type of authority may be referred to as legitimate authority.[12] In a channel of distribution, the owner of products has the right to control all aspects of that product's productions and sale. The owner of products establishes the quality specifications for manufacture of the physical goods and the service standards that surround these goods. This fact is equally true whether the owner of the goods is a production firm, a wholesaler, or a retailer. For example, it is not the manufacturer of All-State tires for Sears, Wizard appliances for Western Auto, or Towncraft clothing for J. C. Penney that determines the quality of these products; rather, it is each retailer cited. So long as the channel leader maintains ownership, he has complete authority for all aspects of promotion and sale.

The owner of products does not have to exercise his right of authority. He can delegate authority by title transfer to some other middleman, but when the sale takes place some leadership authority over the merchandise

---

[12] Frederick J. Beier and Louis W. Stern, "Power In the Channel of Distribution," *Distribution Channels: Behavioral Dimensions*, Louis W. Stern, ed. (Boston: Houghton Mifflin Co., 1969), pp. 92–94.

is also transferred. The question is what choices does the leader have when it comes to delegating control over the product. It would be a mistake for the reader to jump to the conclusion that the new owner has complete leadership authority. In fact, the new owner may have very little authority over the product. We have just established that the owner has complete control over everything he owns, but the question that we must decide in this case is what does the new owner have title to. The reader should remember from an earlier discussion that a product has a real and a symbolic existence. The real product is essentially the physical good and its services, while the symbolic product is embodied in brand. Based on this knowledge, three types of ownership delegation are possible in the channel: (1) an unbranded product can be sold, (2) a manufacturer's brand product can be sold, and (3) a private brand product can be sold.

Sale of Unbranded Products. A leader, say a manufacturer, may sell a product that is unbranded as in the case of staple farm products like wheat, corn, or oats. When this happens, the manufacturer gives up a large measure of his leadership authority because both the real and symbolic product is transferred. The new owner has leadership authority to price, promote, and otherwise sell the product to his choosing. Nevertheless, there has not been a complete delegation of leadership authority in this case, because the manufacturer exercised his right to determine specifications and method of manufacture before the original sale. In short, the manufacturer was a leader so long as the product was under his control. However, once sold, the manufacturer does make a complete delegation for all future sales.

Sale of Manufacturer Brand Products. It frequently happens that a manufacturer relinquishes the product but not the brand. For example, Proctor and Gamble owns a product called *Tide*. When *Tide* is in the Proctor and Gamble warehouse, the company owns both the physical product and the symbolic brand. When P & G sells *Tide* to a retailer, the company gives up ownership over the good but not over the brand. It follows that the retailer cannot have full authority over the resale of *Tide* when that retailer does not have complete ownership. Even if P & G had no product in its warehouse, it would still own the *Tide* brand.

The degree to which the original owner gives up authority in this case depends largely on the strength of the brand. If the brand has strong buyer preference, it may be possible to keep the retailer in line on such things as pricing, promotion, and order sizes. It may even be possible to control, to a degree, the amount of shelf space that the retailer allocates to the product and to competing products. Control is exercised by means of threatening to take away the brand from dealers who do not conform.

If the brand is a very weak one, the manufacturer may be giving up almost complete leadership authority when the product is sold. Since the manufacturer cannot threaten to take the brand away, he has very little control over what the retailer does with his product. With any type of brand, the wholesaler or retailer does not have the right to take action relative to the product that is damaging to the owner of the brand. In other words, one never gives up complete control when he owns the brand.

Private Brand Sales. Private branding occurs when the product is sold along with the brand. In this instance, the manufacturer delegates complete leadership authority to someone else in the marketing channel. The leader even gives up the right to specify original standards and production procedures. The fact is that under private branding, the manufacturer is acting much like an agent for the middleman. The manufacturer has simply been delegated the function of producing, but he has no authority or responsibility beyond that. The term leadership hardly applies to the manufacturer in this situation, and it is the middleman who is acting as a leader.

Economic Power

There is probably no more powerful authority for leadership than that of economic power. To possess economic power over another firm is to have some force, or lever, that can cause the other firm to do your bidding even when it would rather not. Some marketers deny economic power as a basis for leadership authority. They say that leadership is willing motivation and the use of economic power is based on coercion. To them, the use of economic power is the opposite of leadership. The position taken here is that to be motivated is to prefer to do something. It is a desire to perform in some specified manner. It does not matter whether the reason for the preference is based on persuasion or economic power. That economic power is capable of placing a business in a highly motivated state is a fact of leadership. One could even argue that a good leader is one who knows when to use persuasion and when to use coercion; most effective leaders do use both techniques.

The economic power that we speak of may come in diverse forms. Such power is based on such factors as: (1) massive purchasing power, (2) patents, (3) financial strength, (4) physical size, (5) unique techniques, (6) a strong market position, or (7) ability to reward. A company such as Kennicott Copper not only has massive purchasing power, but it also possesses financial strength and a strong market position. Such a company is a natural channel leader. Notice that a company does not necessarily have to use its economic strength. The threat or presence of such strength may be sufficient to assure the leader's position.

Positional Authority

Each channel member is uniquely positioned in the channel, and this placement offers specific advantages to that member. Placement tends to establish identification patterns, and the authority to lead the channel can be based on this placement. Whether you consider an industrial channel or a final consumer channel, some manufacturer, either in the form of a mine or fabricator, is the starting point of that channel. This position is an excellent vantage point for leading the channel because it allows the leader to face in a single direction and deal with members in sequence. The manufacturers' position partly accounts for the fact that this group is so often considered the channel leader. Retailers may be able to exert strong leadership because these firms may directly face a large potential market. The retailer is in an excellent position to know about the market. The wholesaler is strategically located between the manufacturer and the retailer. The ability of the wholesaler to reach large numbers of retailers at relatively low prices may be a strong basis for channel leadership. This fact is particularly true if the wholesaler is large and most manufacturers and retailers in the channel are small.

Technical Skill

The channel leader may derive authority from certain technical abilities that the firm possesses. Technical skill does not mean merely the ability to produce a fine product, although product development is an example of technical proficiency. Any competence possessed in sufficient quantity can be the basis for channel leadership.[13] Technical skill may be based on an efficient management team that is aware of opportunities and able to take advantage of them. Technical skill may be found in demand creation that results from a proficient sales force or an effective advertising department. A firm may have a very strong physical distribution system using regional warehouses and its own fleet of trucks. Very often channel members look up to the firm that has a strong expertise, especially if that expertise lies in some strategic function needed by the entire channel of distribution. It is conceivable that a chain retailer can lead the channel because of the tremendous potential to generate national demand with its strong sales force and regional organization. A voluntary wholesaler, such as IGA, may parlay leadership out if its ability to pull together small independent retailers to gain most of the buying, selling, and management advantages of chain stores. It is also possible to delegate some leadership authority by passing on part of the expertise. This happens in the case of joint advertising or shared delivery.

[13] *Ibid.*, pp. 100–1.

Member Persuasion

Channel leadership authority may be based on the ability of one firm to persuade other channel members. Persuasion is a type of salesmanship, but this factor differs from demand creation discussed above under technical skill. Demand creation involves generating consumer markets, but persuasion is concerned with the leader's ability to influence other member firms. Manufacturers often use persuasion to keep channel members in line on such policies as the quantity of purchase, prices, returned merchandise, discounts taken, and cancellation of orders. The reader should not downgrade the effectiveness of persuasion as a basis for channel leadership; in a person-to-person relationship the ability to persuade another to your point of view is the essence of leadership. Certainly, in a channel of distribution, where relationships between firms are not so personal, it is still a powerful tool. Persuasion typically combines sound logic with an emotional appeal designed to show that the firm's own best interests lie in following the course of action designed by the leader.

Leadership Is Never Absolute

In a channel of distribution, authority to lead is seldom, if ever, absolute. Each member of the channel, except in a completely integrated channel, is an independent businessman. As such, the channel member has free will either to go along with the policies of the leader or to withdraw from the channel. The threat of withdrawal may keep the channel leader from exercising full leadership authority over the member. Members join in power coalitions to oppose the superior power of the leader. From time to time it becomes necessary for a member to withdraw. This is one of the reasons why channel structure is always changing as well as why channel members so often move into and out of the channel.

Not only is authority to lead seldom absolute, but rarely does it come from a single source. Typically, the channel leader has a combination basis for his leadership such as authority and persuasion. For example, General Motors is large, technically proficient, has a large market share, a persuasive sales organization, tremendous financial strength, and the first position in the final consumer channel. United States Steel has a combination basis in the industrial channel. Clearly, the stronger the basis, the firmer the leader's grip on the entire channel.

PARTIAL LEADERSHIP SITUATIONS

So far we have discussed leadership as if it were something that a channel member either had or didn't have. The facts in the situation are seldom that simple. As pointed out earlier, a leader rarely has complete authority over other channel members. In effect, this statement means that leadership is shared. Leadership may be shared with other channel members of the same type as when two manufacturers have some authority on a competitive basis over the same channel, or it may be shared with members of different channel levels, as when a retailer fails to go along with a manufacturer's suggested price list. Actually, three conditions of shared leadership need expansion at this time: dual leadership, multiple channel leadership, and time dimension of leadership.

Dual Channel Leadership

Dual leadership refers to a situation where two or more firms share leadership responsibility in the channel.[14] Three types of dual channel leadership are possible as shown in Figure 16-2.

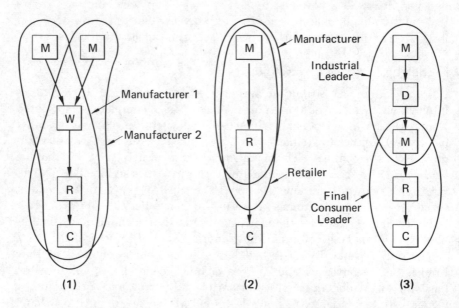

Fig. 16-2. Types of dual leadership.

Example 1 shows a situation in which two leaders exert influence over the same channel. The example shows two manufacturers, but it could just as easily depict two retailers or two wholesalers. In a channel containing Lever Brothers and Del Monte, we find that both these producers exercise leadership control over retail grocery stores. Notice that we do not imply that the degree of leadership over the retailer must be equal

[14] Buckin, *op. cit.*, pp. 142–47.

since this seldom occurs. Both leaders motivate the actions of the retailer.

In example 2 both the retailer and the manufacturer have a basis for leadership. Perhaps both are large, financially strong organizations that possess about equal economic power. This is a situation in which leadership is bargained between two strong firms. For example, Sears may be expected to be the channel leader when dealing with small manufacturers from whom it traditionally purchases private brand products. However, Sears may have to bargain on an equal basis with Mattel over the distribution of this firm's strong brand of toys.

Example 3 illustrates leadership over different parts of a channel of distribution. There is one leader, for example, in the industrial channel and another leader in the final consumer channel. It may happen that the industrial firm is the leader over the manufacturer that has leadership over the remainder of the channel. (In fact, this is the situation shown in the example.) It may be that these two firms bargain about equally with each other but are leaders over their respective channel parts. In other cases this condition may not exist. For example, United States Steel Corporation may be the leader of the channel that produces and distributes steel, but Frigidaire may be the channel leader over the consumer channel that sells final products made from steel.

Multiple Channel Leadership

In the previous discussion we assumed that leadership was something that took place in a single, one-product channel. In our modern society, where a great many firms are multiple producers and/or sellers, this condition may not exist. A single firm may, at any given time, be functioning in several, or even several dozen, channels simultaneously. The ability of a firm to lead in all these channels varies. One might say that A&P is likely to be the overall channel leader of any channel of which this firm is a part. On the other hand who will lead a channel that is made up of A&P, Proctor and Gamble, Campbell's Soup Co., and Bordens? The answer is not so clearcut in this case. Any one of these firms is quite capable of exercising channel leadership over particular parts of the channel at specific times. The same situation exists in a channel that contains Rexall, Schick Safety Razor Co., Revlon, and Andrew Jergens Co. It may be that Rexall coordinates the overall channel but Revlon may be the leader in women's beauty aids, even in Rexall stores.

Time Dimension of Channel Leadership

Just as leadership is not a constant quality between product lines or between different channels, so it is not a constant quality over time. The ability to lead the channel varies, and the variation is due to changing circumstances relative to the basis for leadership previously discussed. Very often a firm's product increases or decreases in popularity over time. Brylcreem is an example of a product that has had significant swings in popularity over time. Chrysler has weathered several financial crises. On the other hand Mattel, a relative unknown in the toy industry a few years ago, jumped to a position of leadership based on well-designed toys effectively advertised, only to find this leadership in trouble because of poor channel policies. Revlon has had a similar jump to prominence in the beauty aids field. The lesson is never to take leadership in a channel for granted. A leader exists to serve both his market and his channel membership; if the leader forgets this even for a minute, he can find himself with no membership to lead.

Risk of Channel Leadership

To be a channel leader is to hold a position of great importance that offers concrete advantages to the leader. Leadership adds prestige to the firm's management and provides a measure of freedom to its activities. Leadership provides some assurance that the firm's policies will be followed, as well as a measure of control over sales, cost, and profits. However, to be a leader has its risks. The leader is by nature out in front—there is no place for him to hide. Mistakes made by the leader are painfully obvious, and effective operating techniques are easily copied. The membership can be terribly unforgiving of ineffective leadership. Furthermore, the leader is often resented for his success, and the membership looks for ways to bring the leader down to their own level. It has been said many times, but it is still true; there is just no place for the leader to go but down. This fact necessitates constant vigilance by the leader.

Channel Domination

It was pointed out previously that authority to lead the channel is never absolute, especially when dealing with independent middlemen who have goals and objectives of their own. However, it is possible for a leader to gain sufficient control over the channel membership to dominate policy. The only alternative for the member may be to get out of the channel. Channel domination exists in a channel when there is no effective way for the members to resist the leader's policies or to protect themselves from the leader's decisions. Influence does not have to be complete for the leader to dominate, but it must be sufficient to assure short-run compliance.

Channel domination may be based on any leadership factor, but the most common are (1) physical size, (2) legal means, (3) financial strength, and (4) brand preference based on promotion. Very frequently the position of domination is formalized through a contract. For example, most franchised agreements tie up the independent middleman sufficiently so that the franchisor has a position of dominance in the channel. Examples can be found in the automobile industry, the franchised restaurant industry, and the franchised hardware industry. The contract merely formalizes an already existing condition.

Channel domination is not necessarily bad for the channel membership. As a matter of fact members may willingly agree to such a position. The reason for agreement lies in profitability. The members may recognize profitable opportunities from product preference, financial help, factory training of employees, advice about profitable operating methods, etc. Channel domination becomes bad when the leader begins to squeeze either the middlemen or the public because of the power position held. This squeeze may come in the form of higher prices to middlemen and customers, a reduction in middlemen's profit margins, reduced product quality, reduced service, highhanded quotas, shipping policies, etc. When this condition occurs, the leader may in the long run destroy his channel of distribution and his own market.

RESPONSIBILITY OF THE CHANNEL LEADER

We have established that the ability of a channel member to make decisions and establish policy for the membership must be based on clear authority. There cannot be authority without responsibility for the firm's actions and we shall now examine the responsibility of the channel leader.

Channel Leader Responsibility Identified

The channel leader is responsible to more groups than he has been prone to recognize in the past. For too long businesses have held the attitude that what is good for the firm is just plain good in itself. When questioned about the billion-dollar electrical conspiracy case in 1960 involving General Electric and Westinghouse, one convicted executive replied, "It's the only way a business can be run." [15] This attitude is beginning to change in many businesses in favor of a broader concept of responsibility. The channel leader has a responsibility to his own business, to the membership of the channel, and to the public.

Leader's Responsibility to Self. There can be no question that the channel leader has a responsibility to meet the company's own objectives as spelled out by the owners and managers. It is unlikely that the business is going to place any other institution's needs before its own, and

[15] Kenneth R. Schneider, *Destiny of Change* (New York: Holt, Rinehart and Winston, Inc., 1968), p. 196.

this is a reasonable position for the firm to take. The channel leader would change the channel before sacrificing his own objective for that of members. However, what the business perceives as its responsibility to self depends on the perceptions held by the members of the organization. The owners, or stockholders, may perceive the organization only in terms of monetary receipts. To this group the objective is profit, growth, dividends, etc. In the case of absentee ownership, the perception of the business may be so narrow that the basic economic function of the firm may be only recognized in a fuzzy manner.

Management and employees often have a deeper commitment to the business. These groups often live or die based on the success of the organization. Thus, management and employees may perceive the firm's responsibility as survival, opportunity for personal achievement, business recognition, monetary reward, security, or advancement. Even among these groups, however, perceptions differ. There are instances where employees by prolonged strike have caused a business to go bankrupt. These employees were willing to sacrifice security and business survival for the principle of monetary reward. It is not unheard of for managers to operate businesses to their personal gain, ignoring their responsibility to owners and employees.

Even within groups there are different perceptions of the firm's responsibility. The engineering department may perceive responsibility as high product quality or engineering efficiency while the marketing department perceives responsibility as sales volume or revenue. A business is a complex entity, and its responsibility to itself cannot be easily dismissed as profit seeking. Every business sees its responsibility in a unique manner according to the people involved.

Leader's Responsibility to Membership.   The channel leader's responsibility to the membership can be summed in the following manner. The leader must meet the channel member's expectations of guidance and control. Whether the leader passes this test of responsibility depends on the perceived roles of leader and member. The management of the member institution has a mental picture of how a leader should act, so also does the management of the leader firm. If the perceptions of role are in harmony the channel should operate relatively smoothly. In some channels, where individual member institutions have small physical facilities or where they are financially insecure, a strong, even dictatorial leader may be necessary for both internal and external relationships. In another channel, where members are more self-sufficient, a democratic leader may be in order.

Many transactions in a channel become routinized, and the problem of leadership responsibility to members becomes critical when the leader steps out of his routine. If the leader suddenly becomes demanding concerning payment, shipment, etc., or starts ignoring situations, such as competitive encroachment, that he has responded to in the past the channel members begin to question his right to lead. Another problem occurs when the channel needs one type of leader but wrongly perceives that it should have a different type. In this situation the leader may be meeting his responsibility, but he is ineffective because of a failure of the membership to understand the situation. An effective leader keeps the membership under willing control at all times.

Nature of Responsibility

The channel leader is responsible for everything that happens in the channel, even though there are practical limitations on the leader's ability to shoulder complete responsibility. However, traditional functions are increasingly shifted around in modern channels.[16] It is, of course, impossible to discuss every aspect of the leader's management responsibility at this time. Leadership responsibility can be divided into two broad areas: (1) general management responsibility and (2) functional area responsibility.

In a functional sense the channel leader is responsible for: (1) establishing product standards, (2) delegating functional authority, and (3) maintaining performance standards. The channel leader decides on the quality, brand, and individual features of the product. The type of product standards established determines the general character of the channel. Some channels handle quality products, some deal with price-oriented products, and some handle a combination of types.

The channel leader is responsible for the delegation of all authority over functions or activities within the channel. These activities may include all or part of the following: pricing; service standards; purchasing; physical distribution methods; promotion; marketing research; and hiring, training, and maintaining employees. This delegation of authority takes place primarily by the sale of products.

The channel leader is also responsible for performance standards within the channel. This means that he determines, within limits, what constitutes good performance by member institutions. Through his evaluation of performance, the leader ascertains whether the members are functioning in accordance with the established standards. Of course, the channel leader attempts voluntary acceptance of the established standards and willing cooperation in their achievement. Voluntary acceptance is

[16] Bert C. McCammon, Jr., Alton F. Doody, and William R. Davidson, "Emerging Patterns of Distribution," *Marketing Channels and Institutions,* Bruce J. Walker and Joel B. Haynes, eds. (Columbus, Ohio: Grid, Inc., 1973), p. 212.

the route to overall channel efficiency and better service to all the publics that the channel serves, but there are occasions when a heavy hand must be employed.

Attitude Toward Responsibility

Truth, morals, and ethics are as important to channel members as to society in general. Just as marketing activities can be performed efficiently or inefficiently, so marketing responsibility can be performed morally and ethically or immorally and unethically. For example, one marketer may price at all the traffic will bear in order to gouge the middleman, while another may cut his profit, give advice, and make loans to small retailers in order to help them mature. Almost every channel member can think of some business in a position of leadership that has, at one time or another, taken advantage of member institutions. With the increased awareness of consumers, the rapid means of communications, and greater scrutiny of business operations, such practices are becoming more difficult.

The question of moral and ethical business leadership is a difficult one. Guidelines are not easy because what is ethical varies from business to business and over time. As a result, there has never been defined an acceptable list of ethical principles. Businessmen, government officials, consumers, and academicians are concerned in a real way about the answers to ethical business questions and the uproar that has already been stirred up is, in itself, sufficient to make business leaders more conscious of the result of their actions when dealing with middlemen.

CRITERIA FOR EFFECTIVE CHANNEL LEADERSHIP

There has never been established any consistent set of personality traits, human characteristics, personality types, or environmental factors that can lead to or clearly define the existence of leadership. Almost any type of person can become a leader; the same can be said for institutions in the channel. Some highly unlikely firms have upon occasion become channel leaders. There are five criteria that, if possessed by the collective management of the marketing institution, can greatly increase the leader's chances of effective administration of the channel team. These criteria are: (1) identification, (2) competence, (3) objectivity, (4) communications, and (5) fairness.

Identification is the ability to relate to the other channel members. This involves the ability to put one's self into the member's position and see the problem out of the eyes of the members. An effective channel leader can understand what a wholesaler means when he says he is in a price squeeze between the manufacturer and the retailers. *Com-*

petence is the channel leader's technical skill. The leader is going to discover that channel members will be much more willing to follow if he is usually correct in his understanding or assessment of the marketing situation.

Objectivity refers to the ability of the channel leader to get to the causes of problems unemotionally. It is the ability to remain calm and impartial in all investigations. *Communications* is the willingness to inform members and to inform in such a manner as to be understood. Effective communications do not go to some members, say, the large ones, and not to others; effective communications are simple, straightforward statements that omit confusion factors. One of the most difficult problems with communication is to recognize its need. *Fairness* is the ability of the channel leader to dispense impartial treatment. A channel leader is not meeting this criteria when he charges two similar channel members different prices or when he gives one a favorable delivery schedule or allows another to return merchandise unreasonably while holding others to the line.

QUESTIONS

1. Compare personal leadership and collective leadership in the methods they use to guide another firm. Give examples of each type.
2. Give examples of the different types of member status and tell how status changes from member to member and channel to channel.
3. Explain the difference in channel leadership and channel domination.
4. Who is the "normal" leader in a channel? How can the leadership role be placed in the other positions in the channel? Give examples of manufacturer, wholesaler, and retailer led channels.
5. How can there be "partial leadership" in a channel? Compare and give an example of each of the three conditions of shared leadership.
6. It has been said that the concept of leadership responsibility is changing. Explain why this is so and give some examples of the change.
7. What are the criteria that increase the chances of channel leadership? Explain how each is applicable.
8. How might the channel leader delegate some of his authority and responsibility to other members of the channel?
9. Explain the process a single retailer may go through in changing channel leadership as the retailer grows in size.
10. Contrast member separation and organizational separation in the manner in which they affect the leadership of a channel.

17

Conflict Management
in Channels

It is characteristic of human nature that individuals who interact agree on some things and disagree on others. This is as true within the channel team as it is within other operating behavioral systems. To be able to preside over a coordinated effort, the channel leader is vitally concerned with the management of both conflict and cooperation. Actually, handling member conflict and motivating members to efficient cooperation may be the leader's most important functions in the channel. When the leader is effective, coordination is the result.

CHANNEL CONFLICT, COOPERATION, AND COORDINATION

Some marketers argue that the very essence of channel leadership is the achievement of coordination among the institutions that make up the channel team.[1] Whether one agrees with this position or not, coordination is certainly an important goal of channels management. Specifically, channel coordination can be defined as *the effective synchronization of human relationships to achieve an efficient performance of necessary functions by the specialized institutions comprising a marketing channel.* The synchronization of human relationships involves the management by the channel leader of conflict, cooperation, motivation,

[1] See: Louis W. Stern and Jay W. Brown, "Distribution Channels: A Social Systems Approach," *Distribution Channels: Behavioral Dimensions*, Louis W. Stern, ed. (Boston: Houghton Mifflin Co., 1969), p. 12. This article argues that the basis for coordination is changing.

and control in the channel. Although the focus of attention in this chapter is on conflict management, a relationship must be established between all four of these aspects of channel coordination.

Conflict is a word easily used, but one seldom defined clearly. As used here, conflict means to clash, to oppose, to disagree, to resist an idea, event, or thing. Thus our definition of channel conflict is *the opposition to goals, ideas, or performance behavior that occurs among the managements of institutions that make up the marketing channel team.*[2] One point of view says that channel conflict can be recognized when two or more members of the distribution system become the object of each other's frustration.[3] The managements of channel institutions may disagree over almost anything. Some of these disagreements are of small consquence and easily worked out, while some are quite serious. Few conflicts can be easily ignored without some consequence on the total team effort.

Cooperation and motivation are defined more carefully in the next chapter, but basically cooperation refers to a willingness of institutions to operate together, while motivation implies a desire to perform with a high degree of skill. Control, of course, can mean the assurance of performance. Thus, to be coordinated, the channel must have members who cooperate and possess a desire to perform with skill in order to achieve some common goal. In a coordinated channel the entire inter-relationships must be controlled, but control is particularly important where conflict is concerned.

The channel leader cannot get at coordination directly, but must approach it indirectly through the performance of other management activities. That is, one does not tell an executive to go out and coordinate the channel of distribution. Rather, the manager is advised to plan, organize, actuate, and control the operations of the various channel members. When these management activities are properly carried out, not only are the marketing functions synchronized, but conflict is reduced and willing motivated effort is achieved. In other words, coordination is the natural result of good management by the channel leader.

Cooperation and Conflict Affect Coordination

In order to function, channel members must interact, but not all interaction is desirable or constructive. Conflict tends to pull the channel membership apart, and cooperation serves to bring the membership together. Both cooperation and conflict are characteristic of all team efforts, but a smooth operating channel typically has more cooperation

---

[2] Based on Louis W. Stern, ed., *op. cit.*, p. 155.
[3] Louis W. Stern and Ronald H. Gorman, "Conflict in Distribution Channels: An Exploration," *Distribution Channels: Behavioral Dimensions, op. cit.*, p. 156.

than conflict. The channel leader must deal with both. Conflict must be handled in such a manner as to make it an integral and useful part of the channel's operation. Cooperation, and along with it motivation, are necessary to keep the channel operating at a high state of readiness. However, cooperative and highly motivated channel members do not result simply from a lack of conflict. These positive member interactions must be built on a solid foundation of sound channel administration and leadership.

Furthermore, conflict and cooperation not only occur in all channels, but they often occur simultaneously. For example, channel members may be cooperating with the leader on such sales problems as pricing, advertising, and credit while there may be conflict among the members and leader over delivery schedules, discounts, and the return of goods to the manufacturer. Another possibility is that some members of the channel are cooperating with the leader while others are in conflict. Still another possibility is that one or more channel members cooperate, but only to the bare minimum. The channel member may be against some leader policy, and he may be attempting to circumvent that policy while cooperating only to the extent necessary.

It is, perhaps, unrealistic when considering institutions to require that every aspect of their interactions be coordinated.[4] The organizations involved, with multiple departments, several management levels, and even different operating units, are simply too complex. Even simultaneous conflict and cooperation have degrees. A channel may be: (1) fully coordinated, (2) partially coordinated, or (3) uncoordinated. Most channels fit the second situation, and even in this case some are more coordinated than others. Full coordination where members agree on everything is an ideal. An uncoordinated channel, when there is no agreement, cannot long survive. Therefore, in a realistic sense, the problem is not to eliminate conflict and acquire complete cooperation. The problem is to manage conflict and cooperation. It can even be argued that some conflict is good for the channel if it results in new ideas, methods, or arrangements that lead to improved efficiency.

Atmosphere for Channel Coordination

Although coordination cannot be obtained directly, the existence of a certain atmosphere greatly improves the manager's chances of obtaining a coordinated channel. There are four elements to this climate. First, there has to be a *desire* on the part of channel members to work together.

---

[4] Frederick H. Sturdivant and Donald L. Granbois, "Channel Interaction: An Institutional-Behavioral View," *Quarterly Review of Economics and Business* (Summer, 1969), pp. 61–68.

Coordination can be achieved by forced relationships, but the success is greater if the parties are agreeable.

Second, there has to be *contact* between the institutions. Interaction is not possible without either direct or indirect contact. *Direct contact* can occur through sales calls, letters, telephone, or executive visits. *Indirect contact* refers to such interaction as advertising, catalogs, pamphlets, or publicity. Personal contact enhances the chances for coordination by fostering two-way communication. The institutions can throw out ideas, relate mutual problems and solutions, and listen to the other fellow's side of the issue. Indirect contact does not offer these opportunities. A channel which depends largely on promotion, price lists, etc., for interaction is not as likely to be coordinated.

Third, there has to be a *reciprocity of ideas* to insure effective coordination of the marketing channel. Not only must each side have ideas, or relate its ideas, but each must listen to the ideas presented by others. The problem of listening is the most difficult. It requires more than hearing words; it requires a positive attitude of sympathy and understanding. The climate for coordination cannot be killed more quickly than by member institutions having closed minds to the problems and solutions advanced by others. It is particularly difficult for channel members to accept the notion that what is good for their firm may not be good for other channel members. For example, a leader may wish to cut margin to a minimum, not realizing that members with a much lower sales volume cannot operate successfully at the lower rate.

Fourth, the atmosphere for coordination is advanced where the channel members have *mutual trust and respect* for one another. It is not that cooperation and coordination cannot occur in some other type of atmosphere, but they are more likely to occur where there is trust. Of course, the best possible way to build trust and respect is simply to deal honestly and straightforwardly with one another. This is an observation easily made but a situation very difficult to obtain in any type of team effort. It is no less crucial because of its difficulty.

TYPES OF CHANNEL CONFLICT

Some authors tend to equate channel competition with channel conflict.[5] We want to be particularly careful to avoid this confusion. Conflict is any opposition or disagreement in the channel, while competition

[5] See: Bruce Mallon, "Conflict and Cooperation in Marketing Channels," *Reflections on Progress in Marketing*, L. George Smith, ed. (Chicago: American Marketing Association, 1964), pp. 65–85; Joseph C. Palamountain, Jr., *The Politics of Distribution* (Cambridge, Mass.: Harvard University Press, 1955), pp. 48–57.

is a specific type of opposition based on two or more firm's attempts to appeal to the same, or similar, markets. While competition may certainly constitute an important type of conflict in the marketing channel, it is an oversimplification to equate conflict with this particular type of interaction.

Horizontal Channel Conflict

Horizontal conflict occurs between middlemen of the same type at the same stage in the marketing channel. An example of horizontal competitive conflict would be two department stores handling the same manufacturer's branded product in relatively close proximity. Horizontal non-competitive conflict is illustrated by two branch managers who disagree on basic price or promotional policy within the integrated firm. Another example is two franchised dealers who bicker over the personal attention paid each by the channel leader. In non-integrated channels, horizontal conflict is more likely to be of the competitive variety. Either type is equally possible in integrated channels.

Vertical Channel Conflict

Vertical conflict occurs between channel members at different levels in the same channel of distribution. It takes place across the market, whereas horizontal conflict occurs on one side of the market. Vertical conflict comes into play any time the wishes of a channel member at one level are in opposition to those at another level. When a manufacturer of a branded product competes with a department store selling the same brand, you have an example of vertical competitive conflict. Another example of vertical competitive conflict occurs when the manufacturer competes for the same market with the wholesaler by means of selling direct to retailers part of the time.

Important types of vertical non-competitive channel conflict also occur, and some are built into channel operations. For example, every channel involves the exchange process where products are transferred for money. Each act of exchange has two parties—a purchaser and a seller—and the purposes of these two parties are in some respects opposed. There is conflict because the seller wants to obtain the most money for his product, and the buyer wants the product at the lowest price. Obviously, there can be no exchange until this conflict is satisfactorily resolved by a price mutually agreed upon. Thus, while the exchange act tends to build competition into the channel, it also contains the basis for cooperation. Other examples of non-competitive conflict occur when: (1) the manufacturer wants to promote a product one way and the dealer desires another; (2) the manufacturer wants the dealer to handle a full line but the dealer wants a restricted line, or (3) the manufacturer wants to sell through wholesalers while the retailer wants to purchase direct. Such differences revolve around channel policy, where each member agrees on the competitive aspects of channel operations, but conflict arises over the methods used.

A principle of competitive conflict that can be applied to both competitive and non-competitive vertical channel conflict is the concept of countervailing power.[6] Simply stated, *countervailing power* means that for every position of original power in the channel there will develop a power position to counteract it. Thus, if the channel leader begins to abuse his position, the membership will enter into activities to counter the leader. Such activities may include coalitions, increased independence, achieving financial strength, etc. The classic example of countervailing power is the development of labor unions to oppose the early abuses of labor by a management. No channel leader, or member, should even undertake action that will in the future restrict the power to act. In short, the channel should avoid situations that lead to countervailing power.

CAUSES OF CHANNEL CONFLICT

Channel conflict arises out of channel interaction. Just as there is a flow of functions within the marketing channel, so there are patterns of possible conflict at every point in the flow where management interaction occurs. There are seven causes of channel conflict that are founded in: (1) roles, (2) issues, (3) perception, (4) expectations, (5) decisions, (6) goals, and (7) communications among the institution in the channel.[7]

Channel Roles

Each channel member, whether leader or follower, has a role to play. The member's role is actually a normative model of behavior that describes that member's place and contribution to the team. The particular role of a member carries with it rights and obligations. A wholesaler or retailer has the right to expect suppliers to deal honestly, to meet shipment dates, to accept damaged merchandise, and to keep them informed among other things. These wholesalers have the obligation to also deal honestly, to meet payments on time, to inspect goods promptly, to place correct orders, and not to make unreasonable claims on the supplier. When a particular channel member continually performs in a prescribed

[6] John K. Galbraith, "The Concept of Countervailing Power," *American Capitalism*, rev. ed. (Boston: Houghton Mifflin Co., 1956), pp. 110–14.

[7] Stern and Gorman, *op. cit.*, pp. 156–75; Bjorn Carlson and Bertil Kusoffsky, "Distributor Brands vs. Producer Brands" (Stockholm, Sweden: The Economic Research Institute at Stockholm School of Economics, 1966), pp. 114–20.

manner, this behavior is taken as customary by the other channel members. Conflict arises when either of the two parties does not behave in the normative manner—that is, he does not live up to the perceived expectation of this role.

Channel Issues

Issues arise out of consideration of value. According to Boulding there is an issue when two channel members want the same scarce resource.[8] Thus, in the channel issues can develop over territorial rights, product lines carried, shelf space allocated, discounts given, etc. For example, manufacturer's agents often are placed in a position of conflict with their principles because the principle takes the large volume customers, the concentrated markets, or high volume products, and leaves the remainder for the agent to handle. The same type of conflict can arise between the manufacturer and the wholesaler.

Channel Perceptions

Perception refers to a particular awareness of concepts, things, or ideas. It is more than observation, since perception refers to the particular interpretation given to that which is observed. Each channel member, operating through the complex mechanism of its management, is likely to have individualistic perceptions of itself and of the actions of other channel members. Three types of perceptions are possible in the marketing channel.

1. Each channel member has perceptions of itself
2. Each channel member has perceptions of the channel leader
3. The leader has perceptions of each channel member

Conflict arises over the differences in perceived needs, motives, and attitudes that each channel member has.[9]

Examples of conflict arising out of each type of perception cited above can be helpful in understanding the problems. First, the manufacturer may perceive his business as a progressive profit-oriented institution. Retailers in this manufacturer's distribution system may perceive themselves as progressive institutions who hold prices down to benefit consumers. Conflict is bound to arise in this situation because of differences in self-perception. Second, member perceptions of the leader can be illustrated by a strong channel leader who is regarded by the retailer as a hard bar-

[8] Kenneth E. Boulding, "The Economics of Human Conflict," *The Nature of Human Conflict*, Elton B. McNeil, ed. (Englewood Cliffs, N. J.: Prentice-Hall, Inc., 1965), pp. 172–73.

[9] Larry J. Rosenberg and Louis W. Stern, "Toward the Analysis of Conflict in Distribution Channels," *Journal of Marketing* (October, 1969), pp. 40–46.

gainer or dishonest merchandiser. When this happens the retailer is always on his guard; he questions every action or undertaking of the manufacturer. This constant badgering leads to strife. If the frustrations become great enough, the members may break off interaction.

Third, leaders also have perceptions of the channel members. Suppose the wholesaler perceives his primary function in the marketing channel as physical distribution and storage. The channel leader, on the other hand, may perceive the wholesaler's primary function as aggressively pushing and promoting the leader's products. Conflict occurs in this case because there is a difference in the leader's perception of the middleman. This latter example describes many actual channel situations. Wholesalers and retailers seldom push the manufacturer's product to that producer's satisfaction. Very often the wholesaler or retailer carry many more lines of products than a single manufacturer. Thus, these middlemen have less vested interest in any single line.

Channel Expectations

Expectations are similar to perceptions, but where perceptions concern present reality, expectations concern future predicted happenings. Expectations have to do with what the middleman perceives likely to happen in the future as a result of present occurrences—similar to the self-fulfilling prophecy. In the example above, because the retailer expects the manufacturer to be a hard bargainer, he tends to take unreasonable positions from which to begin his negotiation. The unreasonable position assumed by the retailer causes the manufacturer to harden his bargaining position. As a result the retailer's expectations are fulfilled since he finds the manufacturer unreasonable to deal with, and conflict between the two channel members is the result. Differences in expected rewards, policies, procedures, etc., can also lead to channel conflict.

Channel Decisions

Decisions must be made by all channel members. Conflict arises when two or more channel members attempt to control specific decisions or the decision making process. Two examples can serve to illustrate this fact. One is the case of a single decision where the channel leader is known. The manufacturer, as a known leader, may want more or better shelf space in a particular retail store. The retailer recognizes the producer as the channel leader but feels the amount of space, or its location, is his own prerogative. Conflict results over this decision although the retailer recognizes the producer's right to lead the channel.

The second case occurs when two channel members each want to be the leader with responsibility over all decision making in the channel. In this case the conflict takes the form of a power struggle for control over the marketing channel. For example, retail grocery stores can get caught in a power struggle between such producers as Lever Brothers and Colgate-Palmolive should such a struggle develop. In most channels some conflict over individual decisions happens all the time. Power struggles are less frequent except in the normal competitive sense.

Channel Goals

Each channel member participates in the team effort for a simple reason—it is to his advantage. The member gains products, cost savings, opportunities, etc., from belonging to the channel that would not otherwise exist for him. Thus, the channel member willingly participates in achieving the channel's overall goal. Despite the obvious advantages, each firm has individual goals as well as its own ideas about how the overall goal can best be achieved. Conflict arises over these differences in goal interpretation. Even when there is conflict, there must be sufficient agreement over goals and their attainment, or the channel cannot long exist, at least not with its present structure.

Channel Communications

Channel conflict is not possible without communications, because communications in some form is the basis for channel conflict as well as co-operation. Yet, it is often the failure to communicate in the expected patterns that is the basis for channel conflict. This failure may even take the form of not communicating when some communications is expected. Communications conflict can occur in any functional area of the business. While manufacturers give lip service to the need for communication between channel members, they are often important creators of conflict because of a lack of communications.[10] Manufacturers fail to communicate organizational changes, new promotion campaigns, price modifications, product innovation. and policy changes. As a result, the middleman feels left out and conflict results.

It is unfair to blame the manufacturer as the only channel member who fails to communicate, however. Manufacturers' agents and selling agents, although they are experts in the market, often fail to communicate this information to their principals. No channel member likes to pass on financial information to others. Retailers and wholesalers do not inform the channel leader of market conditions, customer reactions to the product or advertising, or operating problems. A failure to communicate is one of the more serious causes of conflict in any marketing channel.

[10] Philip McVey, "Are Channels of Distribution What Textbooks Say?" *Journal of Marketing,* Vol. 24 (January, 1960), pp. 61–65.

CHANNEL CONFLICT CONSEQUENCES

There is a natural tendency to assume that all channel conflict is a bad thing. This point of view is not sound. Conflict is as much a part of channel operations as cooperation. Many times the differences that occur lead to stronger bonds of coordination among the membership as a result of the natural give-and-take associated with working out difficult problems. The result can be to maintain the status quo. However, it often happens that conflict results in change or modification in the present conduct of affairs within the channel, and this change often brings channel improvements.

Channel conflict can be either good or bad depending on the managers involved and how the conflict is handled. It can be identified as constructive or destructive. *Constructive conflict* results when members approach their problems with goodwill and a desire to cooperate. Under such circumstances, the results can be constructive even when the parties do not agree. However, constructive conflict may improve the team operation by means of an orderly process of change and innovation undertaken in an atmosphere of give and take. *Destructive conflict* occurs in an atmosphere of distrust and hostility, and it tends to pull the team apart. There is no attempt to improve or to replace that which is destroyed. Most destructive conflict is vindictive.

Constructive conflict is natural among channel members, and it is necessary to the healthy, vigorous growth of an efficient channel of distribution. We can definitely say that constructive conflict is desirable for the marketing channel. Since the result of constructive conflict is to question present methods, challenge future goals and plans, and point to the lack of efficiency in past operations, it sets in motion the whole control process by which change and innovation are introduced into the channel. There are three steps in this process of change. First, there is disagreement over some idea, event, problem, or thing among channel members. Second, this disagreement leads to member search for a mutually agreeable solution. Third, the result of search is compromise, innovation, or renewed faith in the thing originally disagreed upon. Without conflict to set this process into motion there would never be any new methods, or techniques, or products in the marketing channel.

Destructive conflict is not desirable in a channel of distribution; constructive conflict can be managed, destructive conflict cannot. The executive's only choice is to head it off or to divert it, hopefully to some contructive activity. Once set into motion, destructive conflict is very difficult to stop. It has all the symptoms of highly irrational behavior. For example, a retailer drops one of his most profitable product lines because the producer of the line did not recognize the retailer at a trade show. The fact that the retailer is hurting his own profit position as much as, if not more than, he is hurting the manufacturer does not enter into the situation. The retailer does not agree with the manufacturer's behavior; he is not interested in reasons, he simply seeks to strike out. There may be nothing the manufacturer can do to regain this account. In fact, the producer may never know why the account was lost.

Need for Conflict Management

It was demonstrated previously that conflict in the marketing channel has both good and bad aspects. It follows that the function of the channel's manager is not to attempt to eliminate conflict within the channel but to control and channel its incidence into constructive paths.[11] Thus, the problem is a need to keep destructive conflict to a minimum and to emphasize constructive conflict. One of the major problems of the leader, which lies in his own bias, is to recognize when conflict is constructive. Who is to say that a middleman is incorrect, taking an entire channel perspective, when he attempts to get the leader to maintain prices, reduce product outlets, or provide more information on activities or policies. On the other hand, who can say that the member is correct. In most channels, with a strong leader, it is the leader's attitude that prevails. What is good for the leader is deemed to be good for the channel as a whole, but one can easily reason that this point of view is not necessarily true.

Not only does destructive and constructive conflict have to be balanced in the channel, but there must be some balance between conflict and cooperation.[12] The channel does not need members who act strictly in the capacity of "yes" men, but neither does it need those who are constantly acting as the devil's advocate. A certain degree of open mindedness is needed on the part of the leader to accept criticism. The members must know that they have the right to criticize. This right is encouraged by the leader's creation of a proper climate for dissent and discussion. On the other hand, there is a limit to how much dissent the leader can allow. This limit is typically defined as the point at which the leader begins to lose control over the membership. The achievement of balance between conflict and cooperation is difficult. Too much control stifles constructive criticism and too little leads to anarchy.

---

[11] Reavis Cox, Thomas F. Schutte, and Kendrick S. Few, "Toward the Measurement of Trade Channel Perception," *Proceedings of the American Marketing Association*, Fred C. Allvine, ed. (Chicago: American Marketing Association, 1972), pp. 189–93.

[12] Edwin H. Lewis, *Marketing Channels* (New York: McGraw-Hill Book Co., Inc., 1968), p. 64.

RECOGNITION OF CHANNEL CONFLICT

There are three important steps that can be identified in channel conflict management designed to work for the good of the team: (1) recognition of channel conflict, (2) determination of type of management to use, and (3) decision on timing of conflict management.

The first step leading to control of channel conflict is recognition that a problem exists. The recognition of conflict is simpler in face-to-face organizations than in marketing channels where members may be located considerable distances apart. What occurs when conflict is not recognized and dealt with is management by crisis in which the leader organization dissipates its energies putting out fires throughout the channel. Management by crisis tends to lead to destructive conflict and loss of control by the channel leader. There are three important considerations in conflict recognition: (1) create climate for management awareness, (2) monitor conflict indicators, and (3) provide a collection center for conflict data.

Create Climate for Management Awareness

There is no way to control conflict without recognition. Too many problems of human interaction are left to fester either because they are not important enough for the member to report, some manager in the leader organization did not recognize the symptoms, or because leader management did not care. What is needed to overcome these difficulties is an adequate climate for conflict recognition. First, management throughout the channel leader's organization must be made conflict conscious. This can be done by means of indoctrination and education but it must be realized that there are many specific areas of the business which require management education. The manager learns his lesson, he tries to perform in the prescribed manner, but other problems get in the way, and his best intentions soon wear off. The result is continuous spurts of motivation in the several decision areas with long lapses of attention in between. What top management needs is a single device that, when thoroughly indoctrinated into management's attitude, causes prolonged motivation in all the diverse decision areas including conflict control. The motivation should be automatic. Such a device is available in the marketing philosophy previously introduced.[13]

If the various operating levels of management believe in customer or membership satisfaction, and they are backed up by top management,

---

[13] See: Leslie M. Dawson, "The Human Concept: New Philosophy of Business," *Business Horizons*, Vol. 12 (December, 1969), pp. 29–38.

then service begins to become a way of life in all areas of the business including conflict control. In short, management should spend less time attempting to educate and motivate managers to sales volume, research, conflict control, expense management, customer good will, etc., and devote more of its energies to obtaining a total commitment to member satisfaction. Once management begins to think along these lines all the other decision areas are encompassed into the philosophy. The manager begins, on a long-run basis, to recognize conflict situations and deal with them. The channel leader should undertake, where possible, to indoctrinate the dealers on conflict recognition through the marketing philosophy. The same advantages that apply internally to the leader's organization apply to the membership when the marketing philosophy is practiced. Not only should conflict be more readily recognized, but it should be less serious under this circumstance.

Monitor Conflict Indicators

Indicators of possible conflict occur wherever there is contact between the leader of the channel and the membership. Three major sources of conflict information deserve mention.[14] First, the regular *reports of salesmen* should contain some provision for conflict recognition. The information can be written or verbal. The salesman knows attitudes and moods of channel members perhaps better than any other person in the leader organization. Through direct conversation, member businessmen make complaints, point out difficulties, and express dissatisfactions to the salesman. The salesman has the same opportunity to obtain attitudes of the member's employees which often reflect management attitudes that may, or may not, have been expressed to the salesman. Furthermore, the salesman may get hints of conflict by means of observation. He can see what is happening to product shelf space, product handling, pricing, and condition of the product.

Second, the channel leader can check the various *interorganizational reports*. Good examples of reports that can carry hints of conflict are: (1) orders, (2) sales records, (3) margin changes, (4) services and service standards, and (5) returns of merchandise. Most of these records do not necessarily indicate conflict, but they signal that conflict is a possibility. For example, sales or orders may decline for many reasons, including a failure to push the product by the member. A reduction in margin may indicate that the member is not pushing the more profitable lines, but it can also mean an adjustment by the dealer to customer wishes.

[14] Carlos R. Vest, "The Application of Operating Control Systems to Marketing," *New Ideas for Successful Marketing*, John S. Wright and Jac L. Goldstucker, eds. (Chicago: American Marketing Association, 1966), pp. 94–110.

Third, the leader can check on direct *top level dealer contacts*. Salesmen are not the only people in the channel who have direct interaction. Department heads, divisional managers, unit managers, comptrollers, etc., are also in contact with channel members. A great deal can be determined about conflict by the intensity and frequency of complaints, confrontations, and other contacts between these managers. Management should get most concerned when the regular pattern of complaints changes drastically or when there is a trend toward more complaints.

Provide a Collection Center for Conflict Data

Any channel leader may consider a data collection center to accumulate, organize, and interpret possible areas of conflict. The fact is that conflict situations permeate all divisions, departments, and units of the leader's organization that have human contact with member organizations. It is one thing to be attuned to recognize conflict; it is another to have the information necessary for recognition. Even the availability of all conflict indicators previously discussed is not sufficient when they are scattered throughout the leader's business. Clues obtained in one area of the leader's business may pertain to conflict in other areas. For example, the leader's sales department may observe a decrease in orders from a particular firm, but think nothing of it. Orders fluctuate all the time. However, when it is learned from a salesman that the management of this firm was very antagonistic with many references to unfair discounts and poor shipping schedules, the two bits of information can add up to conflict.

The existence of a data collection center would bring this type of information together for evaluation.[15] In small firms, the evaluation may be placed in an existing department such as sales or personnel where there is an interest. It requires no special organizational consideration. The entire collection may be highly informal in such firms. Larger organizations may want to establish a data collection center through which all communications are funneled, including data from the information system, persuasive information, and all other communications requiring systemization. In this case, the process may be highly formal. Either method can be effective depending on the particular needs of the leader.

DETERMINATION OF MANAGEMENT TYPE TO USE

Once the channel leader recognizes a conflict situation, the next decision concerns what appropriate action should be taken. The manner

---

[15] Philip Kotler, "A Design for the Firm's Marketing Nerve Center," *Concepts for Modern Marketing*, Ralph Day, ed. (Scranton, Pa.: International Textbook Co., 1968), pp. 241–57.

of reaction should be designed to prevent destructive conflict and lead to greater coordination between the channel membership.

Acceptance of Member Solution

Channel members know their operation, and they have often considered logical solutions to their needs. Thus, if a channel member complains that the margin is not sufficiently high, or that the product line is too narrow or that the manufacturer does not provide sufficient promotional help, etc., the leader may accept the complaint as valid and make the suggested correction. In a sense, this solution involves a type of participative management by members, and is usually the quickest and easiest for the channel leader. It is also true that acceptance of the member's solution is often the correct action. Whether the leader accepts the member's solution or not, he certainly owes that member the respect of listening to both his problem and his proposed solution. The channel members may be as interested as the leader in the overall success of the channel. These member institutions do consider problems seriously, and they often have excellent ideas due to their particular placement in the channel and their unique experience.

Very often the leader is the instigator of conflict, and the members may accept the leader's ideas after a careful explanation. The leader can cause conflict by announcing new price lists, promotional policies, shipping arrangements, etc. To some degree, the willingness of the membership to follow the leader's advice depends on (1) the logic of the leader's position and (2) the trust the membership has in the leader. There are usually closer working relations in channels that move non-standardized goods than in channels that move staple goods. This is true because there are, typically, fewer types of members, and few members of each type, in the former channel. Control is easier to obtain because interaction is more frequent and direct.

Bargain With Membership

The leader of the channel and the member firms may bargain their differences. Bargaining is used very frequently in channels. It may be formal or informal. Formal bargaining occurs when the two parties who have differences sit down at a specified time and place to discuss the problem. Informal bargaining is more difficult to identify. It does not require face-to-face negotiation and usually takes the form of resistance to policy, written complaints, or slack performance. The manufacturer gets the message and either gives in by making changes or by insisting on compliance. Informal bargaining can occur over long periods of time.

No matter whether formal or informal, the bargaining process in channels involves each side taking a position on the issue or problem and offering solutions and counter-solutions until agreement is reached on a mutually satisfactory course. The essence of bargaining is reasonableness and concession. There can be no effective bargaining when neither side is willing to adjust its position. As one of the most common methods of settling channel problems, bargaining is used when the leader and the membership have good working relations and mutual trust, or when the two parties each have relatively equal economic strength in the channel.

The practice of bargaining is undertaken in channels handling all types of goods. Perhaps the most important point in bargaining, when member firms are aligned against the leader, is how many of the channel members feel the same way. The more members that agree, the more strength they have in dealing with the leader. Even a powerful leader finds it difficult to go against the will of a majority of his channel members. For example, the membership may feel that six delivery dates each month are called for, but the manufacturer, who makes two deliveries, may feel that extra cost of trucks and personnel is prohibitive. The result of bargaining may lead to a compromise on four delivery dates. Of course, an entirely different solution, unsuspected by either party when bargaining began, may be the result. It may be decided that a higher discount rate would induce larger purchases from members and reduce the need for more frequent deliveries. When undertaken with goodwill, bargaining can produce effective solutions to channel problems and improve goodwill among the parties. When bargaining is undertaken by the two parties to prove who has greater strength, it is likely to be destructive to good relationships.

Reorganize the Channel

When a problem arises that cannot be solved in other ways, the manufacturer may simply reorganize the channel. This solution usually involves eliminating channel members that are the source of the problem. The channel can be reorganized in either of two ways. One method is to add or eliminate individual channel members; the other is to add or eliminate all channel members of a particular type. First, the manufacturer can add or drop individual wholesalers or retailers from the channel. The overall channel remains intact since only individual firms are adjusted. When firms are dropped, they are probably replaced with other firms. The elimination of firms often happens in franchise arrangements when the middleman is not following the manufacturer's policies. In cases of selective distribution, manufacturers often drop the poor sellers and the financially unsound firms on an individual basis. The channel leader may add individual wholesalers or retailers in order to increase product sales or widen the market. New marketers would be added, for example, when a manufacturer expanded into new territories or began selling to discount houses not contacted previously.

Second, the manufacturer may reorganize the entire channel membership by adding or dropping member types. A new channel is created by this action, and the former "traditional" channel may no longer be used.[16] Occasionally, the manufacturer may begin to create a new channel, while continuing to sell to traditional middlemen. This policy may bring the separate parts of the dual channel into direct competition.

A good example of this policy can be seen in the rise of the discount house after World War II. Prices were high in the appliance field after the war due to the prevalence of fair trade laws. The resulting high prices, and the reduction in price competition, were limiting manufacturer's sales. The appliance manufacturers wanted to lower price, but retailers would not agree. Negotiation failed: (1) because the retailers did not have to compete in prices on the fair trade items, and (2) because fair trade had led to fat retailer margins. It did not bother the retailer that total channel sales were restricted. After all, the individual manufacturer's product was often only a small part of the retailer's total sales. In this situation, the manufacturers created the discount channel by giving discounts to some retailers who were willing to cut price and trim their operating expenses. The resulting price differential gave the discount houses an advantage in their competition with appliance and department stores. The effect was to lower the price in the "traditional" channel through competition, and to create an entirely new channel of distribution for appliances. It is, of course, easier to reorganize the channel for shopping for specialty goods than for convenience goods. Convenience goods are sold to too many different types of firms.

Force Compliance by Use of Power

Power in a channel is the assurance that one member can cause specific behavior on the part of another member to occur. It is a forced relationship based on dependency. The use of power in a channel to solve problems should be resorted to only when (1) all other means of handling the situation fail, (2) when teaching the membership a lesson, or (3) when there is small chance of reprisals. Yet some attempt to force member compliance is often the channel leader's first thought in a conflict situation. The use of power, which involves the leader forcing his will on the channel members, is very often bad because it suppresses legitimate disagreement, ignores reasonable solutions, and leads to disharmony within the channel.

Power is brought into play by the use of threat, coercion, and eco-

---

[16] Gerald B. Tailman and Bruce Blomstrom, "Retail Innovations Challenge Manufacturers," *Harvard Business Review,* Vol. 41 (September–October, 1962), pp. 130–41.

nomic sanctions. A strong manufacturer can threaten to (1) take back a popular brand, (2) indulge in operational harassment, (3) cease selling to the member, and (4) refuse cooperation on internal problems. Sanctions come in many forms. The manufacturer may reduce his service by such means as calling on the middleman less frequently, taking a hard line on returned merchandise, reducing margin, dropping extras such as joint advertising or discounts. Since the use of power causes distortions in channel policy, it is not recommended as a regular policy. However, the careful use of power can be very effective in a channel. Often, the simple threat of using power may be sufficient to keep the membership in line.

Adjust to the Channel Situation

We have been discussing the manner of reaction as if the channel leader could select the individual reaction in each conflict situation. Very often this is not true. Channel management occurs in a complex environment in which many forces are at work that limit the ability of the channel manager to have his own way. The smart channel leader remains sufficiently flexible to adjust to the changing situation. There are several factors that may directly influence the channel leader's manner of reacting. First, a combination of methods of conflict management is more common than the use of individual means. For example, the parties may bargain, but both the leader and the membership are likely to have some power in the bargaining process. Furthermore, a reorganization of the channel may be a part of the bargaining process.

Second, both the leader and the membership have something to say about the method used. The previous discussion was from the channel leader's point of view. The membership may also initiate change in the channel, and it may be the leader who has to respond. The leader may wish to use power but the members may want to bargain. The leader may even be able to use that power, but whether he does or not depends on how he feels about the channel members and his estimate of future conditions. Third, external circumstances may dictate the method of dealing with conflict. For example, competition may force a solution or the membership may be forced to react in accordance to what is expected of government. In practice, the method of dealing with conflict is never as clearcut as it may sound on paper.

DECISION ON TIMING OF CONFLICT MANAGEMENT

All conflict situations within the marketing channel do not call for immediate leader reaction. It is sometimes proper to delay the reaction. In this section we deal with the subject of conflict timing.

Passive or Positive Leader Action

The channel leader should be on top of every conflict situation among the team, but not every conflict situation requires the leader's direct intervention. It may be better to let the parties calm down and think the problem though before taking action. Some situations may be best left alone entirely. *Positive action* in the marketing channel means that the leader enters directly into the conflict. The conflict itself may be between the leader and one or more dealers, or it may be solely between members. *Passive action* refers to a situation in which the leader does not directly enter into the conflict although he may or may not be involved in it. The leader may play some behind-the-scene role in the confrontation even when taking no positive action.

Whether the channel leader should take positive or passive action depends on several factors. These include the following: (1) whether the leader is directly involved, (2) the type of conflict, (3) seriousness of the differences, (4) needs of the leader for power, prestige, or specific performance, (5) any real knowledge of right or wrong, and (6) potential danger to the channel of distribution.

It is often desirable for the channel leader to play a passive role in a conflict situation where he is not directly involved, where the problem is small, and where the leader has no great stake in the outcome. For example, channel members often try to get the leader involved in their private competitive wars. One retailer will accuse another of unfair advertising, lying, etc., and this retailer asks the manufacturer to intercede and have the other stop the practice. If it is a normal competitive situation and the stakes are not too high, the leader may prefer passive action where both parties are urged to settle the matter. However, if the conflict is explosive, if the leader needs to exert his will, or if the leader has specific helpful knowledge, he may want to make a positive effort to settle the difference even though not personally involved.

It is very difficult for the channel leader to remain passive when his organization is directly involved in the conflict, but it is not impossible. Some retailers may make unreasonable price, shipment, or discount demands on the producer. These demands are sometimes so unreasonable that they do not deserve the manufacturer's reaction, or the producer may quietly let his position be known to the more influential members in the group. However, in most situations, the leader who is directly involved must respond with some positive action. This may be nothing more than a simple explanation of his price or shipment policy. If stronger action is required, the leader may point out the unreasonableness of the retailer's position. A period of negotiation is even possible. The strongest positive action is for the leader to simply state his course of action, and inform the retailer that this policy must be followed without exception. In the case of vertical conflict, the leader is less likely to get involved in competitive rather than non-competitive situations.

The difficult task for any channel leader is to recognize those situations which require passive action and those that demand positive action. There is no simple answer to this question, but it is certainly true that either course should be based on a sound review of the situation and the facts. Some channel leaders tend to thrive on conflict. Their attitude is to become involved in all such activity. This position probably reflects either a very insecure leader, who cannot afford to allow freedom of action within the channel, or a very aggressive management in the leader organization. Aggressiveness alone in conflict situations does not denote good leadership. A more mature leader can sometimes get more done with a hint or a suggestion than a boisterous leader can accomplish with all the dictates available. The best leader is the one that can use conflict to advantage, and get the channel pulling together toward common objectives most of the time.

Immediate or Delayed Leader Action

The timing of the channel leader's reaction to a conflict situation can be crucial. The reaction can be either immediate or delayed. One of the serious mistakes that channel leaders make is to react to every conflict situation immediately and without proper thought. The manufacturers announce a new policy on quantity discounts that requires larger quantity purchases, and a few very small retailers complain bitterly. Rather than immediately rescinding the new discounts, it may be better to assess the importance of these very small retailers to the channel while waiting to see if larger retailers react in the same manner. Suppose the manufacturer introduces a new product that is not an instant success and middlemen begin complaining. It may be better to give the product a chance to prove itself rather than to overreact immediately. There are many instances in the channel when an immediate reaction is called for. If some drastic action occurs, such as a channel member leaving the channel or a disagreement serious enough to affect overall channel performance, then the channel leader must act. Whichever course followed, it must be as carefully considered as possible; action should be based on previously established policies dealing with the type of situation.

RESULTS OF CHANNEL CONFLICT MANAGEMENT

The outcome of conflict management is not always predictable even under the best of circumstances. Sometimes the membership functions smoothly for long periods of time, and at other times it seems that nothing the leader does can get the member firms to pull together. The channel requires overall cooperation but with sufficient constructive conflict to keep it alert and innovative. There are three possible results of the conflict control within marketing channels. They are: (1) channel coordination, (2) channel disintegration, and (3) armed truce.[17]

Channel Coordination

The result of conflict–cooperation management in the marketing channel may be to improve channel coordination. A coordinated channel displays overall cooperation on principle goals, operations, and issues. Most conflict is constructive, and destructive conflict is contained. Member disagreements may or may not be frequent and/or serious, but these disagreements do not greatly impede channel operations. Channel members view disagreement in an adult manner, and seriously work to find constructive solutions. All channel members have a sense of their own importance and feel secure among the membership. The leader tends to be democratic.

Channel Disintegration

It is possible for the management of conflict and cooperation to be so poorly handled as to lead to disintegration of the channel. A disintegrated channel cannot long exist; it must either break up entirely or find some new means of achieving integration, such as a new channel leader. A disintegrated channel is characterized by overall conflict on most major issues with cooperation at a minimum or non-existent. Member disagreements are typically frequent and serious; yet, when they occur, they are either ignored or the members refuse to negotiate effectively. Each member is out to feather his own nest. There is unconstructive leadership, and the channel members feel little sense of security.

Armed Truce

The result of conflict–cooperation management can lead to an armed truce. In this situation there has been no agreement and no solution to channel problems. The parties continue to function together, perhaps out of necessity, but each member pursues his own individual goal, and there is little channel cooperation. This state is characterized by either overall conflict or indifference toward major issues and policies, but with sufficient cooperation to keep the channel functioning at least in the short run. Lines of disagreement have been established, and there may be few new disagreements simply because there is little actual communication outside that which is absolutely necessary. Any security within the chan-

[17] Stern and Gorman, *op. cit.*, pp. 170–72.

nel is strictly personal with each business organization. This situation may exist for fairly long periods of time, but in the end the channel will have to change toward more coordination or more disintegration.

A state of armed truce is not generally healthy for the channel. The channel leader attempts to achieve an integrated channel and to avoid the other two situations. Obviously there are degrees to each, and it is unlikely for a channel leader ever to achieve a completely integrated channel, but if his policies and decisions are sound, a high degree of integration is possible.

QUESTIONS

1. Compare conflict and cooperation as they apply to channels of distribution.
2. Discuss the three types of channel conflict and give an example of how they have affected channels.
3. Discuss destructive and constructive conflict and how they are managed.
4. There are four important reasons for conflict to develop within the marketing channel. Give an example of each as it applies to marketing channels.
5. Discuss when passive action by the channel leader should be used in managing conflict in the channel; when is positive leadership action valuable?
6. Discuss the benefits of both immediate or delayed leader action in reaction to conflict in the channel.
7. When the channel leader reacts to channel conflict he may act in four possible ways. Describe each and give an example of when it would be used.
8. When a problem arises that cannot be solved in other ways a manufacturer may reorganize the channel. Discuss how and why this is done.
9. Assume you are a manufacturer of men's clothes and the retail outlets for your products are not getting good service. What can you do?
10. What should a manufacturer's attitude be toward normal horizontal and intertype competition?

18

Channel Cooperation and Motivation Management

The fundamental concept of Part V has been the necessary achievement of a coordinated channel effort by means of leadership.[1] Coordination was defined earlier as the meshing of human relationships to achieve efficient performance by channel members. In one sense, four separate levels of channel coordination among members can be identified:

1. Controlled conflict
2. Cooperation
3. Motivated effort
4. Cooperative motivation

It is not suggested that the fourth level is synonymous with coordination because coordination is greater than the sum of the parts. Coordination also relates to marketing functions and to control.

The first level of coordination is controlled conflict. A coordinated effort to keep the institutions that comprise the channel team from fighting among themselves is not enough; the channel members must have a positive desire to work together. This desire is what is meant by cooperation, and it constitutes the second level of coordination.[2] Cooperation is a higher state of coordination than controlled conflict because it introduces harmony into the concept of coordination. The third level of co-

[1] Louis W. Stern and Jay W. Brown, "Distribution Channels: A Social Systems Approach," *Distribution Channel: Behavioral Dimensions,* Louis W. Stern, ed. (Boston: Houghton Mifflin Co., 1969), p. 12.

[2] Henry P. Knowles and Borje O. Saxberg, *Personality and Leadership Behavior* (Reading, Mass.: Addison-Wesley Publishing Co., 1971), pp. 88–89.

ordination is motivation, and it ranks above cooperation because it emphasizes the management desire to perform with a high degree of skill at all tasks assigned to the business. The fourth level of coordination is the combination of cooperation and motivation that relates achievement to harmony.

FUNDAMENTALS OF COOPERATION AND MOTIVATION

Cooperation and motivation are terms more often associated with personnel management than with the management of channels of distribution. Yet these terms are precisely suited to the understanding of channels viewed as a marketing team because the success of an individual firm cannot be separated from the success of the group. In this section, we seek to develop the meaning of cooperation and motivation as these terms apply to the marketing channel.

Meaning of Channel Cooperation

Channel cooperation is specifically defined to mean: *the recognition of a harmony of interests in broad goals and policies among businesses comprising a marketing channel that leads to a desire to function as a unit.*[3] Channels of distribution cannot exist without sustained cooperation.[4]

Cooperation is not a concept that requires either personal affection or efficiency, although either or both can be involved. Channel member managers often work in harmony because of the possible reward involved without any feeling of personal friendliness. Very often the managements simply possess neutral attitudes toward each other. They may not come into personal contact often enough to have strong positive feelings one way or another. For example, a retailer's entire feeling for a manufacturer may be based on six calls a year by the manufacturer's salesman. Efficiency, when associated with cooperation, means that the effort of channel members is productive. Such group productivity is not necessary for cooperation. Several channels, all consisting of members equally willing to cooperate, may display varying degrees of productivity. The reason for the variation is that successful effort depends on much more than a willingness to work together.

Voluntary and Involuntary Channel Cooperation

It is a mistake to assume that cooperation must be voluntary. Actually, cooperation can be either voluntary or involuntary. The require-

---

[3] Adapted from: Bruce Mallen, "A Theory of Retailer–Supplier Conflict, Control, and Cooperation," *Journal of Retailing* (Summer, 1963), pp. 24ff.

[4] Wroe Alderson, "Cooperation and Conflict In Marketing Channels," *Dynamic Marketing Behavior* (Homewood, Ill.: Richard D. Irwin, Inc., 1965), p. 239.

ment for cooperation is that channel members consent, or agree, to a meshing of specialized activities. This consent does not have to be willingly given since it can result from pressure being brought to bear on the channel member. For whatever reason, in order to achieve cooperation, the prospect of institutions working together has to be a more attractive alternative than that of not working together. Only to this extent is the cooperation necessarily voluntary. Involuntary cooperation may be obtained by means of coercion or threat. For example, the exclusive agency for a line of bathing suits may dislike the manufacturer's policies but cooperate because of the fear that the brand may be taken away.

Involuntary cooperation is frequently associated with minimum effort and low morale. This point is often well-taken, but the association is not always valid. In the example above, the dealer may work hard to sell the bathing suits after realizing that he has no choice but to cooperate. However, the channel leader seeks to achieve voluntary cooperation because the chances of high morale and enthusiastic performance are much greater.

Motivation as It Applies to Channels

It should be clear to the reader at this point that cooperation among channel members is a desirable, even necessary consideration of channel management, but it may not be enough to assure team success. The missing link is that factor which can change simple cooperation into highly productive activity: motivation. Motivation is an attitude toward work normally associated with the management of individuals, but it has relevance for teams of business. Motivation means striving based on talent.[5] In the channel of distribution, motivation is defined as: *the desire of the business's management to perform its duties within the group, whether its function is to lead or to follow. with a high degree of skill and enthusiasm.*

There are two theories of personal motivation. They are known as Theory X and Theory Y. Scholars who place their faith in *Theory X* believe that man works because he must, in order to obtain the necessities of life. Work itself is seen as undesirable, and man must either be forced or given a strong reward in order to enter into it. Those who believe in *Theory Y* feel that the desire to work, to accomplish, or to excel is innate in man. Work, according to this view, is as natural as play or rest. Of course, the great fallacy is in taking either point of view too literally. While one man must be forced to work, another has to be forced to stop. Most people do not conform to either extreme, but work willingly up to a point beyond which some inducement becomes necessary.

[5] See: Harper W. Boyd, Jr. and Sidney J. Levy, *Promotion: A Behavioral View* (Englewood Cliffs, N. J.: Prentice-Hall, Inc., 1967), pp. 59–60.

It is the same with institutions composed of human managers. Some businesses stay in a highly motivated state, and their managements are known as dynamic. Other firms appear to drift. Most businesses are capable of much more efficient effort than they put forth at any given time. It is this fact that makes it so important for the channel leader to be able to motivate the members of the team to productive effort. The channel leader would be less than human if he did not realize that the manufacturers, wholesalers, retailers, and agents that make up the channel are going to be more motivated at some times than at others. Channel members are also going to be more motivated to perform one task than another. The difference is based on the competence and skills of the managers involved. For example, a firm may be highly motivated to sell but performs storage without great enthusiasm.

Channel Motivation Not Observable

Motivation, like cooperation, is an internal state of mind, and it cannot be directly observed. Motivation must be inferred from behavior, whether the motivation is personal or related to the operation of a business. Business motivation is particularly difficult to observe because of the numbers and differences in people who comprise the organization. Seldom are all operating managers of a business equally motivated.

One major problem in business motivation is that the different parts of the organization require separate types of motivation. For example, the sales department may need pep talks and monetary incentives to keep them in a high state of aggressive excitement. The accounting department may show better results with quiet talks and personal attention aimed at creating care and attention to detail. The shipping and receiving department may need motivation that stimulates physical work, while the research department may require "think" oriented motivation. Managers and salesmen in the field more frequently must be self-motivating, while clerks, foremen, and common laborers expect their motivation to come from supervisors. The complexities of the situation stagger the imagination. Fortunately, a business operates as a series of manageable units, and motivation of the whole can be accomplished if each manager meets his own obligation to his unit.

Because motivation has to be inferred, one tends to look for symptoms of high motivation. The typical indicators in business are sales, error prevention, output, orders, expense reduction, etc. Reliance on these inferences to indicate motivation can be misleading. For example, we tend to attribute high motivation to a business that succeeds or has high sales volume when either of these conditions can be achieved with moderate motivation or less. Some businesses have succeeded because they were in the right place at the right time, and a more motivated management would have accomplished even more. High sales volume may be achieved as a result of excessive expense. Furthermore, a lot of highly motivated business activity is not successful. The problems, perhaps related finances or management talent, are simply too much for the business to overcome even with its best effort. The importance of luck to business success is particularly difficult to determine.

WHY TEAM MEMBERS FAIL TO PERFORM

In the previous section it was demonstrated that both cooperation and motivation affect the performance of the members of the channel team. We now seek to investigate why members of the channel fail to perform, a failure which makes a discussion of cooperation and motivation critical. The three primary causes for team failures are: (1) leader associated reasons, (2) member associated reasons, and (3) market associated reasons.

Leader Associated Reasons

One of the most important leader associated reasons for member failure is indifference. Too often the leader is only interested in his own operation. He may be interested in the result of wholesaler or retailer performance—for example, profit, sales volume, amount spent on advertising, etc.—and not interested in helping the middleman to achieve these goals. Only when the middleman fails to perform satisfactorily does the leader become concerned. He then wants to know the reasons for the failure and attempts to hold the middleman accountable, but it may be too late. Such behavior by the team leader is not designed to inspire the member to cooperate, much less have high motivation. Another leader associated reason for member failure to perform is poor communication.[6] This is sometimes associated with indifference, but it occurs even when the leader is trying to help the channel member.

It often happens that the poor performance of the middleman can be traced to the channel leader's product or service. If the product is no good, it is hard for the middleman to build up enthusiasm for it because the product reflects on the outlet as well as on the manufacturer. It may not be sufficiently bad to drop, but the middleman just does not push it or display it effectively. A final leader associated reason for member failure to perform is poor organization. The channel leader may have the best of intentions and a good product and still fail to stimulate the middleman to cooperate or to perform with enthusiasm. The poor organization may be traced to an ineffective management, lack of financing

6 Knowles and Saxberg, *op. cit.*, pp. 152–53.

or some similar problem, or some specific policy that is ineffective such as a poor selection of marketing channels.

Member Associated Reasons

Channel members are as subject to mistakes as the channel leader. We can classify member associated reasons for failure to perform under two categories: personal and operational. Personal reasons for member failure include member indifference, lack of ability, failure to identify with the leader, and poor self-motivation. Of this group, the most serious, from the leader's point of view, is lack of ability. It is very difficult for the leader to train a middleman who lacks ability because he usually fails before he learns. If a lack of ability is the reason for poor member performance, it may be necessary for the leader to seek another outlet. Indifference is often a symptom of other problems. Member indifference may relate back to the leader's poor product, poor help, or poor communication. Indifference on the part of the middleman may also be due to a failure to appreciate the situation or the opportunity. Indifference can be overcome by the leader. However, every channel member has to be a self-motivator to some degree; the leader cannot provide all the enthusiasm. But enthusiasm is sometimes difficult for a middleman who is beset with bills, poor employees, overstocked shelves, etc.

Operational reasons for poor member's performance include too many products to sell, lack of finances, poor policies or procedures, and ineffective help. Another reason is that the manufacturer's product may not be important to the middleman's total operation. Some of these reasons are more easily dealt with than others. For example, the presence of too many products can be handled by simply letting inventory run down. Of course, the question of which products to drop is not an easy one. One middleman can be highly motivated to sell a large number of products, but some will usually be slighted. Financial and personnel problems have plagued middlemen down through the ages. Manufacturers can often help retailers or wholesalers with financial problems. Some manufacturers provide help and some do little. This help may take the form of financing inventory, providing financial advice, or helping middlemen obtain loans. In addition, the existence of poor policies and procedures can be handled. To help establish guidelines may require direct intervention by the leader, but it can be done. Manufacturers can assist with management problems by providing advice or the use of specialists. Examples can be found in franchising where the parent organization provides regular consulting and practical laboratory work on specific problems. Some manufacturers furnish advice on inventory and/ or accounting control; if nothing else the manufacturer's salesman can listen to the middleman's problems.

Market Associated Reasons

Channel members often fail to perform up to the leader's expectations because of factors associated with the market. Competition is one of the more serious market associated reasons for member failure. Some channel members become discouraged when competition becomes keen and may give up. Other channel members simply cannot compete effectively because of internal or product associated problems, and their performance drops even when their enthusiasm and effort are high. Another market associated reason for failure is change: the market is in a constant state of change which the channel member may not be able to keep up with. A good market today may not be a good one tomorrow and the successful retailer or wholesaler must be able to adjust. Another reason for member failure is lack of information about the market. It is not enough to want to adjust to the market; the channel member must know what is going on in that market. This knowledge requires proper records and forecasting—which many retailers and wholesalers do not have. The market associated reasons for failure to perform are often difficult to counter because of their nature.

CULTIVATION OF CHANNEL COOPERATION

The achievement of cooperation among manufacturers, wholesalers, retailers, and agents in the marketing channel is the level of coordination one step higher than conflict control. Cooperation must be cultivated, even when it is obviously in the best interest of all parties to work together.

The members of a channel of distribution have as many reasons to agree and cooperate as they have to disagree and develop conflicts.[7] In most cases, it is a matter of identifying the common elements in the situation and developing mutual awareness. Reasons for channel cooperation can be divided into general reasons and specific reasons. The *general reasons* for channel cooperation are so named because they apply to all channels.

First, every channel has certain overriding goals that are common to all members. These goals include profit, survival, expansion, industry leadership, market share, etc. While the individual members may disagree on the means of achieving these goals, there is an underlying agreement that the channel group must stand together on the broader issues that relate to these goals. Second, the functions performed by one chan-

---

[7] Daniel Katz, "The Motivated Basis for Organizational Behavior," *Reading In Organizational Theory: A Behavioral Approach,* Walter H. Hill and Douglas Egan, eds. (Boston: Allyn and Bacon, Inc., 1967), p. 177.

nel member cannot stand alone. Each member is dependent on having the other members perform correlative functions. This interdependence necessitates cooperation. The retailer cannot sell without the wholesaler or manufacturer furnishing the products. The manufacturer depends on market information supplied by wholesalers and retailers. Most ordinary tasks such as packaging, dividing, pricing, servicing, and delivering are divided up among the manufacturer, wholesaler, and retailer. There is no way for the channel members to escape the interdependence that exists among themselves. The buyer may attempt to outdo the seller and vice versa, but there is always the understanding that neither could exist without the other.

Third, the anticipation of joint reward that results from efficient co-operative effort is a powerful integrator in the channel.[8] Most channel members realize that, due to the interdependence of functions among members, the efficiency of the entire channel can be increased if each member cooperates. One way in which they cooperate is for each member to perform the functions he is best suited for. Fourth, just as there is joint reward for cooperation, there are joint sanctions for a lack of cooperation. The sanction may be in the form of inefficiency, less profit, exclusion from the channel, etc. This is a negative reason for coopera-tion, but it can be an effective one. Fifth, channel members cooperate as a means of coping with external pressures. These external pressures may be the government, competing channels, or customer pressures. Channel members recognize the power of joint strategy and a solid front when dealing with such pressures.

Specific reasons for channel cooperation may apply to one channel but not to another. They cannot all be listed here, but some of the important ones include: (1) personal friendship between individuals, (2) mutual respect, (3) opportunity for power over other channel members, (4) possibility to influence decision making in the channel, and (5) oppor-tunity for personal gain from the operation. Any one of these reasons can be a powerful factor in channel cooperation. Most relate to individual motivation or needs, and each is difficult to qualify.

Conditions Needed for Channel Cooperation

There is no set of factors that can assure that a group of marketing in-stitutions will cooperate. However, where there is cooperation within a channel of distribution four factors are generally present to some degree.

First, there is *participation* which means that the businesses must agree to associate as a group. At this time no assumption is made concerning the reason for this agreement, only that it exists. It is a fact that there

[8] *Distribution Channels: Behavioral Dimensions,* Louis W. Stern, ed. (Boston: Houghton Mifflin Co., 1969), p. 92.

can be no cooperation with an institution that refuses to participate. In fact, simple agreement is often not sufficient to achieve cooperation, because the participation can be negative. Second, there is *specialization of activities* among members. If a firm can achieve all its objectives internally, there is no need to cooperate with any other firm. In non-integrated channels made up of independent institutions, each performs his specialty, and the fact that each member's specialty differs in some important respects from that of other institutions necessitates cooperation. Cooperation is also necessary in integrated channels, and specialization of activities is equally important. The only difference lies in the fact that such activities as producing, warehousing, buying, selling, and transportation are specialized within the same organization. Just as a channel of independents cannot cooperate without specialization, so a channel of separate organizational divisions cannot cooperate without specialization. Thus, specialization is essential to the existence of cooperation in any channel of distribution.

Third, there is *subordination* in that individual firms must bow to the leader's wishes for cooperation to exist. There must be some final authority to set policy, settle differences, and allocate rewards. Seldom is there cooperation among equals for more than an instant in time unless some member assumes leadership over each decision. This situation does exist in marketing channels where there is no permanent leader.

Fourth, there is *recognition of common objectives.* Cooperation requires the integration of individual firm goals to the broader interests of the team.[9] Channel cooperation is not possible as long as each institution follows its own interests without regard to the needs of the other members. This does not mean that the individual firms cannot have their own goals or objectives; such private goals must complement the overall goals of the channel or the private goal must demur anytime it comes into direct conflict with the overall channel goal. Cooperation is always directed at something specific. That is, it is not random activity, but aims at a specific goal recognized by all channel institutions comprising a single team. The goal can be profit, survival, market share, competitive strength, sales volume, or some other objective.

Types of Cooperative Channel Activities

There are a great many more types of cooperative activities between the members of a marketing channel than we sometimes recognize. A tendency exists to think of cooperation primarily in terms of discounts, factory training, advertising allowances, and credit. The opportunities are far greater as E. B. Weiss demonstrates in Table 18–1. Not all of these types of cooperation are used in every channel of distribution and, indeed,

[9] Alderson, *op. cit.*, pp. 244–58.

Table 18-1   Types of Channel Cooperation

1. Cooperative advertising allowances
2. Payments for interior displays including shelf-extender, dump displays, "A" locations, aisle displays, etc.
3. P. M.'s for salespeople
4. Contests for buyers, salespeople, etc.
5. Allowances for a variety of warehousing functions
6. Payments for window display space, plus installation costs
7. Detail men who check inventory, put up stock, set up complete promotion, etc.
8. Demonstrators
9. On certain canned foods a "swell" allowance
10. Label allowance
11. Coupon handling allowance
12. Free goods
13. Guaranteed sales
14. In-store and window display material
15. Local research work
16. Mail-in premium offers to consumer
17. Preticketing
18. Automatic reorder systems
19. Delivery costs to individual stores of large retailers
20. Studies of innumerable types, such as studies of merchandise management accounting
21. Payments for mailing to store lists
22. Liberal return privileges
23. Contributions to favorite charities for store personnel
24. Contributions to special anniversaries
25. Prizes, etc., to store buyers when visiting showrooms—plus entertainment, of course
26. Training retail salespeople
27. Payments for store fixtures
28. Payments for new store cost or improvements
29. An infinite variety of promotion allowances
30. Special payments for exclusive franchises
31. Payments of part of salary of retail salespeople
32. Deals of innumerable types
33. Time spent in actual selling on retail floor by manufacturer's salesmen
34. Inventory price adjustments
35. Store name mention in manufacturer's advertising

Source: Edward B. Weiss, "How Much of a Retailer Is the Manufacturer," *Advertising Age*, Vol. 29 (July 21, 1958), p. 68.

the evidence is that very few are employed in most channels. They are all available, and the possible combination of types of cooperative activity is almost infinite. Some channels use a wide variety of these cooperative devices. As a general rule, one finds more different types of cooperative activities used in (1) short channels and (2) contractually integrated channels. However, several types of cooperation can be in effect between any two channel members, such as a wholesaler and a retailer, even when cooperative types are generally employed throughout the channel as a whole.

Recognition of Uncooperative Channel Members

It is difficult for the channel leader to recognize uncooperative channel members, but there are clues if the leader seeks them. The initial evidence can be found in an examination of the member's performance records. When a wholesaler or retailer has a low volume of sales or low revenue compared to similar firms in the channel, the leader knows his products are not being effectively promoted. Most manufacturers can determine this information from shipments of goods or from order forms. Where the initial examination shows up suspected uncooperative activity, the channel manager can have his salesman make a call to observe the middleman's operations. The salesman can gain substantial information by observing whether his firm's products have favorable display space, how the products are priced, whether the products have more or less total space than competitor's products. He can also observe the use of the product in feature displays.

The attitude of both the dealer's salesmen and the management of the store can be ascertained during the course of normal conversations by the manufacturer's representative. Any indifference or belligerence can be carefully noted. It is also possible for the manufacturer's salesman to obtain other information. He may be able to discover the middleman's attitude toward competing products. If the salesman is good, he may obtain some notion of the things that are causing problems with the middleman's attitude. The channel manager can follow up the salesman with a personal visit of his own if he needs more information. Personal visits by management are usually undertaken only in the case of important middlemen or unusual circumstances. Such visits serve two purposes. First, the management of the retail or wholesale operation may be willing to open up concerning problems or grievances held against the leader. Second, the retailer is bound to attach some significance to the executive's visit. It may flatter his ego and reassure him of his store's importance to the channel leader. Thus, the visit may go a long way toward patching up the differences that may exist.

Rules for Obtaining Channel Cooperation

If it is suspected that some member or members of the channel are uncooperative, the channel leader will probably take some action to change the situation. There is no single set of rules that can guarantee obtaining channel cooperation. Each situation is unique in some respects, and each channel member responds to different stimuli. Even when the channel leader uses the best methods there is always the possibility that the member will misunderstand the leader's motive. Besides, sometimes the channel member just does not want to cooperate, and there may be little that the leader can do to change the situation. However, there are certain general rules that if followed tend to improve the opportunity for effecting channel cooperation.

First, the leader or his representative should listen to the member's problems, points, or grievances. Not only can the leader learn from listening, but the simple process of airing complaints is often good for relieving a member's tensions. Furthermore, conversation with members provides the leader with positive ammunition to use in solving the problem. Problems or tensions may be brought out that even the member was not aware of, or the member may offer specific suggestions. Second, the leader should work on the specific points of failure indicated rather than hand out general platitudes about doing good work. He should attempt to get to the heart of the problem and work on that problem. The channel manager must be willing to help, and he must demonstrate that willingness. Most middlemen do not need pep talks as much as they need advice on how to handle real problems.

Third, the leader should emphasize opportunities to cooperate. Almost any problem or point of conflict can be turned to advantage if approached in a positive manner. An effective demonstration of common interest may only be needed, or it may be necessary for the leader to offer some concession or suggest some new method of cooperation between the two that can overcome the common problem. For example, if the dealer is having difficulty promoting the product, the leader may suggest advice from someone in the leader's advertising department. If the problem is promotional cost, the leader may offer to help defer advertising cost on his product. If the problem is a lack of understanding of the product qualities, someone from the sales department can demonstrate product performance. Fourth, the leader should reassure the channel member concerning his importance to the leader and to the channel of distribution. Praise for a job well done and reassurance of worth are generally appreciated by everyone, and the channel member is no exception. This point alone is often sufficient to achieve at least the willingness to try to work out problems, if not cooperation ultimately. It may require nothing more than a letter or a word from the salesman. Sometimes financial reward, letters of merit, plaques, or trophies, etc., are used to show appreciation for a job well done.

MOTIVATION OF THE CHANNEL TEAM

Channel motivation is a higher level of coordinated channel effort than cooperation, and the problems of achieving a motivated team effort are somewhat different from those of achieving cooperation. Every single thing that the channel leader does, including the manner of correspondence, the way he talks, and the way salesmen dress, has some effect on the channel member's enthusiasm for his work. Therefore, the problem of creating enthusiasm is never ending and involves all interactions within the channel. Three characteristics of human motivation can be applied to motivation within the marketing channel. First, motivation is an actuator of ability. It is this factor that makes it so important for the channel leader to find the means to keep the membership motivated. Business management that lacks motivation is a business management that is not thinking. A business with opportunity and ability but no motivation cannot perform near its peak. Much of the firm's talent will simply go to waste, and competition is better able to take advantage of the lapses.

Second, high motivation means high morale. The two are inseparable. It is difficult to conceive of a motivated business that does not have high morale, even when the motivation is forced. It is something like the boy whose father makes him dig the flower bed upon threat of a spanking, but who becomes caught up in the enthusiasm of the digging. He becomes motivated from sheer delight of the task. This same feeling of being caught up in the excitement of introducing a new product, putting into effect a different promotional campaign, and creating a new concept for a product can cause high motivation.

Third, motivation is difficult to sustain. It tends to flow and ebb with time, type of work, situation, and the management's mental state. Even the most interesting task has its boring aspects and the challenge of conquest decreases as the task is mastered and becomes routine. Thus, time and circumstance of work tend to diminish management's enthusiasm. Managers become distracted by new and more interesting situations. A considerable amount of variation in channel performance can be explained by the difficulty of sustaining and coordinating motivation among institutions.

The Task Is Basic to Channel Motivation

The work is the single most important factor involved in motivating channel members. Motivation flows basically out of the challenge of the tasks.[10] There are three considerations important in motivating channel members: (1) work must challenge the mind, (2) accomplishment must be associated with work, and (3) the work must be worthwhile.

Work Must Challenge the Mind. In order to motivate the channel member, the job must provide a challenge to his talents. That is to say,

[10] Claude S. George, Jr., *The History of Management Thought* (Englewood Cliffs, N. J.: Prentice-Hall, Inc., 1968), p. 128.

the job must be complex, difficult, and provide for some decision making.[11] Of course, the job has to be suited to the institution's abilities and the general intelligence of its management. What is complex and challenging to one institution may not be so to another. Small independent wholesalers and retailers cannot handle pricing and logistic problems as well as larger, better equipped institutions. The job should be sufficiently complex and challenging to forestall boredom. Too much specialization within the channel is bad. It leads to uninteresting, repetitious, or insignificant tasks that stifle enthusiasm and lead to minimum effort. The mind expands under challenge and becomes lethargic without it. Enthusiasm goes with challenge because it relates to the satisfaction of conquest. Where there is no challenge there is also no need to excel. Decision making accompanies challenge, and no institution is ever so low or unimportant to the team that there should not be some degree of control over how the work is done.

Accomplishment Must Be Associated with Work. To be motivated, the channel members should be provided with some complete task to perform. The personnel of a business become less enthusiastic when specialization becomes so great that they cannot see anything specific they accomplished. It is important to motivation that the business firm or individual complete a product, complete some specific part of the product, or complete some activity or operation necessary to make or distribute the product. The business requires some specific accomplishment to show for its efforts. This accomplishment is the focal point for business pride, and pride is essential to motivation.

A few years ago some automobile manufacturers found that motivation and morale decreased when workers were overspecialized. Each worker was given one simple task, such as turning the same screw on each car. These workers could point to nothing that they had made, and they took no pride in the finished car. Each worker considered his own task insignificant and unimportant. IBM discovered that productivity increased by combining tasks so that each person built a complete unit within a more complex instrument.[12] Each worker could take pride in his unit because the instrument would not work without it. This principle works the same way within the channel. For example, the channel members may be allowed to handle the complete advertising campaign on a local basis, or the local outlet of a retail store chain may be allowed to have control over all merchandise ordered for his store.

---

[11] Martin Patchen, *Participation Achievement and Involvement on the Job* (Englewood Cliffs, N. J.: Prentice-Hall, Inc., 1970), pp. 32–33.

[12] William F. Dowling, Jr. and Leonard R. Sayles, *How Managers Motivate: The Imperatives of Supervision* (New York: McGraw-Hill Book Co., Inc., 1971), pp. 31–32.

The Work Must Be Worthwhile.   The channel member must be provided with meaningful objectives if he is to be motivated. Businesses
need something around which to rally their efforts. The existence of
clear objectives provides understanding of what the challenge is and indicates the worthwhile nature of entering into the endeavor. The objectives may be in the form of performance standards, sales volume, cost
reduction, shipments, or other meaningful goals, but they must be clear,
specific, and available to the channel member.

There are two types of objectives important to motivation. They are
(1) idealistic goals and (2) realistic goals. *Idealistic goals* resemble the
carrot before the donkey. They relate to aspirations rather than expected achievement possibilities. *Realistic goals* are attainable with
reasonable good effort. Realistic goals recognize that a man, or an institution, has good and bad days, and that competitors or the environment work against achievement. Thus, the idealistic goal is reduced by
the leader to account for these factors.

As a principle, idealistic goals should be turned inward on one's self—
the channel leader. They should never be set for members because
others cannot understand the conditions surrounding achievement. For
example, a manufacturer's management may set the internal goal of producing the finest product in the industry. However, this producer cannot
set the goal for a retailer to become the finest distributor in the industry.
One of two things will happen if an idealistic goal is set for channel members. First, the institution may become discouraged because of continual
failure to achieve the goal. Second, the institution may realize that
achievement is not expected and cease to be concerned with the goal. In
either case, motivation is decreased. Realistic goals do motivate others
because they offer pride in accomplishment and good work.

This discussion does not mean that idealistic goals are unimportant,
or that they should not be used. The author feels that the greatest
motivation stems from the idealistic goals that management places on
itself, since the greatest motivation comes from within. That is the whole
point. Successful firms, like successful individuals, are self-motivating
and set higher standards for their activity than any outsider could ever
set for them. It follows that, in the channel, the leader must utilize
realistic goals in his dealings with middlemen, but set an example and
create a climate within which the middlemen can aspire to their own
standards. When properly established, realistic objectives serve as a
standard to be achieved and as a record against which performance can
be compared. In this latter sense, objectives are related directly to
control.

Remuneration Aids Motivation

Some managers feel that the only basis for motivation is monetary
reward. It is the old theory that man will do anything for money.

Some men will, but most people are motivated by a variety of things. The attitude that only money motivates is unsound, and perhaps dangerous, for the channel manager. A manufacturer who considers only monetary reward attempts to motivate the channel by the sole means of the margin, and he ignores other important motivating devices. The relationship between motivation and remuneration is much more complex than the above reasoning recognizes.

Remuneration, or profit, appears to be most important in motivating small wholesalers and retailers. These institutions barely make a sufficient return to survive, and to make a profit is an all-consuming ideal with them. There is simply no time or energy for other objectives in these small businesses. As the business achieves higher levels of profit, its effect as a motivator decreases and other factors become more important. There is a point of diminishing return on the ability of profit to motivate. Most firms seem to have in mind a level of satisfactory profit, and beyond this point profit becomes more secondary as a motivator. As profit decreases, such factors as survival, market share, industry leadership, management security, customer service, etc., become more important. We do not mean that profit is unimportant as a motivator, but we do imply that its effect varies. There is no type of business where some profit is not important as a motivator.

Environment Affects Motivation

The environment in which the work takes place has only a marginal effect on motivation. Military leaders have always known that front line troops, who face death every day, are typically easier to motivate than the rear echelon soldiers who are safe. The front line troops may be in fox holes, without proper clothing, food, or shelter while the rear guard has the best of everything. The difference in the attitude of the two groups lies in the work, not the surroundings. The front line troops have a goal which the rear echelon troops do not have. The front line troops have an important job, a challenge, and they are actively engaged in it. Furthermore, these troops know that the consequences of failure are significant. Under these circumstances the surroundings are unimportant. Workers in experimental circumstances have performed admirably under the most adverse conditions. The Hawthorne studies provide a classic example of this fact.[13] The same reasoning applies to the channel. It is not the type of store, or the intensity of the competition, or the run-down fixtures that cause a channel member to lack motivation. The problem lies in the other factors that we have discussed. Of course, other things being equal, it is nicer to work under pleasant conditions. Thus, if the other factors of channel motivation are present, the surroundings can add enthusiasm to the situation.

[13] George, op. cit., pp. 128–30.

CHANNEL POLICIES TO ACHIEVE MOTIVATION

In the previous section some general principles of channel motivation were developed. This section discusses specific policies designed to achieve high motivation among the channel membership.

Motivation Policies Related to Work

The most important policies designed to motivate channel members stem from the job. To gain motivation from the job, the channel manager must provide a basis for enthusiastic work and then adequately pay the channel member for good performance. The work basis may include such policies as providing a desirable product or brand, relinquishing some control over local promotional campaigns, or cultivating good personnel relationships between middlemen and the manufacturer's sales force. It may also mean giving the middleman more freedom to price, service, and distribute the product. Any policy that can build confidence and pride in working with the manufacturer's product can help build enthusiasm within the channel. The channel manager can build cooperation based on remuneration in two ways. One is to make sure that the middleman obtains a fair, honest margin. The leader may even undertake to sell the middleman on this fact. The other is to develop as many extras in the form of specials, discounts, allowances, etc., as possible to add to the middleman's income. The gaining of remuneration satisfaction is primarily a payment problem.

Organizational Policies

The organization of the channel provides rules important to acquiring motivation from the channel members. Individuals and organizations function better when they know where they stand. The channel leader should work for a clear chain of command, workable policies, and equitable treatment of all channel members. A clear chain of command means that each member should know his position in the channel and how he relates to other members. For example, a wholesaler should know whether the manufacturer is going to encourage retailers to bypass him. A retailer should know whether there are specials or deals that he might qualify for with better effort. Each channel member should be informed of what the manufacturer's policies are and the manner in which they are to be applied. Equitable treatment is particularly important here. The organization should take full advantage of the abilities of its membership and this is especially true in integrated channels. The chain stores ran into difficulty with their retail operations because these outlets were traditionally considered only sales units. The managers had little or no authority over such decisions as product price, inventory width and depth, specific products to carry, service standards, etc. Chains are finding that such authority is better decentralized because it develops better managers, greater pride, and improved efficiency.

Communication Policies

Communication policies for gaining motivation of channel participants include providing information on policies, issues, problems, solutions, and plans to the extent feasible. They also include building confidence and trust among members, relating member duties to the overall channel objective, and encouraging honest, clear feedback. The provision for effective channel communications is as much an attitude as anything else. The channel leader who wants to communicate will observe situations where communication can help, and he will take the necessary steps to inform the membership about these situations. A leader who is uninterested in his membership does not find many opportunities to communicate.

Goal identification is a particularly difficult task in any channel, and it requires constant attention. The members get involved in their own problems and tend to forget how their activities are related to the group. Retailers and wholesalers often fail to realize that there is help available from the leader if they call on him. Communications are used to obtain motivation not only by informing but by inquiring about problems, reminding of the goal, praising good effort, and suggesting changes.

JOINT COOPERATION AND MOTIVATION IN CHANNELS

The point was made earlier that the highest level of coordination within the channel of distribution occurs when cooperation and motivation are both present. While this statement is true, it is in some respects an oversimplification, since it assumes a high degree of both cooperation and motivation to achieve channel objectives.

Types of Channel Cooperation and Motivation

There may be a natural tendency on the part of the reader to assume that cooperation and motivation occur simultaneously within the channel of distribution. The facts of the situation are different as we shall demonstate at this time. Channel member cooperation and member motivation have points in common as well as differences. They are alike in that both cooperation and motivation involve the attitudes of business managers that affect the operation of the channel. They are different in what these attitudes are directed toward. Cooperation involves the attitude a marketing institution takes toward related institutions. Motivation involves an attitude that the marketing firm takes toward the performance of channel operations. Either or both may be present within the channel.

The following four types of combination of cooperation and motivation can occur in the marketing channel.

1. Cooperative   — Motivated
2. Uncooperative   — Motivated
3. Cooperative   — Unmotivated
4. Uncooperative   — Unmotivated

In the first case there is a harmony of interest in the channel and high performance. This is the best condition for the channel. It is perhaps more nearly approached in fully integrated or contractually integrated channels. In the second situation there is a lack of harmony within the channel but high performance by members. Actually, this may or may not be a bad situation. When it occurs in loosely structured long channels, such as found in the hardware, canned food, or basic grain industries, it may work fine. While there is not much cooperation, each separate member does have a high level of performance. Many channels that employ wholesalers fit this description. Of course, if a close relationship among members is required, the high motivation may not be sufficient to offset the lack of cooperation.

In the third case there is harmony in the channel but low performance levels. This situation is generally not as desirable as the second one. The channel members cooperate but, due to poor leadership, poor selection of members, or poor aptitude, they are just not very good at their assigned tasks. The channel may get along, even show profits, but it is not reaching its potential. The chances of failure for individual members or the channel as a whole are great. In the fourth case, there is a lack of harmony and low performance levels. This channel is the most undesirable. It probably cannot exist except in the short run, although the condition may occur when a channel is undergoing change or when a new alternative channel is developing.

Coordination and Motivation Continuum

Not only do coordination and motivation occur in various combinations within marketing channels, but there are degrees in their occurrence. Cooperation and motivation can each be viewed as forming a continuum as shown in Figure 18–1. In a given channel, at a given point in time, one may find high, medium, or low cooperation, and the same reasoning applies to motivation.[14] The ends of the continuum are taken to be

[14] Keith Davis, "Group Behavior and the Organization Chart," *Advanced Management—Office Executive*, Vol. 6 (June, 1962).

Fig. 18–1.   Coordination and motivation continuum.

theoretical extremes that are probably not found in the real world. Seldom, if ever, are the members of a channel in either complete agreement or complete disagreement on either cooperation or motivation, and to find complete agreement on the two in combination staggers the imagination.

A more normal situation is for the channel members to display some coordination while agreeing to disagree to some extent on either or both cooperation and motivation.   At least five channel situations are possible. First, institutions may substantially agree on all important and unimportant points of cooperation and motivation most of the time, but have a measure of disagreement on each type some of the time.   Second, institutions may substantially disagree on all important and unimportant points of cooperation and motivation most of the time, but possess a small degree of agreement on each some of the time.   Third, institutions may substantially agree on major issues of cooperation and motivation, but disagree on minor issues of each.   Fourth, institutions may substantially disagree on major issues, but substantially agree on minor issues of cooperation and motivation.   Fifth, on any issue, important or unimportant, the channel members may be more or less in agreement on cooperation and motivation.

The following is a fairly typical situation in a marketing channel.   A large discount retailer may want a reduced cost price from the manufacturer which the manufacturer does not want to give.   In this case, the two parties are not likely to break up the channel.   They continue to cooperate substantially, but the retailer has a low degree of motivation to perform.   Another example occurs when a wholesaler and manufacturer have very little in common and engage in practically no cooperation, but the wholesaler has a highly motivated sales force that does a good job of pushing the manufacturer's line nevertheless.

Throughout this chapter, cooperation and motivation have been treated in the positive sense of working within the structure of the team to achieve common goals.   Therefore, there may be a tendency on the part of the reader to assume that motivation is more compatible with cooperation than with conflict.   This assumption would be incorrect.   While conflict is opposition within the channel and cooperation is harmony, motivation can refer to the skill and enthusiasm a channel member applies to either of the other two.   Thus, a channel member may be just as highly motivated to oppose policy, obstruct goals, or circumvent marketing functions as another channel member is motivated to cooperate on these goals, policies, and functions. There have been instances when the all-consuming hatred by a wholesaler for the manufacturer consumed so much energy that the wholesaler went bankrupt in the process of attempting to destroy the manufacturer. There is evidence that in some instances a burning hatred is more easily sustained than a desire to cooperate. In any event, conflict can be highly motivated.

IDENTIFICATION OF COORDINATED CHANNELS

The problems associated with channel coordination are difficult to deal with, and they are never completely solved. Leadership is therefore a constant necessity in the marketing channel. To achieve highly motivated cooperation among the institutions that comprise the channel team requires the leader's constant attention. However, there are certain characteristics that tend to identify a coordinated channel of distribution. First, there is team loyalty. A channel tends to be coordinated when the members stand for the leader, and when everyone stands together against all outsiders. Second, there is agreement on major channel objectives. There may be all kinds of minor irritation, even a major one or two, but a channel tends to be coordinated when the members recognize, support and identify with the broad goals of the group. Third, there is disciplined behavior. This consideration means that leader and members alike use temperance, tact, and moderation in all their relationships. It does not mean that there can be no disagreement, force, or hard bargaining within the team, but that opposition, like cooperation, is thought out, applied only when necessary, and only to the proper degree. Fourth, there is pride in workmanship. A coordinated channel tends to be one where everyone takes pride in their specialty. They know its importance to the entire operation. Fifth, there is satisfaction with rewards. Coordination is always more likely when channel members know that their efforts are appreciated.

QUESTIONS

1. Discuss how involuntary cooperation can exist and describe some representative examples.
2. Discuss the possible relationships between channel conflict, cooperation, and motivation and describe an ideal environment using these variables.
3. Explain why team members fail to perform and give examples of the different reasons.
4. Make up a list of possible methods of channel cooperation for a purchase you recently made.

5. How does the channel leader recognize uncooperative channel members and what can he do to correct the situation?
6. What must the channel leader do to motivate and gain cooperation from his channel team?
7. What effect does environment have on motivation?
8. What organizational policies should the channel leader strive for to gain additional motivation from his channel members?
9. A highly motivated channel has certain characteristics. What are they and how do they aid channel cooperation?
10. In a retailer led channel what motivational methods can be used?

19

Control of Team Effort in Marketing Channels

There is no subject concerning the management of marketing channels that is more important than control, for without it there is no way to regulate the performance of the various members of the team, and no sound basis for taking corrective action where needed. Control is important to all leadership activity concerning the interrelationships of behavioral institutions. It has a bearing on the management of conflict as well as the management of cooperation and motivation.

CONCEPT OF CHANNEL CONTROL

The subject of channel control logically begins with a discussion of what is meant by control since the term does not have the same connotation to everyone. Although there are variations in the statements among scholars as to what constitutes control, there is general agreement that control involves some type of regulation of behavior or performance. The channel manager requires a broad definition of control that meets the realities of his management situation. With these two points in mind, the following definition of channel control is used. *Channel control is the process by which actual performance by members is brought into reasonable conformity with desired member performance.*[1] This definition recognizes that control is regulatory, it applies to institutions, and it concerns the performance of the management of the marketing institutions.

[1] Adapted from: Philip Kotler, *Marketing Management,* 2nd ed. (Englewood Cliffs, N. J.: Prentice-Hall, Inc., 1972), p. 752.

The *unit of control* refers to the lowest common denominator to which control is applied. Of course, this unit depends on the type of organization to which it is applied. In general management, the unit of control is the individual. Within a single marketing organization, the unit of control may be departments, product lines, or territories. The unit of control for a complete behavioral team, such as the marketing channel, is the institution or business. This chapter concerns control of the collective management of business firms comprising the marketing channel.

Channel control relates to the manner in which the management of marketing institutions performs its tasks. However, it is too much to expect that actual performance and expected performance can be made to conform exactly. Control is a concept that necessarily involves an understanding of tolerances. Howard points out that behavioral control is similar to quality control in production.[2] If you desire a casting 3.0″ in diameter but the machine is not capable of producing this diameter consistently, you may have to settle for less than perfection. Tolerances between 2.99″ and 3.01″ may be established as satisfactory, and only castings beyond these limits are rejected. It is the same with human performance. Managers are limited by their talent, the situation, etc., but their performance is acceptable so long as it lies within reasonable tolerances of the ideal.

Human or Functional Control in Channels

Among the members of a behavioral team, control can be viewed as applying to human activity or to functions performed. It may be argued that ultimately only people can be controlled because only people can think and respond. However, this position seems to avoid the real issue of control, because people perform activities. The position taken in this book is that control is regulation, and, as such, it can be applied to either people or functions.

In a practical sense, every channel manager knows that sometimes the focus of his attention is on how channel members behave relative to each other, and sometimes his attention is directed at how well each channel member performs his specific duties. It is a matter of whether the emphasis of decision making lies with regulating the human relations or the physical performance. In one real sense, the two are inseparable. For example, the data supplied by the information system can be used as the basis for evaluating a channel member's physical performance relative to other channel members.

The manner of handling control does differ in some important respects when interaction is emphasized rather than functions. In human control,

---

[2] John A. Howard, *Marketing Management*, rev. ed. (Homewood, Ill.: Richard D. Irwin, Inc., 1963), pp. 12–13.

all the emotional techniques of persuasion, reward, and sanctions apply, but in functional control, the techniques are basically mechanical. These techniques involve records, budgets, reports, and audits designed to spot deviations in performance and to suggest possible corrective action.

In this chapter the emphasis is on human control, and it includes the basic interrelationships involved with conflict, cooperation, and motivation discussed in the previous chapters. This discussion brings together the final element of achieving coordination of the marketing channel. Performance of specific activities is introduced to the extent that these activities aid in explaining the control of business attitude or relationships.

Control Sequence and Management Functions

Although there is some agreement among scholars concerning the basic requirement of control, there is less agreement on where control occurs as a part of the management process. Table 19–1 can aid in clarifying this problem. The marketing function of sales management was selected for the illustration because a function is simpler to deal with than an institutional relationship. However, the sales illustration is equally representative of other functions or for the control of member interrelationships.

The historical, and perhaps popular point of view, is that control is the final function of management. The logic of this position rests on the view that management is a process which includes the following sequence: (1) planning, (2) organizing, (3) directing, and (4) controlling.[3] This position is shown on the left side of the table. Management is considered to be pervasive by this view but only because every human activity requires the four steps. The steps themselves are considered to be mutually exclusive of each other. The point of view of a sequence of management steps has merit when describing a specific operation such as sales management. As the table shows, sales management necessitates plans about what to do, organization abilities to get the job done, direction of performance, and the control of results. It is illogical to think that one could direct the sales force before plans were made and the organization provided for. Thus, control is a logical last step in the management process necessary to perform sales management.

There is another position, less popular, concerning the placement of control in management. This view holds that the management functions are not only pervasive to all operations, but are actually pervasive to each other as well.[4] Each function, such as making plans or control, requires

[3] Edwin B. Flippo, *Management: A Behavioral Approach* (Boston: Allyn and Bacon, Inc., 1970), pp. 4–7; Claude S. George, Jr., *The History of Management Thought* (Englewood Cliffs, N. J.: Prentice-Hall, Inc., 1968), pp. 145–46.

[4] George, *op. cit.*, p. 164.

Table 19-1   Management Functions Viewed As Steps in a Process and as Pervasive Activities

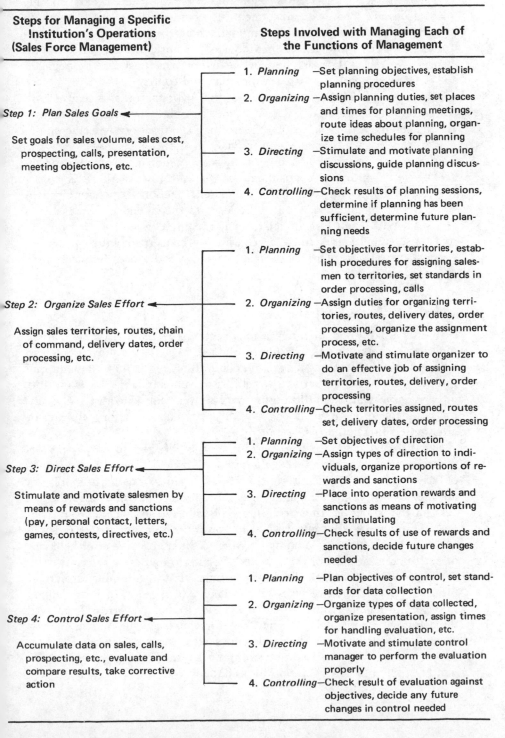

Steps for Managing a Specific Institution's Operations (Sales Force Management)	Steps Involved with Managing Each of the Functions of Management
Step 1: Plan Sales Goals Set goals for sales volume, sales cost, prospecting, calls, presentation, meeting objections, etc.	1. *Planning* —Set planning objectives, establish planning procedures 2. *Organizing* —Assign planning duties, set places and times for planning meetings, route ideas about planning, organize time schedules for planning 3. *Directing* —Stimulate and motivate planning discussions, guide planning discussions 4. *Controlling* —Check results of planning sessions, determine if planning has been sufficient, determine future planning needs
Step 2: Organize Sales Effort Assign sales territories, routes, chain of command, delivery dates, order processing, etc.	1. *Planning* —Set objectives for territories, establish procedures for assigning salesmen to territories, set standards in order processing, calls 2. *Organizing* —Assign duties for organizing territories, routes, delivery dates, order processing, organize the assignment process, etc. 3. *Directing* —Motivate and stimulate organizer to do an effective job of assigning territories, routes, delivery, order processing 4. *Controlling* —Check territories assigned, routes set, delivery dates, order processing
Step 3: Direct Sales Effort Stimulate and motivate salesmen by means of rewards and sanctions (pay, personal contact, letters, games, contests, directives, etc.)	1. *Planning* —Set objectives of direction 2. *Organizing* —Assign types of direction to individuals, organize proportions of rewards and sanctions 3. *Directing* —Place into operation rewards and sanctions as means of motivating and stimulating 4. *Controlling* —Check results of use of rewards and sanctions, decide future changes needed
Step 4: Control Sales Effort Accumulate data on sales, calls, prospecting, etc., evaluate and compare results, take corrective action	1. *Planning* —Plan objectives of control, set standards for data collection 2. *Organizing* —Organize types of data collected, organize presentation, assign times for handling evaluation, etc. 3. *Directing* —Motivate and stimulate control manager to perform the evaluation properly 4. *Controlling* —Check result of evaluation against objectives, decide any future changes in control needed

the performance of all the other functions of management. This position is demonstrated on the right side of the table. In order to make specific plans necessary for sales management, it becomes necessary to engage in the management functions of planning, organizing, directing, and controlling; similarly, in order to provide a specific organization for the sales management task, the same management functions must also be engaged in. This reasoning holds true for direction and control.

There is no need to choose one position over the other because both are correct. The difference does not concern right or wrong, but whether the management function is being described as a part of a specific operation or a pervasive management activity. It is the difference between a plan or planning, providing organization or organizing, direction or directing, and control or controlling. In this latter sense there is no sequence to the performance of management functions by channel members. Such a point of view naturally leads to the conclusion that control is a valid part of all human relationships in the channel of distribution, and the channel leader must be continually concerned with controlling channel operations. This latter point of view is the one emphasized in this chapter.

Locus of Channel Control

It was established in the previous section that control is regulation, and that it occurs in no particular sequence. A convict's movements can be regulated by attaching a ball and chain to his leg *before* allowing him outside, by placing a guard to watch his movements *while* he is outside, or by *rehabilitating* his attitude toward future attempts to run away. By the same token, channel managers can apply control before, during, or after actual functional performance.

Control that occurs before performance is referred to as *pre-performance control.* Such control seeks to condition performance in advance of the actual activity. The term condition is used to mean: to modify in advance of, to pre-affect; condition is a requirement before performance. Control that occurs during performance is referred to as *concurrent control.* This method of control seeks to constrain performance as it is occurring. Constrain is defined as: to rule, to direct, or to restrict behavior or performance. Control that occurs after performance is referred to as *post-performance control.* Post-performance control attempts to correct behavior or performance after occurrence. The term correct is defined to mean: to change from wrong to right or to remove errors from. All three types of control have relevance for the leader in managing the channel of distribution. The leader does not merely select one point in the performance of some activity to apply control; control must be constantly applied in the operation of a channel.

TYPES OF CHANNEL CONTROL

A channel manager is called upon to make several decisions that relate to types of channel control. For example, the leader wants to know whether he can use formal or informal control, positive or negative control, centralized or decentralized control, and partial or complete control. The type of control varies for different channel members and in different situations. The manager's task is made easier if he knows, in advance, the implications of the control types whose use he is contemplating.

Formal and Informal Control

The control of marketing channels may be highly formal or very informal. *Formal control* means that standards of performance, the means to achieve this performance, and consequences are clearly established, usually in such written form as directives, budgets, reports, and memoranda. *Informal control* is usually personal and highly subjective. With informal control, the regulation is based on casual observation or regular daily contact. The individual channel member is more or less expected to do his job; the leader simply puts in a good word or a point of criticism from time to time. Very little is written down. Formal control is more associated with large, complex, integrated channels of distribution. Informal control is typically used with channels displaying wholesalers or agents and those in which the administration of sales effort is not crucial.

Positive and Negative Control

Positive control is reward-oriented and designed to help the channel member by concentrating on benefits that result from improvement in performance.[5] *Negative control* is sanction-oriented and concentrates on the consequences of poor performance. Either type of control can be effective, and either type may be indicated. The managers of some institutions simply do not respond to positive attempts to help, but positive control is generally preferred over negative control. Many managements respond more readily to help and understanding than to criticism. In actual practice, more managements respond best to a combination of positive and negative control, and the two types of control are used jointly. In applying positive or negative control, the channel leader must think of himself as a teacher. He must point out mistakes, but the emphasis should be on demonstrating how to avoid these mistakes in the future and how to improve productivity and profitability to the benefit of the entire channel.

---

[5] William F. Dowling, Jr., and Leonard R. Sayles, *How Managers Motivate: The Imperatives of Supervision* (New York: McGraw-Hill Book Co., Inc., 1971), pp. 176–77.

Centralized and Decentralized Control

Centralized control, in a channel of distribution, means that the leader institution retains all regulatory authority. Control flows directly from the leader to all the individual wholesalers and retailers. *Decentralized control* refers to a situation where the channel leader delegates regulation. This delegation is to the management of operating divisions within a single company or to individual channel members. Decentralized control very much resembles what we refer to as self-control. It means that each individual division of an integrated business, or each independent channel member in non-integrated channels is basically responsible for its own actions. There is little regulation from above, and the channel leader exerts only gentle guidance.

Centralized control tends to concentrate power in the channel leader. There is very little chance for individual member initiative and all performance is strictly accountable. Decentralized control tends toward informality and places a high premium on individual initiative. Centralized control is more likely to occur where the channel is highly integrated, or there is strong manufacturer brand identification, or where the leader faces little competition in administering the channel. Decentralized control tends to occur in longer channels, where there are many essentially similar products, or where the products are convenience goods, or where more than one institution in the channel has power and aspires to be the channel leader.

Partial and Complete Control

Partial control should not be confused with ineffective control. *Partial control* simply means that control is not all-encompassing on the member institution. There are many instances within a channel of distribution where partial control is desirable and quite effective. Any time the leader of the channel delegates authority over pricing, service, or other channel activities, he surrenders some of his ability to regulate overall relationships with that channel member. A delegation simply makes the member more independent, and independence in one area is likely to have its effect in other areas as well. Even so, the delegation may be very worthwhile because of its effects on the member's attitude or because of the overall effect on cost or profits. It should be clear that there is a close relationship between the amount of control and the amount of centralization in the channel.

Very seldom can a channel leader affect *complete control.* Where complete control occurs it is most likely to be associated with either complete ownership of the several stages of the channel or a very tight legal arrangement such as franchising. Partial control, of course, varies all the

way from nearly complete control to practically no control at all. Therefore, partial control is associated with a variety of channel situations.

Interaction of Types of Control

Typically, the manager of a channel of distribution uses more than one
type of channel control simultaneously. For example, one might use formal, positive, centralized control or informal, positive, decentralized control. The type of control varies over time. The channel leader may be
quite formal at one time, say under conditions of high competitive stress,
and rather informal when competition is more typical. He may also use
different types of control on different members in the channel. For example, partial control may apply to trusted channel members but complete control may be used in others.

CONTROL PROCESS IN CHANNELS

In any situation requiring decision making, the manager is wise to follow some logical procedure; such a procedure will have two prime advantages to the decider. First, there is a far better chance that the manager will not overlook some detail that is important to the decision.
Second, following a procedure provides greater assurance that all the
factors involved in the decision receive adequate attention. The control
process is defined as a logical procedure upon which control decisions
can be based. There are several possible reasons why a manager may use
a specific type of control, and he may have only one or two of these
reasons in mind in a decision situation.[6]

1. In the role of a teacher, the channel leader needs to communicate
his likes and dislikes. The leader knows that how he feels about a firm
or a situation affects the attitude and motivation of the channel member
addressed. His task is to emphasize the correct methods while pointing
out how to deal with mistakes.

2. The channel leader needs to know where poor work requires intervention. Even as a teacher, the leader cannot allow poor performance by
a manufacturer, wholesaler, or retailer to endanger the entire channel. If
serious, it must be stopped until the problem can be isolated and the
entire process coordinated again.

3. Control provides the channel leader with necessary information to
make decisions on rewards, channel changes, member status, etc. One
must not forget that, in a real sense, much of control is simple feedback
concerning activities, performances, relationships. Such feedback is not
only useful for correction, but for making vital future decisions which

---

[6] *Ibid.*, pp. 172–74. The five reasons given are modified to meet the needs of a
channels discussion.

may affect the entire channel structure. The leader must make decisions on which members to cultivate, how to divide up rewards, which members to drop or add, how to deal with members in specific situations. All these decisions are related to control

4. The channel leader may want to tie the payment (margin) to channel control. Bonuses, premiums, gifts, etc., may be related directly to control information or performance record.

5. The channel leader uses control to spot undesirable channel trends. A close watch on the operation of various middlemen may discern bad habits, poor performance, long-run market trends, etc., that can be useful to the leader in future planning. No matter what the reason, there is clear evidence that the performance of channels is increased with control.[7] It is important for the channel leader and the membership to recognize this need. Control simply helps to take channel operation out of the realm of chance and give it purpose.

Elements of Channel Control

Control within channels of distribution can be described as a process separate from the management process. The elements of this control process are: (1) plan, (2) performance results, (3) measurements, (4) evaluation, and (5) condition behavior. The information system was concerned only with financial data, and could be easily demonstrated using the income statement. Channel control is concerned with all aspects of the relationship between manufacturers, wholesalers, retailers, and agents, and is not as readily categorized as the information system.

As Figure 19–1 shows, the elements of the control process can be grouped according to whether they are a type of data or a type of activity. Plans and results provide the basic data for channel control (placed in square boxes in Figure 19–1). Measurement, evaluation, and the conditioning of behavior are activities (these are in circles). Measurement and evaluation apply to existing plans or results, while behavior conditioning applies to future plans or results. However, the reader is reminded that the conditioning can be applied before, during, or after either the future plans or the future results. It is important to recognize that the control process can be applied anywhere in relation to the actual operation.

Plans and Results

Whether information fits the category of plans or results has absolutely nothing to do with the information itself—it is entirely a point of view. The information qualifies as *leader plans* if it relates to the future, and

---

[7] Louis P. Bucklin, "The Locus of Channel Control," *Marketing and The New Science of Planning,* Robert L. King, ed. (Chicago: American Marketing Association, 1968), pp. 142–47.

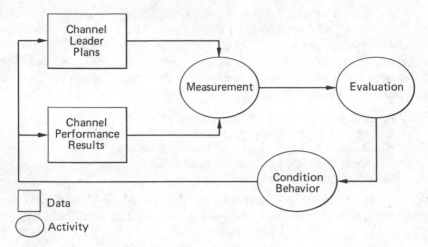

Data

Activity

Fig. 19–1. The elements of channel control. *Source:* Adapted from Ernest I. Hanson, "The Budgetary Control Function," *The Accounting Review* (April, 1966).

it qualifies as *leader results* if it relates to the past. The information should be of the same general type, and in the same general form in either case. If the type of information were not the same it would be impossible to make valid comparisons. Overall team effort in the marketing channel involves creating conformity on at least four basic factors between the leader and the membership. The leader seeks conformity on: (1) channel goals, (2) loyalty to the product line, (3) performance standards, and (4) cooperation with the leader and other members. Such conformity may not be in line with the individual channel member's needs.[8] It is never easy to acquire these types of conformity from channel members, but control is the basic tool that the leader must work with. Performance standards and loyalty to product line are quantifiable, both in the form of plans and operating results. These data can be obtained in many of the forms that we have already discussed and they include sales volume, orders, relative channel cost, dealer profit, inventories on hand, turnover, promotion expenditures, etc.

Channel goals and channel cooperation deal basically with manufacturer, retailer, and dealer attitudes, and this type of information is much more difficult to obtain because of the problems of quantification. Cox, Schutte, and Few suggest that member attitudes are as important as any other type of channel information.[9] Information on attitudes is designed

[8] Louis P. Bucklin, "A Theory of Channel Control," *Journal of Marketing*, Vol. 37 (January, 1973), p. 40.

[9] Reavis Cox, Thomas F. Schutte, and Kendrick S. Few, "Toward The Measurement of Channel Trade Perception," Fred C. Allvine, ed., *Combined Proceedings of the American Marketing Association* (Chicago: American Marketing Association, 1972), pp. 189–93.

to determine not so much what channel members did, but how they feel about policies and procedure of the leader. The leader can compare member attitudes toward his leadership to his own attitude toward his leadership that was used to plan dealer policies. Cox, Schutte, and Few list several types of information on retailer and dealer attitudes that the manufacturer should determine.

> Pricing policies, margins, and allowances
> Extent and nature of the line developed
> New products in the line and their promotion
> Servicing policies, procedures, and results
> Salesman performance

To this list can be added general attitude toward the leader and the other members; willingness to cooperate; and loyalty to the channel in general and the leader in particular.

Activities

Measurement is the first activity of the control process. In the normal sense, measurement includes not only assigning values, but classifying and summarizing the data so that it is in a proper form for evaluation. In many respects, measurement is the most difficult activity of control.[10] It is difficult enough to discover and assign values to such things as dealer attitudes, but perhaps the most difficult aspect of measurement is getting the middlemen to cooperate. Middlemen are secretive about their operations with some justification. They are afraid that either the leader will use the information against them or that the information will leak to competitors. Actually, failure to cooperate on control measurement may be symptomatic of the whole channel's management problem.

Nevertheless, depending on the channel, a considerable amount of information can be measured as a basis for establishing plans and determining results. The basic tools for measuring factual operational data are budgets, standards, accounting record, and forecasts. The methods most often used to obtain information on attitudes are questionnaires, observation, reports, and evaluation sheets.

Evaluation is the second activity of the control process. *Evaluation* is the activity where the plans and the results are brought together and compared. Differences between plans and results are noted, and reasons for these differences are sought. It may be that various factors are thought to have a bearing on the differences observed. Managers must weigh each possibility and determine the most likely causes. Thus, the activity of evaluation is essentially a thought process.

The final activity of the control process is to condition behavior. This

[10] Bucklin, "The Locus of Channel Control," *op. cit.*

action follows directly from the suggestions made in evaluation. The phrase *condition behavior* is used to include behavior modification, constraint, or corrective action as previously discussed. Behavior conditioning is an action taken that is relative to both future plans and performance results. For example, planning goals may have been set too high, and the proper conditioning may be to change future plans to make them more realistic. This need, in turn, may require finding a better method of forecasting or measurement. On the other hand, results may not have measured up to plans because of poor attitude, poor performance, or external considerations. Whatever the cause, methods of affecting behavior during or after the next performance must be discovered and applied. The reader should notice that the application of behavior conditioning actually begins the entire control process over again. This is true because the results of conditioning must be checked in the next cycle. A realistic channel's manager recognizes that control is an endless task—as soon as he gets one problem corrected, another shows up.

METHODS OF CONTROLLING TEAM EFFORT

Relationships among the team tend to revolve around the leader. Everyone in the channel may identify with the leader, but not everyone in the channel identifies with each other. For this reason, the more important channel attitudes and relationships are the ones that exist between the leader and the individual manufacturers, wholesalers, retailers, and agents.

Pre-Performance Control

The idea of pre-performance control is to create a condition, or an atmosphere, in which the manufacturer, wholesaler, or retailer wants to perform in accordance with the leader's wishes. The leader regulates by making the prospect of conformity more desirable than any other prospect. There are several methods available to the channel leader for accomplishing this end. They include the following: (1) use of brand; (2) franchising; (3) dealer service such as factory training, advice, credit, etc.; and (4) establishment of quotas. All of these decisions can be made before the product is sold to middlemen. Pre-performance control tends to be reward-oriented, although this is not true in every case. It is true that service to dealers can occur on a rotating basis concurrent with operations, but the knowledge that certain help will be forthcoming from the leader is a factor of control even when unnecessary.

If the leader can establish a strong brand image with customers—very often before actual physical distribution—then it becomes more desirable for the middleman to push that brand than to push some other brand. It is partly a matter of easier selling and partly a matter of greater profit. Thus, the leader obtains goal identification, brand loyalty, and high performance standards at the same time. The leader may even get improved cooperation among dealers because they each see the brand as desirable. The same type of control can be obtained with the other four methods. The franchising agreement usually includes types of operating policies and acceptable performance standards on these policies.[11] Franchising also creates a close bond between the franchisor and franchisee. The leader, by raising or lowering the margin, can make future sales effort more or less desirable, while quotas establish standards in advance of the performance to be obtained. Quotas typically accompany franchising. The manipulation of margin affects the member's profit position and thus his attitude toward the leader's desires. Generally, the higher the margin, the more willing the member is to cooperate.

Concurrent Control Decisions

Concurrent control decisions relate to constraint. This type of control occurs simultaneously with behavior, and it is designed to perpetuate a favorable attitude toward desired behavior. Concurrent control decisions involve: (1) persuasion, (2) threat, (3) coercion. (4) promotion, (5) deals and extras, and (6) margin. The factors of concurrent control utilize both rewards and sanctions. Most of these control devices can also be used in advance of performance, as when persuasion is used to get a dealer to adopt a new product, but each is more associated with continuing performance.

Persuasion is the same as salesmanship, but it is used to refer to selling a favorable attitude toward the leader's wishes, not to selling products. The leader can attempt to convince the middleman of the high quality of the product, its selling ease, the favorable margin, or the cooperative backup given the middleman's efforts. If the middleman is convinced, then he sees the advantage of performing in the manner desired by the leader, and the leader achieves his desired conformity of goals, loyalty, standards, and cooperation.

The use of threat on the middleman can be equally effective, but the leader must have a sound basis for making the threat. Furthermore, the leader must stand ready to back up any threats made. The leader can threaten to take away the middleman's brand, reduce or eliminate services, reduce margin, eliminate exclusive arrangements, reduce or eliminate extras. Of course, the effectiveness of the threat depends upon the

[11] Bert C. McCammon, Jr., and Albert D. Bates, "The Emergence and Growth of Contractually Integrated Channels in the American Economy," *Economic Growth, Competition and World Markets,* P. D. Bennett, ed. (Chicago: American Marketing Association, 1965), pp. 496–515.

value which the middleman assigns to the above. Coercion is a type of threat based on power.

Promotion is a powerful method of regulating channel performance. The decision by the leader to increase or decrease promotion has a direct effect on sales and the middleman's profits. The cost of promotion is always a problem for middlemen; therefore, a decision by the leader to introduce cooperative advertising can be significant in obtaining desired performance. Promotion is also a powerful tool for building customer preference, a preference that affects branding mentioned in the previous section.

Deals and extras are also methods of obtaining concurrent regulation. Deals and extras in the form of price concessions for purchasing special or odd lot merchandise, the 13 unit dozen, quantity discounts, bonuses, etc., have about the same effect on the dealer as service. Contests and competition among middlemen are often used with deals and prices as the reward for good performance. All of these methods encourage conformity in order not to miss out on the concession. The manipulation of margin affects the channel member's profit position and thus his attitude toward the leader's desires. Margin is an important reward in any marketing channel. Generally, the higher the margin, the more willing the wholesaler or retailer is to follow the leader's wishes in other policy matters. The threat to change margin can be considered a pre-performance control device, since the member may conform to the leader's wishes to keep the margin high.

Post-Performance Control Decisions

Post-performance control is the most widely discussed control; it is correction-oriented and applies directly to past performance. Once the performance has been determined to be faulty or inappropriate, corrections are introduced. The basic tool of post-performance control is retraining. The retraining can be formal or informal. In most instances it is informal and may involve nothing more than having the team leader point out the mistake or perhaps suggest a different or better way to perform a task. Formal training may take considerable time and employ all the tools of teaching, even to setting up classrooms. The retraining of salesmen at schools operated by the personnel department fits this description. Salesmen are often retrained to correct faulty patterns of presentation that develop over time.

The concurrent methods of control, particularly persuasion and threat, may be used for post-performance control. The difference lies in the point of their application. If persuasion or threat are applied during an activity or operation, they are concurrent control, but if they are applied after the operation is completed they are post-performance control.

When applied after, persuasion and threat are used less to correct action and more to affect the attitude toward correction.

CHANNEL CONTROL AND CHANNEL TYPE

There is no way that the author can prescribe which type or types of control are most appropriate to specific marketing channels. The conditions are simply too varied, and even where the same type of channel is used, different controls may be effective. However, some generalizations helpful in guiding the manager with control decisions can be made by relating the methods of control to particular types of marketing channels.

Gravity Channels

A gravity channel is one in which the entire channel operates automatically on the basis of consumer demand. The assumption is that consumers have wants, and they know both what their wants are and how to satisfy them. There is no need for retailers to take any action to attract these consumers. When the consumer purchases, this action depletes retailer stocks and causes the retailer to purchase from wholesalers. The retailer must place orders or he will soon run out of merchandise. The wholesaler's stock is, in turn, depleted by the purchases of the retailer, and this middleman must place orders with the manufacturer. The orders of wholesalers deplete manufacturers' stocks, setting into operation the production necessary to maintain manufacturer inventory levels. The manufacturer initiates the necessary shipments that replace the shortages beginning to occur throughout the channel.

Just as gravity causes the water to flow downhill, so consumer demand causes products to flow through the channel. No action, in the form of promotion, branding, personal selling, or service, is necessary to cause the products to move. Thus, in a gravity channel there is no need for marketing strategy, and no need for channel control. The concept of a gravity channel is reminiscent of pure competition that operates by means of the unseen hand. This type of channel may be approached in the case of some raw materials and unbranded farm products, but it has little relevance to the real world where consumers often do not know what they want or where to satisfy the wants of which they are aware.

Suction Channels

Suction-type channels, sometimes referred to as pull channels, are similar to gravity channels because consumer demand pulls products through the channel by depleting, in order, retailer, wholesaler, and manufacturer inventories.[12] The difference lies in the fact that consumer purchases are not left to chance. The channel leader, or other members of the channel, uses specific strategy to control consumer demand. Figure 19–2 demonstrates the flow of control in a suction channel. However,

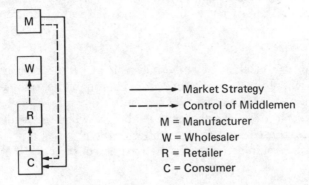

Fig. 19–2.   Suction channel (indirect control).

in a suction channel it is characteristic for all strategy to be directed at the final consumer. At no time is the manufacturer's strategy directed at middlemen. Some examples of the manufacturer's possible consumer strategy are presented below:

1. Brand and package—gives consumers a point of identification
2. Consumer advertising—persuades to action and reassures
3. Product quality—meets specific needs and provides psychic satisfaction
4. Price, regular or sale—induces action, makes purchase possible, and provides psychic satisfaction
5. Consumer service—adjusts product to particular consumer need
6. Warranty—provides security to consumers
7. Retail store atmosphere—personal attention, store location, exterior and interior design, store layout

It is true that no channel member is likely to include all of these factors in a suction strategy, but nevertheless they are all possibilities. One factor that makes channel strategy different among separate channels is the manner in which these factors are combined. There is no question that they can all affect the consumer's willingness to pull products through the channel. There is a direct relationship between the application of manufacturer strategy and that manufacturer's ability to control the actions of middlemen. Where strategy is directed at the

[12] Kenneth R. Davis, *Marketing Management,* 3rd ed. (New York: The Ronald Press Co., 1972), pp. 436–37.

consumer, manufacturer control is indirect, and it also flows up from the consumer. This type of control takes the general form of consumer preference for the manufacturer's products. To the extent that the manufacturer can create brand preference in the mind of consumers by his strategy, the manufacturer can regulate the actions of middlemen. These middlemen cannot afford not to carry brands desired by consumers.

Pressure Channels

A pressure type of channel, sometimes referred to as a push channel, is one in which products are forced down through the channel by the leader. Such a channel occurs when positive pressure to sell products is applied by each successive channel member, or when the leader applies direct pressure to each successive member of the channel, and all control is directed at the middlemen rather than at the consumer.[13] Figure 19–3

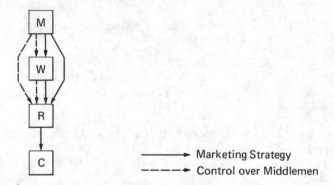

Fig. 19–3. Pressure channel (direct control).

shows the flow of strategy and control in a pressure channel. Several of the important strategy techniques associated with pressure channels are:

1. Advertising and personal selling to dealers—persuades members to the leader's wishes
2. Leader consulting—provides dealer with expertise in areas where he is deficient
3. Leader service to dealers—gains goodwill and close cooperation
4. Margin—provides incentive because of profit
5. Leader deals and extras—offers incentive
6. Contests and bonuses to dealers—provides incentive
7. Threat—forces compliance where enforceable
8. Franchising—provides direct administration of dealer operations

[13] Philip McVey, "Are Channels of Distribution What the Textbooks Say?" *Journal of Marketing*, Vol. 24 (January, 1960), pp. 61–65.

9. Quotas—places pressure to sell all units
10. Point of sales aids—helps dealers sell, fosters cooperation

As with suction policies, not all of these methods will be used, but it is obvious that there are a variety of decision areas available to stimulate middlemen to promote and sell the leader's products aggressively. When a pressure channel is used by the channel's manager, control of middlemen is direct. The manufacturer does not have to depend on goodwill by consumers in a pressure channel. To some degree, according to the techniques used, the channel's manager has direct control over middlemen's operations. The leader can specify what action he seeks from the middleman. Some specific types of control include: price control, operational conformity, submission of control data and reports to the leader, aggressive salesmanship, customer service by dealers, and adherence to the leader's policies. The pressure channel provides much more control over middlemen than does the suction channel.

Push—Pull Channels

Although there are marketing channels that can be characterized as either suction or pressure channels, most channels employ a combination of the two methods to move products.[14] The flow of strategy and control for a push–pull channel is illustrated in Figure 19–4. In practice, the

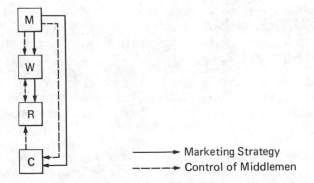

Fig. 19–4. Push-pull channel (direct and indirect control).

channel manager's decision is not whether to use suction or pressure but to determine how much of each in combination can most effectively get the job done. Thus, there can be great differences in the degree to which the two methods are combined. The automobile industry depends more on pressure while the appliance industry depends more on suction. The

[14] "Watering New Markets," *Sales Management Magazine* (September 3, 1965), pp. 29–30, 49.

combinations available to develop marketing strategy are almost infinite, and when one considers the possibilities, the real meaning of differential advantage becomes clear.

Control in the push–pull channel is both direct and indirect. Of course, the techniques used by the channel manager are the same as those described for suction and pressure channels. The combination of control techniques is more effective, but it is also more costly. There is a tendency to associate suction channels with consumer orientation and pressure channels with sales orientation but such a position seems unjustified. As we have pointed out before, an orientation exists in the mind. Any strategy or control device can be employed to benefit consumers or to benefit only the firm's short-run interests.

FACTORS AFFECTING CHANNEL CONTROL

We have considered channel control from several perspectives, and we have gained some understanding of its nature and application to marketing channels. We have also introduced specific types of control into the channel. However, we cannot leave the subject without discussing some of the important factors that influence the manager's use of control.

Leader Type

The application of control to a channel of distribution is as much affected by the type of leader as is channel conflict or cooperation and motivation.[15] Three types of leaders are generally recognized, and each has a direct bearing on control.[16]

1. *Dictatorial leadership.* This type of leader has centralized authority and controls through fear, and he depends primarily on sanctions based on power. The dictatorial leader is command-oriented, and does not allow for any discussion or participation by those led.
2. *Autocratic leadership.* Such a leader has centralized authority, but emphasizes neither rewards nor sanctions as a basis for control. The autocratic leader controls because the members must depend on him for their need satisfaction.
3. *Democratic leadership.* This type of leader utilizes decentralized authority and participation. The democratic leader controls through emphasis on reward and member identification in decision making. He generates self-motivation.

[15] S. G. Huneryager and I. L. Heckmann, *Human Relations In Management*, 2nd ed. (Cincinnati, Ohio: South-Western Publishing Co., 1967), p. 107.

[16] Robert T. Golembiewski, "Three Styles of Leadership and Their Uses," *Personnel*, Vol. 38 (July–August, 1961), pp. 34–45; Huneryager and Heckman, *op. cit.*, pp. 241–48.

Although some managers favor one type over another, there is no clear evidence that any of the three types of leaders is superior. The best leader is the one that gets the job done, and there is evidence that all three types can be successfully used. Among management scholars today, it is popular to favor democratic leadership. The appeal of this method is probably based in our historical conditioning toward the democratic process. Participation and involvement just seems so right to Americans. Unfortunately, businesses are not run by such idealistic principles, and the notion completely leaves out of consideration the ability and the desire of the membership.[17] Some channel members, such as independent retailers and cash-and-carry wholesalers are just not capable of great participation in channels management; a great many wholesalers and retailers also simply do not wish to participate. To these members, participation is a burden that distracts them from their more important responsibilities.

Leadership control must be considered within the total situation. A strong leader can often accomplish results that a democratic leader cannot. One who is clearly in command with no serious challengers has a much greater latitude of control than his opposite. A leader who understands the membership and their problems, and who is concerned about them, is more likely to exercise effective control than one who is unaware. A leader who knows when to use the "carrot" and when to use the "stick" is more prone to exercise effective control over the channel; so also is a leader who understands the entire situation in which the decision must be made. Thus, the important thing for the channel manager to remember is that his leadership is a variable of channel control just as some other factors, and it must be flexible to the needs of his constituents.

Channel Structure

Channel structure and the span of control go hand in hand. Channel structure has two aspects: (1) the number of stages (wholesaler and retailer) in the channel and (2) the number of firms at each stage.[18] Since the span of control refers to the number of institutions that the leader can effectively manage, the relationship is apparent. As a general statement, the more channel levels, the fewer the number of institutions the leader can control at each level, and vice versa. For example, one advantage of using wholesalers is that the leader can reach a large number of households by personal contact with relatively few wholesalers.

[17] William Gomberg, "The Trouble With Democratic Management," *Trans-Action* (July–August, 1966), pp. 30–36; Warren G. Bennis, "A Reply: When Democracy Works," *Trans-Action* (July–August, 1966), pp. 30–36.

[18] Davis A. Revzan, "The Structure of Wholesaling in the United States," *Wholesaling In Marketing Organization* (New York: John Wiley and Sons, Inc., 1961), Chapter 5.

Fortunately, the span of control of a channel manager is greater than the span of control over individual persons. The reason is the greater independence of action by sovereign institutions and the increased importance of self-control by these institutions. Nevertheless, the general rule is: the shorter the channel, the greater the control and the longer the channel, the less the control.[19] The same rule applies to the number of institutions managed at each stage in the channel. The greatest control is found in the channel direct from manufacturer to consumer in which there is a limited number of businesses. Where ownership of all the stages in the channel is not feasible, contractual arrangements, such as franchising, are the next best solution to maintain a favorable span of control.

Control of Middlemen

The type of middleman has a bearing on the ability to maintain channel control. Some middlemen are more independent than others, and some have greater ability than others. For example, a large wholesaler or department store has greater information for decision making than the small independent. Of course, the greater the independence the greater the self-control and the less the regulation that the channel leader can bring to bear. Generally speaking, agents are less independent than such merchants as wholesalers and retailers. These agents are, therefore, easier to control. There are, of course, exceptions to this generalization. For example, the manufacturer's agent handles the output of several principles. There is the problem of competing for his time. When the manufacturer's agent is selling other producer's products, he is not selling yours. In such a case the methods already discussed such as increased margin, persuasion, threat, and brand preference must be used on him in the same way as on a wholesaler or retailer in order to regulate his performance. Even among merchant middlemen some types are easier to control than others.[20] The middleman's size and importance are to be considered. The manufacturer can more easily control a limited-function wholesaler because of his smaller number of items and greater dependence than he can control the full-service wholesaler with his mass of products. A large retailer or a chain retailer is much more difficult to control than a small independent retailer. The difference lies in such considerations as greater economic power, specialized management talent, amount of data for decision making, etc., that the larger middleman possesses.

[19] Louis W. Stern, "The Concept of Channel Control," *Journal of Retailing* (Summer, 1967), pp. 14–20.

[20] Henry Assael, "The Political Role of the Trade Association In Distributive Conflict Resolution," *Journal of Marketing*, Vol. 32 (April, 1968), pp. 21–28.

Influence of Situation

The ability of a leader to control the channel is influenced by the type of situation. Middlemen are more willing to follow the leader's suggestions when products are in short supply, when government intervention is possible, when there are no viable alternatives, or when customers demand the manufacturer's products. Thus, while the channel member may be willing to bow to control at one time, he may be unwilling at another. For example, a retailer may agree to certain prices, service standards, or advertising campaigns. This retailer may follow the manufacturer's wishes most of the time, but fail to comply when involved in a highly competitive situation that requires cutting cost. A dealer may agree to sales control or enforced managerial advice, but resist strenuously any attempt at financial control over his operations. This channel member may feel that finances are a personal matter.

Even a powerful wholesaler or retailer may go along with manufacturer control when it is to his personal advantage, but feel no qualms about simply circumventing control when it is not. This latter situation is one of the more difficult for the channel's manager to handle, and it has no simple solution. The channel leader cannot ignore the influence of the situation when determining channel control.

Financial Factors

Financial considerations influence the ability of the channel leader to control the membership. In part, finances are related to the situation, and in part they are related to economic power. Financial matters are important to both the channel leader and the dealer or retailer where control is concerned. From the leader's point of view, the administration of control is costly. This is especially true if the membership is balky. It takes time and it takes money to make dealer calls, correspond, handle reports, and utilize the telephone to arbitrate problems. Not every aspiring channel leader has the finances to take on the task. Even when finances do not preclude the leader from maintaining control, they may limit the amount or the effectiveness of the control methods utilized. Finances are important to the channel because they relate directly to the channel member's ability to resist control by the leader, or to take an independent attitude toward the leader's control methods.

CRITERIA FOR IDEAL CHANNEL CONTROL

There is, of course, no such thing as an ideal channel control plan. However, a knowledge of the criteria for channel control is useful to management because it provides a standard around which practical control plans can be measured and evaluated. Every control plan is a compromise between what is desirable and what is possible, but the channel manager is better off knowing the types and conditions under which compromise can be made. There are five criteria for an ideal control plan. The plan should be: (1) simple, (2) appropriate, (3) applicable, (4) fair, and (5) effective.

First, simplicity is a preferred ingredient for control. The plan should be clearly thought out and precisely presented. In this way managers can more clearly offer advice, and subordinates can understand what is expected in applying the control. Second, the plan should be appropriate. This criteria means that control should be suited to the problem. Too much control is excessively expensive and too little control is not likely to be effective. In a relatively small, integrated business operation, personal observation may be adequate to control inventory between divisions in the channel, but in a large operation, an elaborate system of reports and budgets may be in order to get the same degree of effectiveness. Complexity for its own sake is never advisable, and where control is concerned too much complexity is likely to obstruct efficiency.

Third, control ideally should be applicable. This criteria means that control should fit the situation. Sometimes the control techniques are excellent, but the control is applied to the wrong problem. For example, elaborate control techniques may be established by channel members to reduce losses from employee theft, but the cost of control is greater than the cost of the theft. Fourth, where people are the unit to be controlled, fairness comes into play as a criteria for ideal control. The control must be fair to the one controlling and to the one controlled. Regulation that is oppressive, vindictive, or overly restrictive is not fair. Control should be used to provide the channel leader with proper information to train, motivate, and excite the channel member to proper behavior.

Fifth, all the criteria for control are useless if the control is not effective. Effectiveness means that the control gets the desired results. Some control is technically very sound but it provides regulation; other control may be technically poor but results in proper regulation. The best control is technically sound and provides for desired regulation at the same time.

QUESTIONS

1. Define and discuss the differences in the four types of control.
2. Make up a problem situation and apply the three steps of the control process in its solution.
3. List the five ways of establishing pre-performance control decisions and give an example of each type.
4. What are the concurrent control decisions? Discuss how they can be used.

5. What are the strategies that are used in a suction channel? Give an example of each.
6. Who is the marketing strategy directed at in a pressure channel? What strategy techniques are associated with pressure channels?
7. What factors may affect middlemen in the channel that have a bearing on the ability of the channel leader to maintain channel control? What can be done to regain control?
8. Discuss the criteria for an ideal control plan. Why is each criteria important?
9. Assume you are the manufacturer channel leader in a push–pull channel and the retailers are not giving your product good shelf position. What can you do about this problem?
10. What type of channel control would be best for a retailer led channel, a manufacturer led channel, and a wholesaler led channel? Why?

20

Special Decisions of
International Channels

This book has focused attention primarily on American channels of distribution. However, with today's mobility of people between nations and the rapid dissemination of information concerning the level of life around the world, there has been a broadening of markets generally. The "have not" nations are developing, some rapidly, and they are no longer willing to be second class citizens in the world market. These countries want to share in the "good life" of their more affluent neighbors. At the same time, today's modern means of transportation and packing have made possible the shipment of even the most perishable of goods to any place in the world. The result is that the world has shrunk, in a relative sense, to within the easy reach of most large corporations. Thus, in the last fifteen years we have observed the rise of the multinational enterprise.

American firms have long sold abroad, but the pattern was to make a sharp distinction between domestic and foreign sales.[1] The new philosophy of the multinational firm is to make no essential distinction between foreign and domestic operations, and many large American corporations are approaching a 50–50 split between domestic and foreign sales. In this chapter we deal with the special channel decision areas that result from foreign marketing.

[1] John Fayerweather, *International Marketing* (Englewood Cliffs, N. J.: Prentice-Hall, Inc., 1965), p. 1.

IMPORTANCE OF INTERNATIONAL MARKETS

It is beyond our scope to provide a detailed study of international markets. However, food, housing, medical care, and the cost of living are basic indicators of the general standard of living within a nation. A look at these indicators can provide some idea of the type and size of potential markets between selected nations.

Food Supply by Nations

Table 20–1 has data on the food supply for selected nations of the world. The various nations demonstrate a wide range of good consumption. Based strictly on calorie intake, Bolivia is the poorest fed nation with 1,760 calories, followed by Indonesia with 1,920 calories. The best fed nations are Ireland with 3,510 calories and the United States with 3,300. Of course, these figures tell very little about the type of food consumed. Generally, the North American and Western European countries are the best fed. The same wide variety noted for calories also applies when the three basic types of food (cereals, potatoes, meat) are reviewed. Some of the low figures for meat consumption reflect cultural factors such as those in Ceylon, India, and Indonesia. In spite of these limiting factors, it is clear that the type of diet shows a wide range between nations. Most nations depend heavily on cereals, and there is some tendency for countries located in cold climates to consume more meat.

Shelter and Health Standards by Nations

The data presented in Table 20–2 shows the wide range of both housing and health standards among the nations of the world. The number of houses tends to vary directly with the population of the nation. For example, India, United States, USSR, Japan, and Brazil rank in that order for the total number of occupied houses. These are also among the most populous nations of the world. As with food, the number of houses occupied does not tell the full story because a house can be either a shack or a mansion. A good measure of the quality of a country's housing is the percentage with piped water and electricity. Again, we notice from Table 20–2 that it is the more affluent Western European and North American nations that rank highest in these factors.

Japan, USSR, India, and the United States lead all nations in the number of hospitals, and the number of hospital beds follows a similar, although not identical pattern. Once again population has to be considered in evaluating the effect of hospitals and beds on the general health of the nation. The ratio of patients per physician adds this dimen-

Table 20-1 Selected Foods—
(Pounds per year, except calories. Relates to net supplies of
deduction for animal feed, industrial purposes, waste, and
terms of flour and milled rice; potatoes include other starchy roots
poultry, and game, is

Country	Year or Period	Calories per Day	Cereals	Pota- toes, etc.	Meat
United States	1970	3,300	142	122	249
Argentina	1969	3,160	208	240	270
Australia	1969/70	(NA)	174	124	237
Austria	1969/70	3,230	204	*155	170
Belgium-Luxemb	1969/70	3,230	176	265	171
Bolivia	1964-66	1,760	192	339[†]	49
Brazil	1970	2,820	219	432[†]	68
Burma	1964-66	2,010	337	5	14
Canada	1970	(NA)	145	173	207
Chile	1970	2,560	258	103	87
China, People's Rep. of[†]	1964-66	2,050	311	199	38
China (Taiwan)	1969	2,620	369	89	60
Columbia	1970	2,140	141	314	73
Denmark	1970/71	(NA)	154	185	(NA)
Ecuador	1970	1,970	151	323	46
Egypt	1968/69	2,770	455	23	25
Ethiopia	1970	1,980	324	66	44
Finland	1970/71	2,940	180	185	99
France	1969/70	3,270	176	216	206
German Dem. Rep[†]	1964-66	3,040	217	308	138
Germany, F. R. of	1969/70	3,180	152	240	177
Greece	1967	2,900	266	130	89
Hungary	1970	3,190	282	166	127
India	1969/70	1,990	309	39	3
Indonesia	1970	1,920	277	197	8
Iran	1964-66	2,030	291	14	30
Ireland	1970	3,510	202	271	184

NA Not available   *Includes plantains and/or bananas.
Source: Statistical Abstracts of the United States, 1973, p. 806.

sion. India has 4.6 persons per physician; followed in order by Japan
with 0.9; United States with 0.7; and the USSR with 0.4. Russia has the
lowest ratio of all nations and India has the highest. The Western
European nations have generally favorable ratios. However, Japan,
one of the more populous nations, ranks among the leaders in the ratio
of persons per physician. Several countries have more favorable ratios

Net Supply Per Person, by Country
foodstuffs for human consumption at the retail level after
processing losses. Excludes alcoholic beverages. Cereals are in
and their root flour equivalent; meat, including edible offals,
dressed carcass weight)

Country	Year or Period	Calories per Day	Cereals	Pota-toes, etc.	Meat
Israel	1969/70	2,990	245	86	125
Italy	1969/70	3,020	284	104	109
Japan	1970	2,470	283	130	39
Khmer Rep	1964-66	2,230	379	13	16
Korea, Rep. of	1969	2,490	460	121	18
Lebanon	1964-66	2,360	266	41	60
Mexico	1964-66	2,620	305	28	44
Netherlands	1970/71	(NA)	147	197	131
Norway	1969/70	2,940	155	214	92
Pakistan	1969/70	2,410	399	38	9
Peru	1968	2,260	216	413*	51
Philippines	1969	2,040	291	71	35
Poland	1964-66	3,140	308	279	111
Portugal	1970	2,920	265	249	76
Romania	1964-66	3,010	402	146	84
South Africa[†]	1964-66	2,730	356	35	91
Spain	1969/70	2,770	245	243	90
Sri Lanka (Ceylon)	1970	2,340	310	56	4
Sweden	1970/71	2,850	135	190	(NA)
Switzerland	1969/70	3,190	175	127	160
Turkey	1964-66	2,760	381	91	31
U.S.S.R.	1964-66	3,180	344	304*	85
United Kingdom	1970/71	3,170	161	225	168
Uruguay	1970	2,740	175	134	230
Venezuela	1970	2,430	203	329*	80
Vietnam, Dem. Rep[†]	1964-66	2,000	331	146	32
Vietnam, Rep. of	1964-66	2,200	391	56	22
Yugoslavia	1968	3,130	401	143	75

[†]FAO estimates.

than the United States including Austria, Belgium, Switzerland, and
Germany.

Cost of Living by Nations

The cost of living is as volatile among nations as we have found for
other factors, and this indicator is important because it erodes the ability

Table 20-2 Housing and Health by Country

| | DWELLINGS | | | HEALTH | | | | | |
| | | | Percentage with | | | Hospitals | | Physicians | | |
Country	Year	Occupied (in thousands)	Piped Water	Electric Lighting	Year	Number	Beds (in thousands)	Number	Persons (in thousands)	Dentists
United States	1970	63,417	94.0	(NA)	1969	7,144	1,649.7	302,966	0.7	101,874
Austria	1970	2,429	(NA)	98.3	1970	(NA)	80.5	13,682	0.5	1,822
Belgium	1961	3,016	76.9	99.6	1968	473	76.8	14,991	0.6	1,844
Brazil	1970	18,086	32.8	46.9	1967	3,238	294.1	47,250	2.0	26,611
Canada	1967	5,034	95.2	(NA)	1968	1,436	212.4	29,659	0.7	6,928
Denmark	1965	1,614	96.7	(NA)	1966-67	170	43.3	7,050	0.7	3,300
Egypt	1960	1,572	39.5	37.8	1968-69	(NA)	68.8	16,219	2.0	1,999
France	1968	15,190	92.8	98.8	1969	(NA)	446.7	68,000	0.7	21,000
Germany, Fed. Rep. of	1968	19,347	99.0	99.0	1969	3,601	677.7	103,410	0.6	31,177
India	1960	79,194	(NA)	(NA)	1965	13,166	291.2	110,884	4.6	(NA)
Japan	1968	24,198	94.9	(NA)	1970	38,919	1,311.7	113,857	0.9	36,367
Korea, Rep. of	1960	4,098	21.4	28.4	1969	219	16.3	13,465	1.2	1,950
Netherlands	1956	2,519	89.6	98.1	1968	(NA)	66.1	15,644	0.8	3,205
Norway	1960	1,075	94.0	(NA)	1969	335	35.5	5,340	0.7	3,175
Peru	1961	1,962	21.1	26.0	1968	315	30.5	6,870	1.9	2,167
South Africa	1960	1,023	(NA)	(NA)	1962	711	87.9	12,743	1.5	1,455
Sweden	1965	2,778	95.2	(NA)	1969	735	118.5	10,380	0.8	6,630
Switzerland	1960	1,580	96.1	(NA)	1969	433	70.7	9,979	0.6	2,501
Turkey	1965	5,538	50.9	68.7	1970	746	72.0	15,886	2.2	3,245
U.S.S.R.	1960	50,900	(NA)	(NA)	1969	26,429	2,567.3	555,400	0.4	87,100
United Kingdom	1966	14,977	93.5	(NA)	1969	2,490	461.1	56,500	0.9	12,500
Yugoslavia	1961	4,082	(NA)	54.5	1970	504	115.0	20,369	1.0	3,001

(NA) Not available.

Source: *Statistical Abstracts of the United States*, 1972, pp. 807–8.

TABLE 20-3 Consumer Price Indexes—Selected Countries, 1965 to 1972

Country	Indexes (1967=100)				Average Annual Percentage Change 1965–1972	Percentage of Price Increase, 1970 to 1972				
	1965	1970	1971	1972		All Goods and Services	Food	Clothing	Rent	Medical Care
United States	94.5	116.3	121.3	125.3	4.1	7.7	6.9	5.3	8.8	9.9
Canada	93.0	112.4	115.6	121.1	3.8	7.8	8.4	4.1	11.4	6.2
Japan	91.5	119.3	126.8	133.0	6.8	11.5	8.8	14.9	18.6	11.2
Austria	94.1	110.6	115.8	123.1	3.9	11.3	9.8*	8.5	24.5	18.7†
Belgium**	93.3	110.7	115.5	121.9	3.9	10.0	8.7	(NA)	(NA)	(NA)
Denmark	86.4	119.1	126.0	134.3	6.5	12.8	16.2	7.8	17.5	13.0
France	94.8	117.1	123.5	131.1	4.7	12.0	15.6	9.8	12.0	8.0
Germany, F. R. of††	94.9	108.2	113.8	120.3	3.5	11.2	10.1	12.6	11.6	17.6
Italy	94.2	109.2	114.4	121.0	3.6	10.8	12.2	12.5	7.7	7.3†
Netherlands	91.4	115.5	124.3	134.3	5.7	16.2	11.6	18.7	19.4	28.7
Norway	92.7	118.0	125.3	134.3	5.4	13.9	13.7	13.9	12.1	18.0
Sweden	90.1	112.0	120.4	127.6	5.1	13.9	19.1	14.9	6.8	28.7
Switzerland	91.8	108.8	115.9	123.7	4.4	13.7	13.4	14.2	17.7	17.4†
United Kingdom	93.9	117.4	128.5	137.6	5.6	17.2	20.9	14.5	20.6	(NA)

NA Not available.   *Includes alcohol and restaurant meals.   †Includes personal care.   **Excludes rent.   ††Includes West Berlin.

Source: *Statistical Abstracts of the United States*, 1973, p. 813.

of the population to purchase (see Table 20–3). Between 1960 and 1971 inflation was greatest in the United Kingdom, followed by Denmark, Norway, and the Netherlands. The United States was among the lowest in annual percentage change. Table 20–3 indicates that even within the same nation, inflation did not have the same effect on the basic necessities of life. The Netherlands and Norway were the only two countries that had a greater percentage increase in food than rent, and only the Netherlands had a greater increase in clothing than in rent. Thus, a large part of the inflation of most countries was due to the relatively higher increases in rent. The particular percentages varied considerably by nations.

U. S. Share of World Markets

The United States is a great exporter nation, and Table 20–4 shows its share of the imports for selected countries of the world. For example,

Table 20–4   U. S. Share of World Markets, 1968

Country	Value of Imports from World in Dollars (millions)	U. S. Share (percentage)
Germany, Fed. Rep.	20,150	10.8%
United Kingdom	18,958	13.4
France	13,929	9.5
Japan	12,988	27.2
Canada	12,446	73.3
Italy	10,253	11.6
Netherlands	9,291	10.9
Switzerland	4,513	9.0
Australia	4,382	26.4
Norway	2,706	7.6
India	2,508	34.9
Brazil	2,132	32.1
Mexico	1,960	63.0
Korea, Rep.	1,468	30.8
Iran	1,386	17.2
Philippines	1,280	32.4
Ireland	1,172	7.4
Israel	1,081	22.7
Pakistan	996	30.1
Taiwan	903	26.6
Turkey	770	15.8
Columbia	643	50.1
Kuwait	611	17.1
Panama	266	39.0
El Salvador	214	28.9

Source: International Commerce, Vol. 76 (February 9, 1970)

Canada obtains over 73 per cent of all its imported goods from the United States, and Mexico obtains 63 per cent. Obviously, good will and proximity help to explain these high percentages. Other nations with high import percentages from the United States include Columbia, Panama, Philippines, Korea, Brazil, and India. The dollar value is even more enlightening. We see that nations with lower percentages often purchase more than nations with higher percentages. The difference, of course, lies in the wealth of the nation and its need for particular products. It is generally the Western European nations and Japan that constitute the best markets for American goods. This pattern is not likely to change much in the near future.

MOTIVES FOR FOREIGN TRADE

The number and types of motives for entering foreign trade are many. Since each business is in some way different, it is natural for them to be motivated in specific ways. Nevertheless, there appear to be five major reasons why a business would seek entry into foreign markets.[2] First, there is the *profit from serving the foreign market*. Our previous discussion suggested that there are almost infinite possibilities for firms to serve and make money on a multinational basis. Second, entry may be based on *surplus production at home*. Foreign markets may be an attractive alternative to laying off workers and closing plants. When entry is based on overproduction at home, it may be either on a short-term or a long-run basis.

Third, *diversification* may be the company stimulus that causes entry into foreign markets. There are many ways of diversification, including adding products, entering new industries, entering new geographic regions, consolidations, and developing foreign markets. Foreign markets in this case provide a hedge against sales decline at home, bring in new revenue, and may offer opportunities for higher profit per sale. Fourth, a business may enter a foreign market because of *political pressure from home.* This pressure may come in many forms, but the most important include the conservation of natural resources, provision of an economic lever on the foreign country, cultivation of friendships abroad, or for military purposes. In any case, the company should find some personal advantage before undertaking foreign trade for political reasons. Fifth, a business may seek foreign markets for *humanitarian reasons*. The opportunity to serve and to aid the people of emerging nations can be a strong motivator in some companies. It is perhaps true that in most

   [2] Philip R. Cateora and John M. Hess, *International Marketing* (Homewood, Ill.: Richard D. Irwin, Inc., 1971), p. 27.

cases a business enters the foreign market for a combination of the reasons cited above.

CHANNEL DEVELOPMENT AND ECONOMIC DEVELOPMENT

It was established in Chapter 2 that there is a direct relationship between the existence of economic systems and the existence of marketing channels. It is equally true that there is a relationship between the stage of economic development of a nation and the general organization of channels of distribution. In a great many nations the relationship develops in two distinct phases. At first, economic development brings about a lengthening of channels of distribution due primarily to the specialization of institutions to meet the needs of increasingly heterogeneous markets. Carson says:

As national markets expand and as new opportunities arise for satisfying consumer demand, greater specialization in distribution is evident both in echelons of distribution and in goods and services handled.[3]

The second phase begins as the nation starts to achieve industrial maturity. Although markets continue to be diversified, business has developed in size, strength, and financial security. At this time there is a tendency for the marketing channel to shorten as the large firms take advantage of integration to increase overall efficiency. Concerning this phase, Carson observes:

When the national markets have matured to the point that basic consumer needs have generally been satisfied and sales promotion becomes of major significance, operational savings are frequently greatest through vertical integration.[4]

Thus, the pattern is toward a lengthening of channels as the nation develops but a compression as the nation reaches maturity.

One study of emerging countries ranked Japan, Brazil, Venezuela, Puerto Rico, Turkey, Egypt, India, and Tropical Africa in that order for economic development.[5] This study found the following generalizations to be true concerning these nations. As a nation develops economically:

1. Levels of distribution, particularly department stores and specialty stores are added
2. Foreign import agents declined
3. Institutional specialization increased

[3] David Carson, *International Marketing* (New York: John Wiley & Sons, Inc., 1967), p. 482.
[4] *Ibid.*
[5] P. W. Bridgman, *Dimensional Analysis* (New Haven: Yale University Press, 1962), pp. 21–22.

4. Wholesalers westernized
5. Manufacturer–wholesaler–retailer activities became specialized in specific firms
6. Wholesale financing decreased but markup increased
7. The average size of store increased
8. Peddlers and open-garden fairs decreased
9. Retail margins increased

When this pattern of channel activity is compared to that described previously, the differences become immediately clear. The American channel is obviously very diversified, but it has also reversed the tendency indicated in (1), (3), and (5) above. Of course, there are exceptions to the rule because, as we have pointed out, the particular channel used is a result of many factors, not just one. It is certainly true that one finds a rather wide variety of channels in both emerging nations and in mature nations.

TYPES OF INTERNATIONAL CHANNEL DECISIONS

In some ways, distribution through international channels is not significantly different from channel operations in home markets. Both markets consist of heterogeneous consumers whose wants must be satisfied. Both markets require the development of specific marketing strategies related to the channel in order to achieve marketing goals and meet the market's requirements.[6] There will be competitive channels to contend with in each case. And in each case, the channels must take into account the environment in which the market resides.

Just as there are similarities in home and international markets, so there are also differences. In a broad sense, these differences are a matter of specific methods and degrees rather than differences of a unique nature. Differences that exist are caused by specific problems of needs, distance, and culture. International channels must respond to these specific differences and the manner of response can be grouped under: (1) decisions of international channel structure, and (2) decisions of international channel operations. Of course, the particular national environment underlies both.

DECISIONS OF INTERNATIONAL CHANNEL STRUCTURE

One of the more important sets of decisions that a business must make concerning international channels involves basic structure. Of course, we

[6] Yoram Wind, Susan P. Douglas, and Howard V. Perlmutter, "Guidelines for Developing International Marketing Strategies," *Journal of Marketing*, Vol. 37 (April, 1973), pp. 14–23.

already possess general knowledge of international channel structure, because when one understands his own nation's distribution system he has the basic knowledge of all distribution systems.[7] However, there are important differences between domestic and international channels and we will now focus our attention on them.

In the broadest terms, the selection of an international marketing channel depends on the same considerations that determine the selection of any channel. These include:

1. Market considerations
2. Product factors
3. Channel member alternatives
4. Company organization and philosophy
5. Competitive conditions
6. Location of production [8]

Business Organizational Philosophy

There is a natural tendency for international channels to be home-oriented and organized for domestic sales in the beginning. The reason is that new businesses are rarely started with the explicit purpose of entering international markets. What is more apt to happen is that a company, already established domestically, has something occur that makes multinational marketing attractive. That something may be excess capacity to produce; a product ideally suited for some foreign country's needs; a foreign-oriented manager; investment opportunity or encouragement from abroad; mineral resources abroad; or a desire to expand markets. No matter what the cause, the decision is typically one of market expansion rather than market introduction.

It is not unusual for a business such as that described above to get involved in the international market cautiously and on a limited basis. In the beginning, the foreign market is viewed as a minor part of the total operation. Figure 20–1 shows a typical *domestically oriented* company. Foreign operations are pushed down in the organization and centralized in the hands of a single executive. Some businesses have been extremely successful with this type of operation, but the experience of most is that such an organization is soon outgrown, or the company begins to lose its market share to more aggressive home or foreign based companies.[9] Several reasons can be cited for the difficulties of domestically oriented foreign sellers, including the following.

---

[7] Cateora and Hess, *op. cit.*, p. 752.

[8] Gordon E. Miracle and Gerald S. Albaum, *International Marketing Management* (Homewood, Ill.: Richard D. Irwin, Inc., 1970), pp. 324–25.

[9] Robert E. Linneman, "A Case for Minimum Marketing Efforts in International Markets," *Mississippi Valley Journal of Business and Economics*, Vol. 1 (Fall, 1965), p. 85.

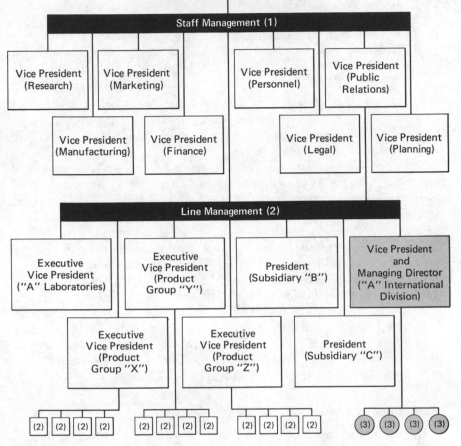

Legend

■ Executives with world-wide responsibility. That is, they are responsible for international activities as well as for domestic activities in the United States and all other countries.

▨ Executives with international (but not world-wide) responsibility. That is, they are responsible for activities involving more than one country, but not the entire world.

Notes

(1) Corporate-staff executives with functional-management responsibility, primarily for United States operations.

(2) Managers of domestic operating divisions (includes such titles as Division Manager, General Manager, Vice President, and President).

(3) Managing directors of foreign companies; responsibility generally (but not always) crosses national boundaries; scope of responsibility centered basically on location of production source or country of incorporation.

Fig. 20–1. Organization structure of Company A—domestically oriented. *Source:* Gilbert H. Clee and Aldred Di Scipio, "Creating a World Enterprise," *Harvard Business Review,* Vol. 37 (November–December, 1959).

1. Organizational problems of communications between home and overseas offices
2. Failure to understand local marketing problems
3. Relative lack of management interest
4. Problems with importing countries including: (a) the desire for industrialization, (b) currency problems, and (c) differences in production cost

The basic problem, of course, is that the domestically oriented company is not really a world enterprise. International executives have little power and the foreign market is considered an appendage rather than an integral part of the organization.

The alternative to the domestically oriented company is *international orientation*. Figure 20–2 demonstrates the organization of such a company. Notice that in this business the overseas operations are specialized on a geographic basis, and the executives report directly to top management. Communications and problems of local adaptation are greatly simplified. Furthermore, the management within each area and country can be recruited and trained locally. This fact adds to understanding and creates goodwill for the organization. The international organization is truly a world business with equal emphasis on sales in all parts of the globe. This type of organization is less likely to develop problems in emerging nations or politically unstable nations because it is identified as an integral part of the country's economy. As a result of the obvious advantages, there has been an increasing tendency for international firms to move in the direction of overseas emphasis.

International Channel Alternatives

The manner of distribution employed by a business selling in foreign markets follows closely whether the organization is domestically or internationally oriented. Figure 20–3 summarizes the alternative international channels of distribution available to an exporting business. A domestically organized firm is likely to utilize direct sales to contact foreign business or direct sales through the domestic sales force. An international oriented organization is more apt to utilize at least some direct sales from overseas facilities.

The reader must bear in mind that the distinction made earlier between a wholesaler and a retailer still holds, and only retailers can sell to final household consumers. Although Figure 20–3 shows direct sales from the producer to the consumer, it is assumed that some dual system such as a branch office or other agency functions in the capacity of a retail unit for the firm.[10]

The only institutions that may not be familiar are exporters and im-

[10] See Chapter 6 for a more complete discussion of this situation.

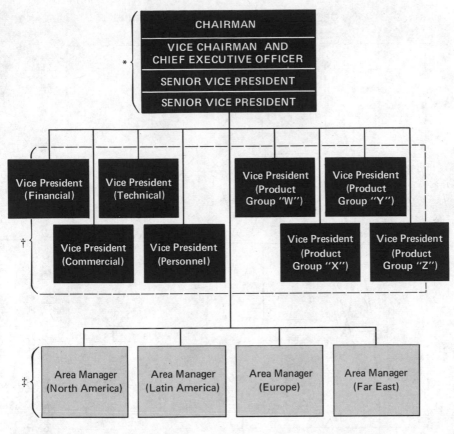

Legend

■ Executives with world-wide responsibility. That is, they are responsible for international activities as well as for domestic activities in all countries.

☐ Executives with international (but not world-wide) responsibility. That is, they are responsible for activities involving more than one country, but not the entire world.

Notes

* Functions as one top-management entity, although Chief Executive Officer has final authority and responsibility for the corporation's performance world-wide; Chairman's position is advisory in nature; Senior Vice Presidents, when directed, act as Deputies of the Chief Executive Officer and are selected to bring supplementary and essential management skills to the top-management entity on a day-to-day basis.

† Comprises the "Strategic Management Board" for the corporation world-wide. These executives, all based at headquarters, exercise strategic planning, decision making, coordination, and control for all functions and all major product lines.

‡ Indicates executives responsible for a geographical area of the world. The responsibility in each case crosses national boundaries and is centered on a manageable area of geography, offering a practical span of control for the Chief Executive thereof. When over-all strategic plans are approved at Headquarters, this "Area Manager" (who may have a title of President, Vice President, Managing Director, or the like) becomes fully responsible for executing the plans, managing company resources and facilities within the geographical area, and achieving operating targets spelled out by the Strategic Management Board.

Fig. 20–2. Organization structure of Company B—internationally oriented.

Source: Same as Fig. 20–1.

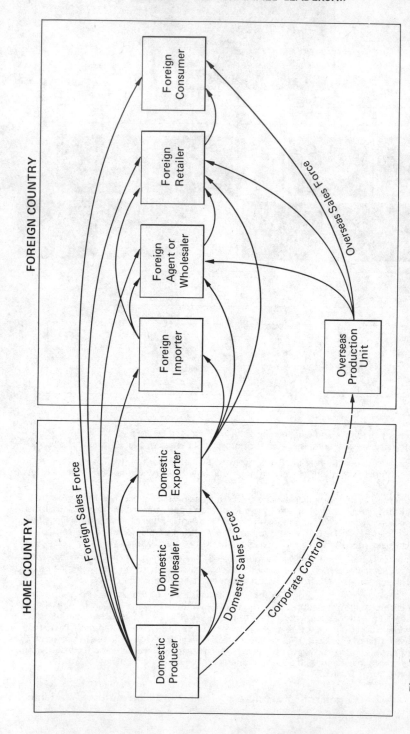

Fig. 20–3. Alternative international channels. **Source:** Adapted from Philip R. Cateora and John M. Hess, *International Marketing*, rev. ed. (Homewood, Ill., Richard D. Irwin, Inc., 1971), p. 753.

porters. Actually, these institutions are simply variations of types that have already been introduced. Some of the same general types of institutions can be involved in both exporting and importing, but the term exporter is used to refer to a business in a shipping nation and the term importer is used to refer to a business in a receiving nation. These institutions are summarized below.

A. Exporters
   1. *Export Merchant.* Operates similar to a full-service wholesaler.
   2. *Export Drop Shipper.* Operates as a domestic drop shipper. Business takes orders, owns merchandise, but does little storing.
   3. *Export Commission House.* An agent who represents foreign buyers in the exporter's home country.
   4. *Export Resident Buyer.* Operates like domestic resident buyers. Represent foreign buyers in the exporter nation.
   5. *Combination Export Manager.* Functions as a domestic selling agent. Takes responsibility for the entire sales department. Resides in the exporter country.
   6. *Manufacturer's Export Agent.* Functions as a domestic manufacturer's agent with limited authority. Located in the exporter nation.

B. Importers
   1. *Import Merchant.* Operates as a full-service wholesaler.
   2. *Brokers.* Agents who seek sources of supply from exporter nations. Located in the receiving nation. Similar to domestic free-lance brokers and purchasing agents.
   3. *Overseas Sales Branch.* Located in the receiving nation but owned by a producer in the exporter nation. May or may not carry stocks.[11]

Decisions of Home or Foreign Production

The basic decision relating to international channel structure is whether to engage in home or foreign production. If domestic production is selected, then the organization can sell directly to overseas firms through use of a domestically controlled but foreign located sales force. The domestic producer can also sell indirectly by means of its domestic sales force. A foreign sales force either requires considerable travel by personnel in the foreign nation, or the salesmen must operate out of some sales offices established overseas. The domestic sales force simply treats the exporter or wholesaler as another domestic market. There is little follow-up after the initial sale. In the case of the foreign sales force, the domestic producer gains control over the entire sales strategy in-

[11] Miracle and Albaum, *op. cit.,* Chapter 15.

cluding salesman effort, promotion, delivery, financing, etc., but increases the cost of reaching the market. The domestic sales force loses some control over strategy after sale to the wholesaler or exporter, but cuts costs of reaching the foreign market. More control is lost if a merchant exporter is used rather than an agent. Cost also varies by the type of middleman who exports.

In either case, domestic sales greatly increases the logistics burden of a domestic producer servicing foreign markets. Products must move from point of manufacture to point of overseas shipment. Railroads, trucks, and air freight—in that order of importance—are involved in the movement. Next, the goods usually must be re-loaded for overseas shipment, mostly by ship lines; however, air freight is increasing as a means of overseas shipment. Then, the goods must be re-loaded once more for shipment to foreign firms, and this movement is primarily by rail or truck. The logistics movement does not necessarily follow the title flow. The problems of matching orders and deliveries is greatly increased with domestic production. Delays in arrivals and resulting "out" conditions can be more frequent.

In the case of overseas production, the channel is essentially the same as in domestic situations. The producing unit can sell through agents, wholesalers, retailers, or direct. The overseas sales force can operate directly from the production plant or out of geographically located branches or sales offices. As a result, the communications problem between the plant and the customer is simplified, and relationships are more casual and direct. This provides a great advantage for the salesman. On the other hand, communication between the overseas unit and the home office is increased and made more difficult. The cost of control increases partly because of the need for more records on sales, orders, expenses, shipments, cost, revenue, calls, and profit.

Logistics is greatly simplified with overseas production. The choices are basically the same as those found for domestic production. There is no need for the extra movement between nations. Thus, there is greater control over delivery schedules, inventories, and cost, and consequently the cost of logistics should be less.

Choice of Internal Foreign Channels

So far, we have treated channel decisions in foreign markets as if they related only to the problems of moving goods and title between nations. There are often tremendous differences between the length and breadth of channels within the different countries.[12] These differences can be

---

[12] George Wadinambiaratchi, "Channels of Distribution in Developing Economies," *The Business Quarterly*, Vol. 30 (Winter, 1965), pp. 74–82.

caused by economic conditions already cited, or by technology, personnel relations, and manufacturing methods.[13]

Figure 20–4 shows typical internal channels of distribution for selected nations in different states of economic and technological development. Compare these channels with the tremendous variety already discussed for the United States and one begins to understand the uniqueness of channel selection in each nation in which a multinational organization operates. Japan has the largest number of levels in their typical channel of distribution, while Egypt has the greatest variety of typical distribution methods. Clearly, the channels manager in international trade must be aware of the differences that exist and adjust his strategy accordingly. It may even be necessary in some cases to develop new channels to serve the foreign market. If the country is changing, the manager must realize the manner of that change so that his channel can be adjusted over time to meet the new needs.

DECISIONS OF FOREIGN CHANNEL OPERATIONS

Not only does the structure of marketing channels differ in foreign markets, but the manner of operation of these channels also differs. The variations are usually based on differences in the social, cultural, economic, and political attitudes of both the customers and the businessmen of the nation in question.[14] Successful foreign marketing requires that the institutions involved in the channel must take into account these differences in decision making.

Type and Size of Firm

Both wholesaling and retailing are important in most economies of the world.[15] However, their nature and size do vary among nations. Western Europe more closely approaches the type and size of firm found in the United States, but even here there are differences. For example, in the United States the supermarket dominates the food industry with approximately 80 per cent of total sales.[16] In the United Kingdom the cooperative is dominant in food retailing and, as a retail type, is more important all over Europe. This type of business accounts for approximately 34 per cent of retail sales in Finland, 15 per cent in Norway, and

[13] Gilbert T. Bowman, "Production Problems in Doing Business Abroad," *Financial Executive*, Vol. 31 (February, 1963), pp. 26–31.

[14] Charles C. Smith, "Business and Cultural Insights to Eastern Europe," *Marketing Education and the Real World*, Boris Becker and Helmut Becker, eds. (Chicago: American Marketing Association, 1973), pp. 171–75.

[15] Roland L. Kramer, *International Marketing*, 2nd ed. (Cincinnati, Ohio: South-Western Publishing Co., 1964), pp. 185–86.

[16] Fayerweather, *op. cit.*, p. 63.

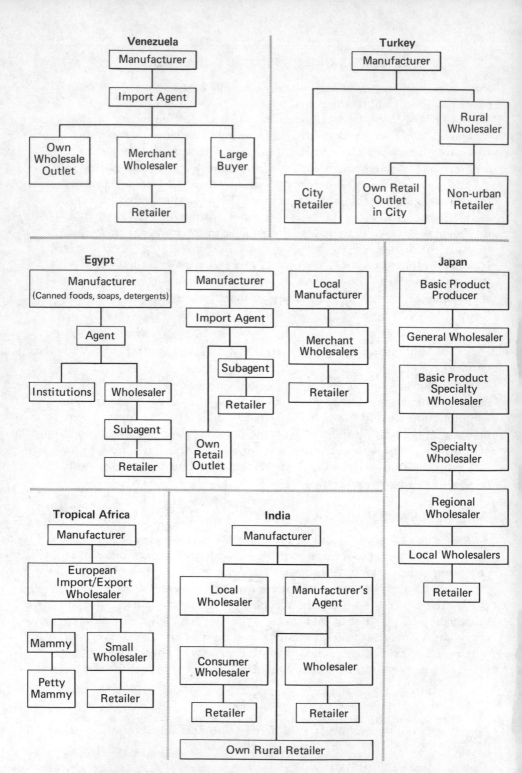

Fig. 20–4. Types and levels of distribution. *Source:* George Wadinambiaratchi, "Channels of Distribution in Developing Economies," *The Business Quarterly,* Vol. 30 (Winter, 1965), pp. 74–82.

14 per cent in Sweden, compared to only about 1 per cent in the United States.[17] Supermarkets are just being introduced into the European market, but they are catching on rapidly. For example, supermarkets increased from none in France in 1956 to 450 by 1965, and the number is still going up.[18] Wholesalers in the Western European market tend to perform more of the financing of retailers than in the United States; they do this in addition to their other distribution function.

Both retailers and wholesalers in foreign markets tend to be small and specialized compared to those in the United States. In Italy, for example, about 88 per cent of all wholesalers employ 6 people or less compared to 59 per cent in the United States.[19] The Italian experience is not so different from many other nations. Retailers overseas tend to be small and specialized. A food retailer in an advanced foreign economy may have only 5,000 square feet of floor space, and in the food stalls of underdeveloped nations less than 100 square feet. In the United States supermarkets often have between 30,000–100,000 square feet. Because of small size and specialization, the number of types of specialty stores is great in foreign countries compared to the assortment of products existing in those countries.

Retail stores overseas tend to be stratified by social class. Exclusive stores exist that cater to only the wealthy, other stores serve the middle class, and still others, cater to the low income consumer. The poor devote more time to shopping and often must visit several of the "hole-in-the-wall" shops to obtain necessary products. The wealthy can often purchase in advance of use and make infrequent shopping trips, but the low income consumer must purchase on a daily basis.

Obviously, an American firm selling abroad must often adjust its policies to meet these differences in operations. Management's thinking on the number and size of stores necessary to cover the market must reflect the situation in the country. The American firm, accustomed to selling through a single large retail to a wide income strata, can fail overseas if it does not take social stratification into account. It may even be necessary to change the form of selling from one type of store to another. For example, an American chain store may need to adopt cooperative methods to sell groceries in England. Where this is necessary, some joint effort with a local organization may be desirable to gain needed experience. On the other hand, the introduction of a new type of firm may be a real competitive advantage, as with the supermarkets in France.

[17] James B. Jeffreys and Derek Knee, *Retailing in Europe* (London: The Macmillan Co., 1962), p. 65.

[18] Michel David, "Developments in the Structure of Distribution in France: A Moderate Degree of Concentration," *Journal of Retailing*, Vol. 41 (Summer, 1965), pp. 34–48.

[19] Fayerweather, *op. cit.*, p. 64.

Assortment and Price Differences

Both product assortments and prices vary considerably among nations. The tendency toward small specialty stores already mentioned restricts the assortments of many nations. This is particularly true of South American, African, and Asian business outside the large metropolitan areas. Assortment restriction is greatest in the emerging nations. One author observes, "In a native market everyone is a specialist—in vegetables, in cloth, in pottery." [20] The reasons for the narrow line probably lie in the cost of inventory and the fact that the specialist wants to keep his merchandise within the bounds of his own management talents.

There are also considerable price differences between countries. Americans take the one-price system for granted, but there are many nations of the world where haggling over the price of most goods, even at retail, is common practice. Some readers may be familiar with this in the North African and South and Central American countries, but it also occurs in small European towns. Margins also greatly differ. They tend to be somewhat higher overseas due primarily to the smaller volume of operations and the different levels in the marketing channel. However, margins do not necessarily have to be higher than those in America. [21]

Price differences do not always reflect quality differences. Where quality is considered overseas, the results are mixed. The larger stores generally have good quality merchandise, and the specialist who caters to middle or upper income groups maintains good quality. However, there are many small stores with little or no quality standards. One can easily determine from these considerations that consumer orientation is not a big factor in foreign sales. American firms must learn to make allowances for the assortment and price problems overseas. It is sometimes difficult to get stores to stock merchandise, and even more difficult to maintain established margins. These factors place a greater burden on the selection of outlets, the control over resale, and maintenance of cost and revenue data. Many foreign wholesalers sell on a limited basis to preferred customers.

Differences in Manner of Service

Service in foreign markets shows a mixed pattern compared to the American experience. There is little self-service. The social and cultural patterns of the people simply do not allow for it. The people of nations such as India, most Middle Eastern countries, and most underdeveloped nations expect to be served. A merchant can spend several

[20] *Ibid.*

[21] See: James C. Abegglen and R. Douglas Norby, 'The World's Newest Mass Market," *The McKinsey Quarterly* (Winter, 1965), pp. 42–52.

minutes catering to the needs of a specific customer. This is even true, to some degree, in European countries. In a great many areas, particularly for the poor, shopping is one of the principle forms of entertainment. It is a chance to get out and meet people and to converse; shopping is not only business, it is also a social activity.

On the other hand, the variety of customer services, such as credit, delivery, market information, store directories, baby sitting pools, etc., is limited in most foreign markets compared to the situation in the United States. Of particular importance is post-purchase service.[22] Institutions that specialize in such services as repair, installation, and consulting are scarce overseas. Thus, the problem for the American firm is to understand the standard of service on the one hand and to prepare for ways to provide service after the sale. The latter in particular may require the establishment of overseas service centers. These centers can be costly, and there may be difficulties in getting people to use them.

Promotional Differences

No matter how one views the situation, promotion is simply not as important in overseas markets as it is in the United States. The de-emphasis of promotion is consistent with our earlier finding on specialization, narrow assortments, negotiation of price, and personal attention. Markets are typically smaller and the seller depends more on reputation than on promotion. Personal sales contact is the primary means of persuasion.

There is evidence that American products overseas have a promotional advantage because foreigners generally have a high opinion of our products. One study of Japanese and American products shows that the Japanese people considered there was definite prestige value in owning American made products.[23] The study shows that American products were rated high for engineering, marketing techniques, technical advancement, mass production, and world-wide distribution. Obviously, there are appeals behind these attitudes that American advertisers can take advantage of in their promotion overseas. The problem is how to get the message across using foreign media.

A major part of the problem of internal foreign communications lies in the firms themselves. We have shown that in the United States the channel functions as a team to a significant degree with considerable cooperation. A great deal of promotion is directed at the middlemen to make them customer-oriented and loyal to the requirements of the channel leader. This is not as true in overseas markets. Each wholesaler and retailer is more likely to function as an individual unit. Secretiveness is

22 See: H. K. Arning, "Business Customs from Malaya to Murmansk," *Management Review*, Vol. 53 (October, 1964), pp. 5–14.

23 Akira Nagashima, "A Comparison of Japanese and U. S. Attitudes Toward Foreign Products," *Journal of Marketing*, Vol. 34 (January, 1970), pp. 68–74.

important in most nations, and the firms do not seek out communications. In other words, there is little loyalty to the channel group. It is said that the stability of demand reinforced by cultural attitudes accounts largely for this lack of promotion. There is a tendency for the business to decrease promotion as it becomes more successful, which is just the opposite of what an American firm would do. The figures below show per capita expenditure on advertising in selected countries.[24]

United States	$67
Canada	34
Sweden	32
Switzerland	26
United Kingdom	25
Australia	24
West Germany	21
Netherlands	15
France	10
Japan	8

One basic problem where promotion is concerned for the American firm selling overseas is to adapt its promotion to the purchase habits of the nation. One author suggests the following rules.

1. You are guests of the country. Act as a guest should.
2. The profits of your enterprise are not solely yours. Your local 'national' employees and the economy of the country should also benefit.
3. Don't try to win over your new customers by completely 'Americanizing' them.
4. Although English is an 'accepted' language overseas, a fluency in the language of your international customer goes further in making sales.
5. Contribute to the country's economy and culture with worthwhile public relations projects.
6. Train the executives you choose to act properly overseas. This goes for their wives too.
7. Don't boast about your company's accomplishments. If you've done a good job, the local press will hear of it.
8. Don't conduct your business from the U. S. Staff your offices with nationals who know what they're doing, and supervise the operation from home.[25]

Problems Associated with Government

One of the basic rules of a market economy is that there must be a stable government with appropriate rules to guide trade. In fact, over the world, some governments are more stable than others, and marketing risk varies in direct proportion to this stability. The recent nationaliza-

---

[24] Charles Cruttenden, "How to Select an Effective Advertising Agency Abroad," *International Management* (June, 1965), pp. 58, 60, 64.
[25] *Printers' Ink*, Vol. 271 (June 3, 1960).

tion of industry in Peru and the threat of nationalization in Panama are examples. In the past, American firms have devoted millions of dollars to developing industries in some countries only to have them taken away when they become profitable. The only real protection is to avoid such countries where the risk is too great.

When an American business opens a channel in a foreign nation, it must expect to operate not only under the letter of the law, but also the spirit of the law of that nation. Nations differ in legal philosophy. Although not condoned, there are nations where the only way to do business is by bribing governmental officials. Such activity may have a cultural background and not even be considered wrong in any real sense by the general population of the nation. The business may have no feasible alternative but to go along with this practice.

There are also many cases where the specific laws of nations differ. For example, in the Netherlands bargain sales are permitted only when a store is actually closing. Germany allows a store to hold mark-down sales only twice a year. There is little consumer protection even in the more advanced nations of Western Europe, and in the underdeveloped countries it is practically nonexistent. Such laws as our Pure Food and Drug acts, Fair Labeling Acts, and Robinson-Patman Acts do not have counterparts in most foreign nations. Goods are sold, even food and meat, with practically no inspection.

Business Efficiency

Business efficiency has a direct bearing on the operation of foreign channels. However, it is difficult to generalize on this topic because so many variables are involved. Business efficiency can be viewed in absolute or relative terms. In relative terms it concerns the economic productivity of the nations involved. When foreign manufacturing and distribution are less productive than American manufacturing and distribution, markets for American companies are opened up. The United States is a heavy exporter of industrial equipment, farm machinery, grain, cotton, electronics equipment, aircraft, automobiles, communications equipment, etc., to nations where we have a comparative productivity advantage. When foreign manufacturing and distribution are more productive than that of America, then American industry becomes the market for foreign products. For example, overseas shipments of steel, shoes, textiles and apparel, and consumer electronics to the United States have been cutting into domestic markets.[26]

In absolute terms there is the cost of doing business in the foreign country where wages and prices may be considerably different from those in America. For example, an American may be able to pay low wages to

26 Cateora and Hess, *op. cit.,* p. 95.

employees in countries such as Iran, Brazil, or Turkey, but at the same time these wages restrict the ability of customers to buy. The answer is not in paying higher wages, but in contributing to the rise in the entire economic condition of the country. If one country pays higher wages it simply leads to internal distortions in the country, unless overall productivity is affected.

Wages can be a significant internal problem for a company using overseas channels. Do you pay overseas employees American scale wages? Most American companies do if the employees are sent from the United States. What if native employees are used? The problem is further compounded if American top management is used, but local people are employed for middle and supervisory management. There is no simple solution where domestic and foreign employees are mixed.

RULES FOR INTERNATIONAL CHANNELS MANAGEMENT

Bryan Houston in the 1960's developed a classic set of rules for managing international channels,[27] and they are paraphrased here. First, management should develop a positive attitude designed to find opportunities to serve customers. Second, management should become thoroughly familiar with its markets. Third, management should make sure that its products are of the highest quality. Foreign markets are becoming too aware to foster poor or second quality products on them. Fourth, management must keep prices competitive. Fifth, the best marketing tools available should be used. These tools particularly include the channel of distribution. It should be carefully thought out, appropriate to the market, and efficient.

QUESTIONS

1. What is the importance of industrial marketing to domestic firms?
2. Compare trends in health and shelter data for the United States and other nations. How does the United States rate?
3. Is it smart for American firms to become involved in international trade? Explain why or why not?
4. There is a relationship between channel development and economic development. Explain this relationship. Contrast channels in emerging countries to channels in established nations.
5. What factors should management take into account when selecting foreign channels? In what ways do they differ from factors involved in selecting domestic channels?
6. What is business organizational philosophy? Discuss the difference in

[27] Bryan Houston, "Five Basic Rules for Success in Developing International Markets," *Export Trade,* Vol. 84 (December 18, 1961).

philosophy of a domestically oriented company and an international oriented company.

7. Why have domestically organized businesses had difficulty overseas? Discuss possible solutions.

8. Compare international channel alternatives. What middlemen are involved that are not involved in domestic channels?

9. Why are internal foreign channels so diverse?

10. How do services differ overseas? What accounts for these differences and how are channels affected? Discuss overseas promotional problems.

Name Index

Subject Index

HF   Walters, Charles
5415.125   Glenn.
.W34
            Marketing
            channels

DATE		
AUG 15 1978		
FEB 2 5 1986		
MAY 6 1986		

101444

© THE BAKER & TAYLOR CO